Research Anthology on Convergence of Blockchain, Internet of Things, and Security

Information Resources Management Association
USA

Volume II

Published in the United States of America by
  IGI Global
  Information Science Reference (an imprint of IGI Global)
  701 E. Chocolate Avenue
  Hershey PA, USA 17033
  Tel: 717-533-8845
  Fax: 717-533-8661
  E-mail: cust@igi-global.com
  Web site: http://www.igi-global.com

Library of Congress Cataloging-in-Publication Data

Names: Information Resources Management Association. editor.
Title: Research anthology on convergence of blockchain, internet of things,
  and security / Information Resources Management Association, editor.
Description: Hershey, PA : Information Science Reference, [2023] | Includes
  bibliographical references and index. | Summary: "This reference book
  describes the implementation of blockchain and IoT technologies to
  better protect personal and organizational data as well as enhance
  overall security, while explaining the tools, applications, and emerging
  innovations in security and the ways in which they are enhanced by
  blockchain and IoT"-- Provided by publisher.
Identifiers: LCCN 2022030165 (print) | LCCN 2022030166 (ebook) | ISBN
  9781668471326 (h/c) | ISBN 9781668471333 (eISBN)
Subjects: LCSH: Blockchains (Databases) | Computer networks--Security
  measures. | Internet of things. | Convergence (Telecommunication)
Classification: LCC QA76.9.B56 R474 2023 (print) | LCC QA76.9.B56 (ebook)
  | DDC 005.74--dc23/eng/20220815
LC record available at https://lccn.loc.gov/2022030165
LC ebook record available at https://lccn.loc.gov/2022030166

British Cataloguing in Publication Data
A Cataloguing in Publication record for this book is available from the British Library.

All work contributed to this book is new, previously-unpublished material. The views expressed in this book are those of the authors, but not necessarily of the publisher.

For electronic access to this publication, please contact: eresources@igi-global.com.

List of Contributors

Table of Contents

Section 2
Development and Design Methodologies

Section 5
Organizational and Social Implications

Section 6
Managerial Impact

Section 7
Critical Issues and Challenges

Preface

Security on the internet has never been more crucial as today an increasing number of businesses and industries conduct their vital processes online. In order to protect information and data, further study on emerging technologies, such as blockchain and the internet of things, is critical to ensure companies and individuals feel secure online and best practices are continuously updated.

Staying informed of the most up-to-date research trends and findings is of the utmost importance. That is why IGI Global is pleased to offer this three-volume reference collection of reprinted IGI Global book chapters and journal articles that have been handpicked by senior editorial staff. This collection will shed light on critical issues related to the trends, techniques, and uses of various applications by providing both broad and detailed perspectives on cutting-edge theories and developments. This collection is designed to act as a single reference source on conceptual, methodological, technical, and managerial issues, as well as to provide insight into emerging trends and future opportunities within the field.

The *Research Anthology on Convergence of Blockchain, Internet of Things, and Security* is organized into seven distinct sections that provide comprehensive coverage of important topics. The sections are:

1. Fundamental Concepts and Theories;
2. Development and Design Methodologies;
3. Tools and Technologies;
4. Utilization and Applications;
5. Organizational and Social Implications;
6. Managerial Impact; and
7. Critical Issues and Challenges.

The following paragraphs provide a summary of what to expect from this invaluable reference tool.

Section 1, "Fundamental Concepts and Theories," serves as a foundation for this extensive reference tool by addressing crucial theories essential to understanding the concepts and uses of blockchain, the internet of things, and security in multidisciplinary settings. Opening this reference book is the chapter "A Holistic View on Blockchain and Its Issues" by Profs. Mohd Azeem Faizi Noor, Saba Khanum, and Manzoor Ansari from Jamia Millia Islamia, India and Prof. Taushif Anwar from Pondicherry University, India, which covers a holistic overview of blockchain and argues about basic operations, 51% attack, scalability issue, Fork, Sharding, Lightening, etc. This first section ends with the chapter "Application of Technology in Healthcare: Tackling COVID-19 Challenge – The Integration of Blockchain and Internet of Things" by Ms. Andreia Robert Lopes from Hovione Farmaciencia, Portugal and Profs. Ana Sofia Dias and Bebiana Sá-Moura of ISEG, Lisbon School of Economics and Management, Portugal, which discusses IoT and blockchain technologies, focusing on their main characteristics, integration benefits, and limitations as well as identifying the challenges that need to be addressed.

Section 2, "Development and Design Methodologies," presents in-depth coverage of the design and development of blockchain and internet of things technologies for their use in security across different industries. This section starts with "Blockchain-Enabled Secure Internet of Things" by Prof. Vinod Kumar from Madanapalle Institute of Technology and Science, India and Prof. Gotam Singh Lalotra of Government Degree College for Women, India, which discusses the blockchain-enabled secure internet of things (IoT). This section ends with "SEF4CPSIoT Software Engineering Framework for Cyber-Physical and IoT Systems" by Prof. Muthu Ramachandran from Leeds Beckett University, UK, which proposes a systematic software engineering framework for CPS and IoT systems as well as a comprehensive requirements engineering framework for CPS-IoT applications which can also be specified using BPMN modeling and simulation to verify and validate CPS-IoT requirements with smart contracts.

Section 3, "Tools and Technologies," explores the tools and technologies used to implement blockchain and the internet of things for facilitating secure operations. This section begins with "Blockchain for Industrial Internet of Things (IIoT)" by Prof. Rinki Sharma from Ramaiah University of Applied Sciences, India, which presents the importance of blockchain in the industrial internet of things paradigm, its role in the different industrial internet of things applications, challenges involved, and possible solutions to overcome the challenges and open research issues. This section ends with the chapter "Cyber Security and Cyber Resilience for the Australian E-Health Records: A Blockchain Solution" by Profs. Shailesh Palekar, Nagarajan Venkatachalam, and Peadar O'Connor from Queensland University of Technology, Australia, which explores how blockchain can be a single digital option that can address both cybersecurity and cyber resilience needs of electronic health records.

Section 4, "Utilization and Applications," describes how blockchain and the internet of things are used and applied in diverse industries for various security applications, such as security. The opening chapter in this section, "Perspectives of Blockchain in Cybersecurity: Applications and Future Developments," by Profs. Muath A. Obaidat and Joseph Brown from City University of New York, USA, aims to provide a neutral overview of why blockchain has risen as a popular pivot in cybersecurity, its current applications in this field, and an evaluation of what the future holds for this technology given both its limitations and advantages. The closing chapter in this section, "Advanced Cyber Security and Internet of Things for Digital Transformations of the Indian Healthcare Sector," by Profs. Esha Jain and Jonika Lamba from The NorthCap University, India, reviews the need for cybersecurity amid digital transformation with the help of emerging technologies and focuses on the application and incorporation of blockchain and the internet of things (IoT) to ensure cybersecurity in the well-being of the business.

Section 5, "Organizational and Social Implications," includes chapters discussing the impact of blockchain and the internet of things on society including how they can be utilized for security purposes across industries. The chapter "Blockchain Technology for IoT: An Information Security Perspective" by Prof. Karthikeyan P. from Thiagarajar College of Engineering, India; Prof. Sasikumar R. of K. Ramakrishnan College of Engineering, India; and Prof. Thangavel M. from Siksha 'O' Anusandhan (Deemed), India presents a detailed investigation of various IoT applications with blockchain implementation. The closing chapter, "Blockchain and IoT Integration in Dairy Production to Survive the COVID-19 Situation in Sri Lanka," by Profs. ruwandi Madhunamali and K. P. N. Jayasena from Sabaragamuwa University of Sri Lanka, Sri Lanka, proposes a dairy production system integration with blockchain and IoT.

Section 6, "Managerial Impact," considers how blockchain and internet of things technologies can be utilized within secure business and management. The opening chapter, "Applying Blockchain Security for Agricultural Supply Chain Management," by Prof. Teresa Edgar from the University of Houston, USA and Profs. Amarsinh V. Vidhate, Chitra Ramesh Saraf, Mrunal Anil Wani, and Sweta Siddarth

Waghmare of Ramrao Adik Institute of Technology, India, provides an overview of blockchain technology and its potential in developing a secure and reliable agriculture supply chain management. The closing chapter, "Blockchain and IoT-Based Diary Supply Chain Management System for Sri Lanka," by Profs. K. Pubudu Nuwnthika Jayasena and Poddivila Marage Nimasha Ruwandi Madhunamali from Sabaragamuwa University of Sri Lanka, Sri Lanka, investigates how blockchain technology can be used in today's food supply chains to deliver greater traceability of assets.

Section 7, "Critical Issues and Challenges," presents coverage of academic and research perspectives on the challenges of using blockchain and the internet of things for various security applications across industries. Starting this section is "A Comprehensive Review of the Security and Privacy Issues in Blockchain Technologies" by Prof. N. Pradeep from Bapuji Institute of Engineering and Technology, India; Prof. Renjith V. Ravi of MEA Engineering College, India; Prof. Mangesh Manikrao Ghonge from Sandip Foundation's Institute of Technology and Research Centre, India; and Prof. Ramchandra Mangrulkar of Dwarkadas J. Sanghvi College of Engineering, India, which covers blockchain's security and privacy issues as well as the impact they've had on various trends and applications. The closing chapter, "Blockchain With IoT and AI: A Review of Agriculture and Healthcare," by Prof. Pushpa Singh from KIET Group of Institutions, Delhi-NCR, India and Prof. Narendra Singh of GL Bajaj Insitute of Management and Research, India, studies the literature, formulates the research question, and summarizes the contribution of blockchain application, particularly targeting AI and IoT in agriculture and healthcare sectors.

Although the primary organization of the contents in this multi-volume work is based on its seven sections, offering a progression of coverage of the important concepts, methodologies, technologies, applications, social issues, and emerging trends, the reader can also identify specific contents by utilizing the extensive indexing system listed at the end of each volume. As a comprehensive collection of research on the latest findings related to blockchain, the internet of things, and security, the *Research Anthology on Convergence of Blockchain, Internet of Things, and Security* provides business leaders and executives, IT managers, computer scientists, hospital administrators, security professionals, law enforcement, students and faculty of higher education, librarians, researchers, and academicians with a complete understanding of the applications and impacts of blockchain and the internet of things. Given the vast number of issues concerning usage, failure, success, strategies, and applications of blockchain and internet of things technologies, the *Research Anthology on Convergence of Blockchain, Internet of Things, and Security* encompasses the most pertinent research on the applications, impacts, uses, and development of blockchain and the internet of things.

Chapter 25
Reinforcement Learning's Contribution to the Cyber Security of Distributed Systems:
Systematization of Knowledge

Christophe Feltus

ⓘD https://orcid.org/0000-0002-7182-8185

Luxembourg Institute of Science and Technology, Luxembourg

ABSTRACT

Reinforcement learning (RL) is a machine learning paradigm, like supervised or unsupervised learning, which learns the best actions an agent needs to perform to maximize its rewards in a particular environment. Research into RL has been proven to have made a real contribution to the protection of cyberphysical distributed systems. In this paper, the authors propose an analytic framework constituted of five security fields and eight industrial areas. This framework allows structuring a systematic review of the research in artificial intelligence that contributes to cybersecurity. In this contribution, the framework is used to analyse the trends and future fields of interest for the RL-based research in information system security.

1. INTRODUCTION

The contribution of artificial intelligence to cyber-security is paramount, given that it has the potential to increase the security level of the defended distributed system (Feltus et al., 2007) up to the state-of-the-art level generally reached by the attackers. In the field of machine learning, the approaches by which the computer program learns to generate output from experiments are classified into three paradigms: supervised, unsupervised and reinforcement learning (RL). In supervised learning, the model is trained using the input data labels, in unsupervised learning, the model is trained using patterns discovered in the input data, and in RL, a software agent learns to react on its own to an environment that it does not yet know (Van Otterlo & Wiering, 2012).

DOI: 10.4018/978-1-6684-7132-6.ch025

Figure 1. RL's mechanism schema

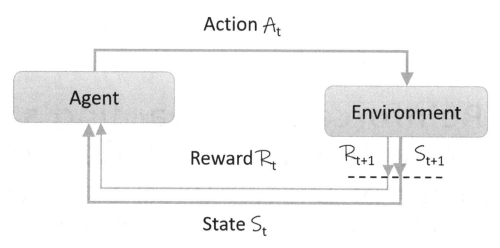

Reinforcement learning involves agents, states (S), and actions per state (A). Agents evolves from state to state when they perform actions. In order to learn how to react, agents make decisions and take action at time t A_t – (Fig.1) with the objective of accumulating rewards (R_t) while avoiding errors. As RL algorithms mostly use dynamic programming techniques, this reward-based environment is typically represented in the of Markov decision processes. These processes reflect a straightforward description of the problem in order to learn to reach a desired goal. In practice, agents continually select actions while the form environment in which they behave responds and presents new situations (Fig. 1)

In contrast to classical dynamic programming methods, RL algorithms have no knowledge of the exact Markov decision processes. Q-Learning [38] is an RL algorithm, whose purpose is to learn the policy that informs agents of the action they have to achieve in determined situations. This policy is optimized and gives all the successive steps necessary to achieve a goal while maximizing the gain of the rewards. Agents that learn the environment must continuously choose between exploiting the knowledge learned and exploring new potential actions to perform. Hence, an important parameter to be considered while defining RL algorithms is the e-greedy, which represents the proportion of exploration vs. exploitation actions (e.g., Li et al., 2018).

Reinforcement learning has already proven to be worthwhile for many fields, such as operations research, multi-agent systems, genetic algorithm or game theory. For some years, it has also been regarded as a strong potential contributor to the security and cyber-security domains (Feltus et al., 2009). However, although reviews of the contributions of machine learning and deep learning to computer security have already been undertaken for very specific fields, like biometry (e.g., Sundararajan & Woodard, 2018), to our knowledge, no systematic deep analysis of the contributions of reinforcement learning to the different fields of cyber-security has ever been completed. This is the aim of this paper. Elaborated from the strategic literature review method (Petersen et al., 2015), the paper will successively answer three knowledge questions:

- *What is the actual contribution of reinforcement learning for the field of cyber-security?*

Answering this question will allow us to identify the fields of cyber-security that most benefit RL-based contributions, as well as the type of contribution and the volume of research dedicated to it. These fields are: malware/intrusion detection, attacker/defender game, security policy elaboration, biometric authentication and software/system protection.

- *Which industrial areas are the most impacted by the RL contribution to cyber-security?*

This question will allow us to determine which industrial areas are the most impacted by the RL-based security contributions, for what purpose and to what amount.

- *What is the trend and future fields of research interests associated to RL contribution to cyber-security?*

Answering this question will support researchers and industries in understanding the potential for further research and development in this field. In the next section, the research method is presented, as well as the trend in regard to the volume of research paper publications. In section 2, the analytic framework is designed based on five relevant security fields and for eight industrial areas. In section 3, the literature is systematically reviewed and classified according to the security fields. In section 4, the evolution of this literature is analyzed and discussed for the industrial areas. Finally, section 5 concludes the paper.

2. ANALYTIC FRAMEWOK

In order to support the systematization-of-knowledge (SoK), a basic analytic framework was designed. This framework is elaborated along two axes: the security field and the industrial area. Its primary goal is to structure the SoK, to detect which security fields get the more contributions from artificial intelligence research, and to identify which industrial area benefits the more from that research. With the support of this framework, the analysis is facilitated first in terms of comparison, e.g.1, comparing which security field receives the more attention from the researchers, e.g.2, comparing which industrial area benefits the more from the research, and second in terms of association (ii), e.g., which security fields are associated to which business areas.

The first axe of the framework addresses the security fields and is composed of the following elements:

- Malware detection and Intrusion detection system
- Attacker-defender game
- Policy management
- Biometric authentication
- Software/system protection

The second axe of the framework addresses industrial areas and is composed of the following elements:

- Information system
- Smart grid
- Cloud computing
- IoT and the 5G
- Critical infrastructure
- Cognitive radio
- Wireless network

All these elements are explained later in the article.

According to Active Design Science Research (ADR – Sein et al., 2011), the development of the framework was carried out in parallel with the review of the literature, by gradually discovering the components of the axes and by refining them iteratively with the reviews in progress. The process corresponds to the activity of discovery / elaboration of a design artefact with secondary data (in this case: literature assets). A first iteration of the framework development was done in this article and, according to ADR, further iterations are needed to refine and improve it. This first iteration consists of using the framework to analyse the contribution of RL to cybersecurity, but it can obviously also be used in the context of other analyses such as the contribution of the GAN or LSTM network to cybersecurity. In this case, the framework will support an analysis extended to the type of AI networks exploited.

3. REVIEW OF THE LITERATURE

3.1 Research Method

We began this review of the literature, according to Petersen et al. (2015), by a systematic investigation of the IEEExplorer database, which includes 5,113,213 records and the ACM database, which includes 2,802,483 records. For both databases, the following search streams were defined:

At the level of IEEExplorer, we refined the number of records by applying the keywords "security", which gives 122,374 records, "IT security" or "cyber-security" which gives 52,938 records, and finally, "reinforcement learning" which gives 9,928 records. By searching both the "security" and "reinforcement learning" keywords together at the abstract level, the result was refined to 164 papers for all dates. Given the recent developments of the RL, we applied a final filter to our research, limiting the papers to the 2010-2020 period, which give us 148 abstracts to read. After reading them, it appeared that there were 92 remaining papers from IEEE worth being considered for the systematic review.

Afterward, we applied the same approach to the ACM Guide to Computing Literature. By looking for the keyword "security" at the abstract level, we obtained 199,113 records, and by looking for the keywords "IT security" or "cyber-security", we obtained 7,707 records. Concerning the keyword "reinforcement learning", it gave 41,079 results. When applying both filters together (that is, "security" and "reinforcement learning") at the abstract level, it gave 655 papers, and when applying the filter only to the 2010-2020 period, it allowed the amount of papers to be limited to 264. After reading the abstracts, only 104 papers appeared relevant for the analysis.

Figure 2. Evolution of the amount of papers addressing RL-based contributions to cyber-security

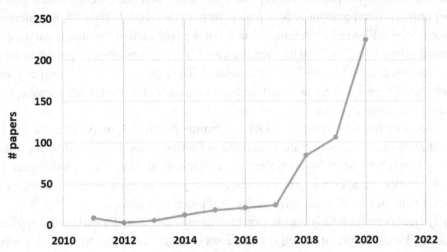

Figure 3. Percentage of type of RL-based contribution by cyber-security field

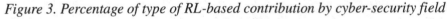

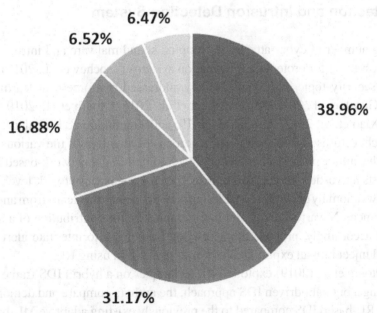

6.47%

6.52%

38.96%

16.88%

31.17%

- Malware detection/IDS
- Attacker/Defender game
- Security policy elaboration
- Biometric authentication
- Software/System protection

In parallel, this selection of papers was applied to Springer, Science Direct, Google Scholar and Web of Science but only a limited amount of new papers were discovered. In the end, this increased the final volume of papers to 312. Figure 2 represents the trend of the evolution of the amount of papers addressing RL-based contributions to cyber-security over the years. The final number of papers to be published in 2020 is not yet known exactly but has been extrapolated. The graph clearly shows an exponential evolution of the volume of papers, which demonstrates the interest that artificial intelligence, and especially RL, represents for security scientists, experts, and professionals.

Among the security fields targeted by the RL are mainly the field of malware detection and intrusion detection for 38.96% of the cases (Figure 3) and the definition of methods used by the attacker and the defender party to protect the distributed system (hereafter named Attacker/defender game) for 31.17%. Other fields of security are also concerned by the RL, such as: security policy management (16.88%), biometric authentication (6.49%) and software/system protection (6.49%).

The security fields in which RL-contributions are foreseeable also depend on the application area in which they occur. Based on the literature review, a set of eight areas was identified, covering most of the cases encountered. These areas are autonomous vehicles (including drones), information systems, smart grids, cloud computing, IoT and 5G, critical infrastructure, cognitive radio, wireless networks. The relative importance of the area of application versus the security field impacted by the RL contribution is further depicted in section 4.

3.2 Malware Detection and Intrusion Detection System

Given the increasing number of cyber-attacks, developing sound malware and intrusion detection systems (IDS) appears essential for protecting information systems (Tsochev et al., 2019). Hence, it is not surprising that this security topic is the most widely addressed reinforcement learning research and development field (Ghosh et al., 2017, Navarro-Lara et al., 2016, Otoum et al., 2019, Sreekesh, 2016, Xiao et al., 2018a, Xiao et. al, 2017, Xing et al., 2019, and Zolotukhin & Hämäläinen, 2018). In this regard, dedicated architectures have been a particular focus of attention of the various research works. In Sreekesh, 2016, the author proposes a novel approach to building a network-based IDS using a ML approach and suggests a two-tier architecture to detect intrusions at the network level. In the proposed architecture, RL allows anomaly detection considering network agents that learn from and make decisions based on the environment. Navarro-Lara et al. (2016) emphasize the contribution of a human expert for threat detection and accordingly, propose the Morwilog framework to integrate alert correlation into security systems and inject human expert feedback into the system using RL.

More recently, Otoum et al. (2019) exploited RL techniques on a hybrid IDS framework in wireless networks. Considering a big data-driven IDS approach, the authors compare and demonstrate the better performances of the RL-based IDS compared to the previously existing adaptive ML-based ones. In the field of autonomous vehicles, Xing et al. exploit a trust evaluation model to support a two-level IDS. Here, an attack warning is established based on (i) trust evaluation with the coverage of a roadside unit, and (ii) the information exchanged between RSUs through the cloud server. Then, an RL-based incentive mechanism reports warnings by stimulating the vehicle (Xing et al., 2019).

In the same vein, Xiao et al. (2018a) investigate and present ways to use deep learning (DL) methods, including RL approaches, to improve methods for mobile crowd sensing and Zolotukhin & Hämäläinen (2018) stress the fact that traditional IDS approaches are unsuitable for IoT networks due to two elements: the limited computational capacity of devices and the diversity of technology (Mayer et al., 2015).

Therefore, an RL agent is proposed as a core component of an IoT defense system in order to evaluate the risk of potential attacks and mitigate them using the most optimal actions. In parallel to this malware detection literature, some authors also address RL contributions to IDS following specific types of malwares to be detected. In Ghosh et al. (2017), to maintain the high-level security of data in the Cloud, RL is incorporated to the Reinforcement Learning Automata for detecting and classifying attacks (Band et al., 2015). Effective rules are generated using learning automata from a vast training set to improve the learning process. Xiao et al. (2017) propose a malware detection scheme with QLearning. This IDS is applied to mobile devices with the aim of deriving the optimal offloading rate without knowing (i) the trace generation and (ii) the radio bandwidth model of other mobile devices. Alongside this, the RL process is accelerated by a post-decision state learning-based scheme, which utilizes the known radio channel model. The simulation of this model shows that the authors' schemes allow a reduction of the detection delay, an improvement of the detection accuracy, and an increase in the utility of mobile devices in dynamic malware detection.

Other malwares are addressed more specifically, such as: jamming attacks, adversarial attacks, eavesdropping, spoofing, (D)DoS, Botnet, ransomware, and some others. The impact of these attacks and their consideration by the RL-based IDS literature is shown in Figure 4 and is discussed in the following sections.

Figure 4. Percentage of attacks considered by the RL-based IDS

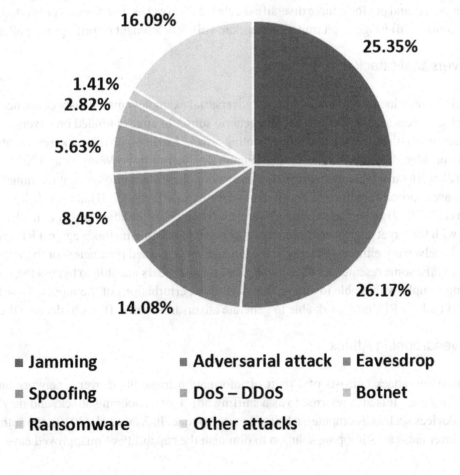

3.2.1 Jamming Attack

Jamming consists of creating interferences within radio channels. In a jamming attack, malicious nodes block legitimate communication by causing intentional perturbations. This type of attack is a subset of denial of service (DoS) attacks (Subsection 3.2.2) but, given that 25.35% of these attacks are considered in the RL-based IDS research, the related literature is reviewed independently in this section, including the solution proposed by Xiao et al. (2018a) that aims to improve mobile crowd sensing security methods, including anti-jamming transmissions. After introducing their solution, the authors propose a detailed discussion of the practical implementations of the related methods.

In Xiao et al. (2018c), the authors investigate attack models (including jamming attacks) for IoT systems and review ML-based IoT security solutions based on RL. Later, Abuzainab et al. (2019) proposed an interference-aware routing protocol to ensure robust communication against jamming. This protocol has the purpose of allowing nodes to avoid communication holes created by jamming attacks. The authors use RL to elaborate a distributed cooperation framework to assess network conditions and make real-time decisions on whether to defend the network against a jamming attack or jam other transmissions. In Sheng et al. (2018) and Min et al. (2018), an RL-based control framework is developed to prevent unauthorized unmanned aerial vehicles (UAV) from entering a target area. The challenge addressed by the authors is to accelerate the learning speed to achieve the optimal UAV control policy. This UAV control scheme enables a target estate to choose the optimal control policy to expel nearby UAVs (e.g., jamming the global positioning system signals). Wang et al. study defense strategies against DRL-based jamming attackers and put forth three diversified defense approaches, to know: (i) proportional-integral-derivative control, (ii) usage of an imitation attacker, (iii) development of orthogonal policies.

3.2.2 Adversarial Attack

ML classifiers are vulnerable to inputs (named adversarial examples) maliciously constructed by adversarial attacks. Adversarial attacks consist of a generic subset of attacks funded on adversarial examples (e.g., a strategically-timed attack and an enchanting attack, Lin et al. (2017)) and represents 26.17% of all attacks considered by the RL-based IDS (Figure 4). According to Wang et al. (2020), adversarial attacks are also effective when targeting neural network policies in reinforcement learning (Wang et al., 2020) and have exposed a significant security vulnerability in ML-models (Huang et al., 2017). Similarly, Inkawhich et al. (2019) present a new class of threat models where the adversary does not have the ability to interact with the target agent's environment, in contrast to existing methods against RL agents that assume that the adversary either has access to the target agent's learned parameters or to the environment. In parallel to this, some researchers have highlighted that intruders are able to bypass the IDS model by constructing samples vulnerable to almost imperceptible perturbations of the inputs. To solve this, Wu et al. (2019) built an RL framework able to generate adversarial traffic flows to deceive the detection.

3.2.3 Eavesdropping Attack

An eavesdropping attack consists of a theft of information transmitted over a network and concerns 14.08% of the cases. It is also referred to as a sniffing attack or a snooping attack, and may concern all connected devices such as a computer, a laptop or a cell phone. In Xiao et al. (2019), the authors develop a physical layer anti-eavesdropping solution to diminish the capability of unapproved eavesdroppers to infer information in the context of visible light communication. Therefore, the authors exploit an RL-based control scheme to discover the theoretically optimal solution of the secrecy rate and, at the same time, define the most efficient beamforming policy against attackers. In the field of internet of things (IoT), Xiao et al. (2018c) discuss the challenge of using ML-based techniques, including RL, to protect user privacy (e.g., against eavesdropping attacks, Feltus et al., 2017). In this regard, the cooperation framework previously explained in Abuzainab et al. (2019) also aims to make decisions on eavesdropping attacks using a dedicated deep RL approach. In another area, to protect wireless networks, Xie & Xiao (2016) apply prospect theory (theory based on the observation that people react differently to potential losses and potential gains - *wikipedia*) to formulate the interaction between a smart attacker and a mobile user. The first makes subjective decisions on the attack model and the second on the security mechanism layer to be applied. This allows the Nash equilibria of the static smart attack game to be derived and a defense strategy based on Q-Learning to be proposed.

3.2.4 Spoofing Attack

A spoofing attack consists of an attacker pretending to be someone else or something else in an attempt to gain the confidence of the defender. By spoofing a system, the attacker attempts to get access to defenders' systems, to steal data, or to spread malwares. This attack was the subject of consideration in 8.45% of the cases. The autopilot system of an autonomous or unmanned aerial vehicle is particularly sensitive to a spoofing attack given, for instance, the physical consequences that being hacked could imply. In Arthur (2019), the author identifies that drones need to identify their intruders and ensure their safe return to home and accordingly, he develops an RL-based adaptive IDS including a self-healing method enforced with a deep-Q network for dynamic route learning. Likewise, in Dai et al. (2018), the authors stress the fact that in vehicular ad hoc networks (VANETs), malicious on board units (OBUs) may potentially try to gain illegal access to other OBUs. To face this situation, Dai et al. propose (i) an indirect reciprocity security framework to evaluate the OBU level of dangerousness to the VANET and (ii) an RL-based action selection strategy, which allow OBUs in the VANET to select a reliable relay OBU or determine whether or not to follow the request of another source OBU.

Bezzo (2018) demonstrated the vulnerability of autonomous cyberphysical systems to cyber-attacks like sensor spoofing, and used RL techniques to determine which sensors are compromised. Therefore, he proposes a reachability-based approach and a Bayesian Inverse Reinforcement Learning technique (Elnaggar & Bezzo, 2018) to leverage the history of sensor data to assess the risk and predict the goal of attack. (Distribute) Denial of Service attack (Distributed) Denial of Service ((D)DoS) attacks concern 5.63% of the cases encountered. It is a typical cyber-attack in which the attacker tries to make the defender system services unavailable in order, mainly, to steal system information. In Zhang et al. (2019), the author analyze the resilience of cyber-physical systems to DoS and define, first, an RL method able to obtain the defense and attack policies at the cyber layer, and second, a dynamical programming method to obtain the physical layer control strategy and judge whether a cyber system is capable of protecting the underlying control system. Malialis et al. (2015) propose Multiagent Router Throttling. This approach aims to defend the system against DDoS attacks and consists of a set of RL agents installed on multiple routers. The goal of these RL agents is to learn to rate-limit or throttle traffic towards a victim server. The particularity of this approach stays in the online learning process and in the incorporation of task decomposition, team rewards and a form of reward shaping (also known as difference rewards) (Grandry et al., 2013).

3.2.5 Botnet Attack

A botnet is a set of devices connected to the internet, compromised by an attacker, which act as a force multiplier to break into the defense system. Generally, botnets are performed in the context of distributed denial of service attacks but their computing power may also be exploited (i) to send large volumes of spam, (ii) to steal large amounts of credentials, or (iii) to spy on persons and organizations. Botnet attacks are consequently addressed by the literature together with D(DoS) attacks. They represent 3.82% of the cases analyzed in this review. In Venkatesan et al. (2017), the authors observe the persistence of modern botnets when they operate in a stealthy manner over along period of time. To reduce the lifetime of stealthy botnets and identify the maximum number of bots, the authors propose an RL-based solution to dynamically and optimally deploy a limited number of defensive mechanisms within the target network, including honeypots and network-based detectors.

3.2.6 Ransomware Attack

A ransomware attack consists of the attacker encrypting important business information stored on the victim's system, and to demand the payment of a ransom in exchange (i) for the data being decrypted and (ii) for the victim regaining access to the system. Hence, ransomware is often motivated by the gain of money usually transferred from the victim to the attacker by bitcoin. This type of attack only targets 2.41% of the cases. Existing ransomware detection approaches usually exploit machine learning, which needs large amounts of data to train the model, like the Domain Generational Algorithm (DGA), a method to quickly generate domains using a mathematical algorithm. DGA has been considered by Cheng et al. (2019) as a relevant technology for detecting ransomwares. However, given the difficulty of getting enough data to train specific models in a short period of time, Cheng et al. have developed a new DGA generation model based on RL and the Long Short Time Memory (LSTM) models. First, LSTM aims to provide the advantage of being able to generate a lot of new data learnt from a short set of real DGA samples and second, reinforcement learning aims to guide the LSTM generation model to be enhanced by evaluating its newly generated domain name. This development aims to create a specific DGA trained with little data without leading to the overfitting of the detection model.

3.2.7 Other Attacks

This review of the reinforcement learning contribution to cyber-security showed that a set of other attacks are also addressed by the scientific community but at a more punctual frequency and sometimes with less validation. These attacks are:

- The bound data injection attack, that Gu et al. (2019) proposes a counter-attack with an active attack-defense model based on game theory and using an RL-based method;
- the forgetting attack, solved by a continual learning RL-based framework (Du et al., 2019);
- the selfish edge attack and the faked service record attack, countered for example, with an RL-based edge central processing unit allocation algorithm in Xiao et al. (2020) and Xiao et al. (2018b).

3.3 Attacker-Defender Game

Attacker-defender games are traditionally developed based on the game theory and aim to study and to analyze situations of interactive decision-making in the field of cyber-security, e.g., Trejo et al. (2016). In Ni & Paul (2019), the attacker-defender game is applied in the smart grid security area and the authors make the hypothesis that most of the existing works in this field only use the one-shot game without considering the dynamic process of the electric power grid. Accordingly, they propose a solution named Dynamic Game for multistage games between the attacker and the defender. This solution is built on RL techniques and aims to identify the optimal attack sequences given determined objectives. For Ni & Paul, these objectives are, e.g., the transmission line outages, the generation loss, and so forth. The principle of the dynamic game is that the attacker learns a sequence of attack actions applying to the transmission lines, although the defender protects a set of selected lines. At each iteration, first, the cascading failure is measured, and second, the line outage and/or generation loss is transmitted as feedback to the attacker, which launches the subsequent action. Aggarwal et al. (2015) analyses the dynamics of cyber-security attacks in terms of actions of attackers and actions of defenders, and investigate the function of some actions taken by the attacker and the defender in a simulated website cyber-attack scenario. Therefore, the authors consider the behavioral game theory and simulate an attacker and defender cyber-security game using an RL model. The objective of the attacker is to hack the website whereas the objective of the defender is to avoid the website to be compromised. The paper demonstrates that the attention to recent outcomes paid by the attackers and the defenders is a relevant parameter concerning the action taken. For instance, the more attention to the outcome paid by the attacker, the more plausible the attacks will be. In Shah et al. (2018), the authors use an RL-based approach to support the defender in making decisions and perform an adversarial evaluation of the latter. To achieve this evaluation, several adversarial alert generation policies were learned, as well as the most relevant response according to the policy of the defender's inspection. They conclude with the finding that the defender's policy is robust to the attacker's best response. Finally, Xiao et al. (2017) investigate the cloud-based malware detection game where application traces of the mobile devices are offloaded on security servers. The authors explains how the Nash equilibrium (NE) is derived from the static malware detection game together with the existence conditions of this NE. This first output strengthens the accuracy of the malware detection (as explained in Section 3.1). The second contribution consists of a Q-Learning based scheme malware detection dedicated to mobile devices exploited to derive the optimal offloading.

3.4 Policy Management

The security policy formalizes the rules and processes for accessing and using the organization's information system, including assets, resources, network and computing power. Defining this policy is becoming extremely challenging given the large amount of information to be considered at the same time and the heterogenic environment in which these information systems exist. In this regard, Wadhawan & Neuman (2018) addresses the elaboration of policy in smart grid, which is exposed to the problem of resource allocations. To this end, the RL-BAGS (Reinforcement Learning-Bayesian Attack Graph for Smart Grid System) tool is defined to support system engineers and to determine, at a regular frequency, the optimal SCAN or PATCH policy concerning a particular function. This tool generates a Bayesian network considering the state of the system and implements two RL algorithms, i.e., Q-Learning and SARSA learning. In the field of network slicing (NS), Chowdhury et al. (2019) observe that the most challenging tasks concern the protection of slices and that RL is an important technology to help solve security problems, especially in network slicing for 5G. Therefore, the authors elaborate the so-called "policy-gradient based model-free RL approach" in order to define and achieve optimal policy for NS considering: (i) the current values and action variables, (ii) the accomplishment of optimal solutions for security improvement, and (iii) the detection of malicious nodes within the NS for 5G. Other relevant research related to the contribution of RL technology for security policies was also highlighted during the review, such as: Zhang et al. (2020) in the field of virtual network embedding, Luong et al. (2019) in the field of communication and networking, or Tozer et al. (2015), which focuses on systems in general and proposes a method which consists of translating the system components and behavior into a multi-objective Markov decision process.

3.5 Biometric Authentication

Biometric identification takes into account all techniques potentially used to digitally identify a person to grant access to a system based on his/her physical or behavioral human characteristics. These techniques include, but are not limited to fingerprints, palm prints, facial/, iris recognition, hand signature, etc. Many of these characteristics have been addressed by deep learning networks like the convolutional neural network (CNN), e.g., Sundararajan & Woodard (2018), but the field of RL is also emerging as potential contributing technology. In Wang et al. (2017), the authors address user authentication for ecommerce transactions and focus their research on facial recognition to identify users' biometric features. They observe that facial recognition is often complicated by facial expressions being hidden and obstructed by lighting changes, thereby limiting the effectiveness of the scheme used to determine the users' identity. Consequently, Wang et al. study the facial recognition process using deep RL approaches, together with CNN, to extract, transform and compare facial features to determine the user identity. In this field of facial recognition, Norouzi et al. (2011) proposes a method for handling occlusion in faces. First, the face is partitioned into blocks and develops a sequential recognition structure. Second, RL is exploited to learn spatial attention control strategy over the blocks. In Hashemi et al. (2018), the authors use a case study of iris scanning to approximate computing in the area of biometric security. Therefore, a flow from an input camera to the iris encoding is designed so that, although it relies on intermediate approximate computational steps, it produces accurate results. According to the authors, the flow consists of a complex pipeline that overall includes eight approximation knobs at both the algorithmic and hardware levels. In this research, RL techniques, together with recurrent neural networks, are used to trade off accuracy with runtime, and to identify the optimal values for the knobs. In the same vein, Nguyen et al. (2017) discusses the evolution of the different architectures for iris recognition. Their analysis advocates that recent advances in deep RL allow the network to generate better instances and may be used to evolve CNN with the aim of generating more performant iris recognition solutions. Other human characteristic detection systems have also been improved using RL techniques, including palm print recognition. In Du et al. (2019), the authors address the "forgetting problem" associated with this type of recognition. The explanation of this problem is that, although there is a high accuracy of recognition on items from sampling datasets, the systems are not able to perform high recognition when applied in practice and when many new users' palm prints are registered in sequence. To solve this problem, a continual RL-based learning framework is proposed to dynamically expand the neural network when facing newly registered prints. This framework shows interesting results and, therefore, demonstrates its utility for countering the forgetting problem, which also occurs in other biometric systems. According to Wiering et al. (2011), RL approaches for biometrics focus mainly on classification tasks. The authors described a new RL framework to solve classification tasks modeled using Markov decision processes and the actor critical learning automaton. This framework is benchmarked with traditional support vector machine (SVM) algorithms and multi-layer perceptrons. The results demonstrate that the RL framework proposed to resolve classification tasks slightly outperforms the multi-layer perceptron and performs as well as the SVM algorithms.

3.6 Software/System Protection

Software and information systems are accessible more than ever via the internet, and are deployed without sufficient testing and for the most part, without fixing bugs before release (Bryant et al., 2017). To cope with this, software or system security has been the focus of attention of researchers and practitioners in order to develop and implement solutions against malicious attacks and other hacker risks, to prevent the software not functioning correctly. Early works in this area looked to embed Q-Learning algorithms in part of the software itself (Randrianasolo & Pyeatt, 2014). This aims to provide a security mechanism to the software so that it has the ability to learn by itself and develop temporary repair mechanisms. In Li et al. (2018), the authors explain that, due to the massive growth of applications, users, and data volumes in the network, traditional mathematical approaches can no longer be applied. For this reason, they propose performing the security Service Function Chaining (SFC) selection with the help of reinforcement learning, specifically Q-Learning. In particular, a reward function is elaborated to make a trade-off among various objectives and, the classical -greedy inspection is shaped to take multiple ranked actions for the defense of varied networks. Determining the right handling granularity of traffic flow, and handling granularity together while mitigating the risk of overloading the forwarding devices is the challenge addressed by Phan et al. (2019). Therefore, the authors propose Q-DATA, an RL-based traffic flow matching control framework that improves the monitoring of the traffic in software-defined net work and that prevents the degradation of performance of the traffic going forward. In Q-DATA, the granularity of the traffic flow is optimized using a Q-Learning approach and support vector machine algorithms are used to derive the forwarding performance status of the network switches. Equally, in Böttinger et al. (2018), the authors observe that, in order to find vulnerabilities in input-processing code, the process enforced to date consists of repeatedly testing the code with fuzzy adapted inputs. Accordingly, they propose exploiting the Markov decision processes to address this testing activity as an RL problem and apply deep Q-Learning algorithms for reward optimizing. This results in the agent learning a policy, which can afterwards generate new higher-reward inputs. Likewise, Wu et al. (2016) propose a mechanism for a security situation, which integrates game theory, analytical methods, and most of all, RL. This mechanism generates higher efficiency and a lower error rate for security situational awareness. From their side, Winterrose et al. (2016) use an RL-based solution to automatically discover and maintain desired operating postures in the security-performance space. The authors demonstrate the utility of their approach, even in the event of changes in the threat environment, and they calculate the right parameters to build the most efficient and adapted response to dynamic adversaries. RL-based approaches for software and system protection have also been envisaged for other security applications, like penetration testing in Ghanem & Chen (2018) that model the system as a partially observed Markov decision process, or Mayadunna & Rupasinghe (2018) that calculate the node trust values for social network users with a dedicated trust framework.

4. LITERATURE ANALYSIS AND DISCUSSION

The review of the literature undertaken in the previous section allows us to survey and analyze the more relevant contributions of RL-based frameworks, techniques and methodologies for the purpose of cyber-security. This analysis has already demonstrated the repartition of the various contributions through five security fields (Figure 3) and the exponential development in the production of contributions since 2019 (Figure 2). In order to frame the analysis and the discussion around these contributions, this section is structured around eight industrial areas of applications: autonomous vehicles (including the drones), information system, smart grid, cloud computing, IoT and 5G, critical infrastructure, cognitive radio, and wireless networks. This classification was decided by sorting the industrial areas addressed by each paper and by selecting and considering the most addressed areas in the classification. Of course, other areas are also impacted and considered in papers, like the blockchain (E.g., Dai et al., 2018 and Xiao et al., 2020). However, in these papers, blockchain is considered a technology to be used in parallel or as a complement to a security field in order to contribute to a specific industrial area. As a consequence, these papers (Dai et al., 2019, Dai et al., 2020, Liu et al., 2018, Liu et al., 2019a, Liu et al., 2019b and Xiao et al., 2020) are reviewed and classified with the security field they complement.

4.1 Autonomous Vehicles

The internet of vehicles, including drones, is developing rapidly (Liu et al., 2019), and necessitates a secure and reliable infrastructure to store and share the massive amount of data it uses and generates, to resolve the problem with high-dimensional and time-varying features (Dai et al., 2020), or to design a secure content caching scheme between vehicles (Dai et al., 2019). The literature related to RL-based contributions for the cyber-security of autonomous vehicles, e.g., (Arthur, 2019, Dai et al., 2019, Dai et al., 2020, Elnaggar & Bezzo, 2018, Gu et al., 2019, Liu et al., 2019a, Min et al., 2018, Sheng et al., 2018, Wu et al., 2019, and Xing et al., 2019), represents 13.7% of the total papers. Figure 5 represents the repartition of papers by security fields. Regarding autonomous vehicles, it is observed that all fields are addressed more or less equivalently. Software/system protection and the IDS are the most significant. In parallel, it is also worth noting that, amongst the types of attacks encountered, the jamming and the spoofing attacks are the ones addressed more, e.g., (Arthur, 2019, Huang et al., 2017, and Sheng et al., 2018). A jamming attack consists, for instance, of generating perturbing interferences against the global positioning system signals, and the spoofing attack, on the other hand, may consist of an attacker taking control of the vehicle, if it is an autonomous car or an unmanned aerial vehicle.

4.2 Information System

Papers addressing the information system, including the network and the servers, are the most frequent with 36.6% of the cases encountered, e.g., Chen et al., 2018, Cheng et al., 2019, Jin & Wang, 2019, Lan et al., 2013, Luong et al., 2019, Randrianasolo & Pyeatt, 2014, Tsochev et al., 2019, and Wang et al., 2020b. As shown in Figure 5, the majority of these papers address malware detection and IDS, but other fields are also considered, such as using a deep RL method for online decision-making to adjust a traffic scheduling policy considering the network security and performance (Jin & Wang, 2019). Another example proposed by Lan et al. consists of adapting the Markov decision process in order to model the adaptive control and, therefore, validate network security in a dynamic network environment (Lan et al., 2013). Yet another example is considered by Chen et al. (Chen et al., 2018), which defines a deep RL-based framework as the automated testing of certificate verification in SSL/TLS implementations. Finally, in the domain of deception technology, which consists of seeking to deceive the attackers by detecting them and defeating them, a recurring problem was the static deployment of policies. To face this, Wang et al. (2020b) used RL and designed a Q-Learning training algorithm to create an optimal policy for deploying the deception resources.

Figure 5. Percentage of papers by security fields for industrial areas

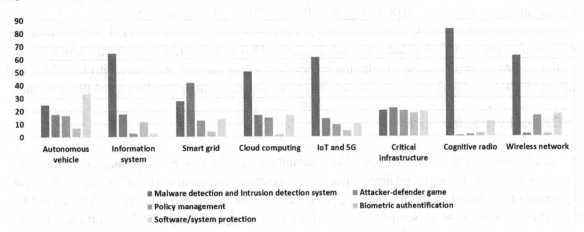

4.3 Smart Grid

Because of the rising occurrence of cyber-physical attacks, the protection of the smart grid against attackers trying to maliciously compromise the cyber-infrastructure and control the physical processes (Liu & Konstantinou, 2019c, and Wadhawan & Neuman, 2018) is gaining more and more attention. The papers dedicated to smart grid compound made up 7.% of the papers reviewed and the field of security most often addressed is the attacker-defender game, e.g., Jiang et al., 2019, and Wadhawan & Neuman, 2018. Other security topics are also considered using RL-based security, like in Jia et al. (2018) where the authors use it to calculate the probability of failure of the network service path, or in Ni et al. (2017) where the authors calculate the minimum number of attacks/actions to reach blackout threshold when an attacker only has limited topological information of the smart grid.

4.4 Cloud Computing

Like smart grid systems, cloud computing relies highly on sharing computing resources and aims to guarantee a high availability and accessibility level of the latter, thereby putting it under threat of major cyber-attacks (Ghosh et al., 2017). Cloud computing is also not the focus of attention for the majority of research work, since 6.02% address it, e.g., Ghosh et al., 2017, Xie & Xiao, 2016, and Xing et al., 2019. Moreover, as highlighted in Figure 5, malware detection and IDS are the main security fields concerned by this research while biometric authentication is rarely a field of interest. Apart from that,

RL contributions for cloud security are the target of other contributions like (Bhargavi & Babu, 2019), which proposes a novel RL-based load balancing algorithm with a so-called "raven roosting policy".

4.5 IoT and The 5G

Recent advances in the Internet of things provide a plethora of opportunities for various industries but also raise security and privacy issues (Xiao et al., 2020, and Zolotukhin & Hämäläinen, 2018). This area is addressed by 21.15% of the research so far; the security field addressing it the most (37%) is malware and intrusion detection systems. More especially, concerning techniques for detection jamming and spoofing attacks, e.g., Bezzo, 2018, Elnaggar & Bezzo, 2018, and Xiao et al. 2018c. However, RL has also tackled other security fields, like Liu et al. (2019b), which proposes a deep RL-based performance optimization framework for blockchain-enabled industrial IoT systems, Liu et al. (2018), which designs an efficient data collection and secure sharing scheme combining deep RL and Ethereum blockchain, and Liang et al. (2020), which proposes a fast deep RL-based detection algorithm for virtual IP watermarks.

4.6 Critical Infrastructure

Critical infrastructure are so called because the continuity of their operations is essential for a given nation in terms of economy, security, and health. These infrastructures represent 4.51% of the cases and Figure 5 shows that the research in this domain, e.g., Liu et al. (2019a), Liu & Konstantinou (2019c), Panfili et al. (2018), and Wadhawan & Neuman (2018), covers all security fields equally. It is worth highlighting two relevant contributions: Panfili et al. (2018), who, in the framework of the ATENA European project, try to define the optimal security configuration by finding the Nash equilibrium of an attack/defense game and Liu & Konstantinou (2019c), who solve a Markov decision process by developing an online reinforcement Q-Learning scheme to model adversarial actions.

4.7 Cognitive Radio

Cognitive radio is defined as the next-generation of wireless communication networks (Koh & Yau, 2014). It aims to exploit underutilized licenses to enhance the quality and efficiency of the radio spectrum, but consequently, it is prone to random attackers, as explained by Singh & Trivedi (2012). It only concerns 1.14% of the cases and the RL-based security contribution is mainly the malware detection (Koh & Yau, 2014, Ling et al., 2015, Singh & Trivedi, 2012, and Yau et al., 2011). Most of the research aims to highlight the added value of RL for this area without proposing complete and sound results at this time.

4.8 Wireless Network

Wireless networks are a type of network from the information system where malicious end-users potentially launch smart attacks (Koh & Yau, 2014, Luong et al., 2019, and Xie & Xiao, 2016).Wireless networks make up 6.85% of the cases. The RL contribution to securing these networks is essentially the field of malware detection, mostly for attacks such as jamming and eavesdropping (Xie & Xiao, 2016).

5. CONCLUSION AND FUTURE WORKS

In this paper, we have systematically reviewed RL-based cybersecurity of distributed system literature in order to answer three knowledge questions. The literature review has followed the method proposed in Petersen et al. (2015) with the aim to review the impact of RL depicted in Feltus (2020) to the industrial fields. After applying filters to the most relevant databases, 312 papers have appeared relevant for scrutiny. The most important findings are that Reinforcement Learning-based contributions to cyber-security, in terms of scientific publications, have been increasing exponentially for the last two years (Figure 2). This literature is spread over five security fields, with the most important two being malware/intrusion detection (38.96%) and the attacker/defender game (31.17%). In terms of types of attacks faced by the IDS, jamming and adversarial attacks are the most frequently addressed, especially in the areas of IoT and 5G, wireless networks and autonomous vehicles, which makes sense, based on the growing interest of these areas and the potential impact of successful attacks. Concerning the industrial areas impacted by the RL-based security contribution, eight of them have emerged from the review and according to the evolution of the publication rate over time, the more important areas are the information system (36.57%), IoT and 5G (23.47%), and autonomous vehicles (13.71%). Other areas also occasionally emerge, like the security of satellite communications but very few papers address them, like Rath & Mishra (2020).

All along the article, the analysis has been structured following the analytic framework presented in section 2. This framework seems to be appropriate to understand the intricacies of RL contributions to cybersecurity. However, according to ADR (Sein et al., 2011), additional iterations are necessary to improve, to refine and to validate the framework. As future works, we foresee improving the framework in other fields of AI like the GAN or the RNN/LSTM.

REFERENCES

Abuzainab, N., Erpek, T., Davaslioglu, K., Sagduyu, Y. E., Shi, Y., Mackey, S. J., Patel, M., Panettieri, F., Qureshi, M. A., Isler, V., & Yener, A. (2019, November). QoS and jamming-aware wireless networking using deep reinforcement learning. In MILCOM 2019-2019 IEEE Military Communications Conference (MILCOM) (pp. 610-615). IEEE. doi:10.1109/MILCOM47813.2019.9020985

Aggarwal, P., Maqbool, Z., Grover, A., Pammi, V. C., Singh, S., & Dutt, V. (2015, June). Cyber security: A game-theoretic analysis of defender and attacker strategies in defacing-website games. In *2015 International Conference on Cyber Situational Awareness, Data Analytics and Assessment (CyberSA)* (pp. 1-8). IEEE. 10.1109/CyberSA.2015.7166127

Arthur, M. P. (2019, August). Detecting Signal Spoofing and Jamming Attacks in UAV Networks using a Lightweight IDS. In *2019 International Conference on Computer, Information and Telecommunication Systems (CITS)* (pp. 1-5). IEEE. 10.1109/CITS.2019.8862148

Band, I., Engelsman, W., Feltus, C., Paredes, S. G., & Diligens, D. (2015). *Modeling enterprise risk management and security with the archimate*. Language, The Open Group.

Bezzo, N. (2018, April). Predicting malicious intention in CPS under cyber-attack. In *2018 ACM/IEEE 9th International Conference on Cyber-Physical Systems (ICCPS)* (pp. 351-352). IEEE. 10.1109/IC-CPS.2018.00049

Bhargavi, K., & Babu, B. S. (2019, December). Load Balancing Scheme for the Public Cloud using Reinforcement Learning with Raven Roosting Optimization Policy (RROP). In *2019 4th International Conference on Computational Systems and Information Technology for Sustainable Solution (CSITSS)* (Vol. 4, pp. 1-6). IEEE.

Böttinger, K., Godefroid, P., & Singh, R. (2018, May). Deep reinforcement fuzzing. In 2018 IEEE Security and Privacy Workshops (SPW) (pp. 116-122). IEEE. doi:10.1109/SPW.2018.00026

Bryant, A. R., Mills, R. F., & Lopez, J., Jr. (2017). *12th International Conference on Cyber Warfare and Security ICCWS 2017*. Academic Press.

Chen, C., Diao, W., Zeng, Y., Guo, S., & Hu, C. (2018, September). DRLgencert: Deep learning-based automated testing of certificate verification in SSL/TLS implementations. In *2018 IEEE International Conference on Software Maintenance and Evolution (ICSME)* (pp. 48-58). IEEE. 10.1109/ICSME.2018.00014

Cheng, H., Fang, Y., Chen, L., & Cai, J. (2019, October). Detecting Domain Generation Algorithms Based on Reinforcement Learning. In *2019 International Conference on Cyber-Enabled Distributed Computing and Knowledge Discovery (CyberC)* (pp. 261-264). IEEE. 10.1109/CyberC.2019.00051

Chowdhury, M. Z., Hossan, M. T., & Jang, Y. M. (2019, May). Applying Model-Free Reinforcement Learning Algorithm in Network Slicing for 5G. In *2019 1st International Conference on Advances in Science, Engineering and Robotics Technology (ICASERT)* (pp. 1-4). IEEE.

Dai, C., Xiao, X., Ding, Y., Xiao, L., Tang, Y., & Zhou, S. (2018, December). Learning based security for VANET with blockchain. In *2018 IEEE International Conference on Communication Systems (ICCS)* (pp. 210-215). IEEE. 10.1109/ICCS.2018.8689228

Dai, Y., Xu, D., Zhang, K., Maharjan, S., & Zhang, Y. (2019, October). Permissioned Blockchain and Deep Reinforcement Learning for Content Caching in Vehicular Edge Computing and Networks. In *2019 11th International Conference on Wireless Communications and Signal Processing (WCSP)*(pp. 1-6). IEEE. 10.1109/WCSP.2019.8928099

Dai, Y., Xu, D., Zhang, K., Maharjan, S., & Zhang, Y. (2020). Deep reinforcement learning and permissioned blockchain for content caching in vehicular edge computing and networks. *IEEE Transactions on Vehicular Technology*, 69(4), 4312–4324. doi:10.1109/TVT.2020.2973705

Du, X., Zhong, D., & Shao, H. (2019, September). Continual Palmprint Recognition Without Forgetting. In *2019 IEEE International Conference on Image Processing (ICIP)* (pp. 1158-1162). IEEE. 10.1109/ICIP.2019.8803748

Elnaggar, M., & Bezzo, N. (2018, June). An IRL approach for cyber-physical attack intention prediction and recovery. In *2018 Annual American Control Conference (ACC)* (pp. 222-227). IEEE. 10.23919/ACC.2018.8430922

Feltus, C. (2020). Current and Future RL's Contribution to Emerging Network Security. In: *7th International Symposium on Emerging Information, Communication and Networks (EICN 2020)*.

Feltus, C., Grandry, E., Kupper, T., & Colin, J. N. (2017, February). Model-driven Approach for Privacy Management in Business Ecosystem. In MODELSWARD (pp. 392-400). doi:10.5220/0006142203920400

Feltus, C., Khadraoui, D., De Remont, B., & Rifaut, A. (2007). Business governance based policy regulation for security incident response. *Proceedings of the International Conference on Risks and Security of Internet and Systems (CRiSIS'2007)*

Feltus, C., Petit, M., & Dubois, E. (2009, November). Strengthening employee's responsibility to enhance governance of IT: COBIT RACI chart case study. In *Proceedings of the first ACM workshop on Information security governance* (pp. 23-32). 10.1145/1655168.1655174

Ghanem, M. C., & Chen, T. M. (2018, October). Reinforcement learning for intelligent penetration testing. In *2018 Second World Conference on Smart Trends in Systems, Security and Sustainability (WorldS4)* (pp. 185-192). IEEE. 10.1109/WorldS4.2018.8611595

Ghosh, P., Bardhan, M., Chowdhury, N. R., & Phadikar, S. (2017). IDS using reinforcement learning Automata for Preserving security in cloud environment. *International Journal of Information System Modeling and Design*, 8(4), 21–37. doi:10.4018/IJISMD.2017100102

Grandry, E., Feltus, C., & Dubois, E. (2013, September). Conceptual integration of enterprise architecture management and security risk management. In *2013 17th IEEE International Enterprise Distributed Object Computing Conference Workshops* (pp. 114-123). IEEE. 10.1109/EDOCW.2013.19

Gu, Z., An, Y., Tan, F., Li, Y., & Zheng, S. (2019, December). A Game Theory Approach to Attack-Defense Strategy for Perception of Connected Vehicles. In *2019 IEEE Symposium Series on Computational Intelligence (SSCI)* (pp. 2587-2594). IEEE. 10.1109/SSCI44817.2019.9002791

Hashemi, S., Tann, H., Buttafuoco, F., & Reda, S. (2018, March). Approximate computing for biometric security systems: A case study on iris scanning. In 2018 Design, Automation & Test in Europe Conference & Exhibition (DATE)(pp. 319-324). IEEE. doi:10.23919/DATE.2018.8342029

Huang, S., Papernot, N., Goodfellow, I., Duan, Y., & Abbeel, P. (2017). *Adversarial attacks on neural network policies.* arXiv preprint arXiv:1702.02284

Inkawhich, M., Chen, Y., & Li, H. (2019). *Snooping Attacks on Deep Reinforcement Learning.* arXiv preprint arXiv:1905.11832

Jia, H., Gai, Y., & Zheng, H. (2018, December). Network Recovery for Large-scale Failures in Smart Grid by Reinforcement Learning. In *2018 IEEE 4th International Conference on Computer and Communications (ICCC)* (pp. 2658-2663). IEEE. 10.1109/CompComm.2018.8780720

Jiang, H., Wang, Z., & He, H. (2019, December). An Evolutionary Computation Approach for Smart Grid Cascading Failure Vulnerability Analysis. In *2019 IEEE Symposium Series on Computational Intelligence (SSCI)* (pp. 332-338). IEEE. 10.1109/SSCI44817.2019.9002979

Jin, Q., & Wang, L. (2019, July). Intranet User-Level Security Traffic Management with Deep Reinforcement Learning. In *2019 International Joint Conference on Neural Networks (IJCNN)* (pp. 1-8). IEEE. 10.1109/IJCNN.2019.8852447

Koh, C. W. K., & Yau, K. L. (2014). *Trust and reputation scheme for clustering in cognitive radio networks.* Academic Press.

Lan, F., Chunlei, W., Qing, M., & Li, L. (2013, November). Dynamically validate network security based on adaptive control theory. In *2013 International Conference on Information and Network Security (ICINS 2013)* (pp. 1-6). IET.

Li, G., Zhou, H., Feng, B., Li, G., & Yu, S. (2018, December). Automatic selection of security service function chaining using reinforcement learning. In 2018 IEEE Globecom Workshops (GC Wkshps) (pp. 1-6). IEEE. doi:10.1109/GLOCOMW.2018.8644122

Liang, W., Huang, W., Long, J., Zhang, K., Li, K. C., & Zhang, D. (2020). *Deep reinforcement learning for resource protection and real-time detection in IoT environment. IEEE Internet of Things Journal.* doi:10.1109/JIOT.2020.2974281

Lin, Y. C., Hong, Z. W., Liao, Y. H., Shih, M. L., Liu, M. Y., & Sun, M. (2017). *Tactics of adversarial attack on deep reinforcement learning agents.* arXiv preprint arXiv:1703.06748

Ling, M. H., Yau, K. L. A., Qadir, J., Poh, G. S., & Ni, Q. (2015). Application of reinforcement learning for security enhancement in cognitive radio networks. *Applied Soft Computing*, *37*, 809–829. doi:10.1016/j.asoc.2015.09.017

Liu, C. H., Lin, Q., & Wen, S. (2018). Blockchain-enabled data collection and sharing for industrial IoT with deep reinforcement learning. *IEEE Transactions on Industrial Informatics*, *15*(6), 3516–3526. doi:10.1109/TII.2018.2890203

Liu, M., Teng, Y., Yu, F. R., Leung, V. C., & Song, M. (2019a, May). Deep reinforcement learning based performance optimization in blockchain-enabled internet of vehicle. In *ICC 2019-2019 IEEE International Conference on Communications (ICC)* (pp. 1-6). IEEE. 10.1109/ICC.2019.8761206

Liu, M., Yu, F. R., Teng, Y., Leung, V. C., & Song, M. (2019b). Performance optimization for blockchain-enabled industrial Internet of Things (IIoT) systems: A deep reinforcement learning approach. *IEEE Transactions on Industrial Informatics*, *15*(6), 3559–3570. doi:10.1109/TII.2019.2897805

Liu, X., & Konstantinou, C. (2019c, June). *Reinforcement learning for cyber-physical security assessment of power systems. In 2019 IEEE Milan PowerTech.* IEEE.

Luong, N. C., Hoang, D. T., Gong, S., Niyato, D., Wang, P., Liang, Y. C., & Kim, D. I. (2019). Applications of deep reinforcement learning in communications and networking: A survey. *IEEE Communications Surveys and Tutorials*, *21*(4), 3133–3174. doi:10.1109/COMST.2019.2916583

Malialis, K., Devlin, S., & Kudenko, D. (2015). Distributed reinforcement learning for adaptive and robust network intrusion response. *Connection Science*, *27*(3), 234–252. doi:10.1080/09540091.2015.1031082

Mayadunna, H., & Rupasinghe, L. (2018, October). A Trust Evaluation Model for Online Social Networks. In *2018 National Information Technology Conference (NITC)* (pp. 1-6). IEEE.

Mayer, N., Grandry, E., Feltus, C., & Goettelmann, E. (2015, June). Towards the ENTRI framework: security risk management enhanced by the use of enterprise architectures. In *International Conference on Advanced Information Systems Engineering* (pp. 459-469). Springer. 10.1007/978-3-319-19243-7_42

Melo. (2001). *Convergence of Q-learning: A simple proof.* Institute of Systems and Robotics, Tech. Rep (2001), 1–4. doi:10.1109/NITC.2018.8550080

Min, M., Xiao, L., Xu, D., Huang, L., & Peng, M. (2018, June). Learning-based defense against malicious unmanned aerial vehicles. In *2018 IEEE 87th Vehicular Technology Conference (VTC Spring)* (pp. 1-5). IEEE. 10.1109/VTCSpring.2018.8417685

Navarro-Lara, J., Deruyver, A., & Parrend, P. (2016, December). Morwilog: an ACO-based system for outlining multi-step attacks. In *2016 IEEE Symposium Series on Computational Intelligence (SSCI)* (pp. 1-8). IEEE. 10.1109/SSCI.2016.7849902

Nguyen, K., Fookes, C., Ross, A., & Sridharan, S. (2017). Iris recognition with off-the-shelf CNN features: A deep learning perspective. *IEEE Access : Practical Innovations, Open Solutions, 6*, 18848–18855. doi:10.1109/ACCESS.2017.2784352

Ni, Z., & Paul, S. (2019). A multistage game in smart grid security: A reinforcement learning solution. *IEEE Transactions on Neural Networks and Learning Systems, 30*(9), 2684–2695. doi:10.1109/TNNLS.2018.2885530 PMID:30624227

Ni, Z., Paul, S., Zhong, X., & Wei, Q. (2017, November). A reinforcement learning approach for sequential decision-making process of attacks in smart grid. In *2017 IEEE Symposium Series on Computational Intelligence (SSCI)* (pp. 1-8). IEEE. 10.1109/SSCI.2017.8285291

Norouzi, E., Ahmadabadi, M. N., & Araabi, B. N. (2011). Attention control with reinforcement learning for face recognition under partial occlusion. *Machine Vision and Applications, 22*(2), 337–348. doi:10.100700138-009-0235-6

Otoum, S., Kantarci, B., & Mouftah, H. (2019, May). Empowering reinforcement learning on big sensed data for intrusion detection. In Icc 2019-2019 IEEE international conference on communications (ICC) (pp. 1-7). IEEE. doi:10.1109/ICC.2019.8761575

Panfili, M., Giuseppi, A., Fiaschetti, A., Al-Jibreen, H. B., Pietrabissa, A., & Priscoli, F. D. (2018, June). A game-theoretical approach to cyber-security of critical infrastructures based on multi-agent reinforcement learning. In *2018 26th Mediterranean Conference on Control and Automation (MED)* (pp. 460-465). IEEE. 10.1109/MED.2018.8442695

Petersen, K., Vakkalanka, S., & Kuzniarz, L. (2015). Guidelines for conducting systematic mapping studies in software engineering: An update. *Information and Software Technology, 64*, 1–18. doi:10.1016/j.infsof.2015.03.007

Phan, T. V., Islam, S. T., Nguyen, T. G., & Bauschert, T. (2019, October). Q-DATA: Enhanced Traffic Flow Monitoring in Software-Defined Networks applying Q-learning. In *2019 15th International Conference on Network and Service Management (CNSM)* (pp. 1-9). IEEE.

Randrianasolo, A. S., & Pyeatt, L. D. (2014, December). Q-learning: From computer network security to software security. In *2014 13th International Conference on Machine Learning and Applications* (pp. 257-262). IEEE.

Rath, M., & Mishra, S. (2020). Security Approaches in Machine Learning for Satellite Communication. In *Machine Learning and Data Mining in Aerospace Technology* (pp. 189–204). Springer. doi:10.1007/978-3-030-20212-5_10

Sein, M. K., Henfridsson, O., Purao, S., Rossi, M., & Lindgren, R. (2011). Action design research. *Management Information Systems Quarterly*, *35*(1), 37–56. doi:10.2307/23043488

Shah, A., Sinha, A., Ganesan, R., Jajodia, S., & Cam, H. (2018). *Two Can Play That Game: An Adversarial Evaluation of a Cyber-alert Inspection System.* arXiv preprint arXiv:1810.05921

Sheng, G., Min, M., Xiao, L., & Liu, S. (2018). *Reinforcement Learning-Based Control for Unmanned Aerial Vehicles.* Academic Press.

Singh, S., & Trivedi, A. (2012, September). Anti-jamming in cognitive radio networks using reinforcement learning algorithms. In *2012 Ninth International Conference on Wireless and Optical Communications Networks (WOCN)* (pp. 1-5). IEEE. 10.1109/WOCN.2012.6331885

Sreekesh, M. (2016, March). A two-tier network based intrusion detection system architecture using machine learning approach. In *2016 International Conference on Electrical, Electronics, and Optimization Techniques (ICEEOT)* (pp. 42-47). IEEE.

Sundararajan, K., & Woodard, D. L. (2018). Deep learning for biometrics: A survey. *ACM Computing Surveys*, *51*(3), 1–34. doi:10.1145/3190618

Tozer, B., Mazzuchi, T., & Sarkani, S. (2015, December). Optimizing attack surface and configuration diversity using multi-objective reinforcement learning. In *2015 IEEE 14th international conference on machine learning and applications (icmla)* (pp. 144-149). IEEE. 10.1109/ICMLA.2015.144

Trejo, K. K., Clempner, J. B., & Poznyak, A. S. (2016, December). Adapting strategies to dynamic environments in controllable Stackelberg security games. In *2016 IEEE 55th Conference on Decision and Control (CDC)* (pp. 5484-5489). IEEE. 10.1109/CDC.2016.7799111

Tsochev, G., Trifonov, R., Yoshinov, R., Manolov, S., & Pavlova, G. (2019, September). Improving the Efficiency of IDPS by using Hybrid Methods from Artificial Intelligence. In *2019 International Conference on Information Technologies (InfoTech)* (pp. 1-4). IEEE. 10.1109/InfoTech.2019.8860895

Van Otterlo, M., & Wiering, M. (2012). Reinforcement learning and markov decision processes. In *Reinforcement Learning* (pp. 3–42). Springer. doi:10.1007/978-3-642-27645-3_1

Venkatesan, S., Albanese, M., Shah, A., Ganesan, R., & Jajodia, S. (2017, October). Detecting stealthy botnets in a resource-constrained environment using reinforcement learning. In *Proceedings of the 2017 Workshop on Moving Target Defense* (pp. 75-85). 10.1145/3140549.3140552

Wadhawan, Y., & Neuman, C. (2018, May). RL-BAGS: A tool for smart grid risk assessment. In *2018 International Conference on Smart Grid and Clean Energy Technologies (ICSGCE)* (pp. 7-14). IEEE. 10.1109/ICSGCE.2018.8556775

Wang, F., Zhong, C., Gursoy, M. C., & Velipasalar, S. (2020a, March). Defense Strategies Against Adversarial Jamming Attacks via Deep Reinforcement Learning. In *2020 54th Annual Conference on Information Sciences and Systems (CISS)* (pp. 1-6). IEEE.

Wang, P., Lin, W. H., Chao, K. M., & Lo, C. C. (2017, November). A face-recognition approach using deep reinforcement learning approach for user authentication. In *2017 IEEE 14th International Conference on e-Business Engineering (ICEBE)* (pp. 183-188). IEEE. 10.1109/ICEBE.2017.36

Wang, S., Pei, Q., Wang, J., Tang, G., Zhang, Y., & Liu, X. (2020b). An Intelligent Deployment Policy for Deception Resources Based on Reinforcement Learning. *IEEE Access : Practical Innovations, Open Solutions, 8*, 35792–35804. doi:10.1109/ACCESS.2020.2974786

Wiering, M. A., van Hasselt, H., Pietersma, A. D., & Schomaker, L. (2011, April). Reinforcement learning algorithms for solving classification problems. In *2011 IEEE Symposium on Adaptive Dynamic Programming and Reinforcement Learning (ADPRL)* (pp. 91-96). IEEE. 10.1109/ADPRL.2011.5967372

Winterrose, M. L., Carter, K. M., Wagner, N., & Streilein, W. W. (2016, June). Balancing security and performance for agility in dynamic threat environments. In *2016 46th Annual IEEE/IFIP International Conference on Dependable Systems and Networks (DSN)* (pp. 607-617). IEEE. 10.1109/DSN.2016.61

Wu, D., Fang, B., Wang, J., Liu, Q., & Cui, X. (2019, May). Evading machine learning botnet detection models via deep reinforcement learning. In *ICC 2019-2019 IEEE International Conference on Communications (ICC)* (pp. 1-6). IEEE. 10.1109/ICC.2019.8761337

Wu, J., Ota, K., Dong, M., Li, J., & Wang, H. (2016). Big data analysis-based security situational awareness for smart grid. *IEEE Transactions on Big Data, 4*(3), 408–417. doi:10.1109/TBDATA.2016.2616146

Xiao, L., Ding, Y., Jiang, D., Huang, J., Wang, D., Li, J., & Poor, H. V. (2020). A Reinforcement Learning and Blockchain-based Trust Mechanism for Edge Networks. *IEEE Transactions on Communications, 68*(9), 5460–5470. doi:10.1109/TCOMM.2020.2995371

Xiao, L., Jiang, D., Xu, D., Su, W., An, N., & Wang, D. (2018a). Secure mobile crowdsensing based on deep learning. *China Communications, 15*(10), 1–11. doi:10.1109/CC.2018.8485464

Xiao, L., Li, Y., Huang, X., & Du, X. (2017). Cloud-based malware detection game for mobile devices with offloading. *IEEE Transactions on Mobile Computing, 16*(10), 2742–2750. doi:10.1109/TMC.2017.2687918

Xiao, L., Sheng, G., Liu, S., Dai, H., Peng, M., & Song, J. (2019). Deep reinforcement learning-enabled secure visible light communication against eavesdropping. *IEEE Transactions on Communications, 67*(10), 6994–7005. doi:10.1109/TCOMM.2019.2930247

Xiao, L., Wan, X., Dai, C., Du, X., Chen, X., & Guizani, M. (2018b). Security in mobile edge caching with reinforcement learning. *IEEE Wireless Communications, 25*(3), 116–122. doi:10.1109/MWC.2018.1700291

Xiao, L., Wan, X., Lu, X., Zhang, Y., & Wu, D. (2018c). IoT security techniques based on machine learning: How do IoT devices use AI to enhance security? *IEEE Signal Processing Magazine, 35*(5), 41–49. doi:10.1109/MSP.2018.2825478

Xie, C., & Xiao, L. (2016, October). User-centric view of smart attacks in wireless networks. In *2016 IEEE International Conference on Ubiquitous Wireless Broadband (ICUWB)* (pp. 1-6). IEEE. 10.1109/ICUWB.2016.7790439

Xing, R., Su, Z., Zhang, N., Peng, Y., Pu, H., & Luo, J. (2019). Trust-evaluation-based intrusion detection and reinforcement learning in autonomous driving. *IEEE Network, 33*(5), 54–60. doi:10.1109/MNET.001.1800535

Yau, K. L. A., Komisarczuk, P., Poh, G. S., & Martin, K. M. (2011, November). On security vulnerabilities and mitigation in the cognition cycle of distributed Cognitive Radio Networks. In *7th International Conference on Broadband Communications and Biomedical Applications* (pp. 132-137). IEEE. 10.1109/IB2Com.2011.6217907

Zhang, P., Wang, C., Jiang, C., & Benslimane, A. (2020). Security-Aware Virtual Network Embedding Algorithm based on Reinforcement Learning. *IEEE Transactions on Network Science and Engineering*.

Zhang, P., Yuan, Y., Wang, Z., & Sun, C. (2019, July). A Hierarchical Game Approach to the Coupled Resilient Control of CPS against Denial-of-Service Attack. In *2019 IEEE 15th International Conference on Control and Automation (ICCA)* (pp. 15-20). IEEE. 10.1109/ICCA.2019.8899933

Zolotukhin, M., & Hämäläinen, T. (2018, November). On Artificial Intelligent Malware Tolerant Networking for IoT. In *2018 IEEE Conference on Network Function Virtualization and Software Defined Networks (NFV-SDN)* (pp. 1-6). IEEE. 10.1109/NFV-SDN.2018.8725767

This research was previously published in the International Journal of Distributed Artificial Intelligence (IJDAI), 12(2); pages 35-55, copyright year 2020 by IGI Publishing (an imprint of IGI Global).

Chapter 26
SEF4CPSIoT Software Engineering Framework for Cyber–Physical and IoT Systems

Muthu Ramachandran

iD https://orcid.org/0000-0002-5303-3100

Leeds Beckett University, UK

ABSTRACT

Cyber-physical systems (CPS) have emerged to address the need for more efficient integration of modern advancement in cyber and wireless communications technologies such as 5G with physical objects. In addition, CPSs systems also needed to efficient control of security and privacy when we compare them with internet of things (IoT). In recent years, we experienced lack of security concerns with smart home IoT applications such as home security camera, etc. Therefore, this paper proposes a systematic software engineering framework for CPS and IoT systems. This paper also proposed a comprehensive requirements engineering framework for CPS-IoT applications which can also be specified using BPMN modelling and simulation to verify and validate CPS-IoT requirements with smart contracts. In this context, one of the key contribution of this paper is the innovative and generic requirements classification model for CPS-IoT application services, and this can also be applied to other emerging technologies such as fog, edge, cloud, and blockchain computing.

INTRODUCTION

Cyber-Physical Systems (CPS) and the Internet of Things (IoT) is on the rapid increase as the demand for such applications is growing exponentially. There is a very strong reason for connecting three technologies such as CPS, IoT, and Cloud as the first two are connected to a cloud for receiving and analysing data. Cloud computing has emerged to provide a more cost-effective solution to businesses and services while making use of inexpensive computing solutions that combines pervasive, Internet, and virtualisation technologies. Cloud computing has spread to catch up with another technological evolution as we have witnessed Internet technology which has revolutionised communication and information superhighway.

DOI: 10.4018/978-1-6684-7132-6.ch026

Cloud computing is emerging rapidly and software as a service paradigm is increasing its demand for more services. However, this new trend needs to be more systematic with respect to developing secure software engineering and its related processes such as requirements, design, development, and test. For example, current challenges that are faced with cybersecurity are: application security flaws and lessons learned which can all be applied when developing applications for CPS and IoT systems. Similarly, as the demand for cloud services increases and so increased importance sought for security and privacy. Cloud service providers such as Microsoft, Google, Salesforce.com, Amazon, GoGrid are able to leverage cloud technology with a pay-per-use business model with on-demand elasticity by which resources can be expanded or shortened based on service requirements. CPS and IoT combined have great potential to evolve new applications such as smart homes, smart cities, smart roads, smart transports, smart grids, etc. Let us take, smart home which can connect several devices such as smart home security cameras, smart home monitoring systems with machine learning to predict abnormalities, smart detection sensors to detect movement in the house when you are away, smart speakers such as Alexa, Google Home, and Siri, smartphone apps connected to home energy supply, smart kitchen utensils such as smart fridge, smart dishwasher, smart oven, smart heating systems, smart radiator valve, etc. However, existing work on smart home applications by Varghese & Hayajneh (2018), Hu, Yang, Lin, & Wang (2020), & Yassein, Hmeidi, Shatnawi, Mardini, & Khamayseh (2019) reported that "the current security mechanisms are insufficient as developer mistakes cannot be effectively detected and notified due to lack of applying systematic software development principles".

There are varying definitions and understanding of these two terms found in the literature as follows: Alur (2015) defines CPS as:

A CPS system is defined as a system consists of computing devices communicating with one another and interacting with the physical world via sensors and actuators. Examples of such systems include smart buildings to medical devices to automobiles.

Whereas (Lin, 2017) defines a CPS system as the interactions between cyber (means sensing, computing, and communicating using current technologies such as Bluetooth, Wifi, etc.) and physical components and also aims to monitor and control the physical components (external world).

McEwen and Cassimally (2014) defines IoT as:

An IoT system consists of any physical objects contains controllers, sensors, and actuators that are connected with the Internet. Examples of such systems include any devices capable of sending and receiving data through the internet such as internet-enabled washing machines, dishwashers, etc.

Whereas (Lin, 2017) defined IoT as a networking infrastructure to connect a massive number of smart devices and to monitor and control devices and IoT forms a horizontal layer support for a vertical layers of CPS connecting a range of applications such as smart city services requires smart transportation, smart energy, smart weather forecasting, smart grid, and smart government councils, etc.

In addition, (Ray, 2018) provides a more systematic review of IoT architectures consisting of components of IoT devices such as connectivity, memory interfaces, processor, graphics, audio and video interfaces, storage interfaces, and i/o interfaces (sensors, actuators, etc.) and also discusses Gartner's prediction of 25 billion devices will be connected to the internet by 2020 which is the current year and it has been a true prediction and still continue to grow rapidly.

Since all CPS and IoT devices are connected via various communication channels and are streaming data enormously to a cloud which enforces the use of big data analytics platforms to analyse to make decisions on smart applications. In this context, (Ahmed et al., 2017) discuss the convergence of big data, analytics techniques, and the role of big data analytics in IoT applications as it streams huge volumes of data.

Likewise, (Faisal, Abdullah, & Sajjan, 2018) propose five layers architecture model for IoT devices such as perception layer (lowest) which provides support for QR, RFID, and wearables devices, followed by Network Layer which provides support for EPC, IPv6, ZigBee, Z-Wave, IPSec, and RPL, followed by Middleware Layer which provides support for CoAP, MQTT, supporting Fog and Cloud, service discovery module by mDNS, Physical Web, and the layer above is the Application layer which provides support for shipments tracking, smart grids, smart homes, smart transport, and smart cities, and the layer above is known as a Business layer which supports SensorML, and Big Data Analytics Platforms such as Apache Spark.

In other words, IoT can also be defined as the network of physical objects or things that are built or embedded with sensors, actuators, software, and connect via the internet which enables these objects to collect and exchange data. Their difference between the CPS and IoT needs to be clarified as the applications being deployed over the years. First of all, let us look at a precursor is known as Embedded systems which have been successfully deployed in wider areas such as aerospace, manufacturing, chemical processes, civil infrastructures, etc. The key difference between the CPS and Embedded system is the inter-connectivity of these networked physical objects whereas IoT often not embedded but interact with physical world objects. A wireless sensor network can be mounted around a river to receive and exchange data amongst them to calculate any abnormal level of river overflow to avoid any natural disasters in the region. Therefore, the security of the CPS and IoT systems are paramount to our research as well as their data has been secured.

Currently, security-related flaws are being found on a daily basis that are fixed by adding security patches. This is simply an unacceptable paradigm for the sustainability of cloud computing. Therefore, we need to develop and build cloud services with build-in security of services (SaaS, PaaS, IaaS), data centers, and cloud servers. The key technical challenges are security and privacy in handling large scale smart applications.

In this context, one of the main purposes of this study is to identify a systematic framework that supports software engineering principles that have been successful for the past fifty years or so and to customize them for the emerging technologies and applications of 'Things'. This article aims to articulate a key set of research problems and questions that need to be addressed and requires further research in this area. The research methodology used for this study is the quantitative and experimental method using BPMN modelling and simulation to validate and verify the proposed requirements engineering framework and a reference architecture for CPS-IoT applications.

This article aims to provide a number of techniques and methods for developing cloud services systematically with build-in security. It will also cover a range of system security engineering techniques that have been adopted as part of a cloud development process. A number of examples of scenarios have chosen from Amazon EC2, to illustrate with, emerging cloud system security engineering principles and paradigm (Ramachandran, 2013 & 2014). This real-world case study has been used to demonstrate the best practices on business process modelling and component-based design for developing cloud services with Build Security In (BSI). BSI techniques, strategies, and processes presented in this article are general systems security principles and are applicable both in a cloud environment and a traditional environment (non-cloud environment). The significant contribution of this research is to illustrate the application of the extended system security method known as SysSQUARE to elicit security requirements, to identify security threats of data as well as integrating build-in security techniques by modelling and simulating business processes upfront in the systems development life cycle.

This article contributes to the foundations of CPS and IoT and how together is needed for large scale secure applications such as smart cities, smart homes, smart transportation, smart health, smart e-Gov, and smart living. However, smart applications need to address the issues of security and privacy with a systematic approach to creating sustainable smart applications that pose a high level of personal and private data such as smart health and smart living. In particular, this paper makes a significant contribution to secure software engineering framework for CPS and IoT driven applications. This paper structured out into five sections: Section 1 Introduction provides the key definitions and terms used in CPS and IoT; Section 2 provides a background literature survey on CPS-IoT architecture and applications and critical evaluation of the approaches; Section 3 provides a secure software engineering framework for CPS and IoT applications; Section 4 proposes an integrated approach to secure service development paradigm and also provides a service component model for CPS and IoT applications, and final Section 5 provides future research directions.

BACKGROUND

Legacy applications have complex interconnections and are connectionless. For example, a sales manager needed to access a real-time stack on the mainframe applications when travelling requires migrating to SOA. IoT (Internet of Things) has emerged to address the need for connectivity and seamless integration with other devices. However, there are potential challenges ahead of meeting the growing need for IoT based applications. This includes design and implementation challenges, various applications and connectivities such as smart objects and wireless sensor networks, data gathering, storing and analyzing in a cloud-based solution, and IoT Security and Privacy issues. Piayre and Seong (2013) discuss an IoT application for a wireless sensor network that is useful in emergency response systems. In addition, CPS systems have a much bigger impact on connected devices, therefore, it is important to understand the clear distinction between these two systems. Table 1 provides features against CPS and IoT systems which considers computational capacity, processing speed, storage capacity, multiple sensor capacity, multiple communication capabilities, mobility, distribution capability, programming, and architectural model that is suitable and secured.

As shown in Table 1 features such as there are high computational capacities and processing speed discovered in CPS than in IoT devices. There is also a high storage capacity discovered in CPS than in IoT devices. There are common multiple input and output sensors and GPSs, wireless communication technologies, and the mobility found in both CPS and IoT devices. Meanwhile, there are plenty of development platforms and tools are available and are supported as a service to the cloud for distributed applications. However, there is a lack of standardization of architectures and hence this paper has proposed a reference architecture model for CPS and IoT Applications which can be integrated to other technologies such as fog, edge, cloud, and blockchain as this integration is needed for large scale applications such as

Table 1. Features of CPS and IoT systems

Features	Cyber-Physical Systems	IoT
Significant computational capacity	high	low
Processing speed	high	low
Storage capacity	medium	low
Multiple sensory input/output devices, such as touch screens, cameras, GPS chips, speakers, microphone, light sensors, proximity sensors	√	√
Multi-communication connectedness using Wifi, GPS, 3-5G, Bluetooth, etc	√	√
Mobility	Mobile CPS	Mobile
High-Level Programming	Java	Java
Distribution Mechanism (Apps Store, Play Store, etc)	√	√
Architectural Design Model	Layer Model, Event-Driven, Web Services	Event-Driven, Web Services

smart cities which requires smart transportation, smart roads, smart grids, smart home, smart living, etc.

CPS and IoT Architectural Design Characteristics: Functions vs. Attributes

Design of software architecture for CPS and IoT systems is the key to achieving long term goal of building a sustainable service which is secure and available. There are numerous characteristics that are expected from such devices and their services. Figure 1 shows a five-layer model for CPS and IoT architectural layers and their properties. The layers are connection layer 1 (providing plug & play capability as shown at the bottom of the triangle), data analytics layer 2, data mining layer 3, presentation/Cognitive layer 4, and finally a configuration layer 5 (as shown at the top of the triangle providing self configurability and composability of services and devices).

IoT has emerged to address connecting everything possible around us and get real data on behaviour otherwise would have not been possible. It all started with RFID technology in the early part of 2000 introduced in the retail market to as product id-tags, in 2010 the technology has been applied to surveillance, healthcare, security, transport, food safety, by 2020 the technology will be used in locating people, products, collecting data on every object, further on it will be applied in teleoperations and telepresence, virtual world, touch and feel, and ability to touch, monitor, and control remote objects, etc.

There are several applications of smartness with the use of the internet and communications technologies such as wireless and data transfer protocols such as 5G and 6G. The smart applications are expected to emerge in combination with cloud, IoT, CPS, Blockchain, etc. The main purpose of these emerging smart applications is to improve the quality of life of people and their environment with the use of ICT. Some of them are Smart Home, Smart City, Smart Vehicle, Smart Road, Smart Transport, Smart Grid,

Smart e-Gov, Smart e-Voting, Smart Land Registry, Smart Waste Management, Smart healthcare, Smart Traffic Control, Smart Environment Control, Smart Disaster, and Emergency Management, Smart Energy, Smart Air Pollution Control, etc. Let us mainly consider some of the key challenges emerging from smart applications. Firstly, smart home poses several technical research challenges such as interoperability, self-management, maintainability, signaling, bandwidth, and power consumption (Yassein et al., 2019). Similarly, (Hakak, Khan, Gilkar, Imran, & Guizani, 2020) have studied the requirement for the use of blockchain technology for smart city applications include security, privacy, fast processing of transactions, and to build trust. Smart city applications also need to be energy efficient for sustainability for the environment when improving the quality of life (Voisin, 2019). Software Platforms have been critically evaluated by (Santana, Chaves, Gerosa, Kon, & Milojicic, 2017) and have proposed a reference architecture. However, existing studies have not been evaluated the proposed frameworks with proven methods.

Figure 1. CPS and IoT Architectural Design Characteristics

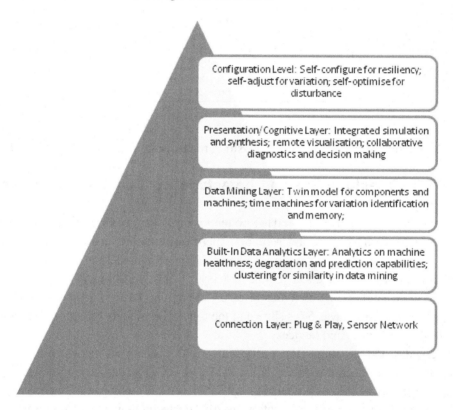

The software platforms include SmartSantander, OpenIoT, Concinnity, Civitas, Gambas, OpneMTC, U-City, etc. and some of the major non-functional requirements for smart city platforms are interoperability, scalability, privacy, context awareness, adaptation, extensibility, and configurability (Santana et al., 2017). Their proposed reference architecture for smart city applications consists of four layers such as cloud & networking layer, Service & IoT middleware layer, followed by big data management layer, and at the top is the application layer. However, existing work has not proposed nor adopted any systematic software engineering approach to developing smart applications using a service-oriented paradigm by integrating the identified non-functional requirements from the beginning of the service development life cycle which is the main significance of this article. The existing reference architecture is specific to smart city and doesn't seem to follow the concept of a service bust which is one of the key principles of service computing and is responsible for coordinating the communications amongst the layers following the smart contracts and non-functional requirements embedded into the smart development platforms.

The following section introduces a systematic approach to developing security-specific system requirements for building BSI right from the requirements phase of the system engineering life-cycle for IoT and CPS based applications.

SECURE SOFTWARE ENGINEERING FRAMEWORK FOR CPS AND IOT (SSEF4CPSIOT)

Current examples of UK cybersecurity attacks on businesses are devastating from the Carphone warehouse (a mobile phone sales business), TalkTalk (a telephone service provider), and Ashley Madison, a dating website where personal data. Ashford (2009) reports UK business spends 75% of the software development budget on fixing security flaws after delivering the product. This is a huge expenditure and it also creates untrustworthiness amongst customers. Andress (2011) provides an excellent literature survey on the basics of information security techniques. The cyclic security principles known as IAA is not limited pattern of solution for developing secure systems. There are other security concepts that form a pattern of solution known as CIA (Confidentiality, Integrity, and Availability). The CIA considers more towards how well we should design supporting those three characteristics of systems including software and services. In addition, Andress (2011) stated the concept of *ParkerianHexad*, which consists of six principles CIA (3) + PAU (3) (Possession or control, Authenticity, and Utility).

Traditionally, security has been added and fixed by releasing security patches on a daily basis by major software vendors. This practice needs to change by systematically identifying and incorporating system security right from requirements. This process is known as *Building In Security (BSI)*. Readers are urged to follow the work by McGraw (2004 & 2006) and Ramachandran (2011). This article contributes towards providing a system engineering process for developing and deploying cloud services systematically. It also provides a classification system for cloud security and cloud data security which are useful for developing and maintaining large scale systems with build in security. Finally, data security has modelled and simulated using business process methodology. The results show effectiveness when we develop systems systematically with good systems engineering principles and tools. Therefore, our main recommendation towards building security in (BSI) strategy is to follow one of our guidelines/ recommendations:

The aforementioned processes and classification, security principles, and security attributes can be used as a framework for capturing security-specific requirements supporting BSI focus by Systems and Software Engineers. In other words, Security requirements = principles of CIA + PAU.

Allen et al. (2008) state that one of the main goals of Software Security Engineering is to address software security best practices, processes, techniques, and tools in every phase and activities of any standard software development life cycle (SDLC). The main goal of building secure software which is defect-free and better built with:

- Continue to operate normally in any event of attacks and to tolerate any failure
- Limiting damages emerging as an outcome of any attacks triggered
- Build Trust & Resiliency In (BTRI)
- Data and asset protection

In other words, secure software should operate normally in the event of any attacks. In addition, it involves the process of extracting security requirements from overall system requirements (includes hardware, software, business, marketing, and environmental requirements) and then also further refined and extracted CPS and IoT security and software and services security requirements gathered for the required CPS and IoT applications. Then the refined CPS and IoT requirements can be embedded and traced across the software development life cycle (SDLC) phases such as requirements, design, development, and testing. This has not explained well in the current works of literature so far. Therefore, this paper has proposed a systematic Software Engineering Framework for CPS and IoT Applications (SEF4CPS-IoT) as shown in Figure 2 and it provides a clear definition of eliciting and integrating security, privacy, and trust requirements across the development lifecycle.

Figure 2. Secure Software Engineering Framework for CPS and IoT Applications (SSEF4CPSIOT)

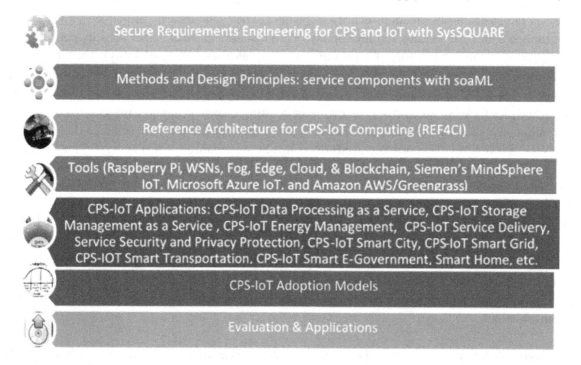

As shown in Figure 2, SEF4CPSIoT consists of a number of phases in the framework namely: Secure RE with SysSQUARE method and BPMN modelling and simulation; Design CPS-IoT services with UML components and with SoAML (an extended UML design model specifically developed for services-orientation); Tools such as Raspberry Pi, WSNs, Fog, Edge, Cloud, & Blockchain, Siemen's MindSphere IoT, Microsoft Azure IoT, and Amazon AWS/Greengrass; CPS-IoT Applications include but not limited to CPS-IoT Data Processing as a Service, CPS-IoT Storage Management as a Service, CPS-IoT Energy Management, CPS-IoT Service Delivery, Service Security and Privacy Protection, CPS-IoT Smart City, CPS-IoT Smart Grid, CPS-IOT Smart Transportation, CPS-IoT Smart E-Government, Smart Home, etc.; CPS-IoT Adoption Models; and approaches to Evaluation & Applications.

Secure requirements engineering process and method with extended sysSQUARE and in addition it proposes a BPMN modelling and simulation for verification and validation of real-world CPS-IoT applications.

Capturing and identifying requirements for security explicitly is one of the challenges in software engineering. Often security is considered as one of the non-functional requirements which have been considered as constraints identified during and after the software has been developed and deployed. However, it has an impact on the functionality of the system. Therefore, we need to be able to specify security requirements explicitly throughout the security-specific life-cycle phases as part of achieving BSI (security requirements, design for security, security testing & securability testing).

Secure Requirements Engineering for CPS and IoT With SysSQUARE

Cloud computing has emerged to address the needs of the IT cost-benefit analysis and also a revolution in technology in terms of reduced cost for Internet data and speed. Therefore, the demand for securing our data in the cloud has also increased as a way of building trust for cloud migration and to benefit business confidence in the cloud technology by cloud providers such as Amazon, Microsoft, Google, etc. Therefore, we also want to make sure our BSI model and strategies are applicable to cloud services as well as traditional systems. Figure 3 shows a model to structure cloud security attributes to develop and integrate BSI across the system development life-cycle.

Figure 3. CPS and IoT security attributes

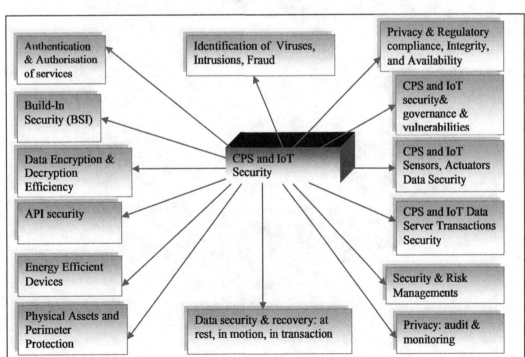

The CPS and IoT security attributes shown in Figure 3, are essential and useful to understand non-functional aspects of services development and service provision. These attributes are also useful for building BSI and maintaining security. As shown in the figure, protecting and securing CPS and IoT systems requires energy-efficient algorithms, efficient data allocation and retrieval algorithms, and a high level of data security using encryption and decryption efficient algorithms. The service availability of these systems is a priority requirement, and often these systems can be developed using readily available APIs such as Google map API, weather forecast APIs, Facebook APIs, Twitter APIs. For example, one could use an IoT to monitor physical premises and send every data to a twitter account using those APIs so that relevant people will be alerted quickly.

Mead (2005) for the SEI's (software Engineering Institute) has identified a method known as SQUARE (Secure Quality Requirements Engineering) which has been extended SysSQUARE (Systems Engineering SQUARE) towards systems security engineering method. The extended and modified sysSQUARE Requirements Engineering Framework is shown in Figure 4 which consists of ten steps starts with agreed definitions, followed by identify Build Security, Privacy, and Trust In (BSPTI) goals, develop BSPTI artifacts, perform risk assessments, identify and select a requirement elicitation technique, Elicit Security & Privacy Requirements, Categorise Security & Privacy Requirements, identify CPS-IoT Application's Data Security & Privacy Requirements, Prioritise Security & Privacy Requirements, and finally Validate, Verify, and Inspect Security & Privacy Requirements using BPMN Modelling and Simulations Tool.

Figure 4. sysSQUARE Requirements Engineering Framework for CPS-IoT Applications

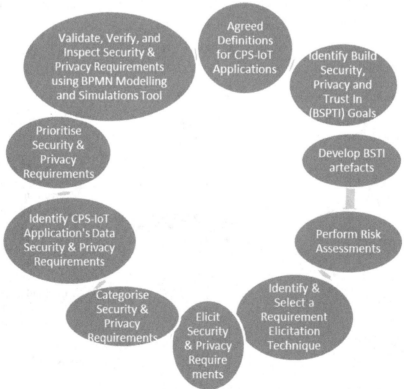

The extended method sysSQUARE consists of ten steps as follow:

- **Agreed Definitions for CPS-IoT Applications:** Which means to define a set of acronyms, definitions, and domain-specific knowledge needs to be agreed by stakeholders. This will help identify and validating security-specific requirements clearly by stakeholders

- **Identify Build Security, Privacy and Trust In (BSPTI) Goals:** Which means to clearly define what is expected of the system with respect to security by business drivers, policies, and procedures

- **Develop BSTI Artefacts:** Which means to develop scenarios, examples, misuse cases, templates for specifications, and forms

- **Perform Risk Assessments:** Which means to conduct a risk analysis of all security goals identified, conduct a threat analysis using any Threat Modelling Tools

- **Identify & Select a Requirement Elicitation Technique:** This includes systematic identification and analysis of security requirements from stakeholders in the forms of *interviews, business process modelling and simulations, prototypes, discussion, and focus groups*. As part of this phase, one has also to identify the level of security, cost-benefits analysis, and organisational culture, structure, and style

- **Elicit Security and Privacy Requirements:** Which includes activities such as producing security requirements document based security-specific principle structure as part of the goal of developing BSI earlier, risk assessment results, and techniques on requirements modelling with software tools such as *business process modelling and simulations, threat modelling, and misuse cases*, etc.

- **Categorise Security & Privacy Requirements:** This includes activities such as classifying and categorising security requirements based on company-specific requirements specification templates and to use our recommended security principles as this will help Systems Engineers to apply BSI and track security-specific requirements for validation & verification at all stages of the systems engineering life-cycle.

- **Identify CPS-IoT Applications Data Security & Privacy Requirements:** This includes activities on extracting and carefully identifying data security and relevant sub-systems such as data centres, servers, cloud VM, and software security, SQL security, and other types of security that are relevant to the data. This separation of concerns allows systems engineers to integrate, track, design, and develop data security as part of enterprise-wide systems development.

- **Prioritise Security & Privacy Requirements:** This includes activities of selecting and prioritising security & privacy requirements based on business goals as well as cost-benefit analysis.

- **Validate, Verify, and Inspect Security & Privacy Requirements Using BPMN Modelling and Simulations Tool:** Which means to conduct requirements validation process using requirements inspection and review meetings and to use business process modelling and simulation tools or any requirements engineering simulation tools to validate security and privacy requirements before the design and implantation of CPS-IoT services. This will provide well-proven security, privacy, trust requirements for a sustainable future of CPS-IoT driven smart applications.

According to the SysSQUARE model, the first phase starts with identifying security requirements that are achievable and agreed by all stakeholders who are involved in the process. The second step focuses mainly on developing a list of all possible security goals as part of the business and functional goals. Thirdly, to develop a list of artefacts that are needed to achieve those security goals. Fourthly, to conduct a detailed risk assessment for each security goal identified and assessed. Clear identification of requirements of the whole application system and extract security requirements. Interact with stakeholders to clarify security requirements and the technology they want to use, and cost implications. Categorisation and prioritisation of security requirements will help achieve realistic goals against business targets. For example, of a network system, we need to separate further two categories of security requirements such as wired and wireless security systems. The SysSQUARE method elicitation of security requirements has been applied to study the behaviour of threat modelling for cloud data security which has been presented in the last section of this article.

This paper has also identified a generic classification framework for CPS-IoT services as shown in Figure 5 based on the identified characteristics as shown in Figure 3.

Figure 5. CPS-IoT Requirements Engineering Classification of Services

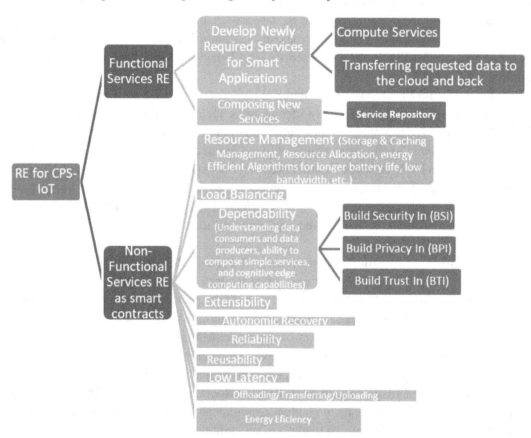

As shown in Figure 5, a generic requirements classification framework is necessary to standardize the identification of both functional services and non-functional service contracts in the modern era of emerging technologies such as fog, edge, cloud, and blockchain-based applications and are needed to be integrated for achieving modern large scale complex but smart applications as smart cities, etc. This RE framework is firstly divided into functional services and non-functional service contracts. The functional services are broadly classified into required services and new services that can be composed using the identified, developed, and deployed in a service repository for CPS-IoT driven applications which is one of the key aspects of this classification framework.

The non-functional services can be a number of simple and coordinated task type services and to design, develop, and deploy as smart contracts and therefore they are reusable services that can also be deposited in the service repository. They are mainly divided into resource management services, load balancing services, dependability and extensibility services, isolation, reliability, reusability, low latency, offloading, transferring & uploading services. In this context, one of the key features of this model is to address BSI, BPI, BTI as part of the dependability of smart services within all CPS-IoT based large scale applications. This follows on to the next phase in the SEF4CPSIoT framework is the reference architecture for designing services for CPS and IoT Applications. A sample data streaming CPS-IoT application has been modelled using BPMN modelling and simulation tool as a first level requirements gathering which is presented in section 3.2.

Process Points Estimation

We also need to estimate the complexity of service level requirements and there have been several approaches such as use case points (UCP) method discussed in (Kusumoto, Matukawa, Inoue, Hanabusa, & Maegawa, 2004), user stories point estimation method in Agile Projects as presented by (Hamouda, 2014) and they have also proposed a set of values for technical complexity factors and Environmental Complexity Factors depending on the nature of applications such as distributed computing, reusability, etc., and service point estimation method in SOA based projects presented by (Gupta, 2013). This paper proposes a concept of process points since SEF4CPSIoT recommends the use of BPMN modelling and simulation to model first level requirements and to validate cost, resource, and performance constraints and smart contracts which can be reusable in the proposed SOA based reference architecture discussed in the following section. In this context, this paper proposes a modified cloud COCOMO model with weighting for cloud computing projects are: a = 2, b = 2.1, c = 3, d = .2. Therefore, the effort and cost estimation equations are:

$$CPS - IoT\ project\ effort\ applied(EA) = a \times (Process\ Points)\ (Human\ Months) \tag{1}$$

$$CPS - IoT development\ time(dt) = c \times (Effort\ Applied)^d\ (Months) \tag{2}$$

$$Number\ of\ Service\ Development\ Engineers\ Required = Effort\ Applied(EA)\ /\ Development\ Time\ (dt) \tag{3}$$

The equations 1-3 provide cloud project effort and cost estimations based on process points which is the sum of all workflows (WF) divided by the total number of BPMN process activities (P):

$$Process\ Points = \sum_{0}^{N} WF\ /\ \sum_{0}^{N} P \times (\text{Technical Complexity Factors (TCF)}) \times (\text{Environmental Complexity Factors (ECF)}) \tag{4}$$

Modified form of Technical Complexity Factors for service and cloud computing applications are presented in Table 2.

Table 2. Technical Complexity Factors for service and cloud computing applications

Metric	Description	Weight
TCF 1	Cloud Computing (new factor introduced)	3
TCF 2	Distributed System	2
TCF 3	Response or throughput performance objectives	*1*
TCF 5	End user efficiency (Online)	*1*
TCF 6	Complex internal processing services	*1*
TCF 7	Reusable services	*1*
TCF 8	Easy to invoke a service	*0.5*
TCF 9	Easy to use and compose new services	*0.5*
TCF 10	Vendor Agnostic Services and Multi-Cloud and Cloud Federation Support	*2*
TCF 11	Easy to change service interfaces	*1*
TCF 12	Concurrent and parallel algorithm supported services	*1*
TCF 13	Build Security In (BSI)	1
TCF 14	Build Trust In (BTI)	1
TCF 15	Build Privacy In (BPI)	1
TCF 16	Build Resiliency In (BRI)	1
TCF 17	API Support (Provide direct access for third parties)	1
TCF 18	Good documentation and software engineering artefacts (requirements, design, and test data available publically)	1
TCF 19	Special user training facilities are required	1
TCF 20	BPMN modelling and simulation used to verify & validate service requirements	1

The modified form of Environmental Complexity Factors (ECF) is presented in Table 3.

Table 3. Environmental Complexity Factors (ECF) for Service and Cloud Computing

Metric	Description	Weight
ECF 1	Familiar with BPMN modelling and simulation	1
ECF 2	Familiar with UML component Modelling	1.5
ECF 3	Familiar with soaML	1.5
ECF 4	Familiar with Service and Cloud Computing Technologies	2
ECF 5	Service Application Experience & Knowledge of the Domain	1
ECF 6	Service-Oriented Programming experience	1
ECF 7	Lead business analyst capability	1
ECF 8	Project Management & Agile Practices capability within the organisation	0.5
ECF 9	Organisational Motivation & Collective Ownership capability	2
ECF 10	Business & Requirements stability & scope	2
ECF 11	Lead software and service Engineers capability & skills level	-1 to +2 (low to high)

Tables 2 and 3 provide a clear estimation technique which is more suitable for service and cloud computing. The example BPMN model for a data streaming service application is presented in the section 3.21. As part of the SEF4CPSIoT framework, the following section presents a reference architecture for CPS and IoT applications which provides the required standardization of the service application development & deployment in a real-world setting.

CPS-IoT Reference Architecture

Systematic approach to integrating validated requirements into the design is one of the best practices of software engineering approach. The proposed design approaches include UML component models, and soaML models for service contracts and architectural design. In order to create an architectural design that reflects CPS-IoT services, we need to identify a standard architecture which is applicable across all smart applications like smart cities, smart transportations, etc. and is known as a reference architecture. Therefore, the reference architecture has been evolved for standardising smart applications with CPS-IoT devices based on a SEF-SCC framework which has been developed for big data driven large scale cloud applications. CPS-IoT Architecture design is the key aspect of the proposed SEF4CPSIoT and it provides a layered structure. Our earlier work in this area has developed a reference architecture for service and cloud computing known as Software Engineering Framework for Service and Cloud Computing (SEF-SCC) (Ramachandran, 2018). This paper has customised the SEF-SCC for CPS-IoT applications which is shown in Figure 6.

Figure 6. Reference Architecture for CPS-IoT (REF4CPSIoT) Applications

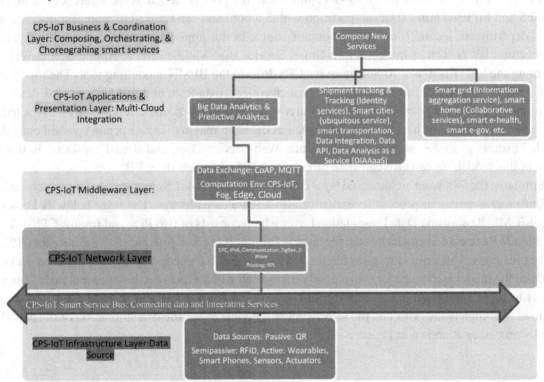

As shown in Figure 6, REF4CPSIoT has been structured namely: the bottom layer is known as CPS-IoT Data Source layer which caters for all sensory and GPS data from CPS-IoT devices; followed by CPS-IoT smart service bus for connecting data and transferring, routing services; followed by Network Layer; followed by Middleware layer; followed by Application layer; followed by a business & coordination layer at the top. However, this paper also proposes a method for validating and verifying CPS-IoT services based on the reference architecture mapping using Business Process Modelling & Simulation which is presented in the following section on validating REF4CPSIoT.

3.2.1. Validating Reference Architecture With Business Process Modelling and Simulation

Business Process Modelling Notation (BPMN) allows to gather and visually model high level business requirements and it allows us to simulate for validating performance, cost, and resource requirements as presented in the SEF4CPSIoT framework. BPMN modelling and simulation allows:

- Visual and simple set of notations which is easy to model business requirements early
- Easy to learn and model
- Simulation provides opportunity to validate the requirements elicitation process
- A number of open-source tools available such as BonitaSoft, Visual Paradigm, Bizaghi, etc.

Figure 7 shows a simple model for a smart data streaming data science application presented in the SEF reference architecture layers represented as *pools* (a pool is a graphical container for partitioning a set of activities from other pools, in this application, the pool is named as the reference architecture for CPS and IoT) and *lanes* (is a sub-partition within a pool and can be used to represent, for example, roles, departments, locations or different organisations. In this application, lanes are used to represent architectural layers such as Infrastructure, Smart Service Bus, Middleware, & Application Layers representing the SEF Reference Architecture for CPS-IoT) in the BPMN modelling tool. The top layer is the CPS-IoT Data Source Infrastructure layer which collects data from multiple CPS and IoT devices in distributed locations. The business process starts with a green filled circle represents an event trigger followed by a number of business activities such as decision making (Data Locator) passed onto three single business processes such as Analytic Data, Web Service Data, and Real-Time Data. In this top layer of this model, we can also calculate process points as there are three PP.

Similarly, the following architectural layer is known as the CPS-IoT Smart Service Bus which consists of four process points or process scenarios or also known as pathways. The layer below is known as CPS-IoT Middleware and Data Presentation Layer which consists of two PPs, and finally, CPS-IoT Application & Business Layer which is the top layer in the presented SEF reference architecture for CPS and IoT applications. This layer is responsible for orchestrating and choreographing new business services.

Once the model is checked for syntactically correct, all BPMN tools do this autonomously. The next step is to input simulation parameters for all business activities, mostly in the form of effort & cost required to complete the tasks and the select simulation view to see the live simulation of the modelled BPMN processes as shown in Figure 8.

Figure 7. BPMN Modelling View for REF4CPSIoT Smart Data Streaming Application

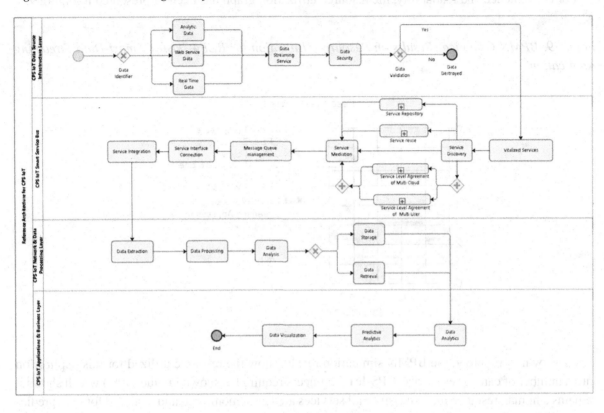

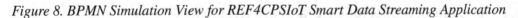

Figure 8. BPMN Simulation View for REF4CPSIoT Smart Data Streaming Application

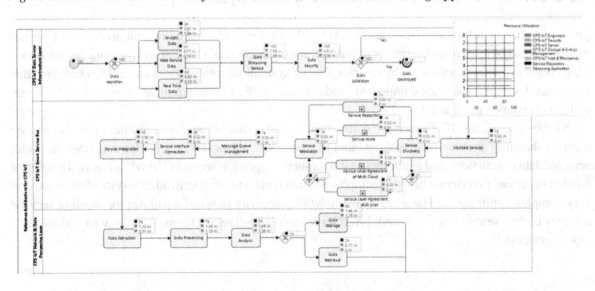

For convenience and readability, the resource utilization graph has been re-presented in Figure 9.

Figure 9. BPMN Graphical Results on Resource Utilisation for REF4CPSIoT Smart Data Streaming Application

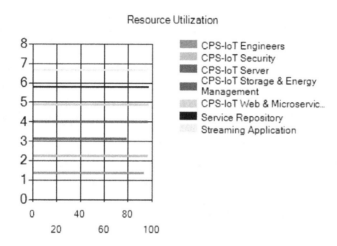

As shown in Figure 9, the BPMN simulation results show the resource utilized for this application into a number of categories such as CPS-IoT Engineers required is shown in blue (90%) which shows it remains a human resource intensive since all services are being monitored and analysed for data predictions by CPS-IoT engineers. It also shows the use high level of service repository when composing new services up to 95% shown in dark blue.

3.2.2. Service Component Model for CPS and IoT Systems

The emergence of IoT's main purpose is to be highly interoperable and being able to connect to smart objects, virtual objects, non-deterministic network environment, etc. This can only be achieved with such a high degree of interoperability is by design CPS-IoT systems on web services and SOA. Therefore, this paper has developed a service component model based on the IoT requirements now and in the future which is presented in Figure 4.

As shown in Figure 10, the service component model provides two types of interfaces that require services shown as semi-arc for accessing input from wireless sensor (IWSN), sensor data (ISensorData), actuator data (IActuator), and environmental data such as location services (IEnvLocData). There are a number of provider services which this component model offers to connect to other services for composing very complex applications. These are IdataAnalytics, ISecurity (a set of attributes for handing secured services in the event of any intrusion), IWebServer and ICloudServer (connecting to web services and cloud services).

Figure 10. Service Component Model for CPS and IoT Systems

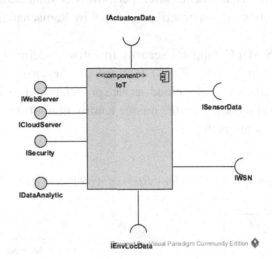

INTEGRATED SECURE AND PRIVACY DRIVEN CPS-IOT SERVICE DEVELOPMENT PARADIGM

The above discussed drawbacks and requirements for a concise method, lead us to develop a model that integrates various activities of identifying and analysing soft-ware security engineering into the software development process, and this new process and its activities is shown in Figure 11. However, this paper focuses on only software security requirements specific activities. According to this model, SSRE (software security requirements engineering) consists of identifying standards and strategies of the organisation with regards to requirements elicitation (including analysis, validation, verification), conducting risk management and mitigation, and identifying software security requirements consists of a further sub-processes of defining security, identifying security strategies, conducting areas and domain scope analysis, business process modeling and simulation, identifying security issues, applying use cases and misuse cases, attack patterns.

Likewise, this model also provides security-specific processes for identifying security threats during design, development, testing, deployment, and maintenance. There are numerous good design principles that can be found in the vast majority of software design literature. However, the following is a list of some of the key design principles that are highly relevant to software security design and are part of our IS-SDLC model:

- Principles of least privilege states to allow only a minimal set of rights (privileges) to a subject that requests access to a resource. This helps to avoid intentional or intentional damage that can be caused to a resource in case of an attack.
- Principles of separation of privilege states that a system should not allow access to resources based on a single condition rather it should be based on multiple conditions that have to be abstracted into independent components.
- Design by incorporating known Common Vulnerability Exposures (CVE, https://cve.mitre.org/).
- Design for resilience to develop a resilience model which supports system sustainability alongside with Building Trust and Security in (BTSI).

- Select software security requirements after performance simulation using BPMN (Business Process Modelling Notation) and is described in detail by Ramachandran.

SSRE activities in our IS-SDLC supports security in software-defined networking (SDN), Cloud computing services (Software as a service (SaaS), Platform as a Service (PaaS), and Infrastructure as a Service (IaaS), Enterprise security includes cloud service providers and service consumers, and design for security principles and techniques. This the unique contribution of this model and for the body of knowledge in software security research.

Figure 11. Integrated secure and privacy service systems development engineering life cycle (IS-SSDLC)

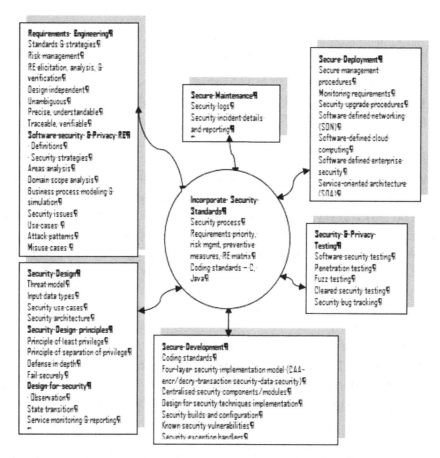

FUTURE RESEARCH DIRECTIONS

This article has presented our approach to developing cloud services for CPS and IoT applications systematically with the use of the Software Engineering Framework for CPS and IoT driven large scale services such as smart cities, smart home, smart transportation, etc. We have developed a number of security-specific components that can be reused and customised because they are components with message interfaces. We have also developed a number of business processes with simulation to pre-inform us about their performances and security measures that can be taken before service implementation and deployment. As we discussed in this article, to make cloud computing as a new technological business model that is highly successful, profitable, and sustainable, we need to ensure cloud security and privacy can be maintained and trusted. Therefore, most of the future research will focus mainly on cloud security-related issues, in particular, some of them are as follows:

- CPS and IoT with Cloud Computing.
- CPS and IoT Development, Tools and Techniques.
- CPS and IoT with Big Data Analytics.
- CPS and IoT with Security issues.
- Control of cloud resources where it is being used and shared and their physical security if this is a hardware resource. In other words, *security concerned with sharing resources and services*.
- Seizure of a company because it has violated the local legislation requirement. Concerns of client's data when it has also been violated. Therefore, forensic investigation of cloud services and cloud data recovery and protection issues will dominate much of the future research.
- Consumer switching for price competition. Storage services provided by one cloud vendor may be incompatible with another vendor's services if a user decides to move from one to the other (for example, Microsoft cloud is currently incompatible with Google cloud).
- Security key encryption/decryption keys and related issues. Which is a suitable technique for a specific service request and for a specific customer data? Who should control? Consumers or providers?
- Cloud service development paradigm. What is the suitable development paradigm for this type of business-driven delivery model?
- CPS and IoT Service security vs. cloud security vs. data security will dominate most of the future research.
- CPS and IoT Privacy related issues. Who controls personal and transactional information?
- Audit and monitoring: How do we monitor and audit service provider organizations and how do we provide assurance to relevant stakeholders that privacy requirements are met when their Personally Identifiable Information (PII) is in the cloud?
- Engineering CPS and IoT cloud services. How do we develop, test, and deploy cloud services? Can we continue to follow traditional methods and processes?
- Business process modelling integrated with cloud service development will emerge and can address business-related issues.
- Integrating data security as part of the systems, software, and services engineering processes.
- Applications such as smart cities, smart transportation, smart grid, smart home, etc.

CONCLUSION

CPS, IoT, and Cloud computing have established its businesses and providing services for connected devices. However, this new trend needs to be more systematic with respect to software engineering and its related processes. For example, current challenges that are witnessed today with cybersecurity and application security flaws are important lessons to be learned. It also has provided best practices that can be adapted. Similarly, as the demand for CPS, IoT, and cloud services increases and so increased importance sought for security and privacy. We can build CPS, IoT, and cloud application security from the start of cloud service development. CPS, IoT, and Cloud computing are multi-disciplinary that include social engineering, software engineering, software security engineering, distributed computing, and service engineering. Therefore, a holistic approach is needed to build services. We need to use the established architectural and service component model that has been proven over the years in many applications.

REFERENCES

Ahmed, E., Yaqoob, I., Hashem, I. A. T., Khan, I., Ahmed, A. I. A., Imran, M., & Vasilakos, A. V. (2017). The role of big data analytics in the Internet of Things. *Computer Networks, 129*, 459–471. doi:10.1016/j.comnet.2017.06.013

Allen, J., Barnum, S., Ellison, R. J., McGraw, G., & Mead, N. R. (2008). *Software security engineering: A guide for project managers*. Addison Wesley.

Alur, R. (2015). *Principles of cyber-physical systems*. MIT Press.

Andress, J. (2011). The Basics of Information Security: Understanding the Fundamentals of InfoSec in Theory and Practice. Syngress (Elsevier).

Aoyama, M. (2002). *Web Services Engineering: Promises and Challenges*. Presented at *International Conference on Software Engineering, ICSE'02*, Orlando, FL. 10.1145/581339.581425

AshfordW. (2009). https://www.computerweekly.com/Articles/2009/07/14/236875/on-demand-service-aims-to-cut-cost-of-fixing-software-security.htm

Bertolino, A. (2006). Audition of web services for testing conformance to open specified protocols. In Architecting systems with trustworthy components. Springer. doi:10.1007/11786160_1

Bias, R. (2009). Cloud Expo Article, Cloud Computing: Understanding Infrastructure as a Service. *Cloud Computing Journal*. Retrieved from http://cloudcomputing.sys-con.com/node/807481

Bonita Soft. (2012). *BOS 5.8. Open source BPMN simulation software*. Retrieved from https://www.bonitasoft.com/resources/documentation/top-tutorials

BPMN2. (2012). *BPMN 2.0 Handbook* (2nd ed.). Future Strategies Inc.

Caminao Project. (2013). *Caminao's Way: Do systems know how symbolic they are?* Modelling Systems Engineering Project. Retrieved June 21 from https://caminao.wordpress.com/overview/?goback=%2Egde_3731775_member_251475288

Cause, G. (2012). *Delivering Real Business Value using FDD*. Retrieved April 26 from http://www.methodsandtools.com/archive/archive.php?id=19

Chesbrough, H., & Spohrer, J. (2006). A research manifesto for services science. *Special Issue on Services Science. Communications of the ACM, 49*(7), 35. doi:10.1145/1139922.1139945

Clarke, R. (2010). *User Requirements for Cloud Computing Architecture*. Presented at the10th IEEE/ACM International Conference on Cluster, Cloud and Grid Computing. 10.1109/CCGRID.2010.20

Cobweb. (2009). Retrieved from https://www.cobweb.com/

CSA. (2010). *Cloud Security Alliance. Domain 12: Guidance for Identity & Access Management V2.1.* Retrieved from https://cloudsecurityalliance.org/guidance/csaguide-dom12-v2.10.pdf

Curbera, F. (2007, November). Component contracts in service-oriented architectures. *IEEE Computer, 40*(11).

EC2. (2012). Retrieved from https://aws.amazon.com/ec2/

Erl, T. (2005). *Service-oriented architecture: concepts, technology, and design.* Prentice hall.

Faisal, A., Abdullah, A., & Sajjan, S. (2018). An Overview of Enabling technologies for the Internet of Things (Q. F. Hassan Ed.). John Wiley & Sons for IEEE.

Farrell, J., & Ferris, C. (2003, June). What are web services? *Communications of the ACM, 46*(6).

Gandhi, B. (2011). *Business Process as a Service (BPaaS) delivered from the cloud.* Retrieved from http://thoughtsoncloud.com/index.php/2011/12/business-process-as-a-service-bpaas-delivered-from-the-cloud/

Gubbi, J., Buyya, R., Marusic, S., & Palaniswami, M. (2013). Internet of Things (IoT): A vision, architectural elements, and future directions. *Future Generation Computer Systems, 29*(7), 1645–1660. doi:10.1016/j.future.2013.01.010

Gupta, D. (2013). *Service Point Estimation Model for SOA Based Projects. Service Technology Magazine, 78.*

Hakak, S., Khan, W. Z., Gilkar, G. A., Imran, M., & Guizani, N. (2020). Securing Smart Cities through Blockchain Technology: Architecture, Requirements, and Challenges. *IEEE Network. IEEE Network, 34*(1), 8–14. doi:10.1109/MNET.001.1900178

Hamouda, A. E. D. (2014). *Using Agile Story Points as an Estimation Technique in CMMI Organizations.* Paper presented at the 2014 Agile Conference.

Helbig, J. (2007, November). Creating business value through flexible IT architecture. *Special Issue on Service-oriented Computing, IEEE Computer, 40*(11).

Hu, H., Yang, L., Lin, S., & Wang, G. (2020). *Security Vetting Process of Smart-home Assistant Applications: A First Look and Case Studies.* Academic Press.

Iaa, S. (2010). *Cloud computing world forum.* Retrieved April 2nd from http://www.cloudwf.com/iaas.html

IBM. (2010). *Eleven habits for highly successful BPM programs.* IBM Thought Leadership White Paper.

IThound. (2010). *Video whitepaper.* Retrieved February 3rd from http://images.vnunet.com/video_WP/V4.htm

Khaled, L. (2010). Deriving architectural design through business goals. *International Journal of Computer Science and Information Security, 7*(3).

Kusumoto, S., Matukawa, F., Inoue, K., Hanabusa, S., & Maegawa, Y. (2004). *Estimating effort by use case points: method, tool and case study.* Paper presented at the 10th International Symposium on Software Metrics, 2004.

Lakshminarayanan, S. (2010, December). Interoperable security service standards for web services. In *IT pro*. IEEE CS Press.

Lin, J., Yu, W., Zhang, N., Yang, X., Zhang, H., & Zhao, W. (2017). A Survey on Internet of Things: Architecture, Enabling Technologies, Security and Privacy, and Applications. *IEEE Internet of Things Journal, 4*(5), 1125–1142. doi:10.1109/JIOT.2017.2683200

Linthicum, D. (2009). *Application design guidelines for cloud computing.* InfoWorld. Retrieved from https://www.infoworld.com/d/cloud-computing/application-design-guidelines-cloud-computing-784?page=0,0

Mather, T., Kumaraswamy, S., & Latif, S. (2009). Cloud Security and Privacy: An Enterprise Perspective on Risks and Compliance. Academic Press.

McEwen, A., & Cassimally, H. (2014). *Designing the Internet of Things*. Wiley.

McGraw, G. (2004, Mar.). Software Security: Building Security. IEEE Security & Privacy.

McGraw, G. (2006). *Software security: building security in.* Addison Wesley.

Nano, O., & Zisman, A. (2007, Nov.). Realizing service-centric software systems. *IEEE Software*.

Naone, E. (2007). *Computer in the cloud, technology review*. Retrieved from https://www.technology-review.com/Infotech/19397/?a=f

NIST. (2009). Retrieved March 22nd from https://csrc.nist.gov/groups/SNS/cloud-computing/index.html

O'Reilly. (2005). *Security Quality Requirements Engineering (SQUARE) Methodology*. Technical Report. CMU/SEI-2005-TR-009. Retrieved from https://www.sei.cmu.edu/library/abstracts/reports/05tr009.cfm

Oh, S. H. (2011). A Reusability Evaluation Suite for Cloud Services. In *Proceedings of the Eighth IEEE International Conference on e-Business Engineering*. IEEE CS Press. 10.1109/ICEBE.2011.27

Oracle. (2012). *Data Security Challenges*. Oracle9i security overview release number 2(9.2). Retrieved November 4th from https://docs.oracle.com/cd/B10501_01/network.920/a96582/overview.htm

OVF. (2010). *Open Virtualization Format (OVF)*. Distributed Management Task Force. Retrieved from https://dmtf.org/sites/default/files/standards/documents/DSP0243_1.1.0.pdf

Paa, S. (2010). *Types of PaaS solutions*. Retrieved April 22nd from http://www.salesforce.com/uk/paas/paas-solutions/

Papazoglou, P. M. (2007). Service-oriented computing: state of the art and research challenges. *IEEE Computer, 40*(11).

Piyare, R., & Seong, R. L. (2013). Towards internet of things (iots): integration of wireless sensor network to cloud services for data collection and sharing. *International Journal of Computer Networks & Communications, 5*(5).

Popović, K., & Hocenski, Z. (2010). Cloud computing security issues and challenges. Presented at MIPRO 2010.

Ramachandran, M. (2008). *Software components: guidelines and applications*. Nova Publishers.

Ramachandran, M. (2011). Software components for cloud computing architectures and applications. In Z. Mahmmood & R. Hill (Eds.), *Cloud Computing for Enterprise Architectures*. Springer. doi:10.1007/978-1-4471-2236-4_5

Ramachandran, M. (2011). *Software Security Engineering: Design and Applications*. Nova Science Publishers.

Ramachandran, M. (2012). Service Component Architecture for Building Cloud Services. *Service Technology Magazine,* (65). Retrieved from http://www.servicetechmag.com/I65/0812-4

Ramachandran, M. (2013). Systems Engineering Processes for the Development and Deployment of Secure Cloud Applications. Encyclopedia of Information Science and Technology.

Ramachandran, M. (2018). SEF-SCC: Software Engineering Framework for Service and Cloud Computing. In M. Zaigham (Ed.), *Fog Computing: Concepts, Principles and Related Paradigms*. Springer. doi:10.1007/978-3-319-94890-4_11

Ray, P. P. (2018). A survey on Internet of Things architectures. *Journal of King Saud University - Computer and Information Sciences, 30*(3), 291-319. doi:10.1016/j.jksuci.2016.10.003

SaaS. (2009). www.saas.co.uk/

Santana, E. F. Z., Chaves, A. P., Gerosa, M. A., Kon, F., & Milojicic, D. S. (2017). Software Platforms for Smart Cities: Concepts, Requirements, Challenges, and a Unified Reference Architecture. *ACM Computing Surveys*, *50*(6), 1–37. doi:10.1145/3124391

Science Group. (2006). *2020 Science Group: Toward 2020 science, tech.report*. Microsoft. Retrieved from http://research.microsoft.com/towards2020science/downloads/T2020S_Report.pdf

Scrugendo, G. (2004). Self-organisation: paradigms and applications, engineering self-organising systems: Nature-Inspired approaches to software engineering. Lecture Notes in CS, 2977.

Sindre, G., & Opdahl, A. L. (2005). Eliciting security requirements with misuse cases. *Requirements Engineering*, *10*(1), 34–44. doi:10.100700766-004-0194-4

Srinivasan, K. M. (2012). *State-of-the-art Cloud Computing Security Taxonomies: A classification of security challenges in the present cloud computing environment*. Presented at International Conference on Advances in Computing, Communications and Informatics, ICACCI '12. 10.1145/2345396.2345474

Taiyuan, S. (2009). A Flexible Business Process Customization Framework for SaaS. Presented at *WASE International Conference on Information Engineering*.

Tondel, I. A. (2008, Jan.). Security requirements for rest of us: a survey. *IEEE Software*.

Tyagi, S. (2006). *RESTful web services*. Retrieved from https://www.oracle.com/technetwork/articles/javase/index-137171.html

Varghese, J., & Hayajneh, T. (2018). *A Framework to Identify Security and Privacy Issues of Smart Home Devices*. IEEE. doi:10.1109/UEMCON.2018.8796765

Venkataraman, T. (2010). *A Model of Cloud Based Application Environment*. Cloud Forum.

Verizon. (2010). Retrieved October 20th from http://www.zdnet.co.uk/news/cloud/2010/10/08/the-cloud-lessons-from-history-40090471/

Voisin, A. (2019). *A Green-by-Design Methodology to Increase Sustainability of Smart City Systems*. IEEE. doi:10.1109/RCIS.2019.8877075

Vouk, M. A. (2008). Cloud computing – issues, research and implementations. *Journal of Computing and Information Technology, 16.*

Wang, L., & Laszewski, G. (2008). *Scientific Cloud Computing: Early Definition and Experience*. Retrieved from http://cyberaide.googlecode.com/svn/trunk/papers/08-cloud/vonLaszewski-08-cloud.pdf

Weiss, A. (2007, December). *Computing in the clouds*. Academic Press.

Wilson, C., & Josephson, A. (2007). Microsoft Office as a Platform for Software + Services. *The Architecture Journal, 13*. Retrieved April 20th from www.architecturejournal.net

Yang, J. (2003). Web service componentisation. *Communications of the ACM, 46*(10), 35. doi:10.1145/944217.944235

Yassein, M. B., Hmeidi, I., Shatnawi, F., Mardini, W., & Khamayseh, Y. (2019). Smart Home Is Not Smart Enough to Protect You - Protocols, Challenges, and Open Issues. *Procedia Computer Science, 160*, 134–141. doi:10.1016/j.procs.2019.09.453

Zhang, L.-J., & Zhou, Q. (2009). *CCOA: Cloud Computing Open Architecture*. Presented at *IEEE International Conference on Web Services*.

This research was previously published in the International Journal of Hyperconnectivity and the Internet of Things (IJHIoT), 5(1); pages 1-24, copyright year 2021 by IGI Publishing (an imprint of IGI Global).

Section 3
Tools and Technologies

Chapter 27
Blockchain for Industrial Internet of Things (IIoT)

Rinki Sharma

Ramaiah University of Applied Sciences, Bangalore, India

ABSTRACT

Over the years, the industrial and manufacturing applications have become highly connected and automated. The incorporation of interconnected smart sensors, actuators, instruments, and other devices helps in establishing higher reliability and efficiency in the industrial and manufacturing process. This has given rise to the industrial internet of things (IIoT). Since IIoT components are scattered all over the network, real-time authenticity of the IIoT activities becomes essential. Blockchain technology is being considered by the researchers as the decentralized architecture to securely process the IIoT transactions. However, there are challenges involved in effective implementation of blockchain in IIoT. This chapter presents the importance of blockchain in IIoT paradigm, its role in different IIoT applications, challenges involved, possible solutions to overcome the challenges and open research issues.

1.1 INTRODUCTION

Industrial Internet of Things (IIoT) refers to the connected industrial applications such as asset monitoring, remote control of machinery and automated quality control systems, to name a few. Apart from these applications, connected cars, buildings and industries also play significant role in IIoT. This segment further spans over smart - retail, - supply chain, - cities, - energy and - agriculture (Schneider, 2017). Such wide array of IIoT applications face numerous challenges in terms of security and scalability. Billions of such connected online devices increase the attack surfaces and give rise to numerous weak areas through which the IIoT systems can be hacked. Current IIoT architecture also has characteristics such as centralized design, the legacy client-server model-based communication, lack of multi-vendor interoperability, and personal identifiable data stored and managed by entities that require trust. These characteristics of IIoT make it vulnerable to attacks and difficult to scale (Sengupta, Ruj & Bit, 2020).

DOI: 10.4018/978-1-6684-7132-6.ch027

Use of blockchain in IIoT environments would help in achieving a tamper proof record of IIoT activities that is auditable in real-time. Blockchain enables in achieving decentralized architecture (thus eliminating single point of attack), distributed network, peer-to-peer communication model and ability to securely process transactions without involving infrastructure costs and risks of centralized model. Blockchain for IIoT can register, certify and track partnership between multiple parties through a supply chain, and verify it in a secure encrypted environment. It can maintain a truly decentralized and trusted ledger of all the transactions in the network. Blockchain allows to maintain a tamper proof record of IIoT device history, particularly for applications where information generation and exchange needs to be trustworthy (Huang et al., 2019).

While blockchain provides numerous advantages to IIoT, there are challenges in successful and effective implementation of blockchain in IIoT. Scalable and deployable blockchain based IIoT solutions still face numerous challenges such as distributed consensus algorithms and data analytics, with privacy preservation. The key challenge is that blockchain is computationally intensive, while the devices in IIoT platform (such as sensors and edge devices) are battery powered, with minimal data storage and processing power. In case of mobile nodes (as in the connected car environment) problem of intermittent connectivity persists. Private key generation and sharing also is a challenge (Zheng et al., 2018).

Numerous blockchain based IIoT solutions and applications have been proposed and developed by the researchers. However, wide adoption of the solutions is an issue in resource constrained IIoT environments. In this chapter, a comprehensive survey and review of the available blockchain based solutions for IIoT is presented. The limitations and challenges of blockchain implementation in different IIoT sectors is discussed. Based on this study, open issues and research avenues for adoption of blockchain technology in IIoT are presented.

The rest of this chapter is structured as follows. Section 2 presents brief introduction of IIoT and its applications. Section 3 introduces the role of blockchain in IIoT and its characteristics that blockchain useful for IIoT. The role of blockchain in different IIoT applications is also emphasized. While blockchain is important for IIoT, its implementation in IIoT poses numerous challenges. The challenges in adoption of blockchain in IIoT are discussed in Section 4. The research opportunities to support blockchain for IIoT are presented and discussed in Section 5. Section 6 concludes the chapter.

1.2 Industrial Internet of Things (IIoT)

The idea behind Internet of Things (IoT) is to enable the devices communicate and take appropriate action without human intervention thus achieving certain level of automation. Industry 4.0, the fourth industrial revolution, combines the customary industrial and manufacturing platforms with contemporary smart communication technology. Use of technology to connect and automate the industry and manufacturing process, obtain data and carry out analytics to augment these processes further, Industrial Internet of Things (IIoT) is used. The authors in (Weyer, Schmitt, Ohmer & Gorecky 2015) distribute the Industry 4.0 operation into three central paradigms as follows, with the aim of achieving reliable and productive industrial environment:

1. Smart product: This paradigm takes control of the resources and orchestrates the manufacturing process to its end

2. Smart machine: This paradigm represents the cyber physical system (CPS) wherein the conventional industrial and manufacturing process transitions into the production lines that are self-organizing, flexible, adaptable and distributed.

3. Augmented operator: This paradigm adds flexibility and capability to the human operator working in the industrial system.

The IIoT is a CPS comprising of machines, computers and people enabling intelligent industrial operations using advanced data analytics to realize transformational business outcomes. Over the years, industrial systems have increased in complexity, leading to inefficient productivity when operated using traditional systems. Present day devices are equipped with sensors, storage, bandwidth and computational power, which allows these industrial machines to be constantly monitored on a large scale. With the help of cloud computing, these devices can be remotely controlled and monitored. Hence IIoT plays a crucial role in present day industrial operations. In most of the cases, IIoT primarily comprises of a network of sensors communicating over wireless medium to each other, or a sink node, or cloud, from where the data can be accessed remotely. Mobility and density of these sensors may lead to increase in network complexity and deterioration in its performance (Sharama, Shankar, & Rajan 2014). Security of data and devices is also a cause of concern in IIoT. However, despite of complexity of implementation and operation, IIoT has gained tremendous popularity in industrial operations.

Some of the industrial application popular for IIoT are:

1. Healthcare
2. Vehicular networks
3. Oil and gas industry
4. Manufacturing
5. Smart building
6. Power industry
7. Smart agriculture
8. Retail and supply chain

This section presents some of the industries to have incorporated the IIoT concepts for enhanced productivity and operation, and the challenges faced by these industries where blockchain can play a crucial role.

Healthcare

IIoT is being actively used in the healthcare industry for applications such as remote patient monitoring, patient rehabilitation, medical waste management, patient fitness and activity tracking, robotic surgery, and in tracing, supply, distribution, monitoring and management of drugs. Numerous smart healthcare devices and systems are commercially available for these purposes (Tyagi, Agarwal & Maheshwari, 2016) and (Sharma, Gupta, Suhas, & Kashyap, 2014).

Vehicular Networks

Autonomous and connected vehicles are equipped with sensors, processing modules and communication units for intra - and inter - vehicle communication. The vehicles communicate with roadside infrastructure and surrounding vehicles for cooperative driving, positioning and navigation. Vehicles form temporary networks known as vehicular ad-hoc networks (VANETs) a subset of mobile ad-hoc networks (MANETs) and communicate over wireless medium with nearby vehicles or roadside units. The topology of MANETs and VANETs is dynamic highly dynamic in nature, leading to connection impairment and interference (Gopinath, Kumar, & Sharma, 2013). Some of the important applications of vehicular networks in IIoT are platooning, road condition updates, e-toll, location-based advertising, retail promotion, infotainment and crowdsensing data (Thriveni, Kumar, & Sharma, 2013).

Oil and Gas Industry

Exploration of oil and gas reservoirs requires high end technology and scientific data. Customary practices involved expensive and unpredictable process of drilling and exploration based on geologist's analysis of the mapping of seafloor. Also, the vast data available on the status and condition of drilling tools, machinery, oil wells, drilling rig was difficult to store and process due to unavailability of sufficient storage and processing resources (Berge, 2018).

Present day oil and gas exploration involves the use of modern sensors, analytics and feedback control systems for enhanced connectivity, monitoring, control and automation (Lu, Guo, Azimi & Huang, 2019). With incorporation of IoT and availability of technological advances such as high bandwidth communication channels, wireless sensors, cloud storage, data analytics and intelligent networking, the process of predictability and exploration of oil and gas reservoirs has become efficient.

Manufacturing

Manufacturing processes can be made more reliable and efficient by integrating IoT. Smart sensors provide optimized asset and inventory management. Constant monitoring of manufacturing process help in achieving agile and energy efficient operations along with reduced machine downtime and operational costs. Some of the advantages achieved by incorporating IoT in manufacturing industry are reduction in operational cost, shorter time-to-market, mass customization, increased safety and reliability (Kiel, Arnold & Voigt, 2017).

Smart Building

Commercial and non-commercial buildings consume volumes of electricity and generate green-house gas emissions. The strategies developed to enhance energy efficiency of the buildings such as improving building insulation and providing better building control systems is difficult to be integrate in old buildings as they were not designed to be energy efficient (Kastner, Kofler, Jung, Gridling, & Weidinger, 2014). IoT plays a major role in efficient energy consumption by these buildings with the help of sensors, actuators and wireless communication. Heating, cooling, air-conditioning, escalators and lighting used in the buildings can be efficiently controlled with the help of sensors depending on the presence of people in the building (Jain, Kaushik, & Jayavel, 2017).

Smart Agriculture

With the help of IoT, smart agriculture helps the farmers with efficient decision making about crops based on weather and soil conditions. Some of the applications of IoT in agriculture are study of climatic conditions, precision farming, smart greenhouse, crop management and data analytics (Brewster, Roussaki, Kalatzis, Doolin, & Ellis, 2017). IoT solutions offer real-time monitoring of weather conditions such as temperature, humidity and rainfall. Based on this information farmers make suitable farming decisions. Precision farming makes the practice of farming more precise and controlled. Precision farming techniques such as livestock management, irrigation management, inventory monitoring, field observation and vehicle tracking increase the farming process manifolds. Solar powered IoT sensors help in real-time monitoring of greenhouse regarding light, temperature, pressure and humidity levels (Gill, Chana, & Buyya, 2017). Data collected by the sensors is stored and analyzed for long term prediction and decision making.

Retail and Supply Chain

Radio Frequency Identification (RFID) tags and sensors are being used in retail and supply chain to make informed decisions about goods and customers. In large retail houses IoT aids location, movement, accounting and stocking of inventory. Based on the sale of certain products, customer-centric decisions can be made to improve sales and customer experience (Jayaram, 2016). The generated consumer data is analyzed to decide the manufacturing status of certain product based on customer demand.

As seen from the above study, the role of IoT present day industry operation is crucial to attain enhanced production and operation efficiency while reducing the machine downtime. While integration of IoT in industrial applications provides numerous advantages, its features such as complex networks, heterogeneous data, support for diverse IoT devices and systems, and decentralization of IoT systems gives rise to the following challenges:

1. Interoperability is difficult to achieve due to heterogeneity among systems and devices.
2. IoT devices primarily comprise of sensor nodes. These nodes are resource constrained with limited processing and battery power.
3. IoT networks are comprises of a mix of static and mobile nodes communicating primarily over a wireless channel. There could be hundreds of diverse IoT sensors and devices communicating over network at a time using different wireless communication protocols. This forms a complex network architecture.

IoT systems are vulnerable to privacy and security as these devices are controlled and communicated through remotely. As the IoT network is decentralized, heterogeneous and comprises of resource constrained mobile nodes communicating over wireless medium, it becomes even more vulnerable to security attacks. Complex authentication and encryption processes are difficult to implement on resource constrained IoT nodes.

1.3 Role of Blockchain in IIoT

The blockchain technology was primarily used for cryptocurrency and secure financial transactions. Over the years, there have been attempts to explore and consider the use of blockchain for other industrial applications. Blockchain is a digital ledger of economic transactions, secured through cryptographic methods. It can be programmed to record the transaction of anything of value. A blockchain is a distributed and decentralized database of transactions that have been executed or shared among the participating nodes. The authors in (Zheng, Xie, Dai, Chen, & Wang, 2018) list decentralization, anonymity, chronological order of data, distributed security, transparency, immutability and stability of trustless environments as the advantages of blockchain. Since it is a distributed ledger, instead of single database or organization keeping transaction records, the records can be made available to other computers anonymously.

1.3.1. Characteristics of Blockchain Helpful for IIoT

- *Distributed database:* Every participating node in the blockchain has access to entire database. Therefore, no single entity has a control over the database. This increases the reliability of the records on database as it can be verified by any node.
- *Transparency:* As the database is distributed, the transactions are visible to everyone. These transactions are indelible once validated by the network.
- *Irreversible records:* If a transaction needs to be changed, then every other block in the chain need to be amended. This makes manipulation of records impossible.
- *Peer-to-peer communication:* In blockchain, all participating nodes are peers, unlike client-server architecture prevalent over Internet. There is no central node in the network. Therefore, very node is capable of communicating with every other node.

With all the above said advantages, blockchain is being considered highly beneficial for secure and trustworthy transactions in IIoT. This section presents the application of blockchain in different aspects of IIoT.

1.3.2 Blockchain for Healthcare

Management of patient data: Remote sharing and exchange of patient health records is vulnerable to security and reliability concerns. The incidents of mismatched patient records can be drastically reduced with the use of blockchain. Conventionally, the patient health records have remained fragmented. Blockchain facilitates the integration of patient health records by providing a structure for securely sharing the data with stakeholders. The stakeholders can access the patient records authentically, securely and reliably. The accessed data can be stored in the cloud for remote access in future. With the use of blockchain, the records of numerous patients can be monitored to identify the spread of diseases over a particular age group or region (Esposito et al, 2018) and (Ekblaw, Azaria, Halamka, & Lippman, 2016).

Drug supply chain: Drug supply and drug counterfeiting are the major issues faced by the pharmaceutical industry. In blockchain, every transaction in the block is timestamped and immutable thus making is easy to track them. The ability of tracking the products by using blockchain allows the pharmaceutical companies to monitor their supply chain to track and detect counterfeit medicines (Clauson, Breeden, Davidson, & Mackey, 2018) and (Jamil, Hang, Kim, & Kim, 2019).

1.3.3 Blockchain for Vehicular Networks

Secure message dissemination: Connected and autonomous vehicular networks are essential for intelligent transportation. In VANETs, the vehicular nodes can join and leave the network dynamically as in MANETs. This dynamic nature of the network also permits the entry of malicious nodes into the network. These malicious nodes can propagate false and untrustworthy information over the network. To overcome this issue of malicious data exchange, blockchain is being considered to support secure and trustworthy message dissemination. The blockchain can store and manage the history of trustworthiness of the messages exchanged and trust levels of the vehicular nodes propagating the messages, as a distributed and reliable solution (Mendiboure, Chalouf, & Krief, 2020) and (Shrestha, Bajracharya, Shrestha, & Nam, 2020).

1.3.4 Blockchain for Oil and Gas Industry

Digitized transactions: Oil and gas companies manage sale of crude oil and land worth millions of dollars. Conventional methods of maintaining records of such transactions has been cumbersome, prone to forgery and illicit activities. The use of blockchain is considered to bring enhanced security, transparency and efficiency in this industry (Berge, 2018) and (Ajao, Agajo, Adedokun, & Karngong, 2019).

Improved trust among parties: A private blockchain network can store the track record of employee and contractor certifications. This can be used to in future by the stakeholders before engaging in any transactions (Lu, Huang, Azimi, & Guo, 2019).

1.3.5 Blockchain for Manufacturing

Enhanced reliability and efficiency of manufacturing process: Incorporating blockchain in the manufacturing process enables the manufacturers with streamlining manufacturing operations, gaining better visibility into the supply chain and tracking the assets with precision. Blockchain is considered to enhance transparency and trust at different stages of manufacturing process such as supply chain monitoring, material provenance, counterfeit detection, identity management, asset tracking, quality assurance and regulatory compliance (Abeyratne & Monfared, 2016).

1.3.6 Blockchain for Smart Building

Efficient power management and billing: With the use of sensors and IoT, smart buildings can control power consumption based on the presence of people in the building. In case of absence of occupants in some area of the building, the power can be turned off, thus saving energy. A building may have different sections having different occupants. Based on the usage by the occupants of different sections of the building, billing can be controlled (Miglani, Kumar, Chamola, & Zeadally, 2020). This helps in efficiently controlling the usage of energy and billing.

1.3.7 Blockchain for Smart Agriculture

Agricultural produce traceability: Farmers, consumers and other stakeholders can maintain and obtain reliable information origins, produce and harvest of the agricultural produce. This enables consumers to trace the journey of the produce and keep a tab on its freshness, leading to timely food consumption and reducing food wastage (Caro, Ali, Vecchio, & Giaffreda, 2018) and (Salah, Nizamuddin, Jayaraman, & Omar, 2019).

Secure transactions and crop insurance: Enables farmers to sell their crops at fair price and benefit from agro commerce and micro-financing. Crop insurance involves communication of information regarding produce, its location and other basic compliance information with carriers. With better visibility about the crops, the participants can obtain reliable information about price, location, quality and state of the product (Tripoli & Schmidhuber, 2018) and (Kim & Laskowski, 2018).

1.3.8 Blockchain for Retail and Supply Chain

Retail and supply chain tracking: By integrating blockchain to the retail and supply chain industry the products can be tracked all the way from manufacturer to consumer. This ensures reliability in supply chain while overcoming the problem of counterfeiting of products. The production details are published in the blockchain by the manufacturer. The transit, logistics and retail details are further updated at the end of logistics partner, warehouse and retailer respectively (Azzi, Chamoun & Sokhn, 2019).

1.4 Challenges With Adoption of Blockchain Technology in IIoT

The IIoT nodes are mainly sensors or other small devices that are resource constrained in terms of storage and computational power. Therefore, adoption of blockchain technology becomes challenging in IIoT, despite of its advantages. Some the main challenges faced by adoption of blockchain in IIoT are as follows (Khan & Salah, 2018) and (Golatowski et al., 2019):

Scalability: The blockchain ledger increases with every transaction. More the number of nodes involved in the blockchain, larger will be the size of the ledger. As IIoT nodes are resource constrained, storage and computation of big ledgers is difficult. This also puts a limit on scale of the blockchain.

Storage: As all the nodes in a blockchain are peers, and there is no central entity to store transaction details and device IDs, this information has to be stored at the nodes itself. For resource constrained IIoT nodes this is a challenge.

Security: While blockchain is secure and robust against hacks, the IIoT applications running over the blockchain platform may not be secure. These connected devices stand huge risk of identity and data theft, device manipulation, data falsification and network manipulation. This calls for the need of mechanisms to identify and prevent the attacks on the IIoT systems.

Processing: Blockchain uses complex encryption and authentication mechanisms. Most of the participating nodes in blockchain may not be equipped with appropriate processing and computation resources required for such complex computations.

Intermittent connectivity: Mobile IoT devices require reliable bidirectional signaling between the IoT devices. Node mobility leads to breakages in connection leading to loss of data or delay in data transfer.

Bandwidth: The surge in the number of IoT devices and the data exchanged between them leads to bottleneck in the network. Reliable data exchange at required data rate requires sufficient bandwidth.

Time - critical applications: Time - critical applications such as healthcare, industrial control, mobility automation and real - time media need high bandwidth, data rate and low latency.

1.5 Research Opportunities to Support Blockchain for IIoT

As discussed in the Section 1.4, while the implementation of blockchain brings in numerous advantages to the field of IIoT, it brings in many challenges as well. This Section presents the research carried out in this field and available research opportunities.

1.5.1 Artificial Intelligence for Blockchain Based IIoT

In spite of blockchain being secure and robust against attacks, the IIoT applications running over blockchain may not be secure. AI can be used to perceive any threats that the blockchain based IIoT system could be vulnerable to. With AI, the application data can be traced and anomalies, fraud, delays and other external events can be detected (Golatowski et al., 2019).

Intelligent AI and ML algorithms are used to detect the presence of attacks in early stages in the IIoT applications and take appropriate action to prevent the damage, such as isolating the attacked component of the blockchain platform to keep the rest of it safe.

To support scalability, AI can increase the block creation rate in case of increasing number of transactions so that the throughput can be increased at the cost of longer confirmation times (Dinh & Thai, 2018).

1.5.2 Security in Blockchain Based IIoT

While the blockchain is secure and robust, the IIoT applications running over it may not be fully secure. Increasing number of connected IIoT devices also increase the number of threats and vulnerabilities of these devices. Attackers exploit these vulnerabilities through various tools and malicious codes. IIoT devices face threats that can be primarily classified under four different categories: Intruder attacks, Denial of Service (DoS), physical attacks and attacks on privacy (Rizvi, Kurtz, Pfeffer, & Rizvi, 2018).

Researchers are working on developing solutions to defend these attacks. In (Ometov et al., 2019) propose the adoption of multi-factor authentication such that multiple heterogenous factors can be combined to control access to IIoT devices and networks. For this, enablers such as hardware tokens, memorable passwords/PINs, fingerprint/palm/eye scanner, facial recognition, voice recognition, data from wearables and behavioral patterns are used. Authors in [38] emphasize the use of AI and ML to identify, predict and defend the security risks for IIoT devices and network. Authors in (Krishnan, Najeem & Achuthan, 2017) have developed a software defined networking (SDN) based framework for securing IoT networks. SDN is considered to be appropriate for providing security to IoT network due to its ability to securely connect millions of connected IoT devices, program dynamically for enforcing custom policies and applications, constant network security monitoring and dynamic network configuration to avoid malicious activity.

1.5.3 SDN and NFV for Blockchain Based IIoT

IIoT involves large number of devices with heterogenous characteristics. The participating devices and related applications have different data rate, throughput and latency requirements. As the participating devices in IIoT are diverse in terms of their capabilities (processor, memory and storage), have different performance requirements, and support different communication standards, traditional networking methods are not suitable for these networks. Use of SDN and NFV can help in achieving cost effective scaling and versatility of IIoT networks. NFV helps in reducing the CAPEX and OPEX cost of the network by sharing the network infrastructure for different services and applications (Ananth & Sharma, 2017) and ((Ananth & Sharma, 2016). It also provides customizability to the network through network slicing and subnet isolation.

As the network scales network bandwidth requirements also increase. SDN can dynamically configure network bandwidth based on network traffic and performance requirements of time-critical applications. Multiple paths can be used for route the data and load balancers can be used for faster data processing (Sharma & Reddy, 2019).

Mobile IIoT applications such as mobile ad-hoc networks (MANETs) and vehicular ad-hoc networks (VANETs) undergo network connectivity issues due to node mobility. Highly dynamic nature of these networks calls for dynamic allocation of network resources for QoS provisioning. The use of SDN in a VANET is explored in (Ku et al., 2014) and (Zhu, Cao, Pang, He, & Xu, 2015).

1.5.4 Big Data for Blockchain Based IIoT

IIoT applications generate thousands of Gigabytes of data per day. Huge digital data is generated by both humans and machines in diverse fields. Volumes of data is used in IIoT to streamline and optimize industrial functions, and to attain transparency in supply chain process. Big data is used to address specific problems in logistics processes (Teslya & Ryabchikov, 2017). In vehicular networks, big data produced from sensors is used to monitor weather and traffic conditions, study driving patterns, advertising and forecasts, and for vehicle diagnostics. The concern is safety and reliability of big data. This is where blockchain plays an important role. Multiple independent nodes in the IIoT blockchain can confirm ledger addition, and detect inconsistent and inaccurate records (Tariq et al., 2019). However, all of these devices are not capable of storing and processing the data. Therefore, advanced, efficient and robust techniques are required to handle such big data in terms of its acquisition, transmission, storage, computation, analytics and processing.

1.5.5 Bandwidth Enhancement for Mobile IIoT

As the IIoT applications gain popularity, data surge for these applications has led to bottleneck in the network. In mobile IIoT applications such as MANETs and VANETs, the node position changes rapidly and continuously. This makes it difficult to maintain the network connectivity. Many researchers are working on increasing the capacity and data rate of wireless communication channels. To increase the distance of wireless communication, contemporary wireless standards and devices use directional antenna (Nitsche et al., 2014). Directional antenna is used to direct energy and extend communication range in these networks (Sharma, Kadambi, Vershinin & Mukundan, 2015) and (Perahia & Gong, 2011). Antenna directivity combined with dual polarization increases network bandwidth, data rate and network throughput to maintain quality provisioning in highly dynamic mobile networks (Sharma, Kadambi, Vershinin & Mukundan, 2015) and (Rinki, 2014). Apart from mobile nodes, time - critical applications such as healthcare, industrial control, mobility automation and real - time media that need high bandwidth, data rate and low latency also get benefitted by dual polarized directional antenna (DPDA) based solutions. Present day wireless standards such as IEEE 802.11 ab, ad and 5G and 6G wireless communication technologies make use of antenna directivity and MIMO (Perahia & Gong, 2011) and (Zhang et al., 2019).

1.6 CONCLUSION

The way of carrying out operations in different industries has changed tremendously with IoT. Increase of IIoT applications calls for secure, reliable and robust IIoT communication. Blockchain technology's decentralized and distributed architecture plays a crucial role in securing IIoT communication and transactions. This chapter presents the role of Blockchain on in present day IIoT applications. The chapter presented the popular IIoT applications and the importance of blockchain in securing these applications. The challenges of adopting blockchain in IIoT are also discussed. A great deal of research is taking place to overcome these challenges. The research opportunities and open research issues in complete adoption of blockchain in IIoT are discussed with the aim to help the researchers in this domain.

REFERENCES

Abeyratne, S. A., & Monfared, R. P. (2016). Blockchain ready manufacturing supply chain using distributed ledger. *International Journal of Research in Engineering and Technology, 5*(9), 1–10. doi:10.15623/ijret.2016.0509001

Ajao, L. A., Agajo, J., Adedokun, E. A., & Karngong, L. (2019). Crypto hash algorithm-based blockchain technology for managing decentralized ledger database in oil and gas industry. *J—Multidisciplinary Scientific Journal, 2*(3), 300-325.

Ananth, M. D., & Sharma, R. (2016, December). Cloud management using network function virtualization to reduce capex and opex. In *2016 8th International Conference on Computational Intelligence and Communication Networks (CICN)* (pp. 43-47). IEEE. 10.1109/CICN.2016.17

Ananth, M. D., & Sharma, R. (2017, January). Cost and performance analysis of network function virtualization based cloud systems. In *2017 IEEE 7th International Advance Computing Conference (IACC)* (pp. 70-74). IEEE. 10.1109/IACC.2017.0029

Azzi, R., Chamoun, R. K., & Sokhn, M. (2019). The power of a blockchain-based supply chain. *Computers & Industrial Engineering, 135*, 582–592. doi:10.1016/j.cie.2019.06.042

Berge, J. (2018, April). Digital Transformation and IIoT for Oil and Gas Production. In *Offshore Technology Conference*. Offshore Technology Conference. 10.4043/28643-MS

Brewster, C., Roussaki, I., Kalatzis, N., Doolin, K., & Ellis, K. (2017). IoT in agriculture: Designing a Europe-wide large-scale pilot. *IEEE Communications Magazine, 55*(9), 26–33. doi:10.1109/MCOM.2017.1600528

Caro, M. P., Ali, M. S., Vecchio, M., & Giaffreda, R. (2018, May). Blockchain-based traceability in Agri-Food supply chain management: A practical implementation. In 2018 IoT Vertical and Topical Summit on Agriculture-Tuscany (IOT Tuscany) (pp. 1-4). IEEE. doi:10.1109/IOT-TUSCANY.2018.8373021

Clauson, K. A., Breeden, E. A., Davidson, C., & Mackey, T. K. (2018). Leveraging blockchain technology to enhance supply chain management in healthcare: an exploration of challenges and opportunities in the health supply chain. *Blockchain in Healthcare Today, 1*(3), 1-12.

Dinh, T. N., & Thai, M. T. (2018). Ai and blockchain: A disruptive integration. *Computer, 51*(9), 48–53. doi:10.1109/MC.2018.3620971

Ekblaw, A., Azaria, A., Halamka, J. D., & Lippman, A. (2016, August). A Case Study for Blockchain in Healthcare:"MedRec" prototype for electronic health records and medical research data. In *Proceedings of IEEE open & big data conference* (Vol. 13, p. 13). Academic Press.

Esposito, C., De Santis, A., Tortora, G., Chang, H., & Choo, K. K. R. (2018). Blockchain: A panacea for healthcare cloud-based data security and privacy? *IEEE Cloud Computing, 5*(1), 31–37. doi:10.1109/MCC.2018.011791712

Gill, S. S., Chana, I., & Buyya, R. (2017). IoT based agriculture as a cloud and big data service: The beginning of digital India. *Journal of Organizational and End User Computing, 29*(4), 1–23. doi:10.4018/JOEUC.2017100101

Golatowski, F., Butzin, B., Brockmann, T., Schulz, T., Kasparick, M., Li, Y., ... Aydemir, Ö. (2019, May). Challenges and research directions for blockchains in the internet of things. In *2019 IEEE International Conference on Industrial Cyber Physical Systems (ICPS)* (pp. 712-717). IEEE. 10.1109/ICPHYS.2019.8780270

Gopinath, T., Kumar, A. R., & Sharma, R. (2013, April). Performance evaluation of TCP and UDP over wireless ad-hoc networks with varying traffic loads. In *2013 International Conference on Communication Systems and Network Technologies* (pp. 281-285). IEEE. 10.1109/CSNT.2013.66

Huang, J., Kong, L., Chen, G., Wu, M. Y., Liu, X., & Zeng, P. (2019). Towards secure industrial IoT: Blockchain system with credit-based consensus mechanism. *IEEE Transactions on Industrial Informatics, 15*(6), 3680–3689. doi:10.1109/TII.2019.2903342

Jain, M., Kaushik, N., & Jayavel, K. (2017, February). Building automation and energy control using IoT-Smart campus. In *2017 2nd International Conference on Computing and Communications Technologies (ICCCT)* (pp. 353-359). IEEE. 10.1109/ICCCT2.2017.7972303

Jamil, F., Hang, L., Kim, K., & Kim, D. (2019). A novel medical blockchain model for drug supply chain integrity management in a smart hospital. *Electronics (Basel), 8*(5), 505. doi:10.3390/electronics8050505

Jayaram, A. (2016, December). Lean six sigma approach for global supply chain management using industry 4.0 and IIoT. In *2016 2nd international conference on contemporary computing and informatics (IC3I)* (pp. 89-94). IEEE.

Kastner, W., Kofler, M., Jung, M., Gridling, G., & Weidinger, J. (2014, September). Building Automation Systems Integration into the Internet of Things The IoT6 approach, its realization and validation. In *Proceedings of the 2014 IEEE Emerging Technology and Factory Automation (ETFA)* (pp. 1-9). IEEE. 10.1109/ETFA.2014.7005197

Khan, M. A., & Salah, K. (2018). IoT security: Review, blockchain solutions, and open challenges. *Future Generation Computer Systems, 82*, 395–411. doi:10.1016/j.future.2017.11.022

Kiel, D., Arnold, C., & Voigt, K. I. (2017). The influence of the Industrial Internet of Things on business models of established manufacturing companies–A business level perspective. *Technovation*, *68*, 4–19. doi:10.1016/j.technovation.2017.09.003

Kim, H. M., & Laskowski, M. (2018). Agriculture on the blockchain: Sustainable solutions for food, farmers, and financing. In *Supply Chain Revolution.* Barrow Books.

Krishnan, P., Najeem, J. S., & Achuthan, K. (2017, August). SDN framework for securing IoT networks. In *International Conference on Ubiquitous Communications and Network Computing* (pp. 116-129). Springer.

Ku, I., Lu, Y., Gerla, M., Gomes, R. L., Ongaro, F., & Cerqueira, E. (2014, June). Towards software-defined VANET: Architecture and services. In *2014 13th annual Mediterranean ad hoc networking workshop (MED-HOC-NET)* (pp. 103-110). IEEE.

Lu, H., Guo, L., Azimi, M., & Huang, K. (2019). Oil and Gas 4.0 era: A systematic review and outlook. *Computers in Industry*, *111*, 68–90. doi:10.1016/j.compind.2019.06.007

Lu, H., Huang, K., Azimi, M., & Guo, L. (2019). Blockchain technology in the oil and gas industry: A review of applications, opportunities, challenges, and risks. *IEEE Access: Practical Innovations, Open Solutions*, *7*, 41426–41444. doi:10.1109/ACCESS.2019.2907695

Mendiboure, L., Chalouf, M. A., & Krief, F. (2020). Survey on blockchain-based applications in internet of vehicles. *Computers & Electrical Engineering*, *84*, 106646. doi:10.1016/j.compeleceng.2020.106646

Miglani, A., Kumar, N., Chamola, V., & Zeadally, S. (2020). Blockchain for Internet of Energy management: Review, solutions, and challenges. *Computer Communications*, *151*, 395–418. doi:10.1016/j.comcom.2020.01.014

Nitsche, T., Cordeiro, C., Flores, A. B., Knightly, E. W., Perahia, E., & Widmer, J. C. (2014). IEEE 802.11 ad: Directional 60 GHz communication for multi-Gigabit-per-second Wi-Fi. *IEEE Communications Magazine*, *52*(12), 132–141. doi:10.1109/MCOM.2014.6979964

Ometov, A., Petrov, V., Bezzateev, S., Andreev, S., Koucheryavy, Y., & Gerla, M. (2019). Challenges of multi-factor authentication for securing advanced IoT applications. *IEEE Network*, *33*(2), 82–88. doi:10.1109/MNET.2019.1800240

Perahia, E., & Gong, M. X. (2011). Gigabit wireless LANs: An overview of IEEE 802.11 ac and 802.11 ad. *Mobile Computing and Communications Review*, *15*(3), 23–33. doi:10.1145/2073290.2073294

Rinki, S. (2014). *Simulation studies on effects of dual polarisation and directivity of antennas on the performance of MANETs* (Doctoral dissertation). Coventry University.

Rizvi, S., Kurtz, A., Pfeffer, J., & Rizvi, M. (2018, August). Securing the Internet of Things (IoT): A security taxonomy for IoT. In *2018 17th IEEE International Conference On Trust, Security And Privacy In Computing And Communications/12th IEEE International Conference On Big Data Science And Engineering (TrustCom/BigDataSE)* (pp. 163-168). IEEE.

Salah, K., Nizamuddin, N., Jayaraman, R., & Omar, M. (2019). Blockchain-based soybean traceability in agricultural supply chain. *IEEE Access: Practical Innovations, Open Solutions*, 7, 73295–73305. doi:10.1109/ACCESS.2019.2918000

Schneider, S. (2017). The industrial internet of things (iiot) applications and taxonomy. *Internet of Things and Data Analytics Handbook*, 41-81.

Sengupta, J., Ruj, S., & Bit, S. D. (2020). A Comprehensive survey on attacks, security issues and blockchain solutions for IoT and IIoT. *Journal of Network and Computer Applications*, 149, 102481. doi:10.1016/j.jnca.2019.102481

Sharama, R., Shankar, J. U., & Rajan, S. T. (2014, April). Effect of Number of Active Nodes and Inter-node Distance on the Performance of Wireless Sensor Networks. In *2014 Fourth International Conference on Communication Systems and Network Technologies* (pp. 69-73). IEEE. 10.1109/CSNT.2014.22

Sharma, R., Gupta, S. K., Suhas, K. K., & Kashyap, G. S. (2014, April). Performance analysis of Zigbee based wireless sensor network for remote patient monitoring. In *2014 Fourth International Conference on Communication Systems and Network Technologies* (pp. 58-62). IEEE. 10.1109/CSNT.2014.21

Sharma, R., Kadambi, G. R., Vershinin, Y. A., & Mukundan, K. N. (2015, April). Dual Polarised Directional Communication based Medium Access Control Protocol for Performance Enhancement of MANETs. In *2015 Fifth International Conference on Communication Systems and Network Technologies* (pp. 185-189). IEEE. 10.1109/CSNT.2015.104

Sharma, R., Kadambi, G. R., Vershinin, Y. A., & Mukundan, K. N. (2015, April). Multipath Routing Protocol to Support Dual Polarised Directional Communication for Performance Enhancement of MANETs. In *2015 Fifth International Conference on Communication Systems and Network Technologies* (pp. 258-262). IEEE. 10.1109/CSNT.2015.105

Sharma, R., & Reddy, H. (2019, December). Effect of Load Balancer on Software-Defined Networking (SDN) based Cloud. In *2019 IEEE 16th India Council International Conference (INDICON)* (pp. 1-4). IEEE.

Shrestha, R., Bajracharya, R., Shrestha, A. P., & Nam, S. Y. (2020). A new type of blockchain for secure message exchange in VANET. *Digital Communications and Networks*, 6(2), 177–186. doi:10.1016/j.dcan.2019.04.003

Tariq, N., Asim, M., Al-Obeidat, F., Zubair Farooqi, M., Baker, T., Hammoudeh, M., & Ghafir, I. (2019). The security of big data in fog-enabled IoT applications including blockchain: A survey. *Sensors (Basel)*, 19(8), 1788. doi:10.339019081788 PMID:31013993

Teslya, N., & Ryabchikov, I. (2017, November). Blockchain-based platform architecture for industrial IoT. In *2017 21st Conference of Open Innovations Association (FRUCT)* (pp. 321-329). IEEE. 10.23919/FRUCT.2017.8250199

Thriveni, H. B., Kumar, G. M., & Sharma, R. (2013, April). Performance evaluation of routing protocols in mobile ad-hoc networks with varying node density and node mobility. In *2013 International Conference on Communication Systems and Network Technologies* (pp. 252-256). IEEE. 10.1109/CSNT.2013.60

Tripoli, M., & Schmidhuber, J. (2018). *Emerging Opportunities for the Application of Blockchain in the Agri-food Industry.* FAO and ICTSD: Rome and Geneva. Licence: CC BY-NC-SA, 3.

Tyagi, S., Agarwal, A., & Maheshwari, P. (2016, January). A conceptual framework for IoT-based healthcare system using cloud computing. In 2016 6th International Conference-Cloud System and Big Data Engineering (Confluence) (pp. 503-507). IEEE. doi:10.1109/CONFLUENCE.2016.7508172

Weyer, S., Schmitt, M., Ohmer, M., & Gorecky, D. (2015). Towards Industry 4.0-Standardization as the crucial challenge for highly modular, multi-vendor production systems. *IFAC-PapersOnLine*, *48*(3), 579–584. doi:10.1016/j.ifacol.2015.06.143

Zhang, Z., Xiao, Y., Ma, Z., Xiao, M., Ding, Z., Lei, X., Karagiannidis, G. K., & Fan, P. (2019). 6G wireless networks: Vision, requirements, architecture, and key technologies. *IEEE Vehicular Technology Magazine*, *14*(3), 28–41. doi:10.1109/MVT.2019.2921208

Zheng, Z., Xie, S., Dai, H. N., Chen, X., & Wang, H. (2018). Blockchain challenges and opportunities: A survey. *International Journal of Web and Grid Services*, *14*(4), 352–375. doi:10.1504/IJWGS.2018.095647

Zheng, Z., Xie, S., Dai, H. N., Chen, X., & Wang, H. (2018). Blockchain challenges and opportunities: A survey. *International Journal of Web and Grid Services*, *14*(4), 352–375. doi:10.1504/IJWGS.2018.095647

Zhu, M., Cao, J., Pang, D., He, Z., & Xu, M. (2015, August). SDN-based routing for efficient message propagation in VANET. In *International Conference on Wireless Algorithms, Systems, and Applications* (pp. 788-797). Springer. 10.1007/978-3-319-21837-3_77

This research was previously published in Blockchain and AI Technology in the Industrial Internet of Things; pages 32-47, copyright year 2021 by Engineering Science Reference (an imprint of IGI Global).

APPENDIX

List of Abbreviations:

5G Fifth Generation
6G Sixth Generation
AI Artificial Intelligence
CAPEX Capital Expenditure
CPS Cyber Physical System
DoS Denial of Service
DPDA Dual Polarized Directional Antenna
ID Identifier
IIoT Industrial Internet of Things
IoT Internet of Things
MANET Mobile Ad-hoc Network
MIMO Multi Input Multi Output
ML Machine Learning
NFV Network Function Virtualization
OPEX Operational Expenditure
PIN Personal Identification Number
QoS Quality of Service
RFID Radio Frequency Identification
SDN Software Defined Networking
VANET Vehicular Ad-hoc Network

Chapter 28
Blockchain Technology– Security Booster

Harsha Kundan Patil

 https://orcid.org/0000-0002-1801-4086

Ashoka Center for Business and Computer Studies, Nashik, India

ABSTRACT

"Blockchain" as the name suggests is the chain of blocks. It is the chunk of digital information (blocks) that are connected through the public databases (Chain). It is nothing but the newer version of file organisation. Blocks store digital information like actual record of any transaction, details of involve entities in the transaction, time stamps, and other metadata of the transactions. Blocks also have unique ids, which are known as hash. Blockchain technology is built using peer-to-peer networking. Anyone who is on network can access the blocks. There is no centralised community to control the blockchain. It is operated by miners, the peoples who lend their computing power to the network to solve the complex computation algorithm problems. These blocks are stored in multiple computers. Due to its distribution and decentralisation, the validation process is broadcast in nature, which provides it "the trusted approach". Blockchain enables security and tamperproof capabilities for storing data and smart contracts. Any tampering of data attempted by a node or user in a block changes the hash of the block. The blockchain technology has the capability to face and provides the solution to fight with the problem of risk and security concern online. In 2008, a mysterious white paper titled "Bitcoin: A Peer to Peer Electronic Cash System", by visionary Satoshi Nakamoto gave birth to the concept of blockchain. The chapter explains the structure of blockchain technology in detail and enlighten the aspects that make blockchain technology the secure concept of today's world.

INTRODUCTION

"Blockchain" as the name suggest is the Chain of Blocks. The Chunk of digital information (Blocks) which are connected through the public databases (Chain). It is nothing but the newer version of the File organisation. Blocks stored digital information like actual record of any transaction, details of involve entities in the transaction, timestamps and other metadata of the transactions. Blocks also has unique id which is known as hash.

DOI: 10.4018/978-1-6684-7132-6.ch028

Blockchain technology is built using peer-to-peer networking. Anyone who is on network can access the blocks. There is no centralised community to control the Blockchain. It is operated by miners; the peoples who lend their computing power to the network to solve the complex computation algorithm problems. These blocks are stored in multiple computers. Figure 1 shows step by step working of Blockchain.

Step1: When any online transaction like purchasing through Amazon occurred and successfully completed the details of transaction is recorded.

Step2: The next step is verification. The details of the transaction verified through network of computers. Thousands of computers connected through global network are utilised for verification process. Which involves verification of purchased article details, transactiontimestamp, cost and parties involved in it.

Step3: After transaction details verified it stored in block with digital signatures of involved parties. One block may contain many verified transactions. The block also have the hash key which gives the unique identification to the block. This block is then added to existing chain of block. So in this way the blockchain grows. Once the block is added to blockchain it is publically available for all.

Each computer which is connected to the blockchain network has their own copy of blockchain and whenever new block added on it the copy of each computer is updated. That means all the computers of the blockchain network have the same copy of network and each time whenever any block is access or added the verifications are done by all connected computers. As we know it is easy to hide from one's eye but difficult to hide from all's eyes. This 360 degree verification of public network makes blockchain very secured.

Concept of Blockchain Technology and its Emergence

Blockchain, the underlying technology behind cryptocurrencies has its origin that stem from a problem of verifying timestamp digitally in the late 1980s and early 1990s. In 1990, Haber & Stornetta published a paper titled 'How to Timestamp a digital Document'. In this paper, they proposed to create a hash chain by linking the issued timestamps together so that the documents get prevented from being either forward dated or back dated, (Haber,1990). Then, Wei Dai one of the noted researchers, introduced the concept of b-money which is used to create money through solving computational puzzles and decentralized consensus. But this proposal lacks implementation details (Dai, 1998). A concept called "reusable proofs of work" was introduced by Hal Finney. This concept combined the ideas of both b-money and computationally difficult Hash cash puzzle by Adam Back for the creation of cryptocurrency.

Block chain technology is having the focus of Ecommerce developer due to its quality of exchange of value units without the need of intermediaries (Nakamoto, 2008). It allow us to secure our digital assets like art or digital data from sensors on a marketplace (Draskovic and Saleh, 2017), or allowing property owners to transfer their land without a notary (Kombe et al., 2017). Technology is also get used to address several other scientific problems (Dhillon, 2016; Golem, 2016; Wolf et al., 2016; Breitinger and Gipp, 2017; van Rossum, 2017; Androulaki et al., 2018) like trust problems in the form of malicious behavior in peer-review processes (Stahel and Moore, 2014; Degen, 2016; Dansinger, 2017), lacking quality and redundancy of study designs (Belluz and Hoffman, 2015), and the restriction of free access to scientific publications (Myllylahti, 2014; Teplitskiy et al., 2017; Schiltz, 2018).

Figure 1. Blockchain Generation

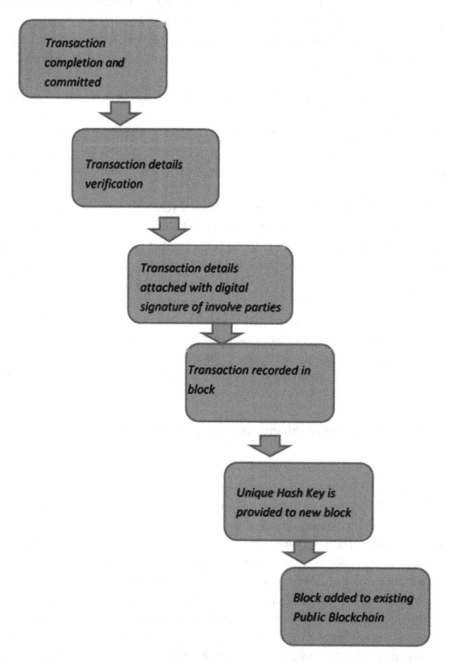

Blockchain Concept

As the world requirements more transformation and digitization, everybody is prepared to receive and adapt new technologies (Dorri et. al. 2016). Blockchain, a new troublesome technology was introduced with its very first modern application termed Bitcoin. The term Blockchain is simply well-defined as the chain of blocks containing encrypted material stored on a decentralized distributed network. This developing technology influences various industries amazingly and its application grows numerously. Blockchain, a shared ledger in which all the data are recorded digitally has a common history and is available to all the participants in the network. This eliminates any fraudulent activity or duplication of transactions. Blockchain is a chain of blocks. Each block covers encrypted information and hashed sticks to previous block, making it problematic to retroactively alter without adapting the entire chain. The first block is called genesis block. Every block contains two components Block header and Block Body.

Block Header

The various components present in the block header is version, Hash of previous block, Merkle root, Timestamp,Target,Nonce.

Public Blockchain

It is a decentralized network in which only the transaction information is totally available to the public. In this type of Blockchain, any user can link the network at any time and they can pile, send and receive data at anywhere and at any time. This feature of Public Blockchain network types it call as Permission less network. The participants in this network gets incentivized and rewarded using the token associated with them. Many decentralized consensus devices such as PoW, PoS are used to make decisions.Public Blockchain networks provide self-governance and higher level of security since all the transaction information are present in all the nodes in the network which makes hacking a particular node impossible.

Private Blockchain

Private Blockchain usually called Permissioned Blockchain are exploits within a institute in which the members need consent in order to join the network. Private Blockchains are more centralized and the transactions are private. The originalities that want to collaborate and share data can make use of private blockchains since it offers more efficiency and faster transactions. The code in this type of blockchain is precisely private and hidden which results in eliminating decentralization and disintermediation. Here, the central-in-charge helps to achieve consensus by giving the mining rights to anyone in the network.

Consortium or Federated Blockchain

A hybrid model between public and private Blockchain in which a number of approved users have control over the network. The term consortium is defined as the group of companies or the group of illustrative individuals who come together to make decisions for the best benefit of the whole network. The consortium blockchain allows only a few selected predetermined parties to verify transactions and to participate in the consensus process instead of allowing any user in the network in case of public blockchain and a single organization in case of private blockchain,(Pilkington, 2016).

Security framework:

Generally redundancy of data is the main source and responsible for generate inconsistency issues in data. But this property is well utilised in Blockchain. The inconsistency generated due to redundancy works as indicator for alteration of block data. Whenever any block data changes the hash key automatically changed which recursively generate inconsistency with trailing blocks.

So if anyone wants to edit block data it indirectly required to alter the hash details of all blocks connected to block chain, which may involve to alteration of millions of computers' blockchain which is very complex to handle. The longest blockchain i.e. Maximum users agreed upon blockchain has been the accepted block chain. This technique known as consensus which accept the longest blockchain when multiple copies of blockchain are available.

By storing data across its network, the blockchain eliminates the risks that come with data being held centrally. Blockchain deploy the encryption methods to strengthen the security of data. After user name password the OTP method is also failed to secure the user data. In blockchain the existing methods are exploiting in a way which overall improved the security of blockchain. The combination of public key and private key worked on blockchain for implementing the security policy of blockchain. Anyone who wants to see the block can see it publically but retrieval of data from block is only possible with the help of private key. If any owner forget the private key of his block it will never be accessible to anyone including himself.

Blockchain and IOT: Security Review

In the era of smartness, smart mobile phone, smart infrastructure, smart devices and smart machines are the leaves of tree named IoT. The heavy acceptance and developments in the area of IoT also attracted hackers as vulnerability of digital data increases. The ecosystem of IoT work in decentralised manner (Atzori et.al., 2010). Data is generated and shared throughout the network and not controlled by any specific device. Due to this distributed data approach, data availability and efficiency of connected devices' service become more rapid, well-organized and reasonable. Rather than working with clod computing or other storage solutions nowadays IoT devices are preferring use of distributed database technology through blockchain concept, (Giusto et. al. 2014).

Conferring to various research reports, there are about 5 billion IoT connected devices which is forecast to upsurge up to 50 billion devices by 2022. The IoT devices shows an important role in changing the current world to smart world. As the number of IoT devices continues to proliferate, data and transaction verification, access control all become important (Christidis et al., 2016). Further, the security holes of IoT upsurges due to the collection of data from various devices at one place, controlling remotely of devices by hackers, handling the devices, lack of ability to find compromised nodes, leakage of sensitive data and other activities. It is an arduous task to overcome the security issues faced by IoT devicesThe problems and security issues with IoT devices could be unlocked if IoT devices becomes decentralized.

Many security experts believe that Blockchain could be the silver bullet needed by the IoT devices to solve its issues. Blockchain when integrated with IoT could improve security and distributed processing power of IoT devices and also solves the problem of cloud-based data monopolyFurther, the blockchain is able to track and process the massive flow of data that pours from myriad of IoT devices. Blockchain and IoT is viewed as a perfect match since blockchain could solve many of the issues associated with IoT devices.

Even if many of the matters of IoT devices are resolved by rapidly accelerating Blockchain technology, the convergence of these two blossoming technologies suffer from certain problems. Since the IoT devices are designed to be light weight and have low processing power, the integration of Blockchain in these devices poses a problem. Also, associated with Blockchain is the scalability issue and sky rocketing fees. So, many companies took convergence of these technologies on their many agenda and starts working on it.

(Elsts, Mitskas, and Oikonomou 2018)IOTA, the Blockchainless cryptocurrency for the Internet of Things is especially being designed for the integration of IoT devices with Blockchain technology. It is a quantum resistant Directed Acyclic Graph (DAG) which works on the top of their own ledger called Tangle. In this graph, nodes are the IOTA transactions and the validation corresponds to edges. Each transaction must validate two other transactions before joining the network. For validation, Proof-of-Work mechanism is used. IOTA is designed to provide zero fee transactions and unique verification process which is able to solve the scalability issues of Blockchain.

DAG differs from other blockchain in such a way that DAG works on 'horizontal' scheme and blockchain is based on 'vertical' scheme and also there are no miners and blocks in DAG, hence the name blocklesschain. The nature of graph is acyclic and also flows in a specific direction. The transactions in IOTA is not duplicated and there is no wait time for the blocks to be confirmed which in turns reduces the sky rocketing transaction fees. Even though, IOTA tries to be a perfect solution, there exists communication overhead of integrating IoT devices with IOTA blockchain.

Following features of Blockchain technology makes more efficient for using in IoT also shows in figure2:

Figure 2. Features of Blockchain, enhancing efficiency of IoT

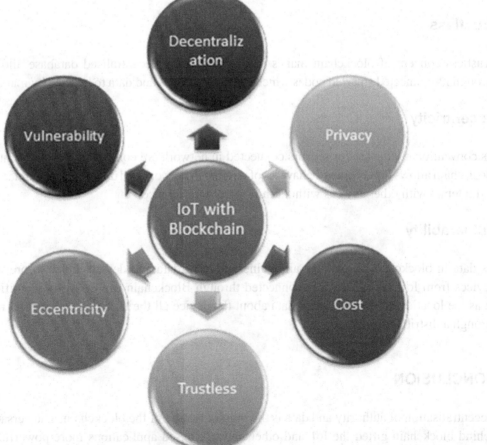

Decentralization

As architecture of IoT and Blockchain is very similar, that is the reason that decentralisation concept of blockchain boosted the use of it in IoT. Blockchain provides the solution for IoT for managing the data and working of all connected devices without any third party. So failure of any device in a network of things never results in unavailability of data.

Privacy

Deployment of blockchain networks concepts in IoT, enhance the privacy of individual device data. As devices are connected in internet, any hacker can easily access the device and can manipulate the data, but due to using of Blockchain technology its consensus protocol prevent such alteration of data records.

Cost

Use of Blockchain Database is major reason for making IoT devices more affordable. Due to cost reduction IoT devices and technology has been implemented in many other domain easily. As no third party is required to maintain and verify the data cost is effectively diminishes. The connected nodes itself taking part in validating the data.

Trustless

Trustless concept of blockchain makes IoT more secure. Decentralised database allows verification through its connected smarted nodes which prevents devices and data to be hack by malicious elements.

Eccentricity

As conventionally devices or sensors connected in network are controlled by some central device. But block chain allows the eccentric behaviour of devices in network and devices can automatically responses and interact with other devices without third party interference.

Vulnerability

As data in blockchain is open for all. Vulnerability of data and devices helps to prevent the theft of devices from IoT. As IoT devices connected through Blockchain can be easily identified and tracked as as the location and management data about the device all the time can be kept and made reachable through a distributed database.

CONCLUSION

Decentralisation of authority and data is the biggest feature of the blockchain. The versatile technology behind blockchain gifted the IoT and other network based applications more powerful, efficient and secure. Nowadays researcher and engineers are deploying blockchain in many domain to enhance the data security. Above discussed features of blockchain not only make IoT application powerful but also helps in every area to strengthen the power of applications.

REFERENCES

Ali, M. S., Dolui, K., & Antonelli, F. (2017). IoT data privacy via blockchains and IPFS. In *International Conference on the Internet of Things*. ACM. 10.1145/3131542.3131563

Androulaki, E., Barger, A., Bortnikov, V., Cachin, C., Christidis, K., De Caro, A., ...(2018). Hyperledger fabric: a distributed operating system for permissioned blockchains. In *EuroSys '18 - Proceedings of the Thirteenth EuroSys Conference*. Porto: ACM. 10.1145/3190508.3190538

Antonopoulos, A. M. (2014). *Mastering Bitcoin* (1st ed.). O'Reilly Media.

Atzori, L., Iera, A., & Morabito, G. (2010). The Internet of Things: A survey. *Computer Networks*, *54*(15), 2787–2805. doi:10.1016/j.comnet.2010.05.010

Banerjee, M., Lee, J., & Choo, K.-K. R. (2017). *A blockchain future to Internet of Things security: A position paper*. Digital Communications and Networks. doi:10.1016/j.dcan.2017.10.006

Banerjee, M., Lee, J., & Choo, K. K. R. (2018). A Blockchain future for internet of things security: A position paper. *Digit. Commun. Networks*, *4*(3), 149–160. doi:10.1016/j.dcan.2017.10.006

Belluz, J., & Hoffman, S. (2015). *The One Chart You Need to Understand Any Health Study*. Vox. Available online at: https://www.vox.com/2015/1/5/7482871/types-of-study-design

Chollet, Castiaux, Bruneton, & Sainlez. (2013). *Continuous interconnected supply chain using blockchain and internet of things supply chain traceability*. Deloitte Blockchain.

Christidis, K., & Devetsikiotis, M. (2016). Blockchains and Smart Contracts for the Internet of Things. *IEEE Access: Practical Innovations, Open Solutions*, *4*, 2292–2303. doi:10.1109/ACCESS.2016.2566339

Conoscenti, M., Torino, D., Vetr, A., Torino, D., & De Martin, J. C. (2016). Blockchain for the Internet of Things: a Systematic Literature Review. *IEEE/ACS 13th International Conference of Computer Systems and Applications (AICCSA)*. 10.1109/AICCSA.2016.7945805

Dai, W. (1998). *B-money*. http://www.weidai.com/bmoney.txt

Dhillon, V. (2016). *Blockchain-Enabled Open Science Framework*. O'Reilly Media. Available online at: https://www.oreilly.com/ideas/blockchain-enabled-open-science-framework

Dhillon, V., Metcalf, D., & Hooper, M. (2017). *"Blockchain in science," in Blockchain Enabled Applications* (1st ed.). Apress. doi:10.1007/978-1-4842-3081-7

Dorri, A., Kanhere, S., & Jurdak, R. (2016). *Blockchain in internet of things: challenges and solutions*. arXiv: 1608.05187

Draskovic, D., & Saleh, G. (2017). *Datapace - Decentralized Data Marketplace Based on Blockchain*. Available online at: https://www.datapace.io/datapace_whitepaper.pdf

Elsts, Mitskas, & Oikonomou. (2018). Distributed Ledger Technology and the Internet of Things: A Feasibility Study. In BlockSys, Shenzhen, China.

Giusto, D., Iera, A., Morabito, G., & Atzori, L. (2014). The Internet of Things. In *20th Tyrrhenian Workshop on Digital Communication*. Springer Publishing Company, Incorporated.

Golem. (2016). *The Golem Project - Global Market for Idle Computer Power*. Available online at: https:// golem.network/crowdfunding

Gord, M. (2016). *Smart Contracts Described by Nick Szabo 20 Years ago now becoming Reality. Bitcoin Magazine*.

Haber, S., & Stometta, W. S. (1991). How to time stamp a digital documents. Journal of Cryptography, 3(2), 99-111. doi:10.1007/3-540-38424-3_32

Huh, Cho, & Kim. (2017). Managing IoT Devices using Blockchain Platform. *ICACT2017*.

Janowicz, K., Regalia, B., Hitzler, P., Mai, G., Delbecque, S., Fröhlich, M., Martinent, P., & Lazarus, T. (2018). On the prospects of blockchain and distributed ledger technologies for open science and academic publishing. *Semantic Web*, 9(5), 545–555. doi:10.3233/SW-180322

Khan & Salah. (2017). IoT security: Review, blockchain solutions, and open challenges. *Future Generation Computer Systems*.

Kombe, C., Manyilizu, M., & Mvuma, A. (2017). Design of land administration and title registration model based on blockchain technology. *Journal of Information Engineering and Applications*, 7, 8–15.

Liang, X., Zhao, J., Shetty, S., & Li, D. (2017). Towards data assurance and resilience in IoT using blockchain. *Conference Paper*. 10.1109/MILCOM.2017.8170858

Macleod, M. R., Michie, S., Roberts, I., Dirnagl, U., Chalmers, I., Ioannidis, J. P., Salman, R. A.-S., Chan, A.-W., & Glasziou, P. (2014). Biomedical research: Increasing value, reducing waste. *Lancet*, 383(9912), 101–104. doi:10.1016/S0140-6736(13)62329-6 PMID:24411643

Myllylahti, M. (2014). Newspaper paywalls–the hype and the reality. *Digit. Journal.*, 2(2), 179–194. do i:10.1080/21670811.2013.813214

Nakamoto, S. (2008). *Bitcoin: A. Peer to Peer. Electronic cash system*. https://bitcoin.org/bitcoin.pdf

Pilkington. (2016). Blockchain technology: Principle and applications. *Research Handbook on Digital Transformations*.

Schiltz, M. (2018). Science without publication paywalls: cOAlition S for the realisation of full and immediate open access. *PLoS Medicine*, 15(9), e1002663. doi:10.1371/journal.pmed.1002663 PMID:30178782

Stahel, P. F., & Moore, E. E. (2014). Peer review for biomedical publications: We can improve the system. *BMC Medicine*, 12(1), 179. doi:10.118612916-014-0179-1 PMID:25270270

Swan. (2015). *Blockchain Blue Print for a new economy*. O'Reilly Media.

Teplitskiy, M., Lu, G., & Duede, E. (2017). Amplifying the impact of open access: Wikipedia and the diffusion of science. *Journal of the Association for Information Science and Technology, 68*(9), 2116–2127. doi:10.1002/asi.23687

van Rossum, J. (2017). *Blockchain for Research - Perspectives on a New Paradigm for Scholarly Communication. Technical report.* Digital Science. doi:10.6084/m9.figshare.5607778

Wolf, M., Wiegand, M., & Drichel, A. (2016). *PEvO (Publish and Evaluate Onchain).* Available online at: https://pevo.science/files/pevo_whitepaper.pdf

Wortner, P., Schubotz, M., Breitinger, C., Leible, S., & Gipp, B. (2019). Securing the integrity of time series data in open science projects using blockchain-based trusted timestamping. *Proceedings of the Workshop on Web Archiving and Digital Libraries (WADL '19),* 1–3.

Zhang, Y., & Wen, J. (2015). *An IoT electric business model based on the protocol of bitcoin. In ICIN.* IEEE.

Zheng, Z., Xie, S., Dai, H., Chen, X., & Wang, H. (2017). *An overview of blockchain technology: Architecture, consensus, and future trends. In Big Data (Big DataCongress).* IEEE International.

This research was previously published in Blockchain Applications in IoT Security; pages 128-139, copyright year 2021 by Information Science Reference (an imprint of IGI Global).

Chapter 29
Blockchain With the Internet of Things:
Solutions and Security Issues in the Manufacturing Industry

Kamalendu Pal

iD https://orcid.org/0000-0001-7158-6481

City, University of London, UK

ABSTRACT

The internet of things (IoT) is ushering a new age of technology-driven automation of information systems into the manufacturing industry. One of the main concerns with IoT systems is the lack of privacy and security preserving schemes for controlling access and ensuring the safety of the data. Many security issues arise because of the centralized architecture of IoT-based information systems. Another concern is the lack of appropriate authentication and access control schemes to moderate the access to information generated by the IoT devices in the manufacturing industry. Hence, the question that arises is how to ensure the identity of the manufacturing machinery or the communication nodes. This chapter presents the advantages of blockchain technology to secure the operation of the modern manufacturing industry in a trustless environment with IoT applications. The chapter reviews the challenges and threats in IoT applications and how integration with blockchain can resolve some of the manufacturing enterprise information systems (EIS).

INTRODUCTION

As a result of changes in the economic, environmental, and business environments, the modern manufacturing industry appears to be riskier than ever before, which created a need for improving its supply chain privacy and security. These changes are for several reasons. First, the increasingly global economy both produces and depends on people's free flow, goods, and information. Second, disasters have increased in number and intensity during the recent decades. Natural disasters such as earthquakes, floods, or

DOI: 10.4018/978-1-6684-7132-6.ch029

pandemic (e.g., coronavirus) strike more often and have a more significant economic impact. Simultaneously, the number of human-made disasters such as industrial sabotage, wars, and terrorist attacks that affects manufacturing supply networks has increased (Colema, 2006). These factors have created significant challenges for manufacturers, the country, and the global economic condition. Simply put, manufacturers must deploy continuous improvement in business processes, which improve both supply chain activities execution and its security enhancement.

Besides, today's manufacturing industry (e.g., apparel, automobile) inclines to worldwide business operations due to the socioeconomic advantage of the globalization of product design and development (Pal, 2020). For example, a typical apparel manufacturing network consists of organizations' sequence, facilities, functions, and activities to produce and develop an ultimate product or related services. The action starts with raw materials purchase from selective suppliers and products produced at one or more production facilities (Pal, 2019). Next, these products are moved to intermediate collection points (e.g., warehouse, distribution centers) to store temporarily to move to the next stage of the manufacturing network and finally deliver the products to intermediate storages or retailers or customers (Pal, 2017) (Pal, 2018).

This way, global manufacturing networks are becoming increasingly complicated due to a growing need for inter-organizational and intra-organizational connectedness that enabled by advances in modern Information technologies (e.g., RFID, Internet of Things, Blockchain, Service-Oriented Computing, Big Data Analytics) (Okorie et al., 2017) and tightly coupled business processes. Also, the manufacturing business networks use information systems to monitor the operational activities in a nearly real-time situation.

The digitalization of business activities attracts attention from manufacturing network management purpose, improves communication, collaboration, and enhances trust within business partners due to real-time information sharing and better business process integration. However, the above new technologies come with different types of disruptions to operations and ultimate productivity. For example, some of the operational disruptions are malicious threats that hinder the safety of goods, services, and ultimately customers lose trust to do business with the manufacturing companies.

As a potential solution to tackle the security problems, practitioners and academics have reported some attractive research with IoT and blockchain-based information systems for maintaining transparency, data integrity, privacy, and security related issues. In a manufacturing data communication network context, the Internet of Things (IoT) system integrates different heterogeneous objects and sensors, which surround manufacturing operations and facilitates the information exchange within the business stakeholders (also known as nodes in networking term). With the rapid enlargement of the data communication network scale and the intelligent evolution of hardware technologies, typical standalone IoT-based applications may no longer satisfy the advanced need is for efficiency and security in the context of the high degree of heterogeneity of hardware devices and complex data formats. Firstly, burdensome connectivity and maintenance costs brought by centralized architecture result in its low scalability. Secondly, centralized systems are more vulnerable to adversaries' targeted attacks under network expansion (Pal & Yasar, 2020).

Intuitively, a decentralized approach based on blockchain technology may solve the above problems in a typical centralized IoT-based information system. Mainly, the above justification is for three reasons. Firstly, an autonomous decentralized information system is feasible for trusted business partners to join the network, improving the business task-processing ability independently. Secondly, multiparty coordination enhances nodes' state consistency that information system crashes due to being a single-point failure is avoidable. Thirdly, nodes could synchronize the whole information system state only by coping the blockchain ledger to minimize the computation related activities and improve storage load. Besides, blockchain-based IoT architecture for manufacturing information systems attracted researchers' attention (Pal, 2020) (Pal, 2021).

Despite the potential of blockchain-based technology, severe security issues have been raised in its integration with IoT to form an architecture for manufacturing business applications. This chapter presents different types of security-related problems for information system design purpose. Below, this chapter introduces first the basic idea of digitation of manufacturing business process. Next, the chapter presents the use of blockchain technology in IoT for manufacturing industry. Then, it discusses the future research directions that includes data security and industrial data breach related issues. Finally, the chapter presents the concluding remarks and future research directions.

DIGITATION OF MANUFACTURING BUSINESS PROCESS

The manufacturing (e.g., apparel, automotive) industry inclines to worldwide business operations due to the financial benefits of the globalization of product design and development. The connecting path from supplier to the customer can include several intermediaries, such as warehouse, wholesalers, and retailers, depending on the ultimate products and markets. Global apparel manufacturing networks are becoming increasingly complicated due to a growing need for inter-organizational and intra- critical strategic asset. Also, manufacturing business networks use information systems to monitor network activities(Pal, 2017) (Pal, 2020). Organizational connectedness, which enabled by advances in modern technologies and tightly coupled business processes. This way, in manufacturing business operational information has been a critical strategic asset.

Figure 1. A diagrammatic representation of manufacturing business process

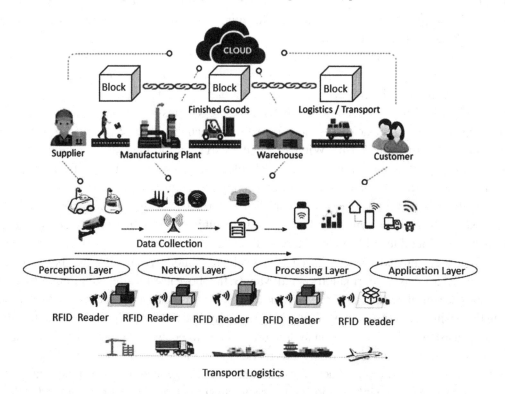

An EIS is to acquire and manage data; and serve as a decision-making system within an enterprise. Therefore, the characteristics of an EIS can be analyzed in the context of decision-making purpose. Figure 1 has illustrated some of data generation sources (e.g., RFID scanner, sensor, security camera, intelligent machine) in a manufacturing environment, which is divided into different layers (e.g., perception layer, network layer, processing layer, application layer). With the evolution of manufacturing system, inputs, outputs, as well as system parameters can be changed with respect to time significantly. One can find that design variables have being increased exponentially with the evolution of manufacturing EIS. The information systems for modern manufacturing systems must accommodate the changes of the IT infrastructure (e.g., IoT, blockchain, SOC) as well as the changes and uncertainties in the system environments.

Evolution of IT Infrastructure

Primary functions of an EIS are (i) to acquire static and dynamic data from objects; (ii) to analyze data based on computer models; and (iii) to plan and control a system and optimize system performances using the processed data. The implementation of a manufacturing system paradigm relies heavily on available IT. In this sub-section, the IT infrastructure related to manufacturing is discussed. IoT has been identified as a critical technology with its great impact on manufacturing industry (Pal, 2021).

IoT becomes foundation for connecting things, sensors, actuators, and other smart technologies. IoT is an extension of the Internet, and IoT technology gives an immediate access to information about physical objects and leads to innovative services with high efficiency and productivity. The characteristics of IoT includes: (i) the pervasive sensing of objects; (ii) the hardware and software integration; and (iii) many nodes. In developing an IoT, objects must be capable of interacting with each other, reacting autonomously to the changes of manufacturing environment (e.g., temperature, pressure).

Radio Frequency Identification (RFID) technology has received massive attention from the manufacturing industry's daily operations as a critical component of the Internet of Things (IoT) world. In RFID-enabled manufacturing chain automation, an EPC (Electronic Product Code) is allocated to an individual item of interest and is attached to an RFID tag for tracking and tracing purpose. RFID tag-attached items are transported from one business activity to another or even move within the manufacturing partners. During the transportation process, individual partner interrogates RFID tags and add business-related contextual information into tags. In this way, involved business partners can check whether the items of interest have passed through the legitimate manufacturing network. If any inappropriateness is traced, such items may be classified as counterfeit products.

Also, the wireless sensor networks (WSNs) are used to provide cloud computing services to enterprises. WSNs are the most important infrastructure for the implementation of IoT. Various hardware and software systems are available to WSNs: (i) Internet Protocol version 6 (IPv6) makes it possible to connect unlimited number of devices, (ii) Wi-Fi and WiMAX provide high-speed and low-cost communication, (iii) Zigbee, Bluetooth, and RFID provide the communication in low-speed and local communication, and (iv) a mobile platform offers communications for anytime, anywhere, and anything. The importance of WSNs to industrial control systems have been discussed by researchers (Araujo et al., 2014). In the research field of WSNs, most ongoing work focuses on energy efficient routing, aggregation, and data management algorithms; other challenges include the large -scale deployment and semantic integration of massive data (Aberer et al., 2014), and security (Gandino et al., 2014).

Cloud computing is also playing an important role in modern manufacturing information system's automation purpose. Cloud computing is a large-scale, low-cost processing unit, which is based on the

IP connection for calculation and storage. The most important characteristics such as on-demand self-service are essential to support a computing cloud for an enterprise in terms of cost reduction, system flexibility, profit, and competitiveness.

A simple IoT architecture composed of devices (e.g., machinery and equipment), networks, cloud-based storage, and information system applications are shown in Figure 1. This architecture consists of four layers, such as perception, network, processing, and application layer. The perception layer consists of electromechanical devices like different types of sensors, RFID tag readers, security surveillance cameras, geographical positioning system (GPS) modules, and so on. These devices may be accompanied by other industrial appliances like conveyor systems, automated guided vehicles (AGVs), and different types of industrial robots for a manufacturing industry context. These devices' primary function is to capture sensory data, monitor environmental conditions and manufacturing assembly areas, and transport materials (e.g., semi-finished, finished products). These collected data needs transportation, and there are different types of data communication protocols (e.g., IPv4, IPv6) responsible for transmitting data to the processing layer. The processing layer consists of dedicated servers and data processing software that ultimately produce management information, and operational managers can act based on the produced information. In this way, the application layer produces user-specific decision information. Few critical IoT based information system applications in the manufacturing industry are smart factory, smart robotics, intelligent supply chain, smart warehouse management.

However, some disadvantages of the centralized IoT information system architecture described above (Ali et al., 2019). A central point of failure could easily paralyze the whole data communication network. Besides, it is easy to misuse user-sensitive data in a centralized system; users have limited or no control over personal data. Centralized data can be tampered with or deleted by an intruder, and therefore the centralized system has lacks guaranteed traceability and accountability.

The vast popularity of IoT based information systems in the manufacturing industry also demands the appropriate protection of security and privacy-related issues to stop any system vulnerabilities and threats. Also, traditional security protections are not always problem-free. Hence, it is worth classifying different security problems classified based on objects of attack that are relevant to IoT based systems. This classification of security-related attacks would help industry-specific practitioners and researchers to understand which attacks are essential to their regular business operations. The different layer specific security related research is shown in Table 1, Table 2, and Table 3.

Blockchain technology is based on a distributed database management system that keeps records of all business-related transactional information that have been executed and shared among participating business partners in the network. This distributed database system is known as a distributed ledger technology (DLT). Individual business exchange information is stored in the distributed ledger and must be verified by most network members. All business-related transactions that have ever made are contained in the block. Bitcoin, the decentralized peer-to-peer (P2P) digital currency, is the most famous example of blockchain technology (Nakamoto, 2008).

The convergence of IoT with blockchain technology will have many advantages. The blockchain's decentralization model will have the ability to handle processing a vast number of transactions between IoT devices, significantly reducing the cost associated with installing and maintaining large, centralized data centers and distributing computation and storage needs across IoT devices networks. Working with blockchain technology will eliminate the single point of failure associated with the centralized IoT architecture. The convergence of Blockchain with IoT will allow the P2P messaging, file distribution, and autonomous coordination between IoT devices with no centralized computing model.

Table 1. Perception layer attacks

Type of attack	Description
Tampering	Physical damage is caused to the device (e.g., RFID tag, Tag reader) or communication network (Andrea et al., 2015).
Malicious Code Injection	The attacker physically introduces a malicious code onto an IoT system by compromising its operation. The attacker can control the IoT system and launch attacks (Ahemd et al., 2017).
Radio Frequency Signal Interference (Jamming)	The predator sends a particular type of radiofrequency signal to hinder communication in the IoT system, and it creates a denial of service (DoS) from the information system (Ahemd et al., 2017).
Fake Node Injection:	The intruder creates an artificial node and the IoT-based system network and access the information from the network illegally or control data flow (Ahemd et al., 2017).
Sleep Denial Attack	The attacker aims to keep the battery-powered devices awake by sending them with inappropriate inputs, which causes exhaustion of battery power, leading to shutting down of nodes (Ahemd et al., 2017).
Side Channel Attack	In this attack, the intruder gets hold of the encryption keys by applying malicious techniques on the devices of the IoT-based information system (Andrea et al., 2015), and by using these keys, the attacker can encrypt or decrypt confidential information from the IoT network.
Permanent Denial of Service (PDoS)	In this attack, the attacker permanently damages the IoT system using hardware sabotage. The attack can be launched by damaging firmware or uploading an inappropriate BIOS using malware (Foundry, 2017).

Blockchain technology offers a mechanism to record transactions, or any digital interaction designed to secure, transparent, highly resistant to outages, auditable, and efficient. In other words, blockchain technology has introduced an effective solution to IoT based information systems security. A blockchain enhances IoT devices to send inclusion data in a shared transaction repository with the tamper-resistant record. It improves business partners to access and supply IoT data without central control and management, which creates a digital fusion.

Software attacks are launched by an attacker taking advantage of the associated software or security vulnerabilities presented by an IoT system is shown in Table 3. This way, a malicious code can attack IoT-based infrastructure applications and create disruption (e.g., repeating the request of a new connection until the IoT system reaches maximum level) of an existing service for the global connectivity.

Blockchain technology offers a mechanism to record transactions, or any digital interaction design to secure, transparent, highly resistant to outages, auditable, and efficient. In other words, blockchain technology has introduced an effective solution to IoT based information systems security. A blockchain enhances IoT devices to send inclusion data in a shared transaction repository with the tamper-resistant record. It improves business partners to access and supply IoT data without central control and management, which creates a digital fusion.

BACKGROUND OF BLOCKCHAIN TECHNOLOGY

The blockchain technology infrastructure has motivated many innovative applications in manufacturing industries. This technology's ideal blockchain vision is tamper evident and tamper resistant ledgers implemented in a distributed fashion, without a central repository. The central ideas guiding blockchain technology emerged in the late 1980s and early 1990s. A research paper (Lamport, 1998) published with the background knowledge of the Paxos protocol, which provided a consensus method for reaching an agreement resulting in a computer network. The central concepts of that research were combined and applied to the electronic cash-related research project by Satoshi Nakamoto (Nakamoto, 2008), leading to modern cryptocurrency or bitcoin-based systems.

Table 2. Network layer attacks

Type of attack	Description
Traffic Analysis Attack	Confidential data flowing to and from the devices are sniffed by the attacker, even without going close to the network to get network traffic information and attacking purpose (Andrea et al., 2015).
RFID Spoofing	The intruder first spoofs an RFID signal to access the information imprinted on the RFID tag (Ahemd et al., 2017). Using the original tag ID, the intruder can then send its manipulated data, posing it as valid. In this way, the intruder can create a problem for the business operation.
RFID Unauthorized Access	An intruder can read, modify, or delete data present on RFID nodes because of the lack of proper authentication mechanisms (Andrea et al., 2015).
Routing Information Attacks	These are direct attacks where the attacker spoofs or alters routing information and makes a nuisance by creating routing loops and sending error messages (Andrea et al., 2015).
Selective Forwarding	In this attack, a malicious node may alter, drop, or selectively forward some messages to other nodes in the network (Varga et al., 2017). Therefore, the information that reaches the destination is incomplete.
Sinkhole Attack	In this attack, an attacker compromises a node closer to the sink (known as sinkhole node) and makes it look attractive to other nodes in the network, thereby luring network traffic towards it (Ahemd et al., 2017).
Wormhole Attack	In a wormhole attack, an attacker maliciously prepares a low-latency link and then tunnels packets from one point to another through this link (Varga et al., 2017).
Sybil Attack	Here, a single malicious node claims multiple identities (known as Sybil nodes) and locates itself at different places in the network (Andrea et al., 2015). This leads to colossal resource allocation unfairly. • Man in the Middle Attack (MiTM): Here, an attacker manages to eavesdrop or monitor the communication between two IoT devices and access their private data (Andrea et al., 2015).
Replay Attack	An attacker may capture a signed packet and resend the packet multiple times to the destination (Varga et al., 2017). This keeps the network busy, leading to a DoS attack.
Denial/Distributed Denial of Service (DoS/DDoS) Attacks	Unlike DoS attack, multiple compromised nodes attack a specific target by flooding messages or connection requests to slow down or even crash the system server/network resource (Rambus).

Table 3. Software layer attacks

Type of attack	Description
Virus, Worms, Trojan Horses, Spyware and Adware	Using this malicious software, an adversary can infect the system to tampering data or stealing information or even launching DoS (Andrea et al., 2015).
Malware	Data present in IoT devices may be affected by malware, contaminating the cloud or data centres (Varga et al., 2017).

Distributed Ledger Technology (DLT) Based Blockchain

The blockchain's initial basis is to institute trust in a P2P network bypassing any third managing parties' need. For example, Bitcoin started a P2P financial value exchange mechanism where no third-party (e.g., bank) is needed to provide a value-transfer transaction with anyone else on the blockchain community. Such a community-based trust is the main characteristic of system verifiability using mathematical modelling technique for evidence. The mechanism of this trust provision permits peers of a P2P network to transact with other community members without necessarily trusting each other. This behaviour is often referred to as the trustless behaviour of a blockchain system. The trustlessness also highlights that a blockchain network partner interested in transacting with another business entity on the blockchain does not necessarily need to know the real identity.

It permits users of a public blockchain system to be anonymous. A record of transactions among the peers is stored in a chain of a data structure known as blocks, the name blockchain's primary basis. Each block (or peer) of a blockchain network keeps a copy of this record. Moreover, a consensus, digital voting mechanism to use many network peers, is also decided on the blockchain state that all network stores' nodes. Hence, blockchain is often designed as distributed ledger-based technology. An individual instance of such a DLT, stored at each node (or peer) of the blockchain network and gets updated simultaneously with no mechanism for retroactive changes in the records. In this way, blockchain transactions cannot be deleted or altered.

Intelligent Use of Hashing

Intelligent techniques are used in hashing the blocks encapsulating transaction records together, which makes such records immutable. In other words, blockchain's transactions achieve validity, trust, and finality based on cryptographic proofs and underlying mathematical computation between different trading-peers (or partners), known as a hashing function. Encryption algorithms are used to provide confidentiality for creating hash function. These algorithmic solutions have the essential character that they are reversible in the sense that, with knowledge of the appropriate key, it must be possible to reconstruct the plaintext message from the cryptographic technique. This way hashing mechanism of a piece of data can be used to preserve the blockchain system's integrity. For example, Secure Hash Algorithm 256 (SHA256) is a member of the SHA2 hash functions currently used by many blockchain-based systems such as Bitcoin.

Figure 2. Immutable hashing mechanism in blockchain

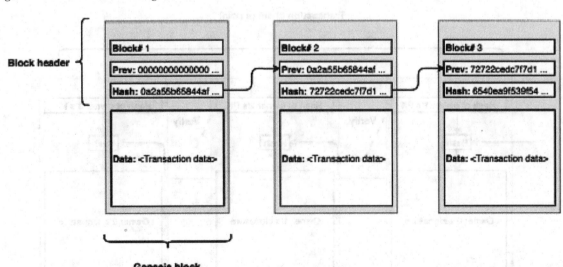

A simplified blockchain is shown in Figure 2. A block consists of four main fields (i.e., block number, previous hash (or prev), hash, data). Block number (e.g., #1, #2, #3) uniquely identify a block. The Prev field contains the previous block's (i.e., the block that comes before it) hash value. It is the way the chain of blocks stays together. The first block in a blockchain is often called the genesis block, is shown by its Prev field initialized to all zeros. The fourth field is the Merkle tree root, a data structure that keeps all the block's transaction-related information. Thus, the block body stores a record of all transactions categorized into input and output. It should be noticed that there is a technical difference between a transaction chain and a blockchain. Every block in a blockchain can contain multiple transaction chains, as shown in Figure 3. In turn, each transaction chain shows the value transferred from one peer of the network to another. Each such transaction chain is sometimes referred to as a digital coin or more usually as a token.

The communication among peer (or user) on blockchain uses a decentralized network in which an individual peer represents a node at which a blockchain client is installed. Once a peer performs a transaction with another peer or receives data from another user, it verifies its authenticity. Afterwards, it broadcasts the validated data to all other relevant nodes for business operation purpose.

Blockchain systems need acceptance and verification by all the chain peers, and this mechanism is known as a consensus. There are different algorithmic solutions available to cope with the distributed nature of this problem.

Distributed Consensus

These distributed consensus algorithms help the blockchain system users say regarding the overall state of the records preserved (or stored) in the blockchain network blocks. This section briefly introduces four of these algorithms, and they are – (i) Proof-of-Work (PoW), (ii) Proof of Stake (PoS), (iii) Practical Byzantine Fault Tolerance (PBFT), and (iv) Delegated Proof of Stake (DPoS).

Figure 3. Diagrammatic representation of transaction chain

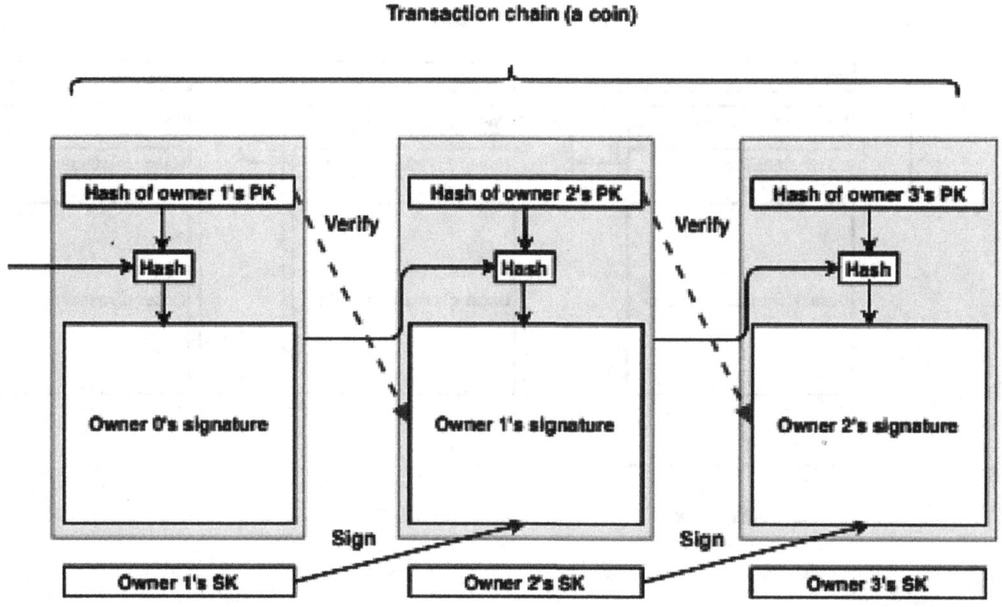

The PoW consensus algorithm is widely popularised by Bitcoin and assumes that all users vote with their "computing power" by solving consensus instances and creating the appropriate blocks. The PoS algorithm uses the existing way of achieving consensus in a distributed system. This algorithm needs the user to prove ownership of an amount of currency. It provides more efficient energy consumption in comparison to PoW. The PBFT consensus algorithm uses a state machine replication method to maintain with Byzantine faults. This algorithm uses an effective authentication method based on public-key cryptography. The DPoS uses a democratic technique to validate a block. It can confirm the transaction quickly.

The blockchain technology is proposed for many manufacturing use-cases where business needs data immutability and P2P consensus, and transaction confidentiality. There are different types of blockchain-based architectures available as industry-specific solution platforms.

Blockchain Technology Architecture in Manufacturing Industry

Blockchain is bringing new technological innovation to business operating models in the manufacturing industry. These business models eventually lead operational managers to develop new processes, which help automate manufacturing functions effectively. This trend is not the cheapest, most effective way to use something, but it is also presumably game-changing for manufacturing industries. As a result, changes occur in the manufacturing network's nature governing a business's relationships with its business partners. In turn, these blockchain-governed business models lead to significant shifts in the competitive structure of manufacturing companies.

Many researchers argue that blockchain technology's effects on manufacturing networks typify this process and usher new business practices using appropriate information systems architecture (Pal, 2020). Before discussing the effect of blockchain technology and its security-related issues, one should note that it is not the first time the manufacturing business network has undergone a revolution. The first occurred at the turn of the nineteenth century, followed by the twentieth century, and formed the manufacturing and distribution model throughout the twenty-first century. Information systems and their architectures play a dominating role in this revolutionary business transformation process. Hence, it is instructive to consider a simple blockchain architecture.

An overview of blockchain architecture is shown in Figure 4. In simple, blockchain can be of three different types: (i) public blockchain, (ii) private blockchain, and (iii) hybrid blockchain. A blockchain is permissionless when anyone is free to be involved in the process of authentication, verification and reaching consensus. A blockchain is permission where its participants are pre-selected. A few different variables could apply to make a permissionless or permission system into some form of hybrid.

The validation occurs to the next layer of the blockchain infrastructure, consensus, where nodes must agree on which transactions must be kept and validated in the blockchain. There are different security measures used to verify transactions within a blockchain system, the most known approaches to research a consensus today are PoW, PoS, and PBFT. Having a good consensus algorithm means better efficiency, safety, and convenience; nevertheless, which consensus an organization should choose depends on the use case.

The upper layer, the computer interface, allows blockchains to offer more functionality to the system. In this part, blockchain stores information on all the transactions that the users have made. For more advanced applications, one needs to store complex states which are dynamically changing, which means that the state shift from one to another once specific criteria are met in this system. These applications have given rise to smart contracts.

Smart contracts are the most transformative blockchain application, which could dramatically change how organizations work. The smart contracts can automate the transfer of assets when the negotiated conditions are met in this application; for example, when a shipment is delivered and verified, the contract will automatically enforce payments.

Figure 4. An overview of blockchain architecture

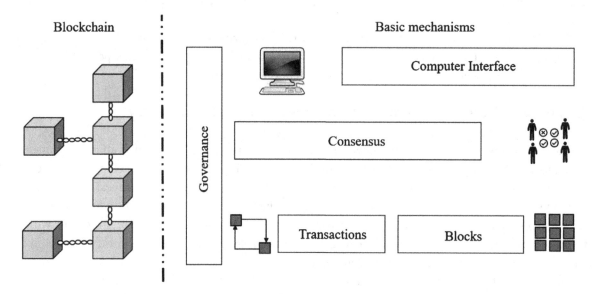

The governance layer (as shown in Figure 4) is human centered in blockchain architecture. Blockchain protocols are affected by inputs from different people who integrate new methods, improve the blockchain protocols, and patch the system.

In blockchain systems assets, monetary values are called tokens, and as stated by Nakamoto (Nakamoto, 2008), these are essential building blocks for the technology. The term tokenization means converting the rights and values of an asset into a digital token. Blockchain technology turns assets into a digitally encoded token that can be registered, tracked, and traded with a private key (Francisco & Swanson, 2017). It means that everything of value can be uploaded as a digital object in the blockchain system.

One of the critical aspects of blockchain technology is the decentralization of its operations. Decentralization means that each transaction in a blockchain transaction system does not need to be validated through a central trusted agency (e.g., bank or other financial organizations). This new validation technique implies that third parties resulting in higher costs and performance bottlenecks at the central services are no longer needed. It is here that consensus algorithms used to maintain data consistency in a distributed network. For an entity to operate in a decentralized network, an organization would be issued a digital identity that it could use in all business interactions.

In blockchain-based information systems, users are anonymous, but their account identifiers are not. Also, all asset transactions are publicly visible. Since blockchain technology users are unknown, it is essential to create trust in this system architecture. To build trust within a blockchain network enabled by four critical characteristics, as described below:

- **Ledger**: One of the essential characteristics of blockchain-based operation is distributed ledger technology (DLT). It is a decentralized technology to eliminate the need for a central authority or intermediary to process, validate or authenticate transactions. Manufacturing businesses use DLT to process, validate or authenticate transactions or other types of data exchanges.
- **Secure**: Blockchain technology produces a structure of data with inherent security qualities. It is based on principles of cryptography, decentralization, and consensus, which ensure trust in transactions. Blockchain technology makes sure that the data within the network of blocks is not tampered with and that the data within the ledger is attestable.
- **Shared**: Blockchain data is shared amongst multiple users of this network of nodes. It gives transparency across the node users in the network.
- **Distributed**: Blockchain technology can be geographically distributed. The decentralization helps to scale the number of nodes of a blockchain network to ensure it is more resilient to predators' attacks. By increasing the number of nodes, a predator's capability to impact the blockchain network's consensus protocol is minimized.

Also, for blockchain-based system architectures that permit anyone to anonymously create accounts and participate (called *permissionless* blockchain networks), these capabilities produce a level of trust amongst collaborating business partners with no prior knowledge of one another. Blockchain technology provides decentralization with the collaborating partners across a distributed network. This decentralization means there is no single point of failure, and a single user cannot change the record of transactions.

SECURITY-RELATED RESEARCH FOR BLOCKCHAIN TECHNOLOGY

Manufacturing businesses have leveraged blockchain technology and its built-in capabilities as an essential component within the software system architecture to provide more secure and dependable computation capability. However, ill-informed, or incorrect design decisions related to the choice and usage of a blockchain, and its components are probably the root cause of potential security risks to the system. For example, adversaries can exploit the envisioned design and verification limitations to compromise the system's security. The system becomes vulnerable to malicious attacks from cyberspace (Sturm et al., 2017). Some of the well-known attacks (e.g., Stuxnet, Shamoon, BlackEnergy, WannaCry, and TRITON) (Stouffer, 2020) created significant problems in recent decades.

The distributed manufacturing industry's critical issues are coordinating and controlling secure business information and its operational network. The application of cybersecurity controls in the operating environment demands the most significant attention and effort to ensure that appropriate security and risk mitigation are achieved. For example, manufacturing device spoofing and false authentication in information sharing (Kumar & Mallick, 2018) are significant problems for the industry. Besides, the heterogeneous nature of diversified equipment and the individualized service requirements make it difficult for blockchain-based P2P business operation (Leng et al., 2020).

In blockchain-based manufacturing business applications, trust and confidentiality among corporate partners play crucial roles in day-to-day operations (Ghosh & Tan, 2020). These issues also get compounded with individual products' personalization requirements across systems, which massively complicates the manufacturing and supply business activities (Mourtzis & Doukas, 2012). The other important issue is related to the manufacturing information system's data storage strategy. The fact is, it is easier to keep data and other files secure on a decentralized server than on a centralized one. With data stored across many computers in multiple locations, the risk of a single-entry point is mitigated and make fewer data accessible at each end. Decentralized platforms can even avoid holding sensitive information altogether, and it makes a better choice for manufacturing information system (Shen, 2002).

A literature survey shows that the techniques and methods of cybersecurity issues have been applied to the field of modern manufacturing information management systems, including traceability of operations (Mohamed & Al-Jaroodi, 2019), cyber-attacks to the digital thread (Sturm et al., 2017). Advanced virus on control system (e.g., Stuxnet) (12), device spoofing and false authentication in data sharing (Kumar & Mallick, 2018), interoperability among heterogenous equipment (Leng et al., 2020), confidentiality and trust between participants (Debabrata & Albert, 2020), information vulnerability and reliability across systems (Mourtzis & Doukas, 2012), and failure of critical nodes in centralized platforms (Shen, 2002).

Leveraging the advantages of integrating blockchain in IoT, academics and practitioners have investigated how to handle critical issues, such as IoT device-level security, managing enormous volumes of data, maintaining user privacy, and keeping confidentiality and trust (Pal, 2020) (Dorri et al., 2019) (Shen et al., 2019). In research work, a group of researchers (Kim et al., 2017) have proposed a blockchain-based IoT system architecture to prevent IoT devices' hacking problems. Besides, blockchain-based technologies are used to protect IoT application vulnerabilities.

Applications on the IoT Devices Management

In IoT, devices management relates to security solutions for the physical devices, embedded software, and residing data on the devices. Internet of Things (IoT) comprises "Things" (or IoT devices) that have remote sensing and data collecting capabilities and can exchange data with other connected devices and applications (directly or indirectly). IoT devices can collect data and process the data either locally or send them to centralize servers or cloud-based application back-ends for processing. A recent on-demand model of manufacturing that is leveraging IoT technologies is called Cloud-Based Manufacturing (CBM). It enables ubiquitous, convenient, on-demand network access to a shared pool of configurable manufacturing business processes information collection and use it service provision.

However, attackers seek to exfiltrate IoT devices' data using malicious codes in malware, especially on the open-source Android platform. Gu et al. (Gu et al., 2018) reported a malware identification system in a blockchain-based system named CB-MDEE composed of detecting consortium chain by test members and public chain users. The CB-MDEE system uses a soft-computing-based comparison technique and more than one marking function to minimize the false-positive rate and improve malware variants' identification ability. A research group (Lee et al., 2017) uses a firmware update scheme based on blockchain technology to safeguard the IoT system's embedded devices.

Applications on the IoT Access Management

Access control is a mechanism in computer security that regulates access to information system. The access control systems face many problems, such as third-party, inefficiency, and lack of privacy. These problems can be address by blockchain, the technology that received significant attention in recent years, and many potentials. Jemel and other researchers (Jemel & Serhrouchni, 2017) report a couple of centralized access control systems problems. This study presents an access control mechanism with a temporal dimension to solve these problems and adapts a blockchain-based solution for verifying access permissions. The attribute-based Encryption method (Sahai & Waters, 2005) also has some problems, such as privacy leakage from the private key generator (PKG) (Hur & Noh, 2011) and a single point of failure as mentioned before. Wang and colleagues (Wang et al.,2018) introduce a framework for data sharing and access control to address this problem by implementing decentralized storage.

Recently, there has been a tremendous investment from the industries and significant interest from academia to solve significant research challenges in blockchain technologies. For example, consensus protocols are the primary building blocks of blockchain-based technologies. Therefore, the threats targeting the consensus protocols become a significant research issue in the blockchain (Pal, 2021), and impact of integrating artificial intelligence (AI) on both IoT and blockchain technology (Atlam et al., 2020).

BLOCKCHAIN SECURITY AND PRIVACY ISSUES

Blockchain technology offers an approach to storing information, executing transactions, performing functions, and establishing trust in secure computing without centralized authority in a networked environment (Minoli & Occhiogrosso, 2018). Although blockchain has received growing interest in academia and industry in recent years, blockchains' security and privacy continue to be at the centre of the debate when deploying blockchain in different industrial applications(Minoli & Occhiogrosso, 2018) (Pal, 2021).

Key Security Risk Areas of Blockchain

The main areas of security on blockchain technology are (i) Ledger, (ii) Consensus Mechanism, (iii) Networking Infrastructure, (iv) Identity Access Management, and (v) Cryptography. A diagrammatic representation is present in the risk areas in Figure 5.

- **Ledger:** The ledger uses to register all transactions and changes in the status of the data. The ledger distributed by intelligent design and shared between the blockchain participating nodes. Two challenging problems (or hazards) generally threaten the applicability of the ledger technology in blockchain applications: (a) unauthorized entry into the ledger; and (b) unauthorized (or improper, or illegal) operations on recorded ledger data.
- **Consensus Mechanism:** A consensus mechanism is a protocol (i.e., set of rules) to ensure that all the blockchain network participants comply with the agreed rules for day-to-day operations. It makes sure that the transactions originate from a legitimate source by having every participant consent to the distributed ledger's state. The public blockchain is a decentralized technology, and no centralized authority is in place to regulate the required act. Therefore, the network requires authorizations from the network participants to verify and authenticate any blockchain network activities. Several consensus mechanisms have introduced considering the requirements of secure digital transactions. However, proof of work (PoW), proof of stake (PoS), and delegated proof of stake (DPoS) are the few consensus protocols used by the industries. In this way, the blockchain relies on the distributed consensus mechanism to establish mutual trust. However, the consensus mechanism itself has a vulnerability, which attackers can exploit to control the entire blockchain. Although a few approaches, e.g., (Muhammad et al., 2018), are highlighted in blockchain-related research to deter and prevent security related attacks. Due to the inherent characteristics of openness, the PoW-based permissionless blockchain networks may not be completely secure.

- **Network Infrastructure:** The network infrastructure threats can detect in nodes being stopped by a malicious attacker using good anticipatory mechanisms. In August 2016, nearly 120,000 Bitcoin (over US $60mn at the time) were stolen from Bitfinex (Nagaraj & Maguire, 2017). Based in Hong Kong, Bitfinex is one of the world's largest digital and cryptocurrency exchanges. The incident exploited security vulnerabilities within individual organizations. The blockchain network itself remained fully functional and operated as envisioned. The incident may have prevented a detailed end-to-end review of security, using scenarios, meaning there would have been a higher chance of identifying risks upfront and mitigating them at that point.
- **Identity Access Management:** Privacy in blockchain enables the client/user to perform transactions without leaking its identification information in the network. Also, blockchain technology uses numerous techniques to achieve the highest level of privacy and authenticity for transactions. As information comes from different users within the blockchain industrial ecosystem, the infrastructure needs to ensure every user privacy and authenticity. Blockchain-based information system often employs a combination of public and private key to encrypt and decrypt data securely.

Figure 5. Various Security Risk Areas of Blockchain

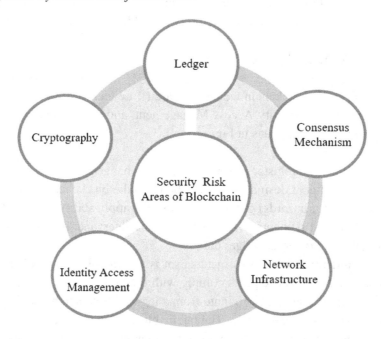

- **Cryptography:** The records on a blockchain are secured through cryptography. Network participants have their private keys assigned to the transactions they make and act as a personal digital signature. If a record is altered, the signature will become invalid, and the peer network will know right away that something has happened. However, there could be software bugs and glitches in cryptography coding. These could include developers' coding mistakes, inappropriate design, and an underlying defect in the cryptography routines.

Safety is an essential aspect of blockchain-based transaction processes. All the data within the blockchain ecosystem needs to be secured and tamperproof. The security ensures that there are no malicious nodes within the blockchain-based enterprise ecosystem. As mentioned earlier, the data inserted into a public ledger or inside the blockchain is distributed to individual users, and everyone maintains their local copy of the blockchain. In that local copy, that individual cannot tamper but upgrade the data and retransmit the network's data. However, for the transaction to be validated, the other nodes should be convinced that the broadcasted information is not malicious, and the system security is ensured.

THREAT MODELS FOR BLOCKCHAIN

This section explains the threat models that are considered by the blockchain protocols in IoT networks. Threat agents are mostly malicious attackers whose intention is to steal corporate vital information, disrupt system functionalities, or create problems for service provisions. Besides, attackers might also be inadvertent entities, such as developers of smart contacts who unintentionally create bugs and designers of blockchain-based system applications who make mistakes in the design or ignore some issues.

Threats facilitate various attacks on assets. Threats arise from vulnerabilities at the network, smart contracts, consensus protocol deviations or violations of consensus protocol assumptions, or application-specific vulnerabilities. Countermeasures safeguard the system from any attacks. These safeguard m involve various security and safety solutions and tools, incentives, reputation techniques, best practices, and so on. Threats and their agents cause risks. They may lead to a loss of monetary assets, a loss of privacy, a loss of reputation, service malfunctions, and disruptions of services and applications (i.e., availability issues).

Blockchain-based information systems owners wish to minimize the risk caused by threats that arise from threat agents. This section presents five types of attacks: *identity-based attacks*, *manipulation-based attacks*, *cryptanalytic attacks*, *reputation-based attacks*, and *service-based attacks*.

Identity-Based Attacks

The emergence of DLT based upon a blockchain data structure has given rise to new approaches to identity management, aiming to upend dominant approaches to providing and consuming digital identities. These new approaches to identity management (IdM) propose to enhance decentralization, transparency and user control in transactions that involve identity information. In identity-based attacks, the attacker forges identity to masquerade as an authorized user to access the system and manipulate it. Again, identity-based attacks can be broadly classified into four different types, and they are (i) Key attack, (ii) Replay attack, (iii)Impersonation attack, and Sybil attack.

- **Key attack:** In blockchain technology, certificates and identities are validated and protected in Hyperledger Fabric by asymmetric cryptography. How each participant chooses to store and protect their private key is up to them. A wide range of wallets and management methods available as Hyperledger Fabric requires no cohesive management scheme. An outside attacker obtaining private key(s) could lead to any number of attacks. To deal with this attack, LNSC (Lightning Network and Smart Contract) protocol (Huang et al., 2018) provides an authentication mechanism between the electric vehicles and charging piles. It uses elliptic curve encryption to calculate the hash functions, ensuring resiliency against the critical leakage attack.

- **Replay attack:** This attack aims to spoof two parties' identities, intercept their data packets, and relay them to their destinations without modification. To resist this attack, LNSC (Huang et al., 2018) uses the idea of elliptic curve encryption to calculate the hash functions. On the other hand, Benin (blockchain-based system for secure mutual authentication) (Lin et al., 2018) uses a fresh one-time public/private key pair.

- **Impersonation attack:** An attacker tries to masquerade as a legitimate user to perform unauthorized operations. As presented in Table II, three methods are proposed to protect against this attack. The elliptic curve encryption idea to calculate the hash functions is proposed by the LNSC protocol (Huang et al., 2018). Wang et al. (Wang et al., 2018) propose a distributed incentive-based cooperation mechanism, which protects the user's privacy and a transaction verification method. On the other hand, Benin (Lin et al., 2018) uses the concept of attribute-based signatures (i.e., legitimate devices can produce a valid signature, and hence any impersonation attempt will be detected when its corresponding authentication operation fails.

- **Sybil attack:** A Sybil attack is when an attacker creates multiple accounts on a blockchain to deceive the other blockchain participants. A successful Sybil attack increases the reputation of some agents or lowers the reputation of others by initiating interactions in the network. These attacks should not be an issue on a permissioned blockchain since the members are clearly identified and wallets are not normally used. TrustChain (i.e., capable of creating trusted transactions among strangers without central control) (Otte et al., 2017) addresses this issue by creating an immutable chain.

- **Whitewashing:** When an agent has a negative reputation, it can eliminate its identity and make a new one. There is no remedy to prevent this behaviour. However, it is suggested in (Otte et a., 2017) to give lower priorities to new identities agents when applying the allocation policy.

- **Service-based attacks:** The attacker try either to make the service unavailable or make it behave differently from its specifications. Under this category, we can find the following attacks:

- **DDoS/DoS attack:** A distributed denial-of-service (DDOS) attack is a prevalent type of network attack against a website, a communication network node, or even a membership service provider. The objective of this attack is to slow down or crash the system. The concentrated attack and subsequent shut down of the system result in a "denial of service" for legitimate users. Denial of Service (DoS) and DDoS are common security problems. DoS attacks on the connectivity of consensus nodes may result in a loss of consensus power, thus preventing consensus nodes from being rewarded. It involves sending a vast number of requests to cause the failure of the blockchain system. CoinParty (Ziegeldorf et al., 2018) proposes the idea of a decentralized mixing service. Liu et al. (Liu et al., 2018) employ a ring-based signature with the Elliptic Curve Digital Signature Algorithm (ECDSA). The resilience against DoS in BSeIn (Lin et al., 2018) is achieved by limiting the block size and using the '*multi-receivers*' encryption technique to provide confidentiality for authorized users.

FUTURE RESEARCH DIRECTIONS

The growth of IoT itself and its advancement in the industrial sector is putting a strain on the computing resources need to maintain the level of connectivity and data collection that IoT devices require (Chan, 2017). This is where service-oriented computing comes into the picture by acting as the backbone of everything IoT offers. Cloud computing, setting up virtual servers, launching a database instance, and creating data pipelines to help run IoT solutions become easier (Chan, 2017). Moreover, data security is an essential concern in such an environment where the cloud can improve security by providing proper authentication mechanisms, firmware, and software update procedures. Besides, the major data attacks that are prevalent in the IoT world today: (i) data inconsistency, which helps an attack on data integrity, leading to data inconsistency in transit or data stored in a central database is referred to as Data Inconsistency (ii) unauthorized access control; and with unauthorized access, malicious users can gain data ownership or access sensitive data., and (iii) data breach or memory leakage refers to disclosing personal, sensitive, or confidential data in an unauthorized manner.

The data breach has posed severe threats to user's personal information in recent years. Researchers are highlighting different aspects of data breach-related issues. One such work (Gope & Sikdar, 2018) on preventing data breach has proposed a lightweight privacy-preserving two-factor authentication scheme for securing the communication between IoT devices. In future, this research will review additional research in the IoT technology and data breach-related issues.

CONCLUSION

The current manufacturing industry operating environment has been extensively scrutinized to determine the primary needs of the enterprise information system's architecture purpose. It is encouraging that the emerging IoT infrastructure can support information systems of next-generation manufacturing enterprises appropriately. Anywhere, anytime, and anything, data collection systems are more than appropriate for gathering and sharing data among manufacturing supply chains resources. IoT technology-based information systems bring different opportunities to advance manufacturing businesses to sustain good system performance in a distributed and globalized environment. However, the application of IoT in executive information systems is at its primitive age; more research is needed in the areas (e.g., modularization, semantic integration, standardization) of encouraging technologies for safe, effective, reliable communication operational decision making.

The domain of global manufacturing communication systems is well suited to a hybrid (i.e., IoT and blockchain) information system architecture approach because of its distributed nature and operating characteristics. From an intelligent manufacturing management perspective, blockchain-based systems' most appealing traits are autonomy, collaboration, and reactivity. Blockchain-based systems can work without the direct intervention of humans or others. This feature helps to implement an automated information system in the global manufacturing industry.

REFERENCES

Aberer, K., Hauswirth, H., & Salehi, A. (2006). *Middleware Support for the Internet of Things*. Available: www.manfredhauswirth.org/research/papers/WSN2006.pdf

Adat, V., & Gupta, B. B. (2017). A DDoS attack mitigation framework for Internet of things. *2017 International Conference on Communication and Signal Processing (ICCSP)*, 2036–2041. 10.1109/ICCSP.2017.8286761

Ahemd, M. M., Shah, M. A., & Wahid, A. (2017). IoT security: a layered approach for attacks and defenses. *2017 International Conference on Communication Technologies (ComTech)*, 104–110. 10.1109/COMTECH.2017.8065757

Airehrour, D., Gutierrez, J. A., & Ray, S. K. (2019). Sectrust-rpl: A secure trust-aware rpl routing protocol for the Internet of things. *Future Generation Computer Systems*, *93*, 860–876. doi:10.1016/j.future.2018.03.021

Al-Turjman, F., & Alturjman, S. (2018). Context-sensitive access in industrial Internet of things (iiot) healthcare applications. *IEEE Transactions on Industrial Informatics*, *14*(6), 2736–2744. doi:10.1109/TII.2018.2808190

Alaba, F. A., Othman, M., Hashem, I. A. T., & Alotaibi, F. (2017). Internet of things security: A survey. *Journal of Network and Computer Applications*, *88*, 10–28. doi:10.1016/j.jnca.2017.04.002

Alccer, V., & Cruz-Machado, V. (2019). Scanning the industry 4.0: A literature review on technologies for manufacturing systems, Engineering Science and Technology. *International Journal (Toronto, Ont.)*, *22*(3), 899–919.

Ali, M. S., Vecchio, M., Pincheira, M., Dolui, K., Antonelli, F., & Rehmani, M. H. (2019). *Applications of blockchains in the Internet of things: A comprehensive survey*. IEEE Commun. Surv. Tutorials.

All, I. F. (2017). *The 5 Worst Examples of IoT Hacking and Vulnerabilities in Recorded History*. Academic Press.

Aman, M. N., Chua, K. C., & Sikdar, B. (2017). A lightweight mutual authentication protocol for IoT systems. *GLOBECOM 2017 - 2017 IEEE Global Communications Conference*, 1–6.

Andoni, M., Robu, V., Flynn, D., Abram, S., Geach, D., Jenkins, D., McCallum, P., & Peacock, A. (2019). Blockchain technology in the energy sector: A systematic review of challenges and opportunities. *Renewable & Sustainable Energy Reviews*, *100*, 143–174. doi:10.1016/j.rser.2018.10.014

Andrea, I., Chrysostomou, C., & Hadjichristofi, G. (2015). Internet of things: security vulnerabilities and challenges. *2015 IEEE Symposium on Computers and Communication (ISCC)*, 180–187. 10.1109/ISCC.2015.7405513

Araujo, J., Mazo, M., Anta, A. Jr, Tabuada, P., & Johansson, K. H. (2014, February). System Architecture, Protocols, and Algorithms for Aperiodic wireless control systems. *IEEE Transactions on Industrial Informatics*, *10*(1), 175–184. doi:10.1109/TII.2013.2262281

Ashibani, Y., & Mahmoud, Q. H. (2017). An efficient and secure scheme for smart home communication using identity-based encryption. *2017 IEEE 36th International Performance Computing and Communications Conference (IPCCC)*, 1–7.

Atlam, H. F., Alenezi, A., Alassafi, M. O., & Wills, G. B. (2018). Blockchain with Internet of things: Benefits, challenges, and future directions. *Int. J. Intell. Syst. Appl.*, *10*(6), 40–48. doi:10.5815/ijisa.2018.06.05

Atlam, H. F., Azad, M. A., Alzahrani, A. G., & Wills, G. (2020). A Review of Blockchain in Internet of Things and AI. *Journal of Big Data and Cognitive Computing*, 1-27.

Azzi, R., Chamoun, R. K., & Sokhn, M. (2019). The power of a blockchain-based supply chain. *Computers & Industrial Engineering*, *135*, 582–592. doi:10.1016/j.cie.2019.06.042

Boyes, H., Hallaq, B., Cunningham, J., & Watson, T. (2018). The industrial Internet of things (iiot): An analysis framework. *Computers in Industry*, *101*, 1–12. doi:10.1016/j.compind.2018.04.015

Cervantes, C., Poplade, D., Nogueira, M., & Santos, A. (2015). Detection of sinkhole attacks for supporting secure routing on 6lowpan for Internet of things. *2015 IFIP/IEEE International Symposium on Integrated Network Management (IM)*, 606–611. 10.1109/INM.2015.7140344

Cha, S., Chen, J., Su, C., & Yeh, K. (2018). A blockchain connected gateway for ble-based devices in the Internet of things. *IEEE Access: Practical Innovations, Open Solutions*, *6*, 24639–24649. doi:10.1109/ACCESS.2018.2799942

Chan, M. (2017). *Why Cloud Computing Is the Foundation of the Internet of Things*. Academic Press.

Chaudhary, R., Aujla, G. S., Garg, S., Kumar, N., & Rodrigues, J. J. P. C. (2018). Sdn-enabled multi-attribute-based secure communication for smart grid in riot environment. *IEEE Transactions on Industrial Informatics*, *14*(6), 2629–2640. doi:10.1109/TII.2018.2789442

Chen, G., & Ng, W. S. (2017). An efficient authorization framework for securing industrial Internet of things. TENCON 2017 - 2017 IEEE Region 10 Conference, 1219–1224. doi:10.1109/TENCON.2017.8228043

Chen, L., Lee, W.-K., Chang, C.-C., Choo, K.-K. R., & Zhang, N. (2019). Blockchain-based searchable encryption for electronic health record sharing. *Future Generation Computer Systems*, *95*, 420–429. doi:10.1016/j.future.2019.01.018

Choi, J., & Kim, Y. (2016). An improved lea block encryption algorithm to prevent side-channel attack in the IoT system. *2016 Asia-Pacific Signal and Information Processing Association Annual Summit and Conference (APSIPA)*, 1–4. 10.1109/APSIPA.2016.7820845

Colema, L. (2006). Frequency of man-made disasters in the 20the century. *Journal of Contingencies and Crisis Management*, *14*(1), 3–11.

De, S.J., & Ruj, S. (2017). Efficient decentralized attribute-based access control for mobile clouds. *IEEE Transactions on Cloud Computing*.

Dorri, A., Kanhere, S. S., Jurdak, R., & Gauravaram, P. (2019). *LSB: A Lightweight Scalable Blockchain for IoT Security and Privacy*. http://arxiv.org/ abs/1712.02969

Esfahani, A., Mantas, G., Matischek, R., Saghezchi, F. B., Rodriguez, J., Bicaku, A., Maksuti, S., Tauber, M. G., Schmittner, C., & Bastos, J. (2019). A lightweight authentication mechanism for m2m communications in industrial IoT environment. *IEEE Internet of Things Journal, 6*(1), 288–296. doi:10.1109/JIOT.2017.2737630

Fernndez-Carams, T. M., & Fraga-Lamas, P. (2018). A review on the use of blockchain for the Internet of things. *IEEE Access: Practical Innovations, Open Solutions, 6,* 32979–33001. doi:10.1109/ACCESS.2018.2842685

Ferran, M.A., Derdour, M., Mukherjee, M., Dahab, A., Maglaras, L., & Janicke, H. (2019). Blockchain technologies for the Internet of things: research issues and challenges. *IEEE Internet Things J.*

Forbes. (2019). Blockchain in healthcare: How it Could Make Digital Healthcare Safer and More Innovative. *Forbes.*

Frustaci, M., Pace, P., Aloi, G., & Fortino, G. (2018). *Evaluating critical security issues of the IoT world: present and future challenges. IEEE Internet Things.*

Gai, J., Choo, K., Qiu, K. R., & Zhu, L. (2018). Privacy-preserving content-oriented wireless communication in internet-of-things. *IEEE Internet of Things Journal, 5*(4), 3059–3067. doi:10.1109/JIOT.2018.2830340

Gandino, F., Montrucchio, B., & Rebaudengo, M. (2014). Key Management for Static Wireless Sensor Networks with Node Adding. *IEEE Transaction Industrial Informatics.*

Gibbon, J., (2018). *Introduction to Trusted Execution Environment: Arm's Trust zone.* Academic Press.

Glissa, G., Rachedi, A., & Meddeb, A. (2016). A secure routing protocol based on rpl for Internet of things. *IEEE Global Communications Conference (GLOBECOM),* 1–7. 10.1109/GLOCOM.2016.7841543

Gomes, T., Salgado, F., Tavares, A., & Cabral, J. (2017). Cute mote, a customizable and trustable end-device for the Internet of things. *IEEE Sensors Journal, 17*(20), 6816–6824. doi:10.1109/JSEN.2017.2743460

Gope, P., & Sikdar, B. (2018). *Lightweight and privacy-preserving two-factor authentication scheme for IoT devices.* IEEE Internet Things.

Granville, K., (2018). *Facebook and Cambridge Analytica: what You Need to Know as Fallout Widens.* Academic Press.

Griggs, K. N., Osipova, O., Kohlios, C. P., Baccarini, A. N., Howson, E. A., & Hayajneh, T. (2018). Healthcare blockchain system using smart contracts for secure automated remote patient monitoring. *Journal of Medical Systems, 42*(7), 1–7. doi:10.100710916-018-0982-x PMID:29876661

Guan, Z., Si, G., Zhang, X., Wu, L., Guizani, N., Du, X., & Ma, Y. (2018). Privacy-preserving and efficient aggregation based on blockchain for power grid communications in smart communities. *IEEE Communications Magazine, 56*(7), 82–88. doi:10.1109/MCOM.2018.1700401

Guin, U., Singh, A., Alam, M., Caedo, J., & Skjellum, A. (2018). A secure low-cost edge device authentication scheme for the Internet of things. *31st International Conference on VLSI Design and 17th International Conference on Embedded Systems (VLSID),* 85–90. 10.1109/VLSID.2018.42

Hei, X., Du, X., Wu, J., & Hu, F. (2010). Defending resource depletion attacks on implantable medical devices. *2010 IEEE Global Telecommunications Conference GLOBECOM 2010*, 1–5. 10.1109/GLO-COM.2010.5685228

Huang, J., Kong, L., Chen, G., Wu, M., Liu, X., & Zeng, P. (2019b). Towards secure industrial IoT: blockchain system with credit-based consensus mechanism. IEEE Trans. Ind.

Huang, X., Zhang, Y., Li, D., & Han, L. (2019a). An optimal scheduling algorithm for hybrid EV charging scenario using consortium blockchains. *Future Generation Computer Systems*, *91*, 555–562. doi:10.1016/j.future.2018.09.046

Huh, J.-H., & Seo, K. (2019). Blockchain-based mobile fingerprint verification and automatic log-in platform for future computing. *The Journal of Supercomputing*, *75*(6), 3123–3139. doi:10.100711227-018-2496-1

Huh, S.-K., & Kim, J.-H. (2019). The blockchain consensus algorithm for viable management of new and renewable energies. *Sustainability*, *11*(3184), 3184. doi:10.3390u11113184

Islam, S. H., Khan, M. K., & Al-Khouri, A. M. (2015). Anonymous and provably secure certificateless multireceiver encryption without bilinear pairing. *Secure. Commun. Netw.,* *8*(13), 2214–2231. https://onlinelibrary.wiley.com/doi/abs/10.1002/sec.1165

Kang, J., Xiong, Z., Niyato, D., Ye, D., Kim, D. I., & Zhao, J. (2019a). Toward secure blockchain-enabled Internet of vehicles: Optimizing consensus management using reputation and contract theory. *IEEE Transactions on Vehicular Technology*, *68*(3), 2906–2920. doi:10.1109/TVT.2019.2894944

Kang, J., Yu, R., Huang, X., Maharjan, S., Zhang, Y., & Hossain, E. (2017). Enabling localized peer-to-peer electricity trading among plug-in hybrid electric vehicles using consortium blockchains. *IEEE Transactions on Industrial Informatics*, *13*(6), 3154–3164. doi:10.1109/TII.2017.2709784

Kang, J., Yu, R., Huang, X., Wu, M., Maharjan, S., Xie, S., & Zhang, Y. (2019b). Blockchain for secure and efficient data sharing in vehicular edge computing and networks. *IEEE Internet of Things Journal*, *6*(3), 4660–4670. doi:10.1109/JIOT.2018.2875542

Karati, A., Islam, S. H., & Karuppiah, M. (2018). Provably secure and lightweight certificateless signature scheme for iiot environments. *IEEE Transactions on Industrial Informatics*, *14*(8), 3701–3711. doi:10.1109/TII.2018.2794991

Khan, F. I., & Hameed, S. (2019). Understanding security requirements and challenges in the Internet of things (iots): a review. *Journal of Computer Networks and Communications*.

Khan, M. A., & Salah, K. (2018). IoT security: Review, blockchain solutions, and open challenges. *Future Generation Computer Systems*, *82*, 395–411. doi:10.1016/j.future.2017.11.022

Kim, J.-H., & Huh, S.-K. (1973). A study on the improvement of smart grid security performance and blockchain smart grid perspective. *Energies*, 11.

Kim, S.-K., Kim, U.-M., & Huh, H. J. (2017). A study on improvement of blockchain application to overcome vulnerability of IoT multiplatform security. *Energies*, *12*(402).

Konigsmark, S. T. C., Chen, D., & Wong, M. D. F. (2016). Information dispersion for trojan defense through high-level synthesis. *ACM/EDAC/IEEE Design Automation Conference (DAC)*, 1–6. 10.1145/2897937.2898034

Kouicem, D. E., Bouabdallah, A., & Lakhlef, H. (2018). Internet of things security: A top-down survey. *Computer Networks*, *141*, 199–221. doi:10.1016/j.comnet.2018.03.012

Li, C., & Palanisamy, B. (2019). Privacy in Internet of things: From principles to technologies. *IEEE Internet of Things Journal*, *6*(1), 488–505. doi:10.1109/JIOT.2018.2864168

Li, R., Song, T., Mei, B., Li, H., Cheng, X., & Sun, L. (2019). Blockchain for large-scale Internet of things data storage and protection. *IEEE Transactions on Services Computing*, *12*(5), 762–771. doi:10.1109/TSC.2018.2853167

Li, X., Niu, J., Bhuiyan, M. Z. A., Wu, F., Karuppiah, M., & Kumari, S. (2018a). A robust ECC-based provable secure authentication protocol with privacy-preserving for industrial Internet of things. *IEEE Transactions on Industrial Informatics*, *14*(8), 3599–3609. doi:10.1109/TII.2017.2773666

Li, Z., Kang, J., Yu, R., Ye, D., Deng, Q., & Zhang, Y. (2018b). Consortium blockchain for secure energy trading in industrial Internet of things. *IEEE Transactions on Industrial Informatics*, *14*(8), 3690–3700.

Lin, C., He, D., Huang, X., Choo, K.-K. R., & Vasilakos, A. V. (2018). Basin: A blockchain-based secure mutual authentication with fine-grained access control system for industry 4.0. *Journal of Network and Computer Applications*, *116*, 42–52. doi:10.1016/j.jnca.2018.05.005

Ling, Z., Liu, K., Xu, Y., Jin, Y., & Fu, X. (2017). An end-to-end view of IoT security and privacy. *IEEE Global Communications Conference*, 1–7. 10.1109/GLOCOM.2017.8254011

Liu, C., Cronin, P., & Yang, C. (2016). A mutual auditing framework to protect iot against hardware trojans. *2016 21st Asia and South Pacific Design Automation Conference (ASP-DAC)*, 69–74. 10.1109/ASPDAC.2016.7427991

Liu, C. H., Lin, Q., & Wen, S. (2019b). *Blockchain-enabled data collection and sharing for industrial IoT with deep reinforcement learning. IEEE Transaction Industrial Informatics*. doi:10.1109/TII.2018.2890203

Liu, J., Zhang, C., & Fang, Y. (2018). Epic: A differential privacy framework to defend smart homes against internet traffic analysis. *IEEE Internet of Things Journal*, *5*(2), 1206–1217. doi:10.1109/JIOT.2018.2799820

Liu, Y., Guo, W., Fan, C., Chang, L., & Cheng, C. (2019a). A practical privacy-preserving data aggregation (3pda) scheme for smart grid. *IEEE Transactions on Industrial Informatics*, *15*(3), 1767–1774. doi:10.1109/TII.2018.2809672

Longo, F., Nicoletti, L., Padovano, A., d'Atri, G., & Forte, M. (2019). Blockchain-enabled supply chain: An experimental study. *Computers & Industrial Engineering*, *136*, 57–69. doi:10.1016/j.cie.2019.07.026

Lu, Y., & Li, J. (2016). A pairing-free certificate-based proxy re-encryption scheme for secure data sharing in public clouds. *Future Generation Computer Systems*, *62*, 140–147. doi:10.1016/j.future.2015.11.012

Machado, C., & Frhlich, A. A. M. (2018). IoT data integrity verification for cyber-physical systems using blockchain. *2018 IEEE 21st International Symposium on Real-Time Distributed Computing (ISORC)*, 83–90. 10.1109/ISORC.2018.00019

Makhdoom, I., Abolhasan, M., Abbas, H., & Ni, W. (2019). Blockchain's adoption in iot: The challenges, and a way forward. *Journal of Network and Computer Applications, 125,* 251–279. doi:10.1016/j.jnca.2018.10.019

Manditereza, K., (2017). *4 Key Differences between Scada and Industrial IoT.* Academic Press.

Manzoor, A., Liyanage, M., Braeken, A., Kanhere, S. S., & Ylianttila, M. (2019). Blockchain-Based Proxy Re-encryption Scheme for Secure IoT Data Sharing. *Clinical Orthopaedics and Related Research.*

Minoli, D., & Occhiogross, B. (2018). Blockchain mechanism for IoT security. *International Journal of Internet of Things,* 1-13.

Mondal, S., Wijewardena, K. P., Karuppuswami, S., Kriti, N., Kumar, D., & Chahal, P. (2019). Blockchain inspired RFID-based information architecture for food supply chain. *IEEE Internet of Things Journal, 6*(3), 5803–5813. doi:10.1109/JIOT.2019.2907658

Mosenia, A., & Jha, N. K. (2017). A comprehensive study of security of internet-of-things. *IEEE Transactions on Emerging Topics in Computing, 5*(4), 586–602. doi:10.1109/TETC.2016.2606384

Naeem, H., Guo, B., & Naeem, M. R. (2018). A lightweight malware static visual analysis for IoT infrastructure. *International Conference on Artificial Intelligence and Big Data (ICAIBD),* 240–244.

ObserveIT. (2018). *5 Examples of Insider Threat-Caused Breaches that Illustrate the Scope of the Problem.* Author.

Okorie, O., Turner, C., Charnley, F., Moreno, M., & Tiwari, A. (2017). A review of data-driven approaches for circular economy in manufacturing. *Proceedings of the 18th European Roundtable for Sustainable Consumption and Production.*

Omar, A. A., Bhuiyan, M. Z. A., Basu, A., Kiyomoto, S., & Rahman, M. S. (2019). Privacy-friendly platform for healthcare data in cloud-based on blockchain environment. *Future Generation Computer Systems, 95,* 511–521. doi:10.1016/j.future.2018.12.044

Oztemel, E., & Gusev, S. (2018). Literature review of industry 4.0 and related technologies. *Journal of Intelligent Manufacturing.*

Pal, K. (2017). Building High Quality Big Data-Based Applications in Supply Chains. IGI Global Publication.

Pal, K. (2018). *Ontology-Based Web Service Architecture for Retail Supply Chain Management.* The 9th International Conference on Ambient Systems, Networks and Technologies, Porto, Portugal.

Pal, K. (2019). Algorithmic Solutions for RFID Tag Anti-Collision Problem in Supply Chain Management. *Procedia Computer Science, 151,* 929–934. doi:10.1016/j.procs.2019.04.129

Pal, K. (2020). *Information sharing for manufacturing supply chain management based on blockchain technology*. In I. Williams (Ed.), *Cross-Industry Use of Blockchain Technology and Opportunities for the Future* (pp. 1–17). IGI Global.

Pal, K. (2021). Applications of Secured Blockchain Technology in Manufacturing Industry. In Blockchain and AI Technology in the Industrial Internet of Things. IGI Global Publication.

Pal, K., & Yasar, A. (2020). Internet of Things and blockchain technology in apparel manufacturing supply chain data management. *Procedia Computer Science*, *170*, 450–457. doi:10.1016/j.procs.2020.03.088

Park, N., & Kang, N. (2015). Mutual authentication scheme in secure Internet of things technology for comfortable lifestyle. *Sensors (Basel)*, *16*(1), 20. doi:10.339016010020 PMID:26712759

Porambage, P., Schmitt, C., Kumar, P., Gurtov, A., & Ylianttila, M. (2014). Pauthkey: A pervasive authentication protocol and key establishment scheme for wireless sensor networks in distributed IoT applications. *International Journal of Distributed Sensor Networks*, *10*(7), 357430. doi:10.1155/2014/357430

Pu, C., & Hajjar, S. (2018). Mitigating forwarding misbehaviors in rpl-based low power and lossy networks. *2018 15th IEEE Annual Consumer Communications Networking Conference (CCNC)*, 1–6. 10.1109/CCNC.2018.8319164

Rahulamathavan, Y., Phan, R. C., Rajarajan, M., Misra, S., & Kondoz, A. (2017). Privacy-preserving blockchain-based IoT ecosystem using attribute-based encryption. *IEEE International Conference on Advanced Networks and Telecommunications Systems (ANTS)*, 1–6. 10.1109/ANTS.2017.8384164

Rambus. (n.d.). *Industrial IoT: Threats and countermeasures*. https://www.rambus.com/iot/ industrial-IoT/

Reyna, A., Martn, C., Chen, J., Soler, E., & Daz, M. (2018). On blockchain and its integration with iot. challenges and opportunities. *Future Generation Computer Systems*, *88*, 173–190. doi:10.1016/j.future.2018.05.046

Sfar, A. R., Natalizio, E., Challal, Y., & Chtourou, Z. (2018). A roadmap for security challenges in the Internet of things. *Digital Communications and Networks.*, *4*(2), 118–137. doi:10.1016/j.dcan.2017.04.003

Shen, M., Tang, X., Zhu, L., Du, X., & Guizani, M. (2019). Privacy-preserving support vector machine training over blockchain-based encrypted IoT data in smart cities. *IEEE Internet of Things Journal*, *6*(5), 7702–7712. doi:10.1109/JIOT.2019.2901840

Shrestha, R., Bajracharya, R., Shrestha, A. P., & Nam, S. Y. (2019). *A new type of blockchain for secure message exchange in vanet*. Digital Communications and Networks. doi:10.1016/j.dcan.2019.04.003

Shukla, P. (2017). Ml-ids: A machine learning approach to detect wormhole attacks in the Internet of things. Intelligent Systems Conference (IntelliSys), 234–240. doi:10.1109/IntelliSys.2017.8324298

Sicari, S., Rizzardi, A., Miorandi, D., & Coen-Porisini, A. (2018). Reatoreacting to denial-of-service attacks in the Internet of things. *Computer Networks*, *137*, 37–48. doi:10.1016/j.comnet.2018.03.020

Singh, M., Rajan, M. A., Shivraj, V. L., & Balamuralidhar, P. (2015). Secure MQTT for the Internet of things (IoT). *5th International Conference on Communication Systems and Network Technologies*, 746–751. 10.1109/CSNT.2015.16

Song, T., Li, R., Mei, B., Yu, J., Xing, X., & Cheng, X. (2017). A privacy-preserving communication protocol for IoT applications in smart homes. *IEEE Internet of Things Journal, 4*(6), 1844–1852. doi:10.1109/JIOT.2017.2707489

SOPHOS. (2015). *49 Busted in Europe for Man-In-The-Middle Bank Attacks*. https://nakedsecurity. sophos.com/2015/06/11/49-busted-in-europe-for-man-in-themiddle-bank-attacks/

Sreamr. (2017). *Streamr White Paper v2.0*. https://s3.amazonaws.com/streamr-public/ streamr-datacoin-whitepaper-2017-07-25-v1_0.pdf

Srinivas, J., Das, A. K., Wazid, M., & Kumar, N. (2018). *Anonymous lightweight chaotic map-based authenticated key agreement protocol for industrial internet of things. IEEE Trans*. Dependable Secure Comput.

Su, J., Vasconcellos, V. D., Prasad, S., Daniele, S., Feng, Y., & Sakurai, K. (2018). Lightweight classification of IoT malware based on image recognition. *IEEE 42nd Annual Computer Software and Applications Conference (COMPSAC), 2*, 664–669. doi:10.1109/TDSC.2018.2857811

Varga, P., Plosz, S., Soos, G., & Hegedus, C. (2017). Security Threats and Issues in Automation IoT. *2017 IEEE 13th International Workshop on Factory Communication Systems (WFCS)*, 1–6. 10.1109/WFCS.2017.7991968

Vechain Team. (2018). *Vechain White Paper*. https://cdn.vechain.com/vechain_ico_ideas_of_ development_en.pdf

Waltonchain. (2021). *Waltonchain white paper v2.0*. https://www.waltonchain.org/en/ Waltonchain_White_Paper_2.0_EN.pdf

Wan, J., Li, J., Imran, M., Li, D., & e-Amin, F. (2019). A blockchain-based solution for enhancing security and privacy in smart factory. *IEEE Transaction*.

Wan, J., Tang, S., Shu, Z., Li, D., Wang, S., Imran, M., & Vasilakos, A. V. (2016). Software-defined industrial Internet of things in the context of industry 4.0. *IEEE Sensors Journal, 16*(20), 7373–7380. doi:10.1109/JSEN.2016.2565621

Wang, Q., Zhu, X., Ni, Y., Gu, L., & Zhu, H. (2019b). *Blockchain for the IoT and industrial IoT: a review*. Internet Things.

Wang, X., Zha, X., Ni, W., Liu, R. P., Guo, Y. J., Niu, X., & Zheng, K. (2019a). Survey on blockchain for Internet of things. *Computer Communications, 136*, 10–29. doi:10.1016/j.comcom.2019.01.006

Wurm, J., Hoang, K., & Arias, O., Sadeghi, A., & Jin, Y. (2016). Security analysis on consumer and industrial IoT devices. *21st Asia and South Pacific Design Automation Conference (ASP-DAC)*, 519–524. 10.1109/ASPDAC.2016.7428064

Xiong, Z., Zhang, Y., Niyato, D., Wang, P., & Han, Z. (2018). When mobile blockchain meets edge computing. *IEEE Communications Magazine, 56*(8), 33–39. doi:10.1109/MCOM.2018.1701095

Xu, L. D., He, W., & Li, S. (2014). Internet of things in industries: A survey. *IEEE Transactions on Industrial Informatics, 10*(4), 2233–2243.

Xu, L. D., Xu, E. L., & Li, L. (2018). Industry 4.0: State of the art and future trends. *International Journal of Production Research*, 56(8), 2941–2962. doi:10.1080/00207543.2018.1444806

Xu, Y., Ren, J., Wang, G., Zhang, C., Yang, J., & Zhang, Y. (2019). *A blockchain-based non-repudiation network computing service scheme for industrial IoT. IEEE Transaction Industrial Informatics.*

Yan, Q., Huang, W., Luo, X., Gong, Q., & Yu, F. R. (2018). A multi-level DDoS mitigation framework for the industrial Internet of things. *IEEE Communications Magazine*, 56(2), 30–36. doi:10.1109/MCOM.2018.1700621

Yang, W., Wang, S., Huang, X., & Mu, Y. (2019a). On the Security of an Efficient and Robust Certificateless Signature Scheme for IIoT Environments. *IEEE Access: Practical Innovations, Open Solutions*, 7, 91074–91079. doi:10.1109/ACCESS.2019.2927597

Yang, Y., Wu, L., Yin, G., Li, L., & Zhao, H. (2017). A survey on security and privacy issues in internet-of-things. *IEEE Internet of Things Journal*, 4(5), 1250–1258. doi:10.1109/JIOT.2017.2694844

Yang, Z., Yang, K., Lei, L., Zheng, K., & Leung, V. C. M. (2019b). Blockchain-based decentralized trust management in vehicular networks. *IEEE Internet of Things Journal*, 6(2), 1495–1505. doi:10.1109/JIOT.2018.2836144

Yao, X., Kong, H., Liu, H., Qiu, T., & Ning, H. (2019). An attribute credential-based public-key scheme for fog computing in digital manufacturing. *IEEE Trans. Ind. Inf.*

Yin, D., Zhang, L., & Yang, K. (2018). A DDoS attack detection and mitigation with software-defined Internet of things framework. *IEEE Access: Practical Innovations, Open Solutions*, 6, 24694–24705. doi:10.1109/ACCESS.2018.2831284

Zhang, H., Wang, J., & Ding, Y. (2019b). Blockchain-based decentralized and secure keyless signature scheme for smart grid. *Energy*, 180, 955–967. doi:10.1016/j.energy.2019.05.127

Zhang, N., Mi, X., Feng, X., Wang, X., Tian, Y., & Qian, F. (2018). *Understanding and Mitigating the Security Risks of Voice-Controlled Third-Party Skills on Amazon Alexa and Google Home.* Academic Press.

Zhang, Y., Deng, R., Zheng, D., Li, J., Wu, P., & Cao, J. (2019a). *Efficient and Robust Certificateless Signature for Data Crowdsensing in Cloud-Assisted Industrial IoT. IEEE Transaction Industry.* doi:10.1109/TII.2019.2894108

Zheng, D., Wu, A., Zhang, Y., & Zhao, Q. (2018). Efficient and privacy-preserving medical data sharing in the Internet of things with limited computing power. *IEEE Access: Practical Innovations, Open Solutions*, 6, 28019–28027. doi:10.1109/ACCESS.2018.2840504

Zhou, R., Zhang, X., Du, X., Wang, X., Yang, G., & Guizani, M. (2018). File-centric multi-key aggregate keyword searchable encryption for industrial Internet of things. *IEEE Transactions on Industrial Informatics*, 14(8), 3648–3658. doi:10.1109/TII.2018.2794442

Ziegeldorf, J. H., Morchon, O. G., & Wehrle, K. (2014). *Privacy in the Internet of Things: Threats and Challenges.* https://arxiv.org/abs/1505.07683

This research was previously published in Enabling Blockchain Technology for Secure Networking and Communications; pages 202-228, copyright year 2021 by Information Science Reference (an imprint of IGI Global).

Chapter 30
Securing the Internet of Things Applications Using Blockchain Technology in the Manufacturing Industry

Kamalendu Pal
https://orcid.org/0000-0001-7158-6481
City, University of London, UK

ABSTRACT

The manufacturing industry tends to worldwide business operations due to the economic benefits of product design and distribution operations. The design and development of a manufacturing enterprise information system (EIS) involve different types of decision making at various levels of business control. This decision making is complex and requires real-time data collection from machines, business processes, and operating environments. Enterprise information systems are used to support data acquisition, communication, and all decision-making activities. Hence, information technology (IT) infrastructure for data acquisition and sharing affects the performance of an EIS significantly. The chapter highlights the advantages and disadvantages of an integrated internet of things (IoT) and blockchain technology on EIS in the modern manufacturing industry. Also, it presents a review of security-related issues in the context of an EIS consisting of IoT-based blockchain technology. Finally, the chapter discusses the future research directions.

INTRODUCTION

Modern manufacturing has got a long history of evolution for several hundred years. The first industrial revolution began in the last part of the 18th century (Lukac, 2015). It symbolized production systems powered by water and steam, followed by the second industrial revolution, which started in the early part of the 20th century with the characteristics of mass labour deployment and manufacturing systems based on electrical power. The third industrial revolution began in the early part of the 1970s with automatic

DOI: 10.4018/978-1-6684-7132-6.ch030

production or manufacturing based on electronics and computer data communication technology. The concept of Industry 4.0 was put forward for developing the German economy in 2011 (Roblek et al., 2016) (Vogel-Heuser & Hess, 2016). Industry 4.0 is characterized by cyber-physical systems (CPS) production based on heterogeneous data and knowledge integration. It is closely related to the Internet of Things (IoT), CPS, information and communication technology (ICT), enterprise information systems (EIS), and integration of EIS. This way, a new generation of CPS controls industrial manufacturing and supply chain management (SCM).

Moreover, because of changes in the economic, environmental, and business environments, the modern manufacturing industry appears to be riskier than ever before, which created a need for improving its supply chain privacy and security. These changes are for several reasons. First, the increasingly global economy produces and depends on people's free flow, goods, and information. Second, disasters have increased in number and intensity during the recent decades. Natural disasters such as earthquakes, floods, or pandemic (e.g., coronavirus) strike more often and have a more significant economic impact. Simultaneously, the number of human-made disasters such as industrial sabotage, wars, and terrorist attacks that affects manufacturing supply networks has increased (Colema, 2006). These factors have created significant challenges for manufacturers, the country, and the global economic condition. Manufacturers must also deploy continuous improvement in business processes, which improve supply chain activities execution and security enhancement.

Besides, today's manufacturing industry inclines worldwide business operations due to the socio-economic advantage of the globalization of product design and development (Pal, 2020). For example, a typical apparel manufacturing network consists of organizations' sequence, facilities, functions, and activities to produce and develop an ultimate product or related services. The action starts with raw materials purchase from selective suppliers and products produced at one or more production facilities (Pal, 2019). Next, these products are moved to intermediate collection points (e.g., warehouse, distribution centers) to store temporarily to move to the next stage of the manufacturing network and finally deliver the products to intermediate storages or retailers or customers (Pal, 2017) (Pal, 2018).

This way, global manufacturing networks are becoming increasingly complicated due to a growing need for inter-organizational and intra-organizational connectedness that enabled by advances in modern Information technologies (e.g., RFID, Internet of Things, Blockchain, Service-Oriented Computing, Big Data Analytics) (Okorie et al., 2017) and tightly coupled business processes. Also, the manufacturing business networks use information systems to monitor operational activities in a nearly real-time situation.

The digitalization of business activities attracts attention from manufacturing network management purpose, improves communication, collaboration, and enhances trust within business partners due to real-time information sharing and better business process integration. However, the above new technologies come with different types of disruptions to operations and ultimate productivity. For example, some of the operational disruptions are malicious threats that hinder the safety of goods, services, and customers' trust to do business with the manufacturing companies.

As a potential solution to tackle the security problems, practitioners and academics have reported some attractive research with IoT and blockchain-based information systems for maintaining transparency, data integrity, privacy, and security related issues. In a manufacturing communication network context, the Internet of Things (IoT) system integrates different heterogeneous objects and sensors, which surround manufacturing operations (Pal, 2019) and facilitates the information exchange within the business stakeholders (also known as nodes in networking term). With the rapid enlargement of the data communication network scale and the intelligent evolution of hardware technologies, typical standalone IoT-based applications may no longer satisfy the advanced need for efficiency and security in the high degree of heterogeneity of hardware devices and complex data formats. Firstly, burdensome connectivity and maintenance costs brought by centralized architecture result in its low scalability. Secondly, centralized systems are more vulnerable to adversaries' targeted attacks under network expansion (Pal & Yasar, 2020).

Intuitively, a decentralized approach based on blockchain technology may solve the above problems in a typical centralized IoT-based information system. Mainly, the above justification is for three reasons. Firstly, an autonomous decentralized information system is feasible for trusted business partners to join the network, improving the business task-processing ability independently. Secondly, multiparty coordination enhances nodes' state consistency that information system crashes are avoidable due to being a single-point failure. Thirdly, nodes could synchronize the whole information system state only by coping with the blockchain ledger to minimize the computation related activities and improve storage load. Besides, blockchain-based IoT architecture for manufacturing information systems attracted researchers' attention (Pal, 2020).

Despite the potential of blockchain-based technology, severe security issues have been raised in its integration with IoT to form an architecture for manufacturing business applications. This chapter presents different types of security-related problems for information system design purpose. Below, this chapter introduces first the basic idea of digitation of manufacturing business process. Next, the chapter presents the use of blockchain technology in IoT for the manufacturing industry. Then, it discusses the future research directions that include data security and industrial data breach-related issues. Finally, the chapter presents the concluding remarks and future research directions.

DIGITATION OF MANUFACTURING BUSINESS PROCESS

Inherent within manufacturing is information creation, communication, and decision making (or action). For example, a design is created via a drawing, design software, or scanning a physical object, creating data. These data are then conveyed to machines that execute the design, bringing it forth from the digital to the physical realm. Ideally, data from the creation process (and subsequent use) is further captured, sparking ongoing cycles between the digital and physical realms. Information Technology (IT) plays an important part in capturing, storing, and processing stored data. Besides, manufacturing business networks use information systems to monitor manufacturing business network activities(Pal, 2017) (Pal, 2020). Organizational connectedness, which enabled by advances in modern technologies and tightly coupled business processes.

There is massive use of IoT devices in the manufacturing industry. However, most IoT devices are easy to attack, and industrial sabotage can be accomplished. Ideally, these IoT devices are limited in computational capability, network capacity, storage, and hence they are much more vulnerable to attacks than other endpoint devices such as smartphones, tablets, or computers. This chapter presents a survey of many security issues for IoT. The chapter reviews and categorizes popular security issues regarding the IoT layered architecture, in addition to protocols used for networking, communication, and management. It also outlines security requirements for IoT along with the existing attacks, threats, and state-of-the-art solutions. Besides, the chapter tabulates and map IoT security problems against existing solutions found in the academic literature. More importantly, the chapter discusses how blockchain technology can be a crucial enabler to solve many IoT security problems. The chapter also identifies open research problems and challenges for IoT security.

Figure 1. A diagrammatic representation of manufacturing business process

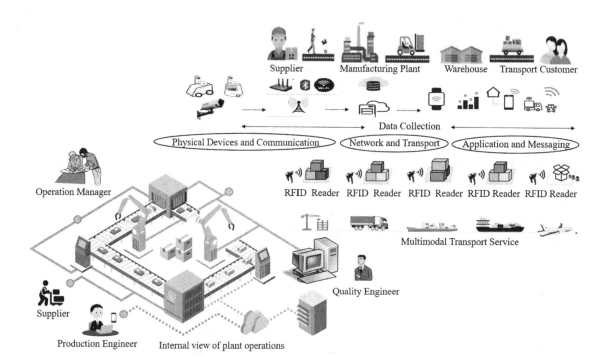

With the quickest increase of smart devices and high-speed data communication networks, IoT-based technology has gained huge popularity for automating manufacturing business processes. This popularity is mainly due to (i) low power consumption in standard IoT devices and (ii) lossy data communication networks having constrained resources. It represents a network where "things" or embedded devices having sensors are interconnected through a private or a public data communication network. The devices in IoT-based technology can be controlled remotely to perform the desired functionality. The information sharing among the devices then occurs through the network, which employs the standard communication protocols. The smart connected devices or "things" range from simple wearable accessories to large machines, each containing sensor chips. For example, the smart warehouse smart robots contain chips that support tracking and analyzing material management data. Similarly, electrical appliances, including machinery and inventory rack tracking robots, can be controlled remotely through IoT devices. The security cameras used for surveillance of a location can be monitored remotely anywhere in the world.

Apart from the industry-specific use, IoT serves the different business process automation needs as well. Different smart electromechanical types of machinery (or devices) perform various business processes functionalities (e.g., detecting transport vehicles movement within manufacturing plants, providing tracking and connectivity in industrial robots, measuring temperature and pressure in highly inhuman conditions). This way, an IoT-based system comprises "Things" (or IoT devices) that have remote sensing and actuating abilities and can exchange data with other connected devices and applications (e.g., directly, or indirectly).

The data collected through these devices may be sent locally or sent to centralized servers or cloud-based applications to perform the real-time processing, monitoring, and improvement of the entire industrial manufacturing systems. In recent years, an on-demand model of manufacturing that is leveraging IoT technologies is called Cloud-Based Manufacturing (CBM) (Rosen et al., 2015) highlighted some of the leading technical themes. CBM provides a convenient, ubiquitous computing environment, on-demand network access to a shared pool of configurable manufacturing resources that can be quickly available for indented service.

The IoT application continues to proliferate due to the evolution of hardware-related issues (e.g., bandwidth improvement using cognitive radio-based networks) to address the underutilization of the frequency spectrum. In addition, the wireless sensor network (WSN) and machine-to-machine (M2M) or cyber-physical systems (CPS) have now evolved as integral parts of the broader concept of the technical term IoT. Consequently, the security-related problems to WSN, M2M, or CPS are lurking a threat for IoT-based manufacturing applications, with the internet protocol (IP) being the central standard for connectivity. The industrial deployment architecture hence needs to be secured from attacks that may create problems for the services provided by IoT and may pose a threat to confidentiality, privacy, and integrity of data. Since the IoT technology-based applications deal with a collection of interconnected data communication networks and heterogeneous devices, it inherits the conventional security issues related to the computer networks. The constrained resources pose extra challenges to IoT security since the small devices or things containing sensors have limited power and memory. As a result, the security solutions need to be adapted to the constrained architectures.

Along with the rapid growth of IoT application and devices in the manufacturing industry, there has been an increasing number of research efforts highlighting security issues in the IoT environment. Some of these research target security issues at a specific layer, whereas other researchers aim at presenting end-to-end security for IoT applications. A research group presented an IoT applications survey and tried to categorize security issues in the application, architecture, communication, and data (Alaba et al., 2017). This proposed categorization for IoT security is different from the conventional layered architecture. The threats on IoT applications are highlighted for the hardware layer, network layer, and application layers. In another survey, a research group (Granjal et al., 2015) highlighted security related issues for the IoT application protocols. The security analyses presented by other research groups (Roman et al., 2011) (Granjal et al., 2008) (Cirani et al., 2013) discuss and compare different critical management systems and algorithmic cryptographic techniques. Besides, other researchers (Butun et al., 2014) (Abduvaliyev et al., 2013) (Mitchell & Chen, 2014) presented a comparative evaluation of intrusion detection systems. The IoT applications in the '*fog computing environment*' were analyzed and presented by few research groups (Yi et al., 2015) (Wang et al., 2015). A systematic survey by Sicari and colleagues (Sicari et al., 2015) provided different aspects of middleware related technical issues (e.g., confidentiality, security, access control, privacy). The authors highlighted trust management, privacy-related issues, authentication, network security, data security, and intrusion detection systems. For edge-computing based applications, including mobile cloud computing, mobile edge computing and computing, identity and authentication, access control systems, network security, trust management, fault tolerance and implementation of forensics are surveyed by a group of researchers (Roman et al., 2016).

Motivated by an increasing number of vulnerabilities, a researcher (Oleshchuk, 2009) presented a survey of privacy-preserving mechanisms for specific IoT applications. The author explained in the research paper the secure multiparty computations to preserving privacy for IoT-based application users. Zhou and collaborative researchers (Zhou et al., 2017) discussed various security threats and possible solutions for cloud based IoT applications. The authors described identity and location privacy, node compromising, layer removing or adding, and critical management threats for IoT using the cloud. In another survey, Zhang and colleagues (Zhan et al., 2014) presented some crucial IoT security issues about unique identification of objects, privacy, authorization, authentication, and the requirement of lightweight cryptographic techniques, malware, and software vulnerabilities. The IoT-A project (IoT-A, 2013) described a reference architecture for IoT that compliance needs implementation for privacy, security, and trust. The used trust model provides data integrity and confidentiality while creating end-to-end data communication through an authentication technique. Besides, to eliminate improper usage of data, the privacy model needs defining access policies and methods for encrypting and decrypting data. The security-related issues are included in a three-layers corresponding to the services, communication, and application. In the same way, the Open Web Application Security Project (OWASP) (OWASP, 2016) introduced ten vulnerabilities for the IoT architecture. Notably, these vulnerabilities include insecure interfaces of entities of the IoT architecture, inappropriate security configuration, physical security, and insecure firmware/software.

IoT ARCHITECTURE AND SECURITY CHALLENGES

IoT becomes the foundation for connecting things, sensors, actuators, and other smart technologies. IoT technology gives an immediate access to information about physical objects and lends to innovative services with high efficiency and productivity. The characteristics of IoT includes: (i) the pervasive sensing of objects; (ii) the hardware and software integration; and (iii) many nodes. In developing an IoT, objects must be capable of interacting with each other, reaching autonomously to the change of manufacturing environment (e.g., temperature, pressure, humidity).

IoT Protocols and Standards

A typical IoT deployment in manufacturing industry contains heterogeneous devices with embedded sensors interconnected through a network, as shown in Figure 1. This architecture consists of three layers, such as physical devices and communication layer, network and transport layer, and application and messaging layer. Radio Frequency Identification (RFID) technology has received massive attention from the manufacturing industry's daily operations as a critical component of the Internet of Things (IoT) world. In RFID-enabled manufacturing chain automation, an EPC (Electronic Product Code) is allocated to an individual item of interest and is attached to an RFID tag for tracking and tracing purpose.

In addition, wireless sensor networks (WSNs) are used to provide computing services to enterprises. WSNs are the essential infrastructure for the implementation of IoT. Various hardware and software systems are available to WSNs: (i) Internet Protocol version 6 (IPv6) makes it possible to connect an unlimited number of devices, (ii) Wi-Fi and WiMAX provide high-speed and low-cost communication, (iii) Zigbee, Bluetooth, and RFID provide the communication in low-speed and local communication, and (iv) a mobile platform offers communications for anytime, anywhere, and anything.

Figure 2 shows a layered architecture with the standard IoT protocols used for manufacturing applications and messaging, and routing or forwarding, physical devices and those for key management and authentication. It shows the standards and protocols for the commonly used low-rate wireless personal area networks (LR-WPANs) (IEEE, 2012) and the recently evolved protocols for the low power wide area network (LPWAN) based protocols.

Figure 2. Common IoT standards and protocols

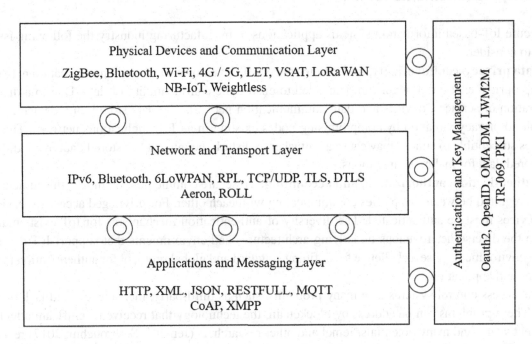

Again, LR-WPANs (i.e., IEEE standard 802.15.15.4) consists of two low-level layers; and they are the Physical Layer and the Medium Access Control (MAC) layer. The physical layer specification is related to communication over wireless channels having diverse frequency bands and data rate. The MAC layer specification is related to mechanisms for channels access as well as for synchronization.

A simple IoT architecture composed of devices (e.g., machinery and equipment), networks, cloud-based storage, and information system applications are shown in Figure 1. This architecture consists of four layers, such as perception, network, processing, and application layer. The perception layer consists of electromechanical devices like different types of sensors, RFID tag readers, security surveillance cameras, geographical positioning system (GPS) modules, and so on. These devices may be accompanied by other industrial appliances like conveyor systems, automated guided vehicles (AGVs), and different industrial robots for a manufacturing industry context. These devices' primary function is to capture sensory data, monitor environmental conditions and manufacturing assembly areas, and transport materials (e.g., semi-finished, finished products). These collected data needs transportation to the processing layer. The processing layer consists of dedicated servers and data processing software that ultimately produce management information, and operational managers can act based on the produced information. In this way, the application layer produces user-specific decision information. Few critical IoT based information system applications in the manufacturing industry are smart factory, smart robotics, intelligent supply chain, smart warehouse management. Besides, the importance of WSNs to industrial control systems have been discussed by researchers (Araujo et al., 2014). In the research field of WSNs, most ongoing work focuses on energy-efficient routing, aggregation, and data management algorithms; other challenges include the large-scale deployment and semantic integration of massive data (Aberer et al., 2014), and security (Gandino et al., 2014).

Security Requirements for IoT

To secure IoT-based information systems applications in manufacturing industry the following issues need to consider.

Data privacy, confidentiality, and integrity: As IoT data moves in a data communication network, an appropriate encryption algorithm is needed to ensure the confidentiality of data. Due to a diverse integration of services, devices and data communication network, the data stored on a device is vulnerable to privacy violation by compromising nodes existing in an IoT applications network. The IoT devices susceptible to attacks may cause an attacker to disturb the integrity of stored data by modifying the stored data for malicious intentions.

Authentication, authorization, and accounting: To secure communication in IoT, the authentication is required between two parties communicating with each other. For privileged access to services, the devices must be authenticated. The diversity of authentication mechanisms for IoT exists mainly due to the diverse heterogenous underlying architectures and environments that support IoT devices. These environments pose a challenge for defining standard and global protocol for authentication in IoT devices and applications.

The access control systems face many problems, such as third-party, inefficiency, and lack of privacy. These problems can be address by blockchain, the technology that received significant attention in recent years, and many potentials. Jemel and other researchers (Jemel & Serrhrouchni, 2017) report a couple of centralised access control systems problems. As there is a third party with access to the data, the risk of privacy leakage exists. Also, a major party is in charge to control the access, so the risk of a single point of failure also exists. This study presents an access control mechanism with a temporal dimension to solve these problems and adapts a blockchain-based solution for verifying access permissions. The attribute-based Encryption method (Sahai & Waters, 2005) also has some problems, such as privacy leakage from the private key generator (PKG) (Hur & Noh, 2011) and a single point of failure as mentioned before. Wang and colleagues (Wang et al.,2018) introduce a framework for data sharing and access control to address this problem by implementing decentralized storage.

IoT Devices Management: In IoT, devices management relates to security solutions for the physical devices, embedded software, and residing data on the devices. Internet of Things (IoT) comprises of "Things" (or IoT devices) that have remote sensing and data collecting capabilities and can exchange data with other connected devices and applications (directly or indirectly). IoT devices can collect data and process the data either locally or send them to centralize servers or cloud-based application backends for processing. A recent on-demand model of manufacturing that is leveraging IoT technologies is called Cloud-Based Manufacturing (CBM). It enables ubiquitous, convenient, on-demand network access to a shared pool of configurable manufacturing business processes information collection and use it service provision.

However, attackers seek to exfiltrate IoT devices' data using malicious codes in malware, especially on the open-source Android platform. Gu et al. (Gu et al., 2018) reported a malware identification system in a blockchain-based system named CB-MDEE composed of detecting consortium chain by test members and public chain users. The CB-MDEE system uses a soft-computing-based comparison technique and more than one marking function to minimise the false-positive rate and improve malware variants' identification ability.

Availability of Services: The attacks on IoT devices may hinder the provision of services through the conventional denial-of-service attacks. Different strategies (e.g., jamming adversaries, sinkhole attacks, replay attacks) are used for deteriorating the quality of service (QoS) to IoT manufacturing application users.

Single points of failure: A huge growth of heterogeneous networks for the IoT-based global manufacturing infrastructure may expose many *'single points of failure'* that may in turn deteriorate the services envisioned through IoT applications. Hence, it is essential to develop a tamper-proof ecosystem for a huge number of IoT devices as well as to provide alternative mechanisms for implementation of a fault tolerant IoT applications network.

Categorization of Security Issues

With the development of ubiquitous computing (e.g., IoT based applications in manufacturing, logistics, and smart grid) uses become widely used in the world (e.g., manufacturing, digital healthcare, smart city). According to statistics website Statista (TSP, 2021), the number of connected devices in industry will drastically increase in coming years. At the same time, with the huge growth of IoT application and devices, security attacks pose a more serious threat for industries. For example, remote adversaries could compromise health services implantable medical devices (3), or smart cars (4), which will create massive economic losses to the world. IoT devices are widely used in industry, military, and other critical operational areas of society. Malicious attackers can jeopardize public and national security. For example, on 21 October 2016, multiple distributed denial of service (DDoS) (5) attacks took place by Domain Name System provider Dyn, which caused the inaccessibility of several websites (e.g., GitHub, Twitter). For example, Stuxnet (6), a malicious computer worm that targeted industrial computer systems were responsible for causing a substantial problem to Iran's nuclear program. The ransomware attack, WannaCry was a worldwide cyberattack in May 2017, which targeted computer systems worldwide. A new variant of WannaCry forced Taiwan Semiconductor Manufacturing Company (TSMC) to temporarily shut down several of its chip-fabrication factories in August 2018 (Wikipedia, 2021). The virus spread to 10,000 machines in TSMC's most advanced facilities.

Inspired by an increasing number of vulnerabilities, predatorial attacks and information leaks, IoT device manufacturers, service-oriented computing service providers, and researchers are working on designing systems to securely control the flow of information between devices, to find out new vulnerabilities, and to provide security and privacy within the context of users and the devices. For example, adversaries can exploit the envisioned design and verification limitations to compromise the system's security. The system becomes vulnerable to malicious attacks from cyberspace (Sturm et al., 2017). Some of the well-known attacks (e.g., Stuxnet, Shamoon, BlackEnergy, WannaCry, and TRITON) (Stouffer, 2020) created significant problems in recent decades.

The distributed manufacturing industry's critical issues are coordinating and controlling secure business information and its operational network. The application of cybersecurity controls in the operating environment demands the most significant attention and effort to ensure that appropriate security and risk mitigation are achieved. For example, manufacturing device spoofing and false authentication in information sharing (Kumar & Mallick, 2018) are significant problems for the industry.

However, disadvantages of the centralized IoT information system architecture issues have been reported by a group of researchers (Ali et al., 2019). A central point of failure could easily paralyze the whole data communication network. Besides, it is easy to misuse user-sensitive data in a centralized system; users have limited or no control over personal data. Centralized data can be tampered with or deleted by an intruder, and therefore the centralized system has lacks guaranteed traceability and accountability.

Table 1. Perception layer attacks

Type of attack	Description
Tampering	Physical damage is caused to the device (e.g., RFID tag, Tag reader) or communication network (Andrea et al., 2015).
Malicious Code Injection	The attacker physically introduces a malicious code onto an IoT system by compromising its operation. The attacker can control the IoT system and launch attacks (Ahemd et al., 2017).
Radio Frequency Signal Interference (Jamming)	The predator sends a particular type of radiofrequency signal to hinder communication in the IoT system, and it creates a denial of service (DoS) from the information system (Ahemd et al., 2017).
Fake Node Injection:	The intruder creates an artificial node and the IoT-based system network and access the information from the network illegally or control data flow (Ahemd et al., 2017).
Sleep Denial Attack	The attacker aims to keep the battery-powered devices awake by sending them with inappropriate inputs, which causes exhaustion of battery power, leading to shutting down of nodes (Ahemd et al., 2017).
Side-Channel Attack	In this attack, the intruder gets hold of the encryption keys by applying malicious techniques on the devices of the IoT-based information system (Andrea et al., 2015), and by using these keys, the attacker can encrypt or decrypt confidential information from the IoT network.
Permanent Denial of Service (PDoS)	In this attack, the attacker permanently damages the IoT system using hardware sabotage. The attack can be launched by damaging firmware or uploading an inappropriate BIOS using malware (Foundry, 2017).

The vast popularity of IoT based information systems in the manufacturing industry also demands the appropriate protection of security and privacy-related issues to stop any system vulnerabilities and threats. Also, traditional security protections are not always problem-free. Hence, it is worth classifying different security problems classified based on objects of attack that are relevant to IoT based systems. This classification of security-related attacks would help industry-specific practitioners and researchers to understand which attacks are essential to their regular business operations. The additional layer-specific security-related research is shown in Table 1, Table 2, and Table 3.

Software attacks are launched by an attacker taking advantage of the associated software or security vulnerabilities presented by an IoT system is shown in Table 3. This way, a malicious code can attack IoT-based infrastructure applications and create disruption (e.g., repeating the request of a new connection until the IoT system reaches maximum level) of an existing service for global connectivity.

Besides, the IoT based application system provides an innovative technology that has become a guiding technology behind the automation of the manufacturing industry and smart computing. The IoT application produces countless digitized services and applications that provide several advantages over existing solutions. The applications and services share some standard features, which include: (i) sensing capabilities, (ii) connectivity, (iii) extensive scale network, (iv) dynamic system, (v) intelligence capabilities, (vi) Big Data processing using traditional data analytics methods, (vii) unique identity of the objects to connect over the computer network, (viii) autonomous contextual and real-time decision making, and (ix) heterogeneity – the IoT system allows different devices and objects to be addressable and communicate with each other over the Internet. These devices come with heterogeneous characteristics, including platforms, operating systems, communication protocols, and other hardware and software components. Despite these heterogeneous characteristics, the IoT system allows all the devices to communicate efficiently and effectively in a manufacturing environment.

Table 2. Network layer attacks

Type of attack	Description
Traffic Analysis Attack	Confidential data flowing to and from the devices are sniffed by the attacker, even without going close to the network to get network traffic information and attacking purpose (Andrea et al., 2015).
RFID Spoofing	The intruder first spoofs an RFID signal to access the information imprinted on the RFID tag (Ahemd et al., 2017). Using the original tag ID, the intruder can then send its manipulated data, posing it as valid. In this way, the intruder can create a problem for the business operation.
RFID Unauthorized Access	An intruder can read, modify, or delete data present on RFID nodes because of the lack of proper authentication mechanisms (Andrea et al., 2015).
Routing Information Attacks	These are direct attacks where the attacker spoofs or alters routing information and makes a nuisance by creating routing loops and sending error messages (Andrea et al., 2015).
Selective Forwarding	In this attack, a malicious node may alter, drop, or selectively forward some messages to other nodes in the network (Varga et al., 2017). Therefore, the information that reaches the destination is incomplete.
Sinkhole Attack	In this attack, an attacker compromises a node closer to the sink (known as sinkhole node) and makes it look attractive to other nodes in the network, thereby luring network traffic towards it (Ahemd et al., 2017).
Wormhole Attack	In a wormhole attack, an attacker maliciously prepares a low-latency link and then tunnels packets from one point to another through this link (Varga et al., 2017).
Sybil Attack	Here, a single malicious node claims multiple identities (known as Sybil nodes) and locates itself at different places in the network (Andrea et al., 2015). It leads to colossal resource allocation unfairly. • Man in the Middle Attack (MiTM): Here, an attacker manages to eavesdrop or monitor the communication between two IoT devices and access their private data (Andrea et al., 2015).
Replay Attack	An attacker may capture a signed packet and resend the packet multiple times to the destination (Varga et al., 2017). It keeps the network busy, leading to a DoS attack.
Denial/Distributed Denial of Service (DoS/DDoS) Attacks	Unlike DoS attack, multiple compromised nodes attack a specific target by flooding messages or connection requests to crash or slow down the system server/network resource (Rambus).

Table 3. Software layer attacks

Type of attack	Description
Virus, Worms, Trojan Horses, Spyware and Adware	Using this malicious software, an adversary can infect the system to tampering data or stealing information or even launching DoS (Andrea et al., 2015).
Malware	Data present in IoT devices may be affected by malware, contaminating the cloud or data centres (Varga et al., 2017).

The convergence of IoT with blockchain technology will have many advantages. The blockchain's decentralization model will have the ability to handle processing a vast number of transactions between IoT devices, significantly reducing the cost associated with installing and maintaining large, centralized data centres and distributing computation and storage needs across IoT devices networks. Working with blockchain technology will eliminate the single point of failure associated with the centralized IoT architecture. The convergence of Blockchain with IoT will allow the P2P messaging, file distribution, and autonomous coordination between IoT devices with no centralized computing model.

However, IoT-based applications' deployment results in an enlarged attack surface that requires end-to-end security mitigation. Blockchain technologies play a crucial role in securing many IoT-oriented applications by becoming security providing manufacturing application. Blockchain technology is based on a distributed database management system that keeps records of all business-related transactional information that have been executed and shared among participating business partners in the network. This distributed database system is known as a distributed ledger technology (DLT). Individual business exchange information is stored in the distributed ledger and must be verified by most network members. All business-related transactions that have ever made are contained in the block. Bitcoin, the decentralized peer-to-peer (P2P) digital currency, is the most famous example of blockchain technology (Nakamoto, 2008).

BACKGROUND OF BLOCKCHAIN TECHNOLOGY

Blockchain technology is based on a distributed database management system that keeps records of all business-related transactional information that have been executed and shared among participating business partners in the network. This distributed database system is known as a DLT. Individual business exchange information is stored in the distributed ledger and must be verified by most network members. All business-related transactions that have ever made are contained in the block. Bitcoin, the decentralized peer-to-peer (P2P) digital currency, is the most famous example of blockchain technology (Nakamoto, 2008).

The blockchain technology infrastructure has motivated many innovative applications in manufacturing industries. This technology's ideal blockchain vision is tamper evident and tamper resistant ledgers implemented in a distributed fashion, without a central repository. The central ideas guiding blockchain technology emerged in the late 1980s and early 1990s. A research paper (Lamport, 1998) published with the background knowledge of the Paxos protocol, which provided a consensus method for reaching an agreement resulting in a computer network. The central concepts of that research were combined and applied to the electronic cash-related research project by Satoshi Nakamoto (Nakamoto, 2008), leading to modern cryptocurrency or bitcoin-based systems.

Distributed Ledger Technology (DLT) Based Blockchain

The blockchain's initial basis is to institute trust in a P2P network bypassing any third managing parties' need. For example, Bitcoin started a P2P financial value exchange mechanism where no third-party (e.g., bank) is needed to provide a value-transfer transaction with anyone else on the blockchain community. Such a community-based trust is the main characteristic of system verifiability using mathematical modelling technique for evidence. The mechanism of this trust provision permits peers of a P2P network to transact with other community members without necessarily trusting each other. This behaviour is commonly known as the trustless behaviour of a blockchain system. The trustlessness also highlights that a blockchain network partner interested in transacting with another business entity on the blockchain does not necessarily need to know the real identity.

It permits users of a public blockchain system to be anonymous. A record of transactions among the peers is stored in a chain of a data structure known as blocks, the name blockchain's primary basis. Each block (or peer) of a blockchain network keeps a copy of this record. Moreover, a consensus, digital voting mechanism to use many network peers, is also decided on the blockchain state that all network stores' nodes. Hence, blockchain is often designed as distributed ledger-based technology. An individual instance of such a DLT, stored at each node (or peer) of the blockchain network and gets updated simultaneously with no mechanism for retroactive changes in the records. In this way, blockchain transactions cannot be deleted or altered.

Intelligent Use of Hashing

Intelligent techniques are used in hashing the blocks encapsulating transaction records together, which makes such records immutable. In other words, blockchain's transactions achieve validity, trust, and finality based on cryptographic proofs and underlying mathematical computation between different trading-peers (or partners), known as a hashing function. Encryption algorithms are used to provide confidentiality for creating hash function. These algorithmic solutions have the essential character that they are reversible in the sense that, with knowledge of the appropriate key, it must be possible to reconstruct the plaintext message from the cryptographic technique. This way hashing mechanism of a piece of data can be used to preserve the blockchain system's integrity. For example, Secure Hash Algorithm 256 (SHA256) is a member of the SHA2 hash functions currently used by many blockchain-based systems such as Bitcoin.

Terminologies in Blockchain

Some private blockchains provide read restrictions on the data within the blocks. Consortium blockchains are operated and owned by a group of organizations or a private community. Blockchain users use asymmetric key cryptography to sign on transactions. The trust factor maintenance within a distributed ledger technology (DLT) can be attributed to the consensus algorithms and the key desirable properties achieved thenceforth. Wüst and Gervais (2018) give a good description of these properties. Some of them are Public Verifiability, Transparency, Integrity. The main terminologies in blockchain have discussed below.

Terminologies in Blockchain:

Blocks: The transactions that occur in a peer-to-peer network associated with a blockchain are picked up from a pool of transactions and grouped in a block. Once a transaction has been validated, it basically impossible to be reverted. Transactions are pseudonymous as they are linked only to the user's public key and not to the user's real identity. A block may contain several hundreds of transactions. The block size limits the number of transactions that can be included in a block. Diagrammatic structure of a blockchain is shown in Figure 3. A block consists of version no., a hash of the previous block, the Merkle root tree to trace the transactions in the block, hash of the current block, timestamp, and nonce value. A blockchain starts with a genesis block.

Mining: Mining is when the designated nodes in the blockchain network called miners collect transactions from a pool of unprocessed transactions and combine them in a block. In mining, each miner competes to solve an equally tricky computational problem of finding a valid hash value with a particular no. of zeroes below a specific target. In Bitcoin mining, the number of zeroes indicates the difficulty of the computation. Many nonce values are tried to arrive at the golden nonce that hashes to a valid hash with the current difficulty level. When a miner arrives at this nonce value, we can say that he has successfully mined a block. This block then gets updated to the chain.

Figure 3. An overview of blockchain architecture

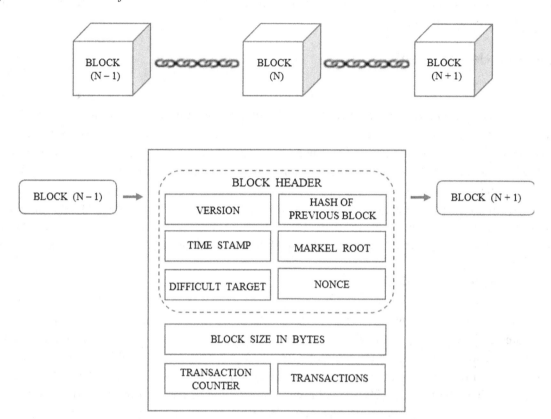

Consensus: The consensus mechanism serves two primary purposes, as given in Jesus et al. (2018): block validation and the most extensive chain selection. Proof-of-Work is the consensus algorithm used in Bitcoin Blockchain. The proof-of-stake algorithm is much faster than Proof-of-Work and demands less computational resources. The Ethereum blockchains use a pure proof-of-stake algorithm to ensure consensus. Besides Proof-of-Work, there are other consensus algorithms such as Proof of Byzantine Fault Tolerance (PBFT), proof- of activity, etc. Anwar(2018) presents a consolidated view of the different consensus algorithms. Proof-of-Work is a signature that indicates that the block has been mined after performing computation with the required difficulty level. The peers can easily verify this signature in the network to ensure a block's validity. The longest chain is always selected as the consistent one for appending the new block.

Smart Contracts: They are predefined rules deployed in the Blockchain network that two parties involved in a settlement must agree to priorly. Smart contracts were designed to avoid disagreement, denial, or violation of rules by the parties involved. They have triggered automatically in the blockchain on the occurrence of specific events mentioned in the rules.

Overall Functioning

Users connect to the blockchain and initiate a transaction signed with their private key. This transaction is sent to a pool of transactions where it resides 63 Securing IoT Applications Using Blockchain until it is fetched into a block by a miner. The miner then generates a new block after gathering transactions from the pool and computing the valid hash of the block. When a miner successfully generates a new block, the new block is broadcast to the nodes in the P2P network. All nodes in the network verify the block using a consensus algorithm, and upon successful validation, update it to their copy of the chain, and the transaction attains completion.

An overview of blockchain architecture is shown in Figure 2. In simple, blockchain can be of three different types: (i) public blockchain, (ii) private blockchain, and (iii) hybrid blockchain. A blockchain is permissionless when anyone is free to be involved in the process of authentication, verification and reaching consensus. A blockchain is permission one where its participants are pre-selected. A few different variables could apply to make a permissionless or permission system into some form of hybrid.

Ledger: One of the essential characteristics of blockchain-based operation is distributed ledger technology (DLT). It is a decentralized technology to eliminate the need for a central authority or intermediary to process, validate or authenticate transactions. Manufacturing businesses use DLT to process, validate or authenticate transactions or other types of data exchanges.

Secure: Blockchain technology produces a structure of data with inherent security qualities. It is based on principles of cryptography, decentralization, and consensus, which ensure trust in transactions. Blockchain technology ensures that the data within the network of blocks is not tampered.

Shared: Blockchain data is shared amongst multiple users of this network of nodes. It gives transparency across the node users in the network.

Distributed: Blockchain technology can be geographically distributed. The decentralization helps to scale the number of nodes of a blockchain network to ensure it is more resilient to predators' attacks. By increasing the number of nodes, a predator's capability to impact the blockchain network's consensus protocol is minimized.

Also, for blockchain-based system architectures that permit anyone to anonymously create accounts and participate (called *permissionless* blockchain networks), these capabilities produce a level of trust amongst collaborating business partners with no prior knowledge of one another. Blockchain technology provides decentralization with the collaborating partners across a distributed network. This decentralization means there is no single point of failure, and a single user cannot change the record of transactions.

Figure 4 represents the outline of how one can manipulate blockchain to ensure security. The figure helps understand the relationship[between offerings such as immutability, province, and so on. Moreover, which aspect is needed to satisfy the specific security requirements in user specifications.

SECURING IoT APPLICATIONS USING BLOCKCHAIN

Blockchain technology uses a new way of managing trust in information systems and their transaction processing capabilities. A transaction processing system gathers and stores data regarding business activity (known as a transaction) and sometimes controls business decisions made as part of a transaction. The transaction is the activity that changes stored data. An individual transaction must succeed or fail as a complete unit; it can never be only partially complete. Since the introduction of the Bitcoin, blockchain technology has shown popularity in other business applications and attracted much attention from academia and industry. The blockchain's interest is its features that provide security, anonymity, and data integrity without any third-party involvement in the transaction control.

Figure 4. Relationship between offering of blockchain and security requirements

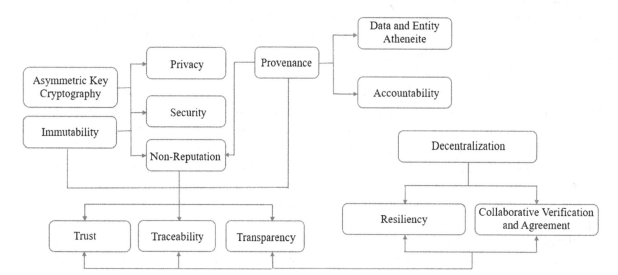

Primary Properties of Digital Blockchain

The information on the blockchain is digitized, getting rid of the requirement for manual documentation. Transactions are structured into blocks for information processing purposes, and standard data communication network protocol ensures that every node (i.e., business partner) receives every transaction in near real-time and uses the same rules. By design, blockchain is distributed and synchronized across the networks and ideal for a multi-organizational business network such as supply chain management.

Decentralization

All blockchain participants (nodes) have their copy of all data in the system and no central authorization organization (e.g., clearing bank). It ensures to have no single point of vulnerability or failure. In the conventional centralized transaction system, each transaction must be validated through a central authority (e.g., bank), needing service fees, time, and performance bottlenecks at the central servers. Besides, there is no central authority in the blockchain network, and no intermediary or authority service fees are required, making the transaction faster. Consensus algorithms maintain data consistency in a decentralized, distributed network (Zheng et al., 2017).

Immutability

The residing data on a blockchain is immutable. Once the participants agreed on a business transaction and recorded it, it is nearly impossible to change or delete or rollback transactions once they are included in the blockchain. If someone subsequently records another transaction about that asset to change its state, the participant cannot hide the original transaction. The provenance of assets deals with any asset, one can tell where it is, where it has been, and what has happened throughout its life (Pattison, 2017).

Consensus

There is a standard algorithm (or mechanism) used to make sure that all participants (or nodes) agree on the validity of transaction data in the system, replacing the requirement for a trusted third party (e.g., bank) for authorization purpose. There must be an agreement among all the participants that the transaction is valid before executing a transaction. The agreement process is known as "consensus", and it helps keep inaccurate or fraudulent transactions out of the blockchain. Blocks that include erroneous transactions could be revealed promptly.

Anonymity in Blockchain

Each participant can interact with the blockchain with a generated address, which does not reveal the user's real identity, but participants can see the transaction (Zheng et al., 2017). Arguably, the bitcoin blockchain cannot guarantee perfect privacy preservation due to its intrinsic constraints, but some other alternative blockchain protocols claim to provide a better privacy protection mechanism.

Traceability

The individual transaction included to a blockchain (i.e., public, or private) is digitally signed and time-stamped that means that participant can trace- back to a specific time for an individual transaction and identify the appropriate party (through their public address) on the Blockchain (Swan, 2015). Therefore, every block is immutably and verifiably linked to the previous block. A complete history can always be reconstructed right back to the beginning (the genesis block).

Related Research on IoT Security and Privacy Using Blockchain

Leveraging the advantages of integrating blockchain in IoT, academics and practitioners have investigated how to handle critical issues, such as IoT device-level security, managing enormous volumes of data, maintaining user privacy, and keeping confidentiality and trust (Pal, 2020) (Dorri et al., 2019) (Shen et al., 2019). In research work, a group of researchers (Kim et al., 2017) have proposed a blockchain-based IoT system architecture to prevent IoT devices' hacking problems.

A group of researchers (Azzi et al., 2019) have introduced a blockchain integrated, IoT based information system for the supply chain management. It provides an example of a reliable, transparent, and secured system. Another group of researchers (Mondal et al., 2019) has reported a blockchain-based food supply chain that uses a proof-of-object (PoO) based authentication method. In this research, RFID tags are attached to the individual food products that are used for tracking purpose throughout their lifecycle within the supply chain network. All the real-time tracking and monitoring data produced are stored in a blockchain-based information system, which monitors food quality.

Francesco Longo and colleagues (Longo et al., 2019) have proposed that an information system consists of blockchain technology for the supply chain management. The system allows the supply chain business partners to share their information among peers with appropriate authentication and integrity.

Practitioners and academics (Pal, 2020) advocated three primary aspects of modern manufacturing: (i) integration of heterogeneous data along with the global operations, (ii) data collection, and (iii) analysis of collected data. Within heterogeneous data integration, service-oriented computing (SOC) plays a dominating role, given that intelligent perception and collection from the various computer networks of physical manufacturing resources and abilities. At the same time, new innovative technologies have emerged. They have wide use in different manufacturing applications, such as the IoT. The data collected by Radio Frequency Identification (RFID) tags and sensors for their underlying assets can help find the essential attributes (e.g., location, condition, availability) that form the essential ingredient for the modern manufacturing system.

Standard IoT systems are built on a centralized computing environment, which requires all devices to be connected and authenticated through the central server. This framework would not be able to provide the needs to outspread the IoT system in globalized operation. Therefore, moving the IoT system into the decentralized path may be the right decision. One of the popular decentralization platforms is blockchain technology.

Blockchain technology provides an appropriate solution to the security mentioned above challenges posed by a distributed IoT ecosystem. Blockchain technology offers an approach to storing information, executing transactions, performing functions, and establishing trust in secure computing without centralized authority in a networked environment. A blockchain is a chain of timestamped blocks connected by special mathematical techniques (i.e., cryptographic hashes) and behaves like a distributed ledger whose data are shared among a network of users. This paper emphasizes how the convergence of blockchain technology with IoT can provide a better manufacturing industry solution.

Blockchain in IoT

With the booming growth of IoT, the number of connected IoT devices and the data generated by them has become a massive bottleneck in meeting Quality-of-Service (QoS) (Ferrag et al., 2019). In this way, blockchain comes into the picture by supporting a decentralized way of storing data and trustful and anonymous transactions. Blockchain technology can thereby be used for tracking and coordinating the billions of connected devices. It can also enable the processing of transactions to allow significant savings for IoT industry manufacturers. This decentralized approach would further eliminate single points of failure, creating a more resilient ecosystem for devices to run on (Ali et al., 2019). The blockchains cryptographic algorithms would also help make consumer data privacy more robust (Makhdoom et al., 2019).

A blockchain is a distributed immutable, verifiable ledger. A typical design of a blockchain consists of a series of transactions that are put into one block. These blocks are then linked so that if a transaction is altered in one block, it must be updated in all the subsequent blocks (Makhdoom et al., 2019). Since the ledger is maintained with many peers, it is challenging to alter a transaction (Ferrag et al., 2019). All the blockchain peers need to agree or validate each transaction to get added to a block (Reyna et al., 2018). Once validated, the block gets updated in the blockchain.

This agreement is achieved with the help of consensus algorithms like Proof of Work (PoW), Proof of Stake (PoS), Delegated Proof-of-Stake (DPoS), Proof-of-Authority (PoA) etc. Blockchain technology is radically reshaping not only the modern IoT world but also the industries. Researchers of late have focused on integrating blockchain into the IoT ecosystem to include distributed architecture and security features. However, before this section discusses how blockchain is bringing about a significant paradigm shift in IoT, we explain the significant features of blockchain as follows (Ali et al., 2019):

- The decentralization offered by Blockchain technology enables two nodes to engage in transactions without a trusted third party. This eliminates the bottleneck of a single point of failure, thereby enhancing fault tolerance.
- All new entries made in the blockchain are agreed upon by nodes using a decentralized consensus algorithm. The design is such that all subsequent blocks in all the peers must be altered to modify an entry in a block. This ensures the immutability of blockchains.
- The audibility property of blockchains ensures transparency by allowing peers to look up and verify any transaction.
- The blockchain peers hold copies of identical replicas of ledger records. Blockchains, therefore, ensure fault tolerance. This property helps maintain data integrity and resiliency in the network.

The benefits of decentralizing IoT are numerous and notably superior to current centralized systems and are discussed below:

§ **Improved Trust and Security:** The distributed and immutable nature of blockchain would eliminate the single point of entry/vulnerability for attackers/hackers. All transactions are cryptographically signed using unforgeable signatures, making them non-repudiable and resistant to attacks.

§ **More Robust:** Decentralization will make IoT more accessible, and damage costs from hacks can be more easily prevented or avoided altogether. Intermediaries that operate for centralized IoT systems will be eliminated through decentralizing IoT, thereby reducing the associated costs.

§ **Autonomy:** Blockchains enable smart devices to act independently according to the pre-determined logic (using Smart Contracts). This would altogether remove intermediary players and central authority.

§ **More trustworthy:** The use of efficient Smart Contracts for communication amongst IoT devices and the decentralization offered by blockchain makes the entire system more trustworthy.

§ **Data provenance:** Since all transactions are recorded on the ledger and signed by the devices/ entities generating data, data provenance can be achieved.

§ **Fairness:** By using native cryptocurrency in blockchain, parties can be incentivized. This makes the IoT system fair.

Despite the advantages (discussed above) that the integration of blockchain into the IoT platform will bring, the traditional blockchains (like Ethereum and Bitcoin) suffer from the following drawbacks too (Popov, 2018):

§ **Scalability:** As the number of IoT devices increases, the amount of data generated will be huge, thereby leading to more storage space to keep the transactions updated in the ledger. This will further lead to high transaction and storage costs.

§ **Communication Overhead and Synchronization:** Since each new transaction that is added to the blockchain needs to be broadcast to all the peers, it involves a lot of communication overhead. Further, all the blockchain peers need to synchronize and maintain the blockchain's duplicate copy, which further adds to the overhead.

§ **Efficiency:** To get a transaction approved, it needs to be verified by all other peers. Thus, the verification algorithm is run multiple times at each of the peers, which drastically reduces operational efficiency.

§　**Energy Wastage:** A majority of the popular blockchain technologies use Proof of Work (PoW) to achieve consensus and are thereby inefficient. They need to perform many computations, thereby leading to energy wastage.

Due to the disadvantages of the traditional blockchain technology, a challenging work direction is to design scalable, computable, and energy-efficient, secure blockchains for IoT applications. The IOTA Foundation has been provided with some examples of works in this direction (Popov, 2018).

The IOTA Foundation (As a distributed ledger technology, IOTA provides a trust layer for any devices connected to the global Internet) was specifically designed for the IoT. It differs from the existing blockchains as it does not use any traditional Blockchain at all. IOTA's main structure is the Tangle, a Directed Acyclic Graph (DAG) (Popov, 2018). The transactions (referred to as sites in Tangle) are stored in a graph format, where the nodes are entities that issue and validate transactions (Popov, 2018). Whenever a new transaction arrives, it is represented by directed edges and must be approved by two previous transactions.

For a node to validate a transaction, it must give Proof of Work, which is successfully executed registers the transaction. This functionality of Tangle allows us to eliminate the need for miners in the network as the node itself acts as a miner now, which further reduces the transaction costs to zero (Popov, 2018). To issue a transaction, users must work to approve other transactions. If a node realizes that a transaction conflicts with the Tangle history, the node will not approve the conflicting transaction, thereby ensuring network security (Popov, 2018). Despite all these, IOTA's Tangle has several advantages, as described below (Popov, 2018):

§　**Scalability:** IOTA addresses this issue by not using a blockchain-based decentralized network instead of opting for their Tangle platform. With IOTA, as the transaction rate increases, scalability also increases, i.e., the more subscribers and transactions the system has, the faster it gets. More importantly, the latency, that is, the time between placing a transaction and validating it, also approaches zero as soon as a specific size is reached.

§　**Centralization of Control:** For a transaction to occur in the Tangle, the previous two transactions must be validated by it. This makes the network faster with increasing use. Thus, IOTA allows each user who has initiated a transaction to act as a miner.

§　**Quantum Computing:** IOTA uses 'exclusively quantum-resistant cryptographic algorithms, making it future-oriented and immune to brute force attacks. Moreover, Tangle holds power to decrease quantum consensus attacks by almost a million times.

§　**Micro Payments:** In traditional blockchain platforms, the concept of mining involves transaction fees (i.e., financial rewards set by the transaction's sender). As a result, even the most minor payment amounts result in high transaction fees. However, in IOTA's Tangle, each site does its PoW to get added to the network, so the concept of transaction fees is completed eliminated.

However, Tangle also has the following disadvantages for which Ethereum, or Bitcoin is preferred over Tangle for commercial use in IoT (Popov, 2018).

REFERENCES

Abduvaliyev, A., Pathan, A. S. K., Zhou, J., Roman, R., & Wong, W. C. (2013). On the vital areas of intrusion detection systems in wireless sensor networks. *IEEE Communications Surveys and Tutorials*, *15*(3), 1223–1237.

Aberer, K., Hauswirth, H., & Salehi, A. (2006). *Middleware Support for the Internet of Things*. Available: www.manfredhauswirth.org/research/papers/WSN2006.pdf

Adat, V., & Gupta, B. B. (2017). A DDoS attack mitigation framework for Internet of things. *2017 International Conference on Communication and Signal Processing (ICCSP)*, 2036–2041.

Ahemd, M. M., Shah, M. A., & Wahid, A. (2017). IoT security: a layered approach for attacks and defenses. *2017 International Conference on Communication Technologies (ComTech)*, 104–110. 10.1109/COMTECH.2017.8065757

Airehrour, D., Gutierrez, J. A., & Ray, S. K. (2019). Sectrust-rpl: A secure trust-aware rpl routing protocol for the Internet of things. *Future Generation Computer Systems*, *93*, 860–876.

Al-Turjman, F., & Alturjman, S. (2018). Context-sensitive access in industrial Internet of things (iiot) healthcare applications. *IEEE Transactions on Industrial Informatics*, *14*(6), 2736–2744. doi:10.1109/TII.2018.2808190

Alaba, F. A., Othman, M., Hashem, I. A. T., & Alotaibi, F. (2017). Internet of things security: A survey. *Journal of Network and Computer Applications*, *88*, 10–28.

Alccer, V., & Cruz-Machado, V. (2019). Scanning the industry 4.0: A literature review on technologies for manufacturing systems, Engineering Science and Technology. *International Journal (Toronto, Ont.)*, *22*(3), 899–919.

Ali, M. S., Vecchio, M., Pincheira, M., Dolui, K., Antonelli, F., & Rehmani, M. H. (2019). *Applications of blockchains in the Internet of things: A comprehensive survey. IEEE Commun. Surv. Tutorials*.

All, I. F. (2017). *The 5 Worst Examples of IoT Hacking and Vulnerabilities in Recorded History*. Academic Press.

Aman, M. N., Chua, K. C., & Sikdar, B. (2017). A lightweight mutual authentication protocol for IoT systems. *GLOBECOM 2017 - 2017 IEEE Global Communications Conference*, 1–6.

Andoni, M., Robu, V., Flynn, D., Abram, S., Geach, D., Jenkins, D., McCallum, P., & Peacock, A. (2019). Blockchain technology in the energy sector: A systematic review of challenges and opportunities. *Renewable & Sustainable Energy Reviews*, *100*, 143–174. doi:10.1016/j.rser.2018.10.014

Andrea, I., Chrysostomou, C., & Hadjichristofi, G. (2015). Internet of things: security vulnerabilities and challenges. *2015 IEEE Symposium on Computers and Communication (ISCC)*, 180–187.

Araujo, J., Mazo, M., Anta, A. Jr, Tabuada, P., & Johansson, K. H. (2014, February). System Architecture, Protocols, and Algorithms for Aperiodic wireless control systems. *IEEE Transactions on Industrial Informatics*, *10*(1), 175–184.

Ashibani, Y., & Mahmoud, Q. H. (2017). An efficient and secure scheme for smart home communication using identity-based encryption. *2017 IEEE 36th International Performance Computing and Communications Conference (IPCCC)*, 1–7.

Atlam, H. F., Alenezi, A., Alassafi, M. O., & Wills, G. B. (2018). Blockchain with Internet of things: Benefits, challenges, and future directions. *Int. J. Intell. Syst. Appl.*, *10*(6), 40–48.

Atlam, H. F., Azad, M. A., Alzahrani, A. G., & Wills, G. (2020). A Review of Blockchain in Internet of Things and AI. *Journal of Big Data and Cognitive Computing*, 1-27.

Azzi, R., Chamoun, R. K., & Sokhn, M. (2019). The power of a blockchain-based supply chain. *Computers & Industrial Engineering*, *135*, 582–592.

Boyes, H., Hallaq, B., Cunningham, J., & Watson, T. (2018). The industrial Internet of things (iiot): An analysis framework. *Computers in Industry*, *101*, 1–12.

Butun, I., Morgera, S. D., & Sankar, R. (2014). A survey of intrusion detection systems in wireless sensor networks. *IEEE Communications Surveys and Tutorials*, *16*(1), 266–282.

Cervantes, C., Poplade, D., Nogueira, M., & Santos, A. (2015). Detection of sinkhole attacks for supporting secure routing on 6lowpan for Internet of things. *2015 IFIP/IEEE International Symposium on Integrated Network Management (IM)*, 606–611.

Cha, S., Chen, J., Su, C., & Yeh, K. (2018). A blockchain connected gateway for ble-based devices in the Internet of things. *IEEE Access : Practical Innovations, Open Solutions*, *6*, 24639–24649.

Chan, M. (2017). *Why Cloud Computing Is the Foundation of the Internet of Things*. Academic Press.

Chaudhary, R., Aujla, G. S., Garg, S., Kumar, N., & Rodrigues, J. J. P. C. (2018). Sdn-enabled multi-attribute-based secure communication for smart grid in riot environment. *IEEE Transactions on Industrial Informatics*, *14*(6), 2629–2640.

Chen, G., & Ng, W. S. (2017). An efficient authorization framework for securing industrial Internet of things. *TENCON 2017 - 2017 IEEE Region 10 Conference*, 1219–1224.

Chen, L., Lee, W.-K., Chang, C.-C., Choo, K.-K. R., & Zhang, N. (2019). Blockchain-based searchable encryption for electronic health record sharing. *Future Generation Computer Systems*, *95*, 420–429.

Choi, J., & Kim, Y. (2016). An improved lea block encryption algorithm to prevent side-channel attack in the IoT system. *2016 Asia-Pacific Signal and Information Processing Association Annual Summit and Conference (APSIPA)*, 1–4.

Cirani, S., Ferrari, G., & Veltri, L. (2013). Enforcing security mechanisms in the IP-based internet of things: An algorithmic overview. *Algorithms*, *6*(2), 197–226.

Colema, L. (2006). Frequency of man-made disasters in the 20the century. *Journal of Contingencies and Crisis Management*, *14*(1), 3–11. doi:10.1111/j.1468-5973.2006.00476.x

De, S. J., & Ruj, S. (2017). *Efficient decentralized attribute-based access control for mobile clouds*. IEEE Transactions on Cloud Computing.

Dorri, A., Kanhere, S. S., Jurdak, R., & Gauravaram, P. (2019). *LSB: A Lightweight Scalable Blockchain for IoT Security and Privacy*. http://arxiv.org/ abs/1712.02969

Esfahani, A., Mantas, G., Matischek, R., Saghezchi, F. B., Rodriguez, J., Bicaku, A., Maksuti, S., Tauber, M. G., Schmittner, C., & Bastos, J. (2019). A lightweight authentication mechanism for m2m communications in industrial IoT environment. *IEEE Internet of Things Journal, 6*(1), 288–296. doi:10.1109/ JIOT.2017.2737630

Fernndez-Carams, T. M., & Fraga-Lamas, P. (2018). A review on the use of blockchain for the Internet of things. *IEEE Access : Practical Innovations, Open Solutions, 6*, 32979–33001.

Ferran, M. A., Derdour, M., Mukherjee, M., Dahab, A., Maglaras, L., & Janicke, H. (2019). *Blockchain technologies for the Internet of things: research issues and challenges*. IEEE Internet Things J.

Forbes. (2019). Blockchain in healthcare: How it Could Make Digital Healthcare Safer and More Innovative. *Forbes*.

Frustaci, M., Pace, P., Aloi, G., & Fortino, G. (2018). *Evaluating critical security issues of the IoT world: present and future challenges*. IEEE Internet Things.

Gai, J., Choo, K., Qiu, K. R., & Zhu, L. (2018). Privacy-preserving content-oriented wireless communication in internet-of-things. *IEEE Internet Things Journal, 5*(4), 3059–3067.

Gandino, F., Montrucchio, B., & Rebaudengo, M. (2014). *Key Management for Static Wireless Sensor Networks with Node Adding. IEEE Transaction Industrial Informatics*.

Gibbon, J. (2018). *Introduction to Trusted Execution Environment: Arm's Trust zone*. Academic Press.

Glissa, G., Rachedi, A., & Meddeb, A. (2016). A secure routing protocol based on rpl for Internet of things. *IEEE Global Communications Conference (GLOBECOM)*, 1–7.

Gomes, T., Salgado, F., Tavares, A., & Cabral, J. (2017). Cute mote, a customizable and trustable end-device for the Internet of things. *IEEE Sensors Journal, 17*(20), 6816–6824. doi:10.1109/JSEN.2017.2743460

Gope, P., & Sikdar, B. (2018). *Lightweight and privacy-preserving two-factor authentication scheme for IoT devices*. IEEE Internet Things.

Granja, J., Silva, R., Monteiro, E., Silva, J. S., & Boavida, F. (2008). Why is IPSec a viable option for wireless sensor networks. *2008 5th IEEE International Conference on Mobile Ad Hoc and Sensor Systems*, 802–807.

Granville, K. (2018). *Facebook and Cambridge Analytica: what You Need to Know as Fallout Widens*. Academic Press.

Griggs, K. N., Osipova, O., Kohlios, C. P., Baccarini, A. N., Howson, E. A., & Hayajneh, T. (2018). Healthcare blockchain system using smart contracts for secure automated remote patient monitoring. *Journal of Medical Systems, 42*(7), 1–7.

Guan, Z., Si, G., Zhang, X., Wu, L., Guizani, N., Du, X., & Ma, Y. (2018). Privacy-preserving and efficient aggregation based on blockchain for power grid communications in smart communities. *IEEE Communications Magazine*, *56*(7), 82–88.

Guin, U., Singh, A., Alam, M., Caedo, J., & Skjellum, A. (2018). A secure low-cost edge device authentication scheme for the Internet of things. *31st International Conference on VLSI Design and 17th International Conference on Embedded Systems (VLSID)*, 85–90.

Hei, X., Du, X., Wu, J., & Hu, F. (2010). Defending resource depletion attacks on implantable medical devices. *2010 IEEE Global Telecommunications Conference GLOBECOM 2010*, 1–5.

Huang, J., Kong, L., Chen, G., Wu, M., Liu, X., & Zeng, P. (2019b). Towards secure industrial IoT: blockchain system with credit-based consensus mechanism. IEEE Trans. Ind.

Huang, X., Zhang, Y., Li, D., & Han, L. (2019a). An optimal scheduling algorithm for hybrid EV charging scenario using consortium blockchains. *Future Generation Computer Systems*, *91*, 555–562.

Huh, J.-H., & Seo, K. (2019). Blockchain-based mobile fingerprint verification and automatic log-in platform for future computing. *The Journal of Supercomputing*, *75*(6), 3123–3139.

Huh, S.-K., & Kim, J.-H. (2019). The blockchain consensus algorithm for viable management of new and renewable energies. *Sustainability*, *11*(3184), 3184.

IEEE. (2012). *IeEEE Standard for Local and metropolitan networks–Part 15.4: LowRate Wireless Personal Area Networks (LR-WPANs), 2012*. IEEE.

IoT-A. (2013). *Internet of Things–Architecture IoT-A Deliverable D1.5–Final architectural reference model for the IoT v3.0, 2013*. http://iotforum.org/wpcontent/uploads/2014/09/D1.5-20130715-VERYFINAL.pdf

Islam, S. H., Khan, M. K., & Al-Khouri, A. M. (2015). Anonymous and provably secure certificateless multireceiver encryption without bilinear pairing. *Security and Communication Networks*, *8*(13), 2214–2231.

Kang, J., Xiong, Z., Niyato, D., Ye, D., Kim, D. I., & Zhao, J. (2019a). Toward secure blockchain-enabled Internet of vehicles: Optimizing consensus management using reputation and contract theory. *IEEE Transactions on Vehicular Technology*, *68*(3), 2906–2920.

Kang, J., Yu, R., Huang, X., Maharjan, S., Zhang, Y., & Hossain, E. (2017). Enabling localized peer-to-peer electricity trading among plug-in hybrid electric vehicles using consortium blockchains. *IEEE Transactions on Industrial Informatics*, *13*(6), 3154–3164.

Kang, J., Yu, R., Huang, X., Wu, M., Maharjan, S., Xie, S., & Zhang, Y. (2019b). Blockchain for secure and efficient data sharing in vehicular edge computing and networks. *IEEE Internet of Things Journal*, *6*(3), 4660–4670.

Karati, A., Islam, S. H., & Karuppiah, M. (2018). Provably secure and lightweight certificateless signature scheme for iiot environments. *IEEE Transactions on Industrial Informatics*, *14*(8), 3701–3711.

Khan, F. I., & Hameed, S. (2019). Understanding security requirements and challenges in the Internet of things (iots): a review. *Journal of Computer Networks and Communications*.

Khan, M. A., & Salah, K. (2018). IoT security: Review, blockchain solutions, and open challenges. *Future Generation Computer Systems*, *82*, 395–411.

Kim, J.-H., & Huh, S.-K. (1973). A study on the improvement of smart grid security performance and blockchain smart grid perspective. *Energies*, 11.

Kim, S.-K., Kim, U.-M., & Huh, H. J. (2017). A study on improvement of blockchain application to overcome vulnerability of IoT multiplatform security. *Energies*, *12*(402).

Konigsmark, S. T. C., Chen, D., & Wong, M. D. F. (2016). Information dispersion for trojan defense through high-level synthesis. *ACM/EDAC/IEEE Design Automation Conference (DAC)*, 1–6.

Kouicem, D. E., Bouabdallah, A., & Lakhlef, H. (2018). Internet of things security: A top-down survey. *Computer Networks*, *141*, 199–221.

Li, C., & Palanisamy, B. (2019). Privacy in Internet of things: From principles to technologies. *IEEE Internet of Things Journal*, *6*(1), 488–505. doi:10.1109/JIOT.2018.2864168

Li, R., Song, T., Mei, B., Li, H., Cheng, X., & Sun, L. (2019). Blockchain for large-scale Internet of things data storage and protection. *IEEE Transactions on Services Computing*, *12*(5), 762–771.

Li, X., Niu, J., Bhuiyan, M. Z. A., Wu, F., Karuppiah, M., & Kumari, S. (2018a). A robust ECC-based provable secure authentication protocol with privacy-preserving for industrial Internet of things. *IEEE Transactions on Industrial Informatics*, *14*(8), 3599–3609.

Li, Z., Kang, J., Yu, R., Ye, D., Deng, Q., & Zhang, Y. (2018b). Consortium blockchain for secure energy trading in industrial Internet of things. *IEEE Transactions on Industrial Informatics*, *14*(8), 3690–3700.

Lin, C., He, D., Huang, X., Choo, K.-K. R., & Vasilakos, A. V. (2018). Basin: A blockchain-based secure mutual authentication with fine-grained access control system for industry 4.0. *Journal of Network and Computer Applications*, *116*, 42 52.

Ling, Z., Liu, K., Xu, Y., Jin, Y., & Fu, X. (2017). An end-to-end view of IoT security and privacy. *IEEE Global Communications Conference*, 1–7.

Liu, C., Cronin, P., & Yang, C. (2016). A mutual auditing framework to protect iot against hardware trojans. *2016 21st Asia and South Pacific Design Automation Conference (ASP-DAC)*, 69–74.

Liu, C. H., Lin, Q., & Wen, S. (2019b). *Blockchain-enabled data collection and sharing for industrial IoT with deep reinforcement learning*. IEEE Transaction Industrial Informatics.

Liu, J., Zhang, C., & Fang, Y. (2018). Epic: A differential privacy framework to defend smart homes against internet traffic analysis. *IEEE Internet of Things Journal*, *5*(2), 1206–1217.

Liu, Y., Guo, W., Fan, C., Chang, L., & Cheng, C. (2019a). A practical privacy-preserving data aggregation (3pda) scheme for smart grid. *IEEE Transactions on Industrial Informatics*, *15*(3), 1767–1774.

Longo, F., Nicoletti, L., Padovano, A., d'Atri, G., & Forte, M. (2019). Blockchain-enabled supply chain: An experimental study. *Computers & Industrial Engineering, 136,* 57–69.

Lu, Y., & Li, J. (2016). A pairing-free certificate-based proxy re-encryption scheme for secure data sharing in public clouds. *Future Generation Computer Systems, 62,* 140–147.

Lukac, D. (2015). The fourth ICT-based industrial revolution "Industry 4.0": HMI and the case of CAE/CAD innovation with EPLAN. *23rd Telecommunications Forum Telfor (TELFOR),* 835-838.

Machado, C., & Frhlich, A. A. M. (2018). IoT data integrity verification for cyber-physical systems using blockchain. *2018 IEEE 21st International Symposium on Real-Time Distributed Computing (ISORC),* 83–90.

Makhdoom, I., Abolhasan, M., Abbas, H., & Ni, W. (2019). Blockchain's adoption in iot: The challenges, and a way forward. *Journal of Network and Computer Applications, 125,* 251–279.

Manditereza, K. (2017). *4 Key Differences between Scada and Industrial IoT.* Academic Press.

Manzoor, A., Liyanage, M., Braeken, A., Kanhere, S. S., & Ylianttila, M. (2019). Blockchain-Based Proxy Re-encryption Scheme for Secure IoT Data Sharing. *Clinical Orthopaedics and Related Research.*

Minoli, D., & Occhiogross, B. (2018). Blockchain mechanism for IoT security. *International Journal of Internet of Things,* 1-13.

Mitchell, R., & Chen, I. R. (2014). Review: A survey of intrusion detection in wireless network applications. *Computer Communications, 42,* 1–23.

Mondal, S., Wijewardena, K. P., Karuppuswami, S., Kriti, N., Kumar, D., & Chahal, P. (2019). Blockchain inspired RFID-based information architecture for food supply chain. *IEEE Internet of Things Journal, 6*(3), 5803–5813.

Mosenia, A., & Jha, N. K. (2017). A comprehensive study of security of internet-of-things. *IEEE Transactions on Emerging Topics in Computing, 5*(4), 586–602. doi:10.1109/TETC.2016.2606384

Naeem, H., Guo, B., & Naeem, M. R. (2018). A lightweight malware static visual analysis for IoT infrastructure. *International Conference on Artificial Intelligence and Big Data (ICAIBD),* 240–244.

ObserveIT. (2018). *5 Examples of Insider Threat-Caused Breaches that Illustrate the Scope of the Problem.* Author.

Okorie, O., Turner, C., Charnley, F., Moreno, M., & Tiwari, A. (2017). A review of data-driven approaches for circular economy in manufacturing. *Proceedings of the 18th European Roundtable for Sustainable Consumption and Production.*

Oleshchuk, V. (2009). Internet of things and privacy preserving technologies. *2009 1st International Conference on Wireless Communication, Vehicular Technology, Information Theory and Aerospace Electronic Systems Technology,* 336–340.

Omar, A. A., Bhuiyan, M. Z. A., Basu, A., Kiyomoto, S., & Rahman, M. S. (2019). Privacy-friendly platform for healthcare data in cloud-based on blockchain environment. *Future Generation Computer Systems*, *95*, 511–521.

OWASP. (2016). *Top IoT Vulnerabilities, 2016*. https://www.owasp.org/index.php/Top_IoT_Vulnerabilities

Oztemel, E., & Gusev, S. (2018). Literature review of industry 4.0 and related technologies. *Journal of Intelligent Manufacturing*.

Pal, K. (2017). Building High Quality Big Data-Based Applications in Supply Chains. IGI Global.

Pal, K. (2018). *Ontology-Based Web Service Architecture for Retail Supply Chain Management*. The 9th International Conference on Ambient Systems, Networks and Technologies, Porto, Portugal.

Pal, K. (2019). Algorithmic Solutions for RFID Tag Anti-Collision Problem in Supply Chain Management. *Procedia Computer Science*, *151*, 929–934.

Pal, K. (2020). Information sharing for manufacturing supply chain management based on blockchain technology. In I. Williams (Ed.), *Cross-Industry Use of Blockchain Technology and Opportunities for the Future* (pp. 1–17). IGI Global.

Pal, K. (2021). Applications of Secured Blockchain Technology in Manufacturing Industry. In *Blockchain and AI Technology in the Industrial Internet of Things*. IGI Global Publication.

Pal, K., & Yasar, A. (2020). Internet of Things and blockchain technology in apparel manufacturing supply chain data management. *Procedia Computer Science*, *170*, 450–457.

Park, N., & Kang, N. (2015). Mutual authentication scheme in secure Internet of things technology for comfortable lifestyle. *Sensors (Basel)*, *16*(1), 20.

Porambage, P., Schmitt, C., Kumar, P., Gurtov, A., & Ylianttila, M. (2014). Pauthkey: A pervasive authentication protocol and key establishment scheme for wireless sensor networks in distributed IoT applications. *International Journal of Distributed Sensor Networks*, *10*(7), 357430.

Pu, C., & Hajjar, S. (2018). Mitigating forwarding misbehaviors in rpl-based low power and lossy networks. *2018 15th IEEE Annual Consumer Communications Networking Conference (CCNC)*, 1–6.

Rahulamathavan, Y., Phan, R. C., Rajarajan, M., Misra, S., & Kondoz, A. (2017). Privacy-preserving blockchain-based IoT ecosystem using attribute-based encryption. *IEEE International Conference on Advanced Networks and Telecommunications Systems (ANTS)*, 1–6.

Rambus. (n.d.). *Industrial IoT: Threats and countermeasures*. https://www.rambus.com/iot/industrial-IoT/

Reyna, A., Martn, C., Chen, J., Soler, E., & Daz, M. (2018). On blockchain and its integration with iot. challenges and opportunities. *Future Generation Computer Systems*, *88*, 173–190.

Roblek, V., Mesko, M., & Krapez, A. (2016). A complex view of Industry 4.0. *SAGE Open*, *6*(2).

Roman, R., Lopez, J., & Mambo, M. (2016). Mobile edge computing, Fog et al.: A survey and analysis of security threats and challenges. *Future Gener. Comput. Syst.*

Sfar, A. R., Natalizio, E., Challal, Y., & Chtourou, Z. (2018). A roadmap for security challenges in the Internet of things. *Digital Communications and Networks.*, *4*(2), 118–137.

Shen, M., Tang, X., Zhu, L., Du, X., & Guizani, M. (2019). Privacy-preserving support vector machine training over blockchain-based encrypted IoT data in smart cities. *IEEE Internet of Things Journal*, *6*(5), 7702–7712.

Shrestha, R., Bajracharya, R., Shrestha, A. P., & Nam, S. Y. (2019). *A new type of blockchain for secure message exchange in vanet*. Digital Communications and Networks.

Shukla, P. (2017). Ml-ids: A machine learning approach to detect wormhole attacks in the Internet of things. *Intelligent Systems Conference (IntelliSys),* 234–240.

Sicari, S., Rizzardi, A., Grieco, L., & Coen-Porisini, A. (2015). Security, privacy and trust in internet of things: The road ahead. *Computer Networks*, *76*(Suppl. C), 146–164.

Sicari, S., Rizzardi, A., Miorandi, D., & Coen-Porisini, A. (2018). Reatoreacting to denial-of-service attacks in the Internet of things. *Computer Networks*, *137*, 37–48.

Singh, M., Rajan, M. A., Shivraj, V. L., & Balamuralidhar, P. (2015). Secure MQTT for the Internet of things (IoT). *5th International Conference on Communication Systems and Network Technologies*, 746–751.

Song, T., Li, R., Mei, B., Yu, J., Xing, X., & Cheng, X. (2017). A privacy-preserving communication protocol for IoT applications in smart homes. *IEEE Internet of Things Journal*, *4*(6), 1844–1852.

SOPHOS. (2015). *49 Busted in Europe for Man-In-The-Middle Bank Attacks*. https://nakedsecurity.sophos.com/2015/06/11/49-busted-in-europe-for-man-in-themiddle-bank-attacks/

Sreamr. (2017). *Streamr White Paper v2.0*. https://s3.amazonaws.com/streamr-public/ streamr-datacoin-whitepaper-2017-07-25-v1_0.pdf

Srinivas, J., Das, A. K., Wazid, M., & Kumar, N. (2018). Anonymous lightweight chaotic map-based authenticated key agreement protocol for industrial internet of things. IEEE Trans. Dependable Secure Comput.

Su, J., Vasconcellos, V. D., Prasad, S., Daniele, S., Feng, Y., & Sakurai, K. (2018). Lightweight classification of IoT malware based on image recognition. *IEEE 42nd Annual Computer Software and Applications Conference (COMPSAC), 2*, 664–669.

Varga, P., Plosz, S., Soos, G., & Hegedus, C. (2017). Security Threats and Issues in Automation IoT. *2017 IEEE 13th International Workshop on Factory Communication Systems (WFCS)*, 1–6.

Vasconcellos, V. D., Prasad, S., Daniele, S., Feng, Y., & Sakurai, K. (2018). Lightweight classification of IoT malware based on image recognition. *IEEE 42nd Annual Computer Software and Applications Conference (COMPSAC), 2*, 664–669.

Vechain Team. (2018). *Vechain White Paper*. https://cdn.vechain.com/vechain_ico_ideas_of_ development_en.pdf

Vogel-Heuser, B. & Hess, D. (2016). Guest editorial Industry 4.0 -prerequisites and vision. *IEEE Transactions, Autom. Sci. Eng., 13*(2).

Waltonchain. (2021). *Waltonchain white paper v2.0.* https://www.waltonchain.org/en/ Waltonchain_White_Paper_2.0_EN.pdf

Wan, J., Li, J., Imran, M., Li, D., & e-Amin, F. (2019). A blockchain-based solution for enhancing security and privacy in smart factory. *IEEE Transaction.*

Wan, J., Tang, S., Shu, Z., Li, D., Wang, S., Imran, M., & Vasilakos, A. V. (2016). Software-defined industrial Internet of things in the context of industry 4.0. *IEEE Sensors Journal, 16*(20), 7373–7380.

Wang, Q., Zhu, X., Ni, Y., Gu, L., & Zhu, H. (2019b). *Blockchain for the IoT and industrial IoT: a review.* Internet Things.

Wang, X., Zha, X., Ni, W., Liu, R. P., Guo, Y. J., Niu, X., & Zheng, K. (2019a). Survey on blockchain for Internet of things. *Computer Communications, 136*, 10–29.

Wang, Y., Uehara, T., & Sasaki, R. (2015). Fog computing: Issues and challenges in security and forensics. *2015 IEEE 39th Annual Computer Software and Applications Conference, 3*, 53–59.

Wurm, J., Hoang, K., Arias, O., Sadeghi, A., & Jin, Y. (2016). Security analysis on consumer and industrial IoT devices. *21st Asia and South Pacific Design Automation Conference (ASP-DAC)*, 519–524.

Xiong, Z., Zhang, Y., Niyato, D., Wang, P., & Han, Z. (2018). When mobile blockchain meets edge computing. *IEEE Communications Magazine, 56*(8), 33–39.

Xu, L. D., He, W., & Li, S. (2014). Internet of things in industries: A survey. *IEEE Transactions on Industrial Informatics, 10*(4), 2233–2243.

Xu, L. D., Xu, E. L., & Li, L. (2018). Industry 4.0: State of the art and future trends. *International Journal of Production Research, 56*(8), 2941–2962. doi:10.1080/00207543.2018.1444806

Xu, Y., Ren, J., Wang, G., Zhang, C., Yang, J., & Zhang, Y. (2019). *A blockchain-based non-repudiation network computing service scheme for industrial IoT. IEEE Transaction Industrial Informatics.*

Yan, Q., Huang, W., Luo, X., Gong, Q., & Yu, F. R. (2018). A multi-level DDoS mitigation framework for the industrial Internet of things. *IEEE Communications Magazine, 56*(2), 30–36.

Yang, W., Wang, S., Huang, X., & Mu, Y. (2019a). On the Security of an Efficient and Robust Certificateless Signature Scheme for IIoT Environments. *IEEE Access : Practical Innovations, Open Solutions, 7*, 91074–91079.

Yang, Y., Wu, L., Yin, G., Li, L., & Zhao, H. (2017). A survey on security and privacy issues in internet-of-things. *IEEE Internet of Things Journal, 4*(5), 1250–1258.

Yang, Z., Yang, K., Lei, L., Zheng, K., & Leung, V. C. M. (2019b). Blockchain-based decentralized trust management in vehicular networks. *IEEE Internet of Things Journal, 6*(2), 1495–1505.

Yao, X., Kong, H., Liu, H., Qiu, T., & Ning, H. (2019). An attribute credential-based public-key scheme for fog computing in digital manufacturing. *IEEE Trans. Ind. Inf.*

Yi, S., Qin, Z., & Li, Q. (2015). Security and privacy issues of fog computing: A survey. *Wireless Algorithms, Systems, and Applications the 10th International Conference on*, 1–10.

Yin, D., Zhang, L., & Yang, K. (2018). A DDoS attack detection and mitigation with software-defined Internet of things framework. *IEEE Access : Practical Innovations, Open Solutions, 6*, 24694–24705.

Zhang, H., Wang, J., & Ding, Y. (2019b). Blockchain-based decentralized and secure keyless signature scheme for smart grid. *Energy, 180*, 955–967. doi:10.1016/j.energy.2019.05.127

Zhang, N., Mi, X., Feng, X., Wang, X., Tian, Y., & Qian, F. (2018). *Understanding and Mitigating the Security Risks of Voice-Controlled Third-Party Skills on Amazon Alexa and Google Home*. Academic Press.

Zhang, Y., Deng, R., Zheng, D., Li, J., Wu, P., & Cao, J. (2019a). *Efficient and Robust Certificateless Signature for Data Crowdsensing in Cloud-Assisted Industrial IoT*. IEEE Transaction Industry.

Zhang, Z. K., Cho, M. C. Y., Wang, C. W., Hsu, C. W., Chen, C. K., & Shieh, S. (2014). IoT security: Ongoing challenges and research opportunities. *Computer Applications, 2014*, 230–234.

Zheng, D., Wu, A., Zhang, Y., & Zhao, Q. (2018). Efficient and privacy-preserving medical data sharing in the Internet of things with limited computing power. *IEEE Access : Practical Innovations, Open Solutions, 6*, 28019–28027.

Zhou, J., Cao, Z., Dong, X., & Vasilakos, A. V. (2017). Security and privacy for cloud-based IoT: Challenges. *IEEE Communications Magazine, 55*(1), 26–33.

Zhou, R., Zhang, X., Du, X., Wang, X., Yang, G., & Guizani, M. (2018). File-centric multi-key aggregate keyword searchable encryption for industrial Internet of things. *IEEE Transactions on Industrial Informatics, 14*(8), 3648–3658.

Ziegeldorf, J. H., Morchon, O. G., & Wehrle, K. (2014). *Privacy in the Internet of Things: Threats and Challenges*. https://arxiv.org/abs/1505.07683

KEY TERMS AND DEFINITIONS

Block: A block is a data structure used to communicate incremental changes to the local state of a node. It consists of a list of transactions, a reference to a previous block and a nonce.

Blockchain: In simple, a blockchain is just a data structure that can be shared by different users using computing data communication network (e.g., peer-to-peer or P2P). Blockchain is a distributed data structure comprising a chain of blocks. It can act as a global ledger that maintains records of all transactions on a blockchain network. The transactions are time-stamped and bundled into blocks where each block is identified by its *cryptographic hash*.

Cryptography: Blockchain's transactions achieve validity, trust, and finality based on cryptographic proofs and underlying mathematical computations between various trading partners.

Decentralized Computing Infrastructure: These computing infrastructures feature computing nodes that can make independent processing and computational decisions irrespective of what other peer computing nodes may decide.

Immutability: This term refers to the fact that blockchain transactions cannot be deleted or altered.

Internet of Things (IoT): The internet of things (IoT), also called the internet of everything or the, is now a technology paradigm envisioned as a global network of machines and devices capable of interacting with each other. The IoT is recognized as one of the most important areas of future technology and is gaining vast attention from a wide range of industries.

Provenance: In a blockchain ledger, provenance is a way to trace the origin of every transaction such that there is no dispute about the origin and sequence of the transactions in the ledger.

Supply Chain Management: A supply chain consists of a network of *key business processes* and facilities, involving end-users and suppliers that provide products, services, and information.

Warehouse: A warehouse can also be called a storage area, and it is a commercial building where raw materials or goods are stored by suppliers, exporters, manufacturers, or wholesalers, they are constructed and equipped with tools according to special standards depending on the purpose of their use.

This research was previously published in IoT Protocols and Applications for Improving Industry, Environment, and Society; pages 234-273, copyright year 2021 by Engineering Science Reference (an imprint of IGI Global).

Chapter 31
The Internet of Things and Blockchain Technologies Adaptive Trade Systems in the Virtual World:
By Creating Virtual Accomplices Worldwide

Vardan Mkrttchian

ⓘ https://orcid.org/0000-0003-4871-5956

HHH University, Australia

ABSTRACT

This chapter presents artificial and natural intelligence technologies. As part of the digital economy of the virtual world program, it is envisaged to increase the efficiency of electronic commerce and entrepreneurship; a similar task has been set by the leadership of the People's Republic of China. At present, thinking in the virtual world and China is radically transforming, along with methodological approaches to the development of trade policy and its tools in the digital economy. It is these circumstances that determine the relevance of the study, the results of which are presented in this chapter. Development of the fundamental foundations for improving the efficiency of electronic commerce and entrepreneurship in virtual world and China based on the virtual exchange of intellectual knowledge using blockchain technology and implementation multi-chain open source platform is the goal. An acceleration of scientific and technological progress in all areas of knowledge raises the task for ensuring the continuous growth of professional skills throughout the whole life.

DOI: 10.4018/978-1-6684-7132-6.ch031

INTRODUCTION IN VIRTUAL WORD AND TRADITIONAL TRADING PROCESS

This chapter is presented author idea use Artificial and Natural Intelligence Technologies. As part of the Digital Economy of the Virtual World program, it is envisaged to increase the efficiency of electronic commerce and entrepreneurship; a similar task has been set by the leadership of the People's Republic of China. At present, thinking in the Virtual World and China is radically transforming, methodological approaches to the development of trade policy and its tools in the digital economy. It is these circumstances that determine the relevance of the study, the results of which are presented in this chapter. Goal research: development of the fundamental foundations for improving the efficiency of electronic commerce and entrepreneurship in Virtual World and China based on the virtual exchange of intellectual knowledge using Blockchain technology and Implementation Multi chain Open Source Platform.

An acceleration of scientific and technological progress in all areas of knowledge raises the task for ensuring the continuous growth of professional skills throughout the whole life. In the traditional trading process, there are several more steps from concluding a contract to delivering an importer. It is difficult, the relevant institutions must carry out a large amount of data exchange, and this work should be. Banking business days, accompanied by a large number of manual reviews and paper documents, as a result of which Efficiency and security are reduced, and there are risks such as letter of credit fraud and soft conditions of the letter of credit. This has led to a gradual reduction in the use of letters of credit. A smart contract is a kind of goal for distribution and testing in an information way.

Over the past few years, information technologies have been able to create a unique environment that can provide resources for the development of global digital commerce, which allows for remote communication with the population on trade issues. This phenomenon has become especially relevant in conditions of forced self-isolation of citizens. Confirmation of this fact is the effect of the corona virus COVID-19. In terms of COVID-19, the population had the greatest demand for products and system solutions for organizing assistance providing video broadcasting, storage and data transfer.

Modern information technologies have allowed the seller and the buyer to quickly interact together at a remote distance from each other in real time. E-mail, instant messengers, Wi-Fi and software and hardware for the development of popular trading applications and technologies have become a significant leader in the market for popular services.

Among the main factors that will ensure positive dynamics in the development of global digital commerce, experts note the proliferation of wearable electronics for commercial use and virtual reality technologies.

This chapter discusses the prospects of Blockchain technology to facilitate the analysis and collection of Big Data using AI and IoT devices used by the People's Republic of China in the modern world by creating Virtual Accomplices' worldwide.

Object of Study

Virtual reality (VR) is a promising tool that can create complex events in the real world (past and present), provoked by traumatic stimuli and controlled by specialists.

VR technology has come a long way from the first experiments in the 50s of the XX century to the modern helmets of virtual reality in the 20s of the XXI century. Two main approaches to the formation of VR systems are known: a virtual room and wearable devices. Wearable VR devices include head-mounted indicators and virtual reality goggles. Currently, the market for virtual devices is formed by the following players by manufacturers: Epson BT-200, Google Glass, Oculus Rift, HTC Vive, Microsoft Hololens, Lumus dk-32, Samsung GearVR, Facebook, Sony, Nokia, etc. Publication and patent the activity of these companies allows us to distinguish four groups of manufacturers, characterized as centers of growth of new knowledge in the field of VR, sustainable research centers, dynamically developing R&D divisions and research engineers. The leading countries in this field are researchers from the USA (46% of the intellectual property market), China (34% of the intellectual property market), Japan (19% of the intellectual property market) and South Korea (13% of the intellectual property market). The market of virtual technologies and simulators in the field of global virtual trade as a whole is widely represented.

Smart contracts allow the absence of third parties. Conduct a trusted transaction. These transactions are track able and irreversible. Thanks to the smart contract technology, the credit intermediary function of the traditional bank is transferred to the smart contract for execution through the smart contract. The verification function, using a computer program to quickly judge the terms of the trading contract, and the next step is to monitor the trading process. As in a typical smart contract trading process between an importer and an exporter Creating a commercial contract based on smart contracts in a blockchain network, importers to financial institutions By providing a deposit, a financial institution registers a guarantee payment in real time to the blockchain network. After the deposit is paid, the exporter will send goods, and the conveyor will send the goods. Downloaded to the blockchain network when a smart contract, transport document and commercial sale are reached. Subject to the same conditions of payment, a financial instruction is issued to the financial institution, and the financial institution may calculate the payment for the importer. Using, thanks to effective blockchain technology, eliminates labor efficiency and low latency, can achieve high-frequency trading around the clock, through smart contracts to eliminate the human factor.

Subject of Study

The People's Republic of China in the modern world by creating Virtual Accomplices' worldwide the blockchain form is mainly divided into a public blockchain alliance. The blockchain consortium is a completely private blockchain (fully private) three, a public blockchain refers to any person in the world, anyone can read it. Anyone can send a transaction, and the transaction can be confirmed, anyone can participate in it. A blockchain process, an alliance blockchain means that its coordinated process is controlled by pre-selected nodes. Blockchain, a completely private blockchain, refers to a zone whose write rights are only in the Joint chapter hands of the Blockchain organization. Among them, the choice of alliance chain technologies is more suitable for creating information technologies for belt and road trade. For the needs of the exhibition, alliance chain nodes are pre-selected, and the pre-selection method can be effective. Eliminate bad, untrusted nodes to protect the blockchain from things like 51% Impact of point attack. In addition, the chain of alliances is not fully decentralized, and its consensus model. To control the alliance, this will contribute to the modernization and expansion of the consensus mechanism in the future. It also facilitates control of the system by the lead organization.

BACKGROUND IN VIRTUAL WORD AND TRADITIONAL TRADING PROCESS

In an environment where technology is a catalyst for new financial ideas, blockchain technology can be integrated into an existing financial system without cost. Currently, the Internet of things and artificial intelligence have become the main form of modern Internet finance, so the future blockchain will certainly develop in the direction of "blockchain + IoT blockchain + artificial intelligence". As the IoT grows geometrically, the cost of computing resources, storage and broadband for centralized services will become inaccessible to operating companies, and blockchain technology can provide direct data transfer for the IoT without the need to create and manage IoT. Secondly, it is necessary to solve the problem of protecting the privacy of the Internet of things. Because the centralized IoT service architecture stores and transmits all information and signals through the central processing unit, excessive data concentration leads to large-scale privacy leaks after information theft. According to blockchain technology, while client data is not controlled by one cloud Service Company, no one can steal data by encrypting the data transfer process, which makes client privacy more secure. Thirdly, it is creating a new business model for the Internet of things. In accordance with the current IoT architecture, clients cannot perform network transactions using another IoT and can conduct financial transactions on only one network or on a trusted network. This limitation significantly reduces the commercial value of the Internet of things. Blockchain technology eliminates trust transactions for direct transactions, for example, a system of "autonomous centralized remote control between centers" jointly developed by IBM and Samsung. The system uses a distributed network to ensure that IoT devices accessing the system can directly communicate and implement complex business logic.

With the continuous improvement of artificial intelligence technology, its application in the financial sector is becoming more and more extensive, including such important activities as account opening, analysis and trading. Therefore, the safety and reliability of artificial intelligence is attracting more attention. Blockchain can be artificially friendly through the following aspects: Firstly, blockchain technology can improve the reputation of artificial intelligence. Blockchain technology can rely on smart contract forms to ensure that during the transaction process, the system automatically creates electronic contracts and leaves irreparable traces. Secondly, the blockchain sharing mechanism will make artificial intelligence more friendly. Any transaction is carried out on the blockchain and must be confirmed by both sides of the transaction, so only two intelligent machines can confirm the transaction at a time. If a party cannot confirm for any reason, the transaction will be automatically canceled. Thirdly, blockchain technology will provide more accurate information for artificial intelligence. The blockchain system can use its own voting mechanism for the scientific classification of information on the Internet: the first level is spam, the second level is informational recommendations, and the third level is informational consent. The blockchain only sends consistent information to artificial intelligence through a rating system to evaluate and improve its accuracy. Fourth, blockchain technology will improve the security mechanism of artificial intelligence. For example, devices can register in a blockchain, perform various hierarchical evaluations using device registration information, provide different functions for different devices, and prevent smart devices from being misused to better exercise common ownership and device usage rights (Wenbin, 2015). The progress of human society and the development of the economy have benefited from the use and creation of tools since ancient times, and various tools have been continuously created. The initial driving force is undeniable from science and technology. In a market economy there will be a periodic cyclical overabundance, and even people's way of life. And the fundamental changes brought about by ideology are the result of large-scale industrial applications of science and technology. " Since the beginning of the 21st century, it has been based on the rapid development and maturity of information technologies such as the Internet and mobile Internet and cloud computing big data, which Ali, Tencent, JD, Baidu, Amazon, Facebook, Apple, Microsoft and Huawei created. A large number of great world-class enterprises have reached many well-known successful entrepreneurs, significantly increasing the efficiency and viability of socio-economic operations. However, the development of science and technology will never stop. Various new technologies are currently undergoing explosive birth and development. The business logic of applying scientific and technical industrialization is also undergoing fundamental changes, that is, from centralized information interaction. If you combine new technologies, such as artificial intelligence, the Internet of things, big data, cloud computing and block-chain, all together in one innovative project form the most effective form of economic activity. In the future, we will enter the era of the true digital economy, and the realization of the digital economy is the result of the merger of these new technologies. Social structural changes will at least completely change the behavior of business people. I think that I am afraid that these new technologies will be "organized and integrated" in various business scenarios. There is an opinion on the market that even "a predictable future = (artificial intelligence + Internet of things + big data) × blockchain". This formula shows that the three main technologies in brackets are "data", that is, deep data mining, massive data collection and transmission in real time and data mining, while a "block chain" provides data protection and trust him. The mechanisms and means of repaying value transactions allow you to safely use the value data required by the three technologies in brackets in the business environment. The right side of this formula actually expresses the product of "Blockchain Technology" and "Virtual Market".

MAIN FOCUS OF THE ARTICLE

Issues, Controversies, Problems

On the right side of the above formula, artificial intelligence is at the forefront because technology essentially embodies a kind of "ability", that is, an ability that allows intelligent machines (computer intelligent systems) to learn and model human thinking. At the same time, the results of the training model of the engine and the working model can be stored on the blockchain, which ensures that the model is not hacked, and the risk of malicious attacks by the commercial applications is further reduced (Li & Ren, 2016). Artificial intelligence technology can provide a glimpse of the future with massive historical data and real-time observations, while the Internet of Things will provide a large amount of real-time data as well as big data to provide sufficient and efficient "fuel" for artificial intelligence.

The data generated by various system sensors will naturally have some real-time data owners, but some data is temporarily unnecessary, so the data owner can desensitize this part of the temporarily unwanted data. Take it and share it with other data developers or developers, so that it can solve the problem of data loss and generate significant income, to offset the cost of the data creation process, and will also generate partial wins. For project founders, having enough data to train AI or ML models will be an endless challenge. Objectively, only large centralized technology companies with a large number of users will be able to get large data sets. However, in decentralized mode, it's very convenient to add more datasets to the artificial intelligence community, which means that IoT devices will make the data sets needed to teach artificial intelligence a big role in real-world business scenarios. Currently, there are many excellent technical research groups involved in collecting training data and the most practical research algorithms and applying these algorithms to the blockchain. Another question: how can we use a large number of unoccupied computing powers distributed in the market to launch AI or ML computing models? The answer is that blockchain technology can make the data market more equitable and efficient. The biggest injustice in the current market environment is that people tend to ignore the minority, but the most necessary thing in machine learning is the minority. Data, data belonging to a minority, will become more valuable, as I wrote in my previous article entitled "Mathematics is the cornerstone of blockchain + AI technology, and mathematics can interpret the value of all business practice." It is mentioned that if you want to increase the accuracy of the machine learning model from 90% to 99%, then you need not the data that has already been studied, but the data that several people should have that are different from the previous ones. For example, the commercial and technical logic, followed by the Ketai Structural Hole Technology Intelligent Eco-Network Investment and Structural Tunnel Financing System, is "(Artificial Intelligence + Internet of Things + Big Data) × Blockchain, which will be artificial intelligence (Such technologies like cognitive computing, intelligent management (IoT), big data and blockchain are combined with the participation of people in the division of labor on connected devices, jointly generated by management data and the operations that these devices can perform to create the first Innovative Intelligent System that "thinks" and is used for commercial purposes in the venture capital market We strongly believe that multicenter, de-mediation, self-organization and data exchange and network synergy are reliable The "intelligent ecosystem system" will be reconstructed from the existing traditional industry in accordance with this new business and technical logic. And this is what the future era of the digital economy needs (Li & Ren, 2016).

Solutions and Recommendations

1. Consensus Mechanism and Performance

A consensus protocol is used to achieve accessibility and consistency in distributed systems. This is a key technology in the blockchain, the main indicators of which include: Typical agreements include BFT consensus presented by PBFT, Nakamoto consensus presented by PoW / PoS, and the new hybrid consensus. Currently, the biggest challenge in consensus agreements is how to strike a balance between safety and efficiency.

Based on the premise of security, there are four ways to increase productivity:

1. Improving the hardware and computing capabilities, from CPU, GPU, FPGA to ASIC, mining equipment is constantly updated, and the general level of computer processing power is also rapidly developing. According to OpenAl analysis, since 2012, the task of teaching artificial intelligence, the computing power used is growing exponentially, and its current speed doubles every 3.5 months (compared with Moore's law, which doubles every 18 months). If computing power goes beyond a certain critical point, the blockchain performance issue may no longer be a problem;
2. The improvement of the consensus agreement system has not changed. Representative methods include reducing the generation interval of blocks, increasing the size of a block, adopting a two-layer chain structure, introducing a lightning-fast network, changing the basic structure of a block + chain, and reducing blocks.
3. Data, a advanced algorithms
4. New data structures, such as the use of directed acyclic graph (DAG) data structures, typical projects have 10TA and ByteBall;
5. New consistent protocols, such as the Thunder Ella algorithm for the PoW mechanism proposed by the researchers, the Algorand protocol and the Ouroboros algorithm for the PoS mechanism, PoS consensus based on the Sleepy model and Proof of Space.

2. Cross Chain

Currently, there are various chains: public, alliance and private. A public chain serves the public, an alliance chain is limited to one alliance, and a private chain serves only one private organization. From a private chain, an alliance chain to a public chain is a decentralization process, and from a public chain an alliance chain to a private chain, this is a centralization process.

During these transformations, various blockchain products will appear for private networks, alliance networks, and government networks. Then, when business interactions between different organizations, how to interact between different chains and chains becomes a big problem. There are currently three cross-chain technologies:

Notary Schemes Side Chains / Relays Hash Lock Technology

Cross-chain technology is the center of the next technological development of the blockchain. In addition, the current private network has a problem with the game, which is who, joins, and each other wants them to join their own blockchain system. Although BaaS (Backend as a Service) can reuse the underlying technology platform, the key is the exchange of data between different business systems and users, as well as collaboration between business systems. If there is no connection between the various systems, it is not possible to reuse core resources such as customers, assets and data.

There a two possible ways to solve this problem:

1.   The government or standardization organizations promote the standardization and standardization of blockchain technology and improve the interaction between different systems;
2.   The government is creating a public service platform. For example, the HKTFP supported by the Hong Kong Monetary Authority is typical. The advantage of this model is that a platform built on the basis of public interests can better resolve disputes between the subject of construction and the management mechanism, as well as open users and scenarios. And public services to achieve the integration of resources, but also easy for government regulation, improve regulatory efficiency.

3. Control Mechanisms

Since the blockchain itself is a natural voting system that contains all the logic necessary to change the validation assembly or update its own rules, and the voting results can be automated, the chain voting mechanism naturally becomes a blockchain ecosystem. The preferred control mechanism currently has a number of chain voting mechanisms, such as EOS, NEO, Lisk, and other systems in the Proof of Equity (DPOS) mechanism, through chain voting to determine who controls the super node that the network is running on or by agreement. Options are voted to determine Essence gas restriction or vote on protocol updates such as Toes.

Disadvantages of the current voting mechanism in the chain:

1.   Low participation in the vote, which leads to two problems. Firstly, the results of the vote reflect only a small number of people's opinions and it is difficult to obtain universal recognition, and secondly, an attacker can vote at low cost.

2. There may be a chapbook-style minority chain management that is detrimental to the interests of ordinary users.

In addition, relying entirely on chain management, he still cannot solve the problem of the main agent of the blockchain ecosystem, and also needs the support of chain supervision, such as legal oversight and a reputation mechanism.

Governments have now begun to take action. For example, the National Network Bureau recently announced the "Regulation on the Management of Information Services of the Blockchain (draft for comments)" and publicly sought public opinion. Of course, this is building a system level. From a technical point of view, how to improve the chain management mechanism is the next step in the study of blockchain technology.

4. Identity Management

Blockchain makes self-sovereign identity possible. By itself, it can be used as a decentralized public key infrastructure (PKI) to make public key authorities more useful and secure. Blockchain can be thought of as a decentralized certification authority that maps support for authentication to a public key.

Smart contracts can also add complex logic, implement cancellation and recovery, and reduce the burden on key management for end users. These technologies push identity ownership from centralized services to end-to-end services between people and make identity itself manageable. This is called autonomy. This approach distracts the data and calculations and transfers them to each individual, which is less economical for hackers because it takes a lot of effort to attack many people one by one.

In the alliance chain, different nodes must be assigned different permissions and they satisfy a certain control. To do this, it is necessary to create a safe and effective mechanism for authentication and identity management.

An authentication mechanism based on biometrics technology or an effective combination of biometrics and cryptography can be used;

An efficient and practical password scheme based on identifiers / attributes can also be used to achieve detailed access control / rights management for nodes / users.

5. Privacy Protection

In a public chain, it is necessary to protect confidential information, such as transaction data, address, identity, etc., and at the same time allow the accounting node to verify the legality of the transaction, and for the alliance chain, when building a privacy protection scheme, it is necessary to take into account the control / tracking of authorization.

Protection of transaction identification and content confidentiality can be achieved with cryptographic primitives and schemes, such as effective knowledge with zero knowledge, commitment and indistinguishable evidence. For example: Zkash uses zk-SNARK to implement a privacy mechanism.

A privacy mechanism based on a cryptographic scheme such as a ring signature, a group signature, and a privacy protection mechanism based on a hierarchical certificate mechanism is also optional. For example:

Montero uses a ring signature scheme to implement privacy protection mechanisms. Hyper ledger Fabric uses a hierarchical certificate mechanism to implement privacy protection mechanisms.

Protecting the confidentiality of transactional contents can also be achieved with an efficient holomorphic encryption scheme or a secure multi-part computing scheme. For example:

Ripple introduces privacy protection for trading channels, introducing a secure multi-user computing solution.

A simple coin protection mechanism can also be used to provide simple privacy protection.

6. Digital Wallet

Currently, digital wallets are trying to move from pure wallet services to environmental portals of digital assets, hoping to gain more market share and develop richer asset management services, mainly in the areas of asset management, asset trading, information aggregation, DApp distribution, etc. .

Asset management can be divided into production of value added, value added management, asset management, asset collection, etc. Asset transactions mainly include a decentralized exchange of digital assets and the exchange of legal currencies, information aggregation - this is mainly information exchange and aggregation of project information, DApp distribution is similar. In a small software store.

Although the entry points and development paths of different wallets are different, and each has its own strengths, the functions of different value-added wallets slightly overlap, because the long-term goals of each other are gradually converging. With the continuous development of the digital asset industry and the continuous improvement of the environment, the digital wallet scene function will become more and more important.

There a three aspects to its future development:

1. ensure the security, openness and convenience of the wallet;
2. Creation of a digital asset management platform based on the demand for added value of assets, providing users with rich financial products and increasing the conversion rate of users;
3. The third is to open the connection between digital assets and the real world, enrich the scenarios of digital assets and create ecology of digital assets.

Security is fundamental. Software technologies can use keyless cryptographic algorithms (a standard white box scheme or create new white box cryptographic algorithms) and code obfuscation methods to allow an adversary to extract basic cryptographic algorithms and key information, or use passwords, an authentication factor encryption algorithm such as personality and biometrics, encrypts and stores the key.

The hardware aspect can be based on the TEE (Trusted Execution Environment) or SE (Security Environment) security module and a technical solution that helps to configure the terminal device, which is one of the important additional directions for protecting a digital wallet.

7. Smart Contracts and Self-organizing Business Models

Smart contracts have the advantages of transparency, reliability, automatic execution and mandatory compliance. Once it is deployed in the blockchain, the code and data of the program are open and transparent, cannot be faked and must be executed in accordance with predefined logic to obtain the expected results, and the execution of the contract will be recorded.

It should be said that blockchain technology and its commercial application mutually reinforce each other. Self-organizing business applications built on smart contracts can help add value to blockchain technology and expand the scope of the encryption economics model.

Although from a technical point of view, a smart contract is just part of the code, it essentially carries a lot of business logic, and even a smart contract is a business model with unlimited imagination. Conversely, the implementation of a self-organizing business model also requires the delicate development of smart contracts, and also requires the support of technical measures, such as improving productivity, increasing security and protecting privacy. In other words, this is both the creation of a business model, and the development of a technical system.

The security of smart contracts is crucial. Due to the openness of smart contracts, their code and content can be obtained using open methods that allow hackers to analyze contracts and attack vulnerabilities. Once the attack is successful, this will result in significant losses. Consequently, there is an urgent need for sophisticated smart contract detection technology to detect, detect, and eliminate vulnerabilities before the contract is chained.

There were many smart contract detection tools or online testing sites, but these tests are still based on experience and there is nothing to be done about unknown contract vulnerabilities.

The formal check method is a possible solution for determining exactly whether a program can work in accordance with the developer's expectations by creating an appropriate model. However, formal verification of smart contracts is difficult, and no suitable solution has been found at this time, and further research is needed.

When applying smart contracts, on the one hand, it is necessary to clarify the possibility of using smart contracts from the legal level, on the other hand, since smart contracts have natural certainty and do not have the flexibility and selectivity of ordinary contracts, therefore, in specific scenarios, in order to establish an intervention mechanism that allows code to pause or stop execution.

FUTURE RESEARCH DIRECTIONS

- **Integration with other technologies:** It is often said that cloud computing, big data, artificial intelligence, blockchain technology, etc. In essence, they are the embodiment of "algorithm + data", and there are no other priorities. Since the essence is the same, mutual integration is inevitable.

For example, an asset securitization scenario requires ongoing disclosure of information from multiple business systems, and also requires a large-scale distributed file storage.

Blockchain technology can ensure the consistency of distributed ledgers on all sides of a transaction by signing a transaction, a consistent algorithm and cross-chain technology to ensure that a transaction is executed in real time and automatically complete real-time information disclosure to ensure accounting. Accounting and accounting are consistent, which greatly improves credit rating of traded products and significantly reduces the cost, which allows information users to receive global information ju about the activities of the enterprise in real time and through it, and receiving global information means information. Mass growth, the best way to store and retrieve the value of information, is becoming the key to the chain.

Therefore, the integration of blockchain technology with distributed file systems, big data analysis, cloud computing, artificial intelligence and other technologies is an important direction for future development.

CONCLUSION

In the presented chapter, the following tasks were solved: the analysis of goods and services of Russia and China was carried out; outline the main policy guidelines and its impact on globalization and regional integration; disclosing the prospects for the development of blockchain technologies in international trade and its impact on the global financial industry; the role of blockchain technology in the development of the global economy is substantiated.

The following research areas were disclosed:

1. The development of international cooperation based on innovative intelligent technologies
   a. Prerequisites for international cooperation on the example of "Belts and Roads". The historical need of the project "One belt – one way"
   b. China's banking industry indicators in the belt and road
   c. Blockchain Technology - the strongest push in international multilateral financial and trade cooperation
   d. Cross-border capital flows: transactional efficiency, risk management, checking the creditworthiness of counterparties
2. Creating conditions for mutually beneficial trade relations in the process of digitalization of national economic systems
   a. Application of blockchain technology in international trade in the context of the "Belt and Road" initiative
   b. Vision of the Alliance Belt and Road Blockchain
   c. Blockchain technology can be combined with more technical means
3. Development of reflective adaptive software for applying Blockchain technology, big data analysis and virtual exchange of intellectual knowledge.

Were disclosed the future direction of blockchain technology: consensus mechanism and performance, cross chain, control mechanism, identity management, privacy protection, digital wallet, smart contracts and self-organizing business models.

REFERENCES

Li, Z., & Ren, X. (2016). Analysis of the impact of blockchain on the Internet finance and its prospects. *Technical Economics and Management Studies*, *10*, 75–78.

Technology illuminates the future - when blockchain technology and adaptive security technology enter social management and economic life. (n.d.). Retrieved October 02, 2019, from http://blog.sina.com.cn/s/blog_67804b9a0102z2gn.html

The fusion of artificial intelligence and blockchain technology represents the future of the digital economy. (n.d.). Retrieved May 14, 2019, from http://www.sohu.com/a/313838766_99985608?qq-pf-to=pcqq.c2c

Wenbin, U. (2015). Principles, models and proposals of banking trading blockchain. *Hebei University Journal, 6*, 159–160.

ADDITIONAL READING

Alguliyev, R. M., Aliguliyev, R. M., & Sukhostat, L. V. (2020). Efficient algorithm for big data clustering on single machine. *CAAI Trans Intell Technol, 5*(1), 9–14. doi:10.1049/trit.2019.0048

Antonopoulos, A. M. (2014). *Mastering bitcoin: unlocking digital crypto-currencies*. O'Reilly Media Inc.

Ash, J. S., Berg, M., & Coiera, E. (2004). Some unintended consequences of information technology in health care: The nature of patient care information system-related errors. *Journal of the American Medical Informatics Association, 11*(2), 104–112. doi:10.1197/jamia.M1471 PMID:14633936

Chang, X., & Han, F. (2016). *Block chain: From digital currency to credit society*. China Citic Press.

Conoscenti, M., Vetr, A., & Martin, J. C. D. (2016) Blockchain for the internet of things: a systematic literature review. In: *Proceedings of the IEEE/ACS 13th international conference of computer systems and applications (AICCSA)*, IEEE, Agadir, Morocco 10.1109/AICCSA.2016.7945805

Devi, D., Namasudra, S., & Kadry, S. (2020). A boosting-aided adaptive cluster-based undersampling approach for treatment of class imbalance problem. *International Journal of Data Warehousing and Mining, 16*(3), 60–86. doi:10.4018/IJDWM.2020070104

Haber, S., & Stornetta, W. S. (1991). How to time-stamp a digital document. *Journal of Cryptology, 3*(2), 99–111. doi:10.1007/BF00196791

Ho, D. C. K., Au, K. F., & Newton, E. (2002). Empirical research on supply chain management: A critical review and recommendations. *International Journal of Production Research, 40*(17), 4415–4430. doi:10.1080/00207540210157204

Huang, G. Q., Lau, J. S. K., & Mak, K. L. (2003). The impacts of sharing production information on supply chain dynamics: A review of the literature. *International Journal of Production Research, 41*(7), 1483–1517. doi:10.1080/0020754031000069625

Hwang, J., Choi, M., Lee, T., Jeon, S., Kim, S., Park, S., & Park, S. (2017). Energy prosumer business model using blockchain system to ensure transparency and safety. *Energy Procedia, 141*, 194–198. doi:10.1016/j.egypro.2017.11.037

Kshetri, N. (2017). Cybersecurity in India: Regulations, governance, institutional capacity and market mechanisms. *Asian Research Policy, 8*(1), 64–76.

Li, S., Wang, G., & Yang, J. (2019). Survey on cloud model based similarity measure of uncertain concepts. *CAAI Trans Intell Technol, 4*(4), 223–230. doi:10.1049/trit.2019.0021

Lin, Q., Yan, H., Huang, Z., Chen, W., Shen, J., & Tang, Y. (2018). An ID-based linearly homomorphic signature scheme and its application in Blockchain. *IEEE Access: Practical Innovations, Open Solutions*, *6*, 20632–20640. doi:10.1109/ACCESS.2018.2809426

Ming, Z., Jun, C., Yuqing, W., Yuanfei, L., Yongqi, Y., & Jinyue, D. (2017). The primarily research for multi module cooperative autonomous mode of energy internet under blockchain framework. *Zhongguo Dianji Gongcheng Xuebao*, *37*(13), 3672–3681.

Namasudra, S. (2017). *An improved attribute-based encryption technique towards the data security in cloud computing*. Concurr Comput Pract Exer., doi:10.1002/cpe.4364

Namasudra, S. (2018). Taxonomy of DNA-based security models. In S. Namasudra & G. C. Deka (Eds.), *Advances of dna computing in cryptography* (pp. 53–68). Springer. doi:10.1201/9781351011419-3

Namasudra, S. (2018). Cloud computing: A new era. *J Fundam Appl Sci*, *10*(2), 113–135.

Namasudra, S., Chakraborty, R., Majumder, A., & Moparthi, N. R. (2020). *Securing multimedia by using DNA based encryption in the cloud computing environment*. ACM T Multi Comput Commun Appl.

Namasudra, S., & Deka, G. C. (2018). *Advances of DNA computing in cryptography*. Taylor & Francis. doi:10.1201/9781351011419

Namasudra, S., & Deka, G. C. (2018). Introduction of DNA computing in cryptography. In S. Namasudra & D. C. Deka (Eds.), *Advances of dna computing in cryptography* (pp. 27–34). Springer. doi:10.1201/9781351011419-1

Namasudra, S., Deka, G. C., & Bali, R. (2018). Applications and future trends of DNA computing. In S. Namasudra & G. C. Deka (Eds.), *Advances of DNA computing in cryptography* (pp. 181–192). Taylor & Francis. doi:10.1201/9781351011419-9

Namasudra, S., Devi, D., Choudhary, S., Patan, R., & Kallam, S. (2018). Security, privacy, trust, and anonymity. In S. Namasudra & G. C. Deka (Eds.), *Advances of DNA computing in cryptography* (pp. 153–166). Taylor & Francis. doi:10.1201/9781351011419-7

Namasudra, S., Devi, D., Kadry, S., Sundarasekar, R., & Shanthini, A. (2020). Towards DNA based data security in the cloud computing environment. *Computer Communications*, *151*, 539–547. doi:10.1016/j.comcom.2019.12.041

Namasudra, S., & Roy, P. (2016). Secure and efficient data access control in cloud computing environment: A survey. *Multiagent Grid Sys Int J*, *12*(2), 69–90. doi:10.3233/MGS-160244

Namasudra, S., & Roy, P. (2017). Time saving protocol for data accessing in cloud computing. *IET Communications*, *11*(10), 1558–1565. doi:10.1049/iet-com.2016.0777

Namasudra, S., & Roy, P. (2018). PpBAC: Popularity based access control model for cloud computing. *Journal of Organizational and End User Computing*, *30*(4), 14–31. doi:10.4018/JOEUC.2018100102

Namasudra, S., Roy, P., Vijayakumar, P., Audithan, S., & Balusamy, B. (2017). Time efficient secure DNA based access control model for cloud computing environment. *Future Generation Computer Systems*, *73*, 90–105. doi:10.1016/j.future.2017.01.017

Sarkar, M., Saha, K., Namasudra, S., & Roy, P. (2015). An efficient and time saving web service based android application. *SSRG Int J Comput Sci Eng*, *2*(8), 18–21.

Swan, M. (2015). *Blockchain: blueprint for a new economy*. O'Reilly Media.

Williams, A. (2016). *IBM to open first blockchain innovation centre in Singapore, to create applications and grow new markets in finance and trade*. The Straits Times Singapore Press Holdings Ltsd. Co.

Wood, G. (2014). *Ethereum: a secure decentralised generalised transaction ledger*. Ethereum Project Yellow Paper.

Xia, Q. I., Sifah, E. B., Asamoah, K. O., Gao, J., Du, X., & Guizani, M. (2017). MeDShare: Trust-less medical data sharing among cloud service providers via blockchain. *IEEE Access: Practical Innovations, Open Solutions*, *5*, 14757–14767. doi:10.1109/ACCESS.2017.2730843

Xue, T., Hongbin, S., & Qinglai, G. (2016). Electricity transactions and congestion management based on blockchain in energy internet. *Power Syst Technol*, *40*(12), 3630–3638.

Zhao, X., Li, R., & Zuo, X. (2019). Advances on QoS-aware web service selection and composition with nature-inspired computing. *CAAI Trans Intell Technol*, *4*(3), 159–174. doi:10.1049/trit.2019.0018

Zheng, Z., Xie, S., Dai, H. N., & Wang, H. (2016). Blockchain challenges and opportunities: A survey. *International Journal of Web and Grid Services*, *14*(4), 314–335.

KEY TERMS AND DEFINITIONS

Blockchain: A continuous sequential chain of blocks (linked list) containing information built according to certain rules.

Digital Economy: Is an economic activity focused on digital and electronic technologies. This includes electronic business and commerce, as well as the goods and services they produce. This definition covers all business, cultural, economic, and social operations performed on the Internet and using digital communication technologies.

EDI (Electronic Data Interchange): A series of standards and conventions for the transfer of structured digital information between organizations, based on certain regulations and formats of transmitted messages.

Electronic Commerce: Financial transactions and transactions carried out through the Internet and private communication networks, during which purchases and sales of goods and services are made, as well as money transfers.

Intellectual Capital: Knowledge, skills and production experience of specific people and intangible assets, including patents, databases, software, trademarks, etc. that are productively used to maximize profits and other economic and technical results.

This research was previously published in Multidisciplinary Functions of Blockchain Technology in AI and IoT Applications; pages 118-136, copyright year 2021 by Engineering Science Reference (an imprint of IGI Global).

Chapter 32
Protection to Personal Data Using Decentralizing Privacy of Blockchain.

Vilas Baburao Khedekar
https://orcid.org/0000-0003-4229-1937
VIT University, India

Shruti Sangmesh Hiremath
Jayawantrao Sawant College of Engineering, India

Prashant Madhav Sonawane
Jayawantrao Sawant College of Engineering, India

Dharmendra Singh Rajput
VIT University, India

ABSTRACT

In today's world, we deal with various online services, where each person deals with various technologies. These technologies are made for people to make our access to the new world easily. There is a tremendous use of online applications, websites which require large storage. Large data is handled by the online systems. The collection of data in the whole world is about 20% in the last few years. The data is captured from the user, controlled by the systems, and operations are performed on data. It requires more system accuracy and protection to personal data. But the person does not know about the data, where and how it is used where it is stored or whether the data is handled by some organisations for their own use or data is been hacked by another person. This chapter explores protection of data using the decentralized privacy of blockchain.

DOI: 10.4018/978-1-6684-7132-6.ch032

INTRODUCTION

In today's world we deal with various online services, where each person deals with various technologies. These technologies are made for people to make our access to new world easily. There is tremendous use of online applications, websites which require large storage. Large data is handled by the online systems. The collection of data in whole world is about 20% in last few years ("Big data, for better or worse: 90% of world's data generated over last two years," 2013). The data is captured from user, controlled by the systems and operations are performed on data. It requires more system accuracy and protection to personal data.

Ex. Email, WhatsApp, Instagram, Facebook, Bank transactions, Real-time estate etc. But the person is unknown about the data, where and how it is used where it is stored or whether the data is handled by some organisations for their own use or data is been hacked by other person (Zyskind & Pentland, 2015). Since the protection towards the personal data is been decreasing day by day. Example- Facebook one of the huge online social network collected 300 petabytes of user data during its inception (PB, n.d.). These leads to illegally accessing personal data for their own purpose without having rights on it.

WHAT IS THE PERSONAL DATA?

Every person deals with various applications nowadays, where each website or application needs authentication of user. He has must create a user id and set password to access the application. He has a unique identity .He keeps his access details up to him, where the data contains login details which he wants to keep private .Personal data is defined as the individual information which is used to identifying a person identity from others . These details may be used to trace the person .The name, identity number, account details, birth date, mothers name, biometrics and various information regarding website access, banking details and medical details is related to an individual. One of these details are enough to identify an individual. These details are not shared with others .These data is kept hidden from public. Only that person can handle or deal with his data .The data is kept private .The data is kept secured .

The Privacy Problem

In various fields, the services deploy applications for users to install. All these applications collect high resolution of personal data. The user is unknown about this process. The person is providing all the data to the applications and allow the applications to deal with his personal data on the system. The application may misuse the authentication details of the user. This results in tracing the user details whenever required . Even the hackers can easily trap the system and get access of the personal details of the system .In agriculture environment the third parties involve between farmers and customers to deal the transaction .This leads to get advantage over the other .The broker earns more profit than farmer.

What Is Blockchain?

Blockchain is a decentralised, distributed, public ledger. Blockchain is defined as collection of blocks. Block is the smallest unit of blockchain which records recent transactions. Every transactions are grouped and stored on a public ledger (*b-money*, 1998). In blockchain, the first block is called as genesis block.

After genesis block the block is added accordingly by using hash of genesis block. Blockchain technology the latest word in financial service has the capacity to store, share and deal with the transactions in a different way. The Satoshi Nakamoto bought Bitcoin and Blockchain over paper in July 2009, the first blockchain was introduced and became popular. Blockchain technology is the one who builds a trust between two member or two entities. When there is a digital transaction between two persons then no a third party involved in transaction system (Nakamoto, 2007). Blockchain provides more security to the data. The aim of blockchain is to build trust among the humans. The trust should be build on both the sides in transaction as between producer and consumer. The blockchain system is build for improving the society, by reducing the frauds as illegal accessing to data and hacking the system .The blockchain is used to build the first cryptocurrency which is Bitcoin. There are various applications on where we can have blockchain technology dealing with the transaction system. The blockchain is updated by itself in each ten minutes.

Figure 1. Blockchain architecture

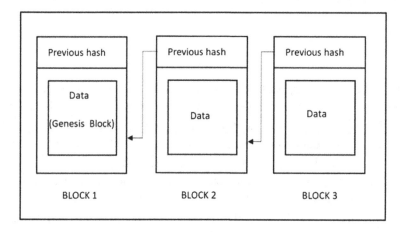

The blockchain provides higher security to the storage system. The data once inserted in the block cannot be changed or deleted. Also the data cannot be updated in the system . A ledger is a list of transactions right from the start of blockchain. Block holds recent copy of ledger which is shared with each member of blockchain over the distributed network. Once the block is verified it becomes a constant part of blockchain. Using the cryptographic functions the data is validated and stored on ledger in the block .To confirm the all transactions reliability .Block time is defined as the time taken by the network to add a block into the blockchain. The block time for bitcoin is 10 minutes. In cryptography the data in encrypted and a hash code is created for every single transaction.

Blockchain technology is made for commercial transactions. The first decentralised cryptocurrency which is made using blockchain is Bitcoin. Today various institutions are changing their transactions systems into blockchain based system. This is due to the reliable and flexible nature of the blockchain .The blockchain technology involves transaction to maintain server networks known as 'nodes'. The computer system which holds blockchain are known as nodes.

The copy of the ledger is sent to the peer-to-peer network off the blockchain. Every system has an updated replica of the ledger on the system (Tosh et al., 2017). The transactions of the blockchain are validated by nodes .If the transactions are valid then the block is added to the ledger. The blockchain makes it easy to use smart contracts such as embedded contracts in computer codes that may implement themselves automatically on the occurrence of various events ("Blockchains and the Internet of Things," n.d.).The blockchain provides high security to personal data by using hashing technique. The main advantage of blockchain are:

1. Data Ownership:

The Blockchain framework mainly ensures that the user can control and own their data. This system makes the user, the owner of their own data with permissions.

2. Data Transparency:

The user is made completely transportable to know where her/his data is being collected and accessed.

Why Blockchain Is Important?

The blockchain has capacity to modify the way data is stored, shared and managed. The most powerful aspects of the technology are the barriers to handle or deleting information which has been added to the chain . The technology is highly secure and is immutable to hacking . It is a decentralized network, so that no one owns the system. It cannot be handled by anyone due to simple structure of blockchain system. The ledger is public so copy of each transaction is stored on each node of the network. If someone wants to use and modify the data of other person it is caught easily because of blockchain. The details of transactions held between the nodes on regular basis are stored on the blockchain . The blockchain system provides encryption of data and verification of data. For a transaction the user is not charged by the system . We can transfer our money from one system to another system. The blockchain system is collection to various terms which ensures the personal data security and storage. The blockchain uses mathematics to create a distributed and secure ledger which enables the transactions without need for third parties (Moubarak & Filiol, 2018).

Aim of Blockchain

The main aim of the blockchain is to build trust among the society (Nakamoto, 2007). The society should be free of fraud systems. The public should be aware of the frauds as illegal accessing of their data by hackers or by the applications .The data should be accessed by that person only to which the data belongs . Others cannot access the details of that person. Brokers and agents are not involved in the transaction. There should be no intermediaries to the transaction .Instead of these there should be end to end transaction. The decision in the peer-to-peer network of blockchain are taken by mechanisms which are decentralised such as Proof of work (POW)(Vukoli, 2016) and proof of stake.

Smart Contracts

In 1997,the smart contracts were designed by Nick Szabo (Szabo., 1997). Smart contracts are defined as the contracts which exist between two entities using automated technique for applying conditions .Rules are defined by the smart contract around the agreement and it enforces automatically the operations .By using computer software the contracts are automatically verified and executed. They help us to have transactions, exchange money anything or shares avoiding the middleman services. This process converts the contracts into code form. Contracts means the agreement signed by two entities with pre-defined conditions. Smart is defined as the process which is automated and executes by its own using computer software. The agreement or a part of agreement are converted in its equivalent code and then send to the nodes of the blockchain. These contracts are called as self executing contracts. These contracts could be stored on blockchain network .These networks of the computer supervises the smart contracts.

The common example is the automated bill payments .In this application the computer software recognizes the details on the barcode and automatically updates the list of parameters in the bill. Then the system charges the credits of the person paying the bill.

On any network the smart contracts can be coded and executed. The computer software deals with the predefined conditions, such that the condition of agreements are agreed by both the entities .

Working of Smart Contracts

1. The code is written for the contact between the two parties. They contact using public ledger.
2. An event is created which hits the strike price and the expiration date.And according to the rules coded the contract executes itself.
3. To maintain the privacy of an individuals position, the blockchain is used by regulators to understand the market activity.

Advantages of Smart Contracts

As the smart contracts are implemented on distributed ledger, it provides advantage to both the parties, like the contracts are distributed on the blockchain network, every node ledger gets updated .The transactions between both the entities are there on the ledger of every node. Hence if one wants to delete or update the transaction, it is not possible to do. Due to the public ledger the transactions can take place easily .The customer and the sender can easily carry out transactions without involving the third parties as brokers or agents and administrators . This also reduces the transactions cost, which were associated with the third parties. Because of smart contracts the industries are benefited mostly. The smart contracts are created on blockchain peer-to -peer network allowing the buyers and sender to transact between them example:To purchase a trade art directly without involving the broker (Nakamoto, 2007). All the documents are encrypted and shared on the network. The document is replicated and stored on each system .There is a backup .The contracts save our money which are taken by the intermediaries. These contracts are cheaper and faster. The contracts also avoid errors.

Decentralised Applications

Decentralised Applications are the applications which run on peer to peer network instead on working with a single computer. DApps are stored on the blockchain system. DApps are blockchain enabled websites. Decentralised applications consist of whole parts front end and backend .Smart contract is a small part of DApp which is mostly written in solidity language. DApps are a kind of the software which cannot be controlled by any entity .In the market these applications have unlimited participants.

DApps Must Satisfy Following Criteria

1. The DApps must be on open platform where each and every one can access and use these applications
2. Using cryptographic techniques all the data should be stored.
3. The application should use cryptographic tokens.
4. Applications should generate tokens.

Advantages of dApps

1. **Autonomy**: No third parties are required for transactions. Brokers and agents are not necessary.
2. **Trust**: The documents are encrypted in ledger. A high security is provided to the data .Trust is build through blockchain.
3. **Backup**: If the documents are lost due to some reasons then there are multiple copies of ledger on nodes of network, from . where we can take details again.
4. **Accuracy**:Smart contracts are faster and cheaper. They avoid errors that arise from manual work.

DApp Examples

1. **Blockverify**: It is a Blockchain based anti counter-feit solution. It identifies counterfeit goods, diverted products, stolen merchandise and fraudulent transactions.
2. **Ripple**: It is a network of institutional payments providers .These providers are such as banks and money services business. The providers use the solutions developed by Ripple.
3. **STORJ**: It is an open source decentralised file storage solution. It uses encryption, file shredding and a hash table of blockchain to store files on peer to peer network.
4. **Cryptokitties**: Due to large processing of transaction the cryptokitties slowed down the Ethereum network in December 2017 (Kharif, n.d.).

Difference Between DAaps and Smart Contracts

The blockchain enabled websites are DApps while connecting to blockchain is allowed by smart contracts .The DApps are similar to web applications which use frontend technologies for user interfacing. Same technologies are used by DApps for rendering the page. Instead of the API the smart contracts are used by the DApps to connect the blockchain.

Issues in Digital Transaction

Centralized Power

The every system is having a central authority which controls the whole system. The central authority has access to deal with transactions in the system .All the transacted currencies are controlled and managed by a central authority .This leads to have chances of extracting data by someone.

- **Blockchain Solution:** Blockchain is defined as public ledger. Every person is assigned the same power. The members of blockchain have equal authority to add block on blockchain.

Private Ledger

The private ledger is mostly used by banking system. The user is unknown about how transactions held in the system are done by him or by other person .The bank may invest these money somewhere else.

- **Blockchain Solution:** Blockchain has a public ledger. Each node of the blockchain receives updated copy of ledger after every 10 minutes .The ledger hold all transaction details right from the start of blockchain .This is a large data which is handled and stored using blockchain. The data is stored in a form that it cannot be manipulated by anyone or any system.

Prone to Hacks

The financial systems are been hacked by someone .The data set is released and the details are stolen (Dai, Shi, Meng, Wei, & Ye, 2017). This leads to problems of account handling by unknown person.

- **Blockchain Solution:** The Blockchain system is immutable to hacking. In blockchain system the data once inserted cannot be deleted or modified (Mense & Flatscher, 2018).

Double Spending

The double spending problems are faced mostly by digital platforms ("Double-spending," n.d.). The transactions using digital platform sometimes may transact money to two account simultaneously.

- **Blockchain Solution:** In Blockchain system the double spending are not allowed .This is due to the basic structure of blockchain.

Transaction Fees

For every transactions the financial systems charge fees near about 2-3% of the transaction amount .This leads to collecting a large amount of money in a single day.

- **Blockchain Solution:** The blockchain doesn't charge any kind of fees on the transaction .Hence we can transfer our money from one system to the other with no charges.

FEATURES OF BLOCKCHAIN

- Decentralised: Every organisation has a centralized authority which handles the systems task. In blockchain all the rights are equally distributed to each member in blockchain.
- Distributed: The blockchain technology is widely spread in peer to peer network, so that all the recent updates can be shared in network easily.
- Public ledger: Blockchain is a public distributed database which holds encrypted ledger. The ledger is in Encrypted format to keep the secured details of the people involved in blockchain technology.
- Trust: Blockchain reduces the need for brokers and agents and can automate the manual tasks.
- Data Security: On Blockchain, interfering the transactions is difficult because of the complex cryptography provided and also of the distributed ledger .The members can have the transaction list of the blockchain and here no one is the head of the other .
- Traceability: A distributed ledger stores the entire ownership history of an transactions.
- Immutable: The data when entered into the blockchain cannot be removed or stolen s because of its basic structure and providing security using cryptographic functions (Moubarak & Filiol, 2018).

TYPES OF BLOCKCHAIN

Public Blockchain

It can be defined as the blockchain which is by people, for people and of the people. Public Blockchain ledgers are visible to every node on internet and any member can verify block of transactions. These blockchain are open and so everyone can read and write on blockchain. Example:Bitcoin, Litecoin. In these examples any person can run, make the transaction, and can know the updates in blockchain ledger.

Private Blockchain

As the name suggest the blockchains are private means the data can be handled by a members . In private blockchain only a person in organisation is allowed to validate, verify and add transactions blocks. Here every member on the internet is only allowed to view. This makes the blockchain centralised but the blockchain is secured using cryptography e.g. Bankchain .

Consortium Blockchain

It is a combination of public and private blockchains. In this blockchain a team of organization verifies transactions and then add. There are more than one in charge in this blockchain. Here we have companies group which come together and take decisions for the network. Eg. r3,EWF.

WORKING OF BLOCKCHAIN

Public Key Cryptography

Public key cryptography has pairs of keys, a private and a public key .A private key is kept secured, and a public key is for the outside network. Encryption means converting normal data into a code. Decryption means again converting code into respective data .If we use private key for encrypting the data then it is necessary to decrypt the data using public key and vice versa.This is called a asymmetric encryption.

Peer-to-Peer Network

Peer-to-peer network is blockchain is used to have a distributed ledger .So that each person in blockchain is connected to other by means of network which is peer to peer. The peer provides disk storage and network bandwidth available to each node. Hence all the data can be shared by using the network. Distributed machines on peer to peer network helps to maintain consistency of their public ledger. This network uses digital signature to validate the transactions.

Blockchain Program

It is the technique of implementation of any solution or use cases. Blockchain can be build by any language. The most preferred default for writing programs in Ethereum blockchain is Solidity. Various other languages such as NodeJS, Kotlin, Python, Javascript, etc. are used to write program in blockchain.

Digital Signatures

The digital signatures are defined as the validation provided to the specific document user (L. Wang, Shen, Li, Shao, & Yang, 2018). They are part of the blockchain protocols. These signatures are used in transactions between the two members of the blockchain (Santra, Aleya, Maji, & Nath, 2016). Similarly using the signature we ensure the security to the sensitive information. They often use asymmetric cryptography (Merkle, 1988).This means the data is shared with other person by using public key.

Nodes

Node is defined as a blockchain device, which carry various functions and are spread over the blockchain network .A node is any electronic device which is connected to the network of internet and has an IP Address. The nodes are arranged in the binary tree format. The nodes can win rewards for validating transactions in blockchain. Node act as a point of communication in the blockchain system.

Hashing

Hashing is defined as a technique of converting a specific input into a output code form .In blockchain system the output depends on the previous transactions of blockchain. Hashing provides high security to the data .This makes blockchain immutable to hacking.

Protocols

A huge set of rules are coded in the blockchain which are known as protocols .The protocols are the program which plays an important role in networking .The blockchain builds trust among the society. The whole transactions operations are automated .The user trusts on protocol that the protocol can handle the transactions over the network and can deal with security of data .The protocol are the backbone of the blockchain network. These are a collection of rules and regulations which explains the transmission process of the blockchain .

Proof of Work

The Proof of work (POW) is a Bitcoin protocol (Salman, Member, Zolanvari, Member, & Erbad, 2018). It is mining process in which the some of the nodes act as miners. The miners validate the transactions by solving some mathematical problems .The solution on this problems are solved on the nodes. The miners which solve the mathematic puzzles, then validate the transactions .Then the miners are rewarded by some currencies

FRAMEWORKS OF BLOCKCHAIN

1. **Ethereum**: It is a decentralised open platform (Salman et al., 2018).It is a public blockchain on which we can develop various decentralised application. In the decentralised way, the contracts are run on the network .The default language for coding in Ethereum is Solidity. .Ethereum blockchains are mainly used for coding in decentralised applications like smart contracts (Salman et al., 2018).
2. **Hyperledger**: Hyperledger is a enterprise blockchain framework. It is a network with various roles .It is not a public chain .It is mostly used for business purpose .It is a global collaboration which is hosted by Linux Foundations.
3. **Corda**: Corda is an open source blockchain created for business right from start. It permits you to build blockchain which transacts in strict privacy.
4. **Quorum**: Quorum is a distributed ledger and a smart contract platform which provides good support for privacy of transaction and privacy for network level.

PROCESS TO ADD BLOCK INTO THE BLOCKCHAIN

- When there is a request for transaction, the transaction is stored on block in ledger
- The block is send to the blockchain network.
- The nodes on the network validate the block, and then the block is approved and verified.
- After the block is verified the it is added in the blockchain.
- The transaction is successful.

Figure 2. Process to add block

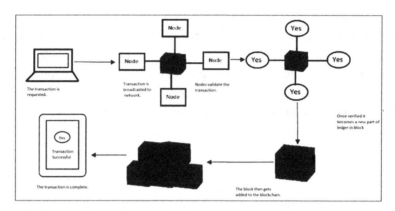

SECURITY TECHNIQUES

Basic Hashing Concept

Hashing technique is specially used to identify a specific element from a group of elements.The main task of hashing is distributing the key-value pairs.

Example:

1. In universities each and every student is assigned a unique rollno which is used to identify the details of that student easily.
2. In library books are assigned a specific number through which it can be identified that either the book is in library on which shelf or it is issued by someone.

In these examples the hashing takes place, where student and the book has their own number. Using hashing technique the larger key are converted into smaller keys, the values are stored in hash table accordingly. Every element is assigned with a key-value pair through which one can search the element in O(1) time complexity.

Hashing is implemented using two ways:

1. An elements are converted into integer which acts as an index, used to store and access data from hash table.
2. The elements stored according to key values from where it can be easily accessed.
   ◦ Hash = hashfunction (key)
   ◦ Index = hash% arraysize

Hash Function: A function which is used to map the data into hash tables using key-value pairs.
Good hashing is achieved by following requirements:

1. It should be easy to compute.
2. The uniform distribution should be provided across the hash table.

3.   Collisions should be avoided.

Hashing in Blockchain

Blockchain uses hashing from proof of work till the verification of file. Hashing is a cornerstone of cryptography .Each block consists of data, hash and hash of previous block and proof of work. Data on block chain is stored in form of amount and persons details.eg Bitcoin system stores details about the sender receiver and the transaction details. A block has a specific hash.The hash can be compared with a fingerprint . It identifies the block and its details in blockchain. Hash is always unique as a fingerprint. When the block is created accordingly the hash code is generated. Changing data or transactions of the block will cause hash to change. So the hashes are more useful when we want to protect our blocks.

The third part of block is previous block hash function, it effectively group of blocks and this technique makes the blockchain more secure. Proof of work is a mechanism which is used during validation of the block. This is a mathematical solution that we attach to block which ensure that it is a valid block. The ledger is produced using software protocol .The mathematical problems can be solved using the protocols. Ledger is distributed over the network. Everyone gets valid copy of the same. If we try to change the ledger it won't get accepted because everyone has a replica of it. Every transaction and every block is highly secured.

Hashing Technique

Hashing means to take a specific input of any length, converting it to a specific output of fixed length. Hash consists of some data structures like pointer and linked list.

Pointers are the variables which store address of another variable.

Linked lists are defined as sequence of blocks containing data which is linked to next block through pointers.

The Hash in blockchain consists of two parts:

- Data of block
- Hash of previous block

1.   Data:

The block is group of recent transactions. All the transactions have an entry on ledger. In blockchain system a block gets added in blockchain after every 10 minutes.

Hence the data is stored on blockchain in block. The recent transaction ledger which is validated by miners and then gets updated on copy of every members system. A miner checks all credits and debits of the user.

2.   Previous block hash:

It is a pointer which will always point to previous block of blockchain. The blockchain has a structure like linked list which consist of data and a pointer of the hash which points to hash of previous block leading to form a blockchain.

Figure 3. Hash key

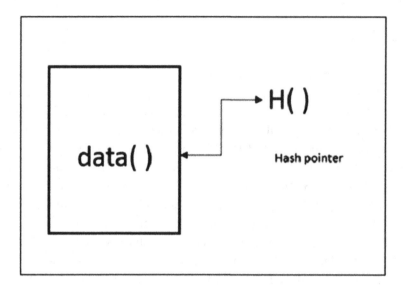

Ex. In Bitcoin system the input transactions are executed using a hashing algorithm known as SHA-256 (Secure Hashing Algorithm-256)[5][14][22], which gives fixed length output. In case of SHA-256 it matter how the input should be, and accordingly the output will be produced of length 256-bits.This becomes very difficult when we are handle with a large data. Instead of remembering the inputs we can remember hash .

Cryptographic Hash Functions

Cryptographic hash functions are special kind of hash functions which has various properties:

1. Deterministic:
    If we parse the input for many times through hash functions the same results are obtained every time.

2. Quick Computation:
    The efficiency of system should be more enough so that the system returns a hash of a particular input quickly.

3. Pre -Imaged Resistance:
    If the hash code of the input is already in system then the same code is also when the input is used every time .So the hash of specific input is always the same.

4. Small changes in input changes the hash:
    The hashing function treats a an individual input to get converted in hash code form.The slight changes in input results a drastic change in hash code.

5. Collision Resistant:
    If collision occur in hashing algorithms, H(A) is equal to H(B) .The system breaks collision resistant as it has 50% chances to break instead of pre imaged resistance.

6. Puzzle Friendly:
    This property has a huge impact on the cryptocurrencies.

    Cryptographic hash functions examples:

1. MD 5 which produces 128-bit hash code .
2. SHA 1 which produces 160-bit hash code.
3. SHA 256 produces 256-bit hash which is by Bitcoin.
4. Keccak-256 which produces 256-bit hash which is used by Ethereum.

Merkle Tree

In blockchain, every single verification of data requires more number of packets which are delivered to the distributed network. Validating a single computer means to compare between an individuals transaction and the entries in ledger and make sure that information is not changed in ledger and individual transaction. This problem is solved by Merkley Tree by hashing the data in record in this ledger (Merkle, 1980).This improves efficiency of blockchain as the small packets are to be distributed across the network. Hash is an algorithm which takes input of variable length and converts it into an output of specific length. Example in Bitcoin, if A wants to send B $150, then its looks like a string of various characters .

"3cbcf3e1075b0b3357140de438336733bd6927cdle78d36cc27834fcce932ad"

Figure 4. Merkle tree

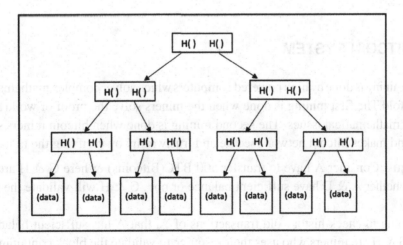

This string is deterministic means that "A->B $150" is always has the same hash output. If there is a minor variation in the input as "A->B $160" the hash code of output is completely different.

In Merkley tree the transactions are hashed using hashing functions. These transactions have their own hash code .The hash codes of two transactions are combined, so that we can remember it well. Similarly the hash code of combination of two transactions are again combined with the other two transactions hash code combination (M. Wang, 2018). Hence it easy to remember the hash code for the combinations of transactions .The hash code which is formed by combinations of hash code of transactions is known as Merkle root. The hash code pointed by arrow in the figure is Merkle root. Root is the combination of two hash codes, and the two hash codes which are further combination of other two hash codes of transactions.

Every Blockchain has a Merkle root which is located in the block header .The contents of block are verified and their consistency using this. If the copy of blockchain of A has similar Merkle root for copy of blockchain of B has same transactions and both A and B are agreed on the ledger. If there is a change in the contents of blockchain it would lead to generating different Merkle roots due to hashing. If there is a dissimilarity in Merkle root then we may request the two sub-hashes, and we can again request the sub-hashes for their hashing code. Hence, we can find out any dissimilarity or fraud in the blockchain by using Merkle root instead of searching the code line to line.

Blockchain Transactions

The transactions are made including information on the time date of members and type of transaction. In the blockchain network each node h as a replica of the ledger .

- Miners verify the transactions after solving complex math puzzles and maintain ledger.
- Mathematical principle ensures that the nodes automatically & continuously agree to current state of ledger and each transaction .
- If changes are done in the transaction the nodes will not reach the consensus and the block is not added to the blockchain.

EXAMPLE: BITCOIN SYSTEM

Mining: Bitcoin mining is done by high powered computers which solver complex mathematical problems. Mining is a two fold.The first mining is done when the miners solve the proof of work(POW),which is solving complex mathematical issues. The second mining is done when bitcoin miners solve computational problem and makes bitcoin network secure and trustworthy by verifying the transactions.

Mining Technique: Consider A have to transfer 500 BTC(Bitcoins) & here G & H are miners .Their job is to verify whether A & D have sufficient balance or not . G & H will validate the transactions of the A & D.

G & H are going to check history old transactions of A, that A has sufficient balance(above 500) for transaction .G & H are miners who uses their resource to validate the block containing transactions.

The transactions has detailed information of the transfer of money from one member to another.Ledger gets updated with respect to every transaction .The details are stored with respect to every transaction as a part of block. Hence, no one can hack the end users money from wallet. After successful transaction the values gets updated in the ledger with respect to everyone which has copy of that ledger.

If the transactions get successful, the ledger gets updated with respect to everyone. Once the block is validated the updated block is added to the blockchain .This solves problem of double spending (Nakamoto, 2007). The total time required for validating is 10 minutes .Miners check credit and debits if the user.

FUTURE TRENDS

1. **Financial Service**: The blockchain in services changes the structure of current financial markets. The markets value will be same as on the network. Some of the financial institutions are trying to make their private blockchains. If banking system is made by blockchain hacking the banking records becomes impossible .This will solve the double spending issues. This reduces bank crisis by a large extent.
2. **Payments and Transfers**: Blockchain are mostly used in payments and transfer system. The currencies are transferred using URL code .Here public and private keys are not necessary, directly by using URL code transfer takes place. The transaction fees are not charged by the network .Easy and safe transfer of money can be done using blockchain.
3. **Healthcare**: In healthcare system blockchain(Mettler & Hsg, 2016) will be useful for storing details of patients on ledger .Getting public key of patient the doctor can access the details of patient. So that every member details are recorded on ledger .Accordingly the doctor would give the person the best treatment .All previous records of the patient will be stored on blockchain and recent data will only be added to the previous block of the patient .
4. **Law Enforcement**: In Law enforcement the blockchain can be used to store the details of the criminals and the crime details .This will reduce the crime strategy in our society. The criminals can be caught easily. The criminal details are updated on network, so we can catch them efficiently wherever they are located .
5. **Voting**: Elections need authentication of voters identity, keeping secure record and trusted tallies. Blockchains are the medium for costing tracking and counting votes without voter fraud and lost records . By using blockchain we get secured data during election and voting. The data will not be hacked due to ledger system. In coming two years blockchain will make elections get handled easily and more securely.
6. **IOT**: This field uses blockchain to transfer the data between the devices without any corruptions and without any interference (Singh, 2016).In IOT the blockchain are used to provide security to the data sensed by the sensors and it provides the best way to store the data .The structure of blockchain is such that no one can hack the data easily. The details of sensed data will be secured.
7. **Online Music**: Recently there are various remakes of the real music .By using blockchain we provide security to the music that they can only hear the music but cannot make changes in the song until we buy the validated copy of the music.

Anyone can access the online music but anyone cannot make modifications with respect to it. If the person pays for the song then all the details can be accessed.

8. **Real Estate**: In Real Estate most of the deals are conducted by an intermediary. This intermediary are the brokers and the agents which deal the process .The buyer and the seller are unknown about each other, the brokers act as bridge between them who charges commission on the transactions by both the sides .the blockchain changes all these frauds .It builds trust among the buyer and seller .The transaction using the blockchain doesn't charge any kind of transaction fees on the members. We can validate and use smart contracts for these deals.

Real Time Applications of Blockchain

1. **followmyvote.com**: This aims to modify the way we vote becoming words first open source online voting system.
2. **Arcade City**: It is a ground work to decentralized right sharing service uber killer.
3. **ShoCard**: It stores your identity onto bitcoins blockchain for easier verification.

CONCLUSION

In every centralised system the user data are accessed by organising system .These data are stored in database of system and they are not secured. Anyone can easily hack the system and access the personal details of members in the system . The blockchain system provides the solution on this problem. It collects information of user and allows the user to have control on their own data .Each user have his own private and public keys for transaction .Each user shares his public key over the decentralised, distributed, public ledger on blockchain So no one can access the details of anyone easily as it is in key form.

Since while transactions the hash code are generated and added on ledgers .Blockchain provides a high security to the personal data of user and as well as on the public network of user. Since, the details are highly secured on blockchain. The laws and regulation systems could be coded into blockchain .In some situations the ledger act as a legal evidence in case of unauthorized transactions. The Merkley tree is used by Blockchain, databases and computer networks to quickly manage the records around the multiple computer systems.

By using blockchain the transactions are validated and verified by the network nodes. The blockchain can be implemented in various fields, such as banking, health and care, voting and real estates . We discussed various future extensions of blockchain which would make the all rounded solution for building trust in society. We conclude that the blockchain provides the best way to provide the security to the data .The security is provided according to the way of storing the data in the blockchain using cryptographic techniques.

REFERENCES

b-money. (1998). Retrieved from http://www.weidai.com/bmoney.txt

Big data, for better or worse: 90% of world's data generated over last two years. (2013). *ScienceDaily*.

Blockchains and the Internet of Things. (n.d.). Retrieved from http://www.postscapes.com/blockchains-and-the-internet-of-things/

Dai, F., Shi, Y., Meng, N., Wei, L., & Ye, Z. (2017). *From Bitcoin to Cybersecurity : a Comparative Study of Blockchain Application and Security Issues.* Academic Press.

Double-spending. (n.d.). Retrieved from https://en.bitcoin.it/wiki/Double-spending

Kharif, O. (n.d.). *CryptoKitties Mania Overwhelms Ethereum Networks Processing.* Retrieved from https://www.bloombergquint.com/technology/cryptokitties-quickly-becomes-most-widely-used-ethereum-app#gs.3m37ft

Mense, A., & Flatscher, M. (2018). *Security Vulnerabilities in Ethereum Smart Contracts.* Academic Press.

Mettler, M., & Hsg, M. A. (2016). *Blockchain Technology in Healthcare The Revolution Starts Here.* Academic Press.

Moubarak, J., & Filiol, E. (2018). *On Blockchain Security and Relevant Attacks.* Academic Press.

Nakamoto, S. (2007). *Bitcoin : A Peer-to-Peer Electronic Cash System.* Academic Press.

Salman, T., Member, S., Zolanvari, M., Member, S., & Erbad, A. (2018). Security Services Using Blockchains : A State of the Art Survey 1. *IEEE Communications Surveys and Tutorials, 1.* doi:10.1109/COMST.2018.2863956

Scaling the Facebook data warehouse to 300 PB. (n.d.). Retrieved from https://code.fb.com/core-data/scaling-the-facebook-data-warehouse-to-300-pb/

Singh, S. (2016). *Blockchain : Future of Financial and Cyber Security.* Academic Press.

Szabo, N. (1997). *Formalizing and securing relationships on public networks.* Academic Press; doi:10.5210/fm.v2i9.548

Tosh, D. K., Shetty, S., Liang, X., Kamhoua, C. A., Kwiat, K. A., & Njilla, L. (2017). *Security Implications of Blockchain Cloud with Analysis of Block Withholding Attack.* Academic Press. doi:10.1109/CCGRID.2017.111

Vukoli, M. (2016). *The Quest for Scalable Blockchain Fabric : Proof-of-Work vs .BFT Replication.* Academic Press. doi:10.1007/978-3-319-39028-4

Wang, L., Shen, X., Li, J., Shao, J., & Yang, Y. (2018). Cryptographic primitives in blockchains. *Journal of Network and Computer Applications.* doi:10.1016/j.jnca.2018.11.003

Wang, M. (2018). *Research on the Security Criteria of Hash Functions in the Blockchain.* Academic Press.

Zyskind, G., & Pentland, A. S. (2015). Decentralizing Privacy : Using Blockchain to Protect Personal Data. 2015 IEEE Security and Privacy Workshops, 180–184. doi:10.1109/SPW.2015.27

This research was previously published in Transforming Businesses With Bitcoin Mining and Blockchain Applications; pages 173-194, copyright year 2020 by Business Science Reference (an imprint of IGI Global).

Chapter 33

Reliable (Secure, Trusted, and Privacy Preserved) Cross-Blockchain Ecosystems for Developing and Non-Developing Countries

Shubham Kumar Keshri
Banaras Hindu University, India

Abhishek Kumar
Banaras Hindu University, India

Achintya Singhal
iD https://orcid.org/0000-0003-0242-2031
Banaras Hindu University, India

K. Vengatesan
Sanjivani College of Engineering, Savitribai Phule University, India

Rakesh S.
iD https://orcid.org/0000-0003-2174-7472
Galgotias University, India

ABSTRACT

The chapter suggests an iterative social system in which individuals and totals use a development, watch its arranged and unintended outcomes, and after that, build new improvements. Blockchain development has the potential to construct productivity, capability, straight imposition, and disintermediation in shared worth or information exchange. This chapter proposes how the blockchain will be implemented in developing and non-developing countries. These countries can use the blockchain for financial services, transportation, healthcare, e-marketplace, etc. And what is the risk and danger of using blockchain in non-developed countries?

DOI: 10.4018/978-1-6684-7132-6.ch033

INTRODUCTION

Every once in a while an innovation goes along that makes a huge difference. To most observers, the most recent to pursue that trend is blockchain. It can possibly revolutionize everything from money to supply chains. Also, blockchain can possibly cross over any barrier between the developed countries and undeveloped countries.

Many people consider of blockchain as the innovation that forces Bitcoin. While this was its unique reason, blockchain is prepared to do a lot more. Despite the sound of the word, there's not only one blockchain. Blockchain is shorthand for an entire suite of distributed record advancements that can be modified to record and track anything of significant worth, from money related transactions, to medical records or even land tiles. What's so unique about blockchain? How about we separate the reasons why blockchain technology stands to revolutionize the way in which we cooperate with one another.

First reason is; the way blockchain tracks and store data, blockchain stores information in batches, called blocks, that are linked to each other in a chronological manner to form a continuous line, a chain of blocks.

Figure 1. Blockchain

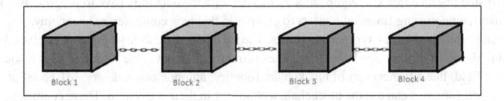

If any person wants to change the existing data of any block, they can't change or rewrite it. Instead the rewritten data is stored in a new block, showing that a changed to b at a particular time and date. It's a non-destructive way to track data changes over time. Presently, here's where things get really interesting. Unlike the traditional record technique initially a book, at that point a database document put away on a network, blockchain was intended to be decentralized and distributed across a large network of computers.

This decentralizing of data minimizes the ability of information tempering and carries us to the *second* factor that makes blockchain one of a kind: it makes trust in the information. Before a block can be added to the chain, few of things need to occur. Initial, a cryptographic puzzle must to be solved, accordingly making the block. Second, the computer that solves the puzzle shares the solution to all the different computers. On the network, this is called proof-of-work (POW). Third, the network will at that point verify and validate this proof-of-work, and if right, the block will be added to the chain. This work will guarantee that we can confide in every single block on the chain. Since the network does the trust working, presently have the chance to interface directly with information in real-time. What's more, that carries us to the *third* reason blockchain innovation is such a distinct advantage: no more mid people (intermediaries). At present, when working with each other, we don't demonstrate the other individual, our money related record or business records. Rather, we depend on trusted intermediaries, for example, a bank or a lawyer, to see our records, and keep that data secret. These intermediaries built trust between the parties and can confirm. This methodology limits risk and hazard, yet additionally adds another progression to the trade, which means additional time and cash spend. As we presently know, all blocks added to the chain have been confirmed to be valid and can't be tempered with. This sort of trusted peer-to-peer cooperation with information can revolutionize the manner in which data can be access, check and execute with each other.

Also, on the grounds that blockchain is a kind of technology, not a network. It tends to be executed from numerous points of view. Some blockchain can be totally open and open to everybody to view and access. Others can be closed to a select group of authorized users, for example, an organization, a banks, or government offices. And there are hybrid public-private blockchain as well. In some, those with private access can see all the data, while the public can see just selected. In others, everybody can see every information, however just a few people have access to new information. An administration, for instance, could utilize a hybrid framework to record the limits of anybody's property, while keeping their own data private or, it could enable everybody to see property records however reserve itself the exclusive authority to update them. It is the combination of all these elements de-centralizing of the information, building trust in the information and enabling us to communicate directly with each other and the information that gives the blockchain technology the possibility to support a large number of the manners in which we connect with each other. In any case, much like the ascent of the internet, this technology will carry with it a wide range of complex strategy questions about administration, international law, security, and financial matters. Here at the centre for International Governance Development, try to bring trusted research that will equip strategy makers with the data they have to progress blockchain advancement, empowering financial matters to prosper in this new computerized economy.

A developed country has all types of resources. The sufficient availability of resources gives strength to the administration of developed countries. These countries are now able to utilize their resources in some other field, like advancement of blockchain, robotics, autonomous industry, IoT based platform. The developed countries can use the blockchain technology in their ecosystem. These countries can use the blockchain in the field of Autonomous Vehicle, Electronic Medical Record, Security and Privacy, Crowd Sensing System, E-Marketplace, Property Rights, Controlling Corruption, and so on.

The undeveloped countries can also use the blockchain technology in their ecosystem. Undeveloped countries basically incorporate those countries that are moderately and comparatively poor socially and financially. These types of countries have no sufficient resources for better advancement of the country. These types of countries may depend on some other developed countries. But the blockchain technology can also be used in undeveloped countries. These countries can initially use the concept of blockchain in the field of education, utilities, finance, government, commerce, and so on.

This report explains about the utility of blockchain in the developed countries as well as undeveloped countries. Also, discuss about the risk arise by using blockchain in undeveloped countries.

Blockchain, the underlying generation at the back of Bitcoin is a unique new way of reaching consensus in a distributed style. At its middle, a Blockchain is only a database that runs on millions of devices simultaneously. The enormous resource pool of devices securing the network prevents malicious actors from enhancing the recorded facts in any way. This gives Blockchain their maximum essential advantage – being absolutely tampered resistant. That is to say, a fact recorded on the Blockchain is everlasting. This makes Blockchain a candidate for a great deal more than simply payments. Information like Land Titles and different asset certificate can also be saved on Blockchain to assist make the statistics tamper-proof.

BLOCKCHAIN TECHNOLOGY IN DEVELOPED COUNTRIES

A large number of the population in the developing world will like to benefit from new blockchain technologies. According to the report of ICT Facts and Figures 2017, 42.9% of households in developing countries use the Internet for different purposes. This percentage of using the internet is growing very rapidly due to the highly demand and use of the smartphones. It can be argued that from multiple points of view, blockchain has a lot of higher offer for the developing world than the developed world. Why? Since blockchain can possibly compensate for an absence of compelling formal foundations—rules, laws, guidelines, and their authorization (Kshetri & Voas, 2018).

How Can Developing Countries Benefit?

The lack of existing infrastructure in developing countries is, in fact, a good thing when it comes to further development. It permits developing countries to skip a couple of cycles of mechanical advancement to bounce to the most developed iteration directly. For instance, nations like Kenya and Tanzania have practically universal telephone get to gratitude to 3G systems. These nations didn't set down copper wires and gave internet access directly via the smartphones. In doing as such, they saved money on the gigantic expenses of setting down copper wires and furthermore had the option to furnish their residents with a vastly superior technology standard. This is called Leapfrogging and has been demonstrated to be enormously effective in developing countries over the most recent couple of years.

In a similar vein, the remote regions of developing countries, which do approach formal banking administrations could jump directly to Blockchain put together arrangements and spare with respect to the enormous expenses of setting up new foundation. Developing countries as of now have a massive system of active smart phones clients on account of the minimal effort information benefits in these nations. Because of the Android cell phone transformation of the previous decade, the measure of cell phone clients in developing countries has skyrocketed, and this gives a novel chance to Blockchains.

CAN BLOCKCHAIN HELP IN DEVELOPING COUNTRIES?

There isn't any doubt about the fact. Blockchains are right here to stay. Blockchains are already allowing us to improve the financial services industry through offering rapid, trust-less payments among peers. But Blockchains are not only for developed countries. In fact, Blockchains might have even extra to make a contribution to emerging markets. Here's a observe how developing countries can more gain even from Blockchain Technology. The developed countries may use the blockchain technology in the field of:

- Autonomous Vehicle
- Electronic Medical Record
- Security and Privacy
- Blockchain based Crowd Sensing System
- E-Marketplace
- Property Rights
- Controlling Corruption etc.

BLOCKCHAIN IN AUTONOMOUS VEHICLE

As per an investigation of the top worldwide automakers, we will see countless vehicles with some self-driving capacity by the mid of 2020s, with the primary vehicles generally being extravagance autos or part of business fleets (Miller, 2018).

What if a vehicle was completely autonomous in every sense of the word? A vehicle could drive itself to refuel or to an electric charging station. Connected vehicle arrangements would advantage from a blockchain and IoT arrangement because of all the more convenient and obvious information caught in the blockchain from vehicle sensors. If the sensors of vehicle feel that any repairing is required then the vehicle, itself derive to the repairing facility. Autonomous vehicle producers would have auspicious access to motor or power train failure data caught on the blockchain and could utilize this data to decide whether failure patterns are happening for the segment (Miller, 2018).

Customers profit by the expanded degree of consideration from the producers of the autonomous vehicle and expanded customer confidence. Producers, designers, controllers, and providers would have suitable perceivability into segment failure on the blockchain and could proactively respond to disappointment inclines all the more rapidly to guarantee buyer safety and fulfilment. The vehicle would safely pay for re-fuelling or fixes quickly without direct human interaction. A permanent record of the refuelling, fixes, and instalments would be recorded on the blockchain and shared by members including vehicle proprietors, makers, fix offices, and financing firms (Miller, 2018).

The IoT stage conjures the fitting blockchain exchange dependent on guidelines attached to the type of received information from the sensors. An open Programming interface combination layer is utilized by the refuelling, charging, parking, or fix facility to summon an exchange on the blockchain when the activity is finished (Miller, 2018).

Figure 2. Blockchain and IoT autonomous vehicle solution.

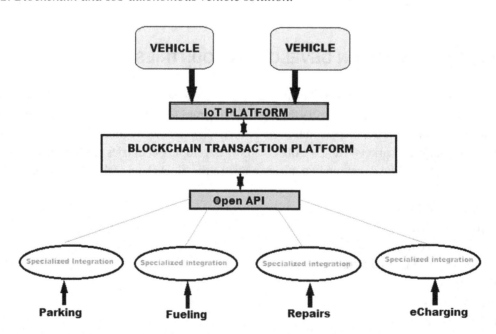

ELECTRONIC MEDICAL RECORD

Diseases spread and suffered more in developing countries than in developed world. Developing nations today are going to innovation as the silver shot or cure. There arises a lot of advancement in the health-care management in terms of Information as well as Communication technology. The electronics health records or electronic medical records (EMR), a key component of medical informatics gives potential solutions for advanced health care (Kamau et al., 2018).

The Electronic Medical Record (EMR) as a key component of medical informatics gives potential solutions for enhanced healthcare. In the world of digitalization, EMR is also a digital version of the record of a patient's paper chart (Crosby et al., 2016). EMR is a very safe system to keep critical and highly sensitive private data and information about patient for diagnosis and treatment the health in the healthcare industry, which need to be frequently distributed and shared among peers such as healthcare providers, insurance companies, pharmacies, researchers,, patient families, among others (Wood et al., 2016).

Patient should not access their own medical data in most of the health care institution. Patients are getting worry with this type of privacy of their own medical report. This problem can be resolve by using the blockchain technology (Stephen & Alex, 2018).

Confidentiality is virtually indisputable in blockchain. With the help of blockchain, data can be completely accessed by the patient as well as patient's can keep eye or track that how the data about his/her health is shared and maintains to fulfil patient's privacy and security of data (Miller, 2018).

The Electronic Medical Report (EMR) should face some challenges and limitations. This system will handle some important challenges at the time of implementing personally control system. It means this personally control information would take the place of hospital record. Some part of this type of personally control record would be downloaded in to the health care institutional record to tribute the previously existing data (Stephen & Alex, 2018).

Because of the encrypted security of the blockchain information, the privacy of the patient is preserved and it is only accessed by the authorized person who has the correct key for decrypt the data (Kamau et al., 2018).

BLOCKCHAIN SECURITY AND PRIVACY

Since blockchain has a feature of decentralization, it provides more privacy and security than any other centralization application. In the blockchain technology, every new created block keeps the track of its previous block. It will give an authentication mechanism during the period of any transaction. Also, there is no any need of any third party to record the information about the transaction in the ledger. By using blockchain technology, all the transactions will be automatically recorded in the ledger without any interference of third party. The data or information stored in the blockchain's ledger is transparent and also immutable (unchangeable), this is the one reason of trustworthy of blockchain. Also, blockchain is free from MITM. MITM means Man in The Middle Attack. Since blockchain doesn't allow any access to any third party (a middle man), so it is protected from MITM (Stephen & Alex, 2018).

Figure 3. Blockchain in Electronic Medical Report, EMR

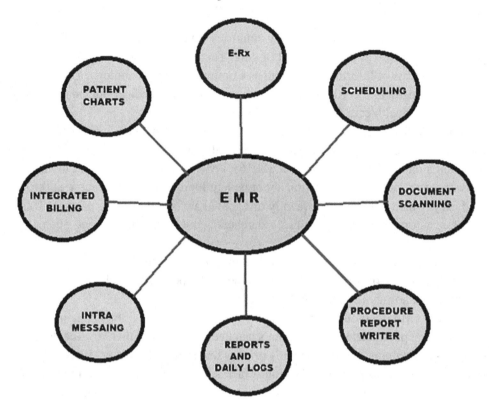

BLOCKCHAIN BASED CROWD SENSING SYSTEM

Blockchain is totally disparate from the traditional architecture, blockchain uses decentralized system, and it has no centralized platform in crowd-sensing process. Instead, by using blockchain technique, the crowd-sensing system is managed by a decentralized system (Huang et al., 2019).

The crowd-sensing process of BCS can be classified into following four steps (Huang et al., 2019):

1)   Requesters post task, at that point verify the rules and send them to correspondence stage, i.e., distribute a brilliant contract that comprises of a few predefined functions.
2)   Users inquiry distributed smart contracts from blockchain and acquire useful detecting task. After the completion of the task, they present the information on correspondence stage, i.e., call explicit function in smart contracts.
3)   By questioning blockchain and tuning in to the correspondence stage, miners get unconfirmed sensing information, and after that look at the quality of information as indicated by guidelines the requester makes. After miners substantiate the quality of detecting information, miners and users will get the rewarded in the wake of pushing handled detecting information into blocks. In general, miners acquire remunerates by contributing figuring power for running smart contracts.
4)   Requesters interfere to the blockchain occasionally. When they choose not to keep gathering information, they can send message to the framework to close this work and get the remained hold

cash from smart contract. As this message will be communicated in the framework, miners and users will at that point stop to work.

As a result of decentralized design of blockchain, BCS doesn't rely upon any third party; there is no single step of failure issue. Additionally, users really need to make security stores, i.e., pay transaction charges to miners, before interest in crowd-sensing task, which proficiently avoids different assaults (Huang et al., 2019).

Figure 4. Blockchain Based Crowd Sensing System

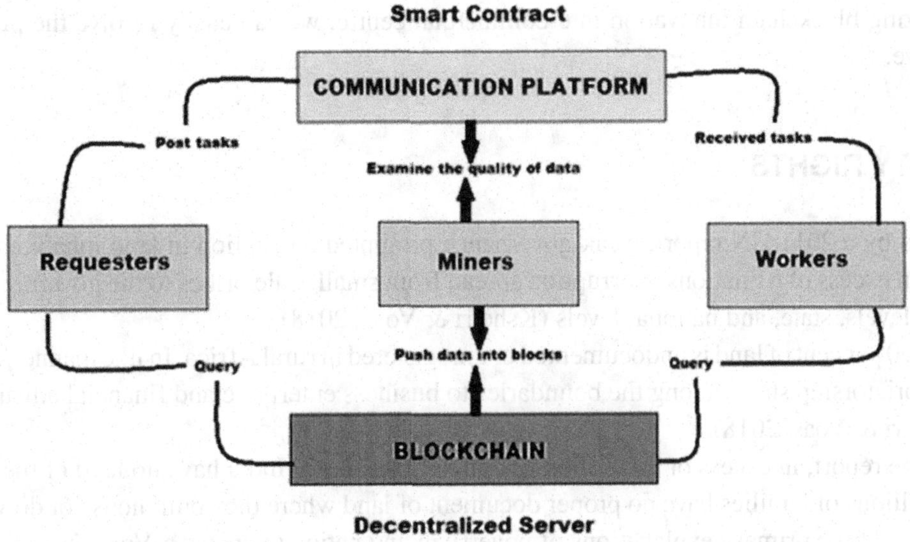

BLOCKHAIN TECHNOLOGY FOR E-MARKETPLACE

The present e-commercial centre environment advanced from internet innovations. It assumes a significant job in the worldwide economy. According to the present condition and circumstance of the e-commercial centre, this part discuss around the accompanying exploration issue (Chang, 2019):

1)   Pervasive computing:

The popularity of cell phones has significantly changed the customer conduct of the present internet based business. From the ad of a game to the buy and conveyance of game tickets and the entering to the stadium should all be possible on a cell phone. Pervasive computing gives access to the context related data for making moment adoptions to the quickly changing versatile online business.

2)   Imposing business model:

There is a great deal of cost based data asymmetry in customary organizations. Significant internet based business stages have caused imposing business model, bringing about high commissions, rate control, and divulgence control. Moreover, user buying conduct is gathered to induce user data, causing security concerns.

3)   Cross-border web based business:

The instalment is ineffective, slow, and expensive for banks and other organizations in cross-border online business transactions. The decentralized blockchain-based electronic commercial centre can offer numerous points of interest for e-commercial centre members, including privacy, trust, minimum transaction expenses, security, and transaction integrity (Chang, 2019).

By utilizing blockchain innovation in e-commercial centre, we can easily resolve the problem discussed above.

PROPERTY RIGHTS

As indicated by a 2011 UN report, weak governance prompted corruption in land inhabitancy and organization in excess of 61 nations. Corruption spread from small scale bribes to the government control at the local levels, state, and national levels (Kshetri & Voas, 2018).

Around 90 per cent of land is undocumented or unregistered in rural Africa. In like manner, an absence of land proprietorship stays among the boundaries to business enterprise and financial advancement in India (Kshetri & Voas, 2018).

As per the report, in excess of 20 million provincial families in India have no land of their own and there are millions of families have no proper document of land where they built house or do work. Lack of land is one of the primary explanations of poverty in any nation (Kshetri & Voas, 2018).

Blockchain can decrease friction and erosion, as well as the expenses related with property registration. It is conceivable to do all or the greater part of the preparing utilizing cell phones. Given this, it is empowering that different activities have been attempted. The US-based stage for land registration, Bitland, reported the presentation of a blockchain-based land vault framework in Ghana, where 78 per cent of land is unregistered. There is a long excess of land-contest cases in Ghanaian courts. Bitland records exchange safely, with GPS facilitates composed portrayals, and satellite photographs. This and comparable procedures are relied upon to ensure property rights and minimise corrupt practices. As of mid-2016, 24 communities in Ghana had expressed interest in the project. Bitland is planning to extend to Nigeria as a team with the OPEC Fund for International Development (Kshetri & Voas, 2018).

In 2017, India's two states, Telangana and Andhra Pradesh states reported designs to utilize blockchain for land registration. Telangana began the registration of land project in the capital city of Hyderabad. In September 2017, it was reported that a total rollout of the program in Hyderabad and close by territories would occur inside a year. In October 2017, the Andhra Pradesh government teamed up with a Swedish start-up, ChromaWay, to make a blockchain-based land registry framework for the arranged city of Amravati (Kshetri & Voas, 2018).

CONTROLLING CORRUPTION

Blockchain makes a carefully designed computerized record of exchanges and offers the record, thus offering straightforwardness. Cryptography takes into consideration access to add to the record safely. It is very troublesome—if certainly feasible—to change or delete information recorded on a ledger. With this component, blockchain makes it conceivable to diminish or dispose of integrity violations, for example, misrepresentation and corruptions while likewise decreasing exchange costs (Kshetri & Voas, 2018).

Blockchain additionally makes it conceivable to create smart ("tagged") property and control it with brilliant contracts. Instances of such properties incorporate physical property (vehicle, house, compartment of metal) and also nonphysical property (shares in an organization). Blockchain-based smart properties just experience activities dependent on the data distributed in a smart contract. On the off chance that property is being utilized as guarantee, the contract probably won't enable the proprietor to expand the same property as a guarantee or security to another bank. Along these lines, the way toward confirming insurance before the credit being made is incredibly streamlined for overseers. Here, a believed exchanging framework is made for smart properties, making credit all the more promptly accessible and less expensive (Kshetri & Voas, 2018).

Since blockchain uses chain of blocks to store any information, it will also store the information about the any priced-based things transparently, which can help us to control corruption.

Blockchain Uses in Developing Countries

Because of the intensely associated nature of the present reality, Blockchain as an innovation can possibly have extensive effects in a moderately short measure of time. This implies developing countries may receive the rewards of the innovation quicker than with past ground-breaking technologies.

Since Blockchains are a type of decentralized, distributed, immutable(changeless) and transparent record, they have the potential to disrupt businesses all through the economy — even in developing markets.

A few instances of such applications are illustrated below (Medium, n.d.):

Figure 5. Applications of Blockchain

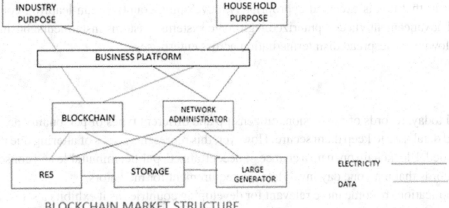

Currency

This is where Blockchain began in. Crypto currencies like Bitcoin and Ethereum have shown the protected utilization of decentralized innovation as a store and move of significant worth.

Developing countries can pilot such currencies in closed, token based frameworks to build transparency in sectors like customs, administration and law.

Goods

Tracking physical goods through the production network is one of the most touted utilizations of blockchain innovation. Firms like Everledger are attempting to implement this by following high worth things like diamonds all through their lifecycle on a worldwide scale. Also, even traditional giants like Walmart are getting into the activity. The organization is trying different things with Blockchains to guarantee food safety all through their inventory network.

Since products provenance is a significant issue in developing countries, this might be a key region of centre as far as executing Blockchain. Parts like nourishment inventory network, government open market deal and customs exchange tracking of import export might be key zones to keep an eye out for.

What's more, Blockchain have likewise been utilized for innovative applications like delivering development aid to that need over the world. A prominent case of this is the way the World Food Program (WFP) utilized blockchain innovation to dispense help to Syrian displaced people living in Jordan.

In the event that International Development Organization like the World Bank and ADB implement token based frameworks to dispense improvement help to nations, at that point it will realize a huge change in transparency in the sector, where as much as 50% of donations may go unaccounted for because of misappropriation and corruption.

Services

Blockchain can possibly change how benefits businesses going from budgetary foundations to lawful foundations work. The mix of Blockchains, smart contracts and Decentralized Autonomous Organizations (DAO) can possibly empower services transactions to happen seamlessly in a decentralized, secure and quick way.

In the event that this is executed appropriately, developing countries can leapfrog counterparts in institutional advancement via computerized legitimate systems, customs instalments, business transactions and allowing widespread disintermediation across enterprises.

Records

Right up 'til today, records of possession, citizenship and different types of personality are put away in incorporated databases to keep them secure. However, this represents issues of altering due to the middle people included. Blockchain open up a chance of decentralized, public, immutable and consensus driven ledger of records that may one day invalidate the requirement for mediators.

These applications become more relevant for developing countries as it exhibits a scope for bringing the whole populace under one stage. It will make giving citizen services like ownership transfers, voter enrolment and sponsorship/tax transfers a lot simpler and progressively transparent.

This can likewise be extended out to organization information, whereby the identity of an organization will be accessible on a blockchain for reference by any stockholder working with the entity. This will permit extraordinary transparency and speed in business exercises and transactions ranging from vendor payments to tax filings.

Possible Advantages of Blockchain Technology for Developing Countries (Energypedia, n.d.)

Compared to developed countries, developing countries are far more likely to be impacted by blockchain technologies. Some of the advantages are listed below:

- Blockchain innovation serves to (re) construct trust among the society (even in reality of weak legislative foundations)
- While many developed countries face the trouble to incorporate blockchain innovation into the legacy infrastructure, this isn't the situation in many developing countries (without a set up framework). Hence, it is a lot simpler to coordinate blockchain innovation.
- Leap frogging the financial area: not having a bank account at a traditional, physical bank but having access to mobile financing options
- Public claimed and shared framework (not to be affected by corrupt politicians and so on.)
- Collaboration is required: This (e) limits manipulation, corruption and fraud.
- There are numerous similitude between the appropriated idea of blockchain and decentralized vitality frameworks like a smaller than expected lattice: prosumers, numerous producers, numerous customers associate and must be synchronised (Runyon, 2017).
- Money remains inside the network: energy producers and consumers don't need to pay a brought together, outside organization. Transactions association charge expenses of 10% or more; blockchain innovation can bring those down to 3%. As per the World Bank, overall settlements are 700 billion USD in 2016 (Rutkin, 2016).
- However, contacting the individuals in remote regions despite everything stays a test. So as to defeat the "last mile", blockchain innovation faces indistinguishable obstacles from in different markets.
- ADB distinguished 4 different ways blockchain innovation can upset the advancement participation area: 1. Limit building and institutional fortifying. 2. Modernizing vitality networks. Blockchain can really assist utilities with staying aware of rising force request in littler, lower-esteem squares. Improve existing vitality industry forms. Respond quicker after disasters (forestalling power outages). 3. Sustainable power source smaller than normal and micro grids. Shared transactions; "prosumers". 4. Green fund and carbon exchanging frameworks. Blockchain can be conveyed to the two plans, which are essential to help the execution of creating part nations' Nationally Determined Contributions under the 2015 Paris Agreement against atmosphere change (Zhai, 2017).

Challenges in Developing Countries

The ultimate numerous many years have shown that the direction to economic prosperity in developing countries depends on having financial services accessible to the poorest people in the society. Micro

Financing is the availability of small loans to terrible marketers and small corporations who've no get right of entry to proper banking offerings. The most deprived sections of the developing countries rely closely on microfinance to growth their economic wealth. Several researches have shown that casual change additionally advantages from the influx of funding similar to in the formal sector. So its miles clean that terrible humans in growing countries want to be supplied avenues to at ease small loans where traditional banking structures may not be willing to installation shop.

Blockchains offer a completely unique possibility here as putting in place Bitcoin wallets does no longer require the same infrastructure as putting in a new physical financial institution store. Since Blockchains run on a allotted network, there's no need for pricey branches to open more workplaces. This saves on expenses for banking that are otherwise passed on to customers inside the shape of fees and switch charges (Medium, n.d.).

BLOCKCHAIN TECHNOLOGY OPPORTUNITIES IN UNDEVELOPED COUNTRIES

Undeveloped countries basically incorporate those countries that are moderately and comparatively poor socially and financially. These countries can possibly advance; however don't have satisfactory access to exhibit day innovation, fundamentally because of absence of infrastructure. On a very basic level, these countries need straightforwardness, security, and responsibility in their procedures, which are all foundations of Blockchain innovation (Ahishakiye et al., 2018).

Blockchain innovation is decentralized and hence eliminates the custodian restraints of any private entity. Every information in the framework are carefully crypt for special distinguishing proof and once posted, a record can never be changed or erased, prompting security. Also, Blockchain idea takes a shot at smart contracts?, wherein transaction happen just if certain pre-set requirements are met, so there will be responsibility of every transactions (Ahishakiye et al., 2018).

Absence of transparency, corruption, and misuse of assets are among the difficulties that international associations face when they provide funds to undeveloped nations. Blockchain offers transparency and unchanging nature. The World Food Program (WFP) tried this innovation in an undertaking called "Building Blocks", in Pakistan and Jordan where weak families got sustenance and money help from the WFP, which was verified and recorded on an open Blockchain through a cell phone interface. Utilizing this strategy, payment was responsible and coordinated with the privileges and the procedure was quicker and progressively precise. Therefore, once Blockchain based technology is copied in other developing nations, the WFP will have straightforwardness and responsibility (Ahishakiye et al., 2018).

The corruption and bribery of authorities happens more oftentimes in undeveloped countries than in developed ones. The use of blockchain on developing and un-developing countries not only can find and resolve the problem of corruption yet in addition lift those nations out of poverty. In spite of the fact that the information governance and security issues stay bigger difficulties, its application to undeveloped nations won't be acknowledged on a huge scale at any point in the near future basically because of two factors: the obstruction of the current authority and absence of framework (Harris, 2018).

DANGERS AND RISKS

In addition to the guarantee that blockchain technology may offer, a comprehension of the orderly dangers and risks is vital. Like any important resources, Bitcoin and blockchain resources can be destroyed, damaged, taken and stolen. The way this can't be confirmed shows the dangers of depending on blockchain innovation as foolproof. Beneath, eight different dangers and risks that blockchain advancements present in the undeveloped nations are portrayed (Harris, 2018):

Manipulation of the Majority Consensus

Blockchain technology creates some potential security issues in undeveloped countries. The most troubling is the probability of a 51percent assault, in which one mining element could snatch control of the blockchain and double-spend recently transacted coins into own account. The issue is the centralization propensity in mining where the challenge to record new exchange blocks in the blockchain has implied that solitary a couple of enormous mining pools control most of the transaction record. Double-spending may likewise still be conceivable in different ways. Another issue is distributed denial of service (DDoS) assaults, which can altogether restrict the chances of mining pools not aligned with an entry that desires to game the framework (Harris, 2018).

In undeveloped nations, especially where the legislature has some incentive to control transaction, the government can present delays in the approval step, permitting government-backed mining elements to give earlier timestamps or to control the majority consensus rule agreement standard utilizing DDoS assaults, making the 51percent assault undeniably bound to happen. This is especially true when the government just permits private and semiprivate blockchains to be executed restricting the adequacy of blockchain transparency (Harris, 2018).

Constraining the Entrance of Miners

Content validation and verification of the transaction is led by clients, this procedure is known as miners who utilize the intensity of their PCs or extraordinarily structured devices to solve numerical equations. This is required for affirming transactions. Thusly, they gain a reward as any digital currency, an amount which is resolved ahead of time. The trouble of equations is extended with the development of mining computational power, with an end goal to keep the time expected to compose the information into a cryptographically-sealed block consistent.

Restricting access of miners to solve this numerical equation is one manner by which a few governments can make validation and verification of transactions far less engaging. Since miners require significant resources, especially electricity, to explain these equations, this effort can draw government consideration rather rapidly (Harris, 2018).

Privacy, Obscurity, and Pseudo-secrecy

Privacy is also an issue. Not all information should be appeared on an open record, accessible for the world to see. Indeed, even in developed nations with solid legal enforcement, one organization may not want its rivals to know the details of its day by day exchanges. This issue is significantly increasingly intense when government transactions are summoned that the government wouldn't like to be transparent.

Second, although private blockchains can improve security issues, transactions between parties in semi-private and open or public blockchains are pseudo-secrecy and not unknown. With enough information, pseudo-secrecy clients can be recognized, and government elements with worries about outside obstruction, which happens in the developing world, can distinguish and follow these clients. This is especially troubling in light of the fact that numerous blockchain clients accept they are anonymous (Harris, 2018).

Issues with Contract Law

Blockchain technology can possibly roll out noteworthy improvements to contract law utilizing self-upholding computerized contracts. These have the advantage of being executed without expecting middle third party to check that the conditions have effectively been met. In this way, in any economy, the legitimate and specialized implications of smart contracts should be considered, especially when disjointed qualities may emerge between genuine contracts and their computerized partners (Harris, 2018).

Guideline

Another test is the uncertain legal structure and government guidelines. Initially, since blockchain arrangements expect crytocurrency to work, it is important to alter the administrative system to perceive Bitcoin and different digital forms of money as a legitimate method for trade. Second, as officially expressed, the courts and different associations need to perceive the administrative parts of smart contracts, which numerous undeveloped nations are reluctant to do (Harris, 2018).

Tax Collection

Another issue is the alteration of tax assessment practice to incorporate the money related exchanges which happen on the blockchain. It is challenging for the most developed countries to follow money related exchanges made between pseudo-anonymous clients and for tax specialists to accurately tax organizations in the sharing economy. Although a move from pay based tax assessment to utilization based tax collection would make these exchanges simpler to pursue, couple of undeveloped government are set up to track such exchanges. These will require a major upgrade of the present tax assessment framework, which not many undeveloped countries are eager to execute rapidly (Harris, 2018).

Scalability and Storage Problem

There are numerous technology issues that presently can't seem to be settled regardless of the advancement of a nation's economy. One issue is identified with the size of blockchain records. Blockchains develop after some time and require proper record management. Indeed, even with open or public blockchains, quickly expanding size issues may prompt record centralization, which focuses to government guideline. This is probably going to influence the future of blockchain technology.

Storage will likewise be an obstacle. Although a blockchain dispenses with the requirement for a central server to store transaction and gadget IDs, the record must be put away on the hubs themselves. In numerous undeveloped nations, the government has a controlling stake in the web. Constraining access to these hubs should be possible through government inclusion, influencing the utility and unwavering quality of a blockchain in those nations (Harris, 2018).

Speed and Veracity of Transaction

Individual blockchain exchanges are delayed in contrast with typical customer instalment norms. The blockchain can't be finished until the new chain and its hash value have been determined and consented to by a majority consensus of clients (Harris, 2018).

Areas where Blockchain will assume a significant job in undeveloped nations incorporate the accompanying as extracted (Ahishakiye et al., 2018):

- *Ease paperwork preparing*. Worldwide compartment dispatching still includes a ton of desk work, costing time and cash. Likewise, paper-based freight documents like the bills are prone to loss, altering and misrepresentation.
- *Identify fake items*. Fake drug is a growing issue for drug store supply chains. This particularly relates to costly, inventive medication like cancer drugs. Drug stores need to make a point to sell "the correct thing" to the customers.
- *Facilitate source tracking*. In the food store network, foodborne episodes are a challenge for retailers. They need to get a speedy review of where the nourishment originated from and which different items are likewise influenced and must be removed from stores.
- *Operate the Internet of Things*. An ever increasing number of strategic items are outfitted with sensors that produce information along the production network e.g., the status of a shipment. This information must be put away in an immutable, available way.
- *Utilities*. Blockchain can enable utilities to stay aware of rising power request in little, lower-value blocks. Improve existing vitality industry forms. Respond quicker after debacles (avoiding power outages).
- *Government*. To record in a transparent manner residents? Votes or legislators? Programs (for checking if guarantees have been kept) or to empower self-governing administration frameworks.
- *Intellectual property*. To confirm the evidence of presence and initiation of a report.
- *Internet*. To decrease oversight, by abusing the changelessness of information put away in the Blockchain.
- *Finance*. To move/ transfer money between two parties without relying upon any outsider like bank.
- *Commerce*. To record goods? Attributes just as their possession, particularly for extravagance products, thus reducing the market of fake/ taken things.
- *Internet of Things*. For instance, by exploiting smart contracts to consequently process information originating from sensors, to give intelligent machines, a chance to interact with one another and independently take activities when explicit circumstances happen.
- *Education*. To store data on qualifications got by students. To diminish employment form fakes; in this specific situation, different entertainers (e.g., colleges, institute, and so forth.) could compose capabilities accomplished by an individual on the Blockchain; HR staff could then effectively get data about when and where a given competency was obtained.

Blockchain technology can solve development problems as it improves existing instruments and enables the development of new ones. Blockchain-based applications particularly address institutional weaknesses and financial inclusion because they restrict deception, corruption and uncertainties. In the future, the blockchain can also be a development vehicle empowering people directly and mitigating power asymmetries.

Poverty and Economic Disparities in Undeveloped Countries

In its "Poverty and Shared Prosperity Report 2016" the World Bank announced that "poverty remains inadmissibly high" with an expected populace of 766 million individuals living on under $1.90 every day in 2013. Numerous nations situated in Sub-Saharan Africa (388.7 million) or South-East Asia (256.2 million) are classified as undeveloped countries. Nevertheless, noteworthy advancement has been made in the previous year's (Luoto et al., 2007). These days, particularly in urban areas, a little accomplished middle class exists which can be a significant fundament for mechanical advancements. Advancement has been distinguished as a way to help improvement in developed and developing countries. All in all, new innovations can carry significant changes to these nations and improve their living conditions. Specifically, blockchain advancements have been proposed as another mechanical answer for some issues in undeveloped countries but has been held to be to somewhat undefined (Ravallion & Chen, 2005).

Weak Institutions

One significant issue of undeveloped countries, and one reason behind why improvement programs regularly don't convey the desired results, is weak institutions. Corruption, for example, is bound to happen in poor areas where an absence of law implementation is watched found that corruption is brought together, with a little gathering of individuals causing an impressive offer and that country zones are especially inclined to corruption. Another issue in undeveloped regions are the low degree of social trust. Key determinants of social trust are characterized as the unwavering quality of lawful foundations and social heterogeneity (Uslaner, 2002). Social trust underpins financial development and improves living conditions for needy individuals through advanced education endeavours, speculation rates and improved administration. Furthermore, training levels ought to be improved. Individuals frequently can't stand to send their kids to class since they come up short on the fundamental monetary capacities which bring about a neediness training trap. In addition, power concentration limits economic improvement on both local and national levels. Local chiefs have incentives for self-centred ruling and frequently catch legislative activities to strengthen social capital and education levels (AbouZahr et al., 2007).

CONCLUSION

Blockchain technology contains three main advantages, namely transparency, distributed architecture and immutability. These all properties of blockchain can help to reduce the fraud and corruption occurring in the developed countries and undeveloped countries. Blockchain can likewise enable financial transaction to occur all the more rapidly and guarantee that aid is distributed with a small chance of robbery and extortion.

These countries can also use the technology of blockchain in various ways, like autonomous vehicle and so on. Blockchain can also use to track and monitor the funds which are transacted for criminal activities like kidnapping. Using this technology all transaction is properly recorded from start to end in immutable fashion.

Even though there are certain limitations of blockchains at present, these are being taken a shot at by a worldwide network and can possibly be explained soon. This will permit the innovation to be executed in frameworks where there is an absence of trust and a requirement for disintermediation.

As a foundational technology that will certainly power new applications in both developed and undeveloped economies, blockchain offers various advantages to economies that can predict and exploit its merit. Undeveloped nations that are impervious to the merits of the blockchain will benefit far not exactly those embrace its advantages.

At last, one of the most energizing viewpoints is that this innovation might be available to developing countries around a similar time as more developed countries adopt them. This has the potential to level the playing field of development to a large extent across countries — both large and small.

REFERENCES

AbouZahr, C., Jha, P., Macfarlane, S. B., Mikkelsen, L., Setel, P. W., Szreter, S., & Stout, S. (2007). A scandal of invisibility: Making everyone count by counting everyone. *Lancet*, *370*(9598), 1569–1577. doi:10.1016/S0140-6736(07)61307-5 PubMed

Ahishakiye, E., Wario, R., & Niyonzima, I. (2018). Developing Countries and Blockchain Technology : Uganda ' s Perspective. *International Journal of Latest Research in Engineering and Technology*, *4*(August), 94–99.

Chang, Y. (2019). Blockchain Technology for e-Marketplace. 2019 IEEE International Conference on Pervasive Computing and Communications Workshops (PerCom Workshops), 429–430. doi:10.1109/PERCOMW.2019.8730733

Crosby, M., Pattanayak, P., Verma, S., & Kalyanaraman, V. (2016). Blockchain technology: Beyond bitcoin. *Appl. Innov.*, *2*, 6–10.

Energypedia. (n.d.). https://energypedia.info/ wiki/Blockchain_Opportunities_for_Social_Impact_in_Developing _Countries#Possible_Advantages _of_Blockchain_Technology_for_Developing_Countries

Harris, C. G. (2018). The risks and dangers of relying on blockchain technology in underdeveloped countries. IEEE/IFIP Network Operations and Management Symposium: Cognitive Management in a Cyber World, NOMS 2018, 1–4. doi:10.1109/NOMS.2018.8406330

Huang, J., Kong, L., Kong, L., Liu, Z., Liu, Z., & Chen, G. (2019). Blockchain-based Crowd-sensing System. *Proceedings of 2018 1st IEEE International Conference on Hot Information-Centric Networking, HotICN 2018*, 234–235. 10.1109/HOTICN.2018.8605960

INC42. (n.d.). https://inc42.com/resources/how-will-blockchain-technology-help-developing-countries/

Kamau, G., Boore, C., Maina, E., & Njenga, S. (2018). Blockchain technology: Is this the solution to EMR interoperability and security issues in developing countries? 2018 IST-Africa Week Conference, IST-Africa 2018.

Kshetri, N., & Voas, J. (2018). Blockchain in Developing Countries. *IT Professional*, *20*(2), 11–14. doi:10.1109/MITP.2018.021921645

Luoto, J., McIntosh, C., & Wydick, B. (2007). *Credit Information Systems in Less Developed Countries: A Test with Microfinance in Guatemala*. University of San Francisco.

Medium. (n.d.). https://medium.com/swlh/what-blockchain-means-for-developing-countries1e-c25a416a4b

Miller, D. (2018). Blockchain and the internet of things in the industrial sector. *IT Professional, 20*(3), 15–18. doi:10.1109/MITP.2018.032501742

Ravallion, M., & Chen, S. (2005). Hidden impact? Household saving in response to a poor-area development project. *Journal of Public Economics, 89*(11-12), 2183–2204. doi:10.1016/j.jpubeco.2004.12.003

Runyon, J. (2017, May 15). How Smart Contracts [Could] Simplify Clean Energy Distribution. Retrieved 10 July 2017, from https://www.renewableenergyworld.com/articles/2017/05/how-smart-contracts-could-simplify-clean-energy-distribution.html

Rutkin, A. (2016, March 2). Blockchain-based microgrid gives power to consumers in New York. Retrieved 10 July 2017, from https://www.newscientist.com/article/2079334-blockchain-based-microgrid-gives-power-to-consumers-in-new-york/

Stephen, R., & Alex, A. (2018). A Review on BlockChain Security. *IOP Conference Series. Materials Science and Engineering, 396*(1). Advance online publication. doi:10.1088/1757-899X/396/1/012030

Uslaner, E. M. (2002). *The Moral Foundations of Trust*. Cambridge University Press.

Wood, W., & Carter, B. Dodd, & Bradley. (2016). How Blockchain technology Can Enhance HER operability. Academic Press.

Zhai, Y. (2017). 4 Ways Blockchain Will Disrupt the Energy Sector. https://blogs.adb.org/blog/4-ways-blockchain-will-disrupt-energy-sector.fckLR

This research was previously published in Opportunities and Challenges for Blockchain Technology in Autonomous Vehicles; pages 115-133, copyright year 2021 by Engineering Science Reference (an imprint of IGI Global).

Chapter 34
Data Security in Clinical Trials Using Blockchain Technology

Marta de-Melo-Diogo

ISEG, Lisbon School of Economics and Management, University of Lisbon, Portugal

Jorge Tavares

NOVA IMS, Universidade Nova de Lisboa, Portugal

Ângelo Nunes Luís

ISEG, Lisbon School of Economics and Management, University of Lisbon, Portugal

ABSTRACT

Blockchain technology in a clinical trial setting is a valuable asset due to decentralization, immutability, transparency, and traceability features. For this chapter, a literature review was conducted to map the current utilization of blockchain systems in clinical trials, particularly data security managing systems and their characteristics, such as applicability, interests of use, limitations, and issues. The advantages of data security are producing a more transparent and tamper-proof clinical trial by providing accurate, validated data, therefore producing a more reliable and credible clinical trial. On the other hand, data integrity is a critical issue since data obtained from trials are not instantly made public to all participants. Work needs to be done to establish the significant implications in security data when applying blockchain technology in a real-world clinical trial setting and generalized conditions of use to establish its security.

INTRODUCTION

Since its discovery, Blockchain is emerging as an innovative technology to provide data transactions and storage in an effective, secure, and timely manner system. This technology has been applied to many sectors of activity, potentializing its features and improving processes and business mindsets.

The health sector is no exception, and many uses of this technology have been reported. Blockchain's full applicability in healthcare is still underway, and many optimizations are needed to be made, not only from a technology development perspective but also concerns about ethical and data protection regulation are raised and need improvement.

DOI: 10.4018/978-1-6684-7132-6.ch034

It is considered essential to mention that the interest in the applicability of blockchain systems in the healthcare sector has been increasing since 2016. More specifically, the number of published articles related to Blockchain in the Pubmed bibliographic database has increased drastically in 2018 (only five studies were published in 2016 and only 16 in 2017), reflecting the potential and growing interest of these systems in the healthcare sector (Mackey et al., 2019). Only 4% of these studies were related to clinical trials, and 32% were related to healthcare data (Mackey et al., 2019).

Particularly in clinical trials, this technology is yet to reach its full potential. Nevertheless, considering the dimension and complexity of a clinical trial network and process interlined, blockchain technology might improve data sharing, management, and access to all key players. However, identifying the risks and threats of applying this technology in such an environment is still amiss, and work needs to be done to establish them in a realistic scenario setting.

Therefore, the purpose of this chapter is to map the current use of blockchain systems in clinical trials, particularly data security managing systems, and its characteristics, such as applicability, interests of use, limitations, and issues, as reported throughout the literature review.

BACKGROUND

Although variations of term have been used before, Blockchain came around in 2008 when this technology was created by Satoshi Nakamoto to support and securely record Bitcoin cryptocurrency transactions (Meunier, 2018; Monrat et al., 2019). Since then, the interest in this technology has increased and soon was applied into other areas of interested such as government, manufacturing, finance, healthcare and distribution (Monrat et al., 2019).

Blockchain is an advanced data structure, designed for storing and sharing information, composed by a growing chain of blocks organized by chronological order (Agbo et al., 2019)(S Chen, Hannah et al., 2019). Each block stores information with digital signatures in a decentralized and distributed network, it allows to record a transaction by binding different blocks connected with chains (S Chen, Hannah et al., 2019) (Abu-elezz et al., 2020) (Monrat et al., 2019). This transaction is validated by a consent algorithm, and therefore, needs no third-party validation to complete an action. The chain continues to grow as new transactions are built and blocks are added into it (Omar, Jayaraman, Salah, Yaqoob, et al., 2020).

Unlike traditional methods, blockchain enables peer-to-peer transfer of digital assets without any intermediaries. All the transactions occur in a decentralized manner that eliminates the requirement for any intermediaries to validate and verify the transactions. Every transaction is regulated by the participants who store and share the information throughout the private key: an unique and individual signature linked to each transaction recorded (S Chen, Hannah et al., 2019).

The digitalization era is reaching almost every industry and is expected that the Distribution Ledger Technology, where technologies such as blockchain, artificial intelligence and Internet of Things are inserted, to reach a market value of $60.7 billion by 2024 (Smetanin et al., 2020).

The features of blockchain, include (Hussien et al., 2019):

- Decentralization, access of information through third parties with multiple copies in multiple locations;
- Consent, the consensus algorithm created controls the access and distribution within a network;
- Immutability: once the information has entered a blockchain no longer can be changed or altered; a

- Auditability and transparency, every transaction information and signature can be traced; interoperability, different systems are connected and communicate in an autonomous manner.

The blockchain platform is distinguished by its key characteristics enabling it to be a promising disruptive technology that reduces the emphasis on traditional data management systems (Omar, Jayaraman, Salah, Yaqoob, et al., 2020). The blockchain is poised to innovate and transform a wide range of applications, including goods transfer (supply chain), digital media transfer (sale of art), remote services delivery (travel and tourism), platforms for example, moving computing to data sources and distributed credentialing.

Healthcare systems are complex and multi-dimensional organizations, involving multiple professionals whin different functions and degrees of access information, multiple organizations of different sectors of activities such as regulatory agencies, insurance companies, suppliers, technical supports and many others. Providing care to a patient involves many professionals and actions, therefore is important that health records are available and updated in time to provide the accurate and appropriate care to each patient at all times. On the other hand, it is also important that every patient owns is medical record and has fully knowledge of the parties that have been granted access to the very same.

Data security and ownership represent two of the most sensitive topics of today's generation. In fact, since the approval of General Data Protection Regulation in 2016 in European Union, when it comes to medical records these two topics became even more important and prominent. Besides this, managing patient data integrity is one of the major concerns for the healthcare industry, combining the need to access each patient characteristics and complete medical records at any time.

The introduction of blockchain systems in healthcare might be the solution to some of the concerns raised in data security and medical records accessibility and might the solution to gather and improve communications and data sharing between every player in the healthcare systems.

Concerning blockchain applications in healthcare, blockchain benefits are the following (Agbo et al., 2019)(Hasselgren et al., 2020):

- Decentralization: Healthcare access is spread to multiple players, such as doctors, hospitals, health insurance companies, pharmacies, etc. This feature of blockchain allows access to multiple stakeholders in a timely manner and provides information sharing in real time.
- Transparency: Given the security and transparency of transactions, information systems and storing systems are very reliable, and therefore provide a solid source of information for healthcare stakeholders. This feature is very important for example, when submitting information to regulatory agencies.
- Data verifiability: every transaction can be check for its integrity and validity. This information is important for healthcare records validation, insurance claim verification and in pharmaceutical supply chain to detect contrafact products.
- Transparency and trust: given the amount of information stored and that every transaction is record, blockchain provide for healthcare providers and stakeholders an ambient of trust and transparency since every information is available to consult.
- Robustness: The blockchain storage method guarantees that data is available and prevented from loss.

- Data ownership: given the levels of access and control of access of a blockchain, through this data storage system, patients are able to a more detailed control of the availability of their medical records to third parties.
- Data security and privacy: once an information has entered in a blockchain it is extremely difficult to alter through maleficent intentions. Additionally, every transaction is recorded in chronological order and is also traceable by its time stamp and user responsible for that action.

Concerning healthcare, blockchain systems can be applied in different areas such as (PwC, 2018) (Deloitte, 2020)(S Chen, Hannah et al., 2019)(Tan et al., 2020) (Smetanin et al., 2020) (Omar, Jayaraman, Salah, Yaqoob, et al., 2020)(Monrat et al., 2019):

- Supply chain: products status can be checked by the supplier at all times. This includes information regarding the transportation route, and more importantly, about controlled factors such as temperature and humidity throughout the transportation, contributing for a better monitorization and assuring the quality and safety of the products delivered. This contribution is especially important when it comes to products that need refrigeration, such as vaccines and biological products. Blockchain systems also improve security and authenticity of the products delivered, tacking the issue of distribution of falsified drugs.
- Precision medicine and medical records: the access of multiple players in healthcare to medical records of a patient in real time not only can improve the care provided, and can also potentiate the uses of precision medicine, since the patient medical records and genomic data can by easy shared between doctors and researchers.
- Data management: Gathering medical records, expenses and reports concerning a medical treatment could be time consuming and an extensive process. Blockchain can improve this field since data sharing would be available and updated by the multiple players making the communication between them more efficient, for example between a hospital and an insurance company.
- Electronic prescription: electronic prescription would be improved by blockchain systems, given the ability of the information can be spread throughout the different services such as hospital-doctor-patient-pharmacy. Patient electronic devices can be also updated with app to monitor the adhesion to therapy, giving precious information to the doctor and pharmacist about the success of the treatment in a timely manner.
- Regulatory compliance: given the security and data authenticity provided by blockchain systems, regulatory compliance and monitorization of records by the regulatory agencies can be improved and in case of no compliance, actions could be performed in a timely manner.
- Research and development: clinical research data throughout every step of a clinical trial could be actively monitored, the information shared between multiple stakeholders have a high classification of security and authenticity, logistical processes can also be improved, such as patient recruitment, payments, consent and authorization, etc.

It is clear that Blockchain technology can bring many improvements for the healthcare sector, in fact, by 2022 it is expected that the blockchain market in healthcare sector is valued in $500 million and those investment would be in the clinical trial management, improvement of sharing electronic records and fulfilling regulatory compliance (Hasselgren et al., 2020).

One of the essential uses of blockchain in the healthcare is, undoubtedly the clinical trials, the theme of this chapter. Specifically, the key features of blockchain technology, such as data provenance, transparency, decentralized transaction validation, and immutability, may contribute to overcome data management issues in clinical trials (Omar, Jayaraman, Salah, Yaqoob, et al., 2020). Areas of clinical trials where blockchain represents an improvement also include patient recruitment, medical data sharing and privacy, data integrity, consent traceability and transparency, as mentioned before (Omar, Jayaraman, Salah, Yaqoob, et al., 2020).

On the other hand, another important topic in authenticity in clinical trials is related to data management. Data could be altered or lost which could represent a major problem in a clinical trial setting creating an untrustworthy environment. In fact, 80% of the assays submitted to FDA are not reproductible due to the presence of various errors, such as fraud, data misrepresentation, and trial misconduct (Petre & Haï, 2018). This is one of the factors that contributes to data obtained from clinical trials not being immediately made public to key-players.

Taking all of this into consideration, to further explore the benefits, disadvantages, threats and opportunities of blockchains in clinical trials in data management, a review as conducted to map this information.

Review Methods

Research Objective

There are several studies reporting the advantages and disadvantages and applicability of blockchains in clinical trials, however the knowledge of those characteristics when applied to data security in clinical trials is lacking.

The role of this review is to map the current utilization of blockchain systems in clinical trials, particularly the data security managing system and its characteristics, such as applicability, interests of use, limitations and issues, as reported in literature.

In this section we report the methodology applied to conduct this review including the selection process.

Research Protocol

To identify potentially relevant publications a search was conducted on November 8th, 2020 in the following online bibliographic databases: PubMed, Science Direct and Google Scholar.

Backward-reference list checking was conducted to identify other relevant references.

The search was conducted using several combination of search terms in order to establish first the amount of information available related to blockchain and to clinical trials or health care sector, and secondly directly related to data security provided by a blockchain in a clinical trial setting. Therefore, several search terms were used and ultimately the search words used to retrieve studies from databases has: "blockchain" AND "Healthcare" AND "Clinical trials" AND "data security".

Data Base Selection Criteria

Search was conducted simultaneously in three data bases: PubMed, Science Direct and Google Scholar.

Pubmed database was considered, as it is one of the leading databases in healthcare content. Google Scholar database was chosen in order to bring different background and variability content sources. Science Direct database was chosen considering the high percentage of peer-review content.

Eligibility Criteria

In this review were included studies and review studies that reported the advantages and disadvantages of use of blockchain in clinical trials particularly in the data security optic. For the purpose of this study were excluded studies that merged blockchain and other technologies not related to the theme of this chapter and that targeted blockchain uses in healthcare other than clinical trials.

Information from magazines with peer-review, newspapers, conference abstracts and book chapters were excluded from this review. Were included studies from 2017 onwards since no relevant information before that year has found in the literature associated with blockchain and its uses in clinical trials.

Additionally, studies that were written in languages other than French and English were excluded. This criteria was established given the authors proficiency in the selected languages.

The study eligibility criteria are described in Table 1.

Table 1. Eligibility criteria of studies included in this work

Inclusion Criteria	Studies that address benefits and/or threats of blockchain in Clinical trials
	Studies from 2017 onwards
	Studies reported in English or French
Exclusion Criteria	Information from magazines, newspapers, conference abstracts and book chapters
	Studies that merged blockchain and other technologies not relevant to the theme of the chapter
	Studies that targeted other uses of blockchain in healthcare other than clinical trials

Study Selection Process

As mentioned above, studies were retrieved from multiple bibliographic databases resulting from a process divided into four phases: (i) screening phase, were multiple search words were used to establish the amount of studies related to the theme; (ii) identification phase, were the citations were retrieved from the several databases; (iii) screening phase, where titles and abstracts of citations were screened to select or exclude articles; (iv) duplicates screening phase, were the citations whom were considered as relevant during screening phase were checked for duplicates; (v) eligibility phase, where the full-texts of articles were read to assess their relevancy to this study.

Data Extraction and Data Synthesis

A summary of the included studies related to the theme of this review were extracted from the selected citations and the articles were categorized by the type of publication. The year of publication was also extracted from the articles.

Search Findings

The number of articles retrieved and consequent process of studies search and selection is described in Figure 1.

Figure 1. Study selection and research process.

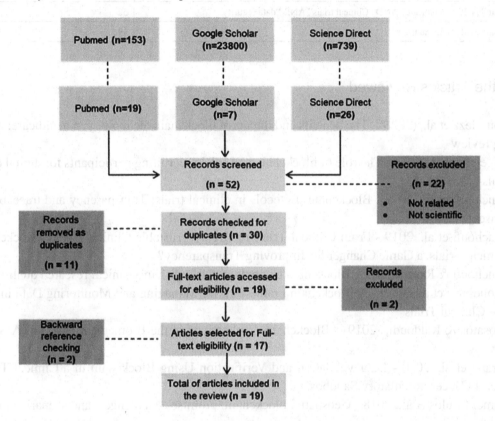

As a result from the initial search with search terms "blockchain" AND "healthcare", a total of 24692 results were obtained gathered from the three bibliographic databases used. After a combination of different search words, as described in Table 2, the search words used ("blockchain" AND "healthcare" AND "clinical trials" AND "data security") produced a total of 52 records to be screened considering the inclusion and exclusion criteria mentioned above. Therefore, these records were screened through their title and abstract and 22 were excluded considering the fact they were not related to the theme or not scientific content. Afterwards, the records were checked for duplicates and 11 records were deleted. A number of 19 records were gathered to check its full text for eligibility and 17 records were considered relevant.

Backward reference was partially conducted to gather additional studies relevant to the theme. Overall, 20 studies were included in this review.

Table 2. Results obtained using the several search terms across the three bibliographic databases (Pubmed, Science Direct and Google Scholar)

Search Terms	Number of Results (n)
"blockchain" AND "Healthcare"	24692
"blockchain" AND "Healthcare" AND "Clinical trials"	1534
"blockchain" AND "Healthcare" AND "Clinical trials" AND "security"	1130
"blockchain" AND "Healthcare" AND "Clinical trials" AND "data security"	52
"blockchain" AND "clinical trials"	19[1]

List of the Articles Reviewed

- Abu-elezz et al., (2020) - The benefits and threats of blockchain technology in healthcare: A scoping review
- Angeletti et al., 2017 - The role of blockchain and IoT in recruiting participants for digital clinical trials
- Benchoufi et al., 2017 - Blockchain protocols in clinical trials: Transparency and traceability of consent
- Benchoufi et al., 2019 - From Clinical Trials to Highly Trustable Clinical Trials: Blockchain in Clinical Trials, a Game Changer for Improving Transparency?
- Benchoufi & Ravaud, 2017. Blockchain technology for improving clinical research quality.
- Choudhury et al., 2019 - A Blockchain Framework for Managing and Monitoring Data in Multi-Site Clinical Trials
- Drosatos & Kaldoudi, (2019) - Blockchain Applications in the Biomedical Domain: A Scoping Review
- Hirano et al., 2020 - Data Validation and Verification Using Blockchain in a Clinical Trial for Breast Cancer: Regulatory Sandbox
- Kamel Boulos et al., 2018 - Geospatial blockchain: promises, challenges, and scenarios in health and healthcare
- Mackey et al., 2019 - 'Fit-for-purpose?' – challenges and opportunities for applications of blockchain technology in the future of healthcare
- Maslove et al., 2018 - Using Blockchain Technology to Manage Clinical Trials Data: A Proof-of-Concept Study
- Monrat et al., 2019 - A survey of blockchain from the perspectives of applications, challenges, and opportunities.
- Omar, Jayaraman, Salah, Simsekler, et al., 2020 - Ensuring protocol compliance and data transparency in clinical trials using Blockchain smart contracts
- Omar, Jayaraman, Salah, Yaqoob, et al., 2020 - Applications of Blockchain Technology in Clinical Trials: Reviewand Open Challenges
- Petre & Haï, 2018 - Opportunities and challenges of blockchain technology in the healthcare industry
- Radanovic et al., 2018 - Opportunities for Use of Blockchain Technology in Medicine

- Tandon et al., 2020 - Blockchain in healthcare: A systematic literature review, synthesizing framework and future research agenda
- Wong et al., 2019 - Prototype of running clinical trials in an untrustworthy environment using blockchain
- Yan Zhuang et al., 2019 - Applying Blockchain Technology to Enhance Clinical Trial Recruitment
- Yu Zhuang et al., 2018 - Applying Blockchain Technology for Health Information Exchange and Persistent Monitoring for Clinical Trials

Characteristics of the Selected Studies

As presented in Figure 2, more than 50% of the studies selected for this article were published afterwards the year of 2019 (5 published in 2019 and 6 published in 2020, therefore 11 of 19 studies selected). Additionally, 4 of the selected studies were published in 2018 and only 3 studies were published in 2017.

Figure 2. Distribution of included studies by year of publication.

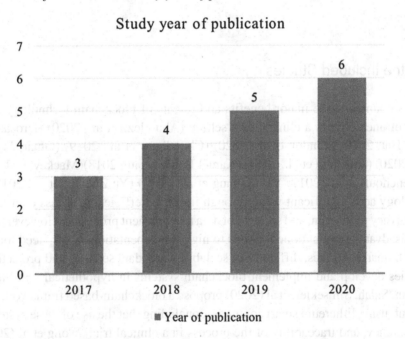

As presented in Figure 3 the selected studies for this article have a heterogenous distribution if the type of publication is considered. In fact, 3 of the studies were classified as articles, 4 as research articles, 4 as reviews, 1 as a paper, 2 as editorials, 1 as method article, 4 as research articles and 3 as proof of concept work.

Figure 3. Study type of publication

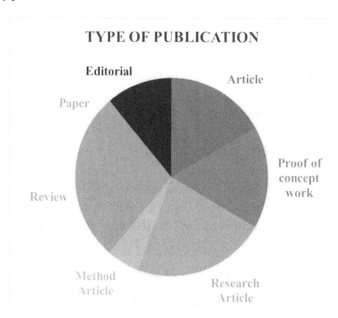

Summary of the Included Studies

Several citations enumerate the major benefits and threats of blockchain technology application in a healthcare system, including in a clinical trial setting (Abu-elezz et al., 2020) (Drosatos & Kaldoudi, 2019) (Petre & Haï, 2018) (Tandon et al., 2020) (Choudhury et al., 2019) (Omar, Jayaraman, Salah, Yaqoob, et al., 2020) (Angeletti et al., 2017) (Kamel Boulos et al., 2018)(Mackey et al., 2019) (Tandon et al., 2020)(Benchoufi et al., 2017; Yan Zhuang et al., 2019) (Yu Zhuang et al., 2018). They reflect that this technology adds significant value through improved efficiency, access control, technological advancement, privacy protection, and security of data management processes. However, in general, there are also some disadvantages mentioned related to high implementations costs, need for robust systems and specialized human resources, difficulty of scalability and data security and protection issues.

Several studies develop and implement blockchain systems in hypothetical real-life clinical trials. Omar, Jayaraman, Salah, Simsekler, et al (2020) propose a blockchain-based framework for clinical trial data management, using Ethereum smart contracts, concluding that the use of these systems assures data integrity, transparency, and traceability of the process in a clinical trial. Wong et al (2019) proposes a blockchain-based system to make data collected in the clinical trial process immutable, traceable, and potentially more trustworthy, and its resilience to data tampering. Maslove et al. (2018) explores the role of blockchain in supporting clinical trials data management and develop a proof-of-concept implementation of a patient-facing and researcher-facing system. Hirano et al (2020) validate a system that enables the security of medical data in a clinical trial using blockchain technology.

Tandon et al (2020) addresses the concerns for the improvement of regulatory compliance and security. Several important aspects are highlighted, particularly that further work needs to be done to address blockchain systems vulnerabilities and robustness, data privacy and authentication in shared storages.

BLOCKCHAIN IN CLINICAL TRIALS

As mentioned before, the interest of the applicability of blockchain systems in the healthcare sector has been increasing since 2016. In fact, this growing interest was also palpable through the research made for this chapter in Pubmed database, using the search words "blockchain" AND "healthcare" 153 results were obtained. This represents an increase of about 139% of the number of citations published in this database since 2018. Additionally, using the search words "blockchain" and "clinical trials" in Pubmed database 19 citations were obtained, which also represents an increasing number of citations since 2018 related to clinical trials and blockchain systems.

Blockchain Advantages and Disadvantages in Clinical Trials

Clinical trials require data and information to be well organized and categorized for the submission of the findings to the regulatory agency for the approval of the drug in test. Such compliance can be time consuming and resource consuming considering the amount of data, number of individuals and entities involved, and therefore it is a process particularly prone to human and system errors.

Blockchain can be the solution for the majority of errors that happen in clinical trials. Therefore, this technology can solve human errors such as: inconsistent data entry (transcription and transposition errors) and missing signatures/authorizations and system errors such as loss of data. Having a blockchain system that allows, in real time, the users in the network to verify, identify and solve the errors, can be a major improvement in clinical trials.

In fact, the most pressing challenges in clinical trials include access and management of clinical trial data; data integrity and provenance for clinical trial processes for regulatory purposes; updating and maintaining patient consent; and patient recruitment and enrolment, reproducibility of results, protocol compliance and data sharing (Mackey et al., 2019) (Omar, Jayaraman, Salah, Simsekler, et al., 2020).

Blockchain systems have the ability of transforming this process by revolutionizing the way data is stored, transmitted and managed throughout the network of participants, investigators and entities engaged in a clinical trial. Therefore, blockchain can lead to the structuration of a global community gathering all the key player involved in a clinical trial setting, such as researchers and patient communities, social networks and Internet of Things data flows with features of individual granularity, decentralization and security and with transparent interactions to ensure easier and more transparent analysis (Benchoufi & Ravaud, 2017). An additional asset is the possibility of a closer monitorization of patient health data tracking and health status (Abu-elezz et al., 2020).

Disadvantages of blockchain system in clinical trials are related to organizational difficulties, such as installations and transactions costs, operability issues and the need of specialized technical resources to manage these systems scalability issues, authorization and security issues, high energy consumption, and slow processing speeds. It is important to emphasize that the interoperability is also one of the major challenges for the blockchain adoption due to the lack of trust between healthcare organizations and lesser number of IT (Information Technology) professionals available to implement the technology. Lack of sufficient technical skills while implementing blockchain technologies may lead to disastrous consequences (Abu-elezz et al., 2020).

The principal advantages and disadvantages of the utilization of blockchain technology in clinical trials is summarized in Table 3.

Table 3. Advantages and disadvantages of blockchain technology used in clinical trials

Advantages	Monitorization
	Transparency
	Immutability
	Decentralization
	Real-time consent
	Real time access to all key players involved
Disadvantages	General access to all key players (need to constrain access depending on its user)
	Implementation system difficulties
	Need of specialized technical resources
	High levels of protection needed
	Implementation costs
	Scalabilities difficulties
	Appropriate software and hardware

Advantages of Blockchain Applied to Data Security in Clinical Trials

Considering the four main assets of blockchain systems in a clinical trial setting monitorization, transparency, immutability, and decentralization, blockchain technology might also prove to be useful in supporting or even supplanting the traditional data infrastructure used in clinical trials. Blockchain enables to establish a permanent record agreed upon by all participating parties, therefore has a tremendous potential to mitigate some of the threats related to data validity.

Taking all of this into consideration, in a real-world setting blockchain technology might have the following characteristics in terms of data security:

- Establish a more difficult precedent to falsifications or adulterations of data, since every transaction is monitored, time-stamped, transparent and in real time;
- Enables permanent recordings, a very desirable asset for clinical trial auditing;
- More compatibility between the results presented to the regulatory agency and later published in scientific publications;
- More efficient volunteer recruitment and protocol attribution;
- More accurate access and recording of data;
- Overall, less time consuming and more, efficient process of data recording, processing and storage.

Ultimately, blockchain systems in terms of data security, specifically, address the questions of data validity, integrity and reproducibility and therefore stands to achieve more confidence and veracity in the results obtained in a clinical trial (Maslove et al., 2018).

Types of Blockchain and Their Applicability in Clinical Trials

Blockchain can be applied in the healthcare sector due to its many characteristics such as immutability, decentralization, traceability and transparency (Abu-elezz et al., 2020). This technology has a potential in protecting sensitive information such as patient related information (medical records and personal information). Therefore, these characteristics have the most relevant interest in the clinical trials setting.

The potential of the Blockchain applicability to clinical trials relies on the type of Blockchain technology used. As described by Abu-elezz et al., (2020) there are three different design types considering their access permissions: public (permissionless), private (permissioned) and hybrid blockchains. Public blockchains allow anyone to participate and allow a complete transparent view to anyone participating in it, and there is no control by any single user on identity. On the other hand, private blockchains are only open for those who are invited to join the network, but nevertheless, the process remains transparent for everyone included in the network. Finally, it is important to characterize the third different type of blockchain. Hybrid Blockchains are a type of blockchains that are flexible because they allow the users to choose the data they want to be made available for the public and the data they want to be kept private for them (Abu-elezz et al., 2020) . To be easily understood, they can be seen as a public blockchain where a private network is hosted, where all of the users only have access to the data that is available for them. Taking all of this into consideration, hybrid blockchains associated with smart contracts could represent a solid method to use in a clinical trial setting since it has the possibility to select a specific amount of data to be available or kept private to the public, as previously mentioned (Kamel Boulos et al., 2018). This platform is more flexible compared to other types of blockchain because it enables the consensus mechanisms to be controlled by selected users in a decentralized manner, which in other hand, makes its structure more vulnerable to information (Omar, Jayaraman, Salah, Yaqoob, et al., 2020).

Smart Contracts

Another major contribution of blockchain technology in a clinical trial setting is the ability to provide in real time consent by the patient to protocol alterations by the sponsor (Petre & Haï, 2018). This process is followed through smart contracts.

Smart contracts are a type of code that is stored, executed, and verified on a blockchain, and also has the ability to act on clinical data sharing, either through storing the data itself or instructions on who can access that data (Maslove et al., 2018)(Kamel Boulos et al., 2018). Smart contracts can play several roles, including encoding the business logic for an application, ensuring that preconditions for action are met before itis executed, and enforcing permissions for an action. As described by Maslove et al. (2018), smart contracts run on a blockchain, they have unique characteristics compared with other types of software. First, the program itself is recorded on the blockchain, which imparts the blockchain's characteristic permanence and resistance to censorship. Second, the program can control blockchain assets. Third, the program is executed by the blockchain, meaning it will always execute as written and no one can interfere with its operation.

Since Smart Contracts all transactions follow rigorous protocols under secure conditions, their use has the possibility to ensure data provenance and create immutable audit trails, and potentially add more integrity and confidence to a clinical trial, by reducing, prevent and detect fraudulent activities and errors (Yu Zhuang et al., 2018).

Benchoufi & Ravaud (2017), described a Smart Contract example applied to a clinical trial setting. In their example, each of the clinical trial steps (trial protocol setup, patient enrollment, data collection, trial monitoring, data management, data analysis, study report, diffusion of results) as described in Figure 4, can be chained together in a preceding order, consolidating a transparent trial and preventing *a posteriori* reconstruction or beautification of data by granting several levels of access. This example represents a piece of code that holds a programmatically written contract between as many parties as needed, without any trusted third party, and that executes algorithmically according to the terms provided by the contracting parties, making the process more automatic, transparent and less prone to falsifications (Benchoufi & Ravaud, 2017).

Blockchain Systems Protection Against Liabilities

Blockchain technology allows the users to track more closely and in real time, the series of events occurring in clinical trials. This is crucial when we are talking about security and protection. By tracing and controlling the processes of clinical trials, Blockchain can prevent frauds or at least discourage them, because they become traceable and averted. But this technology cannot protect against every threat, such as data invention or data falsification since it only protects the information with time stamps and traceability once the information has entered the system (Benchoufi et al., 2019).

Other threats to the validity of clinical trials data stand to undermine the veracity of a clinical trial. These threats could be defined as internal, when they occur within the users of a blockchain, or external, when they came from outside the network of blockchain users, for example in a cyber-attack.

Maslove et al (2018) identified some of these threats. Data can be altered or lost, either accidentally or by nefarious intent; there is a risk that the published analysis is not a true representation of the analysis that was initially planned due for example to lack of monitorization resulting in a bias of the information presented to the regulatory agencies and later published in scientific publications; and lastly, data may be fabricated, manipulated, or duplicated by researchers committing outright fraud.

Some of the functionalities of the Blockchain technology like timestamping, time-ordering and the smart contracts can define a roadmap, that helps tracking errors and frauds. Clinical trials can benefit a lot from using these roadmaps (Benchoufi et al., 2019).

Omar, Jayaraman, Salah, Simsekler, et al., (2020) developed a blockchain-based solution and simulated several data mistakes or internal malicious attempts. These were stopped since the recorded data is validated using consensus algorithms resulting in a tamper-proof system.

As described by Omar, Jayaraman, Salah, Simsekler, et al., (2020) one of the biggest threats to the blockchain technology are the selfish mining external attacks. Blockchains are vulnerable to 51% of these attacks. This generally occurs when malicious blocks are higher than honest blocks in a network. As a result, one of the possibilities is that a new block gets attached to the malicious chain. This strategy is called selfish mining because selfish miners keep their blocks private and reveal them to the public only when the private chain is longer than the current public chain, and thus, it may be accepted by all miners in the network (Omar, Jayaraman, Salah, Simsekler, et al., 2020).

SOLUTIONS AND RECOMMENDATIONS

Clinical trials require data and information to be well organized and categorized for the submission of the findings to the regulatory agency for the approval of the drug in test. Such compliance can be time and resource consuming considering the amount of data, number of individuals and entities involved, and therefore it is a process particularly prone to human and system errors.

In fact, the most pressing challenges in clinical trials include access and management of clinical trial data; data integrity and provenance for clinical trial processes for regulatory purposes; updating and maintaining patient consent; patient recruitment and enrolment, reproducibility of results, protocol compliance and data sharing.

From the review conducted it is possible to point out that the operational benefits of implementing a blockchain technology to conduct a clinical trial are hardly contestable. Indeed, this technology solves many logistical constrains in terms of data sharing, communication between each involved parties and data storage and traceability.

Blockchain certainly represent a technology capable of managing and improving the information system in the healthcare sector and, particularly, in the clinical trial area, by allowing a more transparent, real time and authentic process when submitting a new drug for regulatory approval. Blockchain allows several levels of optimization regarding the organization aspects of a clinical trial (number of participants, number of departments and their areas of action) and in an individual level (the patient has more control and monitorization of his own progression), also.

Reproducibility and data integrity are crucial factors in a clinical trial setting. Regulatory agencies not only shall be able to trace back and identify the players responsible for any information in a clinical trial environment, but also be able to trust the validity of that content. In fact, 80% of the assays submitted to FDA are not reproductible (Petre & Haï, 2018). Blockchain improves the traceability of data and therefore stands to tackle this issue.

Blockchain offers a valuable contribution in addressing this problem since every transaction is validated using consensus algorithms and identity signatures with identification and date stamps.

Notwithstanding, blockchain cannot address a problem that still could affect the integrity and veracity of a clinical trial. In fact, if the information itself introduced in a software is wrong or misleading, this technology cannot address this issue. Blockchain, only, can track this wrong data and timestamp it. There is yet a need to find a solution within the design and operational side of a clinical trial to tackle this question.

Considering the four main assets of blockchain systems in a clinical trial setting, monitorization, transparency, immutability, and decentralization, blockchain technology might also prove useful in supporting or even supplanting the traditional data infrastructure used in clinical trials. Blockchain enables to establish a permanent record agreed upon by all participating parties, therefore has a tremendous potential to mitigate some of the threats related to data validity.

Disadvantages of blockchain system in clinical trials are related to organizational difficulties, such as installations and transactions costs, operability issues and the need of specialized technical resources to manage these systems scalability issues, authorization, security issues, high energy consumption, and slow processing speeds.

Overall, this technology has the ability of producing a clinical trial more transparent and tamper proofing by providing authentic validated data, and therefore, producing a more reliable and credible clinical trial. Nevertheless, there are some technical issues that need to be overcome, such as scalability, implementation costs, the need of technical resources and processing difficulties of implementation and operation. Solving all these issues, we can expect blockchain technology to be fully adopted in clinical trials, with substantial improvements.

FUTURE RESEARCH DIRECTIONS

Work needs to be done to establish the major implications in security data when applying blockchain technology in a real-word clinical trial setting and in generalized conditions of use, since as we move forward through the several phases of a clinical trial more data, more participants and more complexity of results are expected and thereby there is a need of a robust and reliable system to maintain the necessary trust levels to present the findings of a clinical trial to support the process of drug approval to a regulatory agency.

On a regulatory level, it is also important that key regulatory agencies such as FDA and EMA, provide guidelines to construct a blockchain managing system in clinical trials, in order to establish uniformity between the several systems used by different companies and guarantee the overall compliance with ethical, regulatory and safety requirements of a clinical trial.

Covid-19 pandemic lockdown revolutionized the use of technology and overall ability to distance and virtual communication in healthcare. Because of the pandemic, in one year, technology evolved exponentially, in a way never seen before. Given this opportunity, the bases of a digital revolution in healthcare are in order. However, it is important to take into consideration the technology literacy of healthcare professionals and volunteers in clinical trials. In fact, in a survey conducted by HSCB to Bitcoin users about Blockchain, 80% of the percentage of consumers that are familiarized with the term didn't know or fully understand the concept (Radanović & Likić, 2018). Therefore, digital education and technological formation of each player in clinical trials should be a priority to the implementation of blockchain systems. This is essential for the correct adoption of the technology in the clinical trials and if it doesn´t happen, the errors that will occur, can be disastrous.

On the other hand, considering the high level of investment and the need of technological specialized work force to design and run a blockchain system, investments and grants should be also created to incentivize not only the adoption of these systems, but also to educate specialized work force. There aren´t many specialized professionals that know how to work with this technology and that fully understand it, so, this digital formation must be given to the healthcare professionals, in order to have the best results possible. Of course, this formation involves a large investment, so this must be taken into consideration.

Lastly, considering the importance and impact of the data stored in a clinical trial not only on a regulatory level but also on a personal level considering the number of volunteers involved, additional work shall also be made to establish the security of a blockchain system applied in a clinical trial setting to external hazards such as cyber-attacks.

CONCLUSION

Ultimately, blockchain systems represent a technology capable of managing and improving the information organization system in the healthcare sector, specifically in the clinical trial area, by allowing a more transparent, real-time, and exact process when submitting a new drug for regulatory approval. Blockchain allows several optimization levels regarding the organizational aspects of a clinical trial (number of participants, number of departments, and their areas of action) and individual level (the patient has more control and monitorization of his progression). These advantages also reflect data security optic since this technology can produce a more transparent and tamper-proofing clinical trial by providing accurate, validated data, producing more reliable and credible outcomes from the research conducted in a clinical trial. Nevertheless, some technical issues need to be overcome, such as scalability, implementation costs, the need for technical resources, and processing difficulties of implementation and operation of blockchain technology.

ACKNOWLEDGMENT

This research received no specific grant from any funding agency in the public, commercial, or not-for-profit sectors.

REFERENCES

Abu-elezz, I., Hassan, A., Nazeemudeen, A., Househ, M., & Abd-alrazaq, A. (2020). The benefits and threats of blockchain technology in healthcare: A scoping review. *International Journal of Medical Informatics*, *142*(August), 104246. doi:10.1016/j.ijmedinf.2020.104246 PMID:32828033

Agbo, C., Mahmoud, Q., & Eklund, J. (2019). Blockchain Technology in Healthcare: A Systematic Review. *Health Care*, *7*(2), 56. doi:10.3390/healthcare7020056 PMID:30987333

Angeletti, F., Chatzigiannakis, I., & Vitaletti, A. (2017). The role of blockchain and IoT in recruiting participants for digital clinical trials. *2017 25th International Conference on Software, Telecommunications and Computer Networks, SoftCOM 2017*. 10.23919/SOFTCOM.2017.8115590

Benchoufi, M., Altman, D., & Ravaud, P. (2019). From Clinical Trials to Highly Trustable Clinical Trials: Blockchain in Clinical Trials, a Game Changer for Improving Transparency? *Frontiers in Blockchain*, *2*(December), 1–6. doi:10.3389/fbloc.2019.00023

Benchoufi, M., Porcher, R., & Ravaud, P. (2017). Blockchain protocols in clinical trials: Transparency and traceability of consent. *F1000 Research*, *6*, 66. doi:10.12688/f1000research.10531.1 PMID:29167732

Benchoufi, M., & Ravaud, P. (2017). Blockchain technology for improving clinical research quality. *Trials*, *18*(1), 1–5. doi:10.118613063-017-2035-z PMID:28724395

Chen, Jarrell, Carpenter, Cohen, & Huang. (2019). Blockchain in Healthcare: A Patient-Centered Model. *Biomedical Journal of Scientific & Technical Research*, *20*(3), 15017–15022. PMID:31565696

Choudhury, O., Fairoza, N., Sylla, I., & Das, A. (2019). A Blockchain Framework for Managing and Monitoring Data in Multi-Site Clinical Trials. *ArXiv*, 1–13.

Deloitte. (2020). *Intelligent drug discovery About the Deloitte Centre for Health Solutions*. Author.

Drosatos, G., & Kaldoudi, E. (2019). Blockchain Applications in the Biomedical Domain: A Scoping Review. *Computational and Structural Biotechnology Journal*, *17*, 229–240. doi:10.1016/j.csbj.2019.01.010 PMID:30847041

Hasselgren, A., Kralevska, K., Gligoroski, D., Pedersen, S. A., & Faxvaag, A. (2020). Blockchain in healthcare and health sciences—A scoping review. *International Journal of Medical Informatics, 134*(May), 104040. doi:10.1016/j.ijmedinf.2019.104040

Hirano, T., Motohashi, T., Okumura, K., Takajo, K., Kuroki, T., Ichikawa, D., Matsuoka, Y., Ochi, E., & Ueno, T. (2020). Data validation and verification using blockchain in a clinical trial for breast cancer: Regulatory sandbox. *Journal of Medical Internet Research, 22*(6), 1–21. doi:10.2196/18938 PMID:32340974

Hussien, H. M., Yasin, S. M., Udzir, S. N. I., Zaidan, A. A., & Zaidan, B. B. (2019). A Systematic Review for Enabling of Develop a Blockchain Technology in Healthcare Application: Taxonomy, Substantially Analysis, Motivations, Challenges, Recommendations and Future Direction. *Journal of Medical Systems, 43*(10), 320. Advance online publication. doi:10.100710916-019-1445-8 PMID:31522262

Kamel Boulos, M. N., Wilson, J. T., & Clauson, K. A. (2018). Geospatial blockchain: Promises, challenges, and scenarios in health and healthcare. *International Journal of Health Geographics, 17*(1), 1–10. doi:10.118612942-018-0144-x PMID:29973196

Mackey, T. K., Kuo, T. T., Gummadi, B., Clauson, K. A., Church, G., Grishin, D., Obbad, K., Barkovich, R., & Palombini, M. (2019). "Fit-for-purpose?" - Challenges and opportunities for applications of blockchain technology in the future of healthcare. *BMC Medicine, 17*(1), 1–17. doi:10.118612916-019-1296-7 PMID:30914045

Maslove, D. M., Klein, J., Brohman, K., & Martin, P. (2018). Using Blockchain Technology to Manage Clinical Trials Data: A Proof-of-Concept Study. *JMIR Medical Informatics, 6*(4), e11949. doi:10.2196/11949 PMID:30578196

Meunier, S. (2018). Blockchain 101: What is Blockchain and How Does This Revolutionary Technology Work? What is Blockchain and How Does This Revolutionary Technology Work? In *Transforming Climate Finance and Green Investment with Blockchains*. Elsevier Inc. doi:10.1016/B978-0-12-814447-3.00003-3

Monrat, A. A., Schelén, O., & Andersson, K. (2019). A survey of blockchain from the perspectives of applications, challenges, and opportunities. *IEEE Access: Practical Innovations, Open Solutions, 7*, 117134–117151. doi:10.1109/ACCESS.2019.2936094

Omar, I. A., Jayaraman, R., Salah, K., Simsekler, M. C. E., Yaqoob, I., & Ellahham, S. (2020). Ensuring protocol compliance and data transparency in clinical trials using Blockchain smart contracts. *BMC Medical Research Methodology, 20*(1), 1–17. doi:10.118612874-020-01109-5 PMID:32894068

Omar, I. A., Jayaraman, R., Salah, K., Yaqoob, I., & Ellahham, S. (2020). Applications of Blockchain Technology in Clinical Trials: Review and Open Challenges. *Arabian Journal for Science and Engineering*. Advance online publication. doi:10.100713369-020-04989-3

Petre, A., & Haï, N. (2018). Opportunités et enjeux de la technologie blockchain dans le secteur de la santé. *Medecine Sciences, 34*(10), 852–856. doi:10.1051/medsci/2018204 PMID:30451661

PwC. (2018). A Prescription for Blockchain and Healthcare: Reinvent or be Reinvented. *PriceWaterhouseCoopers*, 19. www.pwc.com/us/en/health-industries.html%0A©

Radanović, I., & Likić, R. (2018). Opportunities for Use of Blockchain Technology in Medicine. *Applied Health Economics and Health Policy*, *16*(5), 583–590. doi:10.100740258-018-0412-8 PMID:30022440

Smetanin, S., Ometov, A., Komarov, M., Masek, P., & Koucheryavy, Y. (2020). Blockchain evaluation approaches: State-of-the-art and future perspective. *Sensors (Switzerland)*, *20*(12), 1–20. doi:10.339020123358 PMID:32545719

Tan, L., Tivey, D., Kopunic, H., Babidge, W., Langley, S., & Maddern, G. (2020). Part 2: Blockchain technology in health care. *ANZ Journal of Surgery*, *90*(12), 2415–2419. doi:10.1111/ans.16455 PMID:33236489

Tandon, A., Dhir, A., Islam, N., & Mäntymäki, M. (2020). Blockchain in healthcare: A systematic literature review, synthesizing framework and future research agenda. *Computers in Industry*, *122*, 103290. Advance online publication. doi:10.1016/j.compind.2020.103290

Wong, D. R., Bhattacharya, S., & Butte, A. J. (2019). Prototype of running clinical trials in an untrustworthy environment using blockchain. *Nature Communications*, *10*(1), 1–8. doi:10.103841467-019-08874-y PMID:30796226

Zhuang, Y., Sheets, L. R., Shae, Z., Chen, Y. W., Tsai, J. J. P., & Shyu, C. R. (2019). Applying Blockchain Technology to Enhance Clinical Trial Recruitment. *AMIA ... Annual Symposium Proceedings. AMIA Symposium*, *2019*, 1276–1285.

Zhuang, Yu., Sheets, L., Shae, Z., Tsai, J. J. P., & Shyu, C. R. (2018). Applying Blockchain Technology for Health Information Exchange and Persistent Monitoring for Clinical Trials. *AMIA ... Annual Symposium Proceedings. AMIA Symposium*, *2018*, 1167–1175.

KEY TERMS AND DEFINITIONS

Blockchain: A decentralized, distributed ledger technology that records the provenance of a digital asset.

Clinical Trial: A research study performed in people that are aimed at evaluating a medical, surgical, or behavioral intervention.

Data Security: The process of protecting data from unauthorized access and data corruption throughout all lifecycle.

Decentralization: The transfer of control of an activity or organization to several local offices or authorities rather than one single one.

Immutability: The state of not changing or being unable to be changed.

Traceability: The quality of having an origin or course of development that may be found or followed throughout all lifecycle.

Transparency: The quality of operating in such a way that it is easy for others to see what actions or changes are performed.

Chapter 35
A Cloud–Assisted Proxy Re–Encryption Scheme for Efficient Data Sharing Across IoT Systems

Muthukumaran V.
VIT University, India

Ezhilmaran D.
VIT University, India

ABSTRACT

In recent years, the growth of IoT applications is rapid in nature and widespread across several domains. This tremendous growth of IoT applications leads to various security and privacy concerns. The existing security algorithms fail to provide improved security features across IoT devices due to its resource constrained nature (inability to handle a huge amount of data). In this context, the authors propose a cloud-assisted proxy re-encryption scheme for efficient data sharing across IoT systems. The proposed approach solves the root extraction problem using near-ring. This improves the security measures of the system. The security analysis of the proposed approach states that it provides improved security with lesser computational overheads.

INTRODUCTION

The term Internet of things (IoT) is defined as a network through which the data is collected, processed and analyzed to provide various services using a series of interconnected devices (Zhou et al., 2017 & Abomhara et al., 2014). The growing adoption of IoT techniques makes its application prevalent across various domains, especially with real-life applications. Some of the major applications of IoT system include smart homes, smart cities, transportation, industrial manufacturing, underwater resource management, and healthcare systems. The data generated from the IoT applications are highly voluminous,

DOI: 10.4018/978-1-6684-7132-6.ch035

which the existing IoT devices fail to store and process. This is due to the resource constrained nature of the IoT devices. That is IoT devices possess limited storage and computational capabilities so that it fails to store and process highly voluminous sensor data at real-time. Due to this motive, the IoT devices are integrated with effective middleware's such as cloud computing to outsource storage and computation processes. That is the data collected from IoT devices are stored across the cloud computing infrastructures for further processing and decision-making purposes. In general, IoT devices make use of cloud-based infrastructure (IaaS) services, as it does not only require data storage facilities but also need efficient data processing and computation capabilities (Tao et al., 2014 & Qu et al., 2016). This creates the requirement of efficient security mechanisms for secure management of cloud based IoT systems.

Cloud computing is a unique paradigm offering a wide variety of services across the internet through a series of interconnected computing resources (Youseff et al., 2008). It enables one to store and access confidential data across the internet instead of their local system setups. The NIST definition of cloud computing states that Cloud computing is a model for enabling ubiquitous, convenient, on-demand network access to a shared pool of configurable computing resources (e.g., networks, servers, storage, applications, and services) that can be rapidly provisioned and released with minimal management effort or service provider interaction (Tsai et al., 2010). In other words, the term cloud computing offers on-demand network access services that can be used from anywhere and at any time. The on-demand self-service, broad network access, resource pooling, rapid elasticity, measured services are the key features of the cloud computing systems.

Software as a Service (SaaS), Platform as s Service (PaaS) and Infrastructure as a Service (IaaS) are the three major services provided by the cloud computing systems. The term SaaS offers software services to the cloud users. NetSuite and Salesforce customer relationship management (CRM) are the some of the examples of SaaS. PaaS enables the cloud users to run their applications across cloud computing platforms without the use of their local system setup. Google App Engine and App Stratos are the examples of SaaS. Infrastructure services (IaaS) is otherwise known as Everything as a Service or Hardware as a Service. In IaaS a complete computing platform made up of virtual machines connected to a network is given to the users. Virtual machine (VM) is a software program or an operating system that forms the concept of the IaaS systems. In simple terms, a virtual machine is a guest created from the host machine (another computing environment). A single host can contain multiple virtual machines at a single point of time. Windows Azure and Amazon EC2, Google Compute Engine (GCE) are the best examples of IaaS (JoSEP et al., 2010).

In IaaS, the end users log into the dashboard and raise VM requests. Whenever the cloud server receives the VM request it decides the hypervisor nodes and creates the virtual machine. A virtual machine is configured with the user- defined CPU and storage specifications. Upon the successful creation of the virtual machines, the end users make use of the cloud infrastructure services for an infinite period of time. SaaS and PaaS offer users with the static services to the system users with specified time limits. This dynamic nature of the IaaS services creates the development of high performance and permanent availability measures across the cloud computing environment (Zhang et al., 2010). Thus, the use of proxy re-encryption techniques can reduce the end user overheads and provides improved services to the cloud users.

As, the power of cloud server is finite and the capability of IoT devices are resource constrained in nature. The integration of cloud and IoT systems provide better solution to manage growing amount of IoT device data. In today's world, the applications of IoT is widespread and it ranges from personal data to data sensed from a particular application environment. In such cases, the attacker can easily collect the data from IoT devices and create serious security threats. Therefore, security threats are comparatively greater in the IoT environment rather than normal systems. The advent of modern IoT applications created an increasing amount of importance for the security of the IoT systems (Weber R.H., 2010). IoT security usually deals with sensor data generated, originated or extracted from the IoT network system. One can quantify and measure the security of the IoT systems through the study of IoT network security events. The data that shows abnormality with respect to security, safety, privacy and trust are denoted as IoT security data. In other words, the data that indicates IoT network security events is termed as IoT network security-related data.

However, there exists a vast variety of challenges in secure data collection across IoT cloud systems in the modern era of big data and the next generation of network systems (5G). In the perspective of big data, the quantity of data shared, originated and produced across IoT sensor networks are enormous in amount. The IoT network data possess 5V such as volume, velocity, value, variety and veracity characteristics, which creates tremendous difficulties across IoT cloud systems in terms of security and privacy (Sivaraman et al., 2015 and Kozlov et al., 2012). Further, 5G communications are heterogeneous in nature and support device to device, machine to machine and other communication technologies. In general, 5G networks consists of different types of networks such as wireless sensor Networks (WSN), mobile cellular networks and Mobile Adhoc Networks (MANET) which makes IoT cloud security a difficult process. This is due to the reason that IoT systems work on the basis of WSN, MANET and mobile networks. Thus, in order to evaluate the IoT security features the current IoT security mechanisms for a single network has to be redesigned for large-scale heterogeneous networks. At the same time, the security mechanisms for IoT cloud systems are currently understudied and it is a hot and difficult research topic (Schurgot et al., 2015).

The passive security threats include network attacks on smart devices such as smart televisions and refrigerators. The more aggressive attack includes security threats on vehicle tracking systems and healthcare systems which may even threaten the user's life. Further, the user data collected from IoT devices may lead to various privacy concerns. Even though, the emergence of IoT technologies provide reasonable services in the other hand it has serious security threats. Hence, it is necessary to maintain the property of security across IoT systems without the leakage user's sensitive information's (Hwang et al., 2015 and Bertino et al., 2016).

At present there exists a variety of security mechanisms. However, it is impossible to apply the existing algorithms to the IoT devices. This is due to the reason that the existing security mechanisms are difficult to use in downsized, lightweight, resource constrained IoT devices. Which can complicate the network structure with infinite number of nodes. Rather than introducing lightweight encryption algorithm for IoT devices in this work we define a proxy re-encryption scheme which reduces the number of encryption and decryption counts of the lightweight devices. The proposed approach presents a secure and efficient method of proxy re-encryption to solve twisted root extraction problem using near ring. An overview of the proxy re-encryption scheme is given in figure 1.

The passive security threats include network attacks on smart devices such as smart televisions and refrigerators. The more aggressive attack includes security threats on vehicle tracking systems and healthcare systems which may even threaten the user's life. Further, the user data collected from IoT devices may lead to various privacy concerns. Even though the emergence of IoT technologies provides reasonable services, on the other hand, it has serious security threats. Hence, it is necessary to maintain the property of security across IoT systems without the leakage user's sensitive information's (Hwang et al., 2015 and Bertino et al., 2016).

Figure 1. Proxy re-encryption in IoT systems

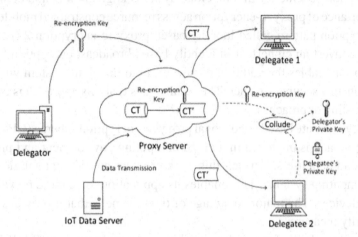

At present, there exists a variety of security mechanisms. However, it is impossible to apply the existing algorithms to IoT devices. This is due to the reason that the existing security mechanisms are difficult to use in downsized, lightweight, resource-constrained IoT devices. Which can complicate the network structure with an infinite number of nodes. Rather than introducing a lightweight encryption algorithm for IoT devices in this work, we define a proxy re-encryption scheme which reduces the number of encryption and decryption counts of the lightweight devices. The proposed approach presents a secure and efficient method of proxy re-encryption to solve the twisted root extraction problem using near ring. An overview of the proxy re-encryption scheme is given in figure 1.

The key contribution of the proposed work is summarized as follows:

1. First, we define a cloud assisted proxy re-encryption scheme for cloud based IoT systems. This reduces the workload of the end users and improves the complexity measures of the system.
2. Next, we briefly design the security analysis of the proposed system. This improves security of the system and prevents various attacks such as chosen ciphertext attack and equivalent private key attack.

The paper is organized as follows: Section 1 provides introduction to the proposed system. Related works are defined in section 2. Section 3 describes the preliminaries and a clear description to the proposed approach is given in section 4. Section 5 provides the security analysis of the proposed approach and section 6 provides conclusion and future directions.

RELATED WORKS

A timing enabled proxy re-encryption scheme for E-health system is given in (Vijayakumar et al., 2018). This work prevents the security threats relating to IoT systems through the implementation of planning empowered intermediary re-encryption techniques. It enables only the authorized users to gain access to the devices for a specific period of time. Further it makes use of both the searchable encryption and proxy re-encryption techniques.

A proxy re-encryption scheme for mobile cloud systems is given in (Zhou et al., 2016). This work emphasizes the importance of proxy re-encryption across resource constrained mobile devices. It provides a new proxy re-encryption pattern called Identity based proxy re-encryption 2 (IBPRE2). It enables a authorized proxy to convert an ciphertext in identity based broadcast encryption to identity based encryption. This approach enables the addition of new users to the cloud system without the decryption of actual data contents in a secured manner. The result states that this approach is comparatively secure and efficient than existing approaches.

A ciphertext policy attribute based conditional proxy re-encryption scheme (CPRE) is given in (Yang et al., 2016). This approach is deployed in a cloud computing environment and provides fine-grained data access to the cloud data users. Further, this work provides an efficient solution to user revocation problem in cloud computing systems. This enables its application to be more prevalent across resource constrained mobile devices. The major advantage of the scheme is that it provides better performance with improved security measures.

A secure data sharing scheme for cloud assisted IoT systems is given in (Mollah et al., 2017). This approach enables the IoT devices to securely share their data across cloud assisted IoT platforms. Further, this approach adopts searching scheme which enables the users to securely search their data cloud assisted IoT platforms. The result shoes that this approach could be efficiently used across IoT systems.

A light weight attribute based encryption scheme for IoT system is given in (Yao et al., 2015). It provides a lightweight attribute based encryption technique with no-pairings for improved security and privacy across IoT systems. The major objective of this work is to achieve secure data sharing and storage across IoT environment. The security of this scheme is based elliptic curve cryptography Diffie-Hellman assumption rather than Bilinear Diffie-Hellman approach. It compares the communication and computational overheads with the existing ABE techniques and provides comparatively better results.

A cloud assisted IoT based healthcare framework was given in (Yeh et al 2015). This approach deals with cloud reciprocity problem and provides efficient solution to it. It makes use of symmetric key cryptographic system across wireless body sensors. This work provides better performance measures.

An efficient identity based revocable proxy re-encryption scheme using cloud computing is given in (Abomhara, M. and Koien, G.M., 2014). In general, Identity based encryption techniques eliminate the need for expensive certificate verification process. However, the process of user revocation remains to be the major issue across certificate based verification techniques. Because, whenever the ciphertext is updated it is difficult to revoke and update the attributes present at the certificate. This work provides an effective solution to the above mentioned issue. It presents a cloud-based revocable Identity-based proxy re-encryption scheme (CR-IB-PRE) with user revocation and delegation properties. In this work, the user access policies are updated by the cloud server in a regular time intervals. That is the cloud server re-encrypt the user data for every particular time interval so that the user revoked cannot access the data for the next period of time interval. This work could be applied to several practical applications such as subscription based cloud storage services and many more. This scheme offers reduced communication and computational efficiencies in comparison to the existing techniques with private key generators. This work makes use of the public key generator to generate a constant size private key and the process of ciphertext update is delegated to the proxy cloud server. The security of the scheme is proven under the standard security model.

Ciphertext-policy Attribute based Proxy Re-encryption Encryption (CP-ABPRE) is given in [26]. Proxy re-encryption is a trusted scheme through which the data owner outsources the access rights to the trusted cloud server to perform the data re-encryption process in a confidential manner. It enables the users with resource constrained devices such as mobile devices to outsource the computational processes. The CP-ABPRE scheme given in this work makes use of proxy re-encryption with attribute based encryption techniques. Such that a proxy server performs the encryption process associated with a access policy to another encryption process with a new access policy. The inability to achieve CCA security remains to be the open problem across the existing proxy re-encryption techniques. This work solves the issue through the integration of dual system encryption technique with selective proof technique. It make use of monotonic access structure with composite order bilinear group which makes this approach to be CCA secure against standard security model. This work is further improved to attain more efficiency during re-encryption key generation and re-encryption phase.

A key-policy attribute based proxy re-encryption scheme was given in (Do et al., 2011). This work is intended to achieve improved data confidentiality and fine grained access control properties across cloud computing environment. It divides the data content in to the header and the body. Further, this approach performs the delegation of decryption process using type based proxy re-encryption process.

A ciphertext policy attribute based encryption with chosen security is given in (Liang et al 2013). This scheme enables a trusted proxy server to perform the data decryption process using attribute based encryption technique. That is the proxy server decrypts the outsourced data associated with an access policy to its corresponding plaintext using attribute based encryption techniques. It assures that the proxy server performs the outsourced decryption in a confidential manner without knowing any information on its underlying identities. Further, this work makes an attempt to solve chosen ciphertext attack. This scheme is constructed using random oracle model with any kind of monotonic access structures. This work is proved to be secure against q-parallel bilinear Diffie-Hellman exponent assumption.

An another approach of proxy re-encryption scheme using ciphertext policy attribute based encryption scheme was given in (Luo et al., 2011). The CP-ABE scheme used in this approach make use of AND-gate policies that supports multiple valued attributes, negative attributes and wildcards. This scheme fulfils the requirement of proxy re-encryption scheme including the properties such as multipurpose, unidirectionality and non-interactivity measures. This approach has master key security through which the data user can decide the necessity of the proxy server to perform the proxy re-encryption process. That is through the use of the master key the data owner can decide whether the proxy server can re-encrypt the data using its associated access policy. Further, this work makes the size of the ciphertext to be constant in length. Even though, this work provides improved security measures still the security threats and computational overheads across the proxy re-encryption techniques remains to be the major issue. This is especially true with the cloud based IoT systems.

It is observed from the literature (Abomhara et al., 2014, Hwang et al., 2015, Sadeghi et al., 2015 and Kawai, Y., 2015) that privacy and security remains to be the major issue across Internet of things. Throughout the paper an effective solution to solve the issue will be discussed in detail.

PRELIMINARIES

Near-Ring

Near-ring is a set R together with two binary operation $+$ and $\bullet$ such that:

1. $(R, +)$ is a group

2. $(R,\bullet)$ is a semigroup
3. $(r_1+r_2)r_3=r_1r_2+r_2r_3$ for all $r_1,r_2,r_3\in R$.

Complexity Assumptions Over Near-Ring

Near-ring Root Extraction Problem:

- **Instance:** Assumed $w\in R$ and an integer $a\geq2$.
- **Objective:** Finding $r\in R$ such that $w=r^a$ if such an r exists.

Twisted Root Extraction Problem (TREP):

- **Instance:** Assumed $\varphi\in End(R)$, $w\in R$ and an integer $a\geq2$.
- **Objective:** Finding a $r\in R$ such that $w=\varphi(ra^j)$.

Computational Diffie-Hellman Problem

Given a near-ring R and a quintuple

$$\left(r_1,r_2,\varphi\left(r_1^a\right)\varphi\left(r_2^b\right),\varphi\left(r_1^c\right)\varphi\left(r_2^d\right)\right)\in R$$

where $a,b,c,d\in R$, the objective is to compute

$$\varphi\left(r_1^a\right)\varphi\left(r_2^b\right).\varphi\left(r_1^c\right)\varphi\left(r_2^d\right).$$

Here $r_1,r_2\in N(R)$, satisfies $N(R_1)\cap N(R_2)=\{1_R\}$ and $r_1r_2\neq r_2r_1$.

Decision Diffie-Hellman Problem

Given a near-ring N and a quintuple

$$\left(r_1,r_2,\varphi\left(r_1^a\right)\varphi\left(r_2^b\right),\varphi\left(r_1^c\right)\varphi\left(r_2^d\right)\right)\in R$$

where $a,b,c,d\in R$, the objective is to decide whether

$$\varphi\left(r_1^a\right)\varphi\left(r_2^b\right).\varphi\left(r_1^c\right)\varphi\left(r_2^d\right)=\varphi\left(r_1^e\right)\varphi\left(r_2^f\right)$$

or not. Here $n_1,n_2\in C(N)$, satisfies $N(R_1)\cap N(R_2)=\{1_R\}$ and $r_1r_2\neq r_2r_1$.

THE PROPOSED SCHEME

Given near-ring R, let $N(R)$ be the set of elements that commute with r i.e., $N(R)=\{r \in R \backslash nr=rn\}$. $N(R)$ is called the normalizer of near-ring in R.

Now suppose that λ is the system parameter, both R_1 and R_2 are two subnear-rings R that satisfy the following conditions:

1. Both $N(R_1)$ and $N(R_2)$ are large enough, say exponential in λ.
2. $N(R_1) \cap N(R_2) = \{1_R\}$ where 1_R is the identity element of R.

Moreover, let

$$H_1 :\rightarrow \{0,1\}^{\lambda+2\mu}, \quad H_2 : R^2 \rightarrow \{0,1\}^{\lambda+2\mu}, \quad H_1 : \{0,1\}^{\lambda} \rightarrow N(R)$$

be the three cryptography hash functions.

Then, our proxy re-encryption scheme consists of the following five algorithms.

Key Generation

On input the security parameter λ, algorithm KeyGen randomly picks $r_1, r_2 \in N(R)$ and $a, b \geq 2$ then outputs the public key $n = \varphi(r_1^a) \varphi(r_2^b)$ and private key (r_1, r_2).

Encryption

On input a message $m \in \{0,1\}^{\lambda}$ and public key n, algorithm Enc constructs the ciphertext $(r,s) \in N \times \{0,1\}^{\lambda+2\mu}$ as follows:

- Randomly picks $\overline{\varphi(r_1^a)}, \overline{\varphi(r_2^b)} \in N$ and let $u = \overline{\varphi(r_1^a)} . n . \overline{\varphi(r_2^b)}$.
- Let $v = H_1(u) \oplus m$.
- Let $\left[\overline{\overline{\varphi(r_1^a)}}, \overline{\overline{\varphi(r_2^b)}}\right] = H_2(v)$.
- Let $w = \overline{\overline{\varphi(r_1^a)}} \cdot u \cdot \overline{\overline{\varphi(r_2^b)}}$
- Let $r = \overline{\overline{\varphi(r_1^a)}} \cdot \overline{\varphi(r_1^a)} \cdot \overline{\varphi(r_2^b)} \cdot \overline{\overline{\varphi(r_2^b)}}$.
- Let $s = H_3(w) \oplus v$.

Decryption

On input a ciphertext $(r,s) \in N \times \{0,1\}^{\lambda+2\mu}$, algorithm Dec outputs a message as follows:

- Let $\bar{w} = \left(r_1^a \right) \cdot t \cdot \varphi \left(r_2^b \right)$
- Let $\bar{v} = H_3 \left(\bar{w} \right) \oplus s.$
- Let $\left(\widehat{\varphi \left(r_1^a \right)}, \widehat{\varphi \left(r_2^b \right)} \right) = H_2 \left(\bar{v} \right).$
- Let $\bar{u} = I_L \left(\widehat{\varphi \left(r_1^a \right)} \right) \cdot \bar{w} \cdot I_R \left(\widehat{\varphi \left(r_2^b \right)} \right),$ where $I_L: R \rightarrow R$ and $I_R: R \rightarrow R$ is the left and right inversion function over the near-ring.
- Let $\bar{m} = H_1 \left(\bar{u} \right) \oplus \bar{v}.$

Re-Encryption Key Generation

On input user A's private key (r_1, r_2) and user B's Private key (r_3, r_4), the re-encryption key $K = (t_1, t_2)$ is defined by:

$$t_1 = \left(\varphi \left(r_3^a \right) \right)^{-1} \varphi \left(r_3^a \right), t_2 = \left(\varphi \left(r_4^b \right) \right)^{-1} \varphi \left(r_4^b \right)$$

Re-Encryption

On input a ciphertext $(r, s) \in R \times \{0,1\}^{\lambda+2\mu}$, algorithm re-encryption calculates $\bar{r} = t_1 \cdot r \cdot t_2$ and then outputs a new ciphertext $(\bar{r}, s).$

Theorem

To prove that the proposed cloud assisted proxy re-encryption scheme is consistent in nature.

Proof

First, the consistency of the decryption process is validated with respect to encryption process. For a valid ciphertext pair $(r, s) \in R \times \{0,1\}^{\lambda+2\mu}$, we have that $\bar{w}$ is appropriately equivalent to its counterpart used across the encryption, i.e.:

$$
\begin{aligned}
\bar{w} &= \varphi \left(r_1^a \right) \cdot r \cdot \varphi \left(r_2^b \right) \\
&= \varphi \left(r_1^a \right) \cdot \overline{\overline{\varphi \left(r_1^a \right)}} \cdot \overline{\varphi \left(r_1^a \right)} \cdot \overline{\varphi \left(r_2^b \right)} \cdot \overline{\overline{\varphi \left(r_2^b \right)}} \varphi \left(r_2^b \right) \\
&= \underline{\underline{\varphi \left(r_1^a \right)}} \cdot \overline{\varphi \left(r_1^a \right)} \cdot \underline{\varphi \left(r_1^a \right)} \cdot \varphi \left(r_2^b \right) \cdot \overline{\varphi \left(r_2^b \right)} \varphi \left(r_2^b \right) \\
&= \varphi \left(r_1^a \right) \cdot u \cdot \varphi \left(r_2^b \right) \\
&= w
\end{aligned}
$$

Thus, we have:

$$\overline{v} = H_3\left(\overline{w}\right) \oplus s$$
$$= H_3\left(w\right) \oplus s$$
$$= v$$

and:

$$\left(\widehat{\varphi\left(r_1^a\right)}, \widehat{\varphi\left(r_2^b\right)}\right) = H_2\left(\overline{v}\right)$$
$$= H_2\left(v\right)$$
$$= \left(\overline{\widehat{\varphi\left(r_1^a\right)}}, \overline{\widehat{\varphi\left(r_2^b\right)}}\right)$$

Therefore, we have:

$$\overline{u} = I_L\left(\widehat{\varphi\left(r_1^a\right)}\right) \cdot \overline{w} \cdot I_R\left(\widehat{\varphi\left(r_2^b\right)}\right)$$
$$= I_L\left(\widehat{\varphi\left(r_1^a\right)}\right) \cdot \overline{\widehat{\varphi\left(r_1^a\right)}} \cdot u \cdot \overline{\widehat{\varphi\left(r_2^b\right)}} \cdot I_R\left(\widehat{\varphi\left(r_2^b\right)}\right)$$
$$= w$$

and:

$$\overline{m} = H_1\left(\overline{u}\right) \oplus \overline{v}$$
$$= H_1\left(u\right) \oplus v$$
$$= m$$

Next, we perform the validation of the decryption process with respect to its encryption process. For a reasonable re-encrypted ciphertext pair $\left(r', s'\right) \in N \times \{0,1\}^{\lambda+2\mu}$, it is already known that it comes from a valid ciphertext (r,s), encrypted under user A's public key n, and a re-encryption key $K=(t_1,t_2)$ in accordance to $r' = t_1 \cdot r \cdot t_2$ and $s' = s$ where, $t_1 = \left(\varphi\left(r_3^a\right)\right)^{-1} \varphi\left(r_3^a\right)$ and $t_2 = \left(\varphi\left(r_4^b\right)\right)^{-1} \varphi\left(r_4^b\right)$, while (r_1,r_2) and (r_3,r_4) are user A's private key and user B's private key, respectively. Now, with knowing B's private key (r_3,r_4) one can at first recover.

Then, subsequent calculating on message m must be correct:

$$
\begin{aligned}
\overline{\overline{w}} &= \varphi\left(r_3^a\right) \cdot r' \cdot \varphi\left(r_4^b\right) \\
&= \varphi\left(r_3^a\right) \cdot t_1 \cdot r \cdot t_2 \cdot \varphi\left(r_4^b\right) \\
&= \varphi\left(r_3^a\right) \cdot \varphi\left(r_3^a\right)^{-1} \cdot \varphi\left(r_1^a\right) \cdot \overline{\varphi\left(r_1^a\right)} \cdot \overline{\overline{\varphi\left(r_1^a\right)}} \cdot \overline{\varphi\left(r_2^b\right)} \cdot \overline{\overline{\varphi\left(r_2^b\right)}} \cdot \varphi\left(r_2^b\right) \cdot \varphi\left(r_4^b\right)^{-1} \\
&= \varphi\left(r_1^a\right) \cdot \overline{\varphi\left(r_1^a\right)} \cdot \overline{\overline{\varphi\left(r_1^a\right)}} \cdot \varphi\left(r_2^b\right) \cdot \overline{\varphi\left(r_2^b\right)} \cdot \overline{\overline{\varphi\left(r_2^b\right)}} \\
&= \varphi\left(r_1^a\right) \cdot \overline{\varphi\left(r_1^a\right)} \cdot \overline{\overline{\varphi\left(r_1^a\right)}} \cdot \overline{\varphi\left(r_2^b\right)} \cdot \overline{\varphi\left(r_2^b\right)} \cdot \overline{\varphi\left(r_2^b\right)} \\
&= \varphi\left(r_1^a\right) \cdot \overline{\varphi\left(r_1^a\right)} \cdot \text{n} \cdot \overline{\varphi\left(r_2^b\right)} \cdot \varphi\left(r_2^b\right) \\
&= \varphi\left(n_1^a\right) \cdot u \cdot \varphi\left(n_2^b\right) \\
&= w
\end{aligned}
$$

Remark

It is evident that the actual encrypted ciphertext and a re-encrypted ciphertext are indistinguishable in nature. Because of the reason that both the ranges of the originally encrypted ciphertexts and the re-encrypted ciphertexts are similar in value. Even with a prior knowledge on corresponding private key, one cannot recognize any difference in decrypting an originally encrypted ciphertext or a re-encrypted ciphertext.

SECURITY ANALYSIS

Security Against Equivalent Private Key Attack

Now, let us consider the relationship that exists between the public key $n \in R$ and the private key $(r_1, r_2) \in R_1 \times R_2$ is very simple: $n = \varphi\left(r_1^a\right) \cdot \varphi\left(r_2^b\right)$, here we must have to be aware of the security threat called equivalent private key attack. That is, if an adversary A can find $\widetilde{\varphi\left(r_1^a\right)}, \widetilde{\varphi\left(r_2^b\right)} \in R$ such that:

$$
n = \widetilde{\varphi\left(r_1^a\right)} \cdot \widetilde{\varphi\left(r_2^b\right)} \tag{1}
$$

holds, then for every given ciphertext (r,s) encryption is performed using the public key n, Such that the adversary A could try to recover the information about the plaintext m through the use of $\left(\widetilde{\varphi\left(r_1^a\right)}, \widetilde{\varphi\left(r_2^b\right)}\right)$. Such that the first step associated with A's decryption process is given as follows:

$$\bar{w} = \widetilde{\varphi\left(r_1^a\right)} \cdot r \cdot \widetilde{\varphi\left(r_2^b\right)}$$
$$= \widetilde{\varphi\left(r_1^a\right)}\widetilde{\varphi\left(r_1^a\right)} \cdot \widetilde{\varphi\left(r_1^a\right)} \cdot \widetilde{\varphi\left(r_2^b\right)} \cdot \widetilde{\varphi\left(r_2^b\right)}\widetilde{\varphi\left(r_2^b\right)}$$

Now, only if:

$$\widetilde{\varphi\left(r_1^a\right)} \in N\left(R_1\right) \text{ and } \widetilde{\varphi\left(r_2^b\right)} \in N\left(R_2\right) \tag{2}$$

the subsequent reduction holds, i.e.:

$$\bar{w} = \widetilde{\varphi\left(r_1^a\right)} \cdot \widetilde{\varphi\left(r_1^a\right)} \cdot \widetilde{\varphi\left(r_1^a\right)} \cdot \widetilde{\varphi\left(r_2^b\right)} \cdot \widetilde{\varphi\left(r_2^b\right)} \cdot \widetilde{\varphi\left(r_2^b\right)}$$
$$= \widetilde{\varphi\left(r_1^a\right)} \cdot \widetilde{\varphi\left(r_1^a\right)} \cdot n \cdot \widetilde{\varphi\left(r_2^b\right)} \cdot \widetilde{\varphi\left(r_2^b\right)}$$
$$= \widetilde{\varphi\left(r_1^a\right)} \cdot u \cdot \widetilde{\varphi\left(r_2^b\right)}$$
$$= w$$

such that the adversary can recover the entire message m. Otherwise, if either $\widetilde{\varphi\left(r_1^a\right)} \in N\left(R_1\right)$ and $\widetilde{\varphi\left(r_2^b\right)} \in N\left(R_2\right)$ the process of decryption will be failed, except with negligible probability, in consideration to the fact that $\widetilde{\varphi\left(r_1^a\right)}, \widetilde{\varphi\left(r_2^b\right)}, \widetilde{\varphi\left(r_1^a\right)}$ and $\widetilde{\varphi\left(r_2^b\right)}$ are randomly distributed in R. Now, through combining the equations (1), (2) and the setting on legitimate private key (r_1, r_2), we have that

$$\varphi\left(r_1^a\right)^{-1} \cdot \widetilde{\varphi\left(r_1^a\right)} \cdot \widetilde{\varphi\left(r_2^b\right)} = \varphi\left(r_2^b\right) \in N\left(R_2\right).$$

With respect to the condition $\widetilde{\varphi\left(r_2^b\right)} \in N\left(R_2\right)$, we have that therefore, $\varphi\left(r_1^a\right)^{-1} \cdot \widetilde{\varphi\left(r_1^a\right)} = 1_R$, i.e. $\varphi\left(r_1^a\right) = \widetilde{\varphi\left(r_1^a\right)}$. Similarly, we have $\varphi\left(r_2^b\right) = \widetilde{\varphi\left(r_2^b\right)}$. That is, over the subnear-ring N_1 and N_2, the solution for the group equation of (1) is defined in unique way under the condition of $N(R_1) \cap N(R_2) = \{1_R\}$. Therefore, the adversary A's probability to execute a successful attack is minimum, under the assumption that the twisted root extraction problem over near-ring N is intractable. In other words, the security of private key is rooted in the hardness of the twisted root extraction problem in near-ring.

Security Against Chosen Plaintext Attack

Now let us consider a scenario that an adversary A, upon the receipt of the public key $n \in R$, given with a challenge ciphertext (r^*, s^*) which is a valid ciphertext under assumption on one of two messages

$m_0^*, m_1^* \in \{0,1\}^{\lambda+2\mu}$ chosen by A himself/herself, and makes an attempt to decide which of the messages is hidden in (r^*, s^*). In accordance to the encryption process, A knows that

$$r^* = \overline{\overline{\varphi\left(r_1^a\right)}} \cdot \overline{\overline{\varphi\left(r_1^a\right)}} \cdot \overline{\overline{\varphi\left(r_2^b\right)}} \cdot \overline{\overline{\varphi\left(r_2^b\right)}}$$

for some unknown $\overline{\overline{\varphi\left(r_1^a\right)}}, \overline{\overline{\varphi\left(r_1^a\right)}}, \overline{\overline{\varphi\left(r_2^b\right)}}, \overline{\overline{\varphi\left(r_2^b\right)}} \in R$. In addition, A have the prior knowledge on the near-ring equation $u = \overline{\varphi\left(r_1^a\right)} \cdot n \cdot \overline{\varphi\left(r_2^b\right)}$, where n is the public key without any awareness to the value u. Suppose that A at first makes a guess on $\overline{\varphi\left(r_1^a\right)}, \overline{\varphi\left(r_2^b\right)}$. Then, A can try the following attack (see Algorithm 1).

Algorithm 1: Chosen Plaintext Attack by Guessing $\overline{\varphi\left(r_1^a\right)}, \overline{\varphi\left(r_2^b\right)}$

$\overline{\varphi\left(r_1^a\right)}, \overline{\varphi\left(r_2^b\right)} \xleftarrow{\$} R$
$\overline{u} \leftarrow \overline{\varphi\left(r_1^a\right)} \cdot n \cdot \overline{\varphi\left(r_2^b\right)}$
for i from 0 to 1 **do**
   $\overline{v} \leftarrow H_1\left(\overline{n}\right) \oplus m_i$
   $\overline{\overline{\varphi\left(r_1^a\right)}}, \overline{\overline{\varphi\left(r_2^b\right)}} \leftarrow H_2\left(\overline{v}\right)$
   $\overline{w} \leftarrow \overline{\varphi\left(n_1^a\right)} \cdot \overline{v} \cdot \overline{\varphi\left(n_2^b\right)}$
   If $s^* = H_3\left(\overline{w} \oplus \overline{v}\right)$ and $r^* = \overline{\overline{\varphi\left(r_1^a\right)}} \cdot \overline{\overline{\varphi\left(r_1^a\right)}} \cdot \overline{\overline{\varphi\left(r_2^b\right)}} \cdot \overline{\overline{\varphi\left(r_2^b\right)}}$ then
      return "SUCCESS: The challenge message is m_i
   end if
   $\overline{v} \leftarrow H_1\left(\overline{u}\right) \oplus m_{i-1}$
   $\left(\overline{\overline{\varphi\left(r_1^a\right)}}, \overline{\overline{\varphi\left(r_2^b\right)}}\right) \leftarrow H_2\left(\overline{v}\right)$
   $\overline{w} \leftarrow \overline{\overline{\varphi\left(r_1^a\right)}} \cdot \overline{u} \cdot \overline{\varphi\left(r_2^b\right)}$
   if $s^* = H_3\left(\overline{w} \oplus \overline{v}\right)$ and $r^* = \overline{\varphi\left(r_1^a\right)} \cdot \overline{\overline{\varphi\left(r_1^a\right)}} \cdot \overline{\varphi\left(r_2^b\right)} \cdot \overline{\overline{\varphi\left(r_2^b\right)}}$ then
      return "SUCCESS: The challenge message is m_{i-1}
   end if
end for
return "FAIL"

From the above attack we can observe, the adversary can validate his/her guess by checking either the equality $s^* = H_3\left(\overline{w} \oplus \overline{v}\right)$, or the equality $r^* = \overline{\overline{\varphi\left(r_1^a\right)}} \cdot \overline{\varphi\left(r_1^a\right)} \cdot \overline{\overline{\varphi\left(r_2^b\right)}} \cdot \overline{\varphi\left(r_2^b\right)}$ instead of both of them. In fact, one of them is true only with negligible probability if the other is false, and for randomly selecting $\overline{\varphi\left(r_1^a\right)}, \overline{\varphi\left(r_2^b\right)}$ both of them are false with a comparatively higher amount of probability, in consideration to the fact that R is large enough. Thus, making a random assumption on $\overline{\varphi\left(r_1^a\right)}, \overline{\varphi\left(r_2^b\right)} \in R$ probability for making a successful attack is negligible.

However, if the adversary A has a knowledge to perform the process of factor r^* over R, then he/she can make a more intelligent attack (see Algorithm 2).

Algorithm 2: Chosen Plaintext Attack Factoring $\overline{\varphi\left(r_1^a\right)}, \overline{\varphi\left(r_2^b\right)}$

$$N = \left\{ \begin{array}{l} \left(\overline{\overline{\varphi\left(r_1^a\right)}}, \overline{\varphi\left(r_1^a\right)}, \overline{\varphi\left(r_2^b\right)}, \overline{\overline{\varphi\left(r_2^b\right)}}\right) : \\ r^* = \overline{\varphi\left(r_1^a\right)}.\overline{\overline{\varphi\left(r_1^a\right)}}.\overline{\varphi\left(r_2^b\right)}.\overline{\overline{\varphi\left(r_2^b\right)}} \end{array} \right\}$$

for $\forall \left[\overline{\varphi\left(r_1^a\right)}, \overline{\varphi\left(r_1^a\right)}, \overline{\varphi\left(r_2^b\right)}, \overline{\varphi\left(r_2^b\right)} \right] \in N$ do

$\overline{u} \leftarrow \overline{\varphi\left(r_1^a\right)} \cdot n \cdot \overline{\varphi\left(r_2^b\right)}$

$\overline{w} \leftarrow \overline{\varphi\left(r_1^a\right)} \cdot \overline{v} \cdot \overline{\varphi\left(r_2^b\right)}$

$\overline{v} \leftarrow H_2\left(\overline{w} \oplus s^*\right)$

    If $\overline{v} = \overline{u} \oplus m_i$ then

        return "SUCCESS: The challenge message is m_i"

    end if

    If $\overline{v} = \overline{u} \oplus m_{i-1}$ then

        return "SUCCESS: The challenge message is m_{i-1}"

    end if

end for

return "FAIL"

Remark

Therefore, on the other sider under the intractability assumption of twisted root extraction problem over the near-ring R, the proposed scheme is resistant towards chosen plaintext attack; similarly, if the twisted root extraction problem of r^* over R is not unique and the total number of solutions are large enough in nature, even without the assumption of intractability, the proposed scheme is highly secure in nature.

Note

The distinctiveness of twisted root extraction problem in public key R over $N(R_1) \times N(R_2)$ does not violate the non-uniqueness of root extraction in r^* over R.

PERFORMANCE ANALYSIS

Security

The proposed approach makes use of near-ring based data sharing method that prevents malicious third-party entities from trapping the data contents, even with the case of wiretapping between the client and the server. Besides, the $t_1 = \left(\varphi \left(r_3^a \right) \right)^{-1} \varphi \left(r_3^a \right), t_2 = \left(\varphi \left(r_4^b \right) \right)^{-1} \varphi \left(r_4^b \right)$ re-encryption key obtained during the user entity A's encryption process is a one-time key and it could not be used continuously by the other user B. Thus, the proposed approach preserves backward secrecy.

Computation Amount

Further, the proposed system offers efficient data sharing facilities with lesser computational complexity measures. This is due to the reason it performs lightweight pairing computation operations across cloud servers that cannot be trusted through re-encryption processes. Further, the proposed approach is more efficient than existing systems such that it re-encrypts only the re-encryption key during re-encryption processes rather than re-encrypting the entire data. Table 1, computation load analysis with the existing approaches and it is observed that the proposed approach is more efficient than existing techniques by means of increased data sharing delay time (Figure 3) during computation. In addition, the amount of computation load based on number of shared members is found to be highly efficient among data sharing groups:

- i-means modular inversion
- m modular exponentiation
- h hash function
- a addition operation
- p pairing operation
- n number of data-sharing group users

Table 1. Comparison of proposed scheme

PRE	Public Information	Illegal User Tracking	Data Sharing Computation	Amount of Sharing
Li et al. (2015)	$(X, T_{X}, g_X), f(k)$	X	$m+h+a$	$O(n(n-1)/2)$
Kar et al. (2011)	$H^{[h]} = \left(R_X^{[h]}, T_X^{[h]} \right)$	O	$m^3+m+3h+2a$	$O(n(n-1)/2)$
Zhou et.al (2017)	$(X, T_{X}, g_X), f(k), g(k)$	O	$2m+h+a$	$O(n(n-1)/2)$
Tao et al. (2014)	(X, T_{X}, g_X)	O	$m+2h+a$	$O(n(n-1)/2)$
Proposed Scheme	(n, e, N, P_k)	O	$4e+1i+6m$	$O(n)$

Communication Traffic

Figure 2 is a graph showing the comparison of the encryption speed of the proposed method and the network using the existing public key encryption. The proposed method takes some computational time. However, the existing method increases the number of encryption operations by the number of nodes, yet the proposed method can pass encrypted data to all nodes on the network with only one encryption operation. Decryption operations are rather similar or faster than the existing method. It is clear that this is more advantageous in an environment where many terminal devices are used (Figure 3).

Figure 2. Comparing the encryption method with the existing network

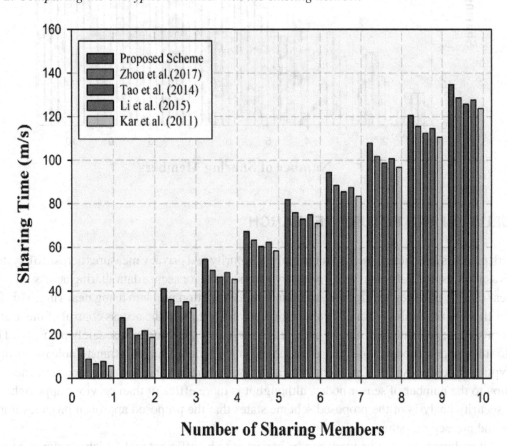

Forward and Backward Secrecy

There is flexible subscription and unsubscription of users in data sharing among groups. Subscribed group members should not know the secret group key used previously, and unsubscribed members should not know the new secret group key. The proposed method is based on the proxy re-encryption scheme for efficient data sharing across IoT system and therefore provide safety in the IoT environment.

Figure 3. Comparing the decryption method with the existing network

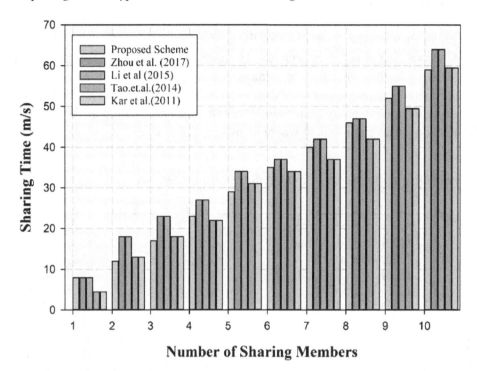

CONCLUSION AND FUTURE RESEARCH

This work presents an efficient method for improved security and privacy measures across IoT systems. It presents a cloud-assisted efficient proxy re-encryption scheme for secure data sharing across IoT systems using near-ring. It provides an effective solution to root extraction problem using near-ring. This further improves the security of the system by enhancing the information of the access control of the user in the cloud atmosphere; delegate information gathered in servers of the cloud can be safely managed. There is a need to study of proposed methods for resolving the unidirectional and non-transferable issues of proxy re-encryption schemes. Another problem to be addressed is the fact that the operation time increases in proportion to the number of sensor nodes, although it is more efficient than previous approaches.

The security analysis of the proposed scheme states that the proposed approach provides improved security and privacy measures.

The protocol proposed in this work can be expected to be efficient and widely deployed in various cloud-based environments. By enabling detailed user access control in cloud environments, sensitive information stored on cloud servers can be managed more safely. The basic purpose of this study is to solve the problems caused by a non-transferable proxy re-encryption scheme. However, a disadvantage of this method is the additional computation in the polynomial equation compared to existing attribute-based encryption methods, since it provides more functions. In the future, this work could be extended to solve security threats across the Blockchain environment.

REFERENCES

Abomhara, M., & Koien, G. M. (2014). Security and privacy in the Internet of Things: Current status and open issues. In *2014 international conference on privacy and security in mobile systems (PRISMS)* (pp. 1-8). IEEE.

Agyekum, O., Opuni-Boachie, K., Xia, Q., Sifah, E. B., Gao, J., Xia, H., ... Guizani, M. (2019). A Secured Proxy-Based Data Sharing Module in IoT Environments Using Blockchain. *Sensors (Basel)*, *19*(5), 1235. doi:10.339019051235 PMID:30862110

Ahene, E., Qin, Z., Adusei, A. K., & Li, F. (2019). Efficient Signcryption With Proxy Re-Encryption and its Application in Smart Grid. *IEEE Internet of Things Journal*, *6*(6), 9722–9737. doi:10.1109/JIOT.2019.2930742

Ali, M., Sadeghi, M. R., & Liu, X. (2020). Lightweight Revocable Hierarchical Attribute-Based Encryption for Internet of Things. *IEEE Access: Practical Innovations, Open Solutions*, *8*, 23951–23964. doi:10.1109/ACCESS.2020.2969957

Belguith, S., Kaaniche, N., & Russello, G. (2018). Lightweight attribute-based encryption supporting access policy update for cloud assisted IoT. In *Proceedings of the 15th International Joint Conference on e-Business and Telecommunications-Volume 1: SECRYPT* (pp. 135-146). SciTePress. 10.5220/0006854601350146

Bertino, E. (2016). *Data Security and Privacy in the IoT* (Vol. 2016). EDBT.

Biswas, A., Majumdar, A., Nath, S., Dutta, A., & Baishnab, K. L. (2020). LRBC: A lightweight block cipher design for resource constrained IoT devices. *Journal of Ambient Intelligence and Humanized Computing*, 1–15.

Cao, M., Wang, L., Qin, Z., & Lou, C. (2019). A Lightweight Fine-Grained Search Scheme over Encrypted Data in Cloud-Assisted Wireless Body Area Networks. *Wireless Communications and Mobile Computing*.

Do, J. M., Song, Y. J., & Park, N. (2011). Attribute based proxy re-encryption for data confidentiality in cloud computing environments. In *2011 First ACIS/JNU International Conference on Computers, Networks, Systems and Industrial Engineering* (pp. 248-251). IEEE. 10.1109/CNSI.2011.34

Eltayieb, N., Sun, L., Wang, K., & Li, F. (2019). A Certificateless Proxy Re-encryption Scheme for Cloud-Based Blockchain. In *International Conference on Frontiers in Cyber Security* (pp. 293-307). Springer. 10.1007/978-981-15-0818-9_19

Fang, L., Li, M., Zhou, L., Zhang, H., & Ge, C. (2019). A Fine-Grained User-Divided Privacy-Preserving Access Control Protocol in Smart Watch. *Sensors (Basel)*, *19*(9), 2109. doi:10.339019092109 PMID:31067751

Fischer, M., Scheerhorn, A., & Tönjes, R. (2019). Using Attribute-Based Encryption on IoT Devices with instant Key Revocation. In *2019 IEEE International Conference on Pervasive Computing and Communications Workshops (PerCom Workshops)* (pp. 126-131). IEEE. 10.1109/PERCOMW.2019.8730784

Ge, C., Liu, Z., & Fang, L. (2020). A blockchain based decentralized data security mechanism for the Internet of Things. *Journal of Parallel and Distributed Computing*, *141*, 1–9. doi:10.1016/j.jpdc.2020.03.005

Huang, C., Liu, D., Ni, J., Lu, R., & Shen, X. (2020). Achieving Accountable and Efficient Data Sharing in Industrial Internet of Things. *IEEE Transactions on Industrial Informatics*, 1. doi:10.1109/TII.2020.2982942

Hwang, Y. H. (2015). IoT security & privacy: threats and challenges. In *Proceedings of the 1st ACM Workshop on IoT Privacy, Trust, and Security* (pp. 1-1). ACM.

Josep, A. D., Katz, R., Konwinski, A., Gunho, L. E. E., Patterson, D., & Rabkin, A. (2010). A view of cloud computing. *Communications of the ACM*, *53*(4).

Kawai, Y. (2015). Outsourcing the re-encryption key generation: flexible ciphertext-policy attribute-based proxy re-encryption. In *International Conference on Information Security Practice and Experience* (pp. 301-315). Springer. 10.1007/978-3-319-17533-1_21

Khashan, O. A. (2020). Hybrid Lightweight Proxy Re-encryption Scheme for Secure Fog-to-Things Environment. *IEEE Access: Practical Innovations, Open Solutions*, *8*, 66878–66887. doi:10.1109/AC-CESS.2020.2984317

Kozlov, D., Veijalainen, J., & Ali, Y. (2012). Security and privacy threats in IoT architectures. In *Proceedings of the 7th International Conference on Body Area Networks* (pp. 256-262). ICST (Institute for Computer Sciences, Social-Informatics and Telecommunications Engineering).

Krishnamoorthy, S., Muthukumaran, V., Yu, J., & Balamurugan, B. (2019). A Secure Privacy Preserving Proxy re-encryption Scheme for IoT Security using Near-ring. In *Proceedings of the 2019 the International Conference on Pattern Recognition and Artificial Intelligence* (pp. 27-32). 10.1145/3357777.3359011

Liang, K., Au, M. H., Liu, J. K., Susilo, W., Wong, D. S., Yang, G., & Yang, A. (2015). A secure and efficient ciphertext-policy attribute-based proxy re-encryption for cloud data sharing. *Future Generation Computer Systems*, *52*, 95–108. doi:10.1016/j.future.2014.11.016

Liang, K., Au, M. H., Susilo, W., Wong, D. S., Yang, G., & Yu, Y. (2014). An adaptively CCA-secure ciphertext-policy attribute-based proxy re-encryption for cloud data sharing. In *International Conference on Information Security Practice and Experience* (pp. 448-461). Springer. 10.1007/978-3-319-06320-1_33

Liang, K., Fang, L., Susilo, W., & Wong, D. S. (2013). A ciphertext-policy attribute-based proxy re-encryption with chosen-ciphertext security. In *2013 5th International Conference on Intelligent Network-ing and Collaborative Systems* (pp. 552-559). IEEE. 10.1109/INCoS.2013.103

Liang, K., Liu, J. K., Wong, D. S., & Susilo, W. (2014). An efficient cloud-based revocable identity-based proxy re-encryption scheme for public clouds data sharing. In *European Symposium on Research in Computer Security* (pp. 257-272). Springer. 10.1007/978-3-319-11203-9_15

Luo, S., Hu, J., & Chen, Z. (2010). Ciphertext policy attribute-based proxy re-encryption. In *International Conference on Information and Communications Security* (pp. 401-415). Springer. 10.1007/978-3-642-17650-0_28

Manzoor, A., Liyanage, M., Braeke, A., Kanhere, S. S., & Ylianttila, M. (2019). Blockchain based proxy re-encryption scheme for secure IoT data sharing. In *2019 IEEE International Conference on Blockchain and Cryptocurrency (ICBC)* (pp. 99-103). IEEE. 10.1109/BLOC.2019.8751336

Mollah, M. B., Azad, M. A. K., & Vasilakos, A. (2017). Secure data sharing and searching at the edge of cloud-assisted internet of things. *IEEE Cloud Computing*, *4*(1), 34–42. doi:10.1109/MCC.2017.9

Pasupuleti, S. K., & Varma, D. (2020). Lightweight ciphertext-policy attribute-based encryption scheme for data privacy and security in cloud-assisted IoT. In *Real-Time Data Analytics for Large Scale Sensor Data* (pp. 97–114). Academic Press. doi:10.1016/B978-0-12-818014-3.00005-X

Qu, T., Lei, S. P., Wang, Z. Z., Nie, D. X., Chen, X., & Huang, G. Q. (2016). IoT-based real-time production logistics synchronization system under smart cloud manufacturing. *International Journal of Advanced Manufacturing Technology*, *84*(1-4), 147–164. doi:10.100700170-015-7220-1

Sadeghi, A. R., Wachsmann, C., & Waidner, M. (2015). Security and privacy challenges in industrial internet of things. In *2015 52nd ACM/EDAC/IEEE Design Automation Conference (DAC)* (pp. 1-6). IEEE. 10.1145/2744769.2747942

Schurgot, M. R., Shinberg, D. A., & Greenwald, L. G. (2015). Experiments with security and privacy in IoT networks. In *2015 IEEE 16th International Symposium on A World of Wireless, Mobile and Multimedia Networks (WoWMoM)* (pp. 1-6). IEEE. 10.1109/WoWMoM.2015.7158207

Shen, J., Deng, X., & Xu, Z. (2019). Multi-security-level cloud storage system based on improved proxy re-encryption. *EURASIP Journal on Wireless Communications and Networking*, (1), 1–12.

Sivaraman, V., Gharakheili, H. H., Vishwanath, A., Boreli, R., & Mehani, O. (2015). Network-level security and privacy control for smart-home IoT devices. In *2015 IEEE 11th International conference on wireless and mobile computing, networking and communications (WiMob)* (pp. 163-167). IEEE. 10.1109/WiMOB.2015.7347956

Su, M., Zhou, B., Fu, A., Yu, Y., & Zhang, G. (2019). PRTA: A Proxy Re-encryption based Trusted Authorization scheme for nodes on CloudIoT. *Information Sciences*.

Tao, F., Cheng, Y., Da Xu, L., Zhang, L., & Li, B. H. (2014). CCIoT-CMfg: Cloud computing and internet of things-based cloud manufacturing service system. *IEEE Transactions on Industrial Informatics*, *10*(2), 1435–1442. doi:10.1109/TII.2014.2306383

Tao, F., Zuo, Y., Da Xu, L., & Zhang, L. (2014). IoT-based intelligent perception and access of manufacturing resource toward cloud manufacturing. *IEEE Transactions on Industrial Informatics*, *10*(2), 1547–1557. doi:10.1109/TII.2014.2306397

Tsai, W. T., Sun, X., & Balasooriya, J. (2010). Service-oriented cloud computing architecture. In *2010 seventh international conference on information technology: new generations* (pp. 684-689). IEEE. 10.1109/ITNG.2010.214

Vijayakumar, V., Priyan, M. K., Ushadevi, G., Varatharajan, R., Manogaran, G., & Tarare, P. V. (2018). E-health cloud security using timing enabled proxy re-encryption. *Mobile Networks and Applications*, 1–12.

Wang, G., Liu, Q., & Wu, J. (2010). Hierarchical attribute-based encryption for fine-grained access control in cloud storage services. In *Proceedings of the 17th ACM conference on Computer and communications security* (pp. 735-737). ACM. 10.1145/1866307.1866414

Wang, X. A., Xhafa, F., Ma, J., & Zheng, Z. (2019). Controlled secure social cloud data sharing based on a novel identity based proxy re-encryption plus scheme. *Journal of Parallel and Distributed Computing*, *130*, 153–165. doi:10.1016/j.jpdc.2019.03.018

Weber, R. H. (2010). Internet of Things–New security and privacy challenges. *Computer Law & Security Review*, *26*(1), 23–30. doi:10.1016/j.clsr.2009.11.008

Xu, P., Jiao, T., Wu, Q., Wang, W., & Jin, H. (2015). Conditional identity-based broadcast proxy re-encryption and its application to cloud email. *IEEE Transactions on Computers*, *65*(1), 66–79. doi:10.1109/TC.2015.2417544

Yang, Y., Zhu, H., Lu, H., Weng, J., Zhang, Y., & Choo, K. K. R. (2016). Cloud based data sharing with fine-grained proxy re-encryption. *Pervasive and Mobile Computing*, *28*, 122–134. doi:10.1016/j.pmcj.2015.06.017

Yao, X., Chen, Z., & Tian, Y. (2015). A lightweight attribute-based encryption scheme for the Internet of Things. *Future Generation Computer Systems*, *49*, 104–112. doi:10.1016/j.future.2014.10.010

Yeh, L.Y., Chiang, P.Y., Tsai, Y.L., & Huang, J.L. (2015). Cloud-based fine-grained health information access control framework for lightweight iot devices with dynamic auditing and attribute revocation. *IEEE Transactions on Cloud Computing, 6*(2), 532-544.

Youseff, L., Butrico, M., & Da Silva, D. (2008). Toward a unified ontology of cloud computing. In 2008 Grid Computing Environments Workshop (pp. 1-10). IEEE. doi:10.1109/GCE.2008.4738443

Zhang, J., Bai, W., & Wang, Y. (2019). Non-interactive ID-based proxy re-signature scheme for IoT based on mobile edge computing. *IEEE Access: Practical Innovations, Open Solutions, 7*, 37865–37875. doi:10.1109/ACCESS.2019.2899828

Zhang, Q., Cheng, L., & Boutaba, R. (2010). Cloud computing: State-of-the-art and research challenges. *Journal of Internet Services and Applications*, *1*(1), 7–18. doi:10.100713174-010-0007-6

Zhou, J., Cao, Z., Dong, X., & Vasilakos, A. V. (2017). Security and privacy for cloud-based IoT: Challenges. *IEEE Communications Magazine*, *55*(1), 26–33. doi:10.1109/MCOM.2017.1600363CM

Zhou, Y., Deng, H., Wu, Q., Qin, B., Liu, J., & Ding, Y. (2016). Identity-based proxy re-encryption version 2: Making mobile access easy in cloud. *Future Generation Computer Systems*, *62*, 128–139. doi:10.1016/j.future.2015.09.027

This research was previously published in the International Journal of Information Technology and Web Engineering (IJITWE), 15(4); pages 18-36, copyright year 2020 by IGI Publishing (an imprint of IGI Global).

Chapter 36
A Reliable Blockchain– Based Image Encryption Scheme for IIoT Networks

Ambika N.

(iD) https://orcid.org/0000-0003-4452-5514

Department of Computer Applications, Sivananda Sarma Memorial RV College, Bangalore, India

ABSTRACT

IoT is used in industrial setup to increase security and provide ease to the user. The manual efforts decrease in this environment. The previous work concentrates on capturing images and transmitting the encrypted image. It uses the Merkle root and blockchain to make the transmission reliable. The suggestion increases reliability to the previous work. The system uses the Merkle root to endorse the key to the transmitting devices. The work increases reliability by 2.58% compared to the previous contribution.

1. INTRODUCTION

Industrial Internet-of-things (IIoT) (Ambika, 2020) (Hossain & Muhammad, 2016) is an aggregation of assembling procedure, checking, and the executive's frameworks. The system manages the availability of industrial facilities like machines and board frameworks required for business activities. IIoT is the contribution of cutting-edge machines and sensors to different ventures. Some examples include aviation, wellbeing (Ambika N., 2020) (Arcelus, Amaya, Jones, Goubran, & Knoefel, 2007) (Chandel, Sinharay, Ahmed, & Ghose, 2016), vitality, and resistance. The framework breaks down leads to a dangerous crisis. In this way, this division requires concentrated consideration and an elevated level of security. It is used across businesses, beginning of the essential assembling segment to signify the magnitude of creation units. It comprises creation, plans of action, client relations, investigate activities, instruction, and overall techniques of advancement.

DOI: 10.4018/978-1-6684-7132-6.ch036

A blockchain (A & K, 2016) (Atlam & Wills, 2019) is a computerized record that contains the whole history of exchanges made on the system. The essential reason for its existence was to wipe out outsiders from cash exchanges by making dependable advanced money transactions. It is a collection of connected obstructs that are combined by hash esteems. All data on the blockchain is perpetual and can't be changed. Many applications have used blockchain in their doings. IIoT is one of them. (Khan & Byun, 2020) is an encryption plot for an IIoT-arranged system processing framework introduced that depends on a blockchain. It begins with the introduction of the web administration of the blockchain for hubs of the system. There are many picture catching gadgets, and every device goes about as a hub. When a device receives the transaction, it commences the chain for preparing the proposed calculation for preliminary checks. It will check that the present time is not as much as that of the message circulation stage and whether the hub is enrolled or not. The Certificate Authority (CA) allocates a computerized personality to each device of the system. If the device has a cryptographically approved advanced testament, mapped by the CA, at that point, it can take an interest in the framework. After beginning checks, it will start with the encryption procedure for the transaction. A hashed exchange ID broadcasted to all the systems. The device that has received hashed ID are the third parties.

The proposal aims to increase reliability. The contribution uses the Merkle root method to generate endorsement keys. The devices register themselves with the auxiliary devices by sharing their credentials. It transmits the encrypted data and the hash value (by using blockchain) to the respective validating node. The endorsement keys calculated by auxiliary devices are attached to the received data before transmitting them. The endorsement keys are derived using the identity of the transmitted device and validating node.

The division of the work is into seven segments. We start by introducing the technologies to the user and a brief paragraph on the contribution. Various authors have provided their insight into the technology is made available in the second division. The third division provides the narration of the Merkle root. The fourth section details the contribution. The details of the analysis are in the fifth section. Future work suggestion is in the sixth segment. The seventh segment contains an outline of the work.

2. LITERATURE SURVEY

The design (Wan, Li, Imran, & Li, 2019) has four layers. The detecting layer comprises of different sorts of sensors and a microcomputer. These gadgets sense information and pre-process the gathered information. The Hub layer parses the transferred information, encodes them, packs them and burdens the equivalent into the database. The capacity layer stores the information gathered by them in the conveyed structure. It synchronizes the information. Firmlayer associates the information securing unit, circulated calculation and information stockpiling innovation. The application layer observes the network and takes care or circumstances like failure forecast. The blockchain utilizes Merkle root to play out its errand. SHA256 and Elliptical curve cryptography calculation is utilized to upgrade security.

The blockchain hubs(Zhao, Li, & Yao, 2019) can be sorted into full hub (FN) and lightweight hub (LN). Full hub can download and check all blocks and exchanges. It can go about as mining hub and make obstructs for the blockchain. Lightweight hub, due to the confine assets stores information on the blockchain. With it, the LN can interface peers running a FN to send and get exchanges. The messages are encoded in CoAP messages. The FN sends back a reaction that can be confirmed by LN by checking its own token while the LN continues to build the exchanges. In IIoT condition, a LN can build up associations with the various intrigued FN to help yield recovery, verification age, updates to the structure, and compromise.

(Zhang, Zhu, Maharjan, & Zhang, 2019), is an edge insight and blockchain enabled 5G IIoT organize for joining and planning appropriated heterogeneous edge assets for modern applications in a proficient and secure way. The creators have built up a cross-area sharing empowered ideal edge asset planning plan to limit the working expenses of the edge hubs while improving limit. In the blockchain enabled it arranges, to proficiently arrive at an edge asset exchange agreement, credit-separated exchange endorsement component for conveyed edge hubs are suggested. The cross-area includes crossing between various asset types and diverse IIoT systems. Three fundamental components of the deep reinforcement learning (DRL) methodology include state, activity, and grant. The state comprises the administration requests of assorted applications in various systems, and the accessible limit of heterogeneous assets of each edge hub. The activity is characterized as edge asset booking techniques, which allot heterogeneous edge assets for different kinds of modern applications created in various systems.

(Xu, et al., 2019), is a blockchain-based nonrepudiation administration provisioning methodology for IIoT situations. The blockchain is utilized as a proof recorder and an administration distribution intermediary. The necessary help program is cut into non-executable parts for conveyance by means of on-chain and off-chain diverts in independent strides. The procedure can lessen the weight of the blockchain and maintain a strategic distance from the program exposure chance. In addition, it implements proof entries of even off-chain practices. The system guarantees the genuine reasonableness of nonrepudiation scheme. The creators planned an assistance confirmation strategy dependent on homomorphic hash strategies, which can accurately approve administrations dependent on negligible lightweight on-chain proof instead of complete help program codes, supporting the centre usefulness of the model.

LightChain(Liu, Wang, Lin, & Xu, 2019) is a savvy manufacturing plant representing the structure of the blockchain framework. The framework comprises of four layers-API layer, LightChain layer, Cache layer, and Storage layer. The light chain layer is comprised of various approval systems to affirm the legitimacy and uprightness of pending (computerized signature approval and connection approval). An API layer offers interfaces for modern control applications. Cache layer is intended to quicken the reactions to different calls. The information stores the pending blocks, and helpful blocks. Capacity layer, ordinarily served by asset rich gadgets, gives determined capacity, administration to the upper layers.

Proof-of-Reputation-X (PoRX)(Wang, Liang, Chen, Kumari, & Khan, 2020) includes a notoriety module which can be incorporated in the PoX conventions. The quintessence of the blockchain accord is to keep up a similar status of the record on various hubs. In every agreement cycle, a certified hub is chosen to refresh the blockchain record. In blockchains the Standard of the agreement is to choose hubs who contribute decisively to the framework based on plentiful assets. Subsequently, with PoRX by the notoriety of hubs in the framework, it can lessen the trouble of PoX agreement, which stays away from the need of ASIC mining machines hazard and the danger of centralization. Identity-based Method incorporates - presumed development, obstruct start process, revelry cycle, motivating force component and Protocol Parameters Update Rule.

(Chen, et al., 2019), is a multi-bounce circulated calculation offloading answer. It considers the information handling undertakings and the digging assignments together for blockchain-engaged IIoT. To address the principal issue introduced, the creators have built up a game-hypothesis based disseminated calculation offloading technique to permit the information preparing undertakings and the mining errands to be offloaded to the Edge servers to accomplish worldwide asset enhancement. To address the subsequent issue introduced, they have defined the offloading issue as a multi-bounce calculation offloading game (MCOG) and plan a dispersed calculation by which the game can rapidly meet to a steady state.

The IIoT Bazaar expects to address these difficulties by applying a decentralized Blockchain organize and the various leveled, conveyed structure of a Fog Computing. Blockchain innovation is utilized to make a commercial centre for the trade of utilizations in which no outsiders should be trusted. The IIoT Bazaar App is the connection between the Edge Devices in the field and the Technician. The experts utilize their cell phones, which have the IIoT Bazaar App introduced, to recognize, distinguish and associate with the Edge Devices. After effective confirmation, the specialists can introduce or uninstall applications utilizing drag and drop activities. Besides, the IIoT Bazaar App gives data about the current status of the Edge Devices and their cooperations with respect to application establishments and updates. The IoT Manager is the core of the design and essential issue of contact. The Dev Store is the interface for the engineers with the IIoT Bazaar biological system. The Warehouse stores the binaries.

In this work, an encryption plot for an IIoT-arranged system processing framework is introduced that depends on a blockchain. The procedure begins with the introduction of the web administration of the blockchain for hubs of the system. There are many picture catching gadgets, and every gadget goes about as a hub. At the point when a hub catches the picture and sends it to the chain for preparing, the proposed calculation will perform introductory checks. It will check that the present time is not as much as that of the message circulation stage and whether the hub is enlisted or not enrolled. The Certificate Authority (CA) allocates a computerized personality to each hub of the system. If the hub has a cryptographically approved advanced testament, mapped by the CA, at that point, it can take an interest in the framework. If the mentioned exchange is as of now prepared, at that point, it is overlooked. After beginning checks, it will begin the encryption procedure for the picture. This picture is prepared, and a hashed exchange ID will be distributed for each picture, which is the key to the whole plan.

The framework foundation(Huang, et al., 2019) is based on DAG-organized blockchain. Every element is a hub in the blockchain-based IIoT framework. There are four segments in the engineering. Remote sensors conveyed in a shrewd industrial facility to gather readings. Every sensor will produce a blockchain account when introduced. The key pair for every gadget is used to sign exchanges. Gateways get the solicitations from different sensors and communicate the exchanges in the knot, they exchange from legitimate sensors that are approved by the chief. The director can oversee the gadgets through propelling an exchange which records public keys of approved IoT gadgets. The knot arrangement is a public blockchain organize where any gathering can get into the system. The credit-based POW instrument to make the tradeoff between productivity and security is proposed. Hubs comply with the framework rules to send exchanges and will build the credit after sometime step by step.

, is a credit-based installment method to help quickness and successive vitality exchanging. Stackelberg games for credit-based advances are used to evaluate the work. All approved EAGs need to review and check exchange records in new squares. It requires some investment to complete the agreement procedure. The process is completed by comparing with the wallet address. At the token mentioning stage, the borrower can apply a token dependent on its credit. During vitality exchanging, the borrower utilizes vitality coins in wallet to complete installation. Every installment Based on the wallet is confirmed and recorded by the nearby credit bank. The credit bank puts the hash estimation of installment related information into prerecording. After a legitimacy span of the token, the borrower will get the most updated token including all hash estimations of the credit-based installment records.

A blockchain-empowered IIoT framework (Liu, Yu, Teng, Leung, & Song, 2019) comprising two sections is suggested. The IIoT arrangement creates exchanges of information and shares the same. The block chain framework manages the exchanges in a secure way. Two sorts of exchanges consistently are made by the savvy gadgets. These exchanges are handed-off to blockchain frameworks for putting away/getting the information into/from the circulated record. To deal with the exchanges created by the youth organize, a block is made, communicated to another block maker, and add the block to their nearby blockchain after an accord is reached on the new block.

An Anonymous Reputation System on a Proof-of-Stake blockchain (ARS-PS)(Liu, Alahmadi, Ni, Lin, & Shen, 2019) is suggested. The contribution permits retailers to build up notorieties by amassing inputs from shoppers. The proposed framework safeguards the commentator namelessness. The individual survey measurements are hidden and just the collected audit insights have been uncovered to people in general by breaking the job of the encryption key administration authority over different council individuals. The blockchain-based engineering that executes the proposed unknown notoriety framework to improve the framework straightforwardness is suggested. In the off-chain rating token stage, the proposed engineering lessens the on-chain stockpiling and calculation overhead.

BPIIoT(Bai, Hu, Liu, & Wang, 2019) is contained on-chain and off-chain organization. All exchanges are handled in the on-chain system (computerized signature). The off-chain organize manages the capacity, complex information preparing, and different issues that blockchain can't explain. The keen agreement is used as the administration agreement by purchasers and assembling assets, giving on-request fabricating administration. Two shrewd application cases, producing gear information sharing and support administration sharing from keen assembling, are executed to clarify the brilliant agreement for the hardware upkeep administration and status information sharing administration. The on-chain organize maintains a strategic distance from the support of outsiders by presenting Secure Multi-Party Computation (SMPC). Information inquiry and computation are dispersed on various hubs, which take an interest in the count without spilling data.

(Seok, Park, & Park, 2019), is a lightweight hash-based blockchain engineering for IIoT. The proposed blockchain organize comprises of "Cell hub" and "Capacity hub", and it works between the field layer and control layer. Field layer of the proposed design relates to level 0 and level 1 in Purdue model. The control layer relates to level 2 in Purdue model. For covering numerous heterogeneous gadgets in an expansion zone, the fields are isolated in a little territory, which is referenced as "Cell". The cell hub makes block of information assembled from associated gadgets and communicate to different hubs in the blockchain for block approval after block mining. After the block approval process, all hubs partaking in block approval sends the arrival message to the capacity hub for notice approving outcomes and afterward block update is prepared. The capacity hub is answerable for overseeing block update and record the board. In the block update process, the capacity hub adds the approved block. The entirety of the prepared exchange can be checked from the conveyed record in the capacity hub.

SCFMCLPEKS+ (Wu, Chen, Wang, & Wu, 2019) utilizes a bilinear guide, ace key, and hash work. The information proprietor's the halfway private key, information client's fractional concealed credential, and worker's incomplete private key DS are registered. Utilizing public, private, and mystery keys, the hidden entryway is determined. The worker's private solution and ciphertext utilization authenticate the check procedure. The proposition improves disconnected watchword speculating assault.

The creators have built up the first CLKS plot with multi-beneficiary watchword scan work (Lu, Li, & Zhang, 2019) for IIoTs. The plan stays away from the excessive bilinear matching. It gives protection catchphrase search. MARCKS plot contains four various elements, in particular: a credential generating center, a distributed storage worker, a sender, and different beneficiaries. The center is accountable for making a lot of shared framework boundaries and a framework ace key. It is likewise answerable for delivering a couple of fractional keys for the sender and every beneficiary. The sender creates and sends the accessible ciphertexts to the distributed storage worker. Each target beneficiary can recover these information ciphertexts by sending the disseminated storage worker an inquiry token determines from the pursuit watchword by utilizing the beneficiary's private key. Finally, the distributed storage worker abuses the pursuit token to find all coordinating ciphertexts that are then gotten back to the beneficiary.

The work (Zhou, et al., 2018) considers assault for Cui's multi-key total accessible encryption, where the aggressor can figure the other approved clients' keys from the unapproved inside client's key. The creators have presented a formalized meaning of record driven total watchword attainable encryption framework, which can be utilized for the IIoT information sharing and approved information search. They formalize two new security models on the Fc-MKA-KSE framework. One catches catchphrase ciphertext security, for example, the lack of definition against particular document picked catchphrase assault, and different catches the hidden entrance security, for example, the vagary against specific record watchword speculating assault. They build a catchphrase reachable encryption conspire in the record driven structure in IIoT sending. At that point, they actualize a model of the proposed plot and assess its presentation. The assessment shows that the ciphertext and secret entrance can figure on the sensor.

The creators planned safe station free certificateless public key encryption with various catchphrases (Ma, He, Kumar, Choo, & Chen, 2017) plot for IIoT sending. It uses two-cycle bunches with a similar request. It chooses a generator and guides it to produce bilinear matching. The framework has four elements- a cloud worker, an information proprietor, a beneficiary, and a credential obtaining unit. It is liable for producing a framework clue and incomplete private keys of both collectors and workers. Information Owner uses the collector's and worker's public solution to encode the information and the file of catchphrases contained in the facts. The information proprietor can store the encoded data and scrambled catchphrase lists in the cloud worker. The recipient is an informed client who acquires his/her incomplete private key from the credential unit. The beneficiary creates the secret entryway of watchwords that he/she wishes to look, sends it to the cloud worker. Cloud Server acquires its halfway private key from key unit. It is answerable for preparing information, for example, registering information, putting away information, and scanning information for the client. The work comprises of eight polynomial-time probabilistic calculations.

The creators develop a light-weight attainable public-key encryption conspire with forwarding protection (Chen, Wu, Kumar, Choo, & He, 2019). It accomplishes both forward preserves and searches effectiveness near that of some down to earth accessible symmetric encryption plans. It keeps away from the requirement for costly credential administration. SPE-FP demonstrates to be ciphertext vague in the irregular prophet model, and it additionally accomplishes forward security. An accessible encryption plot with concealed structure arranges the catchphrase attainable ciphertexts with carefully planned shrouded relations. It lists ciphertexts by the corresponding closed connection between public Head to the first ciphertext. The arrangement has four elements- Certificate Authority (CA), Cloud Server Provider (CSP), Data Owner (DO), and Data Receiver (DR). The correspondence among DO and DR is non-concurrent through a free-channel. There are two channels for corresponds among CSP and DR, where one is a public channel. DO is liable for producing and sending re-appropriated ciphertexts, which incorporate record ciphertexts, file ciphertexts, variant ciphertexts, and catchphrase ciphertexts. CSP entrusts with information stockpiling and recovery, which has practically boundless capacity and calculation limits. DR can give search inquiries by using a catchphrase secret entrance and afterward get all coordinating documents containing the relating watchword.

The information proprietor assembles the catchphrase lists and transfers the information along with the watchword lists to the haze hub (Yu, Chen, Li, Li, & Tian, 2019). The elements of IIoT can present some pursuit tokens called secret entryways to the haze hub looks through the redistributed information relating to catchphrases. The haze hub performs uniformity testing to figure out which parts of the ciphertext coordinate the secret entrance and afterward restores the coordinated share to the element as an output. SE arranges into two classes- symmetric accessible encryption (SSE) and public key encryption with catchphrase search (PEKS). It executes CPoR on a MacBook Pro with 2.3 GHz Intel Core i5 CPU and 8 GB RAM. The calculations run in C ventures upheld by the OpenSSL library. The work area has a 64-piece Win 10 working framework and 8 GB RAM, The processor is Intel Core i5-7400 CPU @ 3.00 GHZ, and the compiler is Visual Studio 2012. The Raspberry Pi 3 is outfitted with Cortex-A53 (ARMv8) 64-piece SoC @ 1.4 GHz CPU and Broadcom BCM2837B0, whose working framework is Raspbian.

The Visual Processing Hub (VPH) in mechanical observation networks (Muhammad, et al., 2018) gathers visual information from visual sensors as video outlines, bringing large volumes of video information. The creators tentatively demonstrated that the aftereffects of vital pictures are multiple times quicker than existing techniques for object discovery. The preliminaries for each casing caught by the visual camera are preliminary for the evacuation of foundation movement and accurate assessment. They estimate by figuring the adjustments in picture block esteems in neighboring casings. The proposed calculation has two significant segments- significant part means to utilize an ongoing 2D disordered guide to create PRNG appropriate for our proposed picture encryption, and the subsequent ones execute one round of stage dispersion measures for the keyframe viable. They utilize a randomized methodology, making it infeasible for assailants to master anything about the first information from the encoded outlines. A 2D strategic balanced sine map (LASM) gives efficiencies and high affectability to starting qualities and sophisticated turbulent conduct of its produced groupings. They set the underlying grades as mystery keys to make assaults ineffectual and futile. Coding the pixels of the keyframe begins with installing genuine disordered pieces into one channel of the sole keyframe. At that point, disarray and dissemination tasks intend to haphazardly change the pixel esteems and mix the pixel positions, individually.

The visual preparation center (VPH) gets visual data from sensors as a video outline in the keen medical care reconnaissance organizations, prompting critical measures of video data. The proposed extraction YOLOv3 calculation for keyframes (Khan, et al., 2020) is lightweight since it is used as a preparation picture dataset and describes to distinguish human presence from the recorded recordings. The utilized methodology proposes a technique to expand discovery accuracy while advancing a continuous cycle by displaying YOLOv3's jumping box, the most representative of single-stage finders. The precision of the model is 88-90% with 1-16 FPS (document every second) on the Intel Core i5-fifth era framework, which is more fitting in regards to the patient's observing in the keen medical services framework. Each communication or development of the patient is precisely distinguished with high exactness and inside the jumping boxes. This extraction cycle utilizes with deferent patients in different clinic wards into the savvy medical services arrangement, and as a came about keyframe. It essentially delivers keyframe from the keyframe extraction model is passed to the lightweight encryption model for additional protected activity. The recommended calculation has two parts. The primary segment that utilizes the most recent cosine transform-based turbulent arrangement (CTC) to produce PRNG proper for our proposed picture encryption and the subsequent one intends to perform three rounds of disarray – dissemination strategies for the keyframe.

The proposed framework (Ahmad, Larijani, Emmanuel, & Mannion, 2018) checks the number of inhabitants and sends information to the distributed computing stage ThingSpeak progressively. Protection attack is consistently a worry for video-based inhabitance observing frameworks when associated with the Internet. They have utilized the Intertwining Logistic guide, and results are likewise contrasted outcomes and NCA map. Analyses use a solitary overhead camera in the T10 office at Glasgow Caledonian University, UK. In the proposed framework, when individuals cross a virtual line, inhabitance (in/out) is estimated, and information transfer to the distributed computing stage, ThingSpeak. The person distinguished in an edge undergoes scrambling.

The proposed model (Elhoseny, et al., 2018) has four consistent cycles. The secret patient's information scrambles utilizing proposed hybrid encryption conspire that creates from both AES and RSA encryption calculations. It hides in a spread picture that uses either 2D-DWT-1L or 2D-DWT-2L and produces a stego-picture. The separated data undergoes unscrambling to recover the first information. The execution completes by using the MATLAB R2015a programming running on a PC with a 2.27 GHz Intel (R) Core (TM) I3 CPU, 8 GB RAM, and Windows 7 as the working framework. The outcomes dependent on six measurable boundaries containing the Peak Signal to Noise Ratio (PSNR Mean Square Error (MSE), Bit Error Rate (BER), Structural Similarity (SSIM), Structural Content (SC), and Correlation.

The calculation introduced joins two clamorous frameworks- Arnold's Cat guide and Duffing conditions (Boutros, Hesham, Georgey, & Abd El Ghany, 2017), for the two phases of confusion based picture encryption. For the disarray stage, pixels rearrangement utilizes an altered two-dimensional Arnold's Cat map. The proposed calculation is executed on Matlab R2016a to investigate its exhibition dependent on the usual security boundaries. The examination performance on three grayscale test pictures of various sizes- Lenna (512×512), Lenna (256×256), and Cameraman (256×256). Histogram examination is performed on the encoded test pictures to envision the distinction in pixels' qualities circulation between the scrambled and the first picture. The connection coefficients allude to the real connection between two contiguous pixels of a figure, evenly, vertically, and tilted. The proposed calculation utilizes 22 distinct boundaries as encryption keys. It assesses its entropy esteem, mean square blunder, top sign to clamor proportion, level of changed pixels' qualities, and power of this change in the code picture concerning the first picture. The commitment is the increasing speed of the proposed encryption plot in a total equipment arrangement reasonable for continuous IoT imaging applications.

The proposed encryption calculation (Wu, et al., 2019) comprises of seven stages containing Initial credential age, Pseudo-arbitrary succession age, Permutation vector age, Confusion, DNA encoding, Diffusion, and DNA disentangling. The information has plaintext alongside two boundaries. It will produce starter certification. The essential ones create two change vectors. The image uses these vectors. The pseudo arrangement and planning rules, two DNA successions are made. These and planning rules generate the figure.

The invisible layer encryption (Lv, Liu, & Sun, 2019) partitions into four sections. Information assortment and Data move part is answerable for routinely gathering information from camera sensors which circulated in savvy urban communities, and putting away in edge server farm or cloud server farm, as per the necessities of IoT applications. The information pre-handling part is principally liable for the preliminary preparation of the gathered information, and recoveries the acquired arrangement of organizing purposes of the prepared article in our social information base. The center of information encryption calculation is answerable for coordinating with the encoded object. After the coordinating is fruitful, our center calculation progressively produces film and passes the film to the information for security information insurance. The framework and Network Monitoring part offer types of assistance.

The plans (Noura, et al., 2018) can partition into two classes-Stream codes and Block figures. The proposed figure plot incorporates a few commitments that prompted a significant level of productivity and security for IoT gadgets contrasted with the ongoing lightweight square codes, late confusing codes. The aging cycle of the dynamic key and the related sub-enters uses in the code. The mystery key is usual between the imparting elements after the shared confirmation step. A pseudo-arbitrary generator produces this Nonce. At that point, the mystery key is Xored, and it is comparing the yield hash to deliver the dynamic credential. It isolates into four distinctive sub-keys that structure the seeds for the distinct code natives and these portray in the accompanying subsections.

The proposition (Abd El-Latif, et al., 2020) is lightweight picture encryption system utilizing one-walker. The introduced arrangement uses the abilities of nonlinear elements of QWs to produce PRNG groupings and build P-boxes. From the start, the first picture is isolated into blocks every one of size 16×16, and afterward, each square is partitioned into two subblocks: right subblock and left subblock. Each subblock previously recombination is permutated and subbed with its own P-box and PRNG that starts from the likelihood appropriation of following up on e-walker on a circle. The encoded blocks are joined together and afterward XORed with another PRNG arrangement to develop the code picture. NIST SP 800-22 tests are applied to research the haphazardness conduct code picture. They comprise of 15 tests on a 106 piece succession.

The SSIR plot (Yan, Chen, & Jia, 2019) empowers the asset compelled customers to move the cycle of preprocessing pictures to cloud cut off and perform looking in cloud workers. It will lessen the expense of the customer. It first needs to build a Hessian grid. It contrasts and its 26 neighbors in the picture space. On the off chance that it is bigger or littler than its neighbors, this point will choose as an intriguing point. The harr wavelet checked in its round neighborhood. That is, in the roundabout neighborhood of the element focuses, the entirety of the level and vertical harr wavelet. The fan shape is pivoted at timespans radians and rehashes this cycle. It has three members. The picture proprietor creates two sets of keys: a public encryption key pair and a mark key pair. The public encryption key uses to scramble the pictures and the element vectors. The mark key uses to approve the customers to play out the picture search over the picture set. Next, through far off verification and neighborhood confirmation, the mystery key of the picture proprietor is moved to the inquiry enclave. The pursuit enclave decodes the encoded inquiry picture, separates the component vectors of the question picture, and runs the hunt calculation on the plaintext. At last, it restores the outcome to the customer.

The gathered data undergoes hashing (Khan & Byun, 2020). Hashing is making a unique mark. If there is a slight change in the data, the entire distinct one will be changed. In the picture encryption measure, a picture modifies into an arrangement of bytes with the goal. It is a helpful procedure to ensure the substance of advanced figures. Diverse cryptographic calculations play out the encryption cycle. Encoded bytes would then be able to be moved to another framework, where it alters to acquire unique qualities utilizing the decoding cycle. For both encryption and decoding measures, we use calculations dependent on some key. The administrator can arrange endorser and non-endorser peers. Since the sensor hubs don't have many force assets to run the mining calculation, a few devices go about as validator hubs. These hubs agree to add another square to the chain. It is an organization that must continue the imitation of a blockchain. It is likewise answerable for preparing the exchange. In an IIoT organization, hubs are battery-or power controlled gadgets perform correspondence and information assortment. The device in the blockchain fuses various squares, state information bases, strategies, and a keen agreement. The condition of the record at given factors and times is spoken to and put away in the state information base.

3. Background

a. **Merkle root -** A Merkle root is a straightforward numerical approach to check the information on a Merkle tree. They are utilized in digital money to ensure information squares went between peers on a shared system. They are key to the calculation required to keep up cryptographic forms of money like bitcoin and ether. A hash tree encodes the blockchain information in a productive and secure way. It empowers by brisk checking of the blockchain information on the distributed organize. Each exchange happening on the blockchain arrange has a hash related with it. These hashes are inserted as a treelike structure with the end goal that each hash is connected to its parent following a parent-kid treelike connection.

Assume that two text messages are hashed at level 1. Let the text be $Text_1$ and $Text_2$. Let the resultant hash value H_1 be derived from hashing of $Text_1$. This is represented in notation (1). Let the resultant hash value H_2 be derived by hashing the text $Text_2$. The same is represented in the notation (2).

$$H_1 \rightarrow hash(Text_1) \tag{1}$$

$$H_2 \rightarrow hash(Text_2) \tag{2}$$

The parent of these two hash values is represented by H_{12}. The same is obtained by hashing both the texts $Text_1$ and $Text_2$. The same is represented in the notation (3).

$$H_{12} \rightarrow hash(Text_1 + Text_2) \tag{3}$$

4. PROPOSED WORK

a. Notations Used in the Work

See Table 1.

b. Assumptions Made in the Work

-   The devices encompass intelligent sensors capable of handling routine. They are liable to get hacked.
-   The work uses two kinds of gadgets –
    -   To sense the environment, process, and forward them to the pre-programmed destination. The loading contains a hashing algorithm (blockchain technology) along with other credentials.
    -   Auxiliary devices/validating devices that can endorse the transmitted data. These devices are capable of building a hash tree using the Merkle root. Only the validating devices are capable of generating the Merkle root tree using the hash algorithm.

Table 1. Notations used in the proposal

Notations used in the proposal	Description
D_i	i^{th} device of the network
Hello	Hello packets
Ack	Acknowledgement
V_i	Validating node/auxiliary node
D_{id}	Device identification
I_d	dimension of the image
R_i	resolution of the image
B_d	bit depth of the image
I_s	Size of the image
T_i	Considered Time

c. Methodology Used in the Proposal

i. *Deployment of the devices* – The deployed devices occupy various locations in the industrial setup. The devices communicate with each other creating a topology. In equation (4), the gadget Di is sending Hello-packet to the device Dj. After receiving the message from the device, Dj sends an acknowledgment to Di. Equation (5) contains the same representation.

$$D_i \rightarrow D_j: \text{Hello} \tag{4}$$

$$D_j \rightarrow D_i: \text{Ack} \tag{5}$$

ii. *Registrations with the auxiliary node/validating node – The devices get* registered at the auxiliary node by providing their identification. In the equation (6) the device D_i is transmitting its identity D_{id} to the validating node V_i.

$$D_i \rightarrow V_i: D_{id} \tag{6}$$

iii. *Deriving the hash value using the blockchain* –The device capturing image calculates the hash value using the blockchain methodology. The following parameters used to derive the hash value – dimension of the image, resolution of the image, bit depth, and size. The corresponding device calculates the hash value using these units and transmits it along with the encrypted data to the respective validation device. In equation (7), the gadget D_i calculates the hash value using the dimension of the image I_d, resolution of the image R_i, bit depth B_d, its size I_s and dispatches it along with encrypted data Data$_i$ to the auxiliary node V_i.

$$D_i \rightarrow V_i: hash(I_d, R_i, B_d, I_s) \| E_x(Data_i) \tag{7}$$

iv. *Deriving the endorsement key for a session* – The auxiliary node uses its and device identification to derive the endorsement key. The construction of the Merkle root uses the identity of the gadget and validating device. Hash$_M$ is the algorithm used to generate the Merkle root tree. In the equation, the device identification D$_{id}$ and validating device identification V$_{id}$ is concatenated. The hash value generation uses the Merkle root tree concept. The device transmits the data to the validating node for endorsement. Equation (8) represents the same. This value is attached to the received message and sent to the destination.

$$V_i \rightarrow hash_M(D_{id} \parallel V_{id}) \tag{8}$$

5. ANALYSIS OF THE WORK

The proposal is the improvement of the previous contribution. (Khan & Byun, 2020), is an encryption plot for an IIoT-arranged system processing framework is introduced that depends on a blockchain. The procedure begins with the introduction of the web administration of the blockchain for hubs of the system. There are many picture catching gadgets, and every gadget goes about as a hub. At the point when a hub catches the picture and sends it to the chain for preparing, the proposed calculation will perform introductory checks. It will check that the present time is not as much as that of the message circulation stage and whether the hub is enlisted or not enrolled. The Certificate Authority (CA) allocates a computerized personality to each hub of the system. If the hub has a cryptographically approved advanced testament, mapped by the CA, at that point, it can take an interest in the framework. If the mentioned exchange is as of now prepared, at that point, it is overlooked. After beginning checks, it will begin the encryption procedure for the picture. This picture is prepared, and a hashed exchange ID will be distributed for each picture, which is the key to the whole plan.

The contribution uses the Merkle root method to generate endorsement keys. The devices register themselves with the auxiliary devices by sharing their credentials. It transmits the encrypted data and the hash value (by using blockchain) to the respective validating node. The endorsement keys calculated by auxiliary devices are attached to the received data before transmitting them. The endorsement keys are derived using the identity of the transmitted device and validating node. Hence the reliability is increased by 2.58% compared to previous work. Figure 1 is used to represent the same.

The work is simulated in NS2. Table 2. Contains the parameters used the work for simulation.

6. FUTURE WORK

The contribution uses the Merkle root method to generate endorsement keys. The devices register themselves with the auxiliary devices by sharing their credentials. It transmits the encrypted data and the hash value (by using blockchain) to the respective validating node. The endorsement keys calculated by auxiliary devices are attached to the received data before transmitting them. The endorsement keys are derived using the identity of the transmitted device and validating node. Hence the reliability is increased by 2.58% compared to previous work. Figure 1 is used to represent the same. As the amount of data transmission increases, the energy in these devices decreases. So, suggestions for Security-centric and energy-centric algorithms are essential in the future.

Table 2. Parameters used during simulation

Parameters used	Description
Number of gadgets installed	4
Number of validating or auxiliary device employed	1
Length of the identity (validating or sensing device)	16 bits
Length of the Hash value obtained (endorsement key)	8 bits
Length of dimension of the image	32 bits
Length of resolution of the image	16 bits
Length of bit depth of the image	12 bits
Length of image size	16 bits
Length of hash value derived (blockchain)	11 bits
Length of data bits	256 bits
Simulation time	60 ms

Figure 1.

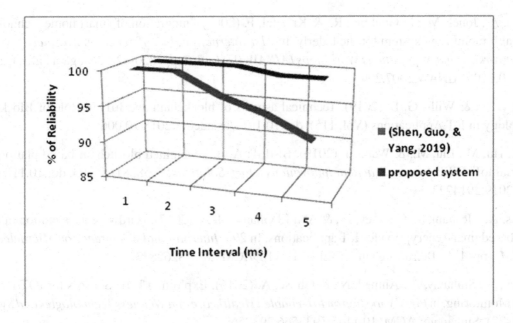

7. CONCLUSION

IoT is used in Industrial setup to increase security and provide ease to the user. The manual efforts decrease in this environment. The previous work concentrates on capturing images and transmitting the encrypted image. It uses the Merkle root and blockchain to make the transmission reliable. The suggestion increases reliability to the previous work. The system uses the Merkle root to endorse the key to the transmitting devices. The usage of the identity of the validating node and the sensing device is made. The work increases reliability by 2.58% compared to the previous contribution.

REFERENCES

A, B., & K, M. V. (2016). Blockchain platform for industrial internet of things. *Journal of software Engineering and Applications, 9*(10), 533.

Abd El-Latif, A., Abd-El-Atty, B., Venegas-Andraca, S., Elwahsh, H., Piran, M., Bashir, A., ... Mazurczyk, W. (2020). Providing End-to-End Security Using Quantum Walks in IoT Networks. *IEEE Access: Practical Innovations, Open Solutions*, 8, 92687–92696. doi:10.1109/ACCESS.2020.2992820

Ahmad, J., Larijani, H., Emmanuel, R., & Mannion, M. (2018). *Secure occupancy monitoring system for iot using lightweight intertwining logistic map. In 10th Computer Science and Electronic Engineering (CEEC)*. IEEE.

Ambika, N. (2020). Encryption of Data in Cloud-Based Industrial IoT Devices. In S. Pal & V. G. Díaz (Eds.), *IoT: Security and Privacy Paradigm* (pp. 111–129). CRC press, Taylor & Francis Group.

Ambika, N. (2020). Methodical IoT-Based Information System in Healthcare. In C. Chakraborthy (Ed.), Smart Medical Data Sensing and IoT Systems Design in Healthcare (pp. 155-177). Bangalore, India: IGI Global.

Arcelus, A., Jones, M. H., Goubran, R., & Knoefel, F. (2007). Integration of smart home technologies in a health monitoring system for the elderly. In *21st International Conference on Advanced Information Networking and Applications Workshops (AINAW'07)* (*vol. 2*, pp. 820-825). Niagara Falls, Canada: IEEE. 10.1109/AINAW.2007.209

Atlam, H. F., & Wills, G. B. (2019). Technical aspects of blockchain and IoT. In Role of Blockchain Technology in IoT Applications (Vol. 115). doi:10.1016/bs.adcom.2018.10.006

Bai, L., Hu, M., Liu, M., & Wang, J. (2019). BPIIoT: A light-weighted blockchain-based platform for Industrial IoT. *IEEE Access: Practical Innovations, Open Solutions*, 7, 58381–58393. doi:10.1109/ACCESS.2019.2914223

Boutros, A., Hesham, S., Georgey, B., & Abd El Ghany, M. A. (2017). Hardware acceleration of novel chaos-based image encryption for IoT applications. In *29th International Conference on Microelectronics (ICM)* (pp. 1-4). Beirut, Lebanon: IEEE. 10.1109/ICM.2017.8268833

Chandel, V., Sinharay, A., Ahmed, N., & Ghose, A. (2016). Exploiting IMU Sensors for IOT Enabled Health Monitoring. In *First Workshop on IoT-enabled Healthcare and Wellness Technologies and Systems* (pp. 21-22). Singapore: ACM. 10.1145/2933566.2933569

Chen, B., Wu, L., Kumar, N., Choo, K. K., & He, D. (2019). Lightweight searchable public-key encryption with forward privacy over IIoT outsourced data. *IEEE Transactions on Emerging Topics in Computing*, 1–1. doi:10.1109/TETC.2019.2921113

Chen, W., Zhang, Z., Hong, Z., Chen, C., Wu, J., Maharjan, S., Zheng, Z., & Zhang, Y. (2019). Cooperative and distributed computation offloading for blockchain-empowered industrial Internet of Things. *Internet of Things Journal, 6*(5), 8433–8446. doi:10.1109/JIOT.2019.2918296

Elhoseny, M., Ramírez-González, G., Abu-Elnasr, O. M., Shawkat, S. A., Arunkumar, N., & Farouk, A. (2018). Secure medical data transmission model for IoT-based healthcare systems. *IEEE Access: Practical Innovations, Open Solutions*, 6, 20596–20608. doi:10.1109/ACCESS.2018.2817615

Hossain, M., & Muhammad, G. (2016). Cloud-assisted industrial internet of things (iiot)–enabled framework for health monitoring. *Computer Networks*, 101, 192–202. doi:10.1016/j.comnet.2016.01.009

Huang, J., Kong, L., Chen, G., Wu, M. Y., Liu, X., & Zeng, P. (2019). Towards secure industrial IoT: Blockchain system with credit-based consensus mechanism. *IEEE Transactions on Industrial Informatics*, 15(6), 3680–3689. doi:10.1109/TII.2019.2903342

Khan, J., Li, J. P., Ahamad, B., Parveen, S., Haq, A. U., Khan, G. A., & Sangaiah, A. K. (2020). SMSH: Secure Surveillance Mechanism on Smart Healthcare IoT System With Probabilistic Image Encryption. *IEEE Access: Practical Innovations, Open Solutions*, 8, 15747–15767. doi:10.1109/ACCESS.2020.2966656

Khan, P. W., & Byun, Y. (2020). A Blockchain-Based Secure Image Encryption Scheme for the Industrial Internet of Things. *Entropy (Basel, Switzerland)*, 22(175), 1–26. doi:10.3390/e22020175 PMID:33285950

Khan, P. W., & Byun, Y. (2020). A Blockchain-Based Secure Image Encryption Scheme for the Industrial Internet of Things. *Entropy (Basel, Switzerland)*, 22(2), 175. doi:10.3390/e22020175 PMID:33285950

Li, Z., Kang, J., Yu, R., Ye, D., Deng, Q., & Zhang, Y. (2017). Consortium blockchain for secure energy trading in industrial internet of things. *IEEE Transactions on Industrial Informatics*, 14(8), 3690–3700. doi:10.1109/TII.2017.2786307

Liu, D., Alahmadi, A., Ni, J., Lin, X., & Shen, X. (2019). Anonymous reputation system for IIoT-enabled retail marketing atop PoS blockchain. *IEEE Transactions on Industrial Informatics*, 15(6), 3527–3537. doi:10.1109/TII.2019.2898900

Liu, M., Yu, F. R., Teng, Y., Leung, V. C., & Song, M. (2019). Performance optimization for blockchain-enabled industrial Internet of Things (IIoT) systems: A deep reinforcement learning approach. *IEEE Transactions on Industrial Informatics*, 15(6), 3559–3570. doi:10.1109/TII.2019.2897805

Liu, Y., Wang, K., Lin, Y., & Xu, W. (2019). A Lightweight Blockchain System for Industrial Internet of Things. *IEEE Transactions on Industrial Informatics*, 15(6), 3571–3581. doi:10.1109/TII.2019.2904049

Lu, Y., Li, J., & Zhang, Y. (2019). Privacy-Preserving and Pairing-Free Multirecipient Certificateless Encryption With Keyword Search for Cloud-Assisted IIoT. *IEEE Internet of Things Journal*, 7(4), 2553–2562. doi:10.1109/JIOT.2019.2943379

Lv, S., Liu, Y., & Sun, J. (2019). IMES: An Automatically Scalable Invisible Membrane Image Encryption for Privacy Protection on IoT Sensors. In *International Symposium on Cyberspace Safety and Security* (pp. 265-273). Guangzhou, China: Springer.

Ma, M., He, D., Kumar, N., Choo, K. K., & Chen, J. (2017). Certificateless searchable public key encryption scheme for industrial internet of things. *IEEE Transactions on Industrial Informatics*, 14(2), 759–767.

Muhammad, K., Hamza, R., Ahmad, J., Lloret, J., Wang, H., & Baik, S. W. (2018). Secure surveillance framework for IoT systems using probabilistic image encryption. *IEEE Transactions on Industrial Informatics*, 14(8), 3679–3689. doi:10.1109/TII.2018.2791944

Noura, H., Chehab, A., Sleem, L., Noura, M., Couturier, R., & Mansour, M. M. (2018). One round cipher algorithm for multimedia IoT devices. *Multimedia Tools and Applications*, *77*(14), 18383–18413. doi:10.100711042-018-5660-y

Seitz, A., Henze, D., Miehle, D., Bruegge, B., Nickles, J., & Sauer, M. (2018). Fog computing as enabler for blockchain-based IIoT app marketplaces-A case study. In *Fifth international conference on internet of things: systems, management and security* (pp. 182-188). Valencia, Spain: IEEE.

Seok, B., Park, J., & Park, J. H. (2019). A lightweight hash-based blockchain architecture for industrial IoT. *Applied Sciences (Basel, Switzerland)*, *9*(18), 1–17. doi:10.3390/app9183740

Wan, J., Li, J., Imran, M., Li, D., & Fazal-e-Amin. (2019). A blockchain-based solution for enhancing security and privacy in smart factory. *IEEE Transactions on Industrial Informatics*, *15*(6), 3652–3660. doi:10.1109/TII.2019.2894573

Wang, E. K., Liang, Z., Chen, C. M., Kumari, S., & Khan, M. K. (2020). PoRX: A reputation incentive scheme for blockchain consensus of IIoT. *Future Generation Computer Systems*, *102*, 140–151. doi:10.1016/j.future.2019.08.005

Wu, T.-Y., Chen, C.-M., Wang, K.-H., & Wu, J. M.-T. (2019). Security Analysis and Enhancement of a Certificateless Searchable Public Key Encryption Scheme for IIoT Environments. *IEEE Access: Practical Innovations, Open Solutions*, *7*, 49232–49239. doi:10.1109/ACCESS.2019.2909040

Wu, T. Y., Fan, X., Wang, K. H., Lai, C. F., Xiong, N., & Wu, J. M. (2019). A DNA Computation-Based Image Encryption Scheme for Cloud CCTV Systems. *IEEE Access: Practical Innovations, Open Solutions*, *7*, 181434–181443. doi:10.1109/ACCESS.2019.2946890

Xu, Y., Ren, J., Wang, G., Zhang, C., Yang, J., & Zhang, Y. (2019). A blockchain-based nonrepudiation network computing service scheme for industrial IoT. *IEEE Transactions on Industrial Informatics*, *15*(6), 3632–3641. doi:10.1109/TII.2019.2897133

Yan, H., Chen, Z., & Jia, C. (2019). SSIR: Secure similarity image retrieval in IoT. *Information Sciences*, *479*, 153–163. doi:10.1016/j.ins.2018.11.046

Yu, Y., Chen, R., Li, H., Li, Y., & Tian, A. (2019). Toward data security in edge intelligent IIoT. *IEEE Network*, *33*(5), 20–26. doi:10.1109/MNET.001.1800507

Zhang, K., Zhu, Y., Maharjan, S., & Zhang, Y. (2019). Edge intelligence and blockchain empowered 5G beyond for the industrial Internet of Things. *IEEE Network*, *33*(5), 12–19. doi:10.1109/MNET.001.1800526

Zhao, S., Li, S., & Yao, Y. (2019). Blockchain enabled industrial Internet of Things technology. *IEEE Transactions on Computational Social Systems*, *6*(6), 1442–1453. doi:10.1109/TCSS.2019.2924054

Zhou, R., Zhang, X., Du, X., Wang, X., Yang, G., & Guizani, M. (2018). File-centric multi-key aggregate keyword searchable encryption for industrial internet of things. *IEEE Transactions on Industrial Informatics*, *14*(8), 3648–3658. doi:10.1109/TII.2018.2794442

This research was previously published in Blockchain and AI Technology in the Industrial Internet of Things; pages 81-97, copyright year 2021 by Engineering Science Reference (an imprint of IGI Global).

Chapter 37
A Survey of Blockchain-Based Solutions for IoTs, VANETs, and FANETs

Maroua Abdelhafidh
https://orcid.org/0000-0003-0626-5598
University of Sfax, Tunisia

Nadia Charef
Canadian University Dubai, UAE

Adel Ben Mnaouer
https://orcid.org/0000-0003-3617-7636
Canadian University Dubai, UAE

Lamia Chaari
University of Sfax, Tunisia

ABSTRACT

Recently, the internet of things (IoT) has gained popularity as an enabling technology for wireless connectivity of mobile and/or stationary devices providing useful services for the general public in a collaborative manner. Mobile ad-hoc networks (MANETs) are regarded as a legacy enabling technology for various IoT applications. Vehicular ad-hoc networks (VANETs) and flying ad-hoc networks (FANETs) are specific extensions of MANETs that are drivers of IoT applications. However, IoT is prone to diverse attacks, being branded as the weakest link in the networking chain requiring effective solutions for achieving an acceptable level of security. Blockchain (BC) technology has been identified as an efficient method to remedy IoT security concerns. Therefore, this chapter classifies the attacks targeting IoT, VANETs, and FANETs systems based on their vulnerabilities. This chapter explores a selection of blockchain-based solutions for securing IoT, VANETs, and FANETs and presents open research directions compiled out of the presented solutions as useful guidelines for the readers.

DOI: 10.4018/978-1-6684-7132-6.ch037

INTRODUCTION

Nowadays, Internet of Things (IoT) (Stoyanova et al.2020) has experienced tremendous opportunities and potential interest from various applications allowing a seamless connection of multiple and diverse devices to the internet in order to exchange efficiently collected data.

With the growth of IoT applications, a rise of Mobile Ad Hoc Networks (MANETs) (Tripathy et al.2020), Vehicular Ad Hoc Networks (VANETs) (Hamdi et al.2020) and Flying Ad Hoc Networks (Mukherjee et al.2018) applications is recognized. MANETs is a network of mobile nodes that are connected wirelessly and characterized by a dynamic network topology. FANET is another class of ad-hoc networks that is a subcategory of VANETs which is a sub form of MANET as illustrated in figure 1.

Figure 1. MANET, VANET, FANET and IoT

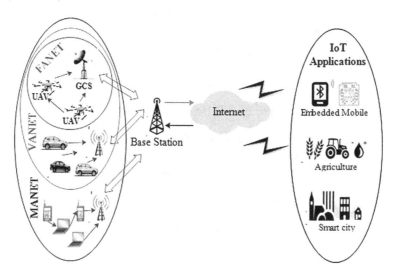

At present, IoT systems are often dependent upon a centralized architecture where information is sent from the connected devices and equipment to a proprietary cloud where the data is processed using analytics and then sent back to those tiny IoT devices to coordinate them as with all centralized systems. All devices are identified, authenticated and connected through cloud servers and the data collected by the devices is stored in the cloud for further processing (Ali et al.2018).

This centralized network architecture cannot be able to respond to the growing needs of the huge IoT ecosystems with the growth of connected devices that will be approximately 75.44 billion, as announced in (Alam2018). This gathered data, stored in centralized servers, can be tampered and consequently lacks traceability. Furthermore, through the current architecture, users have limited control over their data and are made to trust the cloud and have no choice but to rely on their promises of security. Accordingly, IoT security efforts mostly focus on securing point-to-point communication and fall short in addressing security during the lifecycle of data by thinking about this problem of trust. IoT devices need to confidently exchange data without having to rely on an intermediary which adds friction and costs reconciliation problems and all sorts of transactional challenges.

In this context, Blockchain (BC) (Lu2019) is a tailored technology for such problems. It has attracted a tremendous interest from various IoT applications thanks to its distributed nature that implies no single entity controls the ledger, but rather the participating peers together validate the authenticity of records. These records are organized in blocks which are linked together using cryptographic hashes (Ferrag et al.2018). All the BC peers have to validate each record to get added to a block (Reyna et al.2018) in order to be uploaded to the BC. This agreement is achieved through consensus algorithms such as Proof of Work (PoW), Proof of Stake (PoS), Delegated Proof-of-Stake (DPoS), and Proof-of-Authority (PoA). Accordingly, BC keeps track through the data records and achieves a sort of distributed trust that can drastically reduce the cost of verification and bootstrap IoT platform without assigning a lot of market power or much control to one single entity.

Due to this distribution of computing power of resources or IoT devices with BC and its high traceability and trust level, the system designed with BC is much more resilient to attackers.

This technology is currently revolutionizing several IoT applications but still in its early stage of research with VANETs and FANETs.

Several surveys (Wang et al.2020) (Wang et al.2019b) (Fernández-Caramés and Fraga-Lamas2018) (Ferrag et al.2018) have been already proposed to present the IoT security challenges and to explain the integration of BC technology. However, to the best of our knowledge, there is no work on efficient handling of security vulnerabilities of various IoT, VANET and FANET applications by leveraging the benefits offered by BC technology, that has been discussed recently in the literature. In addition, there is no relevant work highlighting the taxonomy of security threats and their BC-based solutions. Hence, our chapter is presenting a synthesis of several BC-based solutions proposed for securing the IoT, VANET and FANET systems considering the inclusion of Edge, Fog and Cloud computing layers in their overall proposed architectures.

The remainder of this chapter is organized as follows: Section II presents the basic concept of IoT, VANETs, FANETs, and BC technology. Section III reviews the related works on the IoT, VANETs, FANETs security vulnerabilities, threats and attacks and proposes two taxonomies of these threats. Section IV studies and discusses a selection of relevant BC-based solutions addressing these security vulnerabilities. Section V highlights future directions and suggests some open research areas related to the effective use of BC for securing the above systems. Section VI concludes the chapter and pinpoints some learned lessons.

To better clarify the acronyms, table 1 reports all the notations used in this chapter.

BACKGROUND

IoT Systems Basic Concepts

Internet of Things (IoT) (HaddadPajouh et al.2019) system represents a platform that combines software and hardware components connected to the internet enabling them to collect and exchange large amount of data. This data is analyzed and processed in order to perform an adequate action or some services offered to the end-user.

Various IoT definitions have been presented in the literature. Gupta et al. (Gupta and Quamara2020) highlighted a things-oriented definition of the IoT without defining the communication protocols by considering it as an interconnection of sensing and devices sharing information across platforms. Bodkhe et al. (Bodkhe and Tanwar2020) presented the IoT from the viewpoint of communication and environment so that devices should be connected in spaces using intelligent interfaces to connect, communicate within the user environment and context. Kavitha et al. (Kavitha and Ravikumar2021) detailed the IoT from a network context. Hence, the devices are connected through the Internet. In conclusion, the IoT is a hybrid infrastructure that associates the digital and physical worlds together through empowering physical things with communication and moderate computing capabilities to allow remote and possibly mobile, access, control and interrogation of these physical things through the Internet. Therefore, it is supposed to define the used entities and the interactions between them considering the communication architecture and scenarios. In an IoT system, it is important to ensure the security and privacy of the system especially with the increase of the number of IoT devices. As mentioned in (Bansal), the authors affirmed that this number will increase progressively to reach 75 billion by 2025. Accordingly, to address the IoT security characteristics, authors in (Hassan et al.2019) (Zarpelão et al.2017) (Sha et al.2018) explained the IoT security requirements (authentication of devices (El-Hajj et al.2019), confidentiality and integrity of data (Garg et al.2020), fault tolerance (Chakraborty et al.2019), heterogeneity (Paul and Jeyaraj2019), access control (Qiu et al.2020), etc), the various possible threats and attacks and they highlighted the proposed solutions.

Table 1. List of Acronyms

Acronym	Meaning	Acronym	Meaning
6LOWPAN	IPv6 over Low -Power Wireless Personal Area Networks	P2P	Peer-to-peer
AHD	Ad-hoc Domain	PoA	Proof-of-Authority
BC	Blockchain	PoET	Proof of Elapsed Time
BLE	Bluetooth Low Energy	PoS	Proof of Stake
DDoS	Distributed DoS	PoW	Proof of Work
DoS	Denial of Service	RFID	Radio Frequency Identification
DPoS	Delegated Proof-of-Stake	RSD	Roadside Domain
DTLS	Datagram Transport Layer Security	RSU	Roadside Unit
FANET	Flying Ah-doc Network	SDN	Software-Defined Networking
GCS	Ground Control Station	SSL	Secure Socket Layer
GPS	Global Positioning System	TLS	Transport Layer Security
HIP	Host Identity Protocol	UAV	Unmanned Aerial Vehicles
IoT	Internet of Things	V2I	Vehicle to Infrastructure
ITS	Intelligent Transportation System	V2V	Vehicle to Vehicle
IVD	In-Vehicle Domain	VANET	Vehicular Ah-doc Network
MANET	Mobile Ad-hoc Network	WEP	Wired Equivalent Policy
OBU	On-board Unit	WSN	Wireless Sensor Network

As addressed in (Dorri et al.2017b) (Dorri et al.2017a), IoT requires a distributed, auditable and scalable solution to ensure its security and privacy. The authors affirmed that the BC technology has the potential to achieve efficiently the IoT security requirements. It is considered as a distributed ledger where data is shared among peer nodes and builds a collective trust between them under a decentralized network. This unified and decentralized nature enables a security measure for IoT.

Blockchain Basic Concepts

Blockchain has been used to revolutionize many IoT applications and it represents a suitable technology that is able to provide a distributed secure ecosystem for the IoT (Kamran et al.2020). It offers a distributed management system in which all nodes can communicate, share information and all together manage the system by means of a distributed consensus among them. This peer-to-peer networking creates a distributed database synchronization which is an attractive feature for IoT to offer auditability and traceability.

As defined by Zheng et al. (Zheng et al.2017), the most important features that justify the increased use of BC technology in several industries and by a majority of researchers are its (i) decentralized infrastructure, (ii) immutability, (iii) ability to control new entries to the network and detect intrusion attempts by applying a decentralized consensus, (iv) It's auditability (to verify the transactions between peers transparently), and (v) their fault tolerance aspect in enabling data replicas records and avoiding data leakage.

Blockchain Structure

A Blockchain is composed of blocks containing the details of transactions within the network. Each block contains information about the current node and previous node, namely, the body and the header, respectively. The body includes the data in form of transactions and the number of transactions inside the block. The header contains a timestamp that indicates when the block was published and a Merkle tree that allows verifying the transactions stored within the body of the block. In addition, it involves the identifier of the previous block. This structure makes it similar to a linked list that ensures the immutability of the BC contents.

Types of Blockchain

Three types of BC, highlighting its privacy levels, are used in different scenarios by presenting various attributes. Table 2 shows a detailed comparison between these types.

- Public Blockchain (Tang et al.2019): is a distributed ledger system that allows to everyone to join the network, publish new blocks, read the transactions data and validate it. Public BCs are called permissionless in that it is very open and permit to anyone to have a copy of the BC. This type is required to manage a large number of anonymous nodes, so it is necessary to mitigate potential malicious behavior. Cryptocurrency networks are examples of such a BC including Bitcoin, Litcoin and Ethereum (Wood et al.2014).
- Private Blockchain (Pahlajani et al.2019): This BC is permissioned and is formed by a set of known transacting parties. All transactions will be validated and controlled by a selected set of nodes. Therefore, a private BC is not as tamper-resistant as a public BC. This type of BC is mainly for

enterprise, use cases and permissioned ledgers will replicate a high degree of confidentiality and accountability and transparency. Hyperledger (Cachin et al.2016) and Ripple (Pilkington2016) are the examples of the private BC.

Table 2. Comparison of Public, Private and Consortium Blockchains

Features	Public Blockchain	Private Blockchain	Consortium Blockchain
Nodes participation in consensus process	All nodes	Only particular participants	Selected nodes in various Organizations
Immutability	Yes	Partial	
Consensus Mechanism	PoS/PoW	multi-party consensus algorithm	
Permissionless	Yes	No	
Transaction speed	Slow	Fast	
Operations	Public read, write, share, validate	Restricted (Approved participants)	
Advantage	Best security of complete trustable transactions.	Emphasize the speed of the system. Highly scalable	● Mitigate some of the risks of a private Blockchain (by removing centralized control) ● Their smaller number of nodes gives them generally much more efficient performance than that of a public Blockchain.

- Consortium Blockchain (Gai et al.2019): called also federated BC. The most notable difference from public and private BC can be notified at the consensus level. It is performed by more than one central entity. Therefore, this system is flexible and decentralized, so that the visibility of the transactions can be limited to validators, searchable by authorized persons, or by all. As private BCs, a consortium BC does not include processing fees. Energy Web Foundation and IBM Food Trust are examples of such BC.

Smart Contracts

Smart contracts (Wang et al.2019a) are tiny computer programs stored inside the BC, used to manage transactions under specific conditions. Therefore, smart contracts are the digital equivalent of traditional contracts in the real world.

They are stored in the BC and inherit interesting properties like immutability and distribution. It is distributed by means that the output of the contract is validated by every node on the network. Tampering with smart contracts becomes almost impossible.

These contracts execute on Ethereum BC's platform that was created and designed to build decentralized applications. These applications are fully trustworthy and transparent because they run on BC. However, smart contracts are not controlled or modified even by developers after the deployment (Praitheeshan et al.2019).

Consensus Algorithms for Blockchain Development

Consensus algorithm is a strategy that a group of computers use to manage which nodes in the network get to set the state of truth that everyone else follows and agrees on. There are different applied consensus algorithms that each one has different properties or tradeoffs in terms of how secure the agreement is:

- Proof of Work (PoW) (Gervais et al.2016): It is the first consensus algorithm that has been developed. It is used to validate transactions and broadcast new blocks to the BC. It helps to protect the network against numerous different attacks. While PoW is a reliable and secure solution for managing decentralized ledger, it is also very resource intensive by consuming a lot of power.
- Proof of Stake (PoS) (Saleh2018): is designed to overcome the drawbacks of the proof of work algorithm. In the Proof of Stake algorithm, each block gets validated before another block is added to the ledger. Miners can participate in the mining process with their coins to stake.
- Proof of Elapsed Time (PoET) (Chen et al.2017): it is a modified form of PoS. Only approved parties selected based on their reputation can become validators. It can be used by private or permissioned BC networks.

Since the network requires identification of the miners, the consensus algorithm ensures a secure login into the system.

VANET Basic Concepts

Technology advancement and the emergence of smart cities have given rise to VANET technology (Lee and Atkison, 2021). VANET is a self organized ad-hoc network that consists of vehicles communicating through Peer-to-peer (P2P) communication or via multihop communication using Wireless technology. The vehicle in VANET contains an On-Board Units (OBU) to communicate with other vehicles and the Roadside Units (RSUs).

VANET is considered a subset of MANET. A major characteristic of VANET is that its topology changes more frequently compared to MANET due to the high speed of the vehicles. Other differences between the two types of network include the large scale of VANET deployment and unlimited power consumption of its node as opposed to MANET (Mokhtar and Azab, 2015).

Communication in VANET can be divided into three domains, namely the Roadside Domain (RSD), Ad-hoc Domain (AHD), and In-vehicle Domain (IVD). Communication at these domains can be classified according to three types of communication: Vehicle to Vehicle (V2V), Vehicle to Infrastructure (V2I), and Intra-Vehicle communication. V2V refers to the ad-hoc communication that occurs between vehicles. On the other hand, V2I describes the communication between vehicles and the RSUs. Intra-vehicle communication is used to define the internal communication of On-board Units (OBUs). VANET is an important technology to establish Intelligent Transportation Systems (ITS) and can play a critical role to enhance the safety and comfort level of drivers and transportation efficiency. VANETs can be used for effective traffic management, provide drivers access to road and environmental conditions, accident prevention and emergency awareness.

FANET Basic Concepts

Flying Ad-hoc Network (Chriki et al.2019) is a sub-class of VANET that is a subcategory of MANET where multiple Unmanned Aerial Vehicles (UAVs) are connected in wireless Ad-hoc Network to cover the monitored area. However, a FANET present specific features that differentiate it from other types of MANET network including the:

- Network connectivity: Connectivity within FANET can be often intermittent due to dynamic behavior of drones, which creates temporary disconnections. The communication link from the source to the destination may be unavailable for an indefinite period, which requires the reactivity of the network to find a backup path and avoid consequent losses to the application flows.
- Mobility model: In FANET, the mobility model depends on various parameters. It is dynamically modified due to the speed of drones, climatic conditions and many other geographical and topographical parameters.
- Strict and constrained deadline: Typically, FANETs are used for real-time applications. Therefore, the control and command messages must be processed in real time by the UAVs in order to avoid loss of control.

Despite the potential importance of FANET-based systems in monitoring and tracking applications, there are still some issues pertaining to stable networking due to the continuous dynamic behavior of drones. Furthermore, resource-constrained drones still need more innovative solutions to address the power scarcity that limits their flying time and consequently can negatively influence the monitoring efficiency. Moreover, various FANET-based systems suffer from security weaknesses that need effective solutions and further investigation. Accordingly, it is required to find a trade-off among security, stability, efficiency, and the network requirements

Similar to VANET, FANET presents three communication domains (Barka et al.2018) including the UAV to UAV communication, UAV to Ground Control Station (GCS) communication, and the hybrid communication.

IOTs, VANETs, AND FANETs: VULNERABILITIES, THREATS, AND ATTACKS

Although the rapid evolution of connected technologies, they are prone to various and critical security concerns. To tackle these challenges, a closer attention should be exclusively given to the emerging IoT, VANET and FANET related vulnerabilities. Accordingly, their related threats and consequent attacks can be highlighted and analyzed in order to define the adequate solutions to cope with these crucial security challenges.

In this section, each system's architecture is defined and explained. In addition, an overview that emphasizes on understanding different security challenges associated with each architecture layer is deeply addressed.

Vulnerabilities, Threats, and Attacks in IoT

IoT Security Architecture

There is no common architecture for the IoT and there are various IoT architecture presented in the literature (Aswale et al.2019) (Manogaran et al.2018). A few of them (Perwej et al.2019) proposed a four-layer architecture including the sensing layer, network layer, service layer and application-interface layer. The majority proposed three-layer architecture (Siegel et al.2017) composed of application, network and perception layers. Therefore, this architecture is considered to cover up the details of the IoT system and the IoT components, from devices, through the connecting network to the end-user through applications.

The perception layer consists of physical objects such as sensors and actuators, nodes, and devices. These devices gather the information from the environment and sense physical parameters. The collected data is then received by the network layer to send it to the application layer which in turn analyzes it in order to deliver specific services to the end-user.

Security vulnerabilities figure at each IoT architecture layer and cause different attacks. It is important to address the security issues in each layer and determine its related vulnerabilities in order to classify their targeted attacks. Alaba et al. (Alaba et al.2017) have surveyed the security threats such as the lack of privacy solutions for defining device location and the packet delay or loss and Distributed Denial of Service (DDoS) attack of Software-defined networking (SDN) architecture used for IoT application. In addition, they provided a taxonomy of IoT security attacks in the application domain (authentication, authorization, exhaustion of resources, and trust establishment), communication channel (MitM attacks, Eavesdropping), and data domain (Data privacy and confidentiality, Micro-probing, tampering of hard components, jamming, Collision, unfairness, exhaustion, replay, meta-data attacks, etc). Frustaci et al. (Frustaci et al.2017) have highlighted the various attacks against IoT system. They have classified them based on the IoT architecture layers (the perception layer including Node Tampering, malicious code injection, DoS attacks, routing attacks, and data transit attacks, the Transportation Layer including Routing Attacks and Data Transit Attacks, and the Application Layer presenting the Data Leakage, DoS Attack and Malicious Code Injection). The authors have investigated the proposed solutions for the highlighted attacks and they have concluded that the perception layer is the most vulnerable level of the IoT system due to the physical exposure of IoT devices, and their constrained resources.

Authors in (Kouicem et al.2018) have introduced the security requirements of various IoT applications (smart grids, healthcare, Transportation systems, smart cities, and manufacturing) in terms of authentication, confidentiality and privacy concerns. Moreover, they have revealed the security challenges for each application (Heterogeneity of communication standards, Scalability issues, Vulnerabilities related to information system technology, devices mobility, etc.). The authors have focused on IoT security solutions by discussing both classical approaches as well as new technologies.

Figure 2 illustrated the taxonomy of IoT security attacks present in each layer.

Perception Layer Vulnerabilities, Attacks and Solutions

This first layer is composed of IoT devices such as smartphones, Radio Frequency Identification (RFID) tags, sensors and actuators. These components sense, gather and measure various physical parameters. The collected data can be stored inside the devices or into a gateway to be processed and analyzed. The major functionalities of this layer are data sensing and data acquisition.

Due to the higher number of devices, their deployment security is an important challenge.

According to (Neshenko et al.2019), the vulnerabilities can be related to IoT devices, affect the confidentiality and the availability of the IoT system and make it victim to various malicious attacks that affect its security objectives and reduce its performance.

As the number of devices is continuously growing and operating autonomously in unattended environments, an attacker can access and manipulate it easily which causes physical damage to the devices and corrupts their control.

Several research works have addressed these vulnerabilities in order to understand their causes, and reveal their effects on the IoT system. Jiang et al. (Jiang et al.2020) have highlighted that the lack of the device encryption can lead to an illegitimate access to the sensed information to be easily extracted and modified. They have suggested security solutions such as proposing strong password-hashing algorithms, and providing transparent system file encryption to protect confidential data.

Nguyen et al. (Nguyen et al.2019) have affirmed that insufficient energy of the devices presents an IoT security challenge. Consequently, attackers try to shutdown the device and waste its limited energy by creating a series of legitimate messages. Therefore, the authors have revealed the importance of energy harvesting techniques to cope with power challenges (Azzabi et al.2017). In addition, they have affirmed that adequate authentication should be important to ensure IoT system confidentiality, interrupt malicious attackers to violate data integrity and save energy consequently.

On the other hand, common perception layer attacks have been elaborated in the literature as illustrated in table 3.

Table 3. Perception Layer attacks, effects and solutions

Attack	Effect	Proposed Solution
Node tempering and Jamming	● Access to sensitive information. ● DoS	● Physical Unclonable Functions based authentication (Aman et al.2017) ● CUTE Mote (Gomes et al.2017)
Sleep Deprivation Attack	Node shutdown	CUTE Mote (Gomes et al.2017)
Eavesdropping	Control data flow	Pervasive Authentication protocol and a Key establishment scheme (PAuthKey) (Porambage et al.2014)
Permanent Denial of Service (PDoS)	Resource Destruction	NetwOrked Smart object (NOS) Middleware (Sicari et al.2018)

Network Layer Vulnerabilities, Attacks and Solutions

This second layer, responsible for transmitting the collected data to the next layer, uses various transmission technologies such as ZigBee (Farahani2011), Bluetooth Low Energy (BLE) (DeCuir2013), 6LoWPAN (Al-Kashoash et al.2019), and LoRaWAN (de Carvalho Silva et al.2017).

At this level, IoT vulnerabilities can be caused by network or protocol weaknesses.

Various research works focus on the ZigBee protocol that ensures the secure communications between devices thanks to the use of symmetric keys shared between nodes (Rana et al.2018). In this context, khanji et al. (Khanji et al.2019) have addressed the various malicious actions employed to compromise

ZigBee-enabled IoT devices due to the unencrypted transmitted keys among nodes. Consequently, attackers can easily access the information and monitor the devices. DoS attack is the major resulting attack. Therefore, the authors have suggested deploying a secure key management process during the key installation to ensure the information confidentiality as highlighted also in (Harbi et al.2019) and (Pandharipande and Newsham2018).

When the Bluetooth technology is used, various vulnerabilities can help attackers to establish a connection with a victim. The authors in (Zeadally et al.2019) and (Antonioli et al.2020) have highlighted that the lack of authentication mechanism and insufficient protections when two devices are paired are the major Bluetooth vulnerabilities that allow an attacker to insert a rogue device between two paired Bluetooth devices and get access to the shared information.

It is recommended to examine the vulnerabilities of 6LoWPAN protocol. As addressed in (Bertin et al.2019), the use of malicious intermediary network nodes is a most known vulnerability of 6LoWPAN networks. It is based on verifying if the neighbor is a node that is authorized to access the Wireless Sensor Network (WSN). Various techniques have been suggested to deal with this vulnerability, including Encryption techniques like Datagram Transport Layer Security (DTLS), host identification technology like Host Identity Protocol (HIP) as affirmed by Benslimane et al. in (Benslimane et al.2018).

The LoRaWan protocol presents various security vulnerabilities leading to diverse attacks. The authors in (Yang et al.2018) (Butun et al.2018) (Butun et al.2019) (Noura et al.2020) have investigated the various LoRaWAN vulnerabilities and security issues including the transmission of different message without rekeying, caching and replay of ACK packets, transmission of falsified gateway beacons to repeatedly wake up sensors. Accordingly, this implies various attacks including replay, eavesdropping, DoS and battery exhaustion.

These network layer vulnerabilities increase the number of security network attacks as detailed in table 4.

Table 4. Network Layer attacks, effects and solutions

Attack		Effect	Proposed Solution
Denial/Distributed Denial of Service (DoS/DDoS) (Sonar and Upadhyay2014)		● Delays data forwarding ● Prevent data to access its required destination	SDN based IoT framework (Yin et al.2018)
Routing Attack (Andrea et al.2015)	Sybil Attack	Malicious node redundancy	Trust aware Protocol (Airehrour et al.2019)
	Sinkhole Attack	Data Alteration	● Authentication ● Intrusion Detection (Glissa et al.2016)
	Wormhole Attack	Packet tunneling	Clustering based Intrusion Detection System (Shukla2017)
	Selective Forwarding attack	Disrupts routing paths and sends incomplete information.	● Hash Chain ● Authentication (Glissa et al.2016) (Pu and Hajjar2018)
Man in the Middle (MiTM)		Data Privacy violation	● Secure MQTT ● Inter-device Authentication (Singh et al.2015)
Replay Attack		● Network congestion ● DoS	Signcryption (Ashibani and Mahmoud2017)
RFID Unauthorized Access		Data Modification	SRAM based PUF (Singh et al.2015)

Application Layer Vulnerabilities, Attacks and Solutions

This third layer is responsible for the collected data analysis and processing. In addition, it is able to provide high-quality services to meet end-users' needs. Different IoT environments (i.e., smart city, healthcare, and industry) can be implemented within this level.

Andrea et al. (Andrea et al.2015) have focused on the security vulnerabilities present in the application layer. It includes the malicious software such as Trojan Horses, Spyware and Adware that infects the system by tampering data and causing DoS attacks. Accordingly, the authors in (Liu et al.2016) have developed a lightweight framework ensuring security techniques in order to eliminate Trojans hardware from IoT devices. They have employed a trusted communication between nodes with encrypted messages to prevent unauthorized parties from accessing the information and allow authorized nodes to verify the forwarded messages. Furthermore, IoT devices data can be victim to different categories of malware. Su et al. (Su et al.2018) have proposed a Lightweight Neural Network Framework that allows to detect accurately malwares from doubtful programs.

At this IoT architecture level, it is necessary to ensure data security by performing data authentication mechanisms, data confidentiality and integrity. The major prevalent data attacks (see table 5) in the IoT system (Aman et al.2018) include the data inconsistency due to the lack of data integrity either that is transmitted or stored in the database, and the unauthorized access to sensitive or confidential data in an unauthorized manner.

Table 5. Application Layer attacks, effects and solutions

Attack	Effect	Proposed Solution
Data Inconsistency	Data Inconsistency	Chaos-based privacy preserving cryptographic scheme along with Message Authentication Code (MAC) (Song et al.2017)
Unauthorized Access	● Lack of Data Privacy ● Confidential data disclosure in an unauthorized manner.	● Attribute-based encryption (ABE) (Zhang et al.2018) ● Improved Secure Directed Diffusion (ISDD) protocol (Sengupta et al.2019) ● Shared secret key with PUF (Gope and Sikdar2018)

Figure 2. Taxonomy of IoT Security Attacks

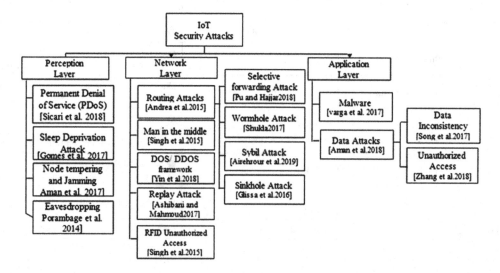

Vulnerabilities, Threats, and Attacks in VANETs

Ensuring security in VANETs is critical due to the sensitive nature of exchanged data, and threats to the privacy and security of users. Moreover, attaining security in VANETs can be challenging as a result of the large number of communication links, the ease to spoof valid IDs, network volatility, the need to achieve a trade-off between liability and privacy, delay sensitivity, large scalability, device heterogeneity in terms of communication and computation capabilities, and multi-hop communication. VANETs are vulnerable to attacks from several entities including: insider attacks such as compromised vehicles and outsider attacks. The attacks can be passive where an eavesdropper tries to capture information exchanged between communicating nodes. It can also be active, where the eavesdropper disguises as a legitimate vehicle and tries to alter the data exchanged (Mokhtar and Azab., 2015).

VANETs are prone to several security issues that differ according to the domain of communication (Hassija et al., 2020). In RSD, DDoS and routing attacks are the most common security issues. In the AHD domain that includes both V2V and V2I, communication is vulnerable to routing and authentication attacks. Authentication attacks happen when attackers use fake IDs to send malicious data. Similarly attackers can use fake IDs in IVD to gain sensitive data or implant false data. The authors in (Mokhtar and Azab., 2015), (Kaur et al., 2018), and (Krishnan and Kumar, 2020) have surveyed VANETs' related security threats. The next subsections summarize the security attacks covered by the three surveys according to five layers, namely, the physical layer, the data link layer, the network layer, the transport layer, and the application layer. The next subsections also touch on some security solutions implemented to address the presented attacks.

Physical Layer Vulnerabilities, Attacks and Solutions

The most common attacks at the level of the physical layer include: jamming attacks, eavesdropping, and DoS, as have been already highlighted with IoT systems.

To solve the jamming attacks, Spread Spectrum Techniques (Hossain et al., 2021) are used to make it difficult to jam or detect a signal. DoS and eavesdropping are caused by malicious vehicles in the network. The presence of malicious vehicles poses threats to the available bandwidth for data transmission in VANET. In the absence of a centralized authority, the attackers can flood the network with a large number of unwanted messages (Kumar and Gupta, 2020). On the other hand, eavesdroppers at the physical layer can perform a traffic interception attack. In this case, the illegitimate nodes listen to the traffic in the network for some time to capture important information. Therefore, a centralized unit is usually required to ensure the security of exchanged data and authentication of communicating vehicles.

Data Link Layer Vulnerabilities, Attacks and Solutions

Attacks at the level of the data link layer can occur by exploiting features of IEEE 802.11p MAC protocol and the Wired Equivalent Privacy (WEP) security algorithm. Common attacks at the data link layer include:

- DoS attacks: attackers exploit the binary exponential backoff scheme where heavily loaded nodes tend to access the channel more frequently causing other nodes to wait for a long time. DoS attacks can also occur when a malicious node takes advantage of the Ready to Send/Clear mechanism by causing interferences to the CTS, data, and ACK packet.

- Privacy and message integrity issue due to the usage of WEP to secure communication in IEEE 802.11p standard.

To address the DoS attacks, a modification has been introduced to the binary exponential backoff scheme where the backoff time is set by the receiver. On the other hand, IEEE 802.11i/WAP has fixed the vulnerabilities in WEP.

Network Layer Vulnerabilities, Attacks and Solutions

The dynamic nature of communicating vehicles in VANETs is the challenge hindering the design of routing protocols that ensure robust and secured communication. Common security threats to VANETs at the network layer include DoS and masquerading attacks. Other attacks include:

- Routing Table Overflow Attacks: involve the creation of routes toward nonexistent nodes to overwhelm the implementation of routing protocol.
- Routing Cache Poisoning Attacks: this includes the malicious manipulation of existing entries in the routing table leading to either undefined subnets or to malicious sites.
- The black hole attack: in this kind of attack, a node advertises itself as a legitimate node. Thus, the node can intercept the packet and drop it.
- Byzantine: this can involve a single malicious node or a set of malicious nodes that create routing loops by forwarding packets over long routes or dropping them.
- Wormhole attacks: involve the collaboration of two nodes to forward data along other legitimate nodes, creating a tunnel to take control of exchanged data.
- Rushing attacks: the attackers can forward packets faster than the legitimate nodes. Therefore, the likelihood that the attacker is part of the selected route is high.
- Location disclosure attack: these attacks involve the collection and leakage of location information.
- GPS Spoofing attacks: the attackers send a false signal instead of the original satellite signal to divert vehicles from the intended trajectory.
- Sybil Attacks: the attacker steals the identity of multiple nodes in VANET to insert malicious data that affect the decision made by legitimate nodes.
- Timing Attacks: the attacker delays the transmission of data, rendering it invalid as it reaches the destination.

To address routing attacks, it is important to ensure the legitimacy of communicating nodes. This is usually achieved by a centralized unit that is responsible for the authentication of participating vehicles in the case of VANETs.

Transport Layer Vulnerabilities, Attacks and Solutions

Common attacks at the level of Transport layer include

- SYN Flooding Attack: the attacker floods vehicles or remote base stations with SYN messages. Therefore, the receiver wastes resources waiting for a half-opened connection, making it unresponsive to legitimate traffic.
- Session Hijacking: happens when a malicious node spoofs the IP address of a legitimate vehicle to hijack its session and perform DoS on a trusted vehicle.
- TCP ACK Storm: occurs after session hijacking where the malicious vehicle storms the trusted vehicle with messages, causing the legitimate vehicle to storm the vehicle whose session was hijacked with ACK packets.

Other attacks at the level of the transport layer which are also relevant to IoT communication include masquerade, man-in-middle, rollback, and replay attacks. To address security's threats at this level, ensuring encrypted end-to-end communication is important. Common solutions to secure end-to-end communication include protocols such as Secure Socket Layer (SSL) (Dastres and Soori2020), and Transport Layer Security (TLS) (Siriwardena2020) that rely on public key cryptography.

Application Layer Vulnerabilities, Attacks and Solutions

Application layer's attacks in VANETs include:

- Malicious Code Attacks: include sending virus, worm, spyware, and trojan horse to vehicles and remote base stations. These types of attacks lead to the destruction of vehicles' applications, interruption of their services' access, and gaining information about legitimate vehicles.
- Repudiation Attacks: involve the refusal to send or receive messages by the attackers.
- Message Tampering Attack: the attacker can modify the content of the message leading vehicles to adapt a different driving behavior.

Common protection mechanisms against application layer's attacks include firewall programs to provide authentication mechanisms and filter packets. To strengthen firewall's operation, Intrusion Detection Systems (Kosmanos et al.2020) are also used to detect spoofed behavior by illegitimate vehicles. Anti-spyware programs are also used to detect spywares. On the other hand, To provide an advanced level of security against data-tampering in VANETs, the authors in (Karimireddy and Bakshi, 2016) propose a hybrid security framework that employs (Rivest–Shamir–Adleman) RSA and (Advanced Encryption Standard) AES to encrypt exchanged messages.

Vulnerabilities, Threats, and Attacks in FANETs

Since FANET is considered as a type of Ad-hoc Network, it is victim to the same security attacks. In addition, it presents new features including the dynamic and distributed environment, the frequent change of network topology because of the high mobility of UAVs, the UAVs limited computing and memory capacities. Accordingly, new security issues can be revealed. It can be either by taking control of the UAVs, interrupting the communication between the UAVs and the GCS, or stealing the collected data that affects its confidentiality and integrity. Therefore, these security attacks can be presented for five security layers as shown in figure 3: Physical layer, Link layer, Network layer, Transport layer and Application layer.

Physical Layer Vulnerabilities, Attacks and Solutions

The majority of works (Sun et al.2019) (Wu et al.2019) (CHAARI et al.2020) focus on eavesdropping, jamming, Spoofing attacks, etc. However, various specific attacks can occur and compromise the UAV functionality including hardware, software attacks. Accordingly, several research works have been suggested to improve the UAVs security. Different techniques are investigated to determine the various UAV components vulnerabilities and understand the possible consequent attacks as explored in (Alhawi2021).

Hardware attacks, as defined by (He et al.2019), occur when an attacker can access the UAV autopilot components, damage or reprogram it, and corrupt the stored data. In addition these attacks threaten on-board sensors such as Global Positioning System (GPS) receivers (Eldosouky et al.2019), IR sensor, camera and radar (Petit et al.2015). These attacks menace the UAV control and affect the survivability of the UAV.

The authors in (Nichols et al.2019) have highlighted that insecure authentication and authorization, the use of malicious hardware, hardcoded passwords and compromised GPS system can allow attackers to access and take control of the UAV components.

On the other hand, Software attacks compromise the software used in the devices such as the operating systems, and open source pilot systems. The SQL injections and insecure authentication are the major UAV software vulnerabilities allowing attackers to extract sensitive information such as credentials and emails and access critical systems to upload malicious codes or firmware (Dahiya and Garg2019).

Various solutions were proposed in order to detect these anomalies such as machine learning techniques (Challita et al.2019), intrusion detection schema (Kacem et al.2017), (Sedjelmaci et al.2017), and hardening the web-based systems used to program the UAVs routes (Pfaff2018).

Table 6. Physical Layer attacks, effects and solutions

Attack		Effect	Proposed Solution
Hardware Attacks (He et al.2019)	GPS Spoofing (Eldosouky et al.2019)	UAV redirection to be effortlessly captured	Intrusion detection schema (Arteaga et al.2019) (Kacem et al.2017) (Sedjelmaci et al.2017)
	On-board Sensor Spoofing (Petit et al.2015)	Mode confusion: False data	Drone sensor spoofing detection (SSDGOF) algorithm (Meng et al.2020)
Software Attacks (He et al.2019) (Dahiya and Garg2019)		False data injection	Authorization and authentication (Iqbal2021)

Data Link Layer Vulnerabilities, Attacks and Solutions

In this layer, the management of links between nodes and the neighbor discovery should be performed rapidly in a dynamic environment in order to hide network topology.

Behzadan et al. (Behzadan2017) have highlighted that accessible network topology allows attackers to find the most vulnerable regions with the maximum connectivity loss between nodes. (Behzadan2016) have suggested the use of covert communications between nodes to hide the network topology from attackers. However, the obtained results demonstrated that the topology can still be determined due to timing analysis attacks. Chen et al. (Chen et al.2017a) have proposed a method to optimize the positioning of UAVs in order to allow an autonomous UAVs path planning by exploiting a finely structured radio map.

On the other hand, to disrupt the data routing process, attackers can inject false bandwidth information into UAV network routing messages causing higher or lower bandwidth than the link really provides (Wei et al.2014).

Network Layer Vulnerabilities, Attacks and Solutions

Various attacks targeting the network layer have been identified and investigated. They aim to disturb the communication between nodes by absorbing network traffic, including malicious nodes in the network, and diverting and controlling network traffic. To achieve these goals, several methods can be adopted by attackers.

Similar to the link layer, the routing layer is also affected by channel jamming and connection deceiving attacks, aiming to increase the lack of UAVs collaboration and hence will disrupt the UAVs' mission and applications. Furthermore, the network performance can be decreased by injecting false messages, or replaying outdated messages. Consequently, the routing information can be disclosed.

To secure the UAV communication in FANET, different solutions have been proposed. Mowla et al. (Mowla et al.2020) have proposed and developed a Reinforcement Learning (RL) mechanism with spatial retreat strategy to ensure a cognitive jamming detection in FANET using various criteria. A Local Learning Mode (LLM) value, calculated by an on-device detection mechanism, is forwarded to an edge server to determine the global learning model value. The latter can be downloaded by the drone to recognize the jamming attack. Zhang et al. (Zhang et al.2019a) have implemented a successive convex optimization methods to improve the security performance. Accordingly, they have controlled the transmission channel and designed a UAVs trajectory to increase the secrecy rate in the uplink and the downlink communications.

Application Layer Vulnerabilities, Attacks and Solutions

UAVs transfer a lot of information that should be secured. The same data attacks (Erroneous data, flood packets, Desynchronization) that have been already detailed with IoT and VANET can occur with FANET applications. To prevent data from being intercepted by the attackers, it should be well verified and protected. Common mechanisms used for such protection are: encryption, authentication and authorization schema, etc (Bhardwaj et al.2020).

BLOCKCHAIN-BASED SOLUTIONS FOR IOT, VANETs AND FANETs SECURITY

Blockchain-Based Solutions for IoT Security

Blockchain-Based Solution for IoT Perception Layer

In order to obtain more secure devices and reliable communication between them, BC technology is used to solve the privacy challenge in IoT devices that are vulnerable to expose user data. Efficient authorization and authentication methods are needed to protect devices from malicious actions and illegitimate access.

Figure 3. Taxonomy of FANET Security Attacks

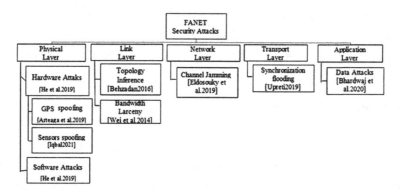

The authors in (Hammi et al.2018) have proposed a BC-based authentication mechanism for IoT called Bubbles-of-Trust. The IoT devices were grouped into clusters named bubbles. Before sharing data, devices are first authenticated. Ethereum is used to control the transactions between devices, validate the implemented public BC, and create secured virtual zones for secure communication. Khalid et al. (Khalid et al.2020) have combined the IoT system with a BC-enabled fog node used for the IoT devices registration and authentication. Each device should register using its corresponding BC-enabled fog node. Then, the information of these devices will be stored in the BC as blocks created for them and transmitted to other devices. Once a device authenticates, the BC-enabled fog node verifies its credentials and validates the authentication if the credentials are valid. Therefore, the device will be able to communicate with the other authenticated devices. Mohanta et al. (Mohanta et al.2019) have suggested a Ethereum BC-based system to establish a secure communication between edge devices and BC through gateways. Single smart contract is used to initialize the network, ensure devices' registration and authentication. The devices are identified by a pair of public/private key and Ethereum address.

Furthermore, key management and encryption methods are explored by several research works to keep the communication more secure and to allow the device authentication. Yazdinejad et al. (Yazdinejad et al.2019) have proposed an-IoT based solution where nodes are divided into clusters. A symmetric encryption is performed with the use of a shared key. The keys are created and distributed by the Cluster Head (CH) to its nodes members. The authors used the Proof-of-Authentication consensus algorithm (Maitra et al.2020) to validate new devices so that only the CH can verify the blocks to decide if the device can be trusted or not without executing the authentication process again.

Blockchain-Based Solution for IoT Network Layer

This layer allows the communication of the nodes and provides a method of propagating the data blocks to the rest of the network. Therefore, to ensure a secure and reliable communication process, the integration of BC is considered important as highlighted in (Zheng et al.2018b). The authors of (Ribeiro et al.2020) have focused on enhancing the LoRaWAN network server performance by coping with its centralized nature. They have proposed a private BC where smart contracts are employed for key management aspects. In the same context, Lin et al. (Lin et al.2017) have developed a trust mechanism that combines BC technology and LoRaWAN IoT technology to build an open and trusted system. This system aims to verify data transactions and their existence at an exact time in the network. In the work addressed in

(Cha et al.2018), the authors have proposed a BC Connected Gateway for BLE enabled IoT devices to maintain user privacy. The BC network is adopted to resolve privacy disputes between IoT application providers and its users by encrypting users' preference and storing it in the network.

On the other hand, researchers aim to solve the security issues in 5G by integrating BC technology. Bera et al. (Bera et al.2020) have presented a secure framework for BC in the 5G-based IoT environment. This framework is based on data management that can resist various attacks. The proposed scheme enables less communication and computation overheads. Zhang et al. (Zhang et al.2019) have designed a BC empowered Industrial IoT framework under the 5G environment. The suggested scheme includes a cross-domain resource scheduling mechanism and a transaction approval mechanism. Accordingly, secure service management and low latency are obtained.

Blockchain-Based Solution for IoT Application Layer

Since protecting user data is of utmost priority, therefore research has been focused on dealing with the aforementioned attacks.

Machado et al. (Machado and Fröhlich2018) have highlighted a three level split BC based architecture to ensure integrity of data stored in remote semi-trusted data storages. On the first level, they have introduced the PoT for Trustful Space Time Protocol (TSTP). The upper levels are responsible for maintaining integrity verification and data availability in semi trusted storages. In one such work, Rahulamathavan et al. (Rahulamathavan et al.2017) have proposed a BC based architecture by incorporating Attribute based Encryption (ABE) with it. Apart from supporting integrity and non-repudiation, the proposed scheme also preserves the privacy of transaction data. The proposed privacy preserving BC based architecture imposes access control to address confidentiality of shared data in the BC and thus provide end to end privacy preserving IoT systems. On the contrary, another work (Zheng et al.2018) has addressed a privacy preserving efficient medical data sharing scheme by utilizing ABE which hides all the attributes in the access control structure by utilizing the attribute bloom filter. The devices encrypt the data and send it to the server where only legitimate users satisfying the access control structure can decrypt the data. Sharma et al. (Sharma and Park2018) have proposed a novel BC based distributed cloud architecture. This architecture is able to gather, classify and interpret the huge amount of data at the edge of the network. This data is stored in the cloud that reduces the traffic load in the core network. Dorri et al. (Dorri et al.2019) have suggested a Lightweight Scalable BC (LSB) based scheme to achieve decentralization as well as end-to-end privacy and security. LSB is explored in a smart home with an overlay network. The latter is organized as clusters to ensure scalability and the public BC is managed by the CHs. Transactions are managed by a Distributed Throughput Management (DTM) scheme that guarantees the throughput and the system security.

Blockchain-Edge/Fog Computing Based Solutions for IoT Security

Other research works highlighted that the use of Edge/Fog Computing (E/FC) strategies with BC can provide more reliable and robust security (Bouachir et al.2020). As confirmed in (Uddin et al.2021), both the Edge and Fog computing systems facilitate the data processing with no need to be stored in the remote cloud. Accordingly, this solution is able to reduce the amount of data forwarded to the remote Cloud. Moreover, BC is required to ensure trust in a distributed Fog network and can be undertaken in highly decentralized environments. Li et al. (Li et al.2018) have proposed a distributed BC-based data storage scheme. Edge devices collect data from IoT devices, register it in the BC to be then forwarded to a Distributed Hash Table (DHT). Here, the BC is used as a trusted entity that manages and protects the stored data that can be accessible only in case of a successful user authentication. The work (Xu et al.2019) has focused on DDoS mitigation in Industrial IoT (IIoT) and have proposed a Multi-Level DDoS Mitigation Framework (MLDMF). It defended DDoS attacks at three levels, i.e. fog, cloud and edge computing levels. The fog, cloud and edge computing levels use a cluster of SDN controllers and applications, SDN-based IIoT gateways and big data along with intelligent computing respectively to analyze network traffic in order to detect and mitigate DDoS attacks. Authors in (Xiong et al.2018) have revealed that it would be very difficult for the resource-limited mobile devices to perform proof of work to reach consensus because of substantial resource requirements. Therefore, they propose a prototype for edge computing where the mobile devices would use the resources of the edge devices to perform complex proof of work operations. Li et al. 2019 (Li et al.2019) have proposed a distributed BC-based data storage scheme using certificateless cryptography. This secure proposed system uses edge devices which collect data from the IoT devices, register the data against that specific IoT device in the BC and finally forward the data to a Distributed Hash Table (DHT). The BC acts as a trusted third party by managing data storage, allowing data protection and also performing user authentication. Authors in (Sharma et al.2017) have designed a BC based distributed cloud architecture by incorporating SDN enabled controller fog nodes at the edge of the network. This flexible architecture is capable of gathering, classifying and analyzing data streams at the edge of the network. This model also brings in an efficient way to offload data to the cloud and reduces delay and also traffic load in the core network. Uddin et al. (Uddin et al.2021) have highlighted that not all BC consensus mechanisms are suitable in a Fog ecosystem due to their limited resources. Hence, PoW is not suitable with Fog miners (Kumar et al.2019) instead of PoS and practical Byzantine Fault Tolerance (pBFT) consensus are appreciated for the Fog network.

Figure 4. Blockchain-based solutions for IoT Security Attacks

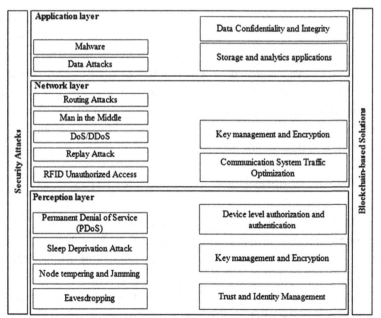

Blockchain-Based Solutions for VANETs Security

The security system used in VANETs must meet the following requirements: data authentication and integrity, data confidentiality, vehicle privacy and anonymity, information accessibility, data non-repudiation, data transfer integrity, vehicle traceability, scalability, efficiency and robustness, protection against forged messages, availability, anti-jamming, protection against impersonation, protection against tampering of in-transit on On-board traffic (Mokhtar and Azab., 2015). To address these requirements, several security solutions have been proposed. However, the main drawbacks of traditional solutions include dependence on a central authority, and low computation and storage capabilities of communicating devices. BC provides a distributed ledger to secure the communication of VANETs against single point of failure and data tempering.

Blockchain-Based Solution for VANETs Physical Layer

At the level of the physical layer, channel accessibility and security are critical factors to facilitate communication in VANETs. Thus, it is important to formulate a solution that guarantees secure communication channels and effective bandwidth utilization. In (Hassija et al., 2020), an advanced BC-based solution is used to store transactions, whereby a distributed Directed Acyclic Graph (DAG) is employed to connect vehicles and RSUs and ensure data immutability. Moreover, to ensure effective bandwidth utilization, an auction-based game-theoretic smart contract is used to govern the communication between requesting vehicles and RSUs.

Blockchain-Based Solution for VANETs Network Layer

Common protection against network layer attacks involves the authentication of communicating nodes and maintaining the privacy of their critical information such as location and identity. Key management mechanisms are important to ensure the legitimacy of communicating nodes. To achieve privacy in VANET, conventional solutions rely on pseudonyms. Pseudonyms are digital certificates used to hide the vehicles' identity. To issue, change, or revoke a vehicle's certificates, a centralized certification authority is required. For fully distributed certificates' management mechanisms, two different BCs are used in (Moussaoui et al., 2021) to issue and revoke vehicles' certificates. Thus, preserving the privacy of the vehicles and the authentication of communicating vehicles. In the proposed solution, vehicles act as the miners in the BC solution to reduce data exchange with the central unit. The authors in (Lu et al., 2018) have proposed a BC-based Anonymous Reputation System (BARS) to preserve the privacy of communicating vehicles. A reputation evaluation algorithm relying on both direct historical interactions and indirect opinions about vehicles is used to identify forged messages and thus decide the legitimacy of communicating vehicles. The public keys are used as pseudonyms in communications to hide information about real identities of the vehicle. Similarly, a key management mechanism has been proposed in (Ma et al., 2020) using BC. A lightweight mutual authentication and key agreement protocol based on the bivariate polynomial is used for the registration, update, and revocation of vehicles' public keys.

In addition to a single point of failure, it's difficult to ensure both the privacy and tractability of vehicles in conventional key management in VANETs. The authors in (Lin et al., 2020) have proposed a Conditional Privacy-preserving Authentication (CPPA) that employs BC technologies to address issues. CPPA implies that the vehicle's identity is hidden from most entities and is available for trusted entities to ensure tractability. BC is used to store vehicles' certificates to be retrieved by other vehicles and RSU for authentication purposes. A smart contract is used to manage the entities that can retrieve the certificates and track vehicles on the network. Moreover, a derivation key algorithm is adapted to reduce the number of pre-stored keys on vehicles' OBUs.

In (Li et al., 2020a), privacy of communicating vehicles' locations is achieved using a k-anonymous algorithm. To address the bottlenecks of a solution that relies on centralized authority to issue the digital certificates, BC is used to build a distributed ledged to store vehicle certificates based on a k-anonymous algorithm. Moreover, a trust management model is used to protect against malicious insiders' attacks. A similar solution is proposed in (Luo et al., 2019). To preserve the privacy of communicating nodes, the authors have suggested a BC enabled trust-based location protecting scheme with a trust management model based on Dirichlet distribution.

Blockchain-Based Solution for VANETs Application Layer

Ensuring data integrity and confidentiality is the main approach to address application layer's attacks in VANET. To provide protection of life-threatening information, the authors in (Shrestha et al., 2020) used a public distributed ledger to store the trustworthiness of nodes and exchanged messages. Moreover, a local BC is used per country to improve scalability and reduce latency. A similar solution is proposed in (El-Salakawy and Abu El-Kheir, 2020), where BC is used for the management of data exchanged to ensure secure communication. Exchanged data using the BC system include safety data and periodic beacons in order to reduce the overhead on the centralized storage unit. Alternatively, the authors in (Dwivedi et al., 2020) have proposed a BC-based decentralized system with an authentication protocol to ensure the legitimacy of communicating vehicles and a consensus mechanism to validate transactions. On the other hand, a fine-grained access scheme is proposed in (Li et al., 2020a). BC integrated with ciphertext-based encryption is used to manage the identity of communicating vehicles and store data. In addition, data access rights are established according to the requester's attribute. The aforementioned solutions help to enhance data immutability and protect against a single point of failure in traditional application security solutions for VANETs. Table 7 depicts the list of BC-based solutions proposed through the literature to address various security requirements in VANETs.

Blockchain-Edge/Fog Computing Based Solutions for VANETs Security

Edge/Fog computing (E/FC) is significant to address the computational constraint of vehicular networks. Employing a BC-based solution to preserve the privacy of vehicles or ensure the immutability of shared data impose a large demand on computational resources. The authors in (Zhang et al., 2018) have proposed a security architecture that consists of three layers, including the perception layer, the edge computing layer, and service layer. While BC is used at the perception and service to protect against data-tempering and the single point of failure, mobile edge computing is helpful to alleviate the computational demand on vehicles due to consensus algorithms. On the other hand, the authors in (Ayaz et al., 2021) have defined a BC-based voting solution that relies on the edge servers to control votes in the proposed Proof-of-Quality-Factor (PoQF) consensus algorithm. The authors in (Tan et al., 2020) have presented an integrated BC and edge computing that is useful to alleviate the computational burden on communicating vehicles and address the issue of interference between regular V2R exchanged data and control messages needed to ensure vehicles' authentication.

Table 7. Blockchain-based solutions for VANETs

Solution	Goal of Solution	Main Addressed Security and Privacy Requirements
(Hassija et al., 2020)	• Ensure Data Immutability • Efficient Bandwidth Utilization	• Data Confidentiality • Efficiency and Robustness
(Dwivedi et al., 2020)	Ensure data immutability	• Data authentication and integrity. • Vehicles' authentication.
(Shrestha et al., 2020)		• Data authentication and integrity • Data Confidentiality • Vehicles' authentication
(Lu et al., 2018)	• Privacy Preservation. • Key Management.	• Vehicle privacy and anonymity • Vehicles' authentication
(Luo et al., 2019)	Preserving Location Privacy	Vehicle privacy and anonymity
(Li et al., 2020a)		Vehicles' authentication
(Ma et al., 2020)	Key management	• Protection against impersonation • Data non-repudiation
(Moussaoui, 2021)		• Vehicles' authentication. • Scalability
(Lin et al., 2020)		• Vehicle privacy and anonymity • Vehicles' authentication • Vehicles' tractability
(Li et al., 2020b)	Access Control	• Data Confidentiality • Vehicle privacy and anonymity • Vehicles' authentication

Blockchain-Based Solution for FANETs Security

Besides the usefulness of FANETs in performing complex missions, it introduces communication security issues between multiple and heterogeneous drones. In this context, recently, BC is being typically introduced into the FANET network to not only manage the event messages and trustworthiness of nodes but also for secure, accurate delivery of data (Noor et al.2020) (Machado and Westphall2021).

Blockchain-Based Solution for FANET Physical Layer

Implementing BC-based solutions ensures the security of FANET devices and makes it impossible to disturb the UAVs hardware or software.

Islam et al. (Islam and Shin2019) have leveraged a BC-based secure data acquisition scheme for UAV swarm (BUS). In this scheme, data is collected and encrypted by IoT devices to be then sent to UAV that validates the transmitter's identity through a hash bloom filter and Digital Signature Algorithm (DSA). Consequently, the UAV forwards the data to the nearest server to prepare and store it in the BC. Simulations were conducted using MATLAB and Python to show the effect of π-hash bloom filters in the server and the UAV, respectively. The result of the simulation shows that BUS is successfully able to filter malicious devices completely. BUS was implemented and the result of experiments proved that utilizing UAV in the assistance of IoT devices ensures extended connectivity and reduces the energy consumption in IoT.

Allouch et al. (Allouch et al.2021) have proposed a lightweight BC-based security solution called Unmanned Traffic Management UTM-chain. The authors have explained and discussed the various UAVs security attacks. In the proposed system, during their flight, the drones constantly update their GPS location and destination address that reduces their vulnerability to GPS attacks. In addition, each UAV has a copy of the BC providing the flight path details which facilitates its flight even in case of communication jamming attack. ; thus, they can continue on its path in case of communication jamming.

Blockchain-Based Solution for FANET Network Layer

Tan et al. (Tan et al.2020) have proposed a secure key management scheme for FANETs that allows drones to generate and update their keys autonomously independently of any central authority. This approach is adapted with heterogeneous FANETs composed of a high-performance CH and other ordinary drones in the network. In order to enhance the scalability level of the proposed scheme, the CH is the only one responsible for the BC management and storage. The authors applied a new fair miner election approach that indicates the producer of the next block easily unlike the difficult process required in PoW consensus algorithm. Furthermore, the cluster key distribution, update process takes into account UAV migration between clusters and malicious UAV revocation tasks. These cluster keys management schemes can perform a secure communication within clusters by identifying impersonation, cloning and internal attacks. On the other hand, the authors have evaluated their scheme by revealing the energy consumption within clusters and comparing the consumption of CH UAVs and UAV members. In addition, the authors have evaluated the relationship between the average processing time of each transaction and the block size as well as the number of UAVs in the system.

Ghribi et al. (Ghribi et al.2020) have proposed a novel consensus-building mechanism for securing communication in a UAV network. This mechanism is based on the integration of BC with the public key cryptographic method of Elliptic Curve Diffe-Hellman (ECDH), a key derivation hash function SHA3 and One-Time Pad (OTP) encryption method. They have designed their scenario for a private BC-based UAV FANET that includes a Ground Control Station GCS, a leader UAV designated by the GCS, and UAV nodes. UAVs can communicate securely with one another using Elliptic-curve Cryptography (ECC) and thus have access to each other's public key.

Khullar et al. (Khullar et al.2020) have defined a decentralized architecture of FANET based on BC and using Practical Byzantine Fault Tolerance (PBFT) for consensus among nodes. They have used a gossip protocol for passing messages among neighboring nodes. For mobility management, authors applied a dynamic peer discovery algorithm so that nodes can disconnect from nodes flying away far from the current node and connect to close nodes. For that, they have used a shared routing table that is constantly updated with the latest location of the corresponding node. Moreover, in order to ensure a decentralized security approach, authors employed a modified version of RAFT consensus algorithm (Mingxiao et al.2017) based on dynamic leader election. The proposed architecture was evaluated by measuring the throughput presenting the valid transactions commitment rate that varies by a small amount and remains approximately constant. In addition, the network latency remains nearly constant with increase in the total number of nodes in the network and the message overload increases in the beginning with the increase in the total number of transmitted transactions but remains approximately constant afterwards.

Blockchain-Based Solution for FANET Application Layer

In FANET, the data integrity and confidentiality guarantee the consistency of collected data and its secure transmission and storage. Liang et al. (Liang et al.2017) have proposed a framework based on a public BC to ensure the secure communication between drones and the integrity of the collected data. They have implemented a prototype of a drone system composed by drones, control system, BC network, cloud database and server. The authors have validated their system using PoW and bitcoin.

Shetty et al. (Shetty et al.2019) have used Cryptographic Hash Functions to enable the integrity of the transmitted data. They have implemented a consensus mechanism in a block mining process to ensure data integrity.

Barka et al. (Barka et al.2019) have proposed a BC-based trust management solution for Unmanned Aerial System (BUAS) in FANET. They aimed to evaluate the trustworthiness of the exchanged messages between UAVs by the use of the Bayesian Inference (BI) approach (Rappel et al.2020) in order to define the truly occurring events and the trusted messages reporting them. To include the trust's offset into the BC by the appropriate GCS, authors combined Proof-of-Work and Proof-of-Stack miner selection. This solution was evaluated using NS-3 simulator and 3D random Waypoint UAV Mobility Model and proved that BUAS can enable high detection ratios exceeding the 95% for different dishonesty ratios with a minimum energy consumption and network overhead.

OPEN RESEARCH

This section provides the list of open research areas that still remain less investigated with regards to IoT, VANET and FANET security based on the major divisions made above:

- **The privacy and integrity of collected data:** The integration of BC with 5G/6G technologies including cloud computing, edge computing, Software Defined Networks, Network Function Virtualization, Network Slicing make the communication more secure against cybersecurity vulnerabilities (Haris and Al-Maadeed2020) (nguyen2020Blockchain).

  Although numerous research efforts have been devoted to BC technology in IoT, VANET and FANET networks, researchers have not yet explored BC-enabled network softwarization (Hu et al.2020).

- **Deep Reinforcement Learning (DRL):** Deep-reinforcement learning techniques can be used to ensure stable communication. In addition, deep-reinforcement learning methods can be used to determine the optimal solution to avoid collisions during real-time path planning and navigation (Azar et al.2021).

  In addition, future research works should develop new DRL techniques allowing with low computation without communication overhead in order to enhance the communication performance between nodes in IoT, VANETs and FANETs.

- **Integration of BC-E/FC:** The BC-E/FC integration becomes widely encouraged in various applications and it is still new in IoT, VANETs and FANETs applications. In fact, the synergy between BC and E/FC can improve the system security and reliability. In addition, to protect the system database, it is recommended to deploy the BC in the cloud. Accordingly, through its cryptographic mechanisms and immutability, the BC can identify the vulnerabilities and protect the database from being altered by the attackers.

Various research works agree about the advantages of this integration, but researchers should take into account various challenges. The BC deployment can increase the system latency. This motivates researchers to find areas of harmony between BC latency, cloud latency in the three emerging IoT, VANETs and FANETs systems. Furthermore, the energy consumption represents a challenge related to BC-based system. In this context, it is highly motivating to propose new consensus algorithms that satisfy the high IoT, VANETs or FANETs systems security with efficient-energy results. Moreover, FANETs and VANETs require efficient mobility control due to the dynamic behavior of nodes (Wan et al., 2019). This issue can be solved by applying E/FC techniques but once the BC has been integrated, it figures again. Therefore, future research works should find solutions for this challenge while keeping the system latency and privacy.

CONCLUSION

With the emergence of IoT, VANET and FANET applications, diverse security vulnerabilities leading to several attacks on devices and collected data have been investigated in recent research works. Therefore, in this work, the basic concepts of IoT, VANET and FANET systems are presented to understand their main functionalities and features. Then, their specific security problems and the solutions proposed in the literature are discussed and a taxonomy of their attacks is defined. The proposed classification would help researchers find the most relevant attacks to their domain of interest. Besides, the comprehensive taxonomy is providing guidelines and hints for understanding the proposed solutions.

In addition, the study presented in this chapter emphasizes the emergence of BC technology as an indispensable and useful paradigm needed to build integrated and robust security solutions for IoT, VANET and FANET systems. Furthermore, BC provides efficient techniques and mechanisms to cope with centralized aspects of these systems. Finally, this chapter provides some open research areas on security issues in IoT, VANETs and FANETs for which BC based solutions are encouraged to be investigated.

REFERENCES

Airehrour, D., Gutierrez, J. A., & Ray, S. K. (2019). Sectrust-rpl: A secure trust-aware rpl routing protocol for the internet of things. *Future Generation Computer Systems*, *93*, 860–876. doi:10.1016/j.future.2018.03.021

Al-Kashoash, H. A., Kharrufa, H., Al-Nidawi, Y., & Kemp, A. H. (2019). Congestion control in wireless sensor and 6lowpan networks: Toward the internet of things. *Wireless Networks*, *25*(8), 4493–4522. doi:10.100711276-018-1743-y

Alaba, F. A., Othman, M., Hashem, I. A. T., & Alotaibi, F. (2017). Internet of things security: A survey. *Journal of Network and Computer Applications*, *88*, 10–28. doi:10.1016/j.jnca.2017.04.002

Alam, T. (2018). A reliable communication framework and its use in internet of things (iot). *CSEIT1835111*, *10*, 450–456.

Alhawi, O. M. (2021). *Finding Software Vulnerabilities in Unmanned Aerial Vehicles* (PhD thesis). University of Manchester.

Ali, M. S., Vecchio, M., Pincheira, M., Dolui, K., Antonelli, F., & Rehmani, M. H. (2018). Applications of blockchains in the internet of things: A comprehensive survey. *IEEE Communications Surveys and Tutorials*, *21*(2), 1676–1717. doi:10.1109/COMST.2018.2886932

Aman, M. N., Chua, K. C., & Sikdar, B. (2017). A light-weight mutual authentication protocol for iot systems. In *GLOBECOM 2017-2017 IEEE Global Communications Conference*, (pp. 1–6). IEEE. 10.1109/GLOCOM.2017.8253991

Aman, M. N., Sikdar, B., Chua, K. C., & Ali, A. (2018). Low power data integrity in iot systems. *IEEE Internet of Things Journal*, *5*(4), 3102–3113. doi:10.1109/JIOT.2018.2833206

Andrea, I., Chrysostomou, C., & Hadji Christofi, G. (2015). Internet of things: Security vulnerabilities and challenges. In 2015 IEEE symposium on computers and communication (ISCC), (pp. 180–187). IEEE.

Antonioli, D., Tippenhauer, N. O., & Rasmussen, K. (2020). Bias: Bluetooth impersonation attacks. In *2020 IEEE Symposium on Security and Privacy (SP)*, (pp. 549–562). IEEE. 10.1109/SP40000.2020.00093

Arteaga, S. P., Hernández, L. A. M., Pérez, G. S., Orozco, A. L. S., & Villalba, L. J. G. (2019). Analysis of the gps spoofing vulnerability in the drone 3dr solo. *IEEE Access: Practical Innovations, Open Solutions*, *7*, 51782–51789. doi:10.1109/ACCESS.2019.2911526

Ashibani, Y., & Mahmoud, Q. H. (2017). An efficient and secure scheme for smart home communication using identity-based signcryption. In *2017 IEEE 36th International Performance Computing and Communications Conference (IPCCC)*, (pp. 1–7). IEEE. 10.1109/PCCC.2017.8280497

Aswale, P., Shukla, A., Bharati, P., Bharambe, S., & Palve, S. (2019). *An overview of internet of things: architecture, protocols and challenges*. Information and Communication Technology for Intelligent Systems.

Ayaz, F., Sheng, Z., Tian, D., & Guan, Y. L. (2021). A Proof-of-Quality-Factor (PoQF)-Based Blockchain and Edge Computing for Vehicular Message Dissemination. *IEEE Internet of Things Journal*, *8*(4), 2468–2482. doi:10.1109/JIOT.2020.3026731

Azar, A. T., Koubaa, A., Ali Mohamed, N., Ibrahim, H. A., Ibrahim, Z. F., Kazim, M., Ammar, A., Benjdira, B., Khamis, A. M., Hameed, I. A., & Casalino, G. (2021). Drone deep reinforcement learning: A review. *Electronics (Basel)*, *10*(9), 999. doi:10.3390/electronics10090999

Azzabi, T., Farhat, H., & Sahli, N. (2017). A survey on wireless sensor networks security issues and military specificities. In *2017 International Conference on Advanced Systems and Electric Technologies (IC_ASET)*, (pp. 66–72). IEEE. 10.1109/ASET.2017.7983668

Barka, E., Kerrache, C. A., Benkraouda, H., Shuaib, K., Ahmad, F., & Kurugollu, F. (2019). Towards a trusted unmanned aerial system using blockchain for the protection of critical infrastructure. *Transactions on Emerging Telecommunications Technologies*, e3706. doi:10.1002/ett.3706

Barka, E., Kerrache, C. A., Hussain, R., Lagraa, N., Lakas, A., & Bouk, S. H. (2018). A trusted lightweight communication strategy for flying named data networking. *Sensors (Basel)*, *18*(8), 2683. doi:10.339018082683 PMID:30111732

Behzadan, V. (2016). *Real-time inference of topological structure and vulnerabilities for adaptive jamming against covert ad hoc networks*. PhD thesis.

Behzadan, V. (2017). *Cyber-physical attacks on uas networks-challenges and open research problems*. arXiv preprint arXiv:1702.01251.

Benslimane, Y., Benahmed, K., & Benslimane, H. (2018). Security mechanisms for 6lowpan network in context of internet of things: A survey. In *International Conference in Artificial Intelligence in Renewable Energetic Systems*, (pp. 49–69). Springer.

Bera, B., Saha, S., Das, A. K., Kumar, N., Lorenz, P., & Alazab, M. (2020). Blockchain-envisioned secure data delivery and collection scheme for 5g-based iot-enabled internet of drones environment. *IEEE Transactions on Vehicular Technology*, *69*(8), 9097–9111. doi:10.1109/TVT.2020.3000576

Bertin, E., Hussein, D., Sengul, C., & Frey, V. (2019). Access control in the internet of things: A survey of existing approaches and open research questions. *Annales des Télécommunications*, *74*(7), 375–388. doi:10.100712243-019-00709-7

Bhardwaj, V., Kaur, N., Vashisht, S., & Jain, S. (2020). Secrip: Secure and reliable intercluster routing protocol for efficient data transmission in flying ad hoc networks. *Transactions on Emerging Telecommunications Technologies*, e4068. doi:10.1002/ett.4068

Bodkhe, U., & Tanwar, S. (2020). Taxonomy of secure data dissemination techniques for iot environment. *IET Software*, *14*(6), 563–571. doi:10.1049/iet-sen.2020.0006

Bouachir, O., Grati, R., Aloqaily, M., & Mnaouer, A. B. (2020). Blockchain based solutions for achieving secure storage in fog computing. In Blockchain-enabled Fog and Edge Computing: Concepts, Architectures and Applications: Concepts, Architectures and Applications. Academic Press.

Butun, I., Pereira, N., & Gidlund, M. (2018). Analysis of lorawan v1. 1 security. *Proceedings of the 4th ACM MobiHoc Workshop on Experiences with the Design and Implementation of Smart Objects*, 1–6.

Butun, I., Pereira, N., & Gidlund, M. (2019). Security risk analysis of lorawan and future directions. *Future Internet*, *11*(1), 3. doi:10.3390/fi11010003

Cachin, C. (2016). Architecture of the hyperledger blockchain fabric. *Workshop on distributed cryptocurrencies and consensus ledgers*, 310.

Cha, S.-C., Chen, J.-F., Su, C., & Yeh, K.-H. (2018). A blockchain connected gateway for ble-based devices in the internet of things. *IEEE Access: Practical Innovations, Open Solutions*, *6*, 24639–24649. doi:10.1109/ACCESS.2018.2799942

Chaari, L., Chahbani, S., & Rezgui, J. (2020). Vulnerabilities assessment for unmanned aerial vehicles communication systems. In *2020 International Symposium on Networks, Computers and Communications (ISNCC)*, (pp. 1–6). IEEE.

Chakraborty, R. S., Mathew, J., & Vasilakos, A. V. (2019). *Security and fault tolerance in Internet of things*. Springer. doi:10.1007/978-3-030-02807-7

Challita, U., Ferdowsi, A., Chen, M., & Saad, W. (2019). Machine learning for wireless connectivity and security of cellular-connected uavs. *IEEE Wireless Communications*, 26(1), 28–35. doi:10.1109/MWC.2018.1800155

Chen, J., Yatnalli, U., & Gesbert, D. (2017a). Learning radio maps for uav-aided wireless networks: A segmented regression approach. In *2017 IEEE International Conference on Communications (ICC)*, (pp. 1–6). IEEE. 10.1109/ICC.2017.7997333

Chen, L., Xu, L., Shah, N., Gao, Z., Lu, Y., & Shi, W. (2017b). On security analysis of proof-of-elapsed-time (poet). In *International Symposium on Stabilization, Safety, and Security of Distributed Systems*, (pp. 282–297). Springer. 10.1007/978-3-319-69084-1_19

Cui, M., Zhang, G., Wu, Q., & Ng, D. W. K. (2018). Robust trajectory and transmit power design for secure uav communications. *IEEE Transactions on Vehicular Technology*, 67(9), 9042–9046. doi:10.1109/TVT.2018.2849644

Dahiya, S., & Garg, M. (2019). Unmanned aerial vehicles: Vulnerability to cyber attacks. In *International Conference on Unmanned Aerial System in Geomatics*, (pp. 201–211). Springer.

Dastres, R., & Soori, M. (2020). Secure socket layer (ssl) in the network and web security. *International Journal of Computer and Information Engineering*, 14(10), 330–333.

de Carvalho Silva, J., Rodrigues, J. J., Alberti, A. M., Solic, P., & Aquino, A. L. (2017). Lorawan—a low power wan protocol for internet of things: A review and opportunities. In *2017 2nd International Multidisciplinary Conference on Computer and Energy Science (SpliTech)*, (pp. 1–6). IEEE.

DeCuir, J. (2013). Introducing bluetooth smart: Part 1: A look at both classic and new technologies. *IEEE Consumer Electronics Magazine*, 3(1), 12–18. doi:10.1109/MCE.2013.2284932

Dorri, A., Kanhere, S. S., Jurdak, R., & Gauravaram, P. (2019). Lsb: A lightweight scalable blockchain for iot security and anonymity. *Journal of Parallel and Distributed Computing*, 134, 180–197. doi:10.1016/j.jpdc.2019.08.005

Dwivedi, S. K., Amin, R., Vollala, S., & Chaudhry, R. (2020). Blockchain-based secured event-information sharing protocol in internet of vehicles for smart cities. *Computers & Electrical Engineering*, 86, 106719. doi:10.1016/j.compeleceng.2020.106719

El-Hajj, M., Fadlallah, A., Chamoun, M., & Serhrouchni, A. (2019). A survey of internet of things (iot) authentication schemes. *Sensors (Basel)*, 19(5), 1141. doi:10.339019051141 PMID:30845760

El-Salakawy, G., & Abu El-Kheir, M. (2020). Blockchain-based Data Management in Vehicular Networks. *2020 2nd Novel Intelligent and Leading Emerging Sciences Conference (NILES)*.

Eldosouky, A., Ferdowsi, A., & Saad, W. (2019). Drones in distress: A game-theoretic countermeasure for protecting uavs against gps spoofing. *IEEE Internet of Things Journal, 7*(4), 2840–2854. doi:10.1109/JIOT.2019.2963337

Farahani, S. (2011). *ZigBee wireless networks and transceivers*. Newnes.

Fernández-Caramés, T. M., & Fraga-Lamas, P. (2018). A review on the use of blockchain for the internet of things. *IEEE Access: Practical Innovations, Open Solutions, 6*, 32979–33001. doi:10.1109/ACCESS.2018.2842685

Ferrag, M. A., Derdour, M., Mukherjee, M., Derhab, A., Maglaras, L., & Janicke, H. (2018). Blockchain technologies for the internet of things: Research issues and challenges. *IEEE Internet of Things Journal, 6*(2), 2188–2204. doi:10.1109/JIOT.2018.2882794

Frustaci, M., Pace, P., Aloi, G., & Fortino, G. (2017). Evaluating critical security issues of the iot world: Present and future challenges. *IEEE Internet of Things Journal, 5*(4), 2483–2495. doi:10.1109/JIOT.2017.2767291

Gai, K., Wu, Y., Zhu, L., Qiu, M., & Shen, M. (2019). Privacy-preserving energy trading using consortium blockchain in smart grid. *IEEE Transactions on Industrial Informatics, 15*(6), 3548–3558. doi:10.1109/TII.2019.2893433

Garg, A., & Mittal, N. (2020). A security and confidentiality survey in wireless internet of things (iot). In *Internet of Things and Big Data Applications* (pp. 65–88). Springer. doi:10.1007/978-3-030-39119-5_5

Gervais, A., Karame, G. O., Wüst, K., Glykantzis, V., Ritzdorf, H., & Capkun, S. (2016). On the security and performance of proof of work blockchains. *Proceedings of the 2016 ACM SIGSAC conference on computer and communications security*, 3–16. 10.1145/2976749.2978341

Ghribi, E., Khoei, T. T., Gorji, H. T., Ranganathan, P., & Kaabouch, N. (2020). A secure blockchain-based communication approach for uav networks. In *2020 IEEE International Conference on Electro Information Technology (EIT)*, (pp. 411–415). IEEE. 10.1109/EIT48999.2020.9208314

Glissa, G., Rachedi, A., & Meddeb, A. (2016). A secure routing protocol based on rpl for internet of things. In *2016 IEEE Global Communications Conference (GLOBECOM)*, (pp. 1–7). IEEE. 10.1109/GLOCOM.2016.7841543

Gomes, T., Salgado, F., Tavares, A., & Cabral, J. (2017). Cute mote, a customizable and trustable end-device for the internet of things. *IEEE Sensors Journal, 17*(20), 6816–6824. doi:10.1109/JSEN.2017.2743460

Gope, P., & Sikdar, B. (2018). Lightweight and privacy-preserving two-factor authentication scheme for iot devices. *IEEE Internet of Things Journal, 6*(1), 580–589. doi:10.1109/JIOT.2018.2846299

Gupta, B., & Quamara, M. (2020). An overview of internet of things (iot): Architectural aspects, challenges, and protocols. *Concurrency and Computation, 32*(21), e4946. doi:10.1002/cpe.4946

HaddadPajouh, H., Dehghantanha, A., Parizi, R. M., Aledhari, M., & Karimipour, H. (2019). A survey on internet of things security: Requirements, challenges, and solutions. *Internet of Things*, 100129.

Hamdi, M. M., Audah, L., Rashid, S. A., Mohammed, A. H., Alani, S., & Mustafa, A. S. (2020). A review of applications, characteristics and challenges in vehicular ad hoc networks (vanets). In *2020 International Congress on Human-Computer Interaction, Optimization and Robotic Applications (HORA)*, (pp. 1–7). IEEE.

Hammi, M. T., Hammi, B., Bellot, P., & Serrhrouchni, A. (2018). Bubbles of trust: A decentralized blockchain-based authentication system for iot. *Computers & Security*, *78*, 126–142. doi:10.1016/j.cose.2018.06.004

Harbi, Y., Aliouat, Z., Refoufi, A., Harous, S., & Bentaleb, A. (2019). Enhanced authentication and key management scheme for securing data transmission in the internet of things. *Ad Hoc Networks*, *94*, 101948. doi:10.1016/j.adhoc.2019.101948

Haris, R. M., & Al-Maadeed, S. (2020). Integrating blockchain technology in 5g enabled iot: A review. In *2020 IEEE International Conference on Informatics, IoT, and Enabling Technologies (ICIoT)*, (pp. 367–371). IEEE. 10.1109/ICIoT48696.2020.9089600

Hassan, W. H. (2019). Current research on internet of things (iot) security: A survey. *Computer Networks*, *148*, 283–294. doi:10.1016/j.comnet.2018.11.025

Hassija, V., Chamola, V., Gupta, V., & Chalapathi, G. S. (2020). *A Framework for Secure Vehicular Network using Advanced Blockchain. In 2020 International Wireless Communications and Mobile Computing*. IWCMC.

He, D. (2019). A survey on cyber security of unmanned aerial vehicles. *Chinese Journal of Computers*, *42*(05), 150–168.

Hossain, M. A., Md Noor, R., Azzuhri, S. R., Z'aba, M. R., Ahmedy, I., Yau, K. L. A., & Chembe, C. (2021). Spectrum sensing challenges & their solutions in cognitive radio based vehicular networks. *International Journal of Communication Systems*, *34*(7). Advance online publication. doi:10.1002/dac.4748

Hu, Q., Wang, W., Bai, X., Jin, S., & Jiang, T. (2020). Blockchain enabled federated slicing for 5g networks with ai accelerated optimization. *IEEE Network*, *34*(6), 46–52. doi:10.1109/MNET.021.1900653

Iqbal, S. (2021). A study on uav operating system security and future research challenges. In *2021 IEEE 11th Annual Computing and Communication Workshop and Conference (CCWC)*, (pp. 759–765). IEEE.

Islam, A., & Shin, S. Y. (2019). Bus: A blockchain-enabled data acquisition scheme with the assistance of uav swarm in internet of things. *IEEE Access: Practical Innovations, Open Solutions*, *7*, 103231–103249. doi:10.1109/ACCESS.2019.2930774

Jiang, X., Lora, M., & Chattopadhyay, S. (2020). An experimental analysis of security vulnerabilities in industrial iot devices. *ACM Transactions on Internet Technology*, *20*(2), 1–24. doi:10.1145/3379542

Kacem, T., Wijesekera, D., & Costa, P. (2017). Key distribution scheme for aircraft equipped with secure ads-b in. In *2017 IEEE 20th International Conference on Intelligent Transportation Systems (ITSC)*, (pp. 1–6). IEEE. 10.1109/ITSC.2017.8317719

Kamran, M., Khan, H. U., Nisar, W., Farooq, M., & Rehman, S.-U. (2020). Blockchain and internet of things: A bibliometric study. *Computers & Electrical Engineering, 81*, 106525. doi:10.1016/j.compeleceng.2019.106525

Karimireddy, T., & Bakshi, A. G. (2016). A hybrid security framework for the vehicular communications in VANET. *2016 International Conference on Wireless Communications, Signal Processing and Networking (WiSPNET)*. 10.1109/WiSPNET.2016.7566479

Kaur, R., Singh, T. P., & Khajuria, V. (2018). Security Issues in Vehicular Ad-Hoc Network (VANET). *2018 2nd International Conference on Trends in Electronics and Informatics (ICOEI)*.

Kavitha, D., & Ravikumar, S. (2021). Iot and context-aware learning-based optimal neural network model for real-time health monitoring. *Transactions on Emerging Telecommunications Technologies, 32*(1), e4132. doi:10.1002/ett.4132

Khalid, U., Asim, M., Baker, T., Hung, P. C., Tariq, M. A., & Rafferty, L. (2020). A decentralized lightweight blockchain-based authentication mechanism for iot systems. *Cluster Computing, 23*(3), 1–21. doi:10.100710586-020-03058-6

Khanji, S., Iqbal, F., & Hung, P. (2019). Zigbee security vulnerabilities: Exploration and evaluating. In *2019 10th International Conference on Information and Communication Systems (ICICS)*, (pp. 52–57). IEEE.

Khullar, K., Malhotra, Y., & Kumar, A. (2020). Decentralized and secure communication architecture for fanets using blockchain. *Procedia Computer Science, 173*, 158–170. doi:10.1016/j.procs.2020.06.020

Kosmanos, D., Pappas, A., Maglaras, L., Moschoyiannis, S., Aparicio-Navarro, F. J., Argyriou, A., & Janicke, H. (2020). A novel intrusion detection system against spoofing attacks in connected electric vehicles. *Array, 5*, 100013. doi:10.1016/j.array.2019.100013

Kouicem, D. E., Bouabdallah, A., & Lakhlef, H. (2018). Internet of things security: A top-down survey. *Computer Networks, 141*, 199–221. doi:10.1016/j.comnet.2018.03.012

Krishnan, P. R., & Kumar, P. A. R. (2020). Security and Privacy in VANET: Concepts, Solutions and Challenges. *2020 International Conference on Inventive Computation Technologies (ICICT)*. 10.1109/ICICT48043.2020.9112535

Kumar, A., & Gupta, N. (2020). A Secure RSU based Security against Multiple Attacks in VANET. *2020 3rd International Conference on Intelligent Sustainable Systems (ICISS)*.

Kumar, G., Saha, R., Rai, M. K., Thomas, R., & Kim, T.-H. (2019). Proof-of-work consensus approach in blockchain technology for cloud and fog computing using maximization-factorization statistics. *IEEE Internet of Things Journal, 6*(4), 6835–6842. doi:10.1109/JIOT.2019.2911969

Lee, H., Eom, S., Park, J., & Lee, I. (2018). Uav-aided secure communications with cooperative jamming. *IEEE Transactions on Vehicular Technology, 67*(10), 9385–9392. doi:10.1109/TVT.2018.2853723

Lee, M., & Atkison, T. (2021). Vanet applications: Past, present, and future. *Vehicular Communications, 28*, 100310. doi:10.1016/j.vehcom.2020.100310

Li, B., Liang, R., Zhu, D., Chen, W., & Lin, Q. (2020). Blockchain-Based Trust Management Model for Location Privacy Preserving in VANET. *IEEE Transactions on Intelligent Transportation Systems*, 1–11. doi:10.1109/TITS.2020.3035869

Li, H., Pei, L., Liao, D., Chen, S., Zhang, M., & Xu, D. (2020). FADB: A Fine-Grained Access Control Scheme for VANET Data Based on Blockchain. *IEEE Access: Practical Innovations, Open Solutions*, *8*, 85190–85203. doi:10.1109/ACCESS.2020.2992203

Li, R., Song, T., Mei, B., Li, H., Cheng, X., & Sun, L. (2018). Blockchain for large-scale internet of things data storage and protection. *IEEE Transactions on Services Computing*, *12*(5), 762–771. doi:10.1109/TSC.2018.2853167

Lin, C., He, D., Huang, X., Kumar, N., & Choo, K.-K. R. (2020). BCPPA: A Blockchain-Based Conditional Privacy-Preserving Authentication Protocol for Vehicular Ad Hoc Networks. *IEEE Transactions on Intelligent Transportation Systems*, 1–13.

Lin, J., Shen, Z., & Miao, C. (2017). Using blockchain technology to build trust in sharing lorawan iot. *Proceedings of the 2nd International Conference on Crowd Science and Engineering*, 38–43. 10.1145/3126973.3126980

Liu, C., Cronin, P., & Yang, C. (2016). A mutual auditing framework to protect iot against hardware trojans. In *2016 21st Asia and South Pacific Design Automation Conference (ASP-DAC)*, (pp. 69–74). IEEE. 10.1109/ASPDAC.2016.7427991

Lu, Y. (2019). The blockchain: State-of-the-art and research challenges. *Journal of Industrial Information Integration*, *15*, 80–90. doi:10.1016/j.jii.2019.04.002

Lu, Z., Liu, W., Wang, Q., Qu, G., & Liu, Z. (2018). A Privacy-Preserving Trust Model Based on Blockchain for VANETs. *IEEE Access: Practical Innovations, Open Solutions*, *6*, 45655–45664. doi:10.1109/ACCESS.2018.2864189

Luo, B., Li, X., Weng, J., Guo, J., & Ma, J. (2020). Blockchain Enabled Trust-Based Location Privacy Protection Scheme in VANET. *IEEE Transactions on Vehicular Technology*, *69*(2), 2034–2048. doi:10.1109/TVT.2019.2957744

Ma, Z., Zhang, J., Guo, Y., Liu, Y., Liu, X., & He, W. (2020). An Efficient Decentralized Key Management Mechanism for VANET With Blockchain. *IEEE Transactions on Vehicular Technology*, *69*(6), 5836–5849. doi:10.1109/TVT.2020.2972923

Machado, C., & Fröhlich, A. A. M. (2018). Iot data integrity verification for cyber-physical systems using blockchain. In *2018 IEEE 21st International Symposium on Real-Time Distributed Computing (ISORC)*, (pp. 83–90). IEEE. 10.1109/ISORC.2018.00019

Machado, C., & Westphall, C. M. (2021). Blockchain incentivized data forwarding in manets: Strategies and challenges. *Ad Hoc Networks*, *110*, 102321. doi:10.1016/j.adhoc.2020.102321

Maitra, S., Yanambaka, V. P., Abdelgawad, A., Puthal, D., & Yelamarthi, K. (2020). Proof-of-authentication consensus algorithm: Blockchain-based iot implementation. In *2020 IEEE 6th World Forum on Internet of Things (WF-IoT)*, (pp. 1–2). IEEE.

Manogaran, G., Varatharajan, R., Lopez, D., Kumar, P. M., Sundarasekar, R., & Thota, C. (2018). A new architecture of internet of things and big data ecosystem for secured smart healthcare monitoring and alerting system. *Future Generation Computer Systems*, *82*, 375–387. doi:10.1016/j.future.2017.10.045

Meng, L., Ren, S., Tang, G., Yang, C., & Yang, W. (2020). Uav sensor spoofing detection algorithm based on gps and optical flow fusion. *Proceedings of the 2020 4th International Conference on Cryptography, Security and Privacy*, 146–151. 10.1145/3377644.3377670

Mingxiao, D., Xiaofeng, M., Zhe, Z., Xiangwei, W., & Qijun, C. (2017). A review on consensus algorithm of blockchain. In 2017 IEEE international conference on systems, man, and cybernetics (SMC), (pp. 2567–2572). IEEE. doi:10.1109/SMC.2017.8123011

Mohanta, B. K., Sahoo, A., Patel, S., Panda, S. S., Jena, D., & Gountia, D. (2019). Decauth: decentralized authentication scheme for iot device using ethereum blockchain. In TENCON 2019-2019 IEEE Region 10 Conference (TENCON), (pp. 558–563). IEEE. doi:10.1109/TENCON.2019.8929720

Mokhtar, B., & Azab, M. (2015). Survey on Security Issues in Vehicular Ad Hoc Networks. *Alexandria Engineering Journal*, *54*(4), 1115–1126. doi:10.1016/j.aej.2015.07.011

Moussaoui, D., Kadri, B., Feham, M., & Ammar Bensaber, B. (2021). A Distributed Blockchain Based PKI (BCPKI) architecture to enhance privacy in VANET. *2020 2nd International Workshop on Human-Centric Smart Environments for Health and Well-Being (IHSH)*.

Mowla, N. I., Tran, N. H., Doh, I., & Chae, K. (2020). Afrl: Adaptive federated reinforcement learning for intelligent jamming defense in fanet. *Journal of Communications and Networks (Seoul)*, *22*(3), 244–258. doi:10.1109/JCN.2020.000015

Mukherjee, A., Keshary, V., Pandya, K., Dey, N., & Satapathy, S. C. (2018). Flying ad hoc networks: A comprehensive survey. Information and Decision Sciences, 569–580.

Neshenko, N., Bou-Harb, E., Crichigno, J., Kaddoum, G., & Ghani, N. (2019). Demystifying iot security: An exhaustive survey on iot vulnerabilities and a first empirical look on internet-scale iot exploitations. *IEEE Communications Surveys and Tutorials*, *21*(3), 2702–2733. doi:10.1109/COMST.2019.2910750

Nguyen, V.-L., Lin, P.-C., & Hwang, R.-H. (2019). Energy depletion attacks in low power wireless networks. *IEEE Access: Practical Innovations, Open Solutions*, *7*, 51915–51932. doi:10.1109/ACCESS.2019.2911424

Nichols, R., Mumm, H., Lonstein, W., Carter, C., & Hood, J. (2019). *Understanding hostile use and cyber-vulnerabilities of uas: Components, autonomy v automation, sensors, saa, scada and cyber attack taxonomy*. Unmanned Aircraft Systems in the Cyber Domain.

Noor, F., Khan, M. A., Al-Zahrani, A., Ullah, I., & Al-Dhlan, K. A. (2020). A review on communications perspective of flying ad-hoc networks: Key enabling wireless technologies, applications, challenges and open research topics. *Drones (Basel)*, *4*(4), 65. doi:10.3390/drones4040065

Noura, H., Hatoum, T., Salman, O., Yaacoub, J.-P., and Chehab, A. (2020). Lorawan security survey: Issues, threats and possible mitigation techniques. *Internet of Things*, 100303.

Novo, O. (2018). Scalable access management in iot using blockchain: A performance evaluation. *IEEE Internet of Things Journal, 6*(3), 4694–4701. doi:10.1109/JIOT.2018.2879679

Pahlajani, S., Kshirsagar, A., & Pachghare, V. (2019). Survey on private blockchain consensus algorithms. In *2019 1st International Conference on Innovations in Information and Communication Technology (ICIICT)*, (pp. 1–6). IEEE. 10.1109/ICIICT1.2019.8741353

Pandharipande, A., & Newsham, G. R. (2018). Lighting controls: Evolution and revolution. *Lighting Research & Technology, 50*(1), 115–128. doi:10.1177/1477153517731909

Paul, A., & Jeyaraj, R. (2019). Internet of things: A primer. *Human Behavior and Emerging Technologies, 1*(1), 37–47. doi:10.1002/hbe2.133

Perwej, Y., Parwej, F., Hassan, M. M. M., & Akhtar, N. (2019). *The internet-of-things (iot) security: A technological perspective and review. International Journal of Scientific Research in Computer Science, Engineering and Information Technology (IJSRCSEIT).*

Petit, J., Stottelaar, B., Feiri, M., & Kargl, F. (2015). Remote attacks on automated vehicles sensors: Experiments on camera and lidar. *Black Hat Europe, 11*, 995.

Pfaff, B. L. (2018). *Overwhelming the SAA System of Delivery UAVs by Drone Swarming* (PhD thesis). Wright State University.

Pilkington, M. (2016). Blockchain technology: principles and applications. In *Research handbook on digital transformations*. Edward Elgar Publishing. doi:10.4337/9781784717766.00019

Porambage, P., Schmitt, C., Kumar, P., Gurtov, A., & Ylianttila, M. (2014). Pauthkey: A pervasive authentication protocol and key establishment scheme for wireless sensor networks in distributed iot applications. *International Journal of Distributed Sensor Networks, 10*(7), 357430. doi:10.1155/2014/357430

Praitheeshan, P., Pan, L., Yu, J., Liu, J., & Doss, R. (2019). *Security analysis methods on ethereum smart contract vulnerabilities: a survey.* arXiv preprint arXiv:1908.08605.

Pu, C., & Hajjar, S. (2018). Mitigating forwarding misbehaviors in rpl-based low power and lossy networks. In 2018 15th IEEE Annual Consumer Communications & Networking Conference (CCNC), (pp. 1–6). IEEE. doi:10.1109/CCNC.2018.8319164

Qiu, J., Tian, Z., Du, C., Zuo, Q., Su, S., & Fang, B. (2020). A survey on access control in the age of internet of things. *IEEE Internet of Things Journal, 7*(6), 4682–4696. doi:10.1109/JIOT.2020.2969326

Rana, S., Halim, M. A., & Kabir, M. H. (2018). Design and implementation of a security improvement framework of zigbee network for intelligent monitoring in iot platform. *Applied Sciences (Basel, Switzerland), 8*(11), 2305. doi:10.3390/app8112305

Rappel, H., Beex, L. A., Hale, J. S., Noels, L., & Bordas, S. (2020). A tutorial on bayesian inference to identify material parameters in solid mechanics. *Archives of Computational Methods in Engineering, 27*(2), 361–385. doi:10.100711831-018-09311-x

Reyna, A., Martn, C., Chen, J., Soler, E., & Dáz, M. (2018). On blockchain and its integration with iot. challenges and opportunities. *Future Generation Computer Systems*, *88*, 173–190. doi:10.1016/j.future.2018.05.046

Ribeiro, V., Holanda, R., Ramos, A., & Rodrigues, J. J. (2020). Enhancing key management in lorawan with permissioned blockchain. *Sensors (Basel)*, *20*(11), 3068. doi:10.339020113068 PMID:32485791

Saleh, F. (2018). Blockchain without waste: Proof-of-stake. *Review of Financial Studies*.

Sedjelmaci, H., Senouci, S. M., & Ansari, N. (2017). A hierarchical detection and response system to enhance security against lethal cyber-attacks in uav networks. *IEEE Transactions on Systems, Man, and Cybernetics. Systems*, *48*(9), 1594–1606. doi:10.1109/TSMC.2017.2681698

Sengupta, J., Ruj, S., & Bit, S. D. (2019). End to end secure anonymous communication for secure directed diffusion in iot. *Proceedings of the 20th international conference on distributed computing and networking*, 445–450. 10.1145/3288599.3295577

Sha, K., Wei, W., Yang, T. A., Wang, Z., & Shi, W. (2018). On security challenges and open issues in internet of things. *Future Generation Computer Systems*, *83*, 326–337. doi:10.1016/j.future.2018.01.059

Sharma, P. K., Chen, M.-Y., & Park, J. H. (2017). A software defined fog node based distributed blockchain cloud architecture for iot. *IEEE Access: Practical Innovations, Open Solutions*, *6*, 115–124. doi:10.1109/ACCESS.2017.2757955

Sharma, P. K., & Park, J. H. (2018). Blockchain based hybrid network architecture for the smart city. *Future Generation Computer Systems*, *86*, 650–655. doi:10.1016/j.future.2018.04.060

Shrestha, R., Bajracharya, R., Shrestha, A. P., & Nam, S. Y. (2020). A new type of blockchain for secure message exchange in VANET. *Digital Communications and Networks*, *6*(2), 177–186. doi:10.1016/j.dcan.2019.04.003

Shukla, P. (2017). Ml-ids: A machine learning approach to detect wormhole attacks in internet of things. In 2017 Intelligent Systems Conference (IntelliSys), (pp. 234–240). IEEE. doi:10.1109/IntelliSys.2017.8324298

Sicari, S., Rizzardi, A., Miorandi, D., & Coen-Porisini, A. (2018). Reato: Reacting to denial of service attacks in the internet of things. *Computer Networks*, *137*, 37–48. doi:10.1016/j.comnet.2018.03.020

Siegel, J. E., Erb, D. C., & Sarma, S. E. (2017). A survey of the connected vehicle landscape—Architectures, enabling technologies, applications, and development areas. *IEEE Transactions on Intelligent Transportation Systems*, *19*(8), 2391–2406. doi:10.1109/TITS.2017.2749459

Singh, M., Rajan, M., Shivraj, V., & Balamuralidhar, P. (2015). Secure mqtt for internet of things (iot). In *2015 fifth international conference on communication systems and network technologies*, (pp. 746–751). IEEE.

Singh, P., Nayyar, A., Kaur, A., & Ghosh, U. (2020). Blockchain and fog based architecture for internet of everything in smart cities. *Future Internet*, *12*(4), 61. doi:10.3390/fi12040061

Siriwardena, P. (2020). Securing apis with transport layer security (tls). In *Advanced API Security* (pp. 69–79). Springer. doi:10.1007/978-1-4842-2050-4_3

Sonar, K., & Upadhyay, H. (2014). A survey: Ddos attack on internet of things. *International Journal of Engineering Research and Development*, *10*(11), 58–63.

Song, T., Li, R., Mei, B., Yu, J., Xing, X., & Cheng, X. (2017). A privacy preserving communication protocol for iot applications in smart homes. *IEEE Internet of Things Journal*, *4*(6), 1844–1852. doi:10.1109/JIOT.2017.2707489

Stoyanova, M., Nikoloudakis, Y., Panagiotakis, S., Pallis, E., & Markakis, E. K. (2020). A survey on the internet of things (iot) forensics: Challenges, approaches, and open issues. *IEEE Communications Surveys and Tutorials*, *22*(2), 1191–1221. doi:10.1109/COMST.2019.2962586

Su, J., Vasconcellos, D. V., Prasad, S., Sgandurra, D., Feng, Y., & Sakurai, K. (2018). Lightweight classification of iot malware based on image recognition. In *2018 IEEE 42Nd annual computer software and applications conference (COMPSAC)*, (vol. 2, pp. 664–669). IEEE. 10.1109/COMPSAC.2018.10315

Sun, X., Ng, D. W. K., Ding, Z., Xu, Y., & Zhong, Z. (2019). Physical layer security in uav systems: Challenges and opportunities. *IEEE Wireless Communications*, *26*(5), 40–47. doi:10.1109/MWC.001.1900028

Tan, H., & Chung, I. (2020). Secure Authentication and Key Management With Blockchain in VANETs. *IEEE Access: Practical Innovations, Open Solutions*, *8*, 2482–2498. doi:10.1109/ACCESS.2019.2962387

Tan, Y., Liu, J., & Kato, N. (2020). Blockchain-based key management for heterogeneous flying ad-hoc network. *IEEE Transactions on Industrial Informatics*.

Tang, H., Shi, Y., & Dong, P. (2019). Public blockchain evaluation using entropy and topsis. *Expert Systems with Applications*, *117*, 204–210. doi:10.1016/j.eswa.2018.09.048

Tripathy, B. K., Jena, S. K., Reddy, V., Das, S., & Panda, S. K. (2020). A novel communication framework between manet and wsn in iot based smart environment. *International Journal of Information Technology*, 1–11.

Uddin, M. A., Stranieri, A., Gondal, I., & Balasubramanian, V. (2021). A survey on the adoption of blockchain in iot: Challenges and solutions. *Blockchain: Research and Applications*, 100006.

Wan, L., Eyers, D., & Zhang, H. (2019). Evaluating the Impact of Network Latency on the Safety of Blockchain Transactions. *2019 IEEE International Conference on Blockchain (Blockchain)*. 10.1109/Blockchain.2019.00033

Wang, Q., Zhu, X., Ni, Y., Gu, L., & Zhu, H. (2020). Blockchain for the iot and industrial iot: A review. *Internet of Things*, *10*, 100081. doi:10.1016/j.iot.2019.100081

Wang, S., Ouyang, L., Yuan, Y., Ni, X., Han, X., & Wang, F.-Y. (2019a). Blockchain-enabled smart contracts: Architecture, applications, and future trends. *IEEE Transactions on Systems, Man, and Cybernetics. Systems*, *49*(11), 2266–2277. doi:10.1109/TSMC.2019.2895123

Wang, X., Zha, X., Ni, W., Liu, R. P., Guo, Y. J., Niu, X., & Zheng, K. (2019b). Survey on blockchain for Internet of Things. *Computer Communications*, *136*, 10–29. doi:10.1016/j.comcom.2019.01.006

Wei, S., Ge, L., Yu, W., Chen, G., Pham, K., Blasch, E., Shen, D., & Lu, C. (2014). Simulation study of unmanned aerial vehicle communication networks addressing bandwidth disruptions. In *Sensors and Systems for Space Applications VII* (Vol. 9085, p. 90850O). International Society for Optics and Photonics.

Wood, G. (2014). Ethereum: A secure decentralised generalised transaction ledger. *Ethereum Project Yellow Paper*, *151*(2014), 1–32.

Wu, Q., Mei, W., & Zhang, R. (2019). Safeguarding wireless network with uavs: A physical layer security perspective. *IEEE Wireless Communications*, *26*(5), 12–18. doi:10.1109/MWC.001.1900050

Xiong, Z., Zhang, Y., Niyato, D., Wang, P., & Han, Z. (2018). When mobile blockchain meets edge computing. *IEEE Communications Magazine*, *56*(8), 33–39. doi:10.1109/MCOM.2018.1701095

Xu, Y., Ren, J., Wang, G., Zhang, C., Yang, J., & Zhang, Y. (2019). A blockchain-based nonrepudiation network computing service scheme for industrial iot. *IEEE Transactions on Industrial Informatics*, *15*(6), 3632–3641. doi:10.1109/TII.2019.2897133

Yang, X., Karampatzakis, E., Doerr, C., & Kuipers, F. (2018). Security vulnerabilities in lorawan. In *2018 IEEE/ACM Third International Conference on Internet-of-Things Design and Implementation (IoTDI)*, (pp. 129–140). IEEE. 10.1109/IoTDI.2018.00022

Yazdinejad, A., Parizi, R. M., Srivastava, G., Dehghantanha, A., & Choo, K.-K. R. (2019). Energy efficient decentralized authentication in internet of underwater things using blockchain. In 2019 IEEE Globecom Workshops (GC Wkshps), (pp. 1–6). IEEE. doi:10.1109/GCWkshps45667.2019.9024475

Yin, D., Zhang, L., & Yang, K. (2018). A ddos attack detection and mitigation with software-defined internet of things framework. *IEEE Access: Practical Innovations, Open Solutions*, *6*, 24694–24705. doi:10.1109/ACCESS.2018.2831284

Zarpelão, B. B., Miani, R. S., Kawakani, C. T., & de Alvarenga, S. C. (2017). A survey of intrusion detection in internet of things. *Journal of Network and Computer Applications*, *84*, 25–37. doi:10.1016/j.jnca.2017.02.009

Zeadally, S., Siddiqui, F., & Baig, Z. (2019). 25 years of bluetooth technology. *Future Internet*, *11*(9), 194. doi:10.3390/fi11090194

Zhang, G., Wu, Q., Cui, M., & Zhang, R. (2019a). Securing uav communications via joint trajectory and power control. *IEEE Transactions on Wireless Communications*, *18*(2), 1376–1389. doi:10.1109/TWC.2019.2892461

Zhang, K., Zhu, Y., Maharjan, S., & Zhang, Y. (2019b). Edge intelligence and blockchain empowered 5g beyond for the industrial internet of things. *IEEE Network*, *33*(5), 12–19. doi:10.1109/MNET.001.1800526

Zhang, N., Mi, X., Feng, X., Wang, X., Tian, Y., & Qian, F. (2018). *Understanding and mitigating the security risks of voice-controlled third-party skills on amazon alexa and google home.* arXiv preprint arXiv:1805.01525.

Zhang, X. D., Li, R., & Cui, B. (2018). A security architecture of VANET based on blockchain and mobile edge computing. *2018 1st IEEE International Conference on Hot Information-Centric Networking (HotICN)*.

Zheng, D., Wu, A., Zhang, Y., & Zhao, Q. (2018a). Efficient and privacy-preserving medical data sharing in internet of things with limited computing power. *IEEE Access: Practical Innovations, Open Solutions*, *6*, 28019–28027. doi:10.1109/ACCESS.2018.2840504

Zheng, Z., Xie, S., Dai, H., Chen, X., & Wang, H. (2017). *An overview of blockchain technology: Architecture, consensus, and future trends. In 2017 IEEE international congress on big data (BigData congress)*. IEEE.

Zheng, Z., Xie, S., Dai, H.-N., Chen, X., & Wang, H. (2018b). Blockchain challenges and opportunities: A survey. *International Journal of Web and Grid Services*, *14*(4), 352–375. doi:10.1504/IJWGS.2018.095647

KEY TERMS AND DEFINITIONS

Blockchain: A decentralized system based on a peer-to-peer network. Each network object keeps a copy of the ledger to avoid having a single point of failure. This technology can be explored in many use cases and used as a secure way to manage and protect all kinds of data.

FANET: A sub-category of the MANET that involves the deployment of a set of drones and ground stations through an ad hoc wireless network.

Internet of Things: Intelligent and autonomous connected objects that communicate with each other via the Internet. It encompasses the areas of the current Information Technology (IT) and uses other technologies such as Cloud Computing, Big data, or even the Blockchains.

MANET: A wireless network and without central entity (unlike a centralized or cellular communication network). It is based on the nodes ability to cooperate and form a network between them.

Security and Privacy: Set of policies and practices adopted to prevent and monitor unauthorized access or modification of an IT operation. It ensures the efficient system functioning.

VANET: A sub-category of MANET which is addressed for traffic management by intelligent transportation systems.

Vulnerabilities and Attacks: Malicious actions exploiting a weakness in a system to achieve a specific goal. These goals could be illegally gaining access to the system, interrupting or disrupting a service, or exploiting system resources.

Chapter 38
IoT Data Compression and Optimization Techniques in Cloud Storage:
Current Prospects and Future Directions

Kaium Hossain

Department of Computer Science & Engineering, Green University of Bangladesh, Dhaka, Bangladesh

Mizanur Rahman

Department of Computer Science & Engineering, Green University of Bangladesh, Dhaka, Bangladesh

Shanto Roy

Department of Computer Science & Engineering, Green University of Bangladesh, Dhaka, Bangladesh

ABSTRACT

This article presents a detailed survey on different data compression and storage optimization techniques in the cloud, their implications, and discussion over future directions. The development of the smart city or smart home systems lies in the development of the Internet of Things (IoT). With the increasing number of IoT devices, the tremendous volume of data is being generated every single day. Therefore, it is necessary to optimize the system's performance by managing, compressing and mining IoT data for smart decision support systems. In this article, the authors surveyed recent approaches with up-to-date outcomes and findings related to the management, mining, compression, and optimization of IoT data. The authors then discuss the scopes and limitations of present works and finally, this article presents the future perspectives of IoT data management on basis of cloud, fog, and mobile edge computing.

DOI: 10.4018/978-1-6684-7132-6.ch038

1. INTRODUCTION

Being called the future of the Internet, IoT is the most popular approach for the business application sector Tan and Wang (2010). It connects physical objects like sensors or devices through the Internet. IoT devices collect data from the environment by using sensors, cameras, radio frequency identifier (RFID) etc. A few basic features of IoT are connectivity, uniqueness, sensing/actuation capability, embedded intelligence and inter-operable communication capability. The concept of the smart city has emerged after IoT took over the scenario with industrial automation process as with utilizing this technology, city life can be smarter and efficient than before Khare and Khare (2018). IoT technology is used almost everywhere like industrial manufacturing Mourtzis et al. (2016), IoT enabled healthcare Roy et al. (2016), smart home Stojkoska and Trivodaliev (2017), smart transportation Whaiduzzaman et al. (2014), smart agriculture Channe et al. (2015) and other smart city approaches.

Every day tremendous volume of data is being generated with the increasing number of IoT devices. Generally these devices have limited processing power and storage capacity which are unable to process or store this big data. Therefore, at this point, a problem has arisen regarding processing power and storage capacity. Another problem for IoT big data is the mining of the data. Because it is quite a big challenge to figure out the actual meaningful data from the large data. The problems are not finished here, the IoT data that are increasing very fast need to be managed more efficiently and requires a more effective storage management system as well. To reduce the required storage space, data need to be compressed with much more compression ratio. And lastly, one of the major challenges is to reduce the energy consumption during processing and transmitting the big data through the IoT-Cloud ecosystem network.

A unified architecture of IoT system is defined in Lv et al. (2017), which contains the brief description of IoT node model, virtual things, the basic service of things and overall hierarchical model of services. To implement a complete IoT system, IoT nodes need to be connected directly to the Internet, and started from the base services, built the IoT application system with the middle layer of the Internet-based services and the base services of things. IoT architecture has seven layers, from bottom to top, the bottom is IoT hardware devices which are divided into two sub-layers, sensing and act device layer and intelligent device layer; the next layer is concerned with the information of things which are physical information layer and logical information layer. After that, the service layer comes up that divided into the IoT basic service layer and service middle layer. At the top is the application layer. A layered architecture of IoT System is shown in the Figure 1.

In this article, we have studied the related researches about the Integration of IoT and Cloud, IoT data storage management, Data mining for IoT, Data compression in IoT and Data Optimization and Energy Consumption in IoT. Therefore, we have discussed some scopes limitations for each section. After that, we have compared the existing works in every section and at last, we have shown some future directions for each and every section.

The main objective of our research work is to show a path to the researchers so that they can get scopes of more research. We have found out the challenges that cannot be solved by the existing research works. Through this paper, we are provoking the researchers to conduct more research works in some particular sectors. We have shown some points where more researches need to be conducted. From this article, researches can get some future directions about that where they should concentrate more on their research.

The rest of the paper is organized as follows: Section 2 discusses the technical advancements on the integration of IoT and Cloud. Section 3 addresses a literature review of IoT data storage management. In Section 4, several data mining techniques for IoT data are presented. Section 5 investigates recent approaches on data compression for IoT data. Then, in Section 6 notable works on data Optimization and energy consumption are summarized. Finally, Section 7 and Section 8 presents an elaborated discussion including issues, challenges, scopes and future direction.

Figure 1. Layered architecture of IoT system

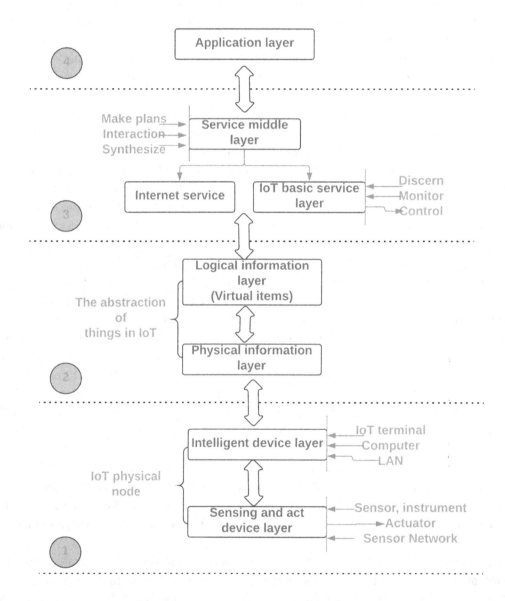

2. IOT-CLOUD ECOSYSTEM

The Cloud Computing (CC) is a service that is delivered through data centers, which are based on virtualization technologies. Cloud computing has virtually unlimited capabilities of storage and processing power. CC provides and delivers the service to clients or users on demand. The major benefit of IoT-Cloud is that it mitigates the limitation of processing power and storage capacity of IoT Celesti et al. (2016). The key issues of IoTCloud which are Protocol support, Energy efficiency, Resource allocation, Identity management, IPv6 deployment, service discovery, quality of service (QoS) provisioning, the location of data storage, Security and privacy, and unnecessary communication of data Aazam et al. (2014). The works require proper research works and evaluation to develop a better model Parwekar (2011). Some paperwork regarding IoT-Cloud are reviewed in the following:

Botta et al. (2014) and Botta et al. (2016) reviewed the literature regarding the integration of Cloud and IoT and derived a temporal characterization of the literature aiming at showing in a qualitative way the temporal behavior of the research and the common interests about the CloudIoT paradigm. In Doukas and Maglogiannis (2012), a platform was presented based on Cloud Computing for management of mobile and wearable health-care sensors, demonstrating this way the IoT paradigm applied on pervasive health-care. In Rao et al. (2012), they described how the IoT and Cloud integration can address the big data issues and proposed a prototype model for providing sensing as a service on the cloud.

Suciu et al. (2013) presented a framework for data procured from highly distributed, heterogeneous, decentralized, real and virtual devices that can be automatically managed, analyzed and controlled by distributed cloud-based services. In Tao et al. (2014), the applications of the technologies of IoT and CC in manufacturing were investigated at first and then concluded that a CC and IoT-based cloud manufacturing (CMfg) service system can ensure easier management in industrial production. In Kumrai et al. (2017), they considered a cloud broker, which is an intermediary in the infrastructure that use to manage the connected things in cloud computing. The cloud broker makes sure to simply find the best deal between the clients and service providers with the maximum profit.

Management applications in healthcare are excellent application area of Cloud-IoT ecosystem. In Gupta et al. (2017), authors discussed the technology in which the IoT based Cloudcentric architecture is used to predict and analyze of physical activities of the users for some common disease like diabetes, blood pressure, heart, and kidney. The architecture is based on the embedded sensors of the equipment rather than using wearable sensors or Smartphone sensors to store the value of the basic health-related parameters. In another work, the limitations of the current Personal health record (PHRs) are examined using the ecosystem hong2017interconnected. They proposed an interconnected PHR system built in accordance with healthcare data communication standards and an IoT Cloud platform.

Whenever we are talking about Cloud Computing there are two things that automatically come in the discussion that are Edge Computing and Fog Computing. A basic block diagram of IoT-Cloud ecosystem is shown in Figure 2

2.1. Edge Computing

Edge computing is a method of optimizing cloud computing systems by performing data processing at the edge of the network, near the source of the data. It reduces the communications bandwidth needed between sensors and the central data-center by performing analytics and knowledge generation at or near the source of the data Xu and Helal (2016). This approach requires griping resources that may not be continuously connected to a network such as laptops, smartphones, tablets, and sensors. Many types of research have been conducted in this sector and still going. Such as in Shi et al. (2016) and Satyanarayanan (2017), they discussed the edge computing primitives and challenges regarding it. And also discussed the vision of edge computing. Different survey works are also done regarding edge computing and different issues regarding it Roman et al. (2018); Abbas et al. (2018).

Figure 2. Basic architecture of IoT-cloud ecosystem

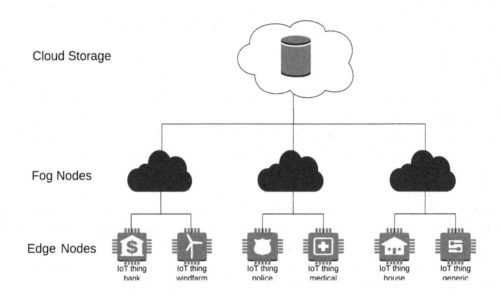

2.2. Fog Computing

Fog Computing is an architecture that uses one or more collaborative end-user clients or near-user edge devices to carry out a substantial amount of storage rather than stored primarily in cloud data centers, communication rather than routed over the Internet backbone, control, configuration, measurement, and management. There are lots of research works have been conducted regarding this topic. Such as in Bonomi et al. (2012), they have discussed the characteristics of fog which are: Low latency and location awareness, Wide-spread geographical distribution, Mobility, Very large number of nodes, the Predominant role of wireless access, the Strong presence of streaming and real-time applications and Heterogeneity. Luan et al. (2015) have marked the main features of Fog computing and described the concept, architecture and design goals of fog computing as well as discussed some of the future research issues from the networking perspective. In Aazam and Huh (2014), they have discussed the concept of fog computing in detail and presented the architecture of Smart Gateway with Fog Computing. Madsen et al. (2013) have considered current paradigms in computing and outlined the most important aspects concerning their reliability. In Stojmenovic and Wen (2014), the motivation and advantages of Fog computing have discussed, and its applications are analyzed in a series of real scenarios, such as Smart Grid, smart traffic lights in vehicular networks and software-defined networks. They have also discussed the state-of-the-art of Fog computing and similar work under the same topic.

3. IOT DATA STORAGE MANAGEMENT

For a large amount of heterogeneous data, there should have an efficient storage management system. Therefore, a functional semantic model Xu et al. (2014) that identifies the acquisition, management, disposing and mining areas of IoT data, based on the data processing function is necessary Cai et al. (2017).

3.1. Heterogeneous Data management

At present, due to versatility in IoT ecosystem, heterogeneous data is being generated. Vlacheas et al. (2013) identified the main issues that may prevent IoT from playing this crucial role, such as the heterogeneity among connected objects and the unreliable nature of associated services. To solve these issues, a cognitive management framework for IoT was presented. In the proposed framework, dynamically changing real-world objects are represented in a virtualized environment. In fact, heterogeneous data require an agile framework that can ensure proper representation, integration and querying over data Dividino et al. (2018).

3.2. Big Data management

With structured data management Jiang et al. (2014) non-structured big data requires proper management as well. Fan and Chen (2010) designed a common data management framework based on SOA to provide a common data management for the IoT ecosystem. In Li et al. (2012), authors designed a storage solution named IoT MDB based on NoSQL (Not Only SQL), by concentrating in a centralized form of data storage. The storage strategies for expressing and organizing IoT data in a uniform manner were proposed, some evaluations were carried out. Later the proposed architecture (IoTMDB) was successfully implemented to the Internet to handle IoT data of huge scale that solves the storage problem of IoT data. Pandey and Subbiah (2016) proposed a new big data storage architecture for facilitating efficient analytics of health informatics big data. The storage architecture consists of an application cluster and a storage cluster. In Xu et al. (2016), they proposed a largescale object-based active storage platform, called Gem, for data analytics in the IoT and explored the utilization of object-based active storage to improve the interaction between data analytics applications and storage systems in the IoT.

3.3. Data Pricing

Smart data pricing (SDP) for IoT requires extensible frameworks so that prices are used to incentivize sensor owners to contribute their data to IoT services, improving the service quality and generating higher revenue from selling IoT services to users Niyato et al. (2016). Moreover, to ensure a privacy preserving trading system, more aspects such as the value of data, comprehensive comparison in market, data identification, digital copyright, etc. (Liang et al., 2018).

3.4. Machine Learning Employed DB

Data science and machine learning (ML) are the base of predictive models. ML is being used a lot in storage management nowadays. In Truong et al. (2017), authors proposed a design of an IoT system that consists of a device able to send real-time environmental data to cloud storage as well as a machine learning algorithm to predict environmental conditions for fungal detection and prevention. In fact, ML based database need to work leveraging past histories of data and utilize new information to change the overall database configurations (Van Aken et al., 2017).

3.5. BlockChain Based Data Storage

BlockChain (BC) provides a trusted decentralized network with collective verifications. It can be utilized as well in storage management for IoT ecosystem. Liu et al. (2017) proposed a BC-based framework for data integrity service. In this framework, they provided a reliable data integrity verification for both the data owners and the data consumers, without depending on any third-party auditor.

4. DATA MINING FOR IOT

As we know that IoT generates a large volume of data, it is necessary to find out the real information from this vast amount of data. Data mining is used to extract information from large volume data generated by the IoT devices. Significant researches have been performed on data mining among which a few works are summarized in the following:

In Watanabe et al. (2003), authors applied variational Bayesian estimation and clustering for speech recognition (VBEC) to an acoustic model adaptation. In Mariscal et al. (2010), authors reviewed the most used and cited data mining and knowledge discovery methodologies and process models and also discussed the advantages and disadvantages of every approach.

In Bin et al. (2010), authors proposed four data mining models for the IoT which are Multi-layer data-mining model, Distributed data mining model, Grid-based data mining model, and Data mining model from a multi-technology integration perspective. They have also discussed several key issues in data mining of IoT. Tsai et al. (2014) discussed the IoT and reviewed the features of data from IoT and data mining for IoT.

In Alguliyev et al. (2016), a new clustering approach was introduced named batch clustering (BC) algorithm. They compared the classic k-means clustering algorithm to the proposed algorithm in order to identify and differentiate the required computation time and objective function. The main focus behind designing the BC algorithm is to maintain the efficiency and quality during clustering large datasets in batches. Kumar et al. (2016) presented a new clusiVAT algorithm and compared it with four other popular data clustering algorithms. The proposed algorithm clusiVAT is based on sampling the data, imaging the reordered distance matrix to estimate the number of clusters in the data visually, clustering the samples using a relative of single linkage (SL), and then non-iteratively extending the labels to the rest of the data-set using the nearest prototype rule.

Singh and Sharma (2017) established the relationship between Data Mining and the IoT. They have discussed the key issues about different data mining models like a collection of data, data abstraction, and aggregation, event filtering etc. Therefore, a new model has been proposed in this paper. In Zhang et al. (2018), they presented a CP high-order probabilistic c-means algorithm (CP-HOPCM) to compress the attributes by applying the canonical polyadic decomposition to the high-order probabilistic c-means scheme. It is basically meant to compress the attributes in the high-order probabilistic c-means algorithm.

Data mining is required in all smart systems from healthcare, agriculture to industrial aspects. As sensors are generating continuous data, it is required to extract only the necessary information.

5. DATA COMPRESSION IN IOT

Data compression has become very important for IoT data which allows to store more data in a small storage space. Data compression not only reduces the need for storage of data but also helps in energy consumption for IoT devices. Because large data sets require more energy for transmission throughout the network. Data compression schemes are categorized into two types- Lossy and Lossless compression techniques.

5.1. Lossy Compressions

In lossy data, compression data are compressed by identifying the important data points and discarding the redundant data. The lossy data compression techniques have better compression efficiency with respect to lossless data compression. In lossy compression algorithms there some errors between the data retrieved from compressed one and original data. Some paperwork regarding lossy data compression is summarized below:

Bose et al. (2016) compared existing lossy data compression algorithms and found out a relation between the performances of these compression algorithms and the sensor data features. Roy et al. (2017) proposed a tokenization-based model that not only compresses IoT data up to 90% but also provides data security in cloud storages. To achieve this, authors built an intermediate node that clusters data from a particular period and then calculates statistical data. Then the data are sent and mapped to distributed storages as token values. The compression basically happens while calculating statistical data and tokenizing using token vaults. Hsu et al. (2017) provided a context-sensitive data compression approach that is adaptable to balance accuracy and storage cost. The main idea of this approach is to reduce the size of the videos by discarding the less changeable sequential frames. This approach has achieved the video compression of the data size down to 60% with 96.5% precision for a sampled IoT video streaming application.

5.2. Lossless Compression

In lossless compression techniques, the original data can be retrieved completely without any error. Some works regarding lossless compression are summarized below:

Danieletto et al. (2012) proposed a novel lightweight approach capable of alleviating both aspects by leveraging on the advantages offered by classification methods to optimize communications and by enhancing information transmission to simplify data classification. In Li et al. (2013), they have presented a novel data compression algorithm PCVQ based on principal component analysis (PCA) and vector quantization (VQ). In Awwad et al. (2013), the performance of the data compression schemes is compared with each other, showing the compression capabilities of each of them under different scenarios.

Vecchio et al. (2014) proposed the lossless compression algorithm (LEC) and tested the proposed approaches on different datasets collected in several real sensor network deployments. Therefore, they showed that in all the datasets, the schemes can achieve significant compression efficiencies. Furthermore, they compared results with existing schemes and showed the performance improvements. In Hadiatna et al. (2016), they obtained the compression ratio (CR) as 50% for the compression method used in the data logger. In the monitoring process with a lot of sensors, the data logger is capable of transmitting and storing data in memory with limited data. The memory capacity of the data logger limited size can increase the size by using the method of data compression.

In some works, both lossy and lossless techniques are used to make a hybrid approach such as In Deepu et al. (2017), authors proposed a novel data compression and transmission scheme for power reduction in IoT enabled wireless sensors. Both lossy and lossless techniques meant to be used here to compress data so that it can enable hybrid transmission mode, support adaptive data rate selection and save power in wireless transmission. It was found to be power reduced to 18% for lossy and 53% for lossless transmission respectively.

6. DATA OPTIMIZATION AND ENERGY CONSUMPTION IN IOT

Most of the IoT data have lower energy power whereas the big data of IoT needs lots of energy during transmission. So, it is very important to develop such infrastructures to save more energy. In this section we have studied and summarized given below:

Wei and Li (2011) proposed a system framework for building energy monitoring and analysis system based on IoT. Tirronen et al. (2012) presented a simple power consumption model for different DRX cycle lengths. Ali and Abu-Elkheir (2012) discussed the IoT data lifecycle and surveyed the current researches that are performed for IoT data management issue. In Chang et al. (2013), they proposed an energy-oriented routing mechanism to improve RPL routing protocol by combining the expected transmission count (ETX) and remaining energy metrics.

In Pielli et al. (2016), the goal was to investigate the trade-offs between energy consumption and data compression at the medium access control (MAC) layer. A TDMA-like scheme was developed based on an optimization framework, which adopts convex and alternate programming to minimize the data distortion and extend the network lifetime simultaneously, under QoS constraints. In Bijarbooneh et al. (2016), they presented a cloud-based solution that utilizes the link quality and spatiotemporal correlation of data to minimize energy consumption by selecting sensors for sampling and relaying data. A multi-phase adaptive sensing algorithm with belief propagation protocol (ASBP) was proposed. The ASBP protocol has found 80% energy-efficient, with the optimal CP active sensor selection and average 5% error in the BP data inference.

One of the big issues of IoT is energy consumption. We know that big data requires more energy to transmit through the network. Even these approaches are also not so efficient enough, the same reason is here also the size of the data. That is why there always a need for more efficient methods than that we have now.

7. APPLICATIONS

7.1. Data Analytics

Data analytics is the process of examining data sets in order to gather information about a particular entity. However, efficient data analytics has become more difficult than ever due to the large volume of data. Right now, there are quality analytics approaches and standards available for the current stage of data. Different approaches for example- people identity verification in cloud using deep neural network

Shovon et al. (2018) requires proper analytics from big data sets. Along with mobile edge and fog computing, it has become a lot easier to analysis and mine data along with compression at expected rate as well.

7.2. Data Modeling

As business analytics is growing fast throughout the world, data modeling is important. All the successful business running right now completely depends on proper data modeling as data is the most valuable asset right now. Efficient technology invention, smart objects and reverse engineering also require proper data modeling achieved through IoT ecosystem.

7.3. Data Visualization

Data visualization is the process of presenting the data graphically. Generated data by IoT ecosystem may be utilized for topological discovery, futuristic model invention or data driven model discovery. Above all, data visualization delivers productive results through graphical representation that is necessary for today's ICT business. Statistical plots, informatics and graphics contribute a lot in data science aspects with descriptive visualization.

7.4. Data Security

Data security is an issue of major concern for IoT-Cloud ecosystem. Proper security of data should be ensured in cloud and mobile computing. Machine learning based ecosystems where systems are feed with continuous training data can ensure blocking of unauthorized activities in cloud. Different cryptographic approaches can be implemented for data security in the ecosystem Badve et al. (2016). Moreover, ensuring secure high performance, multiparty communication can be employed Li et al. (2018). Besides, integrating customized BlockChain based systems are delivering further security in decentralized network without requiring third party management systems.

7.5. Architectural Security

While maintaining data security in Cloud-IoT ecosystems, architectural security seems to be more effective. Adat and Gupta (2018) and Tewari and Gupta (2018) presented the history, background, statistics of IoT and security-based analysis of IoT architecture which shows the vulnerabilities found in recent models. To address the issues, a Cloud Computing Adoption Framework (CCAF) security suitable for business Clouds is presented by Chang et al. (2016). It is a multi-layer security framework based on the development and integration of three major criteria: firewall, identity management, and encryption. Authors found that CCAF multi-layered security could detect and block 99.95% viruses and trojans and could maintain 85% and above of blocking for 100 hours of continuous attacks. Yaseen et al. (2018) discussed the problem regarding collusion attacks for different IoT environments. They also investigated how the mobility of IoT devices is affected by the difficulty of detecting such types of attacks. Therefore, they introduced a model based on Fog Computing infrastructure that keeps track of IoT devices and detects collusion attackers. The model uses fog computing layer for real-time monitoring and detection of collusion attacks in IoT environments.

8. SCOPE, LIMITATIONS AND FUTURE DIRECTIONS

The IoT technology has been integrated with the cloud computing technology to overcome the lack of storage capacity and processing power in IoT ecosystem. Despite the advantages we have by integrating technologies, there arise a lot of issues that require better solutions. Some of those issues are protocol support, energy efficiency, resource allocation, identity management, IPv6 deployment, service discovery, QoS provisioning, the location of data storage, security and privacy, Unnecessary Communication of data etc. We know that the IoT technology is spreading very rapidly and a large volume of data is being generated by the IoT devices which should be handled properly in the future.

IoT enabled smart systems are the primary requirement for futuristic smart cities. Smart systems have been developed considering optimal performance, scalability, connectivity and usability. In order to achieve these performance measurements and security, data appears as the important factor. But with the extension of networks, the amount of data is getting bigger. Therefore, data compression and optimization, energy efficiency approaches, decentralized control systems, integration of new technologies require further research attentions.

New technologies such as BlockChain (BC) and software defined networking have gained tremendous attractions for their features and are being integrated with the current IoT-cloud ecosystem. A novel BC based distributed cloud architecture is proposed in Sharma et al. (2018). It is a distributed cloud architecture based on BC technology that provides lowcost, secure and on-demand access to the most competitive computing environments. The model achieves cost-effective high-performance computing just utilizing a distributed cloud infrastructure. In Nguyen et al. (2017), an SDN-based IoT Mobile Edge Cloud Architecture (SIMECA) is proposed that can deploy diverse IoT services at the mobile edge by leveraging distributed, lightweight control and optimized data planes for IoT communications.

In this paper, we classified the concerns related to IoT operations as cloud-IoT integration, data compression, data mining, storage management and energy efficient approaches. All these fields need unified optimization to ensure overall system developments. While considering improvement of a system, there are two key points- performance and security. In our work, we focused on only the performance-based case-study in Cloud-IoT ecosystem. The taxonomy of IoT operations according to our review has shown in Figure 3:

According to the increase in the volume of data, existing approaches need further development to cope with the future internet architecture. Therefore, all the above-mentioned areas require individual research attention. The limitations and future research scopes are shown in Table 1.

9. CONCLUSION

With approaching towards development of smart systems, IoT has tremendous effect over existing technologies. However, it arises some issues as well. One of the primary concerns of IoT ecosystem is big data management that include storage capacity, processing, optimization, and energy consumption etc. In this article, we discussed these problems in detail with exemplifying some recent works. We also discussed several limitation and area of improvement regarding these topics. Therefore, deducing towards an opinion, it is quite clear that redesigning models and implementing algorithms in middle layers that sit between IoT and Cloud can deliver better result in these arenas.

Figure 3. Taxonomy of IoT operations

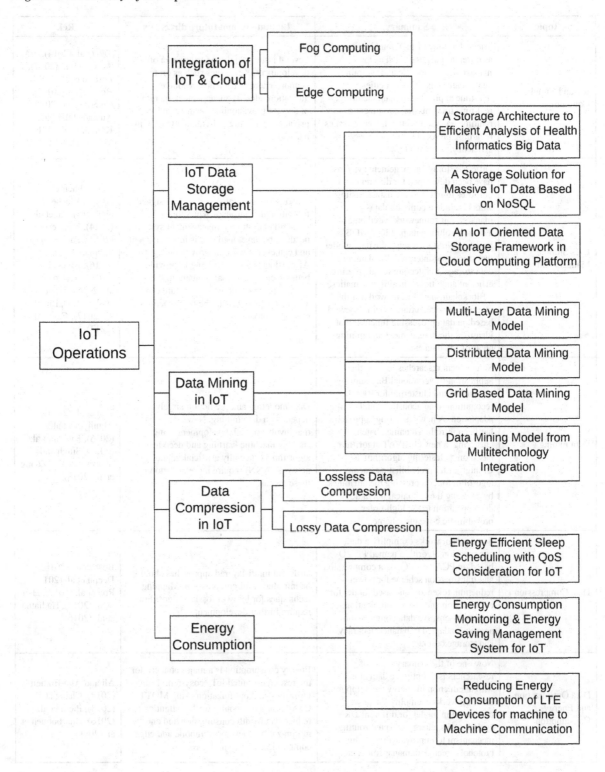

Table 1. Summarized research directions

Topic	Summary	Limitations and future directions	Ref.
IoT and Cloud Computing	The technology of IoTCloud is serving as different purposes such as for management of mobile and wearable health-care sensors, smart cities, real-time applications, manufacturing, real-time transmission equipment of multimedia systems etc. However, issues regarding protocol support, energy efficiency, security etc.	Several issues require a further area of development. Key issues such as protocol support, energy efficiency, resource allocation, identity management, quality of service provisioning, security and privacy etc. require individual attention in particular.	Tao et al. (2014), Aazam et al. (2014), Fortino et al. (2014), Botta et al. (2016), Celesti et al. (2016), Xu and Helal (2016), Kumrai et al. (2017), Yang et al. (2017)
Data Storage Management	Different storage management systems have been developed for different purposes to manage IoT data. Existing works include a common data management framework based on SOA, a storage solution named IOT MDB based on NoSQL, a semantic data model that stores and interprets IoT data, big data storage architecture for facilitating efficient analytics of health informatics, a Blockchain-based framework for data integrity service, a functional framework based on data processing function that identifies the management and mining areas of IoT data etc.	Existing storage frameworks are designed for individual purposes. Therefore, a standard data storage management system needs to be developed that is more efficient and can evolve with the growth of big data. Also, Blockchain is evolving to provide better security and management in this arena. The new storage architecture can be a hybrid approach with the best practices of current approaches.	Abu-Elkheir et al. (2013), Vlacheas et al. (2013), Xu et al. (2014), Jiang et al. (2014), Pandey and Subbiah (2016), Xu et al. (2016), Niyato et al. (2016), Truong et al. (2017), Liu et al. (2017), Cai et al. (2017)
Data mining	Some recent researches involve the application of variational Bayesian estimation and clustering for speech recognition to an acoustic model adaptation. A new clustering approach has been introduced named batch clustering, a new clusiVAT algorithm based on a clustering algorithm, a CP high-order probabilistic c-means algorithm for compressing the attributes by applying the canonical polyadic decomposition to the high-order probabilistic c-means scheme.	Data modeling and prediction largely depends on data mining. New strategies that involve model development using suitable machine learning and deep learning algorithms especially artificial neural network (ANN) require more attention in these arenas.	Tsai et al. (2014), Alguliyev et al. (2016), Kumar et al. (2016), Singh and Sharma (2017), Zhang et al. (2018)
Data Compression	Some recent works exemplify a data compression algorithm named PCVQ based on PCA and VQ, data compression and transmission scheme for power reduction, tokenization-based model for compression and space optimization, a context-sensitive data compression approach adapted to balance accuracy and storage cost etc.	Different multi-layered approaches should be introduced for compression. Mapping techniques for lossy or lossless algorithms require further development.	Bose et al. (2016), Deepu et al. (2017), Roy et al. (2017), Hsu et al. (2017), Hadiatna et al. (2016)
Data Optimization and Energy Consumption	Now one of the primary focus of researchers is to optimize data along with a reduction in energy consumption. Existing works exemplify the power consumption model for different DRX cycle lengths, energy-oriented routing mechanism to improve RPL routing protocol, green data management etc.	Energy consumption is a major concern for the resource-limited IoT ecosystem. Data utilization and optimization using MQTT/ CoAp protocols require further attention to reduce bandwidth consumption and energy minimization. Developed mobile and edge computing can help in this regard.	Ali and Abu-Elkheir (2012), Chang et al. (2013), Pielli et al. (2016), Bijarbooneh et al. (2016)

REFRENCES

Aazam, M., & Huh, E.-N. (2014). Fog computing and smart gateway based communication for cloud of things. In *2014 International Conference on Future Internet of Things and Cloud (FiCloud)* (pp. 464–470). IEEE.

Aazam, M., Khan, I., Alsaffar, A. A., & Huh, E.-N. (2014). Cloud of things: Integrating internet of things and cloud computing and the issues involved. In *2014 11th International Bhurban Conference on Applied Sciences and Technology (IBCAST)* (pp. 414–419). IEEE.

Abbas, N., Zhang, Y., Taherkordi, A., & Skeie, T. (2018). Mobile edge computing: A survey. *IEEE Internet of Things Journal*, 5(1), 450–465. doi:10.1109/JIOT.2017.2750180

Abu-Elkheir, M., Hayajneh, M., & Ali, N. A. (2013). Data management for the internet of things: Design primitives and solution. *Sensors (Basel)*, 13(11), 15582–15612. doi:10.3390131115582 PMID:24240599

Adat, V., & Gupta, B. (2018). Security in internet of things: Issues, challenges, taxonomy, and architecture. *Telecommunication Systems*, 67(3), 423–441. doi:10.100711235-017-0345-9

Alguliyev, R., Aliguliyev, R., Bagirov, A., & Karimov, R. (2016). Batch clustering algorithm for big data sets. In *2016 IEEE 10th International Conference on Application of Information and Communication Technologies (AICT)* (pp. 1–4). IEEE.

Ali, N. A., & Abu-Elkheir, M. (2012). Data management for the internet of things: Green directions. In 2012 IEEE Globecom Workshops (GC Wkshps) (pp. 386–390). IEEE.

Awwad, S. A., Ng, C. K., Noordin, N. K., Ali, B. M., & Hashim, F. (2013). Second and subsequent fragments headers compression scheme for ipv6 header in 6lowpan network. In *2013 Seventh International Conference on Sensing Technology (ICST)* (pp. 771–776). IEEE.

Badve, O., Gupta, B., & Gupta, S. (2016). Reviewing the security features in contemporary security policies and models for multiple platforms. In Handbook of Research on Modern Cryptographic Solutions for Computer and Cyber Security (pp. 479–504). Hershey, PA: IGI Global. doi:10.4018/978-1-5225-0105-3.ch020

Bijarbooneh, F. H., Du, W., Ngai, E. C.-H., Fu, X., & Liu, J. (2016). Cloud-assisted data fusion and sensor selection for internet of things. *IEEE Internet of Things Journal*, 3(3), 257–268. doi:10.1109/JIOT.2015.2502182

Bin, S., Yuan, L., & Xiaoyi, W. (2010). Research on data mining models for the internet of things, In *2010 International Conference on Image Analysis and Signal Processing (IASP)* (pp. 127–132). IEEE.

Bonomi, F., Milito, R., Zhu, J., & Addepalli, S. (2012). Fog computing and its role in the internet of things. In *Proceedings of the first edition of the MCC workshop on Mobile cloud computing* (pp. 13–16). ACM.

Bose, T., Bandyopadhyay, S., Kumar, S., Bhattacharyya, A., & Pal, A. (2016). Signal characteristics on sensor data compression in IoT-an investigation. In *2016 13th Annual IEEE International Conference on Sensing, Communication, and Networking (SECON)* (pp. 1–6). IEEE.

Botta, A., De Donato, W., Persico, V., & Pescap'e, A. (2016). Integration of cloud computing and internet of things: A survey. *Future Generation Computer Systems*, *56*, 684–700. doi:10.1016/j.future.2015.09.021

Botta, A., De Donato, W., Persico, V., & Pescap'e, A. (2014). On the integration of cloud computing and internet of things. In *2014 International Conference on Future Internet of Things and Cloud (FiCloud)* (pp. 23–30). IEEE.

Cai, H., Xu, B., Jiang, L., & Vasilakos, A. V. (2017). IoT-based big data storage systems in cloud computing: Perspectives and challenges. *IEEE Internet of Things Journal*, *4*, 75–87.

Celesti, A., Fazio, M., Giacobbe, M., Puliafito, A., & Villari, M. (2016). Characterizing cloud federation in IoT. In *2016 30th International Conference on Advanced Information Networking and Applications Workshops (WAINA)* (pp. 93–98). IEEE.

Chang, L.-H., Lee, T.-H., Chen, S.-J., & Liao, C.-Y. (2013). Energy-efficient oriented routing algorithm in wireless sensor networks. In *2013 IEEE International Conference on Systems, Man, and Cybernetics (SMC)* (pp. 3813–3818). IEEE.

Chang, V., Kuo, Y.-H., & Ramachandran, M. (2016). Cloud computing adoption framework: A security framework for business clouds. *Future Generation Computer Systems*, *57*, 24–41. doi:10.1016/j.future.2015.09.031

Channe, H., Kothari, S., & Kadam, D. (2015). Multidisciplinary model for smart agriculture using internet-of-things (IoT), sensors, cloud-computing, mobile-computing & big-data analysis, Int. J. *Computer Technology and Application*, *6*, 374–382.

Danieletto, M., Bui, N., & Zorzi, M. (2012). Improving internet of things communications through compression and classification. In *2012 IEEE International Conference on Pervasive Computing and Communications Workshops (PERCOM Workshops)* (pp. 284–289). IEEE.

Deepu, C. J., Heng, C.-H., & Lian, Y. (2017). A hybrid data compression scheme for power reduction in wireless sensors for IoT. *IEEE Transactions on Biomedical Circuits and Systems*, *11*(2), 245–254. doi:10.1109/TBCAS.2016.2591923 PMID:27845673

Dividino, R., Soares, A., Matwin, S., Isenor, A. W., Webb, S., & Brousseau, M. (2018). *Semantic integration of real-time heterogeneous data streams for ocean-related decision making. In Big Data and Artificial Intelligence for Military Decision Making*.

Doukas, C., & Maglogiannis, I. (2012). Bringing iot and cloud computing towards pervasive healthcare. In *2012 Sixth International Conference on Innovative Mobile and Internet Services in Ubiquitous Computing (IMIS)* (pp. 922–926). IEEE.

Fan, T., & Chen, Y. (2010). A scheme of data management in the internet of things. In *2010 2nd IEEE International Conference on Network Infrastructure and Digital Content* (pp. 110–114). IEEE.

Fortino, G., Guerrieri, A., Russo, W., & Savaglio, C. (2014). Integration of agent-based and cloud computing for the smart objects-oriented IoT. In *Proceedings of the 2014 IEEE 18th International Conference on Computer Supported Cooperative Work in Design (CSCWD)* (pp. 493–498). IEEE.

Gupta, P. K., Maharaj, B., & Malekian, R. (2017). A novel and secure IoT based cloud centric architecture to perform predictive analysis of users activities in sustainable health centres. *Multimedia Tools and Applications*, 76(18), 18489–18512. doi:10.100711042-016-4050-6

Hadiatna, F., Hindersah, H., Yolanda, D., & Triawan, M. A. (2016). Design and implementation of data logger using lossless data compression method for internet of things. In *2016 6th International Conference on System Engineering and Technology (ICSET)* (pp. 105–108). IEEE.

Hsu, C.-C., Fang, Y.-T., & Yu, F. (2017). Content-sensitive data compression for IoT streaming services. In *2017 IEEE International Congress on Internet of Things (ICIOT)* (pp. 147–150). IEEE.

Jiang, L., Da Xu, L., Cai, H., Jiang, Z., Bu, F., & Xu, B. (2014). An IoT-oriented data storage framework in cloud computing platform. *IEEE Transactions on Industrial Informatics*, 10(2), 1443–1451. doi:10.1109/TII.2014.2306384

Khare, P., & Khare, A. (2018). Internet of things for smart cities. In Exploring the Convergence of Big Data and the Internet of Things (pp. 96–112). Hershey, PA: IGI Global. doi:10.4018/978-1-5225-2947-7.ch008

Kumar, D., Bezdek, J. C., Palaniswami, M., Rajasegarar, S., Leckie, C., & Havens, T. C. (2016). A hybrid approach to clustering in big data. *IEEE Transactions on Cybernetics*, 46(10), 2372–2385. doi:10.1109/TCYB.2015.2477416 PMID:26441434

Kumrai, T., Ota, K., Dong, M., Kishigami, J., & Sung, D. K. (2017). Multiobjective optimization in cloud brokering systems for connected internet of things. *IEEE Internet of Things Journal*, 4(2), 404–413. doi:10.1109/JIOT.2016.2565562

Li, T., Gupta, B. B., & Metere, R. (2018). Socially-conforming cooperative computation in cloud networks. *Journal of Parallel and Distributed Computing*, 117, 274–280. doi:10.1016/j.jpdc.2017.06.006

Li, T., Liu, Y., Tian, Y., Shen, S., & Mao, W. (2012). A storage solution for massive IoT data based on nosql, In *2012 IEEE International Conference on Green Computing and Communications (GreenCom)* (pp. 50–57). IEEE.

Li, Y., Xi, S., Wei, H., Zhang, Z., & Zhang, C. (2013). A data compression algorithm for the sea route monitoring with wireless sensor network. In *2013 International Conference on Information Science and Cloud Computing (ISCC)* (pp. 153–159). IEEE.

Liang, F., Yu, W., An, D., Yang, Q., Fu, X., & Zhao, W. (2018). A survey on big data market: Pricing, trading and protection. *IEEE Access*, 6, 15132–15154. doi:10.1109/ACCESS.2018.2806881

Liu, B., Yu, X. L., Chen, S., Xu, X., & Zhu, L. (2017). Blockchain based data integrity service framework for IoT data. In *2017 IEEE International Conference on Web Services (ICWS)* (pp. 468–475). IEEE.

Luan, T. H., Gao, L., Li, Z., Xiang, Y., Wei, G., & Sun, L. (2015). Fog computing: Focusing on mobile users at the edge. arXiv:1502.01815

Lv, W., Meng, F., Zhang, C., Lv, Y., Cao, N., & Jiang, J. (2017). Research on unified architecture of IoT system. In *2017 IEEE International Conference on Computational Science and Engineering (CSE) and Embedded and Ubiquitous Computing (EUC)* (Vol. 2, pp. 345–352). IEEE. 10.1109/CSE-EUC.2017.249

Madsen, H., Burtschy, B., Albeanu, G., & Popentiu-Vladicescu, F. (2013). Reliability in the utility computing era: Towards reliable fog computing. In *2013 20th International Conference on Systems, Signals and Image Processing (IWSSIP)* (pp. 43–46). IEEE.

Mariscal, G., Marban, O., & Fernandez, C. (2010). A survey of data mining and knowledge discovery process models and methodologies. *The Knowledge Engineering Review*, *25*(2), 137–166. doi:10.1017/S0269888910000032

Mourtzis, D., Vlachou, E., & Milas, N. (2016). Industrial big data as a result of IoT adoption in manufacturing. *Procedia CIRP*, *55*, 290–295. doi:10.1016/j.procir.2016.07.038

Nguyen, B., Choi, N., Thottan, M., & Van der Merwe, J. (2017). Simeca: Sdn-based IoT mobile edge cloud architecture. In *2017 IFIP/IEEE Symposium on Integrated Network and Service Management (IM)* (pp. 503–509). IEEE.

Niyato, D., Hoang, D. T., Luong, N. C., Wang, P., Kim, D. I., & Han, Z. (2016). Smart data pricing models for the internet of things: A bundling strategy approach. *IEEE Network*, *30*(2), 18–25. doi:10.1109/MNET.2016.7437020

Pandey, M. K., & Subbiah, K. (2016). A novel storage architecture for facilitating efficient analytics of health informatics big data in cloud. In *2016 IEEE International Conference on Computer and Information Technology (CIT)* (pp. 578–585). IEEE.

Parwekar, P. (2011). From internet of things towards cloud of things. In *2011 2nd International Conference on Computer and Communication Technology (ICCCT)* (pp. 329–333). IEEE.

Pielli, C., Biason, A., Zanella, A., & Zorzi, M. (2016). Joint optimization of energy efficiency and data compression in TDMA-based medium access control for the IoT. In 2016 IEEE Globecom Workshops (GC Wkshps) (pp. 1–6). IEEE.

Rao, B. P., Saluia, P., Sharma, N., Mittal, A., & Sharma, S. V. (2012). Cloud computing for internet of things & sensing based applications. In *2012 Sixth International Conference on Sensing Technology (ICST)* (pp. 374–380). IEEE.

Roman, R., Lopez, J., & Mambo, M. (2018). A survey and analysis of security threats and challenges. *Future Generation Computer Systems*, *78*, 680–698. doi:10.1016/j.future.2016.11.009

Roy, S., Rahman, A., Helal, M., Kaiser, M. S., & Chowdhury, Z. I. (2016). Low cost rf based online patient monitoring using web and mobile applications. In *2016 5th International Conference on Informatics, Electronics and Vision (ICIEV)* (pp. 869–874). IEEE.

Roy, S., Shovon, A. R., & Whaiduzzaman, M. (2017). Combined approach of tokenization and mining to secure and optimize big data in cloud storage. In 2017 IEEE Region 10, Humanitarian Technology Conference (R10-HTC) (pp. 83–88). IEEE.

Satyanarayanan, M. (2017). *Edge computing: Vision and challenges*. Santa Clara, USA: USENIX Association.

Sharma, P. K., Chen, M.-Y., & Park, J. H. (2018). A software defined fog node based distributed blockchain cloud architecture for IoT. *IEEE Access*, *6*, 115–124. doi:10.1109/ACCESS.2017.2757955

Shi, W., Cao, J., Zhang, Q., Li, Y., & Xu, L. (2016). Edge computing: Vision and challenges. *IEEE Internet of Things Journal*, *3*(5), 637–646. doi:10.1109/JIOT.2016.2579198

Shovon, A. R., Roy, S., Sharma, T., & Whaiduzzaman, M. (2018). A restful e-governance application framework for people identity verification in cloud. In *International Conference on Cloud Computing* (pp. 281–294). Springer.

Singh, A., & Sharma, S. (2017). Analysis on data mining models for internet of things. In *2017 International Conference on I-SMAC (IoT in Social, Mobile, Analytics and Cloud) (I-SMAC)* (pp. 94–100). IEEE.

Stojkoska, B. L. R., & Trivodaliev, K. V. (2017). A review of internet of things for smart home: Challenges and solutions. *Journal of Cleaner Production*, *140*, 1454–1464. doi:10.1016/j.jclepro.2016.10.006

Stojmenovic, I., & Wen, S. (2014). The fog computing paradigm: Scenarios and security issues. In *2014 Federated Conference on Computer Science and Information Systems (FedCSIS)* (pp. 1–8). IEEE.

Suciu, G., Vulpe, A., Halunga, S., Fratu, O., Todoran, G., & Suciu, V. (2013). Smart cities built on resilient cloud computing and secure internet of things. In *2013 19th International Conference on Control Systems and Computer Science (CSCS)* (pp. 513–518). IEEE.

Tan, L., & Wang, N. (2010). Future internet: The internet of things. In *2010 3rd International Conference on Advanced Computer Theory and Engineering (ICACTE)* (Vol. 5, pp. 376). IEEE.

Tao, F., Cheng, Y., Da Xu, L., Zhang, L., & Li, B. H. (2014). Cciot-cmfg: Cloud computing and internet of things-based cloud manufacturing service system. *IEEE Transactions on Industrial Informatics*, *10*(2), 1435–1442. doi:10.1109/TII.2014.2306383

Tewari, A., & Gupta, B. (2018). Security, privacy and trust of different layers in internet-of-things (IoTs) framework. *Future Generation Computer Systems*. doi:10.1016/j.future.2018.04.027

Tirronen, T., Larmo, A., Sachs, J., Lindoff, B., & Wiberg, N. (2012). Reducing energy consumption of LTE devices for machine-to-machine communication. In 2012 IEEE Globecom Workshops (GC Wkshps) (pp. 1650–1656). IEEE.

Truong, T., Dinh, A., & Wahid, K. (2017). An IoT environmental data collection system for fungal detection in crop fields. In *2017 IEEE 30th Canadian Conference on Electrical and Computer Engineering (CCECE)* (pp. 1–4). IEEE.

Tsai, C.-W., Lai, C.-F., Chiang, M.-C., & Yang, L. T. (2014). Data mining for internet of things: A survey. *IEEE Communications Surveys and Tutorials*, *16*(1), 77–97. doi:10.1109/SURV.2013.103013.00206

Van Aken, D., Pavlo, A., Gordon, G. J., & Zhang, B. (2017). Automatic database management system tuning through large-scale machine learning. In *Proceedings of the 2017 ACM International Conference on Management of Data* (pp. 1009–1024). ACM.

Vecchio, M., Giaffreda, R., & Marcelloni, F. (2014). Adaptive lossless entropy compressors for tiny iot devices. *IEEE Transactions on Wireless Communications*, *13*(2), 1088–1100. doi:10.1109/TWC.2013.121813.130993

Vlacheas, P., Giaffreda, R., Stavroulaki, V., Kelaidonis, D., Foteinos, V., Poulios, G., ... Moessner, K. (2013). Enabling smart cities through a cognitive management framework for the internet of things. *IEEE Communications Magazine*, *51*(6), 102–111. doi:10.1109/MCOM.2013.6525602

Watanabe, S., Minami, Y., Nakamura, A., & Ueda, N. (2003). Application of variational bayesian estimation and clustering to acoustic model adaptation. In *Proceedings 2003 IEEE International Conference on Acoustics, Speech, and Signal Processing (ICASSP'03)* (Vol. 1). IEEE.

Wei, C., & Li, Y. (2011). Design of energy consumption monitoring and energy-saving management system of intelligent building based on the internet of things. In *2011 International Conference on Electronics, Communications and Control (ICECC)* (pp. 3650–3652). IEEE.

Whaiduzzaman, M., Sookhak, M., Gani, A., & Buyya, R. (2014). A survey on vehicular cloud computing. *Journal of Network and Computer Applications*, *40*, 325–344. doi:10.1016/j.jnca.2013.08.004

Xu, B., Da Xu, L., Cai, H., Xie, C., Hu, J., & Bu, F. (2014). Ubiquitous data accessing method in iotbased information system for emergency medical services. *IEEE Transactions on Industrial Informatics*, *10*(2), 1578–1586. doi:10.1109/TII.2014.2306382

Xu, Q., Aung, K. M. M., Zhu, Y., & Yong, K. L. (2016). Building a large-scale object-based active storage platform for data analytics in the internet of things. *The Journal of Supercomputing*, *72*(7), 2796–2814. doi:10.100711227-016-1621-2

Xu, Y., & Helal, A. (2016). Scalable cloud–sensor architecture for the internet of things. *IEEE Internet of Things Journal*, *3*(3), 285–298. doi:10.1109/JIOT.2015.2455555

Yang, J., He, S., Lin, Y., & Lv, Z. (2017). Multimedia cloud transmission and storage system based on internet of things. *Multimedia Tools and Applications*, *76*(17), 17735–17750. doi:10.100711042-015-2967-9

Yaseen, Q., Aldwairi, M., Jararweh, Y., Al-Ayyoub, M., & Gupta, B. (2018). Collusion attacks mitigation in internet of things: A fog based model. *Multimedia Tools and Applications*, *77*(14), 18249–18268. doi:10.100711042-017-5288-3

Zhang, Q., Yang, L. T., Chen, Z., & Li, P. (2018). High-order possibilistic c-means algorithms based on tensor decompositions for big data in IoT. *Information Fusion*, *39*, 72–80. doi:10.1016/j.inffus.2017.04.002

This research was previously published in the International Journal of Cloud Applications and Computing (IJCAC), 9(2); pages 43-59, copyright year 2019 by IGI Publishing (an imprint of IGI Global).

Chapter 39
A Reliable IDS System Using Blockchain for SDN-Enabled IIoT Systems

Ambika N.

ⓘD https://orcid.org/0000-0003-4452-5514

Department of Computer Applications, Sivananda Sarma Memorial RV College, Bangalore,, India

ABSTRACT

The internet of things is the technology that aims to provide a common platform to the devices of varying capabilities to communicate. Industrial internet of things (IIoT) systems can perform better using these devices in combination with SDN network and blockchain technology. The suggestion uses random space learning (RSL) comprising three stages. The random subspace learning strategy is a troupe learning procedure called attributes bagging. It improves forecast and order errands as it utilizes group development of base classifiers rather than a solitary classifier, and it takes arbitrary subsets of properties rather than the whole arrangement of attributes. The system uses the blockchain methodology to secure the system. SDN networks aim to better the transmission of data in industrial IoT devices. Misrouting and forged attacks are some of the common attacks in these systems. The proposal provides better reliability than the previous contribution by 2.7%.

1. INTRODUCTION

The Internet of Things (IoT) (Khan & Salah, 2018) (Ambika, 2020) becomes the fundamental wellspring of changing over things into shrewd, including keen homes, brilliant urban communities, savvy enterprises, and so forth. IoT can interface billions of things simultaneously, which looks to create data sharing necessities that improve our lives. The blockchain idea attempts to interlink the associations or exchanges of information in the groups. The group characterizes as the information structure which incorporates numerous budgetary interchanges.

DOI: 10.4018/978-1-6684-7132-6.ch039

Blockchain (Banerjee, et.al., 2018) members are any individual or foundation that acknowledges convention strings and creates them. The coordinators of these systems and those answerable for programming upkeep don't share the blockchain. Blockchain members are any individual or foundation that acknowledges convention strings and creates them. The coordinators of these systems and those liable for programming upkeep don't share the blockchain. The designated to a gathering of people or elements that can get to information as it were. They can peruse target information and compose as it were. In this manner, an authorized Blockchain is a focal element. For example, a bank that can control the privileges of people and recognize them to take an interest during the time spent in composing information. The Blockchain guarantees higher degrees of security. Web of Things (IoT) (Ambika, 2019) becomes a crucial wellspring of changing over things into brilliant, including intelligent homes, keen urban communities, savvy ventures, and so on.

Software-Defined Network (SDN)(Cherian & Chatterjee, 2018) encourages arranges administrators to program and deal with the system. SDN motivates the IoT system to be overseen powerfully in an asset compelled organize. It gives chances to improve security in IoT (Nagaraj, 2021) systems on SDN (Sahay, et.al. 2019) to forestall, identify, and respond to dangers. The principal usefulness of SDN is to decouple the information planes and control planes in a system. Dynamic in SDN finishes by the control plane, and information sent is taken care of by switches. They come with the customary framework and elevated level calculations used for dynamic operations requiring modern control. SDN requires less administration.

The SDN establishes three significant layers: foundation, controller, and application layers, as the interfaces between progressive layers. The framework layer involves organizing gadgets that perform bundle sending. The first key attribute of SDN is the division of the sending and control planes in systems gadgets. The sending plane actualizes sending usefulness, including the rationale and tables for picking how to manage approaching parcels, in light of qualities, for example, MAC and IP address. The vital activities performed by the sending plane can be portrayed by how it dispatches showing up parcels. It might advance, drop, devour, or duplicate an approaching packet. It might likewise change the bundle in some way before making further moves. For essential sending, the gadget decides the right yield port by playing out a query in the location table in the equipment switch or switch. A parcel drops due to specific filtering. The rationale and calculations programs the sending plane dwells in the control plane. A large number of these conventions and calculations require worldwide information on the system. The control plane decides how the sending tables and rationale in the information plane ought to be customized or configured. Since in a conventional procedure, every gadget has its control plane, the essential undertaking of that control plane is to run directing or exchanging conventions with the goal that all the dispersed sending tables on the gadgets all through the system remain synchronized. In SDN, the control plane is gotten off of the exchanging device and onto an incorporated controller.

Expanding on the possibility of division of sending and control planes, the following attribute of SDN is the simplification of system gadgets, which are then constrained by a brought together framework that runs the executives and control programming. Rather than a large number of lines of entangled control plane programming running on the gadget, permitting the instrument to carry on self-sufficiently, that product is expelled from the device and put in a unified controller. This product-based controller may then deal with the system dependent on more elevated level strategies. The controller gives unrefined directions to the simplified gadgets when proper to permit them to settle on quick choices about how to manage approaching bundles. The incorporated programming based controller in SDN gives an open interface on the controller to take into consideration computerized control of the system. The controller offers a northbound API, permitting programming applications to be connected to the controller, and subsequently permitting that product to give the calculations and conventions that can run the system efficiently. These applications can rapidly and powerfully organize changes as the need emerges. The northbound API of the controller gives a deliberation of the system gadgets and topology. There are three credential benefits that the application engineer ought to get from the northbound API. It changes over to a language structure that is increasingly recognizable to designers. It gives a reflection of the system topology and system layer authorizing the application software engineer to manage the system overall as opposed to singular hubs, and deliberation of the system conventions themselves, concealing the application designer from the subtleties of OpenFlow or BGP.

The proposed system brings better reliability to adding endorsement hash value to the dispatched messages. The message is verified by the server and forwarded by suffixing the endorsement hash value to the data. The evaluated received message brings in reliability to the system by 2.7% than the previous contribution. The received data by the firewall undergo verification against the trail values and aggregated values.

The literature survey follows the introduction in section 2. Assumptions made in the study are in segment 3. The segment four explains the previous architecture. Portion five explains the proposed architecture. Section 6 contains an analysis of the proposed work. Section 7 concludes with a brief explanation of the proposed study.

2. LITERATURE SURVEY

Various contributions are present to authenticate the system in SDN networks. The proposal (Derhab, et al., 2019) focuses on the security of directions in mechanical IoT against fashioned methods and misrouting. The creators propose a security design coordinating with the Blockchain and the Software-characterized arrange (SDN) innovations. The proposed security engineering is an interruption identification framework, RSL-KNN. It joins the Random Subspace Learning (RSL) and K-Nearest Neighbor (KNN) to protect against the produced directions. It focusses on the modern control procedure and a Blockchain-based Integrity Checking System (BICS) (Li, et.al., 2017), which can forestall the misrouting assault, which alters the OpenFlow rules of the SDN-empowered mechanical IoT frameworks. A Blockchain-based Integrity Checking System (BICS), which can guard against the misrouting assault by recognizing in a short timeframe, any messing with the OpenFlow governs and forestalling the execution of the standards.

The proposed arrangement plans to remember the versatility of the particular IoT framework. It is an interruption identification and avoidance instrument by executing an insightful security engineering utilizing Random neural systems (RNNs) (Saeed, et.al., 2016). In the RNN, a sign goes as a driving force between the neurons. On the off chance that the getting signal has a positive potential, it speaks to excite. If the capability of the info signal is negative, it communicates to a hindrance to the accepting neuron. The wise interruption identification arrangements depend on producing a forecast model using the removed element dataset. It confirms the usefulness of the proposed interruption location component. The substantial element dataset is developed by profiling the intelligent controller application, speaking to the framework conduct under ordinary conditions. During the preparation stage, legitimate scopes of the yields produced by the base station handset are recorded, which decides the invalid cases.

(Khan & Herrmann, 2017)makes it conceivable to single out maliciously carrying on units in preparing and vitality inviting way. They utilize a trust the board component that permits gadgets to oversee notoriety data about their neighbors. This system makes it conceivable to single out perniciously carrying on units in handling and vitality in a gracious way. They utilize a trust the board component that permits gadgets to oversee notoriety data about their neighbors. Trust points sent to the outskirt switch total them to notoriety esteems. If terrible notoriety esteem shows a hub as a potential one, the fringe switch expels it from the system and tells the administrator. It calculates Forwarding Check, Ranking Check, and Version Number Check. The hubs likewise forward their trust esteems to the outskirt switch or a group head that totals them to the notoriety esteems in the system or a bunch. Three calculations recommended are Neighbor Based Trust Dissemination (NBTD), Clustered Neighbor Based Trust Dissemination (CNTD), and Tree-Based Trust Dissemination (TTD).

(Fu, et.al 2017) is automata-based IDS of IoT arranges additionally comprise of four significant segments: Event Monitor, Event Database, Event Analyzer, and Response Unit. The authority needs to record the transmitting information into advanced documents and send the records to the IDS Occasion Analyzer. The system occasion portrays as the conceptual activity streams, and such system activities depict with advances of the proposed GluedIOLTS model. Three databases executed are Standard Protocol Library, Abnormal Action Library, and Normal Action Libraries are required. The IDS Event Analyzer contains three essential models: Network Structure Learning Model, Action Flows Abstraction Model, and Intrusion Detection Model. The gathered parcel information ought to be sent to this model first to cause the IDS framework to get a general perspective on the system topologies. The IoT gadgets recognize with the unique ID. It dissects the gathered data of the information bundles, for example, the source IP, goal IP, port number, timestamp, and convention type, the system can recognize the IoT gadgets from the others. The gathered continuous parcels from IoT likewise should be sent to the Action Flows Abstraction Model. Through this model, the bundles designate as indicated by the gadget having a place, meeting ID, timestamps, and convention types perceived through the guides of the Network Structure Learning Model and the Standard Protocol Library.

The work (Hamza, et.al. 2018) creates and actualizes a framework. It interprets MUD strategies to stream decisions, proactively designed into organizing switches. It is as responsively embedded dependent on run-time ties of DNS. The framework involves a handle, whose stream table rules are overseen powerfully by the SDN controller, a parcel investigation motor, and a mark based IDS.

(Lopez-Martin, et.al. 1967) depends on a contingent variational auto-encoder with a particular design that coordinates the interruption names inside the decoder layers. ID-CVAE is a solo strategy prepared in a managed way to utilize the class marks during preparation.

It (Alshahrani, et.al. 2019) is a lightweight verification system that uses dynamic personalities and impermanent keys for IoT hubs in intelligent homes. Three principle members engage with the convention: IoT hub (N), controller hub (CRN), and manufacturer fog node (MFR). A neighborhood IoT arrange is an interconnection of the IoT hubs N (obliged gadgets), and controller hubs CRN. The MFR is a competent processing gadget like a server and can live inside or outside the neighborhood IoT organize. These dynamic personalities and keys are developed from a blend of fixed and variable segments and advancing time-subordinate subdivision. The proposed verification conspire into three stages: the registration stage, enrollment stage, and the confirmation and key trade stage. IoT hub connects with the controller hub CRN for secure unknown shared verification and meeting credential trade.

The work (Singh, et.al. 2019) is a productive lightweight-secure verification convention for human-focused IIoT. The suggestion accepts an enrollment place that essentially produces open and mystery data for a hub when it at first joins the system. After enrollment, the enlistment place isn't required any longer, and propelled forms like shared verification, secure credential trade, and correspondences are autonomously done by hubs included. Secure authentication and encryption is lower calculation and correspondence cost for human-focused IIoT dependent on Guillou-Quisquater's Protocol. It decreases the exponential calculation and augmentation overheads in the verification process. Secure key sharing through the confirmation procedure is dependent on the Diffie-Hellman solution understanding calculation. Device personality approval uses Elliptic Curve computerized signature open key recuperation calculation.

The proposal (Kandi, et.al. 2019) is a profoundly versatile Multi-Group Key Management convention for IoT. It guarantees the forward and in reverse mystery productively recoups from conspiracy assaults, ensures the protected conjunction of a few administrations in a solitary system, and parities the heaps between its heterogeneous gadgets as indicated by their capacities. It has two layers. The upper layer deals with various gatherings and allots hubs to them, as indicated by the administrations to which they buy-in. Then again, the lower layer circulates the devices of each assembly into coherent subgroups to diminish the convention overheads on them. The system isolates into a few gatherings. It will end up with a few further divided subgroups. Each assembly is related to an ID that is exceptional inside the system. It contains then the hubs taking an interest in a given blend of administrations. At the point when a device joins the system, it is doled out to a gathering as indicated by the mix of administrations to which it buys in. Then again, if a present part buys in or withdraws from administrations, it moves from a gathering to another as indicated by its new blend of administrations.

Overhead traffic can make an IDS drop numerous parcels without appropriate assessment, corrupting the security level of its whole conveyed organize. In such a situation, traffic-based trust calculation would become incapable as a result of the loss of bundles. Whitelisted parcels (Meng, 2018) can go straightforwardly to the objective system. Stream-based strategy characterizes parcels into streams and afterward applies an examining procedure to the whole stream as opposed to specific bundles. The blacklist based filtration is On the off chance that the source IP address of approaching bundles coordinates a thing in the process. The relating parcels can be blocked or dealt with regarding predefined security rules. The packet-based strategy utilizes irregularity in the inspecting procedure to forestall synchronization with any instance examples in the rush hour traffic.

(Surendar & Umamakeswari, 2016)a novel exertion at building up an Intrusion Detection and Response System (InDReS) which depends on a requirement based particular model identifies sinkhole assault. Every hub chooses itself as a pioneer hub depending on a probabilistic methodology and communicates its accessibility to all the sensor hubs present in the gathering. It receives the signal quality, which is legitimately relative to the Probability of a sensor node. It decides the pioneer hub and separation between the devices. The pioneer hubs do the collection of the bundles got from all the instruments present in their gathering. The number of parcels missed at the directing layer of 6LoWPAN tallies to decide how adequately the system handles the bundles. The proof worth determines dependent on the likelihood of beta dispersion capacity. The detection system hypothesis applies to every hub. If it is not similar to the edge esteem, the device considers as noxious. The positioning calculation insists that it is a detested hub.

It is (Alexopoulos, et.al. 2020) Communitarian IDS. The crude ready information produced by the screens is put away as exchanges in a blockchain, repeated among the taking a hub of the system. The suspicious devices run an accord convention to ensure the legitimacy of the interchanges before including them in a square. The members are responsible for their activities, as the last is straightforward to the system. The correspondence overhead can be overseen. For example, by putting away hashes of the ready information in the blockchain rather than the crude data. The partaking hubs in the block arrange are either screen units, investigation units, or perform the two undertakings all the while, which is the broadest case. Correspondence between the hubs happens in two sensible layers, in particular the Alert Exchange layer and the Consensus layer. In the Alert Exchange layer, the executed CIDS plays out the ready information scattering process. A Consensus layer is a subset of companions that runs an accord convention and concede to which exchanges. The hubs ought to approach these particular cautions, can take an interest in a different synergistic system, and make various blocks.

(Golomb, et.al. 2018) a lightweight system that uses the blockchain idea to perform disseminated and community-oriented peculiarity identification for gadgets with constrained assets. CIoTA utilizes blockchain to gradually refresh a believed oddity recognition model through self-validation and agreement among IoT gadgets. The framework intends to identify vindictive acts and assemble data about what's going on, and occasionally share an assortment with different specialists. Since a specialist is in the hostile areas, the operator may get bogus talk that brings commotion into the gossipy tidbits passed on to various operators. Each IoT gadget has an operator that keeps up a neighborhood model that uses to distinguish malicious practices in a specific application. A specialist records new Intel by the refreshing nearby models with perceptions of the application's conduct. A specialist shares its Intel nearby operator, like gossip, by adding nearby operators to the chain's incomplete square and afterward sending the chain to neighboring operators in the system. Different specialists will possibly acknowledge this halfway square on the off chance that it is longer than their fractional square, and on the off chance that they can validate the sheltered. A specialist gets the latest knowledge from its kindred operators by supplanting neighborhood specialist with the consolidated model contained inside the freshest shut square.

(Li, et.al. 2019) a nonexclusive system of community-oriented blockchain signature-based IDSs, which can steadily manufacture and update a confided in the signature database in a synergistic IoT condition. In CBSigIDS, every id hub (or blockchain hub) in the consortium blockchain can screen the system traffic, distinguish assaults, and occasionally share a lot of marks (rules) with others. This arrangement is marked by a private key from a hub, to comprehend the wellspring of the accord. Different devices acknowledge these guidelines by checking them against their nearby database.

The authors (Pajouh, et.al., 2016) have exhibited a novel model for interruption identification dependent on two-layer measurement decrease and two-level arrangement module, intended to distinguish noxious exercises, for example, User to Root (U2R) and Remote to Local (R2L) assaults. The proposed model is utilizing segment investigation and direct separate examination of measurement decrease module to spate the high dimensional dataset to a lower one with lesser highlights. They apply a two-level characterization module using Naïve Bayes and Certainty Factor rendition of K-Nearest Neighbor to recognize guilty practices. The proposed model, intended for oddity based interruption location in IoT spine systems, utilizes two-layer measurement decrease and two-level order identification procedures to identify "hard-to-recognize" interruptions, for example, U2R and R2L assaults. Straight Discriminant Analysis (LDA) and Principal Component Analysis to address the high dimensionality issue utilization in the organization. A subset of all chosen highlights is dependent on their viability in the higher arrangement and a subset of new highlights by consolidating existing highlights. Cross-Validation (CV) assesses ideal principals with the least mistakes.

The creator has proposed an interruption discovery and moderation structure, called IoT-IDM (Nobakht, et.al., 2016), to give system-level security to intelligent gadgets sent in home situations. IoT-IDM screens the system exercises of proposed devices inside the home and examines whether there is any suspicious or vindictive movement. When an interruption is recognized, it hinders the gate-device in getting to the injured individual gadget on the fly. The measured plan of IoT-IDM gives its clients the adaptability to utilize AI strategies for discovery dependent on learned mark examples of known assaults. IoT-IDM bridles the appearance of SDN innovation, which offers organize permeability and gives adaptability to arrange, oversee and make sure about the system remotely and the development of AI methods in the discovery of system inconsistency designs. Five key modules used are Device Manager, Sensor Element, Feature Extractor, Detection, and Mitigation.

(Hodo, et al., 2016) centers around the arrangement of typical and dangerous designs of the IoT Network. The multi-layer perception (MLP) is design with three layers of feed-forward Neural Network. The Artificial Neural network (ANN) is utilized as disconnected IDS to assemble and examine data from different pieces of the IoT organize and distinguish a DoS assault on the system. The neurons of the ANN shape complex theories. Assessing the speculations is finished by setting the information hubs in a criticism procedure, and the occasion streams are spread through the system to the yield where it is named ordinary or traded off. At this stage, the inclination plummets push the blunder in the yield hub back through the system by a back-propagation procedure to assess the mistake in the concealed devices. The tendency of the expense – function is determined. Neural system framework experiences preparing to become familiar with the example made in the framework.

The interruption identification design (Sforzin, et.al., 2016) is a little, convenient gadget, pre-bundled with an IDS. The devices move to anyplace in the smart home. It could utilize to ensure intelligent objects. The city organizations could convey it in avenues, squares, college grounds, arenas, or in other swarmed regions, to screen the system traffic of the encompassing territory. It is successfully a compact, on-request, IDS that informs the clients, or the overseers of the system, at whatever point it recognizes a progressing assault or suspicious system exercises. Every gadget will gather assaults' insights locally, and afterward send them to a remote server running a Security Information and Event Management (SIEM) programming, from which organize overseers can perform upkeep or crisis activities.

The intelligent home and the encompassing scene are observed with conduct demonstrating an interruption discovery framework called Behavioral Modeling Intrusion Detection system. (BMIDS) (Arrington, et.al., 2016). The BMIDS utilizes invulnerability roused calculations to recognize whether standards of conduct separated to match the show the deviation from the ideal behavior. The reenactment screens scale all-important movement to check the development of similar conducts models. The BMIDS shows how the catch of IoT sensor information movement linked as a lot of occasion arrangements alongside the reproduced world state gives the parts to build up a numerical portrayal for conduct character. Making conduct models through inescapable framework observes before, and nearby digital-physical framework experimentation with the BMIDS reproduction is cost-proficient, effectively undeniable, and advances self-ruling checking for an autonomic checking system. Additionally, execution estimations can be scaled all the more precisely during the subjective and quantitative examination, delivers the ideal conduct model as portrayed by the predetermined scripted or non-scripted conduct.

The appropriated and lightweight IDS is dependent on an Artificial Immune System (AIS) (Hosseinpour, et.al., 2016). The IDS disseminates in a three-layered IoT structure consisting of the cloud, mist, and edge layers. Because of this engineering, distributed computing obliges the IDS fundamental motor of two sub-motors called a grouping/clustering motor and a training motor. The clustering motor, utilizing solo grouping techniques, separates the essential system traffic into self (typical) and non-self (interruption) bundles as the web-based preparing informational index for our AIS based IDS. The training motor trains a lot of finders dependent on the taking in information acquired from the grouping motor by utilizing a pessimistic choice calculation. These indicators are called essential identifiers. The vital locators after the preparation stage, are put away in a finder archive database at the cloud. It disseminates to the gadgets at the edge of the system. They go about as sensors for IDS that screen the conduct of the edge gadgets. An inconsistency will start a procedure for examining the oddity by delivering a keen information cell.

In SDN, the Data plane comprises switches that are dumb. Each handle is simple equipment with a little capacity to be customized. The rest will be the Control plane. In SDN, controllers are not quite the same as usual systems and OpenFlow switches (Bianco, et.al., 2010). All OpenFlow switches constraints by SDN controller/controllers. The cleverness from controllers moves to the SDN controller. SDN controller can deal with the system, for example, directing information parcels by programming orders. SDN controller (Gheisari, et.al., 2018) isolates it's leveled out IoT gadgets into two classes finishes through grouping techniques. The controller sends a protection class mark of every device to it. The controller sends the encryption strategy IoT gadget should utilize. The IoT gadget applies the relating encryption strategy as its protection conservation technique.

The creators propose a job-based security controller engineering called Rol-Sec(Kalkan & Zeadally, 2017) for the SDN-IoT condition. Each SDN-IoT passage (SDN-IoT GW) speaks with different entryways without considering its own space. It additionally improves organization data transfer capacity of the correspondence connects between the portals and the controllers because the correspondence traffic disseminates. The messages identified with cryptographic activities don't meddle with the progression of control traffic. The interruption controller screens the traffic and deals with the standards for each stream. It can likewise recognize and moderate interruptions that expect to make the framework inaccessible. The solution administrator can be an archive for both symmetric and public keys. The vital dissemination of shared keys is taken care of by this module. This module goes about as a confided in an outsider for both symmetric and public solutions. The controller gives vital administration to the framework. It resembles a catalog that has symmetric keys and shared credential sets. It likewise handles every cryptographic activity requires during administration. The crypto controller offers the accompanying cryptographic types of assistance: uprightness, secrecy, security, confirmation, and personality the board.

STewARD (Boussard, et.al., 2019) permits clients to effortlessly demand from their intelligent home system controller the production of remote programming characterized arrange cuts, to which they allot a necessary trust level utilizing preliminary hazard appraisal. It empowers the arrange controllers to settle on nearby choices in light of worldwide information. By accepting reports on the trust score of gadgets they oversee, controllers can rapidly react to devices. The clients mark gatherings of gadgets utilizing the scale. The component recovers the class of a recently associated device.

Edge computing Architecture (ECA) engineering (Gheisari, et al., 2019) that depends on philosophy for security safeguarding in the IoT-based savvy city condition. ECA has two fundamental subclasses-ontology and nature. It has three security protecting levels. Three focuses on protection safeguarding including security clamor, conceivable deniability, and honest populace. Each IoT gadget sends its ID to the server in the edge cloud. At the point when the protection rules lifetime equivalents to zero, the proprietor of the IoT gadget ought to be changed. At that point, the edge server picks the following appropriate security rule to be applied. We utilize the proprietor of the device to befuddle aggressors more. Something else, the server diminishes one from its protection rule lifetime. The IoT gadget sends its prepared information to the edge cloud as well as to the remote cloud for additional examination. Cloud is a framework that underpins the IoT foundation to accomplish better execution.

IoT botnet discovery and detachment approach (Chaabouni, et.al. 2019) comprise of various smart home systems. These Smart Home systems are associated with employing an Internet association. It utilizes an entrance switch and different IoT gadgets. The methodology is sent inside the entrance switch and comprises the two principle segments checking and detachment. The work has four stages. In the primary phase, the method recognizes the subnet address of the nearby system and outputs for associated IoT gadgets. In the subsequent one, mechanized segregation is performed by composing firewall rules to the entrance switches inside UCI (Unified Configuration Interface) firewall. In the third stage, the Common Vulnerability Enumeration (CVE) online-administration is questioned in standard time interims (default is hourly) to recognize conceivably defenseless administrations and IoT gadgets. These inquiries sift by MAC address prefixes of the found nearby IoT gadgets. The determined port quantities of the past stage are self-improving checking approach in the last phase.

The suggested a lightweight instrument (Maloney, et.al. 2019) to perform security and other gadgets the board refreshes utilizing a golang-based operator. The light-weight specialist is 1.4MB in size and communicates with an IoT gadget's working framework without meddling with other gadget forms. The operator adequately conveys exceptionally focused on updates to an IoT gadget's working framework that doesn't require a framework restart to produce results. It diminishes the danger of bricking a device or meddling with continually running procedures on gadgets expected to work day in and day out. The employed limit administration level shared for digital-physical gadgets are like a vitality conveyance framework. The operator is fit for giving simultaneous procedure execution, not securing intelligent urban areas in an assigned biological system of devices.

The suggested model uses Principal Component Analysis (PCA) (Zhao, et.al 2017) to decrease measurements of the dataset from countless highlights to a modest number. The softmax relapse and k-closest neighbor calculations are applied to build up a classifier. The model comprises of a measurement decrease part and a classifier. PCA is an element extraction instrument, communicates to a subset of new highlights made by anticipating existing highlights to anew measurements. K-closest neighbor calculation uses a classifier without pre-preparing progress.

The engineering (Salman, et.al. 2019) comprises of four segments: highlights extractor, IoT gadget recognizable proof, traffic-type ID, and interruption discovery. The highlights, to be specific, parcel size, timestamp, bearing, and transport convention, are extricated for each system stream. A system stream dictates by the five-tuple- source IP address, source port number, goal IP address, goal port number, and transport convention. The highlights extractor keeps a refreshed rundown of the dynamic streams. When a parcel shows up at the highlights extractor segment, and on the off chance, it has a place with a functioning stream. If there is no dynamic stream for this bundle, another stream inclusion, and the parcel highlights recording. After getting 16 chunks of a similar stream, the stream highlights sent to the classifier. The IoT gadget distinguishing proof part is liable for arranging the devices dependent on their system traffic stream measurable highlights. The traffic-type recognizes proof part targets grouping the produced traffic dependent on the sort. On the off chance, there is confusion between the normal traffic-type from a specific gadget and the generated traffic. The interruption recognition segment has the job of profiling typical gadget conduct and can distinguish strange movement.

(Salman, et.al. 2018) is designed to recognize the gadget type and the traffic type dependent on the created traffic, utilizing AI. When it cultivates, a portal can choose to confine access from/to specific gadgets introducing a few vulnerabilities or identifying some traffic variations from the norm. The work comprises pushing the insight into the system edge. These hubs are mindful extricating stream related highlights, figure measurable stream-based highlights, and send the highlights vectors to a focal controller.

The controller, executing a traffic classifier, a traffic screen, and a security orchestrator, is answerable for gadget and traffic types order, traffic variations from the norm recognition, and security rules design. The system is a little edge system where various sorts of IoT gadgets are associated. Each IoT sub-domain associates with an intelligent programming-based edge. The edge hubs of an IoT area constrains by a controller executing diverse system capacities. The traffic investigation module comprises of three segments: the classifier, the traffic screen, and the security orchestrator. At the point when a parcel shows up at the system edge, the edge hub records the appearance time, the size, the vehicle convention, and the heading (forward or in reverse) of this bundle. The stream characterizes by the arrangement of parcels having the same source port number, source IP, destination port number, destination IP, and transport convention. The edge hub spares a rundown of dynamic streams.

SVELTE (Raza, et.al. 2013) has three fundamental incorporated modules. The principle module, called 6LoWPAN Mapper (6Mapper), assembles data about the RPL organize and reproduces the system in the e6LoWPAN fringe switch (6BR). The subsequent module is the interruption discovery segment that examines the mapped information and identifies an interruption. The third module, a conveyed smaller than usual firewall, is intended to offload hubs by separating undesirable traffic before it enters the asset obliged arrange. The incorporated modules have two comparing light-weight modules in each obliged device. The principal module gives mapping data to the 6BR so it can perform interruption location. The subsequent module works with the firewall. Each compelled hub additionally has a third module to deal with start to finish bundle loss packets.

3. ASSUMPTIONS MADE IN THE WORK

- The server will have all the details of the registered devices.
- The devices send the samples by endorsing the generated hash value.
- The hash value is generated using the device id and the location details. The transmitted message by the devices is verified by the server.
- The adversary is capable of launching forged attacks. These are Assaults that issue produced orders to insightful electronic gadgets, which trigger the execution of undesired activities, for example, power outage.
- The adversary is into redirecting the packets received. Assaults forestall the right directing of orders and other data between the server and the various gadgets. The assault accomplishes by adjusting the stream rules.

4. PREVIOUS WORK ARCHITECTURE

(Derhab, et al., 2019) the architecture consists of a private cloud, IP network, SDN controller, and virtual handle. The cloud has all the parts that offer an incorporated control for ICS as virtual machines. The SDN controller is an application that oversees stream control by utilizing conventions that advice changes where to send information parcels. The OpenFlow convention is a southbound interface between the controller and the sending components, for example, switches. The northbound interface thinks about the correspondence between the controller and the applications.

SD-WAN design decreases the system cost by offering zero-contact organization, i.e., there is no compelling reason to arrange the system gadget by connecting it. The private cloud has all the segments having an incorporated control for ICS as virtual machines, for example, SCADA server, DCS server, and SDN controller. SDN controller is an application that oversees stream control by utilizing conventions. For example, OpenFlow advises changes where to send information parcels. The OpenFlow convention is a southbound interface between the controller and the sending components. The northbound interface thinks about the correspondence between the controller and the applications. Virtual Switch is an application that interconnects numerous virtual machines of the equivalent or various hypervisors. It additionally interconnects these virtual machines with other physical switches.

In the first stage (preparation stage), the authors haphazardly select S characteristic from a lot of F characteristic with the end goal that S ≤ F. The chosen attribute is taken care of to an AI calculation to create a classifier. This activity is rehashed B times, and at each time S, the characteristic is picked aimlessly with substitution to produce an alternate classifier.

In the second stage (testing stage), the yields from every unmistakable student are consolidated by a larger part casting a ballot to acquire the last forecast or characterization result.

The IDS (Ambika & Raju, 2014) is utilizing Random Subspace learning (RSL). The Random Subspace Learning (RSL) strategy is a troupe learning method. It attributes stowing or characteristics sacking. It improves expectation and arrangement undertakings as it utilizes gathering development of base classifiers rather than a solitary classifier, and it takes arbitrary subsets of attributes rather than the whole arrangement of characteristics.

Blockchain-based uprightness checking framework expects to distinguish any infusion of false stream leads in the vSwitches is adopted. The Random Subspace Learning (RSL) strategy is a troupe learning procedure called attributes bagging. It improves forecast and order errands as it utilizes group development of base classifiers rather than a solitary classifier, and it takes arbitrary subsets of properties rather than the whole arrangement of the attribute. The irregular subspace learning process comprises two stages preparing and testing. In the preparation stage, we arbitrarily select a subset. The chosen highlights are taken care of to an AI calculation to produce a classifier. This activity is rehashed B times, and subassembly highlights are picked indiscriminately with substitution to create an alternate classifier. In the testing stage, the yields from every unmistakable student are consolidated by the part casting a ballot to get the last expectation or grouping result.

The blockchain has two hubs- an SDN controller and a firewall. The SDN controller makes squares and offers it to the firewall through the blockchain. The principal device has all the authorizations while the firewall can peruse and get. SDN controller hashes the stream rules and places them in a square circulating to different hubs of the blockchain. At the point when the stream rules arrive at the vSwitch hub, the last update its stream table and spare the principles in the log document. The Firewall gathers the vSwitch logs and gets to the BlockChain to acquire the stream rules sent by the controller. On the off chance that the firewall finds that the two standards, from vSwitch and blockchain, are not comparative, it tells the Administrator to take the countermeasures to fix this bungling.

5. PROPOSED ARCHITECTURE

The suggested RSL architecture follows the same architecture as considered (Derhab, et al., 2019). The proposal is an improvement of the previous contribution. The architecture contains a private cloud, IP network, SDN controller, and virtual switch. The cloud has all the parts that offer an incorporated control for ICS as virtual machines. The SDN controller is an application that oversees stream control by utilizing conventions that advice changes where to send information parcels. The OpenFlow convention is a southbound interface between the controller and the sending components, for example, switches. The northbound interface thinks about the correspondence between the controller and the applications. The proposal used RSL methodology. The method has a trial phase where the subset creation in attack free environment. They provide a set of safe readings. The threat is identified using safe readings. Hence the method provides better reliability than (Derhab, et al., 2019). The procedure has three stages –

5.1. Trial Phase

The devices installed in the environment uses The Random subspace model. Random list R_i is created using attack free environment. This set is treated initial values. The safe readings are made a subset R_s. The treat readings are made as another set R_t.

$$R_s = \{r_{i1}, r_{i2} \ldots \ldots r_{ik}\} \tag{1}$$

$$R_t = \{r_{i(k+1)}, r_{i(k+2)} \ldots \ldots r_{in}\} \tag{2}$$

In the notation (1) the values $r_{i1}, r_{i2} \ldots \ldots r_{ik}$ belong to the safe set R_s. In the notation (2) $r_{i(k+1)}, r_{i(k+2)} \ldots \ldots r_{in}$ belong to the treat value set R_t.

$$R_i \rightarrow R_s \cup R_t \tag{3}$$

In the notation (3), R_i is the combination of safe values R_s and treat values R_t.

$$I_i \rightarrow S_i : R_i = \{r_{i1}, r_{i2} \ldots \ldots r_{in}\} \| E_i \tag{4}$$

$$S_i \rightarrow F_i : R_i = \{r_{i1}, r_{i2} \ldots \ldots r_{in}\} \| E_s \tag{5}$$

In notation (4) the list of values generated during the trial session is dispatched by the device I_i to the server S_i suffixing the endorsement of the device E_i. The endorsements sent by the devices are detached after validation. In notation (5) the list of values generated is communicated by the server S_i to the firewall F_i.

5.2 Training Phase

Another random list is generated by collecting the values from the IoT devices. Let R_j be the set of values collected.

$$I_i \rightarrow S_i : R_j = \{r_{j1}, r_{j2} \ldots \ldots r_{jn}\} \tag{6}$$

Notation (6) represents the list of values generated during the training phase dispatched by the device I_i to the server S_i.

5.3 Testing Phase

The trail values are saved in the server S_i and the firewall F_i. Once the server receives the values during the training phase, it provides a mapping to the values (values of testing phase is mapped to the values in the trail phase). The received message is also made a comparison to other values send by various devices to detect the genuine of the message. The blockchain methodology is adopted similar to (Derhab, et al., 2019).

6. ANALYSIS OF THE WORK

6.1 Reliability

The proposed work uses the endorsement keys verified by the server and the firewall that adds more reliability to the system compared to (Derhab, et al., 2019) by 2.7%. Figure 1 represents the same. The proposed work undergoes three phases namely the trial phase, training phase, and testing phase. The verification is done at server as well as by the firewall. The genuine values are opted by making a comparison to the trail session values and the aggregated values from various devices.

Figure 1. Comparison of the proposed work with (Derhab, et al., 2019)

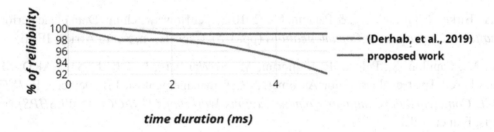

7. CONCLUSION

SDN encourages the IoT system to be overseen powerfully in an asset compelled organize. It gives chances to improve security in IoT systems. The applications can be made on SDN to forestall, identify, and respond to dangers. The Industrial IoT system requires safety to bring in reliability to the system. The proposal has better reliability in adding endorsement hash value to the dispatched messages. The message is verified by the server and forwarded by suffixing the endorsement hash value to the data. The received message evaluates to bring in reliability to the system by 2.7% than the previous contribution. The received data by the firewall undergoes verification against the trail values and aggregated values.

REFERENCES

Alexopoulos, N., Vasilomanolakis, E., Roux, S. L., Rowe, S., & Mühlhäuser, M. (2020). TRIDEnT: towards a decentralized threat indicator marketplace. In *35th Annual ACM Symposium on Applied Computing* (pp. 332–341). Brno Czech Republic: ACM. 10.1145/3341105.3374020

Alshahrani, M., Traore, I., & Woungang, I. (2019). Design and Implementation of a Lightweight Authentication Framework for the Internet of Things (IoT). In *Sixth International Conference on Internet of Things: Systems, Management and Security (IOTSMS)* (pp. 185-194). Granada, Spain: IEEE. 10.1109/IOTSMS48152.2019.8939190

Ambika, N. (2019). Energy-Perceptive Authentication in Virtual Private Networks Using GPS Data. In Security, Privacy and Trust in the IoT Environment (pp. 25-38). Springer.

Ambika, N. (2020). Encryption of Data in Cloud-Based Industrial IoT Devices. In S. Pal & V. G. Díaz (Eds.), *IoT: Security and Privacy Paradigm* (pp. 111–129). CRC Press, Taylor & Francis Group.

Arrington, B., Barnett, L., Rufus, R., & Esterline, A. (2016). Behavioral modeling intrusion detection system (bmids) using internet of things (iot) behavior-based anomaly detection via immunity-inspired algorithms. In *25th International Conference on Computer Communication and Networks (ICCCN)* (pp. 1-6). Waikoloa, HI: IEEE. 10.1109/ICCCN.2016.7568495

Banerjee, M., Lee, J., & Choo, K. K. (2018). A blockchain future for internet of things security: A position paper. *Digital Communications and Networks*, *4*(3), 149–160. doi:10.1016/j.dcan.2017.10.006

Bianco, A., Birke, R., Giraudo, L., & Palacin, M. (2010). Openflow switching: Data plane performance. In *International Conference on Communications* (pp. 1-5). Cape Town, South Africa: IEEE.

Boussard, M., Papillon, S., Peloso, P., Signorini, M., & Waisbard, E. (2019). STewARD: SDN and blockchain-based Trust evaluation for Automated Risk management on IoT Devices. In *INFOCOM 2019-IEEE Conference on Computer Communications Workshops (INFOCOM WKSHPS)* (pp. 841-846). Paris, France: IEEE.

Chaabouni, N., Mosbah, M., Zemmari, A., Sauvignac, C., & Faruki, P. (2019). Network intrusion detection for IoT security based on learning techniques. *IEEE Communications Surveys and Tutorials*, *21*(3), 2671–2701. doi:10.1109/COMST.2019.2896380

Cherian, M., & Chatterjee, M. (2018). Survey of security threats in iot and emerging countermeasures. In *International Symposium on Security in Computing and Communication* (pp. 591-604). Bangalore: Springer.

Derhab, A., Guerroumi, M., Gumaei, A., Maglaras, L., Ferrag, M. A., Mukherjee, M., & Khan, F. A. (2019). Blockchain and Random Subspace Learning-Based IDS for SDN-Enabled Industrial IoT Security. *Sensors (Basel)*, *19*(3119), 3119. doi:10.339019143119 PMID:31311136

Fu, Y., Yan, Z., Cao, J., Koné, O., & Cao, X. (2017). An automata based intrusion detection method for internet of things. *Mobile Information Systems*, 1-14.

Gheisari, M., Pham, Q. V., Alazab, M., Zhang, X., Fernández-Campusano, C., & Srivastava, G. (2019). ECA: An Edge Computing Architecture for Privacy-Preserving in IoT-Based Smart City. *IEEE Access: Practical Innovations, Open Solutions, 7*, 155779–155786. doi:10.1109/ACCESS.2019.2937177

Gheisari, M., Wang, G., Chen, S., & Ghorbani, H. (2018). IoT-SDNPP: A Method for Privacy-Preserving in Smart City with Software Defined Networking. In *International Conference on Algorithms and Architectures for Parallel Processing* (pp. 303-312). Guangzhou, China: Springer. 10.1007/978-3-030-05063-4_24

Golomb, T., Mirsky, Y., & Elovici, Y. (2018). Ciota: Collaborative iot anomaly detection via blockchain. In *Workshop on Decentralized IoT Security and Standards (DISS) of the Network and Distributed Systems Security Symposium (NDSS)* (pp. 1-6). San Diego, CA: NDSS.

Hamza, A., Gharakheili, H. H., & Sivaraman, V. (2018). Combining MUD policies with SDN for IoT intrusion detection. In *Proceedings of the 2018 Workshop on IoT Security and Privacy* (pp. 1-7). ACM. 10.1145/3229565.3229571

Hodo, E., Bellekens, X., Hamilton, A., Dubouilh, P. L., Iorkyase, E., Tachtatzis, C., & Atkinson, R. (2016). Threat analysis of IoT networks using artificial neural network intrusion detection system. In *International Symposium on Networks, Computers and Communications (ISNCC)* (pp. 1-6). IEEE. 10.1109/ISNCC.2016.7746067

Hosseinpour, F., Vahdani Amoli, P., Plosila, J., Hämäläinen, T., & Tenhunen, H. (2016). An intrusion detection system for fog computing and IoT based logistic systems using a smart data approach. *International Journal of Digital Content Technology and its Applications, 10*, 34-48.

Kalkan, K., & Zeadally, S. (2017). Securing internet of things with software defined networking. *IEEE Communications Magazine, 56*(9), 186–192. doi:10.1109/MCOM.2017.1700714

Kandi, M. A., Lakhlef, H., Bouabdallah, A., & Challal, Y. (2019). An Efficient Multi-Group Key Management Protocol for Heterogeneous IoT Devices. In *Wireless Communications and Networking Conference (WCNC)* (pp. 1-6). Marrakesh, Morocco: IEEE. 10.1109/WCNC.2019.8885613

Khan, M. A., & Salah, K. (2018). IoT security: Review, blockchain solutions, and open challenges. *Future Generation Computer Systems, 82*, 395–411. doi:10.1016/j.future.2017.11.022

Khan, Z. A., & Herrmann, P. (2017). A trust based distributed intrusion detection mechanism for internet of things. In *IEEE 31st International Conference on Advanced Information Networking and Applications (AINA)* (pp. 1169-1176). Taipei, Taiwan: IEEE.

Li, W., Tug, S., Meng, W., & Wang, Y. (2019). Designing collaborative blockchained signature-based intrusion detection in IoT environments. *Future Generation Computer Systems, 96*, 481–489. doi:10.1016/j.future.2019.02.064

Liu, B., Yu, X. L., Chen, S., Xu, X., & Zhu, L. (2017). Blockchain based data integrity service framework for IoT data. In *IEEE International Conference on Web Services (ICWS)* (pp. 468-475). IEEE. 10.1109/ICWS.2017.54

Lopez-Martin, M., Carro, B., Sanchez-Esguevillas, A., & Lloret, J. (1967). Conditional variational autoencoder for prediction and feature recovery applied to intrusion detection in iot. *Sensors (Basel)*, *17*(9), 2017. PMID:28846608

Maloney, M., Reilly, E., Siegel, M., & Falco, G. (2019). *Cyber Physical IoT Device Management Using a Lightweight Agent. In IEEE Green Computing and Communications (GreenCom)*. IEEE.

Meng, W. (2018). Intrusion detection in the era of IoT: Building trust via traffic filtering and sampling. *Computer*, *51*(7), 36–43. doi:10.1109/MC.2018.3011034

Nagaraj, A. (2021). *Introduction to Sensors in IoT and Cloud Computing Applications*. Bentham Science Publishers.

Nobakht, M., Sivaraman, V., & Boreli, R. (2016). A host-based intrusion detection and mitigation framework for smart home IoT using OpenFlow. In *11th International conference on availability, reliability and security (ARES)* (pp. 147-156). Salzburg, Austria: IEEE. 10.1109/ARES.2016.64

Pajouh, H. H., Javidan, R., Khayami, R., Ali, D., & Choo, K. K. (2016). A two-layer dimension reduction and two-tier classification model for anomaly-based intrusion detection in IoT backbone networks. *IEEE Transactions on Emerging Topics in Computing*.

Raza, S., Wallgren, L., & Voigt, T. (2013). Real-time intrusion detection in the Internet of Things. *Ad Hoc Networks*, *11*(8), 2661–2674. doi:10.1016/j.adhoc.2013.04.014

Saeed, A., Ahmadinia, A., Javed, A., & Larijani, H. (2016). Intelligent intrusion detection in low-power IoTs. *ACM Transactions on Internet Technology*, *16*(4), 1–25. doi:10.1145/2990499

Sahay, R., Meng, W., & Jensen, C. D. (2019). The application of Software Defined Networking on securing computer networks: A survey. *Journal of Network and Computer Applications*, *131*, 89–108. doi:10.1016/j.jnca.2019.01.019

Salman, O., Chaddad, L., Elhajj, I. H., Chehab, A., & Kayssi, A. (2018). Pushing intelligence to the network edge. In *Fifth International Conference on Software Defined Systems (SDS)* (pp. 87-92). Barcelona, Spain: IEEE. 10.1109/SDS.2018.8370427

Salman, O., Elhajj, I. H., Chehab, A., & Kayssi, A. (2019). A machine learning based framework for IoT device identification and abnormal traffic detection. *Transactions on Emerging Telecommunications Technologies*, 3743. doi:10.1002/ett.3743

Sforzin, A., Mármol, F. G., Conti, M., & Bohli, J. M. (2016). RPiDS: Raspberry Pi IDS—A fruitful intrusion detection system for IoT. In *Intl IEEE Conferences on Ubiquitous Intelligence & Computing, Advanced and Trusted Computing, Scalable Computing and Communications, Cloud and Big Data Computing, Internet of People, and Smart World Congress (UIC/ATC/ScalCom/CBDCom/IoP/SmartWorld)* (pp. 440-448). IEEE.

Singh, J., Gimekar, A., & Venkatesan, S. (2019). An efficient lightweight authentication scheme for human-centered industrial Internet of Things. *International Journal of Communication Systems*, 4189. doi:10.1002/dac.4189

Surendar, M., & Umamakeswari, A. (2016). InDReS: An Intrusion Detection and response system for Internet of Things with 6LoWPAN. In *International Conference on Wireless Communications, Signal Processing and Networking (WiSPNET)* (pp. 1903-1908). Chennai, India: IEEE. 10.1109/WiSPNET.2016.7566473

Zhao, S., Li, W., Zia, T., & Zomaya, A. Y. (2017). A dimension reduction model and classifier for anomaly-based intrusion detection in internet of things. In *IEEE 15th Intl Conf on Dependable, Autonomic and Secure Computing* (pp. 836-843). IEEE.

This research was previously published in IoT Protocols and Applications for Improving Industry, Environment, and Society; pages 173-194, copyright year 2021 by Engineering Science Reference (an imprint of IGI Global).

Chapter 40
BLOFF:
A Blockchain–Based Forensic Model in IoT

Promise Agbedanu

https://orcid.org/0000-0003-2522-891X
University College Dublin, Ireland

Anca Delia Jurcut
University College Dublin, Ireland

ABSTRACT

In this era of explosive growth in technology, the internet of things (IoT) has become the game changer when we consider technologies like smart homes and cities, smart energy, security and surveillance, and healthcare. The numerous benefits provided by IoT have become attractive technologies for users and cybercriminals. Cybercriminals of today have the tools and the technology to deploy millions of sophisticated attacks. These attacks need to be investigated; this is where digital forensics comes into play. However, it is not easy to conduct a forensic investigation in IoT systems because of the heterogeneous nature of the IoT environment. Additionally, forensic investigators mostly rely on evidence from service providers, a situation that can lead to evidence contamination. To solve this problem, the authors proposed a blockchain-based IoT forensic model that prevents the admissibility of tampered logs into evidence.

1. INTRODUCTION

In this era of explosive growth in technology, the Internet of Things (IoT) has become the game changer when we consider technologies like smart homes and cities; smart energy, security and surveillance and healthcare. In a report, Statista predicted that the number of IoT device will reach 75 billion in 2025 (Statista, 2019). The integration of real-world objects with the internet does not only bring numerous advantages but also bring cybersecurity threats to our life, through our interaction with these devices (A. Jurcut et al., 2020). Like any computing technology, IoT is threatened by security issues. Many researchers and device manufacturers are exploring various techniques to ensure the security of IoT devices as well

DOI: 10.4018/978-1-6684-7132-6.ch040

as protect the data generated by these devices. However, according to (Atlam et al., 2017), it is difficult to secure data produce in IoT environments because of the heterogeneity and dynamic features deployed in these devices. It is therefore not surprising that the security of IoT, ranging from the physical security of the devices through to the security of their architecture has become an important area of research for a lot of researchers (A. D. Jurcut et al., 2020).

Currently, several works are being done to ensure data confidentiality, access control, authentication, privacy and trust in IoT environments (Borhani et al., 2020; Braeken et al., 2019; A. Jurcut et al., 2009, 2012; A. D. Jurcut, 2018; A. D. Jurcut et al., 2014; Kumar et al., 2019; Xu et al., 2019). Although a lot of success has been made in the security of IoT using the parameters mentioned above, attackers still find ways to exploit the vulnerabilities that exist in IoT systems (A. D. Jurcut et al., 2020). These billions of IoT devices contain sensitive data, an attribute that makes them attractive to cyber-attacks. The number and the cost of cyber-attacks have been increasing over the years. According to a report by (Morgan, 2017), the damages caused by cybercrimes will cost a whopping 6 trillion dollars by 2021. These attacks need to be investigated; this is where digital forensics comes into play.

Digital forensics helps in acquiring legal evidence that can be used to know more about these attacks, prevent future attacks and most importantly prosecute the perpetrators of these crimes. However, it is not easy to conduct a forensic investigation in IoT systems. According to (Perumal et al., 2015), the heterogeneity and dynamic nature of IoT systems make it practically difficult to use the same frameworks used in traditional digital forensic in IoT environments. It is therefore expedient to develop frameworks that can be used in IoT environments considering their dynamic and heterogeneity nature.

In this chapter, we discuss a blockchain-based model that ensures the verifiability of logs produced in IoT environments. The main idea of this model is to ensure the credibility and authenticity of logs produced by IoT devices during forensic investigations. Our model uses the decentralized approach and the immutability property of blockchain to ensure that logs and other pieces of evidence produced in IoT environments can be verified by forensic stakeholders. Our proposed model prevents Cloud Service Providers (CSPs) or Law Enforcement Agencies (LEAs) from tendering in false evidence during forensic investigations or court proceedings. The proposed model brings the court, LEAs, CSPs and other stakeholders under one umbrella where each stakeholder can verify the authenticity of the evidence presented by any of them. The model also ensures that pieces of evidence are not tampered with during the chain of custody. We start this chapter by providing an introduction to digital forensics in IoT and blockchain. We then continue by describing our proposed model. The benefits of our model are discussed and then we present our conclusion.

2. BACKGROUND

In this section, we present a background of digital forensics, IoT forensics and blockchain.

2.1 Digital Forensics

Several definitions have been given for digital forensics. (Bellegarde et al., 2010) defined computer forensics as "the preservation, identification, extraction, interpretation, and documentation of computer evidence to include the rules of evidence, legal process, the integrity of evidence, factual reporting of the information and providing expert opinion in a court of law or other legal and/or administrative proceedings as to what was found." The concept of digital forensics and computer forensics are closely related with the latter being the subset of the former. The most widely accepted definition of digital forensics is the one proposed during the first digital forensic research workshop and was stated by authors in (James et al., 2015) as "The use of scientifically derived and proven methods toward the preservation, collection, validation, identification, analysis, interpretation, documentation and presentation of digital evidence derived from digital sources to facilitate or further the reconstruction of events found to be criminal, or helping to anticipate unauthorized actions shown to be disruptive to planned operations." Digital forensics involves the application of scientific methods in investigating cyber-crimes (Carrier, 2003). According to (Sumalatha & Batsa, 2016), the methodologies employed in digital forensics to handle electronic evidence has its stems springing out from forensic science.

2.1.1 Digital Forensic Process

There are various stages that digital forensic artifacts undergo before finally being presented in a court for prosecution purposes. (Daniel & Daniel, 2012) stated that the digital forensic is made up of four processes. These processes are identification, collection, organization, and presentation. Similarly, (Zawoad et al., 2015) enumerated the stages of digital forensics as identification, preservation, analysis, and presentation. According to (Hemdan & Manjaiah, 2018), digital forensics involves the application of scientific processes in identifying, collecting, organizing and presenting evidence. Ken Zatyko, the a former director of the US Defense Computer Forensics Laboratory outlined an eight-step process that makes digital forensic a scientific process (Zawoad et al., 2015). These eight steps include (Zawoad et al., 2015): obtaining the search authority, documenting the chain of custody, imaging, and hashing of evidence, validating tools used in the forensic process, analysing evidence, repeating and reproducing to ensure quality assurance, report by documenting the procedures used in the forensic process and then finally, present an expert witness in a court of law.

2.1.2 Evidence Identification

This is the first stage of the forensic process. This stage involves two steps. The first is the identification of the incident and the second is the identification of the evidence. There must be a direct correlation between the incident and the evidence being identified (Daniel & Daniel, 2012).

2.1.3 Evidence Collection

This stage involves the extraction of evidence from different media. The extraction methods may include imaging the original copy of the evidence. This stage also involves preserving the integrity of the evidence (Daniel & Daniel, 2012).

2.1.4 Organization

This stage has two main steps including evidence examination and evidence analysis. Some researchers separate these two steps distinctively. During the evidence examination, the investigator performs a thorough inspection of the data being used as evidence (Daniel & Daniel, 2012). This inspection may involve the use of different forensic tools. These tools are used for extracting and filtering data that is of interest to the investigator and relevant to the investigation process (Zawoad & Hasan, 2015). The analysis phase involves reconstructing events by analysing the data collected. The rationale behind the evidence analysis is to discover any evidential material which will aid the technical as well as the legal perspective of the case (Ademu et al., 2011).

2.1.5 Evidence Presentation

The evidence, after the identification, collection and organization; needs to be presented to a court of law. This stage includes the investigator preparing an organized report to state the findings he or she made during the investigation process (Daniel & Daniel, 2012). These findings are then presented to a court of law with the investigator serving as an expert witness if there is a need to testify (Ieong, 2006).

2.2 IoT Forensics

Unlike the traditional digital forensics, IoT forensics is a new and unexplored area by both industry and academia. Although the purpose of both digital and IoT forensics, is to extract digital information using a scientific approach; the scope available when it comes to information extraction is wider in IoT forensics. According to (Atlam et al., 2017; Raghavan, 2013), IoT forensics is made up of the cloud, network and the device level forensics. Similarly, (Stoyanova et al., 2020) defined IoT forensics as an aspect of digital forensics with the identification, collection, organization, and presentation of evidence happening within the IoT ecosystem. They also broke IoT forensics into Cloud, Network, and Device-level forensics.

2.3 Blockchain

Blockchain, also known as distributed ledger technology is a decentralized and distributed ledger that contains chains of blocks of various transactions joined together by cryptographic hashes. According to (Gaur et al., 2018), the blockchain is "an immutable ledger for recording transactions, maintained within a distributed network of mutually untrusted peers." Any transaction coming from a node is validated by other participating nodes in the blockchain network. After the validation, the set of transactions is added to the block by special nodes called miners as in the case of bitcoin. A miner is a node with sufficient computational power to solve a cryptographic puzzle. Blockchain uses a peer-to-peer (P2P) network. This architecture makes it possible for each node to communicate with a set of neighbour nodes, then each of these nodes also communicate with their neighbour nodes and the communication goes on and on. The blockchain is designed in such a way that any node can join and leave the network at will. Certain key elements are needed in the design and implementation of blockchain technology. These elements are:

1. **Timestamping:** This means that the problem of double-spending in the case of cryptocurrency applications like bitcoin is avoided. Timestamping is achieved by collecting pending transactions into the block and then calculating the hash of the block. This can prove that a transaction existed at the time of creating the block since it is hashed onto the block.
2. **Consensus:** Because new blocks are created and broadcasted by mining nodes, all nodes need to agree on a single version of the block. A distributed consensus helps to decide on which block out of the several variants generated by different nodes would be added to the blockchain.

3. **Data security and integrity:** This property or attribute prevents a malicious node from creating a fake transaction since each transaction is signed by a node or a user using their private key. Similarly, (Gaur et al., 2018) also identifies four blocks within a blockchain framework. These blocks are: the shared ledger, cryptography, consensus, and the smart contracts.

Mining also called proof-of-work (PoW) is used to achieve consensus and to ensure data security and integrity. Mining is done based on the sequence of transactions; a situation can only be changed by redoing the proof-of-work. Mining introduces the difficulty in block generation. There are other methods available ensuring data security and integrity. Some of these methods are proof-of-authority (PoA), proof-of-existence (PoE) and proof-of-concept (PoC). A blockchain can either be permission-less or permissioned. A permission-less blockchain also known as public blockchain allows any node to join and leave at any point in time, whereas private or permissioned blockchain allows nodes to be authenticated before joining the network.

3. RELATED WORK

In this section, we explore some works that are closely related to ours. Blockchain has been widely used in the area of IoT security. However, the concept is still in its exploratory stage when it comes to IoT forensics. (Meffert et al., 2017) proposed a framework that helps evidence acquisition in IoT forensic. Using a centralized approach, the framework is deployed in three nodes namely; controller to IoT device, controller to cloud and controller to controller. Although, the proof of concept used in this work showed that the proposed framework can pull forensic data from IoT devices. However, the centralized nature of their approach makes it difficult to authenticate the evidence captured by the framework. (Li et al., 2019) also used a digital witness approach that allows people to shared logs from IoT devices with guaranteed privacy. The authors used the Privacy-aware IoT Forensics (PRoFIT) model proposed in their earlier work to deploy their digital witness model. The method proposed in their work is to help collect digital evidence in IoT environments as well as ensuring that the privacy of the evidence collected is maintained. The proposed method supports 11 privacy principles captured (Nieto et al., 2018) in their PRoFIT methodology. In their work, (Nieto et al., 2017) proposed a distributed logging scheme for IoT forensics. In this work, the authors used a Modified Information Dispersal Algorithm (MIDA) that ensures the availability of logs generated in IoT environments. The logs are aggregated, compressed, authenticated and dispersed. The distributed approach used in this work only focuses on how logs are stored but not how they are verified. Leveraging the immutability property of blockchain technology, (Noura et al., 2020) proposed an IoT forensics framework that uses a permissioned-based blockchain. This framework enhances the integrity, authenticity and non-repudiation of pieces of evidence.

4. PROPOSED MODEL

In this section, we present our blockchain-based forensic model for IoT (BLOF). In IoT environments, there are three layers. These are the cloud, network and the device layer. Our model leverages the decentralized property of blockchain to ensure that the logs produced in IoT environments are stored on the network and are available for the verification by any of the participating nodes in the network. There are several artefacts to be considered when conducting a forensic investigation. However, our model focuses only on system and event logs. The entities in our model are the Cloud Service Providers (CSPs), Network Devices and the IoT devices. The entities serve as the blockchain nodes in the network. New nodes are added to the network through a key generation process. The public key of a node is appended to a transaction before it is written onto the block. New nodes generate a pair of keys. The CSPs act as the miners in the network. Their computational capacity of CSPs makes them ideal candidates for mining. Our model is made up of a Blockchain Centre (BC), Log Processing Centre (LPC) and User Centre (UC). In the preceding subsections, we discuss each of these components into details. The proposed model is shown in Figure 1.

4.1 Blockchain Centre

The blockchain centre is made up of a distributed ledger where each log is written onto a block after processing. The distributed ledger is made up of all blocks that have been committed to the network. Each block contains a transactional value of hashed values computed from logs. The logs are extracted from the various entities, hashed and written onto the blockchain network as transactions. The nodes in the BC are made up of forensic stakeholders, network and IoT devices and cloud service providers. The blocks are proposed after a consensus has been reached by the nodes.

4.2 Log Processing Centre

This component of our model handles the log processing. The LPC is an Application Programming Interface (API) that sits between entities and the blockchain network. The LPC extracts the logs from the IoT devices, network devices and the cloud layers. The extracted logs are hashed using a SHA-256 hash function and the hashed values are written onto the block as a transaction. We chose to hash the logs because these logs may contain sensitive information. Therefore, it is not advisable to store the logs as plaintext. Secondly, hashing the logs reduces its size which eventually reduces the time needed to process the logs.

Transaction = hash(log)

4.3 User Centre

The user centre is made up of the courts and the forensic investigators. This component of the model makes it possible for forensic investigators to verify the authenticity of logs presented to them by service providers. Additionally, forensic investigators can verify the authenticity of logs even as they are passed on from one investigator to another during the chain of custody. Furthermore, the court can also verify the authenticity of logs presented by prosecutors and decide if such a piece of evidence (log) must be admitted or not. This prevents investigators from tampering with logs to either incriminate innocent people or to exonerate criminals.

5. VERIFICATION OF LOGS

Unlike the traditional digital forensics, investigators solely depend on the CSPs, network and the IoT devices for evidence when it comes to the IoT forensics. This dependence on CSPs may lead to compromising pieces of evidence. Our proposed model does not only ensure the integrity of logs through the use of a decentralized ledger but also allows logs tendered in as evidence to be verified by various stakeholders in the forensic process.

In our proposed model, the forensic investigator still falls on the CSP and IoT devices for the evidence. However, the evidence which in this case is the various logs generated by the cloud instances, network and the IoT devices are hashed after a forensic investigator receives such evidence from a CSP. The hashed value is then compared to the hashes stored as transaction values on the blockchain network. The investigator then searches for the hashed value on the blockchain network. If the hash value exists on the blockchain then the log is accepted by the investigator and forwarded to the court as credible evidence. On the other hand, if the hash value does not exist on the blockchain network then the log is rejected. When the court receives a log from a forensic investigator, the court can determine the credibility of the log by similarly hashing the log and comparing the hashed value to the hash values on the blockchain network. If the value exists, the evidence is accepted by the court. Otherwise, it is rejected. The verification process of our propose model is shown in Figure 2.

For example, Bob who is a forensic investigator receives logs from a CSP intending to present the evidence to a court to prosecute an attacker called Elvan. However, Bob is not sure if the logs provided by the CSP has been tampered with or not. Since the hash of all logs is processed and stored in our blockchain-based model; Bob can verify the authenticity of the logs. Bob first runs the log through a SHA-256 hash function and gets a value (x). He then searches for the transaction (x) on the blockchain network. Bob is one of the participating nodes on the network. If he finds the value (x) as a valid transaction on the network; then the log is genuine and he can then proceed to court and present the log as a piece of evidence. However, if the value (x) is not a valid transaction then Bob must discard that log and rather investigate who made changes to the log. After Bob is presenting the log to the court, the court can also verify the authenticity of the log. The assumption here is that Bob might try to implicate Elvan as the perpetrator of a crime he is innocent of. Similarly, the court runs the log through a SHA-256 hash function and then search for the exact value on the blockchain network. If the transaction value exists, then the court admits the log as evidence and proceeds with hearing the case. Otherwise, the court rejects the evidence and dismisses the case.

6. DISCUSSION

In this section we discuss the advantages of our proposed model, the possible impact it may have on the performance of IoT forensics and then we compare our model to the current existing ones.

Firstly, our proposed model is based on blockchain, making the model a fully decentralized one as compared to a centralized approach discussed in (Meffert et al., 2017). The decentralized characteristic of our model ensures that logs can be verified to determine their authenticity or otherwise. It also prevents service providers and forensic investigators from tampering with logs without being detected. Our model uses the immutability property of blockchain as a leverage to ensure the integrity of logs produced in the IoT environment.

Figure 1. Our proposed blockchain-based IoT forensic model

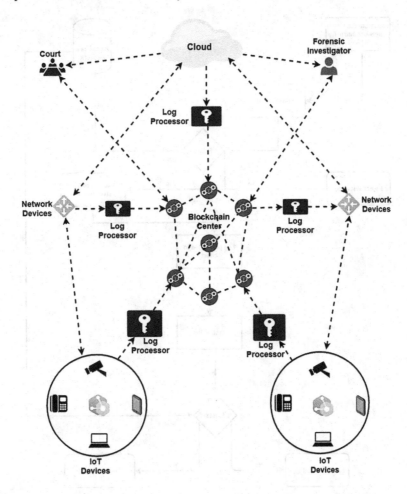

Further, our model offers the advantage of verifiability. This advantage gives the possibility for the forensic stakeholders to verify the authenticity of the logs produced in IoT environments - an advantage that is either not available or not fully explored in the existing related work (Nieto et al., 2018; Nieto et al., 2017; Nieto et al., 2017; Le et al., 2018).

We compare our model with the current work that is closely related to ours, using the following parameters: blockchain-based, verifiability, decentralized, evidence integrity and privacy. In the instance where a model satisfies a parameter, we mark it as a Yes (Y). If it does not satisfy that parameter then we mark it as a No (N). The comparison is shown in Table 1.

We acknowledge the fact that integrating our model into an IoT environment will come with some additional cost in terms of resource usage and computation. In our subsequent work, we intend to evaluate the performance of our model by setting up a testbed to validate the effectiveness of the model.

Figure 2. Verification process of our proposed model

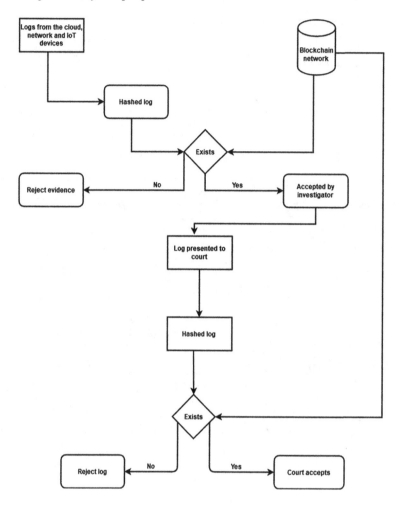

Table 1. Comparing our model to other existing models

Metric	(Nieto et al., 2018)	(Nieto et al., 2017)	(Noura et al., 2020)	(Le et al., 2018)	Our Model
Blockchain-based	N	N	N	Y	Y
Verifiability	N	N	N	N	Y
Decentralized	N	N	N	Y	Y
Evidence integrity	Y	N	Y	Y	Y
Privacy	Y	Y	Y	Y	Y

7. CONCLUSION

Today, IoT has become an integral part of human life. It is integrated into domains such as healthcare, automobile, agriculture, manufacturing industry and household. The world is going to see greater growth in IoT technology with the introduction of 5G network. However, just like any computing technology security of this technology is a concern. With an exponential increase in the number of cyber-attacks, it is important that such crimes are investigated and that the perpetrators are brought to justice. Due to the heterogeneous nature of the IoT environment coupled with the integration of the cloud and the network layer, forensic investigations in an IoT environment is a very challenging task. Further, it is extremely difficult for the stakeholders to determine the authenticity of the evidence they deal with, since in most cases they have to depend on service providers for these pieces of evidence. To ensure that logs presented to forensic investigators are authentic and tamper-free, we proposed a blockchain forensic model that uses a decentralized approach to keep the hashed values of logs produced in IoT environment as transactional records. The proposed model allows any forensic stakeholder to verify the authenticity of the logs they are working with. This model ensures that innocent people are not framed up and culprits are not exonerated by interested parties during a forensic investigation. For future work, we seek to perform an experimental validation to ascertain the computational impact our model will have in an IoT environment. Additionally, exploring ways of storing logs within our model is another area that is of interest to us.

REFERENCES

Ademu, I. O., Imafidon, C. O., & Preston, D. S. (2011). A new approach of digital forensic model for digital forensic investigation. *International Journal of Advanced Computer Science and Applications*, 2(12), 175–178.

Atlam, H. F., Alenezi, A., Walters, R. J., Wills, G. B., & Daniel, J. (2017). Developing an adaptive Risk-based access control model for the Internet of Things. *2017 IEEE International Conference on Internet of Things (IThings) and IEEE Green Computing and Communications (GreenCom) and IEEE Cyber, Physical and Social Computing (CPSCom) and Ieee Smart Data (SmartData)*, 655–661. 10.1109/iThings-GreenCom-CPSCom-SmartData.2017.103

Bellegarde, M., Orvis, M., & Helba, S. (2010). *Ethical Hacking and Countermeasures: Attack Phases*. EC-Council Press.

Borhani, M., Liyanage, M., Sodhro, A. H., Kumar, P., Jurcut, A. D., & Gurtov, A. (2020). Secure and resilient communications in the industrial internet. In *Guide to Disaster-Resilient Communication Networks* (pp. 219–242). Springer. doi:10.1007/978-3-030-44685-7_9

Braeken, A., Liyanage, M., & Jurcut, A. D. (2019). Anonymous lightweight proxy based key agreement for iot (alpka). *Wireless Personal Communications*, 106(2), 345–364. doi:10.100711277-019-06165-9

Carrier, B. (2003). Defining digital forensic examination and analysis tools using abstraction layers. *International Journal of Digital Evidence*, 1(4), 1–12.

Daniel, L., & Daniel, L. (2012). Digital forensics for legal professionals. *Syngress Book Co, 1*, 287–293.

Gaur, N., Desrosiers, L., Ramakrishna, V., Novotny, P., Baset, S., & O'Dowd, A. (2018). *Hands-On Blockchain with Hyperledger: Building decentralized applications with Hyperledger Fabric and Composer*. Packt Publishing. https://books.google.co.za/books?id=wKdhDwAAQBAJ

Hemdan, E. E., & Manjaiah, D. H. (2018). *CFIM : Toward Building New Cloud Forensics Investigation Model*. Academic Press.

Ieong, R. S. C. (2006). FORZA–Digital forensics investigation framework that incorporate legal issues. *Digital Investigation*, *3*, 29–36. doi:10.1016/j.diin.2006.06.004

James, J. I., Shosha, A. F., & Gladyshev, P. (2015). Digital Forensic Investigation and Cloud Computing. In *Cloud Technology* (pp. 1231–1271). IGI Global., doi:10.4018/978-1-4666-6539-2.ch057

Jurcut, A., Coffey, T., & Dojen, R. (2012). Symmetry in Security Protocol Cryptographic Messages—A Serious Weakness Exploitable by Parallel Session Attacks. *2012 Seventh International Conference on Availability, Reliability and Security*, 410–416. 10.1109/ARES.2012.39

Jurcut, A., Coffey, T., Dojen, R., & Gyorodi, R. (2009). Security Protocol Design: A Case Study Using Key Distribution Protocols. *Journal of Computer Science & Control Systems*, *2*(2).

Jurcut, A., Niculcea, T., Ranaweera, P., & LeKhac, A. (2020). *Security considerations for Internet of Things: A survey*. ArXiv Preprint ArXiv:2006.10591.

Jurcut, A. D. (2018). Automated logic-based technique for formal verification of security protocols. *Journal of Advances in Computer Network*, *6*, 77–85. doi:10.18178/JACN.2018.6.2.258

Jurcut, A. D., Coffey, T., & Dojen, R. (2014). Design requirements to counter parallel session attacks in security protocols. *2014 Twelfth Annual International Conference on Privacy, Security and Trust*, 298–305. 10.1109/PST.2014.6890952

Jurcut, A. D., Ranaweera, P., & Xu, L. (2020). Introduction to IoT Security. *IoT Security: Advances in Authentication*, 27–64.

Kumar, T., Braeken, A., Jurcut, A. D., Liyanage, M., & Ylianttila, M. (2019). AGE: Authentication in gadget-free healthcare environments. *Information Technology Management*, 1–20.

Le, D.-P., Meng, H., Su, L., Yeo, S. L., & Thing, V. (2018). Biff: A blockchain-based iot forensics framework with identity privacy. *TENCON 2018-2018 IEEE Region 10 Conference*, 2372–2377.

Li, S., Choo, K.-K. R., Sun, Q., Buchanan, W. J., & Cao, J. (2019). IoT forensics: Amazon echo as a use case. *IEEE Internet of Things Journal*, *6*(4), 6487–6497. doi:10.1109/JIOT.2019.2906946

Meffert, C., Clark, D., Baggili, I., & Breitinger, F. (2017). Forensic State Acquisition from Internet of Things (FSAIoT): A General Framework and Practical Approach for IoT Forensics Through IoT Device State Acquisition. *Proceedings of the 12th International Conference on Availability, Reliability and Security*, 56:1-56:11. 10.1145/3098954.3104053

Morgan, S. (2017). *Cybercrime Report, 2017*. Academic Press.

Nieto, A., Rios, R., & Lopez, J. (2017). A methodology for privacy-aware IoT-forensics. *2017 IEEE Trustcom/BigDataSE/ICESS*, 626–633.

Nieto, A., Rios, R., & Lopez, J. (2018). IoT-forensics meets privacy: Towards cooperative digital investigations. *Sensors (Basel)*, *18*(2), 492. doi:10.339018020492 PMID:29414864

Noura, H. N., Salman, O., Chehab, A., & Couturier, R. (2020). DistLog: A distributed logging scheme for IoT forensics. *Ad Hoc Networks*, *98*, 102061. doi:10.1016/j.adhoc.2019.102061

Perumal, S., Norwawi, N. M., & Raman, V. (2015). Internet of Things(IoT) digital forensic investigation model: Top-down forensic approach methodology. *2015 Fifth International Conference on Digital Information Processing and Communications (ICDIPC)*, 19–23. 10.1109/ICDIPC.2015.7323000

Raghavan, S. (2013). Digital forensic research: Current state of the art. *CSI Transactions on ICT*, *1*(1), 91–114. doi:10.100740012-012-0008-7

Statista, R. D. (2019). *Internet of Things-Number of connected devices worldwide 2015-2025*. Statista Research Department. Statista. Com/Statistics/471264/Iot-Number-of-Connected-Devices-Worldwide.

Stoyanova, M., Nikoloudakis, Y., Panagiotakis, S., Pallis, E., & Markakis, E. K. (2020). A Survey on the Internet of Things (IoT) Forensics: Challenges, Approaches and Open Issues. *IEEE Communications Surveys and Tutorials*, *22*(2), 1191–1221. doi:10.1109/COMST.2019.2962586

Sumalatha, M. R., & Batsa, P. (2016). Data collection and audit logs of digital forensics in cloud. *2016 International Conference on Recent Trends in Information Technology (ICRTIT)*, 1–8. 10.1109/ICRTIT.2016.7569587

Xu, L., Jurcut, A. D., & Ahmadi, H. (2019). Emerging Challenges and Requirements for Internet of Things in 5G. *5G-Enabled Internet of Things*.

Zawoad, S., & Hasan, R. (2015). A trustworthy cloud forensics environment. *IFIP Advances in Information and Communication Technology*, *462*, 271–285. doi:10.1007/978-3-319-24123-4_16

Zawoad, S., Hasan, R., & Skjellum, A. (2015). OCF: an open cloud forensics model for reliable digital forensics. *2015 IEEE 8th International Conference on Cloud Computing*, 437–444.

This research was previously published in Revolutionary Applications of Blockchain-Enabled Privacy and Access Control; pages 59-73, copyright year 2021 by Information Science Reference (an imprint of IGI Global).

Chapter 41
Identification of a Person From Live Video Streaming Using Machine Learning in the Internet of Things (IoT)

Sana Zeba

ⓘ https://orcid.org/0000-0003-1311-7817

Department of Computer Engineering, Jamia Millia Islamia University, New Delhi, India

Mohammad Amjad

Department of Computer Engineering, Jamia Millia Islamia University, New Delhi, India

ABSTRACT

In this paper, the authors develop an efficient face recognition algorithm from images or live video streaming for IoT systems based on K-nearest neighbor and support vector machine learning to recognize the person from the local database and extract the features of the face. Because of the complexity of the conditions, there might be some factors of facing errors like the size; the angle; the distance from the ear, nose, and eyes; etc. This sustainable machine learning-based IoT system is designed for sovereign face recognition with features extraction with improved accuracy near about 96%. The experimental study is done to test the performance of the face recognition in the changes of number of persons in video or images. Finally, this manuscript recognized persons from live video or images with accuracy approximately 96% by using the SVM and KNN classifiers and discussed with the block diagram and proposed algorithm.

DOI: 10.4018/978-1-6684-7132-6.ch041

INTRODUCTION

An Evolutionary and Emerging technology, the Internet of Things (IoT) generates new scopes and opportunities in engineering and science applications for cracking humans' problems. Without the interference of human beings, different emerging technologies make our life fully or partially automated. (Kumar & Mallick, 2018) Face recognition algorithm considers as an important factor in various areas such as identification, authentication of the persons, identification of criminals, security, and privacy of sovereign information of users in IoT applications. The Internet of Things (IoT) environment is the collection of computing devices, mechanical object, and digital machines thing, object, electronic devices which can communicate and access the data among devices from anywhere in the network (Haque et al., 2021). Each thing or objects have unique identifiers (UIDs) for identification purpose. Recently, IoT applications had one major problem which is the security of applications because of their rapid growth, heterogeneities of devices, and complex nature. Security is a big concern and needs to tackle in the network because of its nature.

Recent Biometric technology is based on face recognition and image processing concepts. The biometric research field has not only become common in computer vision, but it is also become popular in neuroscientists and psychologists due to its secure nature. (Balla & Jadhao, 2020) The biometric credentials enable users to use users' physical traits like the face, retina, eyes, nose, fingers, voice and gait, etc. instead of PINs or passwords as accessing any critical IoT systems or a database. The Biometric approach is based on the perception of replacing "one thing you have with you" with "who you are," which has been realized as a safer paradigm to preserve private information. (Ferrag et al., 2019) Biometric identification and authentications are applied in the sectors where security is the main concern like a residential area, airports, banks lockers, ATM, air frontier and crossing the borders, etc.

Face recognition system has been used in different small-scale applications to identify the face from the captured image or group of images. In this paper, the idea behind developing an IoT application with a face recognition concept that recognizes only trained data that are stored in the database. Through this recognition IoT system, only authorized users can enter or access any sovereign information and prevent any fraud or crimes remotely. This system used the K-nearest neighbor and Support Vector Machine classification algorithm to recognize the face from the captured images and extract the features of the faces. The main contribution of this system is to recognize the faces from the trained database and categorized the recognized database based on different parameters like odd coming time, covering faces, etc. for securing and preventing criminal activities through the IoT system.

This paper is systemized as follows. Section2 explains previous work review on the IoT and face recognition in ML, Section 3 discusses some preliminaries related to the IoT and Face Recognitions algorithms KNN, SVM, LBPH. Section4 discusses the research gaps; section 5 defines the problem statements related to the data analysis of IoT with face recognition. Section6 proposed the ML-based face recognition methodology of the problem and the section7 evaluate the result and comparison analysis of the proposed solution. Section 8 discussed some future work and section9 gives a conclusion of the overall research work.

RELATED WORK

In this segment, the summary of the previously published literature related to the security problems of the IoT system is presented, Blockchain Technology in IoT and solutions of the IoT problems using Blockchain. This literature review has the main focus on the following aspects of the Security provisioning of IoT Network:

Erwin Adi1 et al. (Adi et al., 2020), have given a critical review to generate IoT-data for machine learning and the challenges of the IoT environment. Besides this, the author proposed a framework to permit to adaptively learn with IoT applications and present a case study in real-time daily life applications. At last, they have discussed the key issues that affect upcoming intelligent IoT applications. Syeda Manjia Tahsien et.al. (Tahsien et al., 2020a), has given a comprehensive review of Internet of Things (IoT) architecture with machine learning and also discussed the possible attacks of IoT systems. In the paper, comprehensive comparison of security in IoT and ML-based secure IoT system up to 2019. Sherali Zeadally et. al.(Zeadally & Tsikerdekis, 2020), has explored about how to improve the security of IoT system at the host and network levels with the machine learning and investigate the potential learning algorithm while enhancing security challenges of IoT devices. They have been also discussed the strength and shortage of machine learning algorithms in IoT environments. Zhu Hongpeng et.al. (Zhu, 2020) has proposed image quality assessment methods that used the multi-feature fusion technique based on IoT for evaluating the faces of images. Mehedi Masud et.al. (Masud et al., 2020) has suggested an automatic face recognition model in a cloud environment based on a tree-based deep model that has computationally less costly without cooperating the accuracy. Tanya Sinha et.al.(Tanya Sinha, Abhisekh Ghosh, 2020) has proposed an attendance system framework with face recognition to maintain accuracy, remove proxy and make the attendance procedure more efficient. Similarly, Syeda Manjia Tahsiena et.al.(Tahsien et al., 2020b) have also performed a survey of IoT architecture and discussed a comprehensive review on recognition approaches with corresponding importance in terms of security of IoT. Amit Sagu et.al.(Amit Sagu, 2020) has given a survey on existing concerns; security challenges as well as explores several approaches, features, factors of techniques and compares several techniques. Timmy Schenkel et. al. (Schenkel et al., 2019) has proposed a report that has compared the several recognition approaches on the several datasets (ORL, LFW) such as Eigenface with KNN, Convolutional Neural Network (CNN), Fisherface with KNN, SVM at the same conditions. LI MAO et.al. (Mao et al., 2019), have given the concept of detecting crime behaviors through the developed novel framework of face recognition. This occludes recognition algorithm has three phases like face detection, tracking, verification of faces. Gaussian algorithm for face detection, CNN model used deep feature for tracking the particular face and design dictionary novel learning approach for verification of faces. Also discussed future work to enhance this approach with detect head recognition algorithms and detect faces of all sexes, ages, etc. Salma Abdel Magid et.al.(Abdel et al., 2019), has discussed the feasibility of image classification using devices of the IoT Network and studying the performance of its. The author has explored numerous factors like resolution, dataset size, algorithm phase, algorithm types of images, and their relationships themselves. Design an approach to predict the energy consumption when the device performs the image classification by using three machine learning concepts which are Gaussian process, regression, and random forests. Suraj Pawar et.al. (Pawar et al., 2018), has proposed an energy and cost-efficient solution IoT system and face detection algorithm for home security. The author has also discussed major problems of the current IoT system like power failure, high cost, and high maintenance required in case of providing high-level security in the system. This proposed system can detect motion and triggers the system using PIR (Passive Infrared) sensor and Ultrasonic used for distance measurement which calculates the position of the person. Nazrul M. Ahmad et.al.(Ahmad et al., 2018), has presented an initiative to improve identity management (IDM) by integrating blockchain and face recognition tactics in an integrated cloud-based IoT application. In the use case of this paper, face recognition is used as an entry point to the service of the system. Printing activities are performed when the user's information is digitally verified via distributed immutable blockchain and smart contract used to keep track of the user's information printing activities. Prayag Bhatia et.al.(Bhatia et al., 2018), has proposed an effective face recognition IoT system. The IoT system has created the local database for the members of family houses and used Local Binary Pattern Histograms for recognizing the person from the created local database. Jiang Lu et.al. (Lu et al., 2018), have built an automated face recognition system. The developed system can capture pictures and execute face detection algorithms. There are two main steps required in this algorithm: first has a cascade classifier for face detection and second has spatial correlation for result improvement. Sandesh Kulkarni et.al.(Kulkarni et al., 2017), has introduced a project that identified the person to open the door lock based on personal identification basis. The proposed system has performed the detection and recognition in real-time for opening the door lock. This project exploits the basic web camera, and the internet connection to create a door that unlocks the door itself via facial recognition. This introduced the project enhances mainly five features: security, safety, control, and monitoring to home automation. In the future, proper designing in the face recognition algorithm requires and needs to develop new algorithms. Dwi Ana Ratna Wati et.al.(Ana & Wati, 2017), has introduced a system that has examined the performance of face detection in numerous variations of distance, light intensity, light position angles, person's accessories, and shirt color. Ravi Kishore Kodali et.al.(Kodali et al., 2017), has focused on built a smart home IoT system that sends alerts to the owner of the system by using the Internet in case of any intrude and also raises an alarm. Jiakailin Wang et.al. (Wang et al., 2016), has presented a real-time face recognition system for home security service which has been applied to recognize the person's face in front and give a warning when the identity of the captured image person is unfamiliar. Yasser Alsouda et. al.(Alsouda, n.d.), has explored various parameters of SVM and KNN algorithms to calculate optimal classification of the sound sample in the dataset. The proposed method used SVM, KNN algorithm, and MFCC for feature extraction. For implementation used Raspberry Pi Zero W and do experiments with numerous environments sounds like car horn, street music, and jackhammer. The dataset of this experiment contains sound sample and train the 3000-sound sample of KNN (k=1) on Raspberry Pi Zero W device.

PRELIMINARIES

Internet of Things

In terms of the Internet of Things (IoT), every linked device in the network is considered a thing of the network. Every object has consisted with sensors, actuators, and microprocessor embedded system and each object transmit and communicate with each other without a human to a computer or human to human interaction. This communication may be in a short-range or wide-range network.

For short-range communication used wireless technologies like Bluetooth, Wi-Fi, ZigBee and for wide-range applications used mobile networks such as LoRa, GSM, GPRS, 3G, WiMAX, LTE, 4G, and 5G, etc. Various IoT applications are Smart Home, Smart City, Traffic System, Health Monitoring

System, Parking System, Smart Attendance System, and Online Mode Education System, etc. Due to the enormous usage of IoT systems in different applications, it is crucial to maintain the security of the system properly and keep the cost low of its devices. Moreover, devices should be able to do tasks depending on the numerous applications like the preprocessing of data, data acquisition, and M2M communication, etc.

Security and privacy of the data or information is the biggest challenge of IoT applications. Security parameters are such as integrity, confidentiality, availability, authorization, and authenticity. Four layered architecture of Internet of Things system shown in figure 1.

- **Perception Layer:** It is also called the sensor layer and it is the topmost layer. Acquisition of data done from this layer through sensor devices and actuators.
- **Network Layer:** This layer of the IoT system performs the operations such as routing, switching and transferring, etc.
- **Middleware Layer:** The middleware Layer or Support layer is responsible for processing and manipulating data.
- **Application Layer:** The application layer is the most important. This layer confirms the integrity and authenticity, etc. of the data.

Figure 1. Layered Architecture of IoT

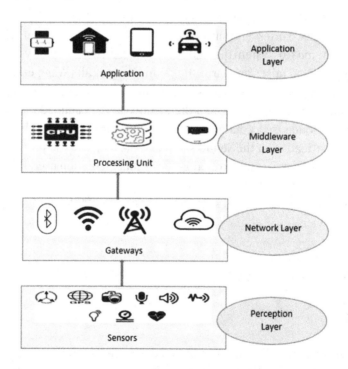

Machine Learning

Machine Learning (ML) in the field of research has been capable of learning without being directly programmed by the computer. Although it is closely connected to artificial intelligence (AI), ML is not a novel concept. Computers are trained to perform various operations around the ML algorithms, such as regression, sorting, extraction of features, clustering and pattern recognition, etc.

In the last few years, Machine Learning has been advanced curiously for the Internet of Things security purposes. Therefore, ML procedures can be used to protect IoT applications from any unauthorized activities, malware, and various attacks at the very early stage with analyzing the behaviors. Additionally, ML provided the appropriate solutions for maintaining the security of resource-constrained IoT applications. Machine Learning used statistics for making the prediction or classification about something from the massive amount of data.

ML techniques of AI have included many methods such as supervised learning, unsupervised learning, semi-supervised learning, and reinforcement learning which can be applied to prevent any fraud or thefts and also detect attacks in the IoT applications. (Sagu & Gill, 2020) Below Figure 2, represent the various learning methods.

Figure 2. Machine Learning Methods

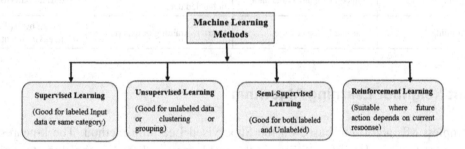

Supervised Learning

The supervised approach is the most common technique in machine learning of all techniques, where it is educated using labeled examples such as an input where the target output is identified (19). This learning is categorized specifically as both grouping and regression. In such applications, supervised learning is mostly used. Where future events have been predicted based on historical data. Two phases of supervised learning are the training and testing phases.

Unsupervised Learning

Unsupervised learning deals with data that has no historical labels. This type of learning works on train unlabeled data. (Sagu & Gill, 2020) Based on data testing, it attempts to define trends and do data clustering or forecast potential values. The unsupervised learning base system is not stated the "right answer." This learning algorithm only figures out what is being shown.

Semi-Supervised Learning

For related implementations, such as supervised learning, this method of learning is important. For training and research, uses both unlabeled and labeled information. Semi-supervised learning can be used for classification, regression, and prediction. Hence, it is a combination of both supervised and unsupervised learning.

Reinforcement Learning

In this learning method, using the trial-and-error concept that which actions profit the greatest reward. The output of the problem is predicted on the set of tuning parameters. There are three main components which are agent, environment, and actions.

Table 1. Different Machine Learning Method

Supervised Learning	Unsupervised Learning	Semi-supervised Learning	Reinforcement Learning
Based on Input and Output	Based on Only Input	Based on Input and Output or Only on Input	Based on Input and Feedback
Trained using labeled data	Trained using unlabeled data	Trained using labeled or unlabeled data	Used trial-and-error concept
Learning by training	Learning by experience.	Learn by training or experience.	The Learn by exploring the agent, environment, and actions.

K-Nearest Neighbor Learning Algorithm

It is the simplest ML algorithm based on the Supervised Learning method. The k-nearest neighbor algorithm is a method for classifying objects in the problem space based on the closest training in classification or identification but it is mostly used for classification problems. This algorithm guesses the similarity between the new data point with available point cases and puts the new data into the class that is most analogous to the available classes. K-NN algorithm stores all the presented data points based on the likeness.

K-NN algorithm well defined with two properties which are:

- **Lazy learning algorithm:** KNN is often referred to as a lazy learning or instance-based learning algorithm since there is no specialized testing process and all data points are used for training when conducting classification.
- **Non-parametric learning algorithm:** KNN is referred to as non-parametric learning because there is little to speculate about the underlying data points.

In our research, we favored using the KNN learning algorithm because it can be trained with the lesser dataset and realize better results in a minimum time with minimum hardware requirements.

Support Vector Machine Learning Algorithm

Support vector machines (SVM) are versatile supervised learning algorithms with classification and regression in all characteristics. But mostly, it is more powerful for classification problems. Firstly, the

SVM algorithm was introducing in 1960, but it was refined in 1990. SVM algorithm creates a plane between two classes called a hyperplane.

Support vector machines have two types which are:

- **Linear Support vector machines:** In Linear SVM is classified a dataset with a single line into two classes. It means linear SVM used linearly divisible data.
- **Non-linear Support vector machines:** It is recommended for non-linearly divided data, which means a dataset cannot be divided by using a straight line.

The key objective of the approach of the support vector machine is to find an N-dimensional space hyperplane (where N is the number of features) that categorizes the data points distinctly. Some major SVM-related principles are:

- **Support Vectors:** It is the closest data point to the hyperplane.
- **Hyperplane:** As a space plane or decision plane that is divided between several object points with distinct groups.
- **Margin:** It is known as the distance between two lines of different classes between the nearest data points.

Local Binary Patterns (LBP)

LBP specifies the local binary patterns used as the operator to describe the presence of images in the local texture. (Wang et al., 2016). It is an efficient and simple texture operator, which labels each pixel of images with neighbor pixels and also reflects the result in a binary pattern. LBP was firstly described in 1994 and further, it is joint with the histograms concept. LBP with the histogram called Local Binary Patterns Histogram algorithm (LBPH) to improve the performance of face detection.

Local Binary Patterns Histogram (LBPH) algorithm has extracted the features from an input picture and match them with a database image. This LBPH algorithm was proposed in 2006. It is used a local binary operator. The LBPH algorithm is used for OpenCV. This operator tags the pixels of a face by comparing with the center value of a 3×3 neighborhood for every pixel. If the value of the neighbor pixel is greater than the pixel of the center, then it is written as 1, otherwise 0. The basic steps involved in this algorithm are:

1. Creating the face dataset
2. Acquisition
3. Feature extraction
4. Classification of faces

RESEARCH GAP

The IoT system is a very rapidly increasing technology and needs to develop smart IoT applications for handling security and prevent any unauthorized activities of the system. However, there are so many research gaps to developing such an IoT-based face detection and recognition IoT application. On the behalf of literature study, we have identified major gaps or shortages of the ML-based IoT recognition system. Some research gaps related to ML-based IoT system has discussed below:

1. Delay in processing time due to complicated computation in actual implementations of facial recognition algorithms.
2. Strong false positive rate due to the effects of inaccurate face recognition.
3. Most of the current face detection systems are detecting only standard, and unshaded faces.
4. Until now, there has been no well-organized approach for processing and handling data generated by IoT devices connected through the internet for handling any criminal activities of users in a distributed manner.
5. Design an algorithm for detecting users through the arbitrary posture of face recognition and preventing any criminal or suspicious actions in the departments.

PROBLEM STATEMENTS

Everything in our life at fingertips because of the amendment of various technologies days to day. (Balla & Jadhao, 2020) However, we want to know about visitors of the numerous visiting places such as home, office, airport, ATM, etc. at the same because of security reasons. Hence, we need to track everything's for up to date ourself with smart Internet of Things (IoT) for various scenarios simultaneously like:

1. Entry of unofficial persons at the office location.
2. Entry of workers or any unknown at home.
3. Entry at the bank locker locations.
4. Violating the security rules at ATM, Airport, Malls.
5. Burglar identification at home, ATM, Jeweler's shop, Warehouse.
6. Safety of Research laboratories, etc.

Hence, we need to develop a smart IoT application for monitoring and tracking the locations remotely. This paper has a major contribution to handle these problems recording face recognition of users in IoT system through images, video clip, and as well as live video streaming as well as. Major problems handle in this paper is:

1. Detect the images from live videos with different postures.
2. Design an algorithm to detect and recognition of faces from images and live video streaming as well in a different posture.
3. Reduce the delay in processing time faced due to the complex computation of face recognition algorithms in real applications.
4. Discussed the proposed algorithm-based system with the proper block diagram with various steps.
5. Improve Accuracy of recognition of faces through images or live video.

PROPOSED METHODOLOGY

Block Diagram of Proposed Methodology

The major components of the face recognition approach are image gathering, face detection, feature extraction, and face recognition as shown in Figure 3. For implementing the system, we used the face recognition API based on dlib's face recognition approach and the web came as camera hardware. The proposed solution can be divided into various parts such as Face detection, Feature Extraction, Trained the Recognizer, and then recognizing the faces from images as well as live video streaming. Videos or live streaming are nothing but it is collection of images arrange with respect to time. So, we divide the live video as frame by frame similar to images and match them same as e we did with images.

After detection of faces creates the local database and comparing the detected faces with the local database for recognizing them. This proposed solution was done with the "Open-Source Computer Vision Library (OpenCV)", pickle, imutils, etc. This proposed solution was done with the "Open-Source Computer Vision Library (OpenCV)", pickle, imutils, etc. OpenCV package was designed for efficient computation and with the feature to focus on real-time applications. The complete face recognizes Internet of Things (IoT) system has worked on the various distinct steps which are shown in figure 3:

1. Live video streaming or Image Capture
2. Face Detection
3. Feature Extraction
4. Trained the Recognizer
5. Face Recognition

Figure 3. Steps in Face Recognition for IoT system

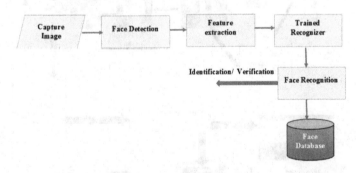

1. **Live Video Streaming or Image Capturing:** Firstly, we have a required set of images or videos for processing any machine learning algorithm. Webcam of PC or computer used for capturing the images.
2. **Face Detection:** An effective object detection classifier Haar Cascade Classifier is based on haar features, and it has developed by Paul Viola and Michael Jones. In the proposed approach using embedding, the model is used for mapping an image into a 128-dimensional vector. Videos are

nothing but pictures that are arranged in time. So, we split pictures frame by frame and balance them as we did with pictures.

3. **Feature Extraction:** OpenCV package comes with the detector as well as a trainer for live video as well as images. OpenCV is used for extracting the images features like eyes, nose, mouth, and ear, etc., and used SVM as well as to classify the images or video through the pixels range value. After extracting the features and making face embedding, which creates embed_dictt dictionary of image embed information and stores it into pickle file.

4. **Trained the Recognizer:** We make the face or live streaming embeddings with face_recognition. face_encodings method. Dissimilar vectors of same-person images or video clips are identical to each other or in group form in the vector space. We've stored them in a qualified pickle file after creating face embedding.

5. **Face Recognition:** Here, we have again created face embeddings from the live video streaming and images frame. Further, matched the embedding of new faces to the saved embedding of the pickle file. If the new image embedding's have closed to their embedding's in the embedded vector space, then we can identify the entity from both live streaming and images. For checking the frame closed vector value with the embedded value used the threshold value with KNN learning.

The block diagram of the proposed IoT system demonstrates in figure 4 which shows all phases in experimental form. The proposed system used webcam camera hardware for capturing the images or video. Block diagram is shown in Figure 4.

Figure 4. Block Diagram of Face Recognition in Live Video Streaming

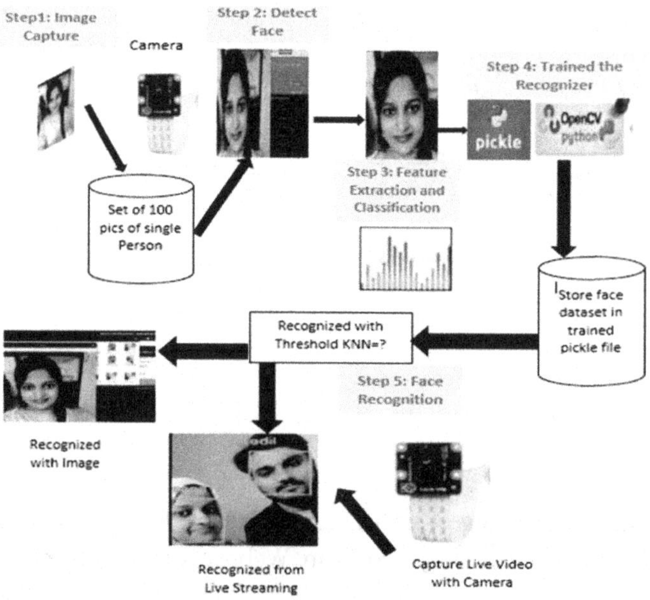

Flow Chart of Proposed Methodology

Figure 5 displays a flowchart of the proposed IoT system for face recognition. The webcam image or video capture (real images) is handled by the face recognition module. Later it performs the mapping of the video images into vector form. Both the proposed algorithm as well as flow chart has discussed below to clarify the working of the proposed system in detail.

Figure 5. Flowchart of Face Recognition in IoT system

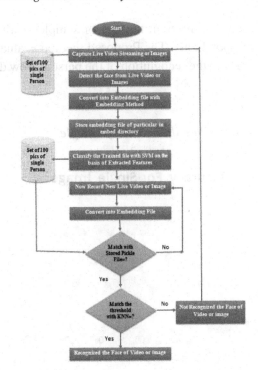

PERFORMANCE EVALUATION

To test the efficiency of the proposed face recognition technique in live video streaming and photos, as well, much real-time testings' done and the results are concise separately for both images and live video as follows:

- **Datasets:** In this segment, discussed datasets that were utilized in the experiments for system testing. For the experiments, used self-created datasets that have 50 images per sample and used 10 samples. Hence, the total 500 images and also maintain group images of each sample. While for the comparative analysis of the proposed algorithm used ORL datasets that have contained 40 subjects and 10 images of each subject (Masud et al., 2020).

- • **Training process:** We have trained the recognizer and recognized some images and live videos of known persons in the database. For testing's purposed collects single person image with the different set of images. The maximum number of sets of images gives the better accuracy of a system.

Performance Evaluation Through Images

For image recognition testing we performed on the two bases.

Accuracy in Single Person Image

The single-person image is stored in a different number of samples with various postures of images and calculates the accuracy correspondingly. The Proposed method evaluates that a greater number of sample images gives more accuracy to the recognition of the person. Now draw the summary of a result in this case.

Figure 6. Accuracy of Single Person with Different no of Sample

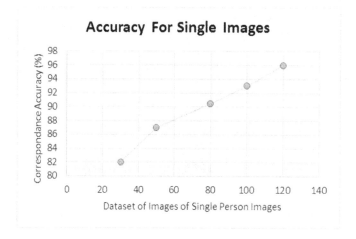

Accuracy in Group of Person Image

Group images of different persons stored in a different number of samples having two persons, three persons, or more than three persons in a single image. Images are having with varying a position of images and calculate the accuracy correspondingly. The Proposed method evaluates that a greater number of people in a group sample images little to reduce the accuracy of face recognition of the different person in the group. Now draw the summary of a result in this case.

Figure 7. Accuracy of Group Image with Different no of Groups Image

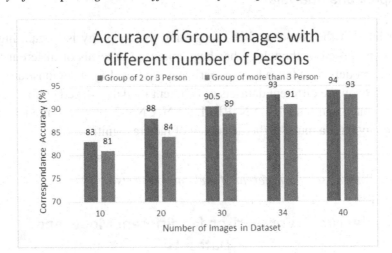

Performance Evaluation Through Live Video

Record the live video correspondence of different persons such as a single person, two people, etc., and stored it. The Proposed method evaluates that a greater number of persons in a video reduce the accuracy rate of recognition. Now draw the summary of a result in this case.

Figure 8. Accuracy of Live Video with Different no of Persons Video

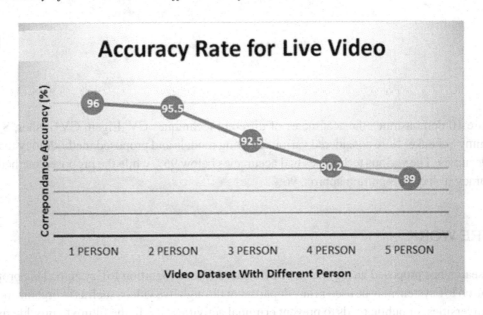

Accuracy Comparisons Analysis

One of the major aims of the proposed face recognition methodology is to gain high accuracy. The performance of the proposed methodology has been analyzed in terms of different factors. Different previously proposed models were taken for comparison purposes. Fig. 9 demonstrates the performance of the different models on the different datasets of different models (Masud et al., 2020).

Figure 9 demonstrates four models CNN_RBM, CNN, CNN-2, proposed model, and among all the proposed methodology have a much higher accuracy of face recognition.

Figure 9. Accuracy Comparison for different Model and Datasets

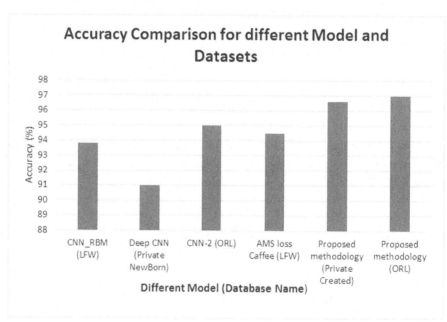

Figure 10 demonstrates the accuracies of different techniques CV_Eigen, CV_Fisher, S_Eigen_K, etc. Timmy Schenkel Here considered various existing models and proposed methodology that achieved better accuracy. The various techniques had accuracies below 95% while the proposed methodology had an accuracy of face recognition approx. 96%.

FUTURE WORK

This research has proposed an algorithm of ML-based face recognition IoT system. This proposed face recognition IoT system may be used in any department through live videos such as in organizations, industries, universities, or public roads to prevent criminal activities, etc. In the future to provide more strong security in the system then combine face recognition algorithm with the encrypted password of users.

Figure 10. Accuracy Comparison of Various Techniques

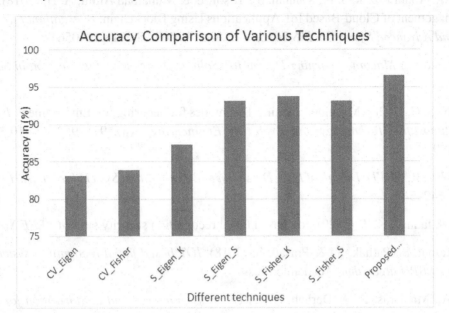

CONCLUSION

The face recognition IoT system was proposed in this paper. This paper explores how live video face recognition with machine learning could enhance IoT security. There were performing evaluations through single images, group of images, and video streaming. This paper presents a reliable face recognition IoT system through live video streaming a well as images in the different postures. The face recognition IoT framework was proposed with the aid of pickle, python, and machine learning algorithms. Experimental studies indicate that facial recognition can be done with an average accuracy of 96% for the images while in the case of live video it is approx. 95%. Comparison analyses were performed of different models and available face databases. Accuracy of proposed face recognition has calculated approx. 96% in case of a created database of single-person video or image, while there is bit decrease accuracy in case of more than 3 person's video. The proposed recognition system has achieved around 97% accuracy using publicly available ORL databases. These conclusions prove the efficiency of the proposed face recognition system. Although the performance of face recognition of more than 5 group images or video through the proposed system still needs to improve for increasing accuracy in the future.

REFERENCES

Abdel, S., Francesco, M., & Behnam, P. (2019). Image classification on IoT edge devices : Profiling and modeling. *Cluster Computing*, 9. Advance online publication. doi:10.100710586-019-02971-9

Adi, E., Anwar, A., Baig, Z., & Zeadally, S. (2020). Machine learning and data analytics for the IoT. *Neural Computing & Applications*, 32(20), 16205–16233. doi:10.100700521-020-04874-y

Ahmad, N. M., Abdul Razak, S. F., Kannan, S., Yusof, I., & Muhamad Amin, A. H. (2018). Improving Identity Management of Cloud-Based IoT Applications Using Blockchain. *International Conference on Intelligent and Advanced System, ICIAS 2018,* 1–6. 10.1109/ICIAS.2018.8540564

Alsouda, Y. (n.d.). *A Machine Learning Driven IoT Solution for Noise Classification in Smart Cities.* Academic Press.

Amit Sagu, N. S. G. (2020). Machine Learning Techniques for Securing IoT Environment. *International Journal of Innovative Technology and Exploring Engineering, 9*(4), 977–982. doi:10.35940/ijitee. D1209.029420

Ana, D., & Wati, R. (2017). *Design of Face Detection and Recognition System for Smart Home Security Application.* 342–347.

Balla, P. B., & Jadhao, K. T. (2020). IoT based facial recognition security system. *IEEE Xplore,* 1–4.

Bhatia, P., Rajput, S., Pathak, S., & Prasad, S. (2018). *IOT based facial recognition system for home security using LBPH algorithm.* Academic Press.

Ferrag, M. A., Maglaras, L., & Derhab, A. (2019). *Authentication and authorization for mobile IoT devices using bio-features: Recent advances and future trends.* Academic Press.

Haque, M. A., Haque, S., Kumar, K., & Singh, N. K. (2021). A Comprehensive Study of Cyber Security Attacks, Classification, and Countermeasures in the Internet of Things. In *Digital Transformation and Challenges to Data Security and Privacy* (pp. 63–90). IGI Global. doi:10.4018/978-1-7998-4201-9.ch004

Kodali, R. K., Jain, V., Bose, S., & Boppana, L. (2017). IoT based smart security and home automation system. *Proceeding - IEEE International Conference on Computing, Communication and Automation, ICCCA 2016,* 1286–1289. 10.1109/CCAA.2016.7813916

Kulkarni, S., Bagul, M., Dukare, A., & Gaikwad, P. A. (2017). Face Recognition System Using IoT. *International Journal of Advanced Research in Computer Engineering & Technology, 6*(11), 1720–1723.

Kumar, N. M., & Mallick, P. K. (2018). Blockchain technology for security issues and challenges in IoT. *Procedia Computer Science, 132,* 1815–1823. doi:10.1016/j.procs.2018.05.140

Lu, J., Fu, X., & Zhang, T. (2018). A smart system for face detection with spatial correlation improvement in IoT environment. *2017 IEEE SmartWorld Ubiquitous Intelligence and Computing, Advanced and Trusted Computed, Scalable Computing and Communications, Cloud and Big Data Computing, Internet of People and Smart City Innovation,* 1–4. doi:10.1109/UIC-ATC.2017.8397550

Mao, L., Sheng, F., & Zhang, T. (2019). Face Occlusion Recognition With Deep Learning in Security Framework for the IoT. *IEEE Access: Practical Innovations, Open Solutions, 7,* 174531–174540. doi:10.1109/ACCESS.2019.2956980

Masud, M., Muhammad, G., Alhumyani, H., Alshamrani, S. S., Cheikhrouhou, O., Ibrahim, S., & Hossain, M. S. (2020). Deep learning-based intelligent face recognition in IoT-cloud environment. *Computer Communications, 152,* 215–222. doi:10.1016/j.comcom.2020.01.050

Pawar, S., Kithani, V., Ahuja, S., & Sahu, S. (2018). Smart Home Security Using IoT and Face Recognition. *Proceedings - 2018 4th International Conference on Computing, Communication Control and Automation, ICCUBEA 2018*, 1–6. 10.1109/ICCUBEA.2018.8697695

Sagu, A., & Gill, N. S. (2020). Machine Learning Techniques for Securing IoT Environment. *Machine Learning Techniques for Securing IoT Environment.*, 4(4), 977–982. doi:10.35940/ijitee.D1209.029420

Schenkel, T., Ringhage, O., & Branding, N. (2019). *A Comparative Study of Facial Recognition Techniques: With focus on low computational power*. Academic Press.

Sinha, T., & Ghosh, A. (2020). Attendance System with Face Recognition. *International Journal of Engineering and Advanced Technology*, 9(4), 799–804. doi:10.35940/ijeat.D7710.049420

Tahsien, S. M., Karimipour, H., & Spachos, P. (2020a). Machine learning based solutions for security of Internet of Things (IoT): A survey. *Journal of Network and Computer Applications*, 161(April), 102630. Advance online publication. doi:10.1016/j.jnca.2020.102630

Tahsien, S. M., Karimipour, H., & Spachos, P. (2020b). Machine Learning Based Solutions for Security of Internet of Things (IoT). *Survey (London, England)*, 161, 102630. Advance online publication. doi:10.1016/j.jnca.2020.102630

Wang, J., Zheng, J., Zhang, S., He, J., Liang, X., & Feng, S. (2016). A face recognition system based on local binary patterns and support vector machine for home security service robot. *Proceedings - 2016 9th International Symposium on Computational Intelligence and Design, ISCID 2016, 2*, 303–307. 10.1109/ISCID.2016.2079

Zeadally, S., & Tsikerdekis, M. (2020). Securing Internet of Things (IoT) with machine learning. *International Journal of Communication Systems*, 33(1), 1–16. doi:10.1002/dac.4169

Zhu, H. (2020). Image quality assessment model based on multi-feature fusion of energy Internet of Things. *Future Generation Computer Systems*, 112, 501–506. doi:10.1016/j.future.2020.05.037

This research was previously published in the International Journal of Mobile Computing and Multimedia Communications (IJMCMC), 12(3); pages 44-59, copyright year 2021 by IGI Publishing (an imprint of IGI Global).

Chapter 42
Security and Privacy for Electronic Healthcare Records Using AI in Blockchain

Ramani Selvanambi

Vellore Institute of Technology, Vellore, India

Samarth Bhutani

Vellore Institute of Technology, Vellore, India

Komal Veauli

Vellore Institute of Technology, Vellore, India

ABSTRACT

In yesteryears, the healthcare data related to each patient was limited. It was stored and controlled by the hospital authorities and was seldom regulated. With the increase in awareness and technology, the amount of medical data per person has increased exponentially. All this data is essential for the correct diagnosis of the patient. The patients also want access to their data to seek medical advice from different doctors. This raises several challenges like security, privacy, data regulation, etc. As health-related data are privacy-sensitive, the increase in data stored increases the risk of data exposure. Data availability and privacy are essential in healthcare. The availability of correct information is critical for the treatment of the patient. Information not easily accessed by the patients also complicates seeking medical advice from different hospitals. However, if data is easily accessible to everyone, it makes privacy and security difficult. Blockchains to store and secure data will not only ensure data privacy but will also provide a common method of data regulation.

DOI: 10.4018/978-1-6684-7132-6.ch042

INTRODUCTION

Blockchain technology began from Bitcoin, giving stability against failure and cyber assaults. It utilizes technologies, for example, hash chains, digital signatures, and consensus mechanism to record bitcoin exchanges by building dispersed, shared database in decentralized way. Such technologies make interactions secure by providing services like distributed storage, non-repudiation, time-based traceability for exchange substance, which frame a vital framework. Albeit, at first developed for bitcoin, it was later understood that this innovation could also profit in different fields. It was then implemented in different fields, for example, healthcare, fintech, computational law, review, notarization, et cetera by outlining different keen contracts in view of blockchain. This paper includes the way in which blockchain can be used to solve the above-mentioned problem and make electronic healthcare data storage easier and more secure.

As to Bitcoin, (Nakamoto, 2008) Pierro depicts each Bitcoin as a number, and that these numbers are the response for a condition. Each new response for the condition makes another bitcoin and the exhibition of creating an answer is assigned "mining." Once mined, a bitcoin can be traded or exchanged, and each trade produces a segment into the blockchain's activity log. This is regularly suggested as a "record." What makes the blockchain champion is that the record isn't guaranteed or taken care of by one association, yet rather every trade drove has a copy of the focal points of that trade set aside on every PC that was a piece of the trade.

(Ekblaw et. al., 2016) study shows that clinical data is not, at this point restricted to compose news, study of images, and testing blood sample. Genomic information and to facilitate gathered by wearable gadgets, for example, arm bands and watches installed with sensors, are progressively aggregated. Whenever abused viably, the accessibility of the new types of information may prompt superior healing choices and results and might likewise be analyzed by medical coverage organizations offer limits designed for "solid" conduct. Further advantages emerge in the domain of computerized reasoning. (Zhang et. al., 2017) at the point when given the suitable information, this can gather patterns from the information that are then used to produce populace level knowledge, thus accomplish populace wellbeing overall. These new information designs, nonetheless, will require cautious combination to permit suitable examination while keeping up quiet protection and protection from programmers.

(Crosby, 2016) identifies that despite the fact that digitization of wellbeing records has been set up in the overall specialist (GP) area for more than 30 years (though inadequate with regards to fundamental information sharing and trading capacities), optional consideration has not yet effectively accomplished this true norm. Appropriated record innovation, started and exemplified by the bitcoin blockchain, is growingly affecting IT conditions in which compliance to authoritative guidelines and support of open trust is progressively foremost, and it might be utilized in acknowledging digital objective. The point of this survey be to sum up the proof identifying with the execution of blockchain to oversee electronic wellbeing records (EHRs) in addition to examine whether this might get better productivity of record the executives.

(Danbar, 2012) said it is additionally significant that the target of this survey isn't simply to distinguish the utilization or the instances of blockchain based application in medical services, yet in addition to comprehend the constraints and difficulties for the blockchain-based medical care applications just as the momentum patterns regarding the specialized methodologies, strategies, and ideas utilized in building up these applications (defeating the restrictions) in a vision to unwind the territories for prospect examination. Also, this audit covers numerous new equipment that has not been distributed by the hour of the past surveys. As eminent before, the utilization of blockchain in medical care is a generally new worldview which is developing quickly.

The remainder of the paper discusses the vulnerabilities in present healthcare data storage system and how these can be overcome using blockchain. Each vulnerability is discussed along with how it affects the security and access of data in section 3. Centralized data has been a popular data storing approach in healthcare; however, alternative approaches have not been explored. Further, section 4 explains the basic working of blockchain. Terminologies such as "distributed ledger technology" and "SSL certificate" are explained. It also explains the decentralized storage and traceability of blockchain. Section 5, the final section, discusses the integration of blockchain in healthcare and how its use can transition the healthcare storage for the better.

Inspiration and Contribution

As opposed to the referenced documents, this proposed work depicts an orderly audit plus investigation of the cutting edge blockchain investigation in the ground of medical care. The aim of this work is likewise to show the expected use of block chain in medical care and to give you an idea about the difficulties and likely bearings of research in blockchain. This orderly audit just incorporates research that presents another arrangement, calculation, strategy, philosophy, or design in the ground of medical services. Audit form research, conversations of potential use as well as utilizations of blockchain, and various not significant distributions are avoided.

LITERATURE REVIEW

Few education institutes, organizations have linked blockchain technologies into teaching, and largely universities and organizations use it to help managers learn and learn the summative assessment of outcomes. This technology is able to calculate the entire transcription. In official learning environment, these include learning content and results, as well as academic performance and academic statements. In these areas, in the leisure learning environment, data on research engagement, competence, web-based learning, and additional single premiums are included. This information can be securely placed and arranged in a blockchain in a fitting manner.

Decentralization points to procedures for the identification, storage, support and dissemination of information on blockchains, which depend on the framework of the dissemination. In this arrangement, the faith flanked by the communicating hubs is achieved through science and technology to a certain extent than the gathering of associations.

Traceability includes that every exchanges on the blockchain are planned in sequential requests, while squares identify two consecutive squares by cryptographic hashing. In this way, each exchange can be identified by looking at the square data connected by the hash key. Blockchain technology is permanent for two reasons. From one point of view, all exchanges are placed in a square where one hash key joins the past square and a hash key indicates the square behind. Chaos of any exchange produces various hashes and is therefore recognized by the various centres that run similar approval calculations. Then, the blockchain is a shareable open record, placed on many hubs, and all records are constantly being adjusted. Effective changes require changes to more than 51% of system records.

(Mettler M, 2016) Blockchain technology and encryption funds cannot distinguish any blockchain organization with digital currency attributes. The essence of blockchain technology is peer-to-peer exchange, which does not include outsiders, which means that all exchanges do not require the cooperation of outsiders. The dissemination of advanced funds that rely on blockchain technology has been resolved. In the Bitcoin the age of advanced cash is achieved through the use of explicit mining calculations and is limited by pre-characterized formulations. Therefore, problems such as swelling or falling do not occur. In the Blockchain version 2.0 and version 3.0 applications, a mix of different exercises, like management exercises, teaching exercises, plus money-related exercises, can make these non-currency practice cash assets.

VULNERABILITIES IN HEALTH CARE DATA STORAGE

Current Infrastructure

Currently, there are a number of different health data frameworks that store individual patient information in a large health data warehouse. These data systems are ordered in a variety of ways. In order to solve the problem of connecting a unique health information storage system, various standards have emerged. In the current agreement, to hand is no extensively recognized agreement, the issue of information trading is again a real problem.

Centralized Data Storage

A centralized framework can provide the information you need in a fairly smooth way, with a focus on centralization itself. Excessive authorization in the hands of the central government has led to a complex licensing system that includes the possibility of data breaches and information disclosure.

Multiple Devices

Medical institutions are equipped with a variety of gadgets. As healthcare workers use their gadgets for expert purposes, it becomes more and more complex. Customers, IT increases the risk of security, which is now diverse and difficult to explain.

Embedded Devices

Even if the problem is solved, the connection is prone to problems. The same seamless connection enables tracking and logging to easily open healthcare IT networks to various forms of cyber threats, including viruses.

Patient data availability

Information is one of the most significant resources in the creation of medical care frameworks. Getting to this advantage makes a great deal of issues. Members inspired by this information are basically patients, care suppliers and outsiders who can utilize this information for various interests. Locale ought to give clear rules with regards to which outsiders, under what conditions and for what reason. Currently, the regulations are unclear and inconsistent, so if the healthcare system even contains any solutions, it usually contains inconsistent solutions.

Interoperability

Wellbeing information is dynamic and broad, and consistent trade of wellbeing information across wellbeing data frameworks would be invaluable. As it would not be reasonable regarding speed, stock-piling limit, or supportability to repeat all wellbeing records on each PC in the blockchain organize, rather activist blockchain as a strategy in the direction of oversee right of entry control (savvy indenture the board) by efficiently putting away a list of all clients' wellbeing accounts and connected metadata. Every occasion information is put to the EHR by a specialist (portable application), a metadata pointer to this be further added to the blockchain, whilst the information are put away safely resting on cloud. A complete file of a specific patient's accounts is put away in a solitary area alongside related metadata, paying little heed to the whereabouts of the clinical information. The blockchain, with this made sure about file of records, at that point guides approved people to the cloud-based information, along these lines permitting the prompt trade of data between endorsed experts, while likewise keeping an unchanging record of those pursuers.

(Ivan D, 2016) described the method that blockchain relies upon open source programming moreover has potential focal points, as prosperity trust can use the open application programming border to fuse data, give them ideal induction to correct information in a setup which can be used by them. Trying interoperability is moreover a key part of the Health Information Technology for Economic and Clinical Health Act, inferred 2011; American clinical consideration providers have been known cash related spurring powers to display critical usage of EHRs.

Health

Quick admittance to a far reaching group of patient information permit specialists to get patients devoid of the necessitate hang tight for the appearance of past outcomes. The accessibility of brief as well as more continuous information would permit doctors to make specific treatment plans based on results and treatment adequacy. Day by day wellbeing information would likewise draw in a patient added in their medical services, and get better quiet consistence a notable test in the domain. The capacity of custom-ized medication, consequently, is better with this interoperability, as a solitary passageway for every one constant wellbeing information is made for every patient. Information accumulated from handheld sensors and portable applications would add data on the dangers and advantages of medicines, in addi-tion to persistent announced result process.

Reliability

The unchanging nature of a blockchain that comes as of connecting the hash of resulting squares conveys by means of characteristic trustworthiness because squares can't be revised devoid of the coordinated effort of a larger part of hubs. This is critical to keeping up a genuine documentation of patient supplier communications just as information starting from gadgets, the two of which could impact clinical choices as well as those including protection. A framework that permits patients to maintain ownership of their clinical pictures, alongside a permanent chain of guardianship. Impermanent tokens are able to be made by blockchain clients and voted for onto those, for example, medical concern suppliers, life insurance provider agencies, giving brief access to patients.

The voucher is free of the information, contain just approval orders, and is checked and approved previous to the necessary information are sent. Respectability may likewise be kept up by the utilization of outside evaluators, who may confirm framework exactness continuously and reflectively. Expected approaches to improve the respectability are to utilize daze marks, which fortify assurance from altering just as affirming the sender's and watcher's characters, or to utilize marks from different specialists.

Security

(Guo, 2018) explained touchy information must be remained careful from spies and interlopers. Penetrates negatively affect the open view of the medical services field and take steps to obstruct future exploration through more tough administrative limitations. The WannaCry assault of May 2017 contaminated a large number of PCs around the world. One prior assault in US States focused on electronic health records specifically, requesting a huge number of dollars in recover. A blockchain is safer than heritage techniques, which give patients with qualifications. It accomplishes these belongings by the utilization of open key cryptography. This includes creating an open and private key for every client utilizing a single direction encryption work, known as a hash. It's absolutely impossible for anybody yet the beneficiary to observe data conveyed over the blockchain, as it is made sure about by their secret key.

WORKING OF BLOCKCHAIN

The blockchain is essentially a decentralized, digitized, open record that includes all the cryptocurrency exchanges and uses known to distributed ledger technology. (Underwood, 2016) mentioned the use of a centralized architecture and simple login is an important part of a regular system. There is not much money available for investment security, and all of these efforts can be made if employees and customers can use it to modify or destroy it. Blockchain offers powerful opportunities and solves a single point at a certain time. With the help of blocking, the security system used in the organization can provide users with useful devices and distributed public key information structures. This security system provides a specific SSL certificate for each device. The production of the certificate was carried out on the blockade, which made it impossible for the manufacturer to use the fake certificate.

Decentralized Storage

Blockchains prevent users from placing their computers on their computers in their network. Still, they can be sure that this product will not collide. In the real world, if someone who is not the owner of a component (such as a component) tries to block the component, the entire system excludes a block that can prevent it from being distinguished from other components. If this type of block is located by the system, it simply excludes the block from the block and identifies it as valid.

Traceability

Every task performed on a private or public block is done in a time and digitally signed manner. This way you can complete each task in a public place and then find the corresponding features on the block. This situation relies on non-repudiation: some people have not proved that their signal is the authenticity of the document. This blocking feature increases the reliability of the system and encrypts the user with each check.

BLOCKCHAIN IN HEALTHCARE

The constantly updated distributed database brings much reward to healthcare industry. The reward is more than ever exciting as multiple parties want to access the same data. For example, medical treatment in areas of aged care or chronic disease is a predetermined field of application in which blockchain technology can create added value. (Broderson et. al., 2016) the number of media disruptions involved in the treatment of patients involved in various mediators, media changes, numerous clinical health facts and incompatible IT interfaces may result in prolonged with supply wide correlations Certification and information flow for medicinal stakeholders.

(Yue et. al., 2016) the implementation of blockchain in healthcare will work similarly to how a bitcoin transaction takes place. The patient and the doctor will be the two parties involved in the transaction and all the medical data of the patient will be stored in the form of chains with hash functions for extraction of data. This will enable the patient or the doctor to extract data whenever necessary. Blockchain will also provide data security as the medical information is only accessible by the parties involved and does not require authorization by a third party. Since it is decentralized, it also prevents access of data by any third party. All the information is traceable and is time-stamped for ease of availability of healthcare information.

A US company is effectively engaged with this region and, accordingly, delivered the Gem Health network dependent on the Ethereum technology. This mutual organization foundation; diverse medical services specialists can get to similar records. These likewise allow the making of another polish of Blockchain based applications in medical care that would open squandered assets and healing issues. (Peterson et. al., 2016) Consequently, the Gem wellness network speaks to medical services environmental factors that consolidate the two organizations, people and specialists and which, simultaneously, upgrade understanding focused on care while tending to operational execution issues. This organization is a case of a Blockchain approach that offers all pertinent clinical partners straightforward and clear admittance to bleeding edge treatment data. Additionally, the Swiss computerized wellbeing, fire up, adopts a drastically new strategy with regards to the treatment of information exchanges and the sharing of individual wellbeing information. This start company offers its clients a stage on which they can store and deal with their wellbeing data in a safe situation.

(Banerjee et. al., 2018), the Blockchain library model sponsorships the ability to create and change essentially all through the blockchain lifetime by including new individuals with varying legitimate connections. Its advancement is particularly useful for recording the steady and predictable improvement of trades. EHR structure, there is an upper bound on the quantity of records, which is the quantity of occupants it serves. People improvement is by and large more slow than the advancement of the quantity of monetary trades, for the model, in the Bitcoin technology. Chain structure in blockchain also maintains the ever-creating clinical files by keeping up a reliably creating associated summary of clinical records; in which each square contain a details of timestamp and an association with a past square.

(Mannaro et. al., 2018) an elective arrangement would be a Blockchain containing pointers to off-chain information; the metadata which are related with the pointers be able to incorporate data requisite for following interoperability. With this methodology, paper information, counting imaging test outcome, might be put away off-chain. With regards to the sharing of imaging test result, a couple of creators proposed putting away encoded wellbeing data legitimately on the Blockchain; in any case, putting away the scrambled imaging investigations of all patients would bring about a tremendous Block chain, that is excessively huge for a hub which is running on a cell phone or an advanced computer unit to extract, store up, approve.

(Kleinaki et. al., 2016) the size of the blockchain is difficult which is under dynamic investigation and it is demonstrated to be a restricting element in any event, for chains that store basic conditional information, considerably less the monstrous hinders that might be required to put away clinical studies. When blockchain keeps on developing, the versatility of the framework might be undermined in light of the fact that just clients who have enormous extra rooms and high computational force will have the option to participate in Blockchain as diggers or complete hubs. To defeat this subject, this technology commonly bolsters 3 kinds of hubs: Complete hubs, light hubs, and document hubs:

Complete Hubs: It is the measure of each exchange and stores each square in the Blockchain.

Light Hubs: It is possible to ensure trades instead of running a full framework centre. Customers should simply maintain a copy of the square headers of the best confirmation of work chain, which can be acquired by addressing framework centre points till they obtain the best lengthy chain. By taking care of the square header, a light centre can watch that a trade is not adjusted devoid of submitting colossal fragments of blockchain memory. Light centres can in like manner contact the data they want.

Document Hubs: It stores each exchange with square on the technology blockchain. Likewise, they store up exchange receipts and the whole position tree.

CONCLUSION

This paper has shown how the use of blockchain in the healthcare industry for the use of storing data can help solve the various problems. Although this technology has been around for a few years, it has still not been utilized to its full potential. Integrating blockchain with healthcare information storage will not only provide the much-needed security but will also enable patients to access their data without the presence of a middle man. This omission of a middle party prevents many errors and security faults which are otherwise common. Migrating the existing network to blockchain could initially be expensive. However, as shown above, the overall advantages of this outweigh the limitations by a large degree. This technology opens new doors to the working and management of the healthcare industry.

Today, some of the people own belongings but can't establish possession or rights, like intellectual property disputes. It might cause clashes with others. Some business information, for example, auxiliary outlines, corporate plans, perhaps taken. The innovation of blockchain can be utilized to secure these asset benefits by putting away information in a block chain network. Blockchain innovation shields instructors' encouraging plans from being usurped, along these lines improving the security of protected innovation insurance. Security implies that every center keeps the whole record, including all information aside from the genuine element. So as to secure protection, the client's particular distinguishing proof is totally demonstrated by the ID number. This implies blockchain innovation can ensure the protection of brokers as just they will have the private key.

REFERENCES

Banerjee, M., Lee, J., & Choo, K. K. R. (2018). A blockchain future for internet of things security: A position paper. *Digital Communications and Networks*, *4*(3), 149–160. doi:10.1016/j.dcan.2017.10.006

Brodersen, C., Kalis, B., Leong, C., Mitchell, E., Pupo, E., Truscott, A., & Accenture, L. (2016). *Blockchain: Securing a new health interoperability experience*. Accenture LLP.

Crosby, M., Pattanayak, P., Verma, S., & Kalyanaraman, V. (2016). Blockchain technology: Beyond bitcoin. *Applied Innovation*, *2*(6-10), 71.

Dankar, F. K., & El Emam, K. (2012, March). The application of differential privacy to health data. In *Proceedings of the 2012 Joint EDBT/ICDT Workshops* (pp. 158-166). 10.1145/2320765.2320816

Ekblaw, A., Azaria, A., Halamka, J. D., & Lippman, A. (2016). A Case Study for Blockchain in Healthcare:"MedRec" prototype for electronic health records and medical research data. Proceedings of IEEE open & big data conference, 13.

Fan, K., Ren, Y., Wang, Y., Li, H., & Yang, Y. (2017). Blockchain-based efficient privacy preserving and data sharing scheme of content-centric network in 5G. *IET Communications*, *12*(5), 527–532. doi:10.1049/iet-com.2017.0619

Gordon, W. J., & Catalini, C. (2018). Blockchain technology for healthcare: Facilitating the transition to patient-driven interoperability. *Computational and Structural Biotechnology Journal*, *16*, 224–230. doi:10.1016/j.csbj.2018.06.003 PMID:30069284

Guo, R., Shi, H., Zhao, Q., & Zheng, D. (2018). Secure attribute-based signature scheme with multiple authorities for blockchain in electronic health records systems. *IEEE Access: Practical Innovations, Open Solutions*, *6*, 11676–11686. doi:10.1109/ACCESS.2018.2801266

Ivan, D. (2016, August). Moving toward a blockchain-based method for the secure storage of patient records. In *ONC/NIST Use of Blockchain for Healthcare and Research Workshop. Gaithersburg, Maryland, United States: ONC/NIST* (pp. 1-11). Academic Press.

Kleinaki, A. S., Mytis-Gkometh, P., Drosatos, G., Efraimidis, P. S., & Kaldoudi, E. (2018). A blockchain-based notarization service for biomedical knowledge retrieval. *Computational and Structural Biotechnology Journal*, *16*, 288–297. doi:10.1016/j.csbj.2018.08.002 PMID:30181840

Kuo, T. T., Kim, H. E., & Ohno-Machado, L. (2017). Blockchain distributed ledger technologies for biomedical and health care applications. *Journal of the American Medical Informatics Association*, *24*(6), 1211–1220. doi:10.1093/jamia/ocx068 PMID:29016974

Lohr, K. N., & Donaldson, M. S. (Eds.). (1994). *Health data in the information age: use, disclosure, and privacy*. National Academies Press.

Mannaro, K., Baralla, G., Pinna, A., & Ibba, S. (2018). A blockchain approach applied to a teledermatology platform in the Sardinian region (Italy). *Information*, *9*(2), 44. doi:10.3390/info9020044

Mettler, M. (2016, September). Blockchain technology in healthcare: The revolution starts here. In *2016 IEEE 18th international conference on e-health networking, applications and services (Healthcom)* (pp. 1-3). IEEE.

Nakamoto, S. (2008). *Bitcoin: A peer-to-peer electronic cash system*. Retrieved from https://bitcoin.org/ bitcoin.pdf

Peterson, K., Deeduvanu, R., Kanjamala, P., & Boles, K. (2016, September). A blockchain-based approach to health information exchange networks. In *Proc. NIST Workshop Blockchain Healthcare* (*Vol. 1*, No. 1, pp. 1-10). Academic Press.

Pilkington, M. (2016). Blockchain technology: principles and applications. In *Research handbook on digital transformations*. Edward Elgar Publishing. doi:10.4337/9781784717766.00019

Wang, H., & Song, Y. (2018). Secure cloud-based EHR system using attribute-based cryptosystem and blockchain. *Journal of Medical Systems*, *42*(8), 152. doi:10.100710916-018-0994-6 PMID:29974270

Yue, X., Wang, H., Jin, D., Li, M., & Jiang, W. (2016). Healthcare data gateways: Found healthcare intelligence on blockchain with novel privacy risk control. *Journal of Medical Systems*, *40*(10), 218. doi:10.100710916-016-0574-6 PMID:27565509

Zhang, P., White, J., Schmidt, D. C., & Lenz, G. (2017). *Applying software patterns to address interoperability in blockchain-based healthcare apps*. arXiv preprint arXiv:1706.03700

Zyskind, G., & Nathan, O. (2015). Decentralizing privacy: Using blockchain to protect personal data. In 2015 IEEE Security and Privacy Workshops (pp. 180-184). IEEE.

This research was previously published in Applications of Artificial Intelligence for Smart Technology; pages 90-102, copyright year 2021 by Engineering Science Reference (an imprint of IGI Global).

Chapter 43
Use of Internet of Things With Data Prediction on Healthcare Environments:
A Survey

Gabriel Souto Fischer
Universidade do Vale do Rio dos Sinos - Unisinos, São Leopoldo, Brazil

Rodrigo da Rosa Righi
(iD) https://orcid.org/0000-0001-5080-7660
Universidade do Vale do Rio dos Sinos - Unisinos, São Leopoldo Brazil

Vinicius Facco Rodrigues
(iD) https://orcid.org/0000-0001-6129-0548
Universidade do Vale do Rio dos Sinos - Unisinos, São Leopoldo, Brazil

Cristiano André da Costa
Universidade do Vale do Rio dos Sinos - Unisinos, São Leopoldo, Brazil

ABSTRACT

Internet of Things (IoT) is a constantly growing paradigm that promises to revolutionize healthcare applications and could be associated with several other techniques. Data prediction is another widely used paradigm, where data captured over time is analyzed in order to identify and predict problematic situations that may happen in the future. After research, no surveys that address IoT combined with data prediction in healthcare area exist in the literature. In this context, this work presents a systematic literature review on Internet of Things applied to healthcare area with a focus on data prediction, presenting twenty-three papers about this theme as results, as well as a comparative analysis between them. The main contribution for literature is a taxonomy for IoT systems with data prediction applied to healthcare. Finally, this article presents the possibilities and challenges of exploration in the study area, showing the existing gaps for future approaches.

DOI: 10.4018/978-1-6684-7132-6.ch043

INTRODUCTION

Internet of Things (IoT) is a computational concept where physical objects and ``things'' are connected through a network structure and are part of the internet activities in order to exchange information about themselves and about objects and things around themselves (Singh & Kapoor, 2017). The development of this paradigm is in constant growth because of the continuous efforts of the research community since IoT allows unlimited applications to solve unlimited needs in all spheres of life. Thus, in a not-so-distant future, everything in our homes, workplaces, and study will have a unique internet address and, through the network, it will be possible to monitor and control any of our "things" (Singh & Kapoor, 2017). According to Sarhan (2018), IoT is used in various domains, such as airports, military, and healthcare. IoT enables the devices to interact not only with each other but with services and people on a global scale (Akeju, Butakov, & Aghili, 2018). The world is undergoing an unprecedented technological transformation that evolves isolated systems to ubiquitous internet-enabled "things" capable of generating and exchanging large amounts of valuable data. The IoT is a new reality that is completely changing everyday life. In addition, it also promises to revolutionize healthcare applications, enabling a more personalized, preventive and collaborative way of caring for patients (Pinto, Cabral, & Gomes, 2017).

According to Senthilkumar, Manikandan, Devi and Lokesh (2018), IoT remote health monitoring systems have advantages over traditional health monitoring systems. Patients can use health sensors 24 hours a day for monitoring. A nurse or doctor can observe a patient for a limited time by day, but critical health issues can occur at any moment. Based on this, 24/7 monitoring of health facts is crucial, and it is necessary. In this context, IoT assisted patients can be accessed for medical staff over the internet and by other systems, the health state of a patient can be supervised uninterruptedly, being possible to detect health risk situations at the right time, in order to be possible to apply the appropriate countermeasures. Also, IoT can support to collect health records that can be used to generate statistic information correlated to a health condition. Using these statistics, surveillance and risk drawing of diseases can be completed using remote health data. According to Singh (2018), using IoT, systems are able to analyze and predict health disorders in early stage through Data Prediction techniques applied to generated data.

There are people who, when they have a health problem, can make an appointment in a clinic with a doctor they trust. Other people decide to go to the most appropriate hospital for their needs. In other cases, the health situation is so critical that the only alternative is to go as quickly as possible to hospital care. Thus, hospitals and healthcare environments are extremely important service points for the general population to perform one of the most important tasks: to ensure medical treatment. There are many environments, resources and processes within a hospital to accomplish this task. Thus, it becomes interesting to have effective control over how these resources and processes are being used and executed in order to identify optimization points. This becomes even more necessary when it comes across the Brazilian reality, where hospitals are increasingly crowded with people to attend. When a hospital or emergency care unit is opened, usually it takes a long time until it exceeds its service capacity. If it were possible to identify when the points of care and resources would have a demand higher than their ability to attend, it would be possible to establish action plans to minimize or perhaps even eliminate these bottlenecks in the healthcare environments systems. However, how can one analyze and define when this moment is about to arrive? Relying only on the judgment of people who work with these resources, with no efficient way of recording their uses, and no statistically reliable prediction system can become a problem, with a high probability of errors in their evaluation.

In this context, in order to identify the state of the art for IoT systems with Data Prediction applied to healthcare and to discuss the main open issues, this work surveys the main contributions of the scientific community over the last years. The main objective of this work is to review the use of Internet of Things combined with Data Prediction in healthcare literature and describe the existing models. As a way of mapping this study scenario, we used the systematic literature review methodology to choose the studies (Roehrs, Costa, Righi, & Oliveira, 2017). As a result, were reviewed scientific studies published in the last years, selected the most significant approaches, and thoroughly surveyed the use of IoT combined with Data Prediction in the healthcare field. Also, was developed an updated and wide taxonomy for IoT systems with Data Prediction applied to healthcare and indicated challenges and possibilities for future study. Contributions were also proposed in the field from the study of related works, which are an updated taxonomy and an updated vision about main challenges and possibilities about the use of IoT with Data Prediction applied to healthcare.

This article is organized as follows: Section 2 presents the background, bringing other surveys in this scenario, and gaps in their approaches. Section 3 presents the article selection process through a systematic literature review for Health IoT systems, bringing a comparison between the selected studies. Section 4 presents the state of the art for the Internet of Things combined with Data Prediction in healthcare literature. This section also describes a taxonomy proposed in this work for IoT systems with Data Prediction applied to healthcare. Section 5 presents the possibilities and challenges for exploring the Internet of Things paradigm and Data Prediction techniques to improve healthcare processes and, finally, Section 6 presents the conclusions and proposed future works.

BACKGROUND

The use of Data Prediction combined with IoT applied to healthcare has several uses and a lot of potentials and can help to identify diseases and risk situations before they happen. After a literature review, only surveys that address the Internet of Things and healthcare in a common context were found. When the search was extended for Data Prediction, few surveys were found that bring some question related to forecast techniques. This is the case of the review conducted by Darshan and Anandakumar (2015) on the usage of IoT in the healthcare system and did not address the use of Data Prediction in any of the reviewed articles. The relation of the research with prediction is in the results since as the authors did not find an approach for prediction of chronic disorders in wearable devices context, they proposed a methodology for this. Another study is a survey conducted by Meharouech, Elias, and Mehaoua (2015) on ubiquitous healthcare. The focus of the research was on the use of ubiquitous devices for the health area, and some of the studies addressed, provided approaches for the mobility prediction of patients. Based on this, it can be noted that although there are surveys that address the use of IoT in the health area, there are still no surveys which combine Data Prediction in this area of study, that means there is no global view of it in the literature. Although there are taxonomies such as the one proposed by Meharouech et al. (2015), they focus only on IoT in the healthcare area and do not address Data Prediction.

ARTICLE SELECTION

This section presents a systematic review of the literature to identify and provide the state of the art of academic research in the healthcare area, related to the concept of Internet of Things, focusing on Data Prediction to predict and prevent problems. This type of literature review was selected to summarize the technology in relation to this topic, in a way that does not require in-depth analysis and synthesis. For this systematic literature review, the following activities were used, as reviewed by Roehrs et al. (2017):

1. **Research Questions:** Presents the research questions elaborated for this systematic review;
2. **Search Strategy:** Describes the explored libraries and the strategy to collect the data;
3. **Article Selection:** Define the steps taken to filter and select the studies;
4. **Quality Assessment:** Describe the quality assessment of the selected studies;
5. **Data Extraction:** Compare the selected papers and research questions.

Research Questions

According to Roehrs et al. (2017), the definition of research questions is one of the most important parts of any systematic literature review. This study aims to identify and classify the technology related to IoT use in healthcare combined with Data Prediction; the resources, problems, challenges, and solutions that are currently being considered; and the research opportunities that exist or are emerging. For this work, two types of questions were defined: General Question (QG) and Specific Questions (SQ). Table 1 shows the research questions raised for this search of works related to the research theme of this document.

Table 1. Research questions

Group and Identifier	Question
General Question	
GQ1	How would the taxonomy for IoT systems with Data Prediction applied to healthcare appear?
Specific Question	
SQ1	What are the data that are included in an IoT system with Data Prediction applied to healthcare?
SQ2	What are the technologies and standards that apply to IoT systems with Data Prediction applied to healthcare?
SQ3	Which are the techniques or methods used to input information into IoT systems with Data Prediction applied to healthcare?
SQ4	What are the goals of IoT systems with Data Prediction applied to healthcare?
SQ5	What are the architecture models of IoT systems with Data Prediction applied to healthcare?

The proposed General Question brings a broad classification related to the IoT systems with Data Prediction for the healthcare area. GQ1 refers to classifying and defining a taxonomy for existing IoT systems with Data Prediction applied to healthcare. To improve the filtering process of the studies, in order to guide and facilitate the process of identifying the answer for GQ1, some Specific Questions were defined. SQ1 seeks to identify the types of data an IoT system with Data Prediction applied to healthcare can contain. SQ2 investigates the types of standards that are used for IoT systems with Data Prediction applied to healthcare. SQ3 seeks to show how information is inserted into the proposed systems. SQ4 investigates what are the goals that IoT systems with Data Prediction applied to healthcare have. SQ5 focuses on architecture models for IoT systems with Data Prediction applied to healthcare.

Search Strategy

The next step was to identify a set of studies related to research questions. In this process, the search keywords and the definition of the search scope were defined. These words were defined to obtain research results focused on the theme of this systematic review. Therefore, the Search String located in Textbox 1 was defined for the search and selection of articles in electronic academic databases.

Textbox 1. Search string

```
((prediction OR analytics OR forecast OR time serie) AND (Internet of Things
OR IoT OR sensors) AND (health OR healthcare OR hospitalar OR clinical))
```

To cover a large number of related studies, several electronic scientific libraries were selected as the basis for research on the articles, listed in Table 2. According to Roehrs et al. (2017), these portals are some of that cover the most relevant journals and conferences of the computer science area. The period utilized for search in the electronic databases was between 2010 and 2018.

Table 2. Electronic databases for article search

Acronym	Electronic Database Name
ACM	ACM Digital Library
Google Scholar	Google Scholar
IEEE	IEEE Xplore Digital Library
IET	IET Digital Library
PubMed	National Center for Biotechnology Information, U.S. National Library of Medicine
ScienceDirect	Elsevier B. V. ScienceDirect
Wiley	Wiley Online Library

Article Selection

After all articles were found in the electronic databases using the Search String, were carried out a process of removing articles that would not be relevant to this research, in order to keep only those that would be more representative to the theme. Thus, all works that did not address the use of Internet of Things combined with Data Prediction to prevent problems in healthcare were removed. Therefore, the following exclusion criterion was defined for article selection:

Exclusion Criterion 1: Article does not address the use of Internet of Things in healthcare.
Exclusion Criterion 2: Article does not address Data Prediction techniques to prevent problems.

According to Roehrs et al. (2017), an important step in the systematic review is the definition of the filtering process of the articles. As a result, the following steps were defined for the filtering and selection process: (I) Filter by Title, (II) Filter by Abstract, and (III) Filter by Full Text. First, the titles of the articles were analyzed, so that those who did not address the Internet of Things and Health were excluded, according to Exclusion Criterion 1. After, the abstract of the remaining articles was analyzed so that the articles that do not address the use of IoT in healthcare could be excluded, according to Exclusion Criterion 1. At the same stage, are also excluded the articles in which nothing was found in their abstracts regarding Data Prediction, according to Exclusion Criterion 2. Finally, the texts of the articles filtered in the previous stages were read and the exclusion criterion was applied again, removing those that did not address the proposal of that systematic review.

Quality Assessment

According to Roehrs et al. (2017), it is essential to evaluate the quality of the selected papers, in order to verify if it is really relevant to the study. Thus, the selected articles were evaluated in relation to the parameters used by Roehrs et al. (2017): the purpose of the research, contextualization, literature review, related works, methodology, results obtained and the conclusion, related to the proposed objectives, and an indication of future works. Based on this, Table 3 was elaborated, presenting the quality criteria in the form of questions to which the selected articles were submitted for validation of their quality.

Table 3. Quality assessment criteria

Identifier	Criteria
C1	Does the article clearly show the purpose of the research?
C2	Does the article adequately describe the research context through a literature review?
C3	Does the article present the related work to the main contribution?
C4	Does the article have a description of a proposed architecture or research methodology?
C5	Does the article present results for the research?
C6	Does the article present a study conclusion related to the research objectives?
C7	Does the article present some future work, improvements or some future study?

Data Extraction

In order to gather the information about the paper previously raised, a comparison was made between the chosen articles and the research questions. Table 4 shows how they were compared, bringing each item of the related papers to the research, in order to have a better way to extract details of the articles and understand how studies have addressed issues related to the research questions proposed in the systematic literature review performed in this paper.

Table 4. Review of articles with research questions

Section	Description	Research Questions
Metadata		
Title	Title of article	GQ1, SQ1, SQ2, SQ5
Abstract	Summary of paper with method and results	GQ1, SQ1, SQ2, SQ5
Keywords	Words representing the article content	GQ1, SQ1, SQ2, SQ5
Article		
Introduction	Section introducing the addressed problem	All questions
Background	Section presenting concepts about the article them	All questions
Method	Presents the proposed scientific methodology	All questions
Results	Covers results acquired after evaluation	All questions
Discussion	Compare article results with the literature	SQ2-SQ5
Conclusion	Relate objectives and hypotheses	SQ2-SQ5

Selected Studies

In Table 5 all selected articles are presented, bringing: (I) An identifier for each of them, (II) Author names in bibliographic reference format, (III) The article Publisher, and (IV) Type of publication, which may be Journal Article or Conference Article. The papers were sorted in ascending order by year of publication and, after, order by alphabetical order of authors' names.

Performing the Quality Assessment

In Figure 1 the satisfied Quality Criteria are presented for each of the selected works, based on the Quality Assessment Criteria proposed in Table 3. The criteria satisfied by each article are shown on the vertical axis, and the articles themselves on the horizontal axis, according to the Identifiers previously defined. After this quality assessment, it may be noted that most of the articles could reach 6 or 7 quality criteria.

STATE OF THE ART

Based on the selected articles, it was possible to identify that there are currently several fronts and approaches when the objective is to predict issues related to the health of a patient using the Internet of Things and Data Prediction concepts. Through the articles surveyed it was possible to see that it is not only possible to use the technology for this, as it is already being used in several approaches in the scientific community. Most of the IoT systems with Data Prediction applied to healthcare researched focus on the monitoring of the patient's health conditions, in order to generate alerts if any risk situations are identified. These systems are able to predict when the patient's vital signs will be at risk, identify health problems and diseases, and environmental risk situations for patients. Table 6 presents a comparison between the collected papers, relating some of their main characteristics.

Table 5. Selected studies

Identifier	Authors (Year)	Publisher	Type
A01	Kwon, Shin, Shin, and Kim (2010)	IEEE	Conference
A02	Kan, Chen, Leonelli, and Yang (2015)	IEEE	Conference
A03	Kang, Adibi, Larkin, and Luan (2015)	IEEE	Conference
A04	Orimaye, Leong, Lee, and Ng (2015)	IEEE	Conference
A05	Jouini, Lemlouma, Maalaoui, and Saidane (2016)	IEEE	Conference
A06	Azimi et al. (2017)	ACM	Journal
A07	Chen, Chen, Wu, Hu, and Pan (2017)	Elsevier	Journal
A08	Robben, Englebienne, and Kröse (2017)	IEEE	Journal
A09	Zamanifar, Nazemi, and Vahidi-Asl (2017)	Elsevier	Journal
A10	Ali et al. (2018)	Elsevier	Journal
A11	Basanta, Huang, and Lee (2018)	IEEE	Conference
A12	Bhatia and Sood (2018a)	Elsevier	Journal
A13	Bhatia and Sood (2018b)	Springer	Journal
A14	Farahani et al. (2018)	Elsevier	Journal
A15	Gondalia et al. (2018)	Elsevier	Journal
A16	Huang, Zhao, Zhou, and Jiang (2018)	IEEE	Journal
A17	Kumar, Lokesh, Varatharajan, Babu, and Parthasarathy (2018)	Elsevier	Journal
A18	Manogaran et al. (2018)	Elsevier	Journal
A19	Paudel, Dunn, Eberle, and Chaung (2018)	AAAI	Conference
A20	Sood and Mahajan (2018)	IEEE	Journal
A21	Tan and Halim (2018)	Taylor & Francis	Journal
A22	Thakur et al. (2018)	MDPI	Journal
A23	Verma, Sood and Kalra (2018)	Springer	Journal

Figure 1. Satisfied quality criteria for each selected article

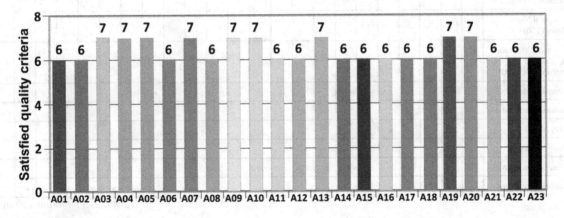

Table 6. Comparative between characteristics of the articles

Characteristics	Reference Articles																						
	A01	A02	A03	A04	A05	A06	A07	A08	A09	A10	A11	A12	A13	A14	A15	A16	A17	A18	A19	A20	A21	A22	A23
Presents mechanisms for security such as																							
Authentication and Authorization of users						•				•	•	•	•	•			•						•
Data encryption						•					•		•	•			•	•					•
Patient privacy											•			•									
Uses the following techniques																							
Cloud Computing		•	•			•					•	•	•	•	•	•	•	•		•	•		•
Fog Computing						•							•	•				•		•			
Data Prediction	•	•	•	•	•	•	•	•	•	•	•	•	•	•	•	•	•	•	•	•	•	•	•
Uses the following techniques to perform prediction																							
Artificial Intelligence				•		•	•			•		•	•		•		•		•	•	•	•	•
Big Data														•					•				
Probability and statistics	•	•	•		•			•	•		•					•		•	•			•	
Use the following prediction algorithms and models																							
Adaptative Boosting (AdaBoost)																			•			•	
Artificial Neural Networks (ANN)							•					•								•	•		
Decision Tree																			•				
Fuzzy Logic									•								•						
K-Means clustering															•								
K-Nearest Neighbors																			•			•	•
Linear Discriminant Analysis																			•				
Random Forest																			•			•	
Support Vector Machines (SVM)				•		•													•			•	
Temporal Naive Bayes (TNB)													•										
Disease Combination Appearance Probability (DCAP)	•																						
Bayesian inference			•													•							
Gaussian function		•																					
Grey Model					•																		
Hidden Markov									•														
Linear Regression								•															
Logistic Regression																			•	•		•	

continues on following page

Table 6. Continued

Characteristics	Reference Articles																						
	A01	A02	A03	A04	A05	A06	A07	A08	A09	A10	A11	A12	A13	A14	A15	A16	A17	A18	A19	A20	A21	A22	A23
Multi Criteria Decision Making Analytical Hierarchy Process (MCDM–AHP)											•												
Regression Forest.,								•															
Performs prediction for the following cases																							
Future status of vital signs and conditions of the patient's health	•		•		•	•		•		•		•	•							•		•	•
Anticipate risk situations for patients							•								•								
Identify the patient's future location				•					•														
Identify the incidence of diseases in future		•								•							•	•	•	•	•		•

Based on the Research Questions defined in Research Questions Section, was performed the data extraction process of the selected articles in order to determine the State of the Art of Internet of Things and Data Prediction in healthcare systems. Next, are presented the General Question and the Specific Questions used to help answer the General Question, along with the answers found for each of them.

GQ1: How Would the Taxonomy for IoT Systems With Data Prediction Applied to Healthcare Appear?

Were investigated several studies that work with the concept of Internet of Things and Data Prediction applied to situations in the healthcare area. When analyzing the selected articles, it was possible to propose a taxonomy based on important characteristics of the models, in order to help in the classification, comparison, and evaluation of different IoT systems for health. In addition, this classification can provide an overview of possible alternatives in terms of objectives, content, and architectures. The proposed taxonomy is summarized in Table 7, divided into three groups: (I) Structures, (II) Functions and (III) Architecture. Next to each item have a brief description.

Figure 2 presents the proposed taxonomy, bringing the entire classification for IoT systems with Data Prediction applied to healthcare. The next sections of this article present the subclassifications proposed in Table 7, showing how this taxonomy was proposed, also presenting which studies have used each of the structures, functions, and architectures proposed in this work.

Table 7. IoT systems with data prediction applied to healthcare taxonomy summarized

Group	Description
Structures	Data and technologies used in IoT systems with Data Prediction
Data	Data found in the systems (See Table 8)
Technologies	Technologies that can be applied in the systems (See Table 9)
Functions	Describes the main objectives and characteristics present in the systems
Data Source	Techniques for input information in the systems (See Table 10)
Objectives	Represents the aim of the systems (See Table 11)
Architecture	Architecture types (See Table 12)
Models	Describes the architecture models
Prediction	Presents which prediction models were used

Figure 2. IoT systems with data prediction applied to healthcare taxonomy

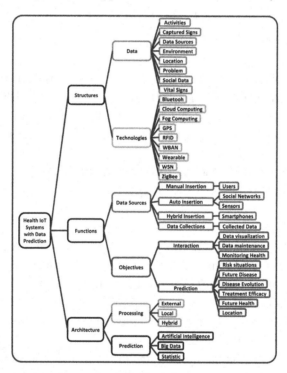

SQ1: What are the Data That are Included in an IoT System With Data Prediction Applied to Healthcare?

To answer this question were analyzed all previously selected articles. The types of data that are included in IoT systems with Data Prediction applied to healthcare are described in Table 8. The data types found are as follows: (I) Activities that a particular patient may be performing, (II) Status of the environment where the patient is located, (III) Data sources, internal or external, with information on diseases, treatments, diagnoses and others, (IV) Data captured through Social Networks, (V) Location of the patient in an environment in any instant of time, (VI) Patient's vital signs captured by the system in real time and (VII) Patient's vital signs captured by examinations and measurements, subsequently inputted into the system. Table 8 lists all data types found and a brief description of each of them.

Table 8. Data found in IoT systems with data prediction applied to healthcare

Data	Description	Reference Articles																						
		A01	A02	A03	A04	A05	A06	A07	A08	A09	A10	A11	A12	A13	A14	A15	A16	A17	A18	A19	A20	A21	A22	A23
Activities	Activities that the patient is performing			•			•		•			•	•	•		•				•				
Captured signs	Vital signs not captured by the system					•			•					•					•		•		•	•
Data sources	Data sources with information on diseases, treatments and related		•				•	•			•	•	•					•	•		•			•
Environment	Status of the patient's environment			•					•			•	•	•		•	•		•	•				•
Location	Where the patient is in an environment			•	•		•	•	•	•						•			•	•				
Problem	Identified health problem	•	•	•		•	•		•		•	•							•	•	•	•		•
Social Data	Social media data							•																
Vital signs	Body function Status	•	•	•			•			•	•	•	•	•	•	•	•		•		•	•	•	•

SQ2: What are the Technologies and Standards That Apply to IoT Systems With Data Prediction Applied to Healthcare?

Many studies use own formats to organize the data they use so that there is not always a standard among them. Thus, there are many technologies that can be used for IoT systems with Data Prediction applied to healthcare. However, in order to answer this question, were analyzed the open industry standards and other technologies that are used in these articles. As there are numerous technologies in this aspect, it was decided to list only those used by more than one article studied. Table 9 presents them, some of them being: Bluetooth, Cloud and Fog Computing, Global Positioning System (GPS), Radio Frequency Identification (RFID), Wireless Body Area Network (WBAN), Wearables, Wireless Sensor Network (WSN), and ZigBee.

SQ3: Which are the Techniques or Methods Used to Input Information Into IoT Systems With Data Prediction Applied to Healthcare?

Another result of this systematic literature review was the identification of the techniques used by the IoT systems with Data Prediction applied to healthcare to perform the insertion of data and information into the applications. Table 10 presents the techniques for insertion of the data in the systems proposed in these articles, bringing a description of each of these techniques. The techniques are divided into four main groups: Data Collection (T1), where the data is inserted through previously created collections of data; Auto Insertion (T2), where information is captured automatically through some techniques and entered into the application; Manual Insertion (T3), where information must be entered manually into the application; Hybrid Insertion (T4), where the same technique can enter information in the system either manually or automatically.

Table 9. IoT systems with data prediction applied to healthcare related technologies

Technology	Description	Reference Articles																						
		A01	A02	A03	A04	A05	A06	A07	A08	A09	A10	A11	A12	A13	A14	A15	A16	A17	A18	A19	A20	A21	A22	A23
Bluetooth	Wireless technology standard	•	•										•		•									
Cloud Computing	Technology for delivery of on-demand computing resources over the internet		•	•			•					•	•	•	•	•			•		•	•		
Fog Computing	Cloud geographically close to the user for latency-sensitive applications						•							•	•				•		•			
GPS	satellite-based radio navigation system														•						•			
RFID	Standard for identification		•							•		•	•	•	•						•			
WBAN	Sensor network		•	•				•	•															
Wearable	Wearable											•	•	•	•	•		•	•					•
WSN	Sensor network							•							•									
ZigBee	Suite of high level communica-tion protocols	•												•	•	•								

Table 10.

Technique	Description	Reference Articles																						
		A01	A02	A03	A04	A05	A06	A07	A08	A09	A10	A11	A12	A13	A14	A15	A16	A17	A18	A19	A20	A21	A22	A23
Data Collection (T1)																								
Collected Data	Previously developed works fed databases that were used by some articles in their processes			•		•		•					•	•				•	•	•		•	•	•
Auto Insertion (T2)																								
Social Networks	Data are captured directly from patients' social media							•																
Sensors	Information captured by sensors is added in applications	•	•	•	•	•	•	•	•	•	•	•	•	•	•	•	•	•	•	•	•	•	•	•
Manual Insertion (T3)																								
Users	Users can manually enter information into systems					•			•												•			
Hybrid Insertion (T4)																								
Smartphones Apps	Smartphone applications can be sources of information inputs					•							•											

SQ4: What are the Goals of IoT Systems With Data Prediction Applied to Healthcare?

This research question presents the main goals or objectives of IoT systems with Data Prediction applied to healthcare. Table 11 presents the objectives found for the articles analyzed in this systematic literature review. It was concluded that the objectives can be divided into two categories: Interaction (O1), that are related to the way of the system will interact with the patients and other users, and Prediction (O2), which are related to the predictions that the system intends to perform in order to prevent in advance life-threatening situations which patients may be exposed.

Table 11. Objectives related to the form of interaction with the system and to the predictions that the system intends to perform

Objectives	Reference Articles																						
	A01	A02	A03	A04	A05	A06	A07	A08	A09	A10	A11	A12	A13	A14	A15	A16	A17	A18	A19	A20	A21	A22	A23
Interaction (O1)																							
Objective patient data visualization in a query tool	•		•											•	•	•	•		•		•		
Objective the maintenance of patient data for themselves or/and for other users of the system, manually																							
Objective monitoring of the health conditions of the patient, in order to generate alerts when a problem identified	•	•	•	•	•	•	•	•	•	•	•	•	•	•				•				•	•
Prediction (O2)																							
Predict risk situations that patients may be exposed							•																
Predict heart disease		•				•					•						•	•	•	•	•		•
Predict future conditions or vital signs of patients' health	•		•		•	•		•		•			•	•	•	•			•			•	•
Predict where the patient will be next, in order to prepare the sensors installed in the healthcare environment to collect the patient information in a non-invasive way				•					•														

SQ5: What are the Models of Architecture of IoT Systems With Data Prediction Applied to Healthcare?

This last specific question aims to identify the main models of architectures used by IoT systems with Data Prediction applied to healthcare in their implementations. After analyzing the articles, were defined two main architecture groups (as shown in Table 12): Processing (A1), which presents the data processing architectures, which are classified in Local, External or Hybrid, and Prediction (A2), which presents the techniques used for the Data Prediction architecture, such Artificial Intelligence, Big Data, and Probability and statistics.

Table 12. Models of data processing and prediction

Model	Description	Reference Articles																						
		A01	A02	A03	A04	A05	A06	A07	A08	A09	A10	A11	A12	A13	A14	A15	A16	A17	A18	A19	A20	A21	A22	A23
Processing (A1)																								
Local	Data is processed locally				•	•				•										•			•	
External	Processing occurs on external server		•					•	•		•	•				•		•						
Hybrid	Data is processed in parts locally and in parts on an external server	•		•			•						•	•	•		•		•		•	•		•
Prediction (A2)																								
Artificial Intelligence	Performed through Artificial Intelligence techniques							•			•		•			•		•		•	•	•	•	•
Big Data	Performed through Big Data techniques													•		•		•						
Probability and Statistics	Performed using probability and statistics techniques	•	•	•	•	•	•		•	•		•		•		•			•	•	•		•	

CHALLENGES AND POSSIBILITIES

It was possible to observe that there are currently several fronts and approaches when the goal is to take care of the health of patients using the Internet of Things concept, and not only this but to anticipate problem situations through Data Prediction techniques. Several systems use different techniques to achieve the same goals. When looking at these systems, it is possible to note that concepts such as Cloud Computing, Fog Computing, Artificial Intelligence, Big Data, Probability, and Statistics are at the top of the world's health research. However, few of these approaches have effective mechanisms to deal with the issue of security in the digital age. And those who have them do not always rely on extremely secure protocols and systems. Some applications do not make use of adaptive computing resources like Cloud Computing, using own resources and own servers that end up becoming single points of failure and, because of that dependability, if a single service stops working, the entire application will fail.

Furthermore, there are many techniques for analyzing the future status of the patient's health conditions, but practically none to predict the evolution of the diseases that the patient already has. The approaches are very focused on analyzing patient health conditions and focus very little on risk situations in the environment where the patient is inserted. Even in this regard, neither approach attempts to analyze the use of hospital resources and, consequently, to predict when these resources will become insufficient for patients care. Thus, it is possible to say that the technology needed to better explore the Internet of

Things concept and Data Prediction in healthcare environments exists and is already used today, but there are few approaches that can merge concepts into one to solve several of the problems raised.

Distributed Environments and Dependability

As can be seen, only half of the approaches studied make use of Cloud Computing and the other half operate on own, apparently centralized, servers. One of the main problems of working with a centralized environment is dependability, that is, with the system running on a single server, if it fails, the entire application will fail. Often, there are several services and servers to perform all the tasks, which makes the problem even worse, because if any one of them fails, the whole application stops working, and will have several services and servers running, but nothing to process.

In this context, a possibility of exploration would be to create techniques and systems capable of operating over distributed environments, with data replication and redundancy of services and servers. One way to do this would be by using the Cloud Computing concept, maintaining the Health IoT application with Data Prediction in a cloud instance. However, one of the major problems of IoT is a large amount of data generated by the most diverse sensors. This way, transmitting all the data to the cloud can take considerable time, and until the data is processed by the application, the problem that is waiting to be predicted will already have happened. Thus, another possibility of exploration would be to propose systems that use Fog Computing, that is, clouds closer to the user, making the transmission occur faster and, in this context, to create techniques to pre-process the data in an appropriate way, eliminating noise and sending only what is needed for the main cloud to perform data processing.

Also, in this context of distributed applications, another possibility of exploration would be to define techniques for virtualization of services, that is, to define techniques to instantiate virtual machines to meet the processing demand, and to perform load balancing between them. Thus, the system would become able to increase and decrease the capacity as required. In this possibility, ways could be proposed to identify when a system is close to reaching its processing limit, to trigger a new virtual machine and, at the same time, to identify the underutilization of the system to disable virtual machines. Also, in this context, techniques could be proposed to divide the tasks between the machines appropriately.

Internet of Things Standards and Technologies

One of the major problems and challenges for the Internet of Things is the absence of standards for data. The proposed systems have different ways of storing data, performing processing, and making it available to users. Data captured by one application can hardly be used by another. The few data that can be used, need an intermediate processing, only to carry out the translation of the same between the applications. Some approaches used the CoAP for data transfer. Others have used ontologies to store the knowledge acquired by the application and others have made web-services. Regarding the network, has the use of LoWPAN, WSN, and WBAN. One of the most used standards was the WBAN, presented in five of the articles. The few standards presented in the articles are not being used even for half of the studies studied. One of the premises of the Internet of Things is precisely the fact that all things and sensors capture full-time data to be used by the most diverse applications, but if there is no portability between them, would have only sensor systems and not a true Internet of Things.

In this context, a great possibility of exploration and studies would be to propose standards for the Internet of Things in health's area. Thus, standard architectures for systems could be proposed, for all research to follow the same path that works. Another idea would be to propose standards for the data captured by the sensors, so any data captured by any sensor of any application could be used by any other application. Even in this context, another possibility could be the proposal for data standards handled by these applications. In this way, the output data of an approach could be used as input to any other approach. Thus, the systems proposed by several future studies would have the capacity to exchange information between them in a natural and intuitive way, to effectively realize a collaborative Internet of Things, utilizing the full potential of technology.

SECURITY AND PRIVACY

Another point to be highlighted after analyzing the articles is the issue of security and privacy. Few approaches have been concerned with the safety of patient data. And even fewer have been able to implement adequate systems to address this problem. The security and privacy problem is extremely critical to the Internet of Things. With data being generated about users, and the objects that belong to them, the amount of information that can be generated is incalculable. In addition, in most cases, this information can be classified as confidential, since users would not like to make it available to third parties. Thus, the need to provide resources to deal with the security and privacy of data captured is extremely valuable to the scientific and industrial approaches.

In this context, a possibility of exploration would be systems capable of implementing an efficient and transparent layer of security to the users, that can protect the data of the same of a simple, but safe, way. Currently, one of the technologies that have been gaining a lot of prominences when it comes to data security is Blockchain. Blockchain provides an interesting approach to maintaining reliable databases on untrusted networks. Initially, it was used in Bitcoin proposed by Nakamoto (2008) as a data structure, becoming a technological solution that provides security in distributed systems (Jin, Zang, Liu, & Lei, 2017). According to Kuzuno and Karam (2017), Blockchain is an electronic records book that keeps a public record of all transactions processed in full transparency without revealing the identity of the transmitter and receiver. In this way, systems that use Blockchain are extremely secure and can become what is needed to provide adequate security for the IoT and to protect user data in that environment.

Prediction on Healthcare Environments

Most of the studied approaches focus on predicting future patient health conditions. Based on this predictive strategy, applications are able to inform patients, doctors, and family members when bad situations will happen so that preventive measures are taken. In this way, risk situations can be minimized and even avoided depending on the prediction time. However, not only the vital signs are important when talking about the health of a patient. People are exposed to various situations that may endanger their health. And besides, one of the most common problems, when someone seeks hospital care, is the precarious situation of emergencies in Brazil.

In this context, one of the possibilities of exploration would be to propose systems capable of predicting external factors that influence the health of patients in hospitals. The goal is to capture information from the environment where the patient is inserted, in order to anticipate problems that may affect him. One possibility would be to analyze the resources that a given hospital has and uses to attend to the public, to identify underutilization or overuse of them and, based on past use, to predict when a given resource will be insufficient to meet the demand. In this way, hospital systems are aware of which features are insufficient, what resources are left over, and what resources are going to become insufficient, can they optimize processes, perhaps by eliminating unnecessary resources, and focusing on acquiring those that really are or will be needed.

CONCLUSION

The objective of this study was to discuss the main issues regarding the use of Data Prediction combined with IoT applied to healthcare and identify the concepts of technology in this area. Differently of others works, this survey does not address only the use of IoT in the healthcare field, but also the use of IoT combined with Data Prediction in order to anticipate and mitigate problems in this area of study. In this context, it was able to identify and propose a broad taxonomy for the scope of work, and an updated view of challenges and possibilities for future studies in this area. Thus, the main objective was completely fulfilled. However, this survey is limited to the use of IoT and Data Prediction techniques applied to the healthcare area. Furthermore, this work just contemplates articles published in electronic scientific libraries, not analyzing other types of work, such as technical or industrial approaches.

It is expected that the taxonomy proposed in this work can help in the classification of different systems using the Internet of Things concept combined with Data Prediction for solving problems in healthcare, serving as a baseline of studies for the scientific community in general. It is hoped that, with this taxonomy, future approaches will be able to identify gaps in healthcare systems, and show ways for future new approaches in the area, improving the future research potentiality. It is also hoped that this research can help hospital IT teams and researchers to propose systems and approaches that can help treat patients in a more automated way with techniques that can predict health problems and prevent them.

As future work was envisioned the development of a model for controlling processes in a healthcare environment, using the Internet of Things paradigm, to record the use of resources by healthcare environment processes, being able to evaluate and predict when the demand for some resource will exceed the capacity of use of the same resource. Therefore, it would be necessary to define which sensors to use and which places they should be allocated, in order to perform data capture for some time. With a good amount of data, Data Prediction techniques could be applied to identify patterns and predict, with a good degree of confidence, the overuse of some resource. Finally, was expected to implement the system in a real healthcare environment, in order to have real data for a better validation of the proposed model.

ACKNOWLEDGMENT

This work was partially supported by the following Brazilian agencies: CNPq; FAPERGS; and CAPES.

REFERENCES

Akeju, O., Butakov, S., & Aghili, S. (2018). Main factors and good practices for managing BYOD and IoT risks in a K-12 environment. *International Journal of Internet of Things and Cyber-Assurance*, *1*(1), 22–39. doi:10.1504/IJITCA.2018.090161

Ali, F., Islam, S. R., Kwak, D., Khan, P., Ullah, N., Yoo, S., & Kwak, K. S. (2018). Type-2 fuzzy ontology–aided recommendation systems for iot–based healthcare. *Computer Communications*, *119*, 138–155. doi:10.1016/j.comcom.2017.10.005

Azimi, I., Anzanpour, A., Rahmani, A. M., Pahikkala, T., Levorato, M., Liljeberg, P., & Dutt, N. (2017). HiCH: Hierarchical Fog-Assisted Computing Architecture for Healthcare IoT. *ACM Transactions on Embedded Computing Systems (TECS)*, *16*(5s), 174:1-174:20. doi:10.1145/3126501

Basanta, H., Huang, Y. P., & Lee, T. T. (2018). Intuitive IoT-based H2U healthcare system for elderly people. In *Proceedings of the 2016 IEEE 13th International Conference on Networking, Sensing, and Control (ICNSC)*, Mexico City, Mexico (pp. 1-6). IEEE. doi:10.1109/ICNSC.2016.7479018

Bhatia, M., & Sood, S. K. (2018). A comprehensive health assessment framework to facilitate IoT-assisted smart workouts: A predictive healthcare perspective. *Computers in Industry*, *92-93*, 50–56. doi:10.1016/j.compind.2017.06.009

Bhatia, M., & Sood, S. K. (2018). Exploring Temporal Analytics in Fog-Cloud Architecture for Smart Office HealthCare. *Mobile Networks and Applications*. doi:10.100711036-018-0991-5

Chen, J., Chen, H., Wu, Z., Hu, D., & Pan, J. Z. (2017). Forecasting smog-related health hazard based on social media and physical sensor. *Information Systems*, *64*(Supplement C), 281–291. doi:10.1016/j.is.2016.03.011

Darshan, K. R., & Anandakumar, K. R. (2015). A comprehensive review on usage of internet of things (iot) in healthcare system. In *Proceedings of the 2015 International Conference on Emerging Research in Electronics, Computer Science and Technology (ICERECT)* (pp. 132-136). Mandya, India: IEEE. 10.1109/ERECT.2015.7499001

EndNote. (2017). Retrieved from https://endnote.com/

Farahani, B., Firouzi, F., Chang, V., Badaroglu, M., Constant, N., & Mankodiya, K. (2018). Towards fog-driven iot ehealth: Promises and challenges of IoT in medicine and healthcare. *Future Generation Computer Systems*, *78*(Part 2), 659–676. doi:10.1016/j.future.2017.04.036

Gondalia, A., Dixit, D., Parashar, S., Raghava, V., Sengupta, A., & Sarobin, V. R. (2018). IoT-based Healthcare Monitoring System for War Soldiers using Machine Learning. *Procedia Computer Science*, *133*, 1005–1013. doi:10.1016/j.procs.2018.07.075

Huang, Y., Zhao, Q., Zhou, Q., & Jiang, W. (2018). Air Quality Forecast Monitoring and Its Impact on Brain Health Based on Big Data and the Internet of Things. *IEEE Access: Practical Innovations, Open Solutions*, *6*, 78678–78688. doi:10.1109/ACCESS.2018.2885142

Jin, T., Zhang, X., Liu, Y., & Lei, K. (2017). BlockNDN: A Bitcoin Blockchain Decentralized System over Named Data Networking. In *Proceedings of the 2017 Ninth International Conference on Ubiquitous and Future Networks (ICUFN)*, Milan, Italy (pp. 75-80). IEEE. 10.1109/ICUFN.2017.7993751

Jouini, R., Lemlouma, T., Maalaoui, K., & Saidane, L. A. (2016). Employing grey model forecasting gm(1,1) to historical medical sensor data towards system preventive in smart home e-health for elderly person. In *Proceedings of the 2016 International Wireless Communications and Mobile Computing Conference (IWCMC),* Paphos, Cyprus (pp. 1086-1091). IEEE. 10.1109/IWCMC.2016.7577210

Kan, C., Chen, Y., Leonelli, F., & Yang, H. (2015). Mobile sensing and network analytics for realizing smart automated systems towards health internet of things. In *Proceedings of the 2015 IEEE International Conference on Automation Science and Engineering (CASE),* Gothenburg, Sweden (pp. 1072-1077). IEEE. 10.1109/CoASE.2015.7294241

Kang, J. J., Adibi, S., Larkin, H., & Luan, T. (2015). Predictive data mining for converged internet of things: A Mobile Health perspective. In *Proceedings of the 2015 International Telecommunication Networks and Applications Conference (ITNAC),* Sydney, Australia (pp. 5-10). IEEE. 10.1109/ATNAC.2015.7366781

Kumar, P. M., Lokesh, S., Varatharajan, R., Babu, G. C., & Parthasarathy, P. (2018). Cloud and IoT based disease prediction and diagnosis system for healthcare using Fuzzy neural classifier. *Future Generation Computer Systems, 86,* 527–534. doi:10.1016/j.future.2018.04.036

Kuzuno, H., & Karam, C. (2017). Blockchain explorer: An analytical process and investigat0ion environment for bitcoin. In *Proceedings of the 2017 APWG Symposium on Electronic Crime Research (eCrime),* Scottsdale, AZ (pp. 9-16). IEEE. 10.1109/ECRIME.2017.7945049

Kwon, O. Y., Shin, S. H., Shin, S. J., & Kim, W. S. (2010). Design of u-health system with the use of smart phone and sensor network. In *Proceedings of the 2010 Proceedings of the 5th International Conference on Ubiquitous Information Technologies and Applications,* Sanya, China (pp. 1-6). IEEE. doi:10.1109/ICUT.2010.5677830

Manogaran, G., Varatharajan, R., Lopez, D., Kumar, P. M., Sundarasekar, R., & Thota, C. (2018). A new architecture of Internet of Things and big data ecosystem for secured smart healthcare monitoring and alerting system. *Future Generation Computer Systems, 82,* 375–387. doi:10.1016/j.future.2017.10.045

Meharouech, A., Elias, J., & Mehaoua, A. (2015). Future body-to-body networks for ubiquitous healthcare: a survey, taxonomy and challenges. In *Proceedings of the 2015 2nd International Symposium on Future Information and Communication Technologies for Ubiquitous HealthCare (Ubi-HealthTech),* Beijing, China (pp. 1-6). IEEE. 10.1109/Ubi-HealthTech.2015.7203330

Nakamoto, S. (2008). *Bitcoin: A Peer-to-Peer Electronic Cash System.* Retrieved from https://bitcoin.org/bitcoin.pdf

Orimaye, S. O., Leong, F. C., Lee, C. H., & Ng, E. C. H. (2015). Predicting proximity with ambient mobile sensors for non-invasive health diagnostics. In *Proceedings of the 2015 IEEE 12th Malaysia International Conference on Communications (MICC),* Kuching, Malaysia (pp. 6-11). IEEE. 10.1109/MICC.2015.7725398

Paudel, R., Dunn, K., Eberle, W., & Chaung, D. (2018). Cognitive Health Prediction on the Elderly Using Sensor Data in Smart Homes. In *Proceedings of The Thirty-First International Flairs Conference (FLAIRS-31),* Melbourne, FL (pp. 317-322). AAAI.

Pinto, S., Cabral, J., & Gomes, T. (2017). We-care: An iot-based health care system for elderly people. In *Proceedings of the 2017 IEEE International Conference on Industrial Technology (ICIT),* Toronto, Canada (pp. 1378-1383). IEEE. 10.1109/ICIT.2017.7915565

Robben, S., Englebienne, G., & Kröse, B. (2017). Delta features from ambient sensor data are good predictors of change in functional health. *IEEE Journal of Biomedical and Health Informatics, 21*(4), 986–993. doi:10.1109/JBHI.2016.2593980 PMID:27455530

Roehrs, A., da Costa, C. A., Righi, R. da R., & de Oliveira, K. S. F. (2017). Personal Health Records: A Systematic Literature Review. *Journal of Medical Internet Research, 19*(1), e13. doi:10.2196/jmir.5876 PMID:28062391

Sarhan, Q. I. (2018). Internet of things: A survey of challenges and issues. *International Journal of Internet of Things and Cyber-Assurance, 1*(1), 40–75. doi:10.1504/IJITCA.2018.090162

Senthilkumar, T., Manikandan, B., Devi, M. R., & Lokesh, S. (2018). Technologies Enduring in Internet of Medical Things (IoMT) for Smart Healthcare System. *International Journal of Scientific Research in Computer Science. Engineering and Information Technology, 3*(5), 566–572.

Singh, K. J., & Kapoor, D. S. (2017). Create your own internet of things: A survey of iot platforms. *IEEE Consumer Electronics Magazine, 6*(2), 57–68. doi:10.1109/MCE.2016.2640718

Singh, P. (2018). Internet of Things based Health Monitoring System: Opportunities and Challenges. *International Journal of Advanced Research in Computer Science, 9*(1), 224–228. doi:10.26483/ijarcs. v9i1.5308

Sood, S. K. & Mahajan, I. (2018). IoT-Fog based Healthcare Framework to Identify and Control Hypertension Attack. *IEEE Internet of Things Journal,* 1-8. doi:10.1109/JIOT.2018.2871630

Tan, E. T., & Halim, Z. A. (2018). Health care Monitoring System and Analytics Based on Internet of Things Framework. *Journal of the Institution of Electronics and Telecommunication Engineers,* 1–8. do i:10.1080/03772063.2018.1447402

Thakur, S. S., Abdul, S. S., Chiu, H.Y., Roy, R. B., Huang, P. Yu., Malwade, S., Nursetyo, A. A., & Li, Y. C. (2018). Artificial-Intelligence-Based Prediction of Clinical Events among Hemodialysis Patients Using Non-Contact Sensor Data. *Sensors, 18*(9), 2833:1-2833:16. doi:10.3390/s18092833

Verma, P., Sood, S. K., & Kalra, S. (2018). Cloud-centric IoT based student healthcare monitoring framework. *Journal of Ambient Intelligence and Humanized Computing, 9*(5), 1293–1309. doi:10.100712652-017-0520-6

Zamanifar, A., Nazemi, E., & Vahidi-Asl, M. (2017). Dmp-iot: A distributed movement prediction scheme for IOT health-care applications. *Computers & Electrical Engineering, 58*(Supplement C), 310–326. doi:10.1016/j.compeleceng.2016.09.015

This research was previously published in the International Journal of E-Health and Medical Communications (IJEHMC), 11(2); pages 1-19, copyright year 2020 by IGI Publishing (an imprint of IGI Global).

Chapter 44
Cyber Security and Cyber Resilience for the Australian E–Health Records:
A Blockchain Solution

Nagarajan Venkatachalam
🆔 https://orcid.org/0000-0002-5545-0549
Queensland University of Technology, Australia

Peadar O'Connor
Queensland University of Technology, Australia

Shailesh Palekar
Queensland University of Technology, Australia

ABSTRACT

Cybersecurity is a critical consideration for all users of electronic health records (EHR), particularly for patients. With the advent of Healthcare 4.0, which is based on the internet of things (IoT) and sensors, cyber resilience has become a key requirement in ensuring the protection of patient data across devices. Blockchain offers crypto-enforced security, data immutability, and smart contracts-based business logic features to all the users in the network. This study explores how blockchain can be a single digital option that can address both the cybersecurity and cyber resilience needs of EHR. The effective use lens is adopted to analyze how blockchain can be leveraged to meet cybersecurity needs while the novel use lens is adopted to analyze how blockchain can be leveraged to address cyber resilience needs originating from IoT. Based on the analysis, this study proposes two Hyperledger-based security models that contribute to individual privacy and information security needs.

DOI: 10.4018/978-1-6684-7132-6.ch044

INTRODUCTION

Electronic Health Records (EHRs) have been widely adopted for exchanging health information between stakeholders (hospitals, labs, insurance companies, government, and patients) in health systems (Del Fiol et al. 2020; Fragidis and Chatzoglou 2018). However, most EHRs still use the traditional client-server architecture for storing and exchanging data. Hence, with client-server-based controls, any errors in controlling data confidentiality, integrity, and accessibility (CIA) can result in significant loss of privacy and increase security threats to all stakeholders whereby the data become vulnerable to cyberattacks and other intruders (Tanwar et al. 2020). In Australia, the lack of adequate investments in cyber-security protocols and security solutions in health systems, use of old legacy computing systems by hospitals, lack of health-management training in cyber security, and the lack of mandatory reporting of cyberattacks are key reasons that make health systems vulnerable (Offner et al. 2020).

On the other hand, health care is transitioning toward Healthcare 4.0, which involves rapid and disruptive technological changes for aligning with Industry 4.0 initiatives. These include building cyber-physical systems and interoperability, and cyber-security solutions. Big data, cloud computing, and Internet of Things (IoT) are identified as the three digital pillars supporting Healthcare 4.0 transformations (Aceto et al. 2020) wherein the key objectives are (i) the continuous, simple, and bi-directional exchange of information; and (ii) accurate monitoring of health conditions and intake of medicines. Personalized health care, telepathology, telemedicine, disease monitoring, and assisted living are core areas of health and economic constraints addressed by the three pillars (Aceto et al. 2020). However, high-impact risks, such as (i) security concerns related to sensitive information and the digital devices storing the information; (ii) compromising privacy and ethical issues relating to ownership, dissemination, and sharing of information; and (iii) poor monitoring of information and system use, highlight serious concerns about the massive drive toward Healthcare 4.0 (Aceto et al. 2020). Based on the abovementioned dynamics, it is imperative that protecting the privacy and security of individual health records and health-related data, as well as securing the bi-directional exchange of information, are critical for realizing the benefits offered by EHR and Healthcare 4.0. For example, a recent survey on the security requirements for IoT-based healthcare systems identified cyber security and cyber resilience as key requirements that need to be addressed for developing and adopting new digital solutions (Nasiri et al. 2019). Based on the above, this study proposes a blockchain-enabled solution to address both requirements.

Blockchain offers an immutable audit trail of data and provides a consistent view for all network participants. The early success of blockchain, with the first disruptive innovation called Bitcoin (Nakamoto 2008), has evolved significantly toward frameworks such as Ethereum and Hyperledger. The power of these blockchain tools enables the enforcement of crypto security and reliable data exchanges between participants. Strategic management scholars refer to blockchain as a "foundational institutional technology" (Davidson et al. 2018), as it represents a digital-transaction ledger containing value exchanges between two peers. Blockchain also guarantees asset ownership for all individuals in the network through intelligent and trusted consensus protocols (Catalini 2017; Pilkington 2016) without the need for traditional centralized governance structures. Hence, this technology has been applied to improving information storage and distribution in supply chains, the finance sector, and other professional services, such as health care. In the health industry, ongoing studies have investigated how blockchain can be leveraged to address the needs of Healthcare 4.0 (Angraal et al. 2017; Griggs et al. 2018); (Gupta et al. 2019; Tanwar et al. 2020). These studies have highlighted the urgent need for developing robust and reliable digital infrastructures to address serious flaws and deficiencies in cyber-security and cyber-resilience protocols. To address the abovementioned security needs, this study undertakes a comprehensive review of blockchain case studies in health services. Further, it addresses two key research questions:

1. How can blockchain be leveraged to address the cyber-security needs of EHRs?
2. How can blockchain be leveraged to address the cyber-resilience needs of EHRs?

This chapter is organized as follows. First, we review literature that examines the concepts of cyber security and cyber resilience, privacy implications in EHRs, and the effective and novel use of cyber security and cyber resilience. Next, we explore Healthcare 4.0, including the changing industry landscape based on the integration of IoT and wearable devices with cloud and big-data services. Further, we examine how blockchain technology works, and how it can provide a secure solution for recording EHRs using Hyperledger Fabric. This is followed by an assessment of the solution for cyber-security and cyber-resilience tenets. Finally, future research areas and the study's conclusion are presented.

LITERATURE REVIEW

Cyber Security and Cyber Resilience

The CIA triad is often referred to when defining information security (IS), as it forms a simple model that can be applied to other domains beyond the information technology (IT) industry. However, it limits the security aspects when dealing with digital information in cyberspace (Warkentin & Orgeron, 2020, p. 3). Nasiri et al. (2019) show that the CIA triad model can be utilized for (i) protection of information, including authentication (i.e., validating who is accessing the information); (ii) authorization (i.e., controlling access to the information); (iii) non-repudiation (i.e., proving who took what action); and (iv) data freshness (i.e., ensuring access to all information). Combined with the CIA triad, these additional tenets are frequently used as pillars that define cyber security (Geusebroek, 2012, p. 25). However, cyber-security models often focus on control of access to information and ignore the complexity of modern IT infrastructures, such as cloud services and the IoT. For example, a business owner deploying IoT may not often know the location of information and the devices storing it, or how access to such devices and information can be obtained. Thus, increased complexity opens new pathways for potential attacks that can affect the operability of information systems and devices. Researchers have urgently called for a secure, scalable, and immutable solution for health data, particularly in the wake of a multitude of information system attacks in the health sector, including the WannaCry availability compromise of the National Health Service in the UK, and the Medijack integrity attacks that infected networked medical devices (Stamatellis et al., 2020, p. 2).

To understand cloud- and IoT-compromised vectors, Nasiri et al. (2019) state that new tenets are required to maintain reliability (how information sources can be made more reliable), configurability (how components can be changed without compromising the information system), autonomy (whether the components are self-healing, self-optimizing, and self-protecting), adaptability (how elements can be repurposed as demands change), repairability (how elements can detect faults and correct them), safety (where a compromised element can potentially cause physical harm), survivability (where the system can continue operating when some of the elements are compromised), and performability (where the information system can still meet the needs, even if some parts of its system are compromised). The collection of these tenets used in combination with cyber-security tenets is referred to as cyber resilience. This definition relating to IoT also fits well with Harman et al.'s (2019, p. 1) interpretation of cyber resilience, which relates to how quickly an organization can restore its services after an attack.

Blockchain for E-Health

Blockchain is a digital representation of a utility based on the seven layers of the Open-System Interconnection model. It is a network-wide distributed database (*Data layer*), where the data are replicated across a set of nodes connected by a peer-to-peer network (*Network layer*; (Pilkington 2016). The network is customizable through a communication messaging protocol (*Transport layer*) that uses cryptography (*Session layer*) for protecting user identities and guarantees the transactions data (*Presentation* and *Application layers*) associated with the asset value of all participating members (Glaser 2017). Due to this integrated combination, blockchain offers security, privacy, transparency, reliability, access flexibility, and decentralization of transactional data stored in the chain for all participants in the network (Seebacher and Schüritz 2017; Tapscott and Tapscott 2017; Yaga et al. 2019).

Health and technology scholars have explored how blockchain can be leveraged for tele-surgery (Gupta et al. 2019), remote and automated patient monitoring (Griggs et al. 2018), and e-health data storage and distribution (Tanwar et al. 2020). However, these studies assume that cryptography methods inherent in blockchain automatically provide the necessary CIA triad needs. This study posits that such assumptions need to be evaluated and validated. Hence, the first research question is posed to address this need.

Gajek et al. (2020) explore how air-gapped devices can be compromised by the Stuxnet attack through the use of USB drives containing compromised firmware updates. This type of attack can produce serious issues if applied to health-related life-saving devices, and can be further amplified if elements are networked together. Additionally, Gajek et al. (2020) argue that blockchain can offer an intelligent solution where a digital twin of the firmware can be recorded in the ledger, thereby allowing the device to remotely and automatically validate the new firmware while ensuring the integrity of the firmware and avoiding any security compromises. A similar concept is explored by Harman et al. (2019) in which backups of data are hashed, and the hashes are stored on a blockchain solution, providing irrefutable proof of whether or not the stored backup has been tampered with. Such an application can be applied to e-health through the recording of EHRs.

Effective Use of Blockchain for CIA Compliance

Effective use is defined as using the system in a way that helps its users to attain the goals for using the system (Burton-Jones and Grange 2013). For example, a network of affordances of information systems and IT artifacts can enable a hospital to achieve its goals with EHRs and realize specific benefits (Burton-Jones and Volkoff 2017). Though a system may offer many features, the user can leverage those that they specifically need. This helps in achieving system benefits by using the system within their routines more effectively. This study illustrates how blockchain can be used to address CIA compliance for all EHR users. Further, it postulates that protecting the privacy affordance of EHR users (e.g., doctors, patients, hospitals, labs, insurance companies) is necessary to maximize the usage of EHR in healthcare. In this context, since effective use can be the enabler for actualizing a specific affordance (Burton-Jones and Volkoff 2017), this study adopts the effective-use lens to illustrate how privacy of individual affordance can be realized and protected through the efficient use of blockchain.

Novel Use of Blockchain for Cyber Resilience

The novel-use lens is an effective way to analyze how users can:

- Take advantage of previously used features for accomplishing additional tasks.
- Engage features that were not previously accessed.
- Use features and extensions of a specific technology (Bagayogo et al. 2014).

Novel use is also referred to as the enhanced use of IT wherein the analysis focuses on the use of technology after implementation. Scholars have elaborated on how novel use can leverage the fit between digital technologies characteristics and specific users' needs for particular tasks (Beaudry et al. 2020). In this study, the novel use of blockchain (as the IT) is analyzed through blockchain features to scrutinize cyber-resilience needs. Novel use of IT can also disrupt and transform entire work processes by enabling conditions that allow users to realize the full potential of new technology innovations (Bagayogo et al. 2014). This study illustrates how IS needs for protecting data in Healthcare 4.0 can be realized through the novel use of blockchain. Considering the Healthcare 4.0 and IoT-based IS needs, it proposes a solution through the novel use of blockchain to address the IS needs of Healthcare 4.0 data.

Electronic Health Records: The Question of Individual Privacy

Although the benefits of EHRs are numerous (Kierkegaard, 2011, p. 503), privacy remains a key concern for both the subjects and stakeholders of the records. Privacy refers to personal information stored in information systems and is defined by the Australian Privacy Act of 1988 as "information or an opinion about an identified individual, or an individual who is reasonably identifiable" (Privacy Act 1988, p. 25). Simply put, it refers to information that defines who someone is. EHRs contain sensitive and private data related to a user's (e.g., patient's) physical and mental health, medications, treatments, and even religious beliefs. Therefore, protection of data privacy and compliance with standards are of paramount importance, as users of such records place trust in such systems. The document AS ISO 279911:2011, published by Standards Australia, highlights the need for cyber-security tenets to be applied to secure the information contained in EHRs (Standards Australia, 2011, p. 5). It further states that such systems should be resilient in facing attacks, failures, and disasters. This can be difficult to control and manage in simple air-gapped computer networks where the risk of breaching privacy remains high, given that many individuals interact with the data. The risk of breaching privacy expands considerably when information is moved into networked cloud and IoT environments (Nasiri et al., 2019).

Industry 4.0, Healthcare 4.0, and a Secured Collaboration Quest

The IoT, along with Internet of Services (IoS) and physical systems connected in cyberspace, are generally considered key components of the Industry 4.0 concept (Thuemmler & Ba, 2017). These empower industries to evolve by providing customized solutions to specific user and client scenarios. As the concept extends into healthcare, it has triggered a new phase known as Healthcare 4.0, wherein individual health information is directly connected to autonomous IoT systems (Thuemmler & Ba, 2017, pp. 30–31). For example, Al-Odat et al. (2018) show through IoT architecture how insulin pumps can track patient measurements and upload data to cloud storage, which helps medical practitioners to remotely monitor the patient's health. This big data can also be used for providing insights into conducting large-scale medical studies. As the volume of data increases, so does the complexity of collecting, processing, and storing the information (Klonoff, 2017, p. 647). New computing methods (e.g., fog, edge computing) help in analyzing voluminous data. Cisco has forecast that, by the end of 2021, there could be an estimated 700 million edge-hosted containers (Cisco, 2020, p. 4). The increased complexity and diversity of networks make the security of elements and the information carried and stored within them crucial.

Individual Privacy Questions?

Assessing how data should be treated by various IoT devices is complex. In this context, the IS CIA triad helps in assessing the data interaction points. For example, it can help in understanding (i) how data can be stored so that only authorized users can access it, thereby keeping the data private; (ii) how data can be accessed; (iii) how medical practitioners can know that it is complete; and (iv) whether or not the data have been accessed by other individuals. Depending on the specificity of the data collected, and how it is collected, ethical and legislative protocols are required to answer the above questions.

Long-Term Quest: Clinical Notes for Collaborative Health Care

In addition to the data-volume issues of big data, EHRs are designed to address two distinct needs. First, they serve as a means to capture the patient's narrative as useful data with the clinical notes from general practitioners, specialist physicians, and nurses. Second, they are historical and legal references related to research, management, and quality assurance (Bansler et al. 2016). The clinical notes about a patient in EHRs constitute the working document that records the core narrative of medical care, which unfolds over time (Hobbs 2003). Hence, EHRs should be designed to enable collaboration between primary health care providers to address the individual patient's health care over a period of time. Despite the benefits gained from the historical analysis of EHR data, many questions persist, for example, how can medical narratives be stored in EHRs (note: this problem is compounded by the individual privacy questions identified in the earlier section)?

IoT, Cloud, and Big Data: Information Security Challenges

With IoT devices, the data collected can be accessed and stored on numerous Internet-connected devices, and each element can be questioned (for assessment) from an IS perspective. For example, if the data are collected on a fog computing device, will the device owner have access to the data? How can one determine whether the stored data file is the latest version of those data? When can an IoT-enabled device, such as a cardiac defibrillator, take remedial action on a patient's condition (Klonoff, 2017, p. 650)? Based on the above, it is critical to record (i) a command provided to the device, (ii) who provided the command, and (iii) the data associated with the decision. In other words, the system needs to be auditable such that accountability is maintained, the data trail is immutable, and the reputability of events is clear. Conversely, if the records are intended for big-data analysis, then they must be deanonymized so that the privacy of the patient is retained even if the data are in use.

BLOCKCHAIN FOR ELECTRONIC HEALTH RECORDS

This study positions blockchain as a faithful representation for (i) protecting individual privacy and (ii) ensuring the IS of transactional exchanges and the value of assets stored in the blockchain.

Effective Use of Blockchain for Protecting Individual Privacy

The Bitcoin blockchain solution has demonstrated that irrefutable data records can be stored publicly while typically maintaining users' privacy. However, Henry et al. (2018, pp. 38–39) highlight that it is possible to heuristically link users to transactions. Other blockchain models offer increased privacy, such as the Hawk model proposed by Kosba et al. (2016), which uses smart contracts to obfuscate the data stored within the public Ethereum blockchain, or the Sony educational solution that protects data on the IBM blockchain cloud utilizing a private Hyperledger Fabric solution (Grech & Camilleri, 2017, p. 59). Adlam and Haskins (2018) highlight how a permissioned blockchain, such as Hyperledger Fabric, can store EHRs in a distributed blockchain, allow access to medical practitioners at multiple hospitals, and contribute to the data using protected channels built into the blockchain architecture.

What Is Blockchain and How Does It Work?

The generally accepted classification of blockchain is an immutable decentralized digital ledger distributed to a group of networked peer nodes. The ledger is made up of a chain of blocks, with each block containing verifiable data, and a linkage that proves the block is in sequence and accurate. How the data are distributed among networked peers depends on the mechanism developed for chain implementations, which is called a "consensus mechanism." The information stored in the blocks and the consensus mechanism vary across implementations and the type of blockchain (e.g., public/permission-less, private/permissioned).

The public Bitcoin block architecture described by Nakamoto (2008) is summarized in Figure 1. It contains a group of transaction records between two entities, plus a SHA-256 cryptographic hash of each transaction (Nakamoto, 2008). The block also contains a header containing a cryptographic hash of the transaction hashes (known as a Merkle root hash), which proves the integrity of the block. The header also includes a hash of the previous block in the chain and an integer (called a nonce), which is

Figure 1. Bitcoin block details

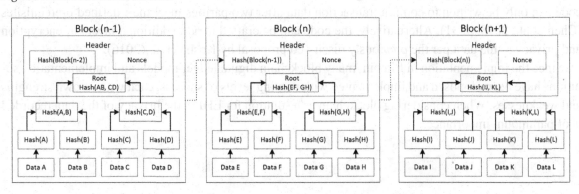

calculated by the mathematical algorithm defined by the consensus mechanism (Nakamoto, 2008, p. 3; Grech & Camilleri, 2017, pp. 121–122).

As new blocks are created and distributed among network peers, the peers need to validate that the new block is suitable to be added to the chain. This is achieved using the aforementioned consensus mechanism. There are three common methods of achieving consensus: (i) proof of work (PoW), (ii) proof of stake (PoS), and (iii) proof of authority (PoA; Parisi, 2020; Ma & Fang, 2020, pp. 21–22; Grech & Camilleri, 2017, p. 127).

Public and permission-less blockchain solutions, such as Bitcoin and Ethereum, use a PoW consensus mechanism (Parisi, 2020). These chains have an indefinite number of peers in the network, can be accessed by anyone, and have no central authority. The open nature of the network presents a challenge in determining whether or not a new block should be added to the chain. The PoW mechanism requires the peer creating the new block to perform a complex mathematical task. The effort of calculation is deemed as suitable proof that the block proposal can be assessed by other peers in the network. Additionally, the PoW mathematical challenge defined by the architecture becomes more complex as the chain grows. If a peer faces a conflict in assessing multiple blocks, then the block with the greater challenge is considered the superior block by the peer (Nakamoto, 2008, p. 3; Grech & Camilleri, 2017, pp. 121–122). The complexity of this permission-less configuration has several drawbacks, including an increasing cost to write the chain, a limit on how quickly data can be written to the chain, and that anyone can read the data stored on the chain (addressed by a permissioned blockchain solution).

The PoS mechanism can be used in permission-less blockchain solutions (Ma & Fang, 2020, pp. 21–22; Grech & Camilleri, 2017, p. 127). In the PoS option, stakeholders of the network are trusted proportionally, based on their commitment and investment in the network and validated by their digital certificates (Parisi, 2020; Grech & Camilleri, 2017, p. 127).

Permissioned blockchains, such as Hyperledger, create an authority to govern what and how blocks can be added to the chain. They are often referred to as "private blockchains" managed by a single organization, or "consortium blockchains" managed by a group of consenting organizations (Parisi, 2020). The authority is defined by the participating organizations that use digital certificates to prove that the peer proposing the block has the requisite authority. This mechanism is referred to as PoA and allows for faster processing of blocks at a consistent cost to the peers. Permissioned chain solutions usually restrict access to the data stored on the chain, which can assist in protecting the privacy of the data, although some privacy can be achieved on public blockchains using techniques such as smart contracts.

A few blockchain models include the ability to execute a set of code stored on-chain, such as Ethereum's smart contracts (Parisi, 2020). The code can be customized to user needs and is written specifically for the chain technology, the data being stored, and the users' needs. For example, the smart contract code can only be written to commit transaction data after two parities meet their defined prerequisites (Chen et al., 2018, p. 31). Alternatively, the code can be crafted to add additional layers of encryption and privacy to the data per the previously discussed proposal by Kosba et al. (2016).

Since the implementation in Bitcoin, many blockchain digital ledger models and implementation solutions have been proposed and implemented with varying levels of success, each with its own strengths and weaknesses. When considering blockchain as a solution for EHRs, the privacy of the data recorded is of paramount importance.

SOLUTIONS AND RECOMMENDATIONS

Novel Use of Blockchain for Protecting Information Security

A Permissioned Blockchain EHR Solution

Blockchain may be an ideal solution for protecting EHRs collected and stored in IoT networks. It also addresses many concerns raised by the cyber-security and cyber-resilience tenets. Hyperledger Fabric is a permissioned blockchain model released by the Linux Foundation that can be configured with various security and consensus modules. A well-configured model can store patient data privately while providing the ability to manage access to a wide range of clients using a combination of attribute-based access controls (ABAC), well-defined roles in the membership service provider (MSP) service module, and use of private state databases within the blockchain ledger.

Hyperledger Fabric can have multiple channels defined within the peer network, wherein organizations can communicate with each other and share digital ledgers. However, the channels keep the data independent from others that may utilize the same peers and networks (Hyperledger Fabric, 2020). Channel separations allow for multiple solutions to be implemented on the same platform and peer network without sharing data between the solutions or clients. Figure 2 shows how two health authorities can create their own ledger solutions on a common network while storing their EHR on peers without sharing them with other authorities. Separating the data into different channels increases the overhead managing the network across multiple channels. Additionally, the solution does not easily permit the sharing of data within the ledger with other clients. Although the solution maintains confidentiality of the patient data by restricting access to the managed private channels, it limits the availability and integrity tenets, as the data are not available to those off chain or those that are not authorized, and the data cannot be easily verified by others.

Figure 2. Hyperledger Fabric channel separation (adapted from Hyperledger Fabric, 2020)

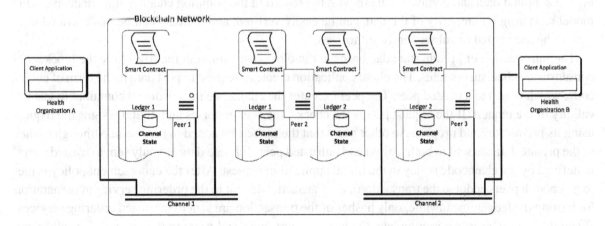

The private data-collection feature of Hyperledger Fabric offers an alternative solution, whereby private state databases can be created within digital ledgers. Figure 3 highlights how different organizations can share a common channel, although private data are distributed only to trusted peers.

Figure 3. Hyperledger Fabric private state ledgers (Hyperledger Fabric, 2020)

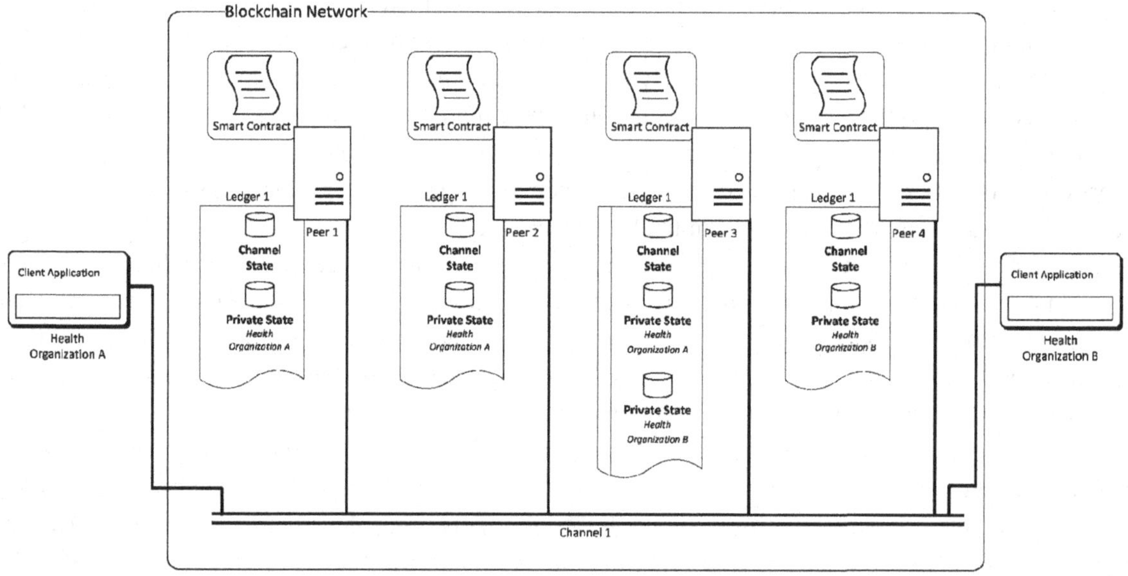

Digital signatures (or hashes) of the private data are created and distributed to both trusted and untrusted peers in the common channel-state databases, as shown in Figure 4. Where required, discrete records of private data can be shared with untrusted peers and clients. Because all peers in the network have a copy of the digital signature of the records, the shared private data can be easily verified by hashing the supplied data and comparing them with the record in the common channel-state database. This model reflecting the integrity of the data can be easily verified, and the data can be made available to those who are trusted or subsequently authorized.

The introduction of private state databases in the blockchain solution modifies how the blockchain consensus mechanism operates. The client application creates a request to post data in the form of chaincode, which is sent to a trusted peer. The peer executes the chaincode in an isolated container to test the validity of the request. If the request passes the checks, the peer endorses and digitally signs the request using its private key and proposes to other peers that the request be added to the chain. Although hashes of the private data are sent to both trusted and untrusted peers, private data are only sent to trusted peers, as defined by the chaincode policy in the initial application request. After the endorsement policy is met (e.g., enough peers endorse the transaction), the transaction is sent to the ordering service in preparation for writing the ledger; meanwhile, only hashes of the transaction are sent to untrusted ordering services. When the ordering service is complete, the hash sets are sent to all peers in the network for validation, and are subsequently written to the channel-state databases for every peer in the channel. The private data are distributed to any trusted peer that does not yet have a copy of the data, and each of the peers

Figure 4. Private data collection for Health Organization A (adapted from Hyperledger Fabric, 2020)

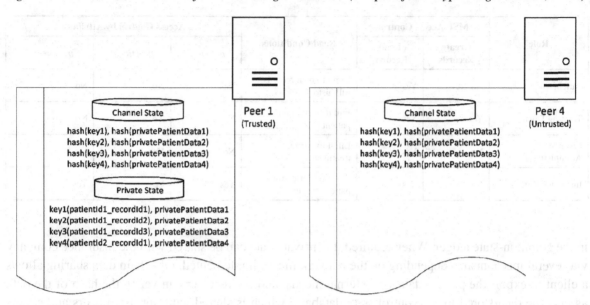

commit the records to the private state database within the ledger. This solution maintains the confidentiality of the patient data, as only authorized clients, services, and peers have access to the actual data.

Suitable access controls underpin the privacy of the described blockchain solution. Two primary factors provide this control, namely, the MSP and the configuration of the ABACs. The MSP stores the public keys of peers and defines what elements and actions are permitted within the network (Hyperledger Fabric, 2020). It can define roles for the permissions a particular actor has within the network or on a particular node. For example, the MSP can store the trusted peers in a particular organization or a client that is a member of an organization. ABACs can enhance the MSP to define permissions in a more granular manner for each organization and for elements within the blockchain network.

Let us now look at how a combination of an MSP and ABACs can assist with managing permissions of EHRs for a patient undergoing treatment at a hospital. In this context, we define four roles: patient, doctor, the hospital practice administrator, and a health insurance company. The doctor (treating the patient), or other medical practitioners involved in the patient's treatment, can create a new EHR for the patient. They should be able to read all of the patient's past and current EHRs, as governed by the MSP. Likewise, patients should be able to read their own EHRs from previous and current treatments, but only those records requiring a *patientId* attribute control. A hospital practice administrator should be able to read a patient's EHR for treatment at the practice, but only those records requiring a *practiceId* attribute control. A health insurance company can review the specific treatment records as part of a patient claim, should the patient consent to disclosing the records, but only those requiring *patientId*, *practiceId*, and *treatmentId* attribute controls for sharing specific private data. These roles, access rights, and permissions are summarized in Table 1.

In the scenario described in Table 1, it is implied that the health insurance company is treated as a trusted client for EHRs, and that the data are protected by the ABAC privileges. An alternate solution is to create additional untrusted peers and establish data collections for the insurance company, meaning the insurance company would not have direct access to the private state data, except for the hashes stored

Table 1. Example of an MSP and ABACs for an EHR for patient treatment in a hospital

Role	MSP Access Control		Read Conditions	Access Control by Attribute		
	Create Records	Read Records		*patientId*	*practiceId*	*treatmentId*
Patient	No	Yes	Limit to own records, full history	Yes	No	No
Treating Doctor	Yes	Yes	Full history of any patient being treated	No	No	No
Practice Administrator	No	Yes	Limit to current treatment	No	Yes	No
Insurance Company	No	Yes	Selective based on patient consent	Yes	Yes	Yes

in the common-state ledger. When required, the private data can be shared with the insurance company via several mechanisms, depending on the network model implemented. Off-chain data sharing allows a client to export the private data via external means, and the receiver can verify the hash of the data against the data stored in the control-state database, which is shared with untrusted peers and clients within the network (Hyperledger Fabric, 2020). Alternatively, private data can be shared with another collection within the network, where the data are copied to the untrusted collection private state data (Hyperledger Fabric, 2020). Again, the private data copied can be validated using the hash data stored in the common-state ledger. This solution carries less risk of losing the shared private data, as it is shared only within the blockchain network.

Given the Hyperledger Fabric configuration proposed in Figures 3 and 4, and with the MSP and ABACs proposed in Table 1, the key question is: How does the model address the cyber-security and resiliency tenets namely confidentiality, integrity, availability, authorization, non-repudiation, configurability, autonomy, adaptability, repairability, safety, survivability and performability? Next, we elaborate on how these tenets are addressed by the solution.

Confidentiality is achieved by protecting data in a permissioned blockchain ledger, with encrypted private state databases, clearly defined roles and access attributes, and managed by the owning organization. The data can be stored in privately managed networks or cloud services so the appropriate level of controls can be enacted on the private state databases to provide much-needed confidentiality of the EHR.

Integrity is enacted with multiple layers of data hashing within the blockchain, providing certainty that the data are correctly recorded, and that shared hashes of private data are validated by others if they should be shared. The integrity of the solution is inherent in the design of blockchain, whereby the whole chain can be verified at any time, in its entirety, as the header of each block includes a hash of the previous block.

Availability is achieved through the use of multiple peers that store the data so that any single peer failure will not affect the availability of the data. As each trusted node contains a full copy of the private state databases, and each untrusted node contains a copy of the entire hash ledger, availability can be extended as much as desired by adding more trusted and untrusted nodes in the network, and selecting high-reliability services, such as cloud data storage solutions. This means that the EHR can be made available practically anywhere, at any time, if it is provided enough capacity.

Authorization is ensured through the use of digital certificate infrastructure to certify each actor and network element with protection built in via the MSP. The consortium holds the responsibility for defining who may have access to the system in the MSP and can define record-level permissions through the use of well-designed ABACs. Using the model proposed, each patient, doctor, or other actor must first prove who they are and then be assessed on what rights they have for each EHR.

Non-repudiation relates to the idea that blockchain ledgers are immutable through the use of multi-stage data hashing and peer sharing, ensuring that the EHR history is accurately reflected. Put simply, once the record is entered in the database, it cannot be changed without this change being noticed, as the hash on the blockchain will not match the record in the private state database.

Configurability means that the model is highly configurable to the environment, where elements, actors, services and access controls can be set up as required, and altered during operation by the network administrators, with the consensus of those forming the network. This means that, as the medical industry and user demand evolves, so can the solution. New types of records and data sources can be added at a later time if the primary solution is well designed. For example, should a new type of wearable monitor be created with custom data requirements, a new private state database can be established and linked to the channel-state database, as the channel state will only record the hash of the new database records being incorporated.

Autonomy means that the network is designed to continue operating even if a number of peers are under attack, compromised, or otherwise faulty. By harnessing reputable cloud service providers, each node of the solution can be designed to withstand a large range of issues before they are compromised.

Adaptability indicates that elements can be added, changed, and removed without impacting the basic operations of the network. This can apply to the entire node elements of the network or the individual components.

Repairability means that the Fabric modules implemented can change based on the consensus mechanisms, the level of encryption, and the level of fault tolerance permitted during the acceptance of new data blocks.

Safety is protected in that optional safety features can be accounted for in the chaincode, if required.

Survivability and performability are achieved if the minimum number of trusted peers are operational in the network (as defined by the MSP and chaincode).

There are many ways in which blockchain digital ledger technologies can be implemented for EHRs. For example, the above solution can be enhanced with the use of in-hospital IoT smart-monitoring devices. If the devices are configured with the suitable digital certificates, authorizations, and network connections, then the *patientId* can be input into the devices, and the monitoring data can be automatically sent to the blockchain as new EHR data.

Guo et al. (2019) propose a different model wherein smart health devices can cryptographically communicate and store data at edge nodes, while a Hyperledger Fabric blockchain facilitates access to the data while logging access requests. Protection of the data is enforced by the edge node using ABACs. This is only accessible if the correct decryption key and data address are supplied in a one-time, self-destructing uniform resource locator provided by smart contracts built into the blockchain. Such a system can provide non-repudiation and auditability access to the data, control who and how the data are accessed, and guarantee the freshness of the data.

FUTURE RESEARCH DIRECTIONS

Patient data analysis in EHRs has been growing over the past few decades. However, the adoption and use of new and emergent information technologies to analyze and manage the data vastly differ between developed and developing countries. There are three distinct areas where scholars can extend their research and investigations.

First, this study introduced cyber-security and resilience models based on blockchain use that cater to the challenges posed to the IoS and the IoT. Future investigators can evaluate and validate these models as well as identify new factors that need to be added to handle the hyper-dynamic volatility of IoT-enabled health care in Healthcare 4.0.

Second, current designs of EHRs are proving to be a challenge in enabling collaboration between physicians and specialists for recording and tracking clinical notes data. This arises due to the complexity of processes related to storing and sharing relevant data and individuals' privacy considerations. Though this study provides a model to address this gap, future work could investigate how collaboration-related problems and scans can be addressed by standardizing data stored in blockchain.

Third, as the adoption and implementation of EHRs vary extensively between developed and developing countries, privacy and security considerations of EHR data also fluctuate based on capital funding and other government-related priorities. Scholars can investigate how blockchain-based EHRs can address the needs of developing countries, such as India and Brazil.

In addition, more research is required to analyze how diverse data sources can be secured, and how consistent levels of security are achieved across systems before a universal solution is attained and adopted.

CONCLUSION

IS is a constantly evolving requirement for systems adopted by public and private enterprises and entities. As the complexity of network elements and the volume of data increase, so do the requirements for protecting the data. EHRs can provide revolutionary improvements in patient care and medical research, as the healthcare industry evolves toward Healthcare 4.0. However, technological advances should not compromise patient privacy and data security to achieve their intended outcomes. Therefore, any solution must focus on and mandate the core privacy and IS principles as intrinsic pillars of the design.

A suitable private/consortium blockchain-implementation model with ABACs can address the cyber-security CIA tenets demanded by IS protocols by separating patient records into managed private state databases, while recording irreversible hashes of the records in a common channel-state blockchain. Such a solution can also manage access at the data-record level to address authorization issues, with non-repudiation built into the core design of blockchain. Additionally, the solution can help tackle cyber-resiliency issues, such as survivability, reliability, maintainability, and adaptability, which are particularly useful as the realm of EHRs evolve rapidly with new IoT services and security demands.

REFERENCES

Aceto, G., Persico, V., & Pescapé, A. (2020). Industry 4.0 and health: Internet of Things, big data, and cloud computing for Healthcare 4.0. *Journal of Industrial Information Integration*, *18*, 100129. doi:10.1016/j.jii.2020.100129

Adlam, R., & Haskins, B. (2019). A permissioned blockchain approach to the authorization process in electronic health records. In *2019 International Multidisciplinary Information Technology and Engineering Conference (IMITEC)*, (pp. 1-8). IEEE 10.1109/IMITEC45504.2019.9015927

Al-Odat, Z. A., Srinivasan, S. K., Al-qtiemat, E., Dubasi, M. A. L., & Shuja, S. (2018). *Iot-based secure embedded scheme for insulin pump data acquisition and monitoring*. arXiv preprint arXiv:1812.02357.

Angraal, S., Krumholz, H. M., & Schulz, W. L. (2017). Blockchain technology: Applications in health care. *Circulation: Cardiovascular Quality and Outcomes*, *10*(9), e003800. doi:10.1161/CIRCOUT-COMES.117.003800 PMID:28912202

Bagayogo, F. F., Lapointe, L., & Bassellier, G. (2014). Enhanced use of IT: A new perspective on post-adoption. *Journal of the Association for Information Systems*, *15*(7), 3. doi:10.17705/1jais.00367

Bansler, J. P., Havn, E. C., Schmidt, K., Mønsted, T., Petersen, H. H., & Svendsen, J. H. (2016). Cooperative epistemic work in medical practice: An analysis of physicians' clinical notes. *Computer Supported Cooperative Work*, *25*(6), 503–546. doi:10.100710606-016-9261-x

Beaudry, A., Vaghefi, I., Bagayogo, F., & Lapointe, L. (2020). Impact of IT user behavior: Observations through a new lens. *Communications of the Association for Information Systems*, *46*(1), 15. doi:10.17705/1CAIS.04615

Burton-Jones, A., & Grange, C. (2013). From use to effective use: A representation theory perspective. *Information Systems Research*, *24*(3), 632–658. doi:10.1287/isre.1120.0444

Burton-Jones, A., & Volkoff, O. (2017). How can we develop contextualized theories of effective use? A demonstration in the context of community-care electronic health records. *Information Systems Research*, *28*(3), 468–489. doi:10.1287/isre.2017.0702

Catalini, C. (2017). How blockchain technology will impact the digital economy. *Blockchains Smart Contracts Internet Things*, *4*, 2292-2303. https://ide.mit.edu/sites/default/files/publications/IDE%20Research%20Paper_v0517.pdf

Chen, L., Xu, L., Gao, Z., Lu, Y., & Shi, W. (2018). Tyranny of the majority: On the (im)possibility of correctness of smart contracts. *IEEE Security and Privacy*, *16*(4), 30–37. doi:10.1109/MSP.2018.3111240

Cisco. (2020). *2020 Global Network Trends Report*. https://www.cisco.com/c/m/en_us/solutions/enterprise-networks/networking-report.html

Davidson, S., De Filippi, P., & Potts, J. (2018). Blockchains and the economic institutions of capitalism. *Journal of Institutional Economics*, *14*(4), 639–658. doi:10.1017/S1744137417000200

Del Fiol, G., Kohlmann, W., Bradshaw, R. L., Weir, C. R., Flynn, M., Hess, R., Schiffman, J. D., Nanjo, C., & Kawamoto, K. (2020). Standards-based clinical decision support platform to manage patients who meet guideline-based criteria for genetic evaluation of familial cancer. *JCO Clinical Cancer Informatics*, *4*(4), 1–9. doi:10.1200/CCI.19.00120 PMID:31951474

Fragidis, L. L., & Chatzoglou, P. D. (2018). Implementation of a nationwide electronic health record (EHR). *International Journal of Health Care Quality Assurance*, *31*(2), 116–130. doi:10.1108/IJHC-QA-09-2016-0136 PMID:29504871

Gajek, S., Lees, M., & Jansen, C. (2020). IIoT and cyber-resilience: Could blockchain have thwarted the Stuxnet attack? *AI & Society*. Advance online publication. doi:10.100700146-020-01023-w

Geusebroek, J. (2012). *Cyber Risk Governance-Towards a framework for managing cyber related risks from an integrated IT governance perspective* (Master's thesis). Institute of Information and Computing Sciencem, Utrecht University.

Glaser, F. (2017). *Pervasive decentralisation of digital infrastructures: A framework for blockchain enabled system and use case analysis*. doi:10.24251/HICSS.2017.186

Grech, A., & Camilleri, A. F. (2017). *Blockchain in education*. Publications Office of the European Union. doi:10.2760/60649

Griggs, K. N., Ossipova, O., Kohlios, C. P., Baccarini, A. N., Howson, E. A., & Hayajneh, T. (2018). Healthcare blockchain system using smart contracts for secure automated remote patient monitoring. *Journal of Medical Systems*, *42*(7), 130. doi:10.100710916-018-0982-x PMID:29876661

Guo, H., Li, W., Nejad, M., & Shen, C. C. (2019, July). Access control for electronic health records with hybrid blockchain-edge architecture. In *2019 IEEE International Conference on Blockchain (Blockchain)* (pp. 44-51). IEEE. 10.1109/Blockchain.2019.00015

Gupta, R., Tanwar, S., Tyagi, S., Kumar, N., Obaidat, M. S., & Sadoun, B. (2019). Habits: Blockchain-based telesurgery framework for Healthcare 4.0. *2019 International Conference on Computer, Information and Telecommunication Systems (CITS)*, 1–5. 10.1109/CITS.2019.8862127

Harman, T., Mahadevan, P., Mukherjee, K., Chandrashekar, P., Venkiteswaran, S., & Mukherjea, S. (2019). Cyber resiliency automation using blockchain. *2019 IEEE International Conference on Cloud Computing in Emerging Markets (CCEM)*, 51–54. 10.1109/CCEM48484.2019.00011

Henry, R., Herzberg, A., & Kate, A. (2018). Blockchain access privacy: Challenges and directions. *IEEE Security and Privacy*, *16*(4), 38–45. doi:10.1109/MSP.2018.3111245

Hobbs, P. (2003). The Use of Evidentiality in Physicians' Progress Notes. *Discourse Studies, 5*(4), 451-478.

Hyperledger Fabric. (2020a). *Blockchain network, 2.2*. https://hyperledger-fabric.readthedocs.io/en/release-2.2/network/network.html

Hyperledger Fabric. (2020b). *Membership Service Provider, 2.2*. https://hyperledger-fabric.readthedocs.io/en/release-2.2/membership/membership.html

Hyperledger Fabric. (2020c). *Private Data, 2.2.* https://hyperledger-fabric.readthedocs.io/en/release-2.2/private-data/private-data.html#what-is-a-private-data-collection

Kierkegaard, P. (2011). Electronic health record: Wiring Europe's healthcare. *Computer Law & Security Review, 27*(5), 503–515. doi:10.1016/j.clsr.2011.07.013

Klonoff, D. (2017). Fog computing and edge computing architectures for processing data from diabetes devices connected to the medical Internet of Things. *Journal of Diabetes Science and Technology, 11*(4), 647–652. doi:10.1177/1932296817717007 PMID:28745086

Ma, Y., & Fang, Y. (2020). Current status, issues, and challenges of blockchain applications in education. *International Journal of Emerging Technologies in Learning, 15*(12), 20–31. doi:10.3991/ijet.v15i12.13797

Nakamoto, S. (2008). Bitcoin: A peer-to-peer electronic cash system. *Bitcoin.* https://bitcoin.org/bitcoin.pdf

Nasiri, S., Sadoughi, F., Tadayon, M. H., & Dehnad, A. (2019). Security requirements of Internet of Things-based healthcare system: A survey study. *Acta Informatica Medica, 27*(4), 253. doi:10.5455/aim.2019.27.253-258 PMID:32055092

Offner, K., Sitnikova, E., Joiner, K., & MacIntyre, C. (2020). Towards understanding cybersecurity capability in Australian healthcare organisations: A systematic review of recent trends, threats and mitigation. *Intelligence and National Security, 35*(4), 556–585. doi:10.1080/02684527.2020.1752459

Parisi, A. (2020). *Securing blockchain networks like Ethereum and Hyperledger Fabric* (1st ed.). Packt Publishing.

Pilkington, M. (2016). Blockchain technology: Principles and applications. In F. X. Olleros & M. Zhegu (Eds.), *Research handbook on digital transformations* (pp. 1–39). Edward Elgar. doi:10.4337/9781784717766.00019

Privacy Act. 1988 (Cth) part ii.6 (Austl.). (1988). https://www.legislation.gov.au/Details/C2014C00076

Seebacher, S., & Schüritz, R. (2017). Blockchain technology as an enabler of service systems: A structured literature review. *International Conference on Exploring Services Science*, 12–23. https://link.springer.com/chapter/10.1007/978-3-319-56925-3_2

Stamatellis, C., Papadopoulos, P., Pitropakis, N., Katsikas, S., & Buchanan, W. (2020). A privacy-preserving healthcare framework using Hyperledger Fabric. *Sensors (Basel), 20*(22), 1–14. doi:10.339020226587 PMID:33218022

Standards Australia. (2011). *Information security management in health using ISO/IEC 27002 (AS ISO 27799-2011).* Techstreet Enterprise.

Tanwar, S., Parekh, K., & Evans, R. (2020). Blockchain-based electronic healthcare record system for Healthcare 4.0 applications. *Journal of Information Security and Applications, 50*, 102407. doi:10.1016/j.jisa.2019.102407

Tapscott, D., & Tapscott, A. (2017). How blockchain will change organizations. *MIT Sloan Management Review, 58*(2), 10.

Thuemmler, C., & Bai, C. (2017). Health 4.0: Application of industry 4.0 design principles in future asthma management. In C. Thuemmler & C. Bai (Eds.), *Health 4.0: How virtualization and big data are revolutionizing healthcare* (pp. 23–37). Springer International Publishing. doi:10.1007/978-3-319-47617-9_2

Warkentin, M., & Orgeron, C. (2020). Using the security triad to assess blockchain technology in public sector applications. *International Journal of Information Management*, *52*, 1–8. doi:10.1016/j.ijinfomgt.2020.102090

Yaga, D., Mell, P., Roby, N., & Scarfone, K. (2019). *Blockchain technology overview*. doi:10.6028/NIST.IR.8202

This research was previously published in the Handbook of Research on Advancing Cybersecurity for Digital Transformation; pages 61-78, copyright year 2021 by Information Science Reference (an imprint of IGI Global).

Section 4
Utilization and Applications

Chapter 45
Perspectives of Blockchain in Cybersecurity:
Applications and Future Developments

Muath A. Obaidat

Center for Cybercrime Studies, City University of New York, USA

Joseph Brown

City University of New York, USA

ABSTRACT

In recent years, blockchain has emerged as a popular data structure for use in software solutions. However, its meteoric rise has not been without criticism. Blockchain has been the subject of intense discussion in the field of cybersecurity because of its structural characteristics, mainly the permanency and decentralization. However, the blockchain technology in this field has also received intense scrutiny and caused to raise questions, such as, Is the application of blockchain in the field simply a localized trend or a bait for investors, both without a hope for permanent game-changing solutions? and Is blockchain an architecture that will lead to lasting disruptions in cybersecurity? This chapter aims to provide a neutral overview of why blockchain has risen as a popular pivot in cybersecurity, its current applications in this field, and an evaluation of what the future holds for this technology given both its limitations and advantages.

INTRODUCTION

As an emergent technology, blockchain has been a crux of discussion and experimentation in many fields. One among these is cybersecurity - a fast-moving, ever-changing industry which is constantly at the mercy of changing norms. The blockchain technology did not emerge with cybersecurity solely in mind, but rather as a means of decentralizing data while maintaining trust between users. However, as blockchain grew in notability, its purpose expanded to academia and commerce, where it quickly

DOI: 10.4018/978-1-6684-7132-6.ch045

developed in the cybersecurity area as well because of its intrinsic characteristics, commonly cited as immutability and decentralization.

Cybersecurity is a field which demands evolution at a more frequent rate than its constituent industries. As other technological norms evolve in tandem, cybersecurity must evolve at a relative rate in order to ensure the safety of - or alternatives to - such norms. To adhere to both the ever-changing norms of technology as well as the constant race for improved soundness and convenience for security, cybersecurity remains a field which is constantly evolving. As new architectures and protocols enter the public consciousness, such concepts always find their way into the sphere of cybersecurity discussion and research. Can these concepts be utilized to improve security? What implications do such concepts have for the field? One of these concepts is blockchain. The spur in discussion and research about blockchain has largely been fueled by both a desire for innovation as well as changing logistical cybersecurity structures which have already been considered as standard, such as the client-server or third-party authentication models. Blockchain stands as a contrast to historical architectures and security methodologies, and thus has brought some renewed hopes for researchers and businesses for the future, while others remain skeptical of its applicability.

The introduction of any elements considered ground-breaking or game-changing into a field, brings its own problems. These elements do exist in isolation, but alongside an omnipresent race for innovation, notability, or attracting the attention of investment without care for the integrity of proposed solutions. In the past few years, blockchain has shifted from a once curious concept into a pivotal discussion point in the fields of software, computer science, and cybersecurity. The exponential growth in popularity of blockchain has drawn rigorous debate; some voices purport blockchain to be a universal solution for filling prior gaps in historical fields, while others believe blockchain is simply a passing fad. As mentioned above, in cybersecurity especially, blockchain has remained a hot button yet also a controversial topic.

This chapter aims to present an investigation into the place of blockchain within the current field of cybersecurity, and evaluate its possible presence in the field in the future. The organization of this chapter is broken into three sections as follows. The first section outlines the characteristics of blockchain as they pertain to cybersecurity, discussing both the advantages of the blockchain architecture as well as the limitations and liabilities that its implementation could propose. The second section uses the first as a springboard to both discuss and evaluate the most popular currently discussed applications of blockchain within the cybersecurity field. The third section discusses the future implications of what impact blockchain will have on the cybersecurity field; it discusses both what opportunities blockchain has created which may continue to be influential in the future, as well as what issues a blockchain-centric future for cybersecurity may create.

CHARACTERISTICS OF BLOCKCHAIN

The usages of blockchain within cybersecurity and other perpendicular fields such as finance, typically lean on the core architectural traits of blockchain rather than more tangential extrapolations of its functionalities. Possible usages of blockchain within the field which have been promoted both by studies and private firms have included digital identity management, including digital signatures which is a direct derivative of the inherent functionality of the data structure. There are typically five core architectural characteristics of blockchain: *decentralized, immutable, anonymous, cryptographically encrypted,* and *trust-based.* Each of these elements has their own extrapolations within the field of cybersecurity (Yeasmin, 2019; Yassein, 2019). Brief explanation is as follows:

- **Decentralization** refers to the structure of inter-node communication within a blockchain network. This is dependent in part on the type of blockchain deployed, which is discussed within sections below. Decentralization, in general, typically means there is no centralized authority for assignment of permissions and storage.
- **Immutability** typically is a guarantee that data retains integrity and cannot be modified once stored; this is achieved in blockchain through the mutual agreement upon data between ledgers.
- **Anonymity** is facilitated in part through the decentralized nature of blockchain. Since there is no central authority, identities are distinct only through their communication, not their identity. Since blockchain is typically built on asymmetric encryption, identities are based around keys rather than being tied to personal identifiable information. It should be noted that the anonymity facilitated by blockchain is not a lack of identity, but rather a lack of publicly centralized identity. The identity which exists is tied to a key rather than to an individual. This distinction is what allows smart contracts to exist. Theoretically, blockchain applications can eliminate anonymity by assigning identities to keys, but this would done be through a middleware implementation, not through an inherent function of blockchain itself.
- **Cryptographic encryption** is a self-evident facet, as blockchain is built on asymmetric encryption between ledger storage and clients. Data within the ledger is encrypted while respective clients possess needed keys for decryption and management of their own data.
- **Trust**-based is a slightly more complicated characteristic. Trust refers to the overall integrity and legitimacy of actions between authorities manipulating data within a wider network. *Trust* is built differently, depending on blockchain structure; "proof" mechanisms are used for facilitating *access control*, which is the basis of trust.

While these traits may overlap with fundamental concepts within cybersecurity, one striking issue which researchers have struggled with is the imprecise nature of blockchain. As a result of its vast usage and asymmetric, decentralized deployments from a wide variety of sources and usages, it is hard to universally consider any non-theoretical traits as standard. This lack of standardized foundations has meant that, especially in a concrete field such as cybersecurity (where standardized information, outcome, and reliability are apropos to applicability), blockchain can be hard to coherently develop solutions with or to study consistently. This has led to a strong nuance in research, which has in turn led to a strong communal desire for general classification for the purpose of further judging accessibility and applicability (Yassein, 2019).

The architecture of blockchain itself is not singular; there are different categories for the structure of ledgers, such as the nature of visibility, or for what algorithm is used to guarantee trust. As such, some architectures are not suited for all applications in all given fields, and some are better suited than others. Intense research has been done for lending credence to the applicability of blockchain, both for the more generalized universal concept of blockchain itself, as well as the differentiations between variant architectures. This has been referred to as *blockchain applicability framework*. In this framework, the functionality of an application is contrasted with various variables to determine how its ecosystem fits (or fails to fit) not just into a blockchain itself, but also into individual categorizations of blockchain (such as public or private). It is divided into five domains; *data and participation, technical attributes, security, trust parameters,* and *performance/efficiency.* Each of these domains is constituted by several sub-domains, which themselves are structured around the aforementioned variables to determine the needs of a given system (Gourisetti, 2019).

Blockchain Architecture

Blockchain's extrapolation differs slightly depending on the architecture of the ledger. Although there are some elements which may overlap between categorizations, some categories of blockchain are best suited for certain applications over others, depending on the needs of the individual ecosystem.

Types of Blockchain

There are three main types of blockchain, each with its own distinct structures. These include *public, "consortium",* and *private.* Refer to Figure 1. In a public blockchain, every node within the ledger participates in verification, and thus creates a decentralized data structure. Public blockchains are permissionless, with every node carrying equal participation. This category of blockchain is typically deployed in ecosystems where every node is considered equal, most popularly, in cryptocurrencies. In a consortium blockchain, there are distributed permissions, unlike a public version. As a result, it is partially centralized; however, this creates a more secure environment, as the permissioned nodes allow relative security functionality. As such, the trust process is not universally mutual, but permissioned. Lastly, a private blockchain is one which is fully centralized. These blockchains are strictly permissioned and typically reserved for dictation by a central organization. Certain functionalities, such as read or write permissions, are controlled by centralized preference. As a result of centralization however, data is not guaranteed full integrity; thus, data tampering may occur in some environments, which may present an issue depending on the purpose the blockchain is meant to fulfill (Yeasmin, 2019; Gourisetti, 2019; Yassein, 2019).

Figure 1. Visualization of blockchain architectures; from left to right: public, private, consortium.

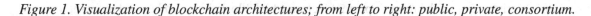

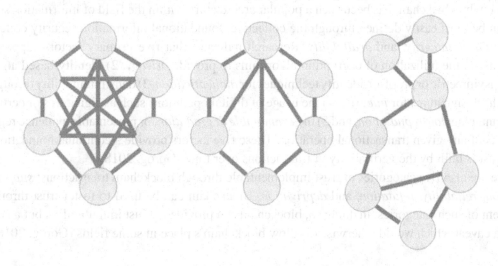

Consensus Algorithms

As mentioned above, blockchain is built on the facilitation of trust between nodes. Within a given network, trust is one of the most important characteristics of any deployed system in cybersecurity. In order to build trust, blockchain architectures implement internal schemes called *consensus algorithms*, which are fundamental blueprints for how nodes communicate within a wider architecture. There are various different algorithms which can be used, and the choice of one over another typically relies on both the functionality as well as the category of blockchain in question. As such, choosing the correct algorithm, much like choosing the correct category of blockchain, is vital to an application's functionality. These algorithms are used for fostering both reliable data integrity as well as the distribution of access control among nodes. There are three popular versions of *consensus algorithms*: *proof of work, proof of stake,* and *proof of authority*. In a *proof of work* algorithm, iterative blocks are created through challenges which are exponentially hard to create, but easy to verify. Thus, nodes must work to create a proof, creating an environment in which blocks are probabilistically near impossible to modify, and also work in an iterative chain manner. In a *proof of stake* algorithm, the trust is distributed. Nodes compete by offering relative proportions of their stake in a system in order to be selected as valid. Selected nodes then verify transactions as valid. *Proof of authority* works as a modified version of *proof of stake;* in addition to competing for validation, the identity of the node itself is put at stake when competing for validation.

As such, limited nodes maintain authority for approval at any given time. It is important to note that these are not the only forms of consensus algorithms; there are at least a dozen popular other ones which have been employed by various blockchain applications. Other forms of consensus algorithms may include *proof of burn*, an algorithm where authority is proven by burning an amount of a stake in a system from a node. However, the three algorithms mentioned above are typically the most common in wider extrapolatable discussions (Yeasmin, 2019; Gourisetti, 2019).

Trust Factors

As seen above, trust is one of the most important factors which blockchain can be used to facilitate. This is, in part, why blockchain has been such a popular architecture within the field of information security. Trust can be most easily defined through the collective, foundational information security concepts of *confidentiality, integrity,* and *availability*. Research indicates that five primary factors support these operations: 1) the utilization of encryption algorithms to provide *privacy*, 2) identity-based algorithm through asymmetric or proof-of-identity techniques for *authentication*, 3) data immutability through storage and hash signatures for *integrity,* 4) the usage of digital operations such as signatures or certificates for guaranteeing *non-repudiation*, and 5) the *examinable degradation*, or presentable evidence regarding the norms of any given transactional operation. These five factors provide a continual foundation from which trust is built by the verifiability of transactions over time (Gorog, 2018).

There are also five categories of trust implementable through blockchain transactions: *suppression, validation, reliability, refutation,* and *deprivation*. Blockchain can be used to foster trust through the fulfillment of such categories; in doing so, blockchain can provide not just immutability, but also traceability, a caveat which would otherwise disallow blockchain's place in some fields (Gorog, 2018).

Smart Contracts

These are another important aspect of blockchain architecture. Similar to how anonymity and encryption are features which are derivative of intrinsic qualities of blockchain, smart contracts are derivative of both blockchain's inherent features of identity management and integral data storage. It is a protocol pre-baked into the transactional structure of the architecture. They allow for permanent, immutable agreements to take place between parties, which are then stored encrypted on the blockchain ledger (Yeasmin, 2019; Abbas, 2019). These contracts happen between nodes on a ledger, and facilitate guaranteed transactions, as well as the permanency of signatures between two parties. This feature is related to *"Digital Signatures"*, another aspect of blockchain architecture which facilitates an important need within the cybersecurity field. *Digital signatures* are related to identity management, and allow for a node - presumably held by a consistent entity - to sign transactions. It is most commonly facilitated through asymmetric cryptography (Huynh, 2019).

CURRENT CYBERSECURITY PARADIGMS

The goal of cybersecurity can be succinctly summarized as managing risk and protecting assets. A popular subcategory, *information security*, can be summarized with three facets: confidentiality, integrity, and availability of data (Andriole, 2020). Researchers have noted that because of the exponential growth in reliance on technology, the demand for innovative cybersecurity tools and protocols has grown. Because of the timely presence and popularity of blockchain, it has become a popular staple within proposed cybersecurity whitepapers and studies. Some still ask, however, has blockchain proven itself as a pivotal concept to warrant such attention? Some academics, as well as business people, say it may be too early to tell, but the infant state of blockchain may foretell a future explosion of popularity, similar to the previous rise of cloud computing and cloud-based solutions (Andriole, 2020).

Blockchain's looming presence in cybersecurity has mimicked its place within the wider private business sector. Because of its trending and attractive nature to investors, blockchain has largely been proposed as a solution for bridging gaps and solving unresolved issues in the field, regardless of the actual viability of it within that sub-category. This has also been a result of unproven theory; many business pitches and studies which tout blockchain have not provided proof-of-concept or deployed solutions, and have simply existed as quantifiably vague theory. However, with that having been said, this does not mean that blockchain cannot separately be a useful tool within the cybersecurity field aside from the above also being true. Four particular usages of blockchain have been more popularly touted as extrapolatable features: data integrity and confidentiality aside from human oversight, previously discussed data immutability and mutuality between nodes, scalability of usership, and permanency of user identities (Sharma, 2019).

Application Determinacy

Due to the explosion of proposals, a need has emerged for determining if blockchain is truly needed for a given solution. Prior research has recommended a four-step process for assessing the applications of emerging technology, under which blockchain would fall. The steps include: 1) technology's background, 2) technology's potential impact, 3) pilot demonstration identification, and 4) planned demonstration development (Andriole, 2020). In the cybersecurity field, many applications of blockchain have stalled at step three; there is an abundance of discussion about the theorized impact of blockchain as well as the traits of it as an emerging technology, as well as theoretical applications within localized fields, but many theories have not manifested in active demonstrations. In the business sector, there have been more demonstrations of blockchain technology, but many have not managed to fully extrapolate the concept to where such demonstrations are more practical to use than current traditional methodologies.

Cryptocurrency and Tokens

It would also be impossible to discuss blockchain's current applicative presence without discussing cryptocurrency, and cryptocurrency's place in cybersecurity (Mohanta, 2019). While cryptocurrency is not a topic inherently related to cybersecurity, extrapolations of concepts introduced by cryptocurrency have found some level of integration - or at least discussion - within the field. This has been partially bolstered by the rise of features such as smart contracts popularized by the Ethereum platform (Polvora, 2020). Such extrapolations, besides smart contracts, have included ideas of permissioned policies and/or access controls based on relative token holding (Polvora, 2020). Such discussion has been largely influenced by ICOs, or "Initial Coin Offerings", that are preliminary investment rounds of cryptocurrency ecosystems which mimic public company stock offerings. Ideas have included distributed token holdings, which in turn relate to relative access control or permissions in relation to an application's ecosystem. Since the tokens are possessed immutably by wallets tied to specific identities, the owner of such identity can be considered to have concrete relative control as such (Polvora, 2020). Despite being in early stages, there has still been some level of proof-of-concept of many of these techniques. While there has, to some degree, been proof of such working - at least on small levels, in whitepapers, or in nascent stages - worries have still stemmed from various issues, such as identities being more at risk if compromised through tangential means (such as phishing or otherwise), as well as other more typical worries such as the previously discussed limitations of blockchain networks, which still ring true here.

Blockchain vs. Cloud Computing

Blockchain has drawn significant comparisons to cloud computing. Refer to Figure 2 for virtualization for Cloud distributed computing. Cloud-based security solutions have grown significantly in popularity over the last decade and have targeted similar solutions in similar fields. Unlike blockchain, however, cloud computing solutions at times amplify narrow vulnerabilities, or can even create new surfaces of attack, like centralized data storage or shared access control. Blockchain has been proposed as a solution for replacing more centralized cloud-computing structures with decentralized architectures and eliminating vulnerabilities in turn. This is not to say that blockchain is fully impenetrable, but rather that the surfaces of attack are greatly distilled in comparison to simple cloud-computing solutions; this is partially because of the lack of singular points of entry on most implementations of blockchain architectures (Kshetri, 2017).

Figure 2. Visualization of Cloud Computing

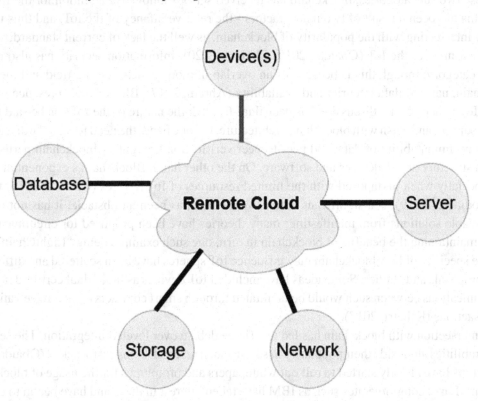

CYBERSECURITY SOLUTIONS AND DISCUSSION

Current applications of blockchain, whether in cybersecurity or in wider fields, are hard to evaluate in full, which in turn has led to segmented evaluations of their usage. This is because current designs vary greatly, and thus have made implementation as well as deployment and maintenance, difficult. Unlike many current systems, blockchain's relative infancy combined with its requirement of high levels of sophisticated technical knowledge and complex setup requirements make it harder to be adopted widely (Vance, 2019). This has raised questions, particularly in the field of cybersecurity where concrete knowledge of what one is working with is of utmost importance. Despite the constant desire for innovation within the field, precedent is also very important within the industry among professionals, and the lack of large-scale precedent for blockchain's usage has been a detriment to the spread of its adoption. This is not to say, however, that there have not been successful test cases or proof-of-concepts, simply that the wider application of blockchain within cybersecurity has been handicapped because of unfamiliarity and decency, as well as lack of historical usages proving its usefulness over more traditional implementations and architectures.

Blockchain and the Internet of Things

While there has been a general explosion in the popularity of blockchain, it has seen particular exponential interest in two cybersecurity fields: information security and Internet of Things (IoT) security.

Out of these two subcategories, blockchain has received serious innovative attention for the Internet of Things. This has been a result of two major factors - the relative infancy of the IoT, and thus its timely popularity intersecting with the popularity of blockchain, as well the lack of current standardization and security measures for the IoT (Obaidat, 2019; Obaidat, 2020). Information security has also remained a popular category; though this is because of an overlap in motives between the field and the features of blockchain, namely, data integrity and availability (Ahram, 2017). Blockchain's presence within the sphere of IoT cybersecurity discussion has been dual-faceted: the nature of the IoT can be said to simultaneously support and clash with blockchain architecture. On one hand, the need for standardized identity management, immutability of data, and peer-to-peer verification brought by blockchain perfectly suits the design structure of IoT devices and software. On the other hand, Blockchain's exponential resource usage, especially when juxtaposed with the limited resources of IoT devices (Obaidat, 2019; Hassebo, 2018; Khodjaeva, 2019), is a significant hurdle. While this has been an obstacle, it has not fully prevented possible solutions from manifesting; many theories have been proposed for circumventing this issue and maintaining the benefits of blockchain in turn, one such example being "LightChain" (Doku, 2019). The specifics of how blockchain may influence IoT spheres have been scattered and differ greatly between proposals and studies. Some ideas have included IoT devices as individual certified nodes, and all communications between such would be facilitated through smart contracts to guarantee validity, and track transactions (Kshetri, 2017).

IoT's intersection with blockchain has led to a fierce debate over leveled integration. The severity of IoT vulnerabilities alongside their popularity has led to such research being fast-tracked (Obaidat, 2019). Many startups have already started to roll out whitepapers and prototypes for the usage of blockchain in IoT systems. Large conglomerates such as IBM have taken interest in these and have begun to distribute blockchain services for supply chains to rely on. These inter-business facilitations have elevated blockchain to industrial level discussion. Blockchain-based protocols have been proposed for the deployment of such architectures as safeguards in industrial systems which rely on wireless communications. The use of blockchain to validate identities between sources has made it an important discussion point for devices that vitally rely on communication from a select source of valid entities (Kshetri, 2017). The intersection of IoT and blockchain proposals, however, have not been without issue; depending on the infrastructure of blockchain implementation, which would be determined by the type of blockchain, there are possible privacy issues, considering the vast amount of data collected and transferred between IoT devices. There are already large concerns about IoT device interactions in this regard which have not been solved by consensus yet, especially considering an industry-wide lack of standardization. Blockchain's integration with the IoT does not inherently solve these issues and may open up new issues because of its ledger-based distribution structure. Possible solutions to this have included tiered networks with individual private blockchains connected to wider public blockchains, distributed with fine-grained access controls. These architectures, however, have largely not been tested. Blockchain has been proposed also as a management platform for IoT devices, essentially functioning as a middleware for managing data, establishing permanent identities, and tokenizing privileges (Ali, 2019).

Facilitation of API Functionalities

Blockchain's cybersecurity functionality is by no means limited to IoT devices; blockchain as a non-IoT data management platform has also been tested separately as another popular means. Due to its node-based structure as well as its immutable nature, blockchain has been used as a platform for simplifying user management, particularly in relation to cloud-based applications. This assists in facilitating access control, as well as bolstering user authentication methods and implementing single sign-on capabilities. Blockchain has also been proposed methodically through other approaches, one being an "API Approach", where blockchain functions as an API to facilitate other functionalities rather than acting as a functional platform in and of itself. Some of these usages have included DevOps, cloud integration, and data analytics, particularly for apps, businesses, and ads (Ahram, 2017). As mentioned before, this may echo traits of cloud platforms. Much capacity has been given to comparing facets of cloud computing and blockchain platforms. Research has noted that some cloud platforms follow "zero trust" security models, and, similar to blockchain, fully employ encrypted transactional models. Blockchain, as a decentralized model for the most part (outside of modified architectures such as consortium), does lack the segmented control schemes which cloud computing allows, such as administrator oversight. However, blockchain arguably employs better identity management and data immutability, at the cost of compromising that client nodes bear more serious implications because of such. However, with current technology, hacking into a blockchain node would be significantly harder, as attacks would be limited to brute-forcing or client hijacking, both of which have a far lower rate of success than man-in-the-middle, masquerade, or replay style attacks. However, both models are still susceptible to attacks based on human error, such as phishing or social engineering (Kshetri, 2017).

Given the above evaluations of blockchain functionalities, it is not hard to see how most current applications of blockchain are comparable to current applications of cloud computing. However, there are nuances between the two which may affect which is more viable for an application (or user/enterprise, in turn) to utilize. Cloud computing relies on a third party with physical infrastructure, while blockchain is decentralized through a ledger, but may be facilitated through a third-party vendor. These options may fit different companies differently: some may want a third party for validatory oversight, while others may want to eliminate middlemen. Similarly, physical infrastructure may suit some, while ledger-based immutability may be better for other companies. Blockchain and cloud computing are very similar, however, not on all fronts. For example, while both carry nuances in how they are permissioned, blockchain can be selected to operate as permission-less, while this would be a risk under most cloud computing paradigms. Other nuances between the two, such as the level of encryption, would be left up to individual organizations to evaluate depending on target and vendor specifications. Both still face challenges, however; cloud computing is a less recent and more developed standard, while blockchain still faces early implementation issues such as lack of security mechanisms. In theory, both face resource management issues, albeit for different reasons - blockchain because of the exponential growth of needed resources for transactions and ledger-size, while cloud computing because of limited hardware resources for storage and speed (Kshetri, 2017).

Identity Management

Another functional usage of blockchain is the facilitation of digital certificates and signatures, an inherent attractive feature of its architecture. Refer to Figure 3. As such, its implementation has been simplified, but has not largely been deployed en masse. Many private companies have started either developing or rolling out solutions in this light, but, because of a race for innovation, these competing brands have largely crowded each other out from reaching wider accessibility. Larger brands such as Facebook or Twitter, however, have announced their own initiatives for developing blockchain-based solutions, some of which have intersected desires for immutable identity management and signatures (Ahram, 2017).

Popular applications of digital certification have promised a functionality for replacing notarization and have hinted at ideas for replacing infrastructure for intangible assets such as copyrights or licenses, as well as storage for public and private records, and taking advantage of smart contracts for implementation of arbitration and real-life contracts. Current implementations of many of these practices leave systems open to data tampering or theft; blockchain solutions promise to bolster cybersecurity standards for storage and transaction through increased confidentiality and integrity. Many private companies have undertaken these ideas already but have yet to break into the mainstream for further serious consideration (Alexander, 2019).

Figure 3. Visualization of digital signing and signature verification process

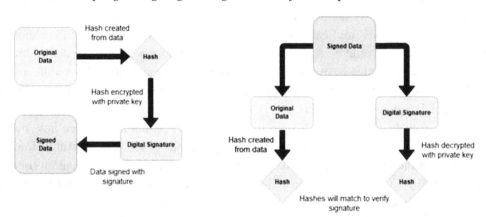

Other Applications

Further deployments of blockchain include email and endpoint security. The insecurity of current emailing services and protocols has remained an issue for multiple years; blockchain has been proposed as an alternative, and unlike many claims, has been backed by proof-of-concept tests. Blockchain has posed itself as a decentralized solution for email because of immutable transaction records and identity nonrepudiation. Current issues of message authenticity, from which phishing and fraud emails currently stem, could be eroded by the implementation of blockchain systems. Endpoint security, on the other hand, ties into the aforementioned intersection of Blockchain's popularity in relation to IoT security. Most IoT devices lack endpoint security measures, thus increasing the need for effective measures. Blockchain has been proposed as a solution primarily because attacks against blockchain-based architecture are weakened by the distributed architecture of blockchain, especially if data validation nodes are used. Much like email, use cases have been deployed for this as well, which have shown promising results (Vance, 2019).

Advantages of using blockchain for the above mentioned applications have a level of nuance between implementation but, beyond decentralization, also present certain advantages which suit some purposes over others; this includes trust between nodes, local-remote synchronization, availability of unchangeable data, and cross-node synchronization. In applications which require communication between individual nodes, or applications which rely on synchronization, blockchain has become an important discussion pivot. This is very easy to see in its popularity in the IoT, but also applies to other fields, such as fields looking to synchronize clients without reliance on a centralized database. Peer to peer communicative clients, which still require a level of trust certification, have found blockchain to be a suitable solution. However, for larger peer networks, the resource consumption and scaling performance issues with blockchain have remained a discouraging disadvantage (Yassein, 2019).

Functionality Challenges

Besides the inconsistencies between deployments of blockchain, other issues have been discussed widely in academic research of Blockchain's capabilities, especially in regards to security and privacy. Issues which the blockchain architecture possesses include balancing authority with integrity/data consistency, proportional control in a ledger's network by users, and exponential size of operations and size. Balancing confidentiality with the connective nature of blockchain has also remained an issue. Blockchain's immutability can be a double-edged sword as well, in the case of mistakes from users or organizations. The exponential cost and size of blockchain ledgers, as previously mentioned, has remained a massive issue, even for enterprise organizations (Yassein, 2019).

Various solutions have been proposed for solving many of these limitations, such as further deployment of encryption techniques, as well as the implementation of new data structures (Yassein, 2019). The infancy and lack of standardization of blockchain has been a catalyst in many of these limitations (Ahram, 2017). Blockchain is not only a complex system in and of itself, but also it does not suit a "plug and play" style of development. This is a potential drawback for two reasons. Firstly, as blockchain is a relatively nascent architecture, it discourages many from adopting such because of it being unproven. However, the lack of adoption, in turn, means a lack of widespread security mechanisms have been tested or developed on a wide scale basis, in comparison to traditional methods which are more easily tested. The complex and intended large, decentralized nature of blockchain makes proof-of-concepts hard to evaluate in low-density or testing environments (Kshetri, 2017). However, as blockchain matures as an architecture, many of these issues are expected to be solved, especially as it attracts more academic attention for research (Ahram, 2017; Kshetri, 2017).

Common Attacks and Threats

A variety of attacks also exist because of intrinsic features of blockchain networks. "Majority" attacks, as exemplified in Figure 4, remain an issue in many networks, which can occur when a node controls the majority of stakes in a given environment. Similarly, "selfish mining" has remained an issue, where miners participate in creating blocks on a private branch and then only broadcast them to the public network once the chain is longer than the public network, thus replacing them (Abbas, 2019; Huynh, 2019). Distributed Denial of Service (DDoS) attacks are also a threat to blockchain networks. This may occur when a dishonest node uses a large number of other nodes to attempt to overwhelm requests on the rest of the blockchain ledger (Huynh, 2019; Oksiiuk, 2020).

It is also important to note that, while blockchain bolsters authentication measures, because of its integrity of permanency and ability to foster digital signature and identity management, the immutable status of identities on a blockchain also brings its own worries. While authentication strength is partially dependent on the strength of cryptographic implementation, there are tangential vulnerabilities which may call for greater worry than their non-blockchain counterparts. Primarily, phishing and social engineering carry more grave risks for blockchain authentication than they do for other authentication procedures. This is because of the immutable, permanent nature of identities on a blockchain; if information regarding an identity is compromised, depending on the nature of the Blockchain's implementation, it may be permanently compromised (Oksiiuk, 2020).

Figure 4. Example of a "majority" attack in a blockchain, where malicious blocks outweigh original blocks, and thus overwrite them.

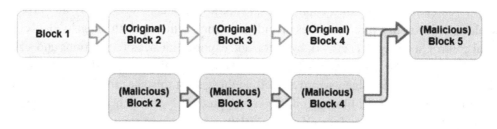

Limitations

Blockchain is commonly brought up in information security discussions for "big data" applications but suffers from some limitations which are often ignored. Firstly, block capacity is a large limitation. Wider implementations of blockchain have low block capacities, and while larger blocks can store more data, they cause significant performance and scaling issues. Smaller blocks, on the other hand, are reliable, but obviously limit the actual space for records. Secondly, because blockchain is a distributed ledger, the storage mechanism for large blockchains often does not take into account that ledgers are copied to the side of all users. This is, of course, dependent on implementation: some may circumvent this by using vendors or applications which simply facilitate access to a blockchain rather than distributing client nodes. Nevertheless, this remains an issue for some implementations; while this data is encrypted, it still opens data to data mining and other attacks depending on how the ledgers are actually accessed. It also means that attackers can potentially store permanent malicious data in a ledger (Dai, 2017).

FUTURE TRAJECTORIES AND DISCUSSION

Blockchain's future is still unclear; the technology is bright and is still drawing much attention and investment but is also mired by limitations and worries which have not been verifiably solved yet, despite their continual subjection to academic debate. Future applications of blockchain within the cybersecurity sphere will largely depend on the scale under which blockchain protrudes into the wider technical sphere. Both private and public (governmental) entities have commissioned research for enterprise implementations, but many of such remain, as aforementioned, confined to theorization or small-scaling testing rather than large-scale deployment. Most cybersecurity implications of where blockchain may shine in the future lies in either information security derivative functionalities or the facilitation of trust between transacting entities (Gorog, 2018).

Studies largely fall into two camps when considering which path blockchain may take in the future. One position is an optimistic view of integration on the public, communal level, replacing the foundations of many inter-entity communications (Aggarwal, 2019). On the other hand, a more pessimistic view which either passes off blockchain as a fad or instead proposes that current limitations on blockchain application architecture are enough to prevent it from being further pervasive in the future. Much discussion derivative of the former point does not necessarily agree with the possibility of blockchain's ability to constitute such functionality. When it comes to the integration of blockchain with concepts such as contracts, financial transactions, or other communal activities, there is not much debate as to *if* such integration can be done, but rather if it *should* be done (Aggarwal, 2019). There is much technical consensus on how these concepts could be implemented, but there is less consensus from an organizational standpoint insofar as the realistic measures under which such applications could be deployed.

Propositions and Frameworks

Research has indicated that future public implementations of blockchain must be open, transparent, and auditable, in order to circumvent worries which may otherwise manifest from the nature of the architecture. Most research on the future of blockchain in cybersecurity, and in wider fields to an extent, has indicated that the strongest promises of the architecture come from its facilitation of decentralization, and the ability for mutual, decentralized validation without the need for arbitrary authority (Oksiiuk, 2020). Such future implementations of blockchain may not be restricted solely to using public architectures but will have to pay close attention to caveats in individual blockchain categorizations according to the need of their applications. For example, applications which seek better privacy protections and better performance are more likely to depend on consortium blockchain models (Cai, 2018). It is important to note, however, that moving forward, the usage of the prior mentioned "blockchain applicability framework(s)" will be vital for this reason. Incorrect blockchain application may result not just in decreased performance but also in heightened security risks.

Developing decentralized applications is a lucrative measure with a high demand but presents unique challenges. It requires extra scrutiny, which blockchain may not be fully self-sufficient to handle. When dealing with the trust and assets of enterprises at high levels in particular, decentralized applications must be evaluated as holistically secure. This means that individual parts of the architecture - the consensus algorithm, the category of blockchain, and even the separate structure of the application - must all be given strict security and performance guidelines (Cai, 2018). Future opportunities for blockchain in this light may not just present themselves as innovations utilizing blockchain but rather as innovations built off of blockchain perpendicularly aimed at making blockchain utilization more accessible and/or secure to either users or to commercial or governmental enterprises.

Blockchain-as-a-Service

Future implementations of blockchain may replicate the current usage of cloud providers. Referring to Figure 5, just as cloud-based cybersecurity applications are provided as a *service*, alongside the rise of SaaS (Software-as-a-Service), PaaS (Platform-as-a-Service), and IaaS (Infrastructure-as-a-Service) models, research has indicated that the future of blockchain may popularize the model of *Blockchain-as-a-Service* (Andriole, 2020). This concept heavily ties into prior mentions of comparisons between blockchain and cloud computing; the similarity in service model and focused solutions also creates similarities on this front. Unlike cloud computing, however, a vendor would facilitate access rather than facilitate hosting. This is slightly different from the current cloud-computing model because a vendor is also liable for the actual maintenance of the core foundations of the platform. While the core functionality would be dependent on both the category of blockchain and consensus algorithm deployed, in this evolved model, a vendor would simply act as a front end for providing access to a ledger and, at best, moderate data on the application layer rather than the underlying data structure of blockchain. Some studies have noted that the rise of peer-to-peer ecosystems and contractor ("gig") platforms could be similarly bolstered by implementations of blockchain. This would be because of the identity management functionality of the architecture as well as the decentralized structure, the implementation of cryptocurrencies and tokens, and, most importantly, the smart contract functionality. Such implementations would likely mimic "as-a-service" infrastructures (Fraga-Lamas, 2019).

Figure 5. Comparison of service infrastructures.

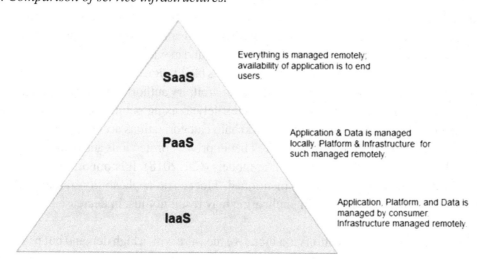

Blockchain as Infrastructure

As previously discussed, there is much discussion over Blockchain's possible place in replacing and/or aiding the foundational architectures of communal and legal activities, such as securing the integrity and availability of inter-entity contracts or providing a secure basis for voting (Aggarwal, 2019). While there has not been practical mass application of most of such proposals to date, surveyed and commissioned research has pinpointed that blockchain could be utilized as a cybersecurity tool for securing government level infrastructural needs; research into such has been commissioned by multiple governments, including the UK for energy infrastructure, the US for secured domestic messaging between officials and for identity certification, and Australia for securing communication between entities inside of wider "smart cities" (Vance, 2019). Blockchain has also been proposed as a means of securing voting from malicious influence; proposals have stated that blockchain would bolster risk reduction through identity validation as well as increase the speed of digitization while minimizing infrastructural interactions (Alexander, 2019). On this government level, blockchain has been proposed not only for civilian level transactions but also for trans-active systems on an infrastructural level. For example, the integration of blockchain into power grids may allow for permissioned, traceable, and immutable records of transactions which provide a higher security than otherwise purely centralized mechanisms often currently deployed. Smart contracts have been proposed as having a strong usage in infrastructural concerns, both akin to power grids as mentioned prior, as well as other societal needs, such as field devices or generators (Li, et al., 2019).

Elsewhere, blockchain has persisted in discussions of infrastructural means through the proposals for usage of ensuring trust and cybersecurity for complex energy transactions and data exchanges (Mylrea, 2017). Researchers have pointed out that, not only are many grids centralized but also that interconnectivity alongside current outdated technological means has made both energy grids as well as associated electrical infrastructure, greatly insecure. As cities move toward visions of smart cities, securing infrastructure becomes increasingly important as new vectors of attack become available. Blockchain's ability to create a decentralized "Energy Internet of Things" makes systematic attacks on infrastructural grids harder by decentralizing vulnerabilities. The usage of smart contracts may also increase resilience and more reliably track energy transactions within infrastructure. Researchers note that the integration of blockchain will also help both single out anomalous entities or transactions within a system and allow for a more streamlined intersection of infrastructural needs such as electricity and the reporting of data. These ideas have been tested on a small scale within testbeds but have not yet been extrapolated to apply to large cities. Much like other specialized, large-scale theories, these concepts are often found trapped in a limbo of not being able to be deployed because of a lack of proof but also not carrying proof because of their need for large-scale deployment in order to create such (Mylrea, 2017).

Specialized Usage

New opportunities regularly arise, such as those recently proposed within the automotive economy (Fraga-Lamas, 2019). The integration of blockchain within the sphere of automotive technology intersects with the recent rise of the intelligent automotive economy. The term "intelligent automotive" does not just apply to autonomous cars: it applies to any car with onboard technology for data processing. Many newer models of cars feature on-board computers, with some relying at least partially on cloud-based information. Given the absolute need for safety as a priority within an automobile, as computer systems are embedded in them, the need for cybersecurity arises. Cybersecurity for automotive may apply to different categorizations, not only the traditional categories of preventing cyber-attacks and ensuring reliability and validity of cloud information, but also new functionalities such as ensuring the validity of parts and protecting against counterfeits, and protecting the integrity of the production process. Studies say that blockchain may be utilized for the prevention of counterfeits through blockchain-based certificates; meanwhile, integrity during production processes may be facilitated through the usage of smart contracts. Other such benefits that blockchain may bring to smart-automobiles, essentially mimic the benefits blockchain brings to other integrations, namely information integrity and security through encryption, standardization, and decentralization (Narbayeva, 2020).

Whether or not blockchain can meet other more specialized purposes is still undecided. A significant amount of research has been dedicated to these more focused fields, as seen above, despite the otherwise scattered nature of scouting opportunities for blockchain to fulfill. Much like the considerations given to blockchain as a foundation for securing communal activities, much of the question of integration does not lay on *how* or *why*, but rather *if*. Surveyed research has found a significant number of benefits for blockchain, and, without a doubt, there will be continued discussion, especially for as long as a standard fails to exist otherwise for the IoT. Given the virtues and wide discussion of blockchain in relation to these narrow implementation ideas, there is much reason to think optimistically about their future. However, non-technical factors, such as business considerations, must also be taken into account in this regard (Ali, 2019).

Open Research and Current Challenges

As previously mentioned, if blockchain is to be deployed as massively accessible architecture, future implementations of blockchain will still have various hurdles to overcome which have not yet been solved. The most important of these includes the lack of scalability of blockchain - not of usership but instead with regards to processing transactions and consumption of resources. Furthermore, there are some privacy concerns within blockchain, e.g. those originating from the public nature of ledgers. Research has also indicated that bootstrapping could pose an issue for blockchain applications, as related to large commercial enterprise files and frameworks (Sharma, 2019). Accessibility is generally held back in a technical fashion; accessibility for blockchain must also be improved at a user-derivative level. As mentioned in the evaluation section, blockchain has been handicapped in its adoption because of the complexity surrounding its development, deployment, and maintenance. Experts in the cybersecurity field believe that, because of the importance of concrete understanding of employed metrics and concepts, the future of blockchain applications will be dependent on its ability to develop user friendly adaptations (Vance, 2019).

Performance

Many of the previously discussed limitations of blockchain, particularly in regards to performance and exponential resource usage, remain serious concerns for widespread adoption in the future. While individual implementations may not find these limitations as stifling due to their scope, many company products and academic studies which purport blockchain as a solution, intend for such to be deployed on a massive scale. Currently, these issues are generally incurred on wide scales and create worries in many of the organizations and clients who otherwise may be apt to adopt such innovative measures. The direct adoption, as well as the further discussion, of blockchain has not been fully blockaded by these issues. The reason being that there has been a significant interest in solving the issues, but progress has nonetheless been significantly slowed down. Many conclude that before blockchain can reach peak cybersecurity implementation in both the general public and within individual private sectors, these issues will have to be solved (or alternatively, at least addressed in part), due to them eclipsing the benefits blockchain otherwise brings (Alexander, 2019). These worries carry over to many of the more focused implementation ideas which outline blockchain as a solution, such as the previously discussed IoT, and thus may prove to be some of the biggest hurdles which blockchain will need to overcome before seeing wider implementation even within these narrow pigeonholes (Ali, 2019).

User Identification

While it has been previously discussed that decentralization, and thus strengthened anonymity measures, are possible future strengths for the Blockchain platform, this is a double-edged sword. Anonymity also implies a lack of traceability which may be a worry when considering the facilitation of illegal activity through blockchain. Since cybersecurity also involves offensive tactics rather than just defensive, blockchain architectures may hinder the ability of law enforcement to enforce laws regarding illegal transactions; alternatively, because of data permanency, the ability to hinder or delete the spread of illegal materials online (Oksiiuk, 2020).

Accessibility and Propagation

The future of blockchain's implementation in cybersecurity especially, parallel to its dependence on user accessibility, will also be heavily determined by the quality of research which discusses the concept. Academics have noted that claims about blockchain are tricky to make. For example, blockchain carries a reputation for immutability of data but is also vulnerable to majority or 51% of the attacks, which allows data to be modified. This creates concerns as to whether claims for the concept are fully understood and justified in how they are propagated between researchers, developers, governments, and business people. Current dissonances, for example, in claims of blockchain being fully immutable would be technically false because of the existence of these attacks. Nevertheless, such claims continue to be made (Vance, 2019).

As with the aforementioned topics, it is likely conclusive that, given the current status of blockchain as well as the consensus drawn around certain points, the future of blockchain will lie in specialized implementations rather than as a replacement for systems constituting historical methods and foundations. This is not to say that blockchain would not provide theoretical strengths in its implementation for these systems; rather, the viability of such will be likely limited to theory rather than practice. However, this is also not an ultimate conclusion but rather an evaluation of the current status of blockchain and its implementations which notes their highly volatile nature (Fraga-Lamas, 2019).

Applicability

The benefits of implementation within many of these new opportunities typically overlap with those proposed for other such systems. For example, we earlier discussed the possible usage of blockchain as a foundation for further technical standardization of communal activities (Fraga-Lamas, 2019). Many of these overlaps, even within these specialized systems, as seen with the above explanation of automotive integration, typically boil down to the same infrastructural benefits and limitations; these being standardization, identity management, and information security benefits, alongside limitations of scalability, complexity, and maintenance, amongst many others. Given that many of these benefits overlap concretely, it is hard to conclude whether blockchain is actually benefiting the individual fields or whether the field is simply absorbing the nature of blockchain. In other words, the discussion has often fallen on pivots of *"How would this function on blockchain?"* rather than *"How would this benefit from blockchain?"* Hence both the vague generality and the benefits being traits of blockchain rather than improved traits of the individual fields. It is important to note that this is not necessarily universal; fields such as the IoT have had far more conclusive discussion on the purpose and individualized benefits of blockchain implementation. However, from a wider generalized perspective, this harkens back to the early mentions of the *"blockchain applicability framework"*. The question is often not what traits of blockchain could be integrated with an application but rather if the application benefits enough from blockchain to render its integration as being worthwhile.

Summary of Open Research and Debate

To summarize, current research challenges in blockchain typically can be boiled down to six categories (Mohanta, 2019):

- Efficiency of distributed systems in regards to wider scalability
- Correct distribution of trust and/or permission between nodes without compromising usability and cybersecurity, depending on the architecture of the blockchain
- Exponential resource usage
- Universality of smart contract designs
- Task scheduling on blockchain networks
- Efficient validation of data between nodes as networks grow exponentially in size.

Several other discussed challenges also exist; however, such is the complexity of blockchain and its relative nascence (Fraga-Lamas, 2019) as well as the existence of prior mentioned cyber-attacks (Oksiiuk, 2020). Lastly, the actual applicability of blockchain itself for certain functionalities over others remains a debate, hence the discussed existence of applicability frameworks (Gourisetti, 2019).

CONCLUSION

Blockchain is an exciting, relatively new architecture which has spurred a significant interest in both public and private sectors, particularly regarding its possible place within the cybersecurity field. However, despite the significant proposed innovation and sheer amount of discussion taking place, there is still no consensus as to what the future may hold for wider implementation. There is certainly a significant amount of both research and theory for projecting that the future of blockchain is bright. However, these promising implementations are held back by current limitations for which there is yet to be a consensus on how to fix, such as scalability and exponential resource usage. Specialized niches, especially within narrow uses such as IoT security, show the most promise for blockchain as an application structure.

Researchers mostly agree that the future of blockchain will largely be dependent on the ability of the architecture to adapt to the needs of enterprises which wish to adopt it. While there is much consensus as to the security benefits the adoption of blockchain may bring, questions about its detractions or about the sheer complexity and maintenance of its implementation, particularly on a wide-scale, have acted as a barrier for it penetrating further within the sphere of cybersecurity. As discussed within this chapter, the universality of Blockchain's benefits have led to discussion about the actual benefits of blockchain, rather than if Blockchain's usage actually suits an application or if blockchain itself just carries certain traits which applications adopting it would adopt in turn. These have led to frameworks being developed for the purpose of determining whether or not blockchain is actually needed. Some may say the excitement surrounding blockchain has, in part, obscured its adoption, because through its wider proposals for almost all forms of cybersecurity gaps, specialized sectors, for which its implementation is better suited, have received less attention.

While blockchain continues to receive much attention, its place in cybersecurity is still uncertain. Although the benefits of the architecture may be inarguable, propositions of its integration beckon logistical and theoretical questions. Most importantly, the questions arise as to: should blockchain be integrated just because it can be? and do the benefits of blockchain outweigh the complexity and downsides? Unfortunately, there is no universal answer to such questions. Instead, the answers are largely determined by the individual factors of the application in question. Just as with the wider cybersecurity field, no matter what benefits may be innate to blockchain, the individual nuances and caveats of deployments are more determinate factors for integration than the supposed benefits of what is being integrated itself. As a result of this, it is no surprise that the proposed integrations of blockchain, which shine the most, are those which come from specialized systems, such as the Internet of Things. These systems do not benefit from blockchain solely because of the traits of blockchain but instead because the nature of such systems intersect with the structure and functionalities made available by blockchain architecture.

REFERENCES

Abbas, Q. E., & Sung-Bong, J. (2019). A Survey of Blockchain and Its Applications. *2019 International Conference on Artificial Intelligence in Information and Communication (ICAIIC)*, 1–3. 10.1109/ICAIIC.2019.8669067

Aggarwal, S., Chaudhary, R., Aujla, G. S., Kumar, N., Choo, K.-K. R., & Zomaya, A. Y. (2019). Blockchain. *Journal of Network and Computer Applications*, *144*, 13–48. doi:10.1016/j.jnca.2019.06.018

Ahram, T., Sargolzaei, A., Sargolzaei, S., Daniels, J., & Amaba, B. (2017), Blockchain technology innovations. *2017 IEEE Technology Engineering Management Conference (TEMSCON)*, 137–141. 10.1109/TEMSCON.2017.7998367

Alexander, C. A., & Wang, L. (2019), Cybersecurity, Information Assurance, and Big Data Based on Blockchain. 2019 SoutheastCon, 1–7. doi:10.1109/SoutheastCon42311.2019.9020582

Ali, M. S., Vecchio, M., Pincheira, M., Dolui, K., Antonelli, F., & Rehmani, M. H. (2019). Applications of Blockchains in the Internet of Things. *IEEE Communications Surveys and Tutorials*, *21*(2), 1676–1717. doi:10.1109/COMST.2018.2886932

Andriole, S. J. (2020). Blockchain cybersecurity. *IT Professional*, *22*(1), 13–16. doi:10.1109/MITP.2019.2949165

Cai, C., Duan, H., & Wang, C. (2018). Tutorial: Building Secure and Trustworthy Blockchain Applications, 2018 IEEE Cybersecurity Development. SecDev. doi:10.1109/SecDev.2018.00023

Dai, F., Shi, Y., Meng, N., Wei, L., & Ye, Z. (2017), From Bitcoin to cybersecurity: A comparative study of blockchain application and security issues. *2017 4th International Conference on Systems and Informatics (ICSAI)*, 975–979. 10.1109/ICSAI.2017.8248427

Doku, R., Rawat, D. B., Garuba, M., & Njilla, L. (2019). LightChain: On the Lightweight Blockchain for the Internet-of-Things. *2019 IEEE International Conference on Smart Computing (SMARTCOMP)*, 444–448, 10.1109/SMARTCOMP.2019.00085

Fraga-Lamas, P., & Fernandez-Carames, T. M. (2019). A Review on Blockchain. *IEEE Access: Practical Innovations, Open Solutions*, *7*, 17578–17598. doi:10.1109/ACCESS.2019.2895302

Gorog, C., & Boult, T. E. (2018). Solving Global Cybersecurity Problems by Connecting Trust Using Blockchain. *2018 IEEE International Conference on Internet of Things (IThings) and IEEE Green Computing and Communications (GreenCom) and IEEE Cyber, Physical and Social Computing (CPSCom) and IEEE Smart Data (SmartData),* 1425–1432. 10.1109/Cybermatics_2018.2018.00243

Gourisetti, S. N. G., Mylrea, M., & Patangia, H. (2019). Evaluation and Demonstration of Blockchain. *IEEE Transactions on Engineering Management,* 1–15. doi:10.1109/TEM.2019.2928280

Hassebo, A., Obaidat, M. A., & Ali, M. (2018). *Commercial 4G LTE Cellular Networks for Supporting Emerging IoT Applications in Internet of Things.* Mechatronics and their Applications International Conference, as a part of the Advances in Science and Engineering Technology Multi-Conference (ASET), Dubai, UAE.

Huynh, T. T., Nguyen, T. D., & Tan, H. (2019). A Survey on Security and Privacy Issues of Blockchain Technology. *2019 International Conference on System Science and Engineering (ICSSE),* 362–367. 10.1109/ICSSE.2019.8823094

Khodjaeva, M., Obaidat, M. A., & Salane, D. (2019). Mitigating Threats and Vulnerabilities of RFID in IoT through Outsourcing Computations Using Public Key Cryptography. In *Security, Privacy and Trust in the IoT Environment.* Springer-Cham.

Kshetri, N. (2017). Blockchain privacy. *Telecommunications Policy, 41*(10), 1027–1038. doi:10.1016/j.telpol.2017.09.003

Li, Z., Bahramirad, S., Paaso, A., Yan, M., & Shahidehpour, M. (2019). Blockchain. *The Electricity Journal, 32*(4), 58–72. doi:10.1016/j.tej.2019.03.008 PMID:32524086

Mohanta, B. K., Jena, D., Panda, S. S., & Sobhanayak, S. (2019). Blockchain privacy. *Internet of Things, 8,* 100107. doi:10.1016/j.iot.2019.100107

Mylrea, M., & Gourisetti, S. N. G. (2017). Blockchain for smart grid resilience: Exchanging distributed energy at speed, scale and security. Resilience Week. doi:10.1109/RWEEK.2017.8088642

Narbayeva, S., Bakibayev, T., Abeshev, K., Makarova, I., Shubenkova, K., & Pashkevich, A. (2020). Blockchain Technology. *Transportation Research Procedia, 44,* 168–175. doi:10.1016/j.trpro.2020.02.024

Obaidat, M. A., Khodjaeva, M., Obeidat, S., Salane, D., & Holst, J. (2019). Security Architecture Framework for Internet of Things. IEEE 10th Annual Ubiquitous Computing, Electronics & Mobile Communication Conference (UEMCON), 154-157. doi:10.1109/UEMCON47517.2019.8993096

Obaidat, M. A., Obeidat, S., Holst, J., Al Hayajneh, A., & Brown, J. (2020, May). A Comprehensive and Systematic Survey on the Internet of Things: Security and Privacy Challenges, Security Frameworks, Enabling Technologies, Threats, Vulnerabilities and Countermeasures, in Computers Journal. *MDPI, 9,* 44.

Oksiiuk, O., & Dmyrieva, I. (2020). Security and privacy issues of blockchain technology. *2020 IEEE 15th International Conference on Advanced Trends in Radioelectronics, Telecommunications and Computer Engineering (TCSET),* 1–5. 10.1109/TCSET49122.2020.235489

Pólvora, A., Nascimento, S., Lourenço, J. S., & Scapolo, F. (2020). Blockchain. *Technological Forecasting and Social Change, 157,* 120091. doi:10.1016/j.techfore.2020.120091

Sharma, M. (2019), Blockchain for Cybersecurity: Working Mechanism, Application areas and Security Challenges. *2019 2nd International Conference on Intelligent Computing, Instrumentation and Control Technologies (ICICICT), 1*, 1182–1187. 10.1109/ICICICT46008.2019.8993204

Vance, T. R., & Vance, A. (2019). Cybersecurity in the Blockchain Era: A Survey on Examining Critical Infrastructure Protection with Blockchain-Based Technology. *2019 IEEE International Scientific-Practical Conference Problems of Infocommunications, Science and Technology (PIC S&T)*, 107–112. 10.1109/PICST47496.2019.9061242

Yassein, M. B., Shatnawi, F., Rawashdeh, S., & Mardin, W. (2019). Blockchain Technology: Characteristics, Security and Privacy; Issues and Solutions. *2019 IEEE/ACS 16th International Conference on Computer Systems and Applications (AICCSA)*, 1–8, 10.1109/AICCSA47632.2019.9035216

Yeasmin, S., & Baig, A. (2019). Unblocking the Potential of Blockchain. *2019 International Conference on Electrical and Computing Technologies and Applications (ICECTA)*, 1–5. 10.1109/ICEC-TA48151.2019.8959713

ADDITIONAL READING

Hasanova, H., Baek, U., Shin, M., Cho, K., & Kim, M. (2019). A survey on blockchain cybersecurity vulnerabilities and possible countermeasures. *International Journal of Network Management, 29*(2), e2060. doi:10.1002/nem.2060

Zhang, X., Li, R., & Cui, B. (2018). A security architecture of VANET based on blockchain and mobile edge computing. 2018 1st IEEE International Conference on Hot Information-Centric Networking (HotICN). 10.1109/HOTICN.2018.8605952

KEY TERMS AND DEFINITIONS

Access Control: A fundamental concept of cybersecurity facilitated through the regulation of who and/or what can view, maintain, and use individual resources within a system.

Availability: A principle of cybersecurity which states that authorized users should be able to not only access systems as needed, but also perform needed tasks and data transactions.

Cloud Computing: A method of distributed computing in which a network of remote servers are used to remotely provision, manage, store, and process rather than using local systems.

Confidentiality: A principle of cybersecurity which dictates that only those who should be able to have access to certain data, should be able to access it.

Cryptocurrency: A decentralized, blockchain-based system of digital currency assets where digital coins are stored in distributed ledgers, and units are generated through strongly protected cryptographic means.

End-Point Security: A method of protecting system networks which relies on the security of bridged devices participating in a network.

Immutability: The ability for data to exist within a source while maintaining definition and inarguable integrity, for connected systems to transmit such data without error.

Integrity: A principle of cybersecurity which dictates that data should be insured to be both accurate and untampered with, from any unauthorized entities.

Internet of Things (IoT): The interconnected web of devices spread between internet-connected computers and processors embedded within everyday systems, which receive and transmit data.

Peer to Peer (P2P): A method of networking in which a network is distributed across interconnected nodes for whom resources are shared, without a centralized source, thus coordinating outside of a traditional client-server model.

Transaction: An event between at least two systems or participants where a sequence of information is sent and received by participating entities.

This research was previously published in Industry Use Cases on Blockchain Technology Applications in IoT and the Financial Sector; pages 109-131, copyright year 2021 by Engineering Science Reference (an imprint of IGI Global).

Chapter 46
Conceptual Insights in Blockchain Technology:
Security and Applications

Anup Bihari Gaurav
Maulana Azad National Institute of Technology, India

Pushpendra Kumar
iD https://orcid.org/0000-0001-7555-2625
Maulana Azad National Institute of Technology, India

Vinod Kumar
iD https://orcid.org/0000-0002-3495-2320
Madanapalli Institute of Technology and Science, India

Ramjeevan Singh Thakur
Maulana Azad National Institute of Technology, India

ABSTRACT

The global popularity of digital cryptocurrencies and research in a decentralized system have led to the foundation of blockchain, which is fundamentally a public digital ledger to share information in a trustworthy and secure way. The concept and applications of blockchain have now spread from crypto-currencies to various other domains, including business process management, smart contracts, IoT, and so on. Cryptocurrency is a mechanism designed to work for the online secure payments system using cryptography. Cryptography maintains confidentiality, integrity, and authentication. Cryptocurrency has come as a novel way of making payments that keep all the transactions secure and safe, which avoids any type of intermediaries such as a bank. This chapter will shed light on the concept of blockchain technology, security, and its applications in various domains.

DOI: 10.4018/978-1-6684-7132-6.ch046

INTRODUCTION

The system refers to organisation of different elements which collectively works for a common purpose. In the case of database and computer networking environment, this can be categorised in three basic types as Centralized System, Decentralised System, and Distributed System.

Centralized System: A centralized system has complete reliance on single point which could be turn out to be a complete failure for all associated system if the single point failures occur. Fig. 1 refers to the schematic diagram of centralized system (J. Yli-Huumo, et al., 2016).

Decentralised System: A decentralised system don't have any central authority in this system each node can take independent decisions. Decentralised system gives freedom for lower level component to compute local information to accomplish global goal (i.e. Transaction). Fig. 2 refers to the schematic diagram of decentralized system.

Distributed System: The distributed system is a network of autonomous components that cooperate, coordinate to achieve a common goal. It help in resource sharing and provide user a view of a single network. They share resources such as software (file, databases, and links), hardware (printer, processor, memory). Fig 3. Refers to the schematic diagram of distributed system (Z. Zheng et al., 2017)

The blockchain is a decentralized computation and information sharing platform that enables multiple authoritative domains, who don't trust each other, to cooperate, coordinate and collaborate in a rational decision making process.

The decentralised system which exists in blockchain system provides consistent database support for every transactions that happens. It is an open, distributed ledger that can record transactions between two parties efficiently and in a verifiable and permanent way (Chen, G., *et* al. 2018).

Figure 1. Centralized System

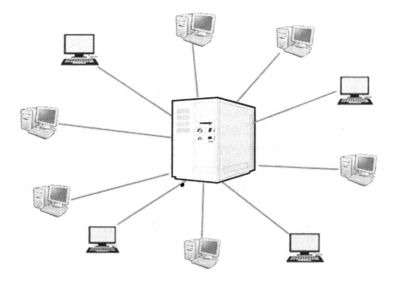

Figure 2. Decentralized System

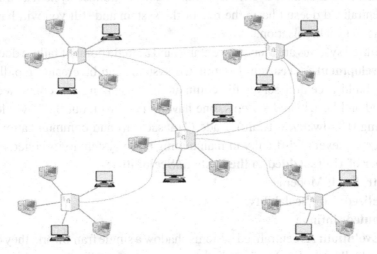

Figure 3. Distributed System

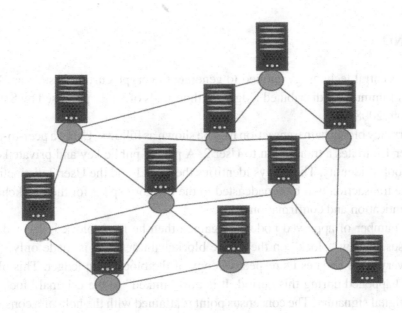

Pros And Cons Of Distributed, Centralised, Decentralised Systems

1. **Maintenance /Points of Failure**:
   a. Decentralized have more but still finite numbers of failure.
   b. Distributed systems are the most difficult to maintain.
   c. Centralized systems are easy to maintain as there is only a single point of failure.
2. **Fault Tolerance / Stability**:
   a. **Centralized** systems can be highly unstable and intolerable due to single point failure may ruin the whole working system.

b. **Decentralized** are stable system as compared to centralized system as if failure of the leader in decentralized doesn't harm the rest of the system and still you will have a stable network working in synchronisation.

c. **Distributed** systems are much more stable and a single point of failure doesn't do much harm.

3. **Ease of Development / Creation**: Centralized systems can be created rapidly, and in easy way just have to build a central server for commanding/managing the connected components. For Decentralized and Distributed systems, one have to first work out the lower level details like resource sharing (Hardware/Software), trade (Transaction) and communications (Network) and it imposes a certain level of difficulty in maintaining these system to its coherent state.

4. **Max Number of Users Added to the System/ Scalability**:

a. **Decentralized:** Moderate

b. **Centralized:** Low scalability

c. **Distributed:** Infinite

5. **Diversity / Evolution:** As centralized systems shadow a single framework, they don't have diversity and grow gradually. But for distributed systems and decentralized systems, once the elementary infrastructure is in place, evolution is remarkable.

BACKGROUND

Blockchain is the central technology applied to generate the cryptocurrency, such as Bitcoin, through the maintenance of immutable distributed ledgers in thousands of nodes proposed by Satoshi Nakamoto in 2008 (Nakamoto 2008).

The cryptocurrency blockchain transaction may be shown as follows- Using a peer-to-peer blockchain network, the User 1 initiates a transaction to User 2. A pair of public key and private key is taken as a cryptographic proof of identity. These keys identifies the User 1 and the User 2 distinctively within the network. Now the transaction will be broadcasted to the memory space for the blockchain network for transaction authentication and confirmation.

If an assured number of approved nodes are gained then he fresh block is created; this is said as reaching consensus. A new "block" on the whole blockchain network is made only if the consensus is reached and every node updates its respective copy of the blockchain ledger. This block has all the transactions that happened during this period. It is now "linked" to the original block in the network with the help of digital signature. The consensus point is attained with the help of a consensus algorithm and this process is called mining.

2.1 A Simplified View Of Blockchain

The simplified view of how the blockchain technology works is mentioned below and the how blocks are chained is shown in the schematic diagram of Figure 4.

- Every single node maintain a local copy of global data sheet.
- The system guarantees the consistency among the local copies of ledger
- The local copies at every node is identical.
- The local copies are always modified based on the global information.

- The transaction is maintained over a public ledger, which is a database of historical information available at every local node within a system. This information is utilised for future computations.

Figure 4. A simplified view of blockchain

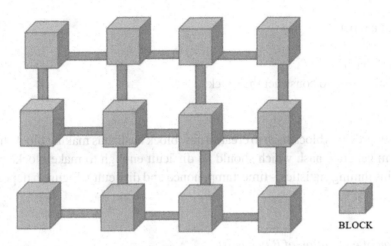

2.2 Securing Data Cryptographically Within A Block

Block: A block is a container data structure which contain series of transactions. Each transaction within a block is digitally signed and encrypted and verified by the peer node of blockchain network. Cryptography security ensures that only authorised participant will be able to view information on the ledger. Fig.5 shows the transaction information that is contained in the blockchain.

Figure 5. Transaction information in blockchain

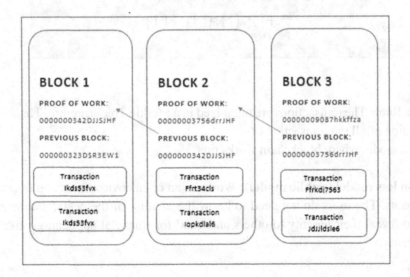

A single block of bitcoin can contain more than 500 transactions on average. A block contain two component

- Block header
- List of transaction

Metadata about a block

1. Previous block hash
2. Mining statistics used to construct the block
3. Merkle tree root

Every block uses previous block hash to create a new block hash thus making blockchain tamperproof. Mining mechanism generate hash which should be difficult enough to make blockchain tamperproof. The header contains mining statistics – timestamp, nonce and difficulty. Figure 6 depicts the generation of Block Hash.

Figure 6. Depiction of generation of Block Hash

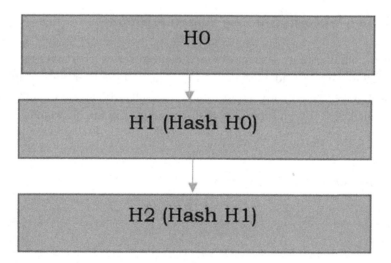

Merkle Tree Root: The transactions are organized in a Merkle Tree structure. The root of the Merkle tree is a verification of all the transactions.

There are two model where blockchain works on

1. **Permission less model (public model):** Works in an open environment and over a large network of participants. The users do not need to know the identity of the peers, and hence the users do not need to reveal their identity to others and good for financial applications like banking using cryptocurrency.

2. **Permissioned model (private model):** Blockchain can be applied just beyond cryptocurrency. The underlying notions of consensus, security and distributed replicated ledgers can be applied to even closed or permissioned network settings.

2.3 Bitcoin

Bitcoin are cryptocurrency that are generated by a complex algorithm using peer to peer network in a process referred as mining that require extensive computing resources.

Bitcoin is a decentralized digital currency without a central bank or single administrator authority Bitcoin can be sent from user-to-user on the peer-to-peer bitcoin network without the need of intermediaries. Bitcoin has many unique attributes that differentiate it from traditional currencies as it didn't require a central authority to handle transaction, and incurring cost related with it. Bitcoin also allows business to take and make payments much more easily than through usual mode of channels for payments like PayPal and credit cards. Bitcoin allows merchants to avoid the fees associated with these services, enabling frictionless transactions.

Bitcoins are not minted as traditional currency it have been generated at a predetermined rate. The program used to generate Bitcoin runs on a peer to peer network and requires very powerful computer system to operate.

Mining a Bitcoin is a result of powerful computers solving cryptographic problems in tandem with other similar computers. The computer that gets the solution will be awarded the bitcoin and the computers that are jointly solving the problems are recorded as "proof of work". Miners in the bitcoin network collect transaction for 10 minutes and start mining the proof of work. The probability of getting a proof of work is low as it is uncertain which miner will be able to generate the block. Mining bitcoin requires massive computational power of host machine and they consider to have value (F. Tschorsch & B. Scheuermann 2016).

Bitcoin uses public key cryptography to make and verify digital signatures. Spending bitcoin in a network require verification of ownership on all of the thousands of nodes in the network this prevent tampering with blockchain, double spending, attacks (Sybil, Dos services).

Proof of work: Proof of work is a process of producing data that's hard to get but easy to verify. In blockchain proof of work is about solving mathematical problems having certain level of difficulty (D. Kraft, 2016).

ISSUES AND CHALLENGES IN BLOCKCHAIN TECHNOLOGY

Blockchain technology is a revolutionary concept in the computer science and it has a variety of applications in different fields likes – banking, management, IoT's, Identity applications etc. There are still numerous challenges that are still being faced by the blockchain technology.

Lack of legal regulations: One of the major obstacle in the pursuance of blockchain technology in entrepreneurial activity. Some people are using without any obvious regulatory framework in the grey area comfortably. May countries around the world are in the way of designing the suitable laws for blockchain technology. It is expected that in a few years many country will allow to flourish business using blockchain technology with proper legal framework (A. Natchkebia, 2018)

Huge consumption of energy: In this technological functioning, a very complex and long running complex computation occurs which requires lots of computing infrastructure as a result they also need huge consumption of electrical energy (A. Natchkebia, 2018).

Cost to set up: There exists a challenge in the setting up the functional infrastructure for the blockchain technology. The system bears the complex setup which also costly tool (A. Natchkebia, 2018).

Public Perception: The prime problem in the way of the success of Blockchain is the public perception. The folks don't consider it be a portion of conventional functioning. Most of the folks consider that this technology will not last long. The characteristics like the absence of governance, easy admittance to become a member of public Blockchain spoils the image of Blockchain in public perception (A. Natchkebia, 2018).

Moreover, if a transaction has been committed in blockchain technology then the transaction roll back is not possible. Congestions generation due to cypto mining in the communication network is a big issue. All these discussed factors poses as challenges for the development of this new Technology.

APPLICATIONS OF BLOCKCHAIN TECHNOLOGIES

Blockchain technology has the wide variety of applications in the present time. The major applications of this technology has been discussed as below:

A. Cryptocurrency

1. **Bitcoin (BTC):** Bitcoin is cryptocurrency that is generated by a complex algorithm using peer to peer network in a process referred to as mining which require extensive computing resources, they have changeable value to open market, they are exchanged via a 34 character alphanumeric address that the user maintain. Managing transactions and issuing of bitcoin is carried out collectively by the network. It is exposed to all, anybody can take part in it.
2. **Litecoin (LTC):** Litecoin is another kind of open source global payment network, it is fully decentralised in nature and without any central authority Litecoin uses a peer-to-peer network to allow instant transactions. It is the internet currency incurring near-zero cost payments to anyone in the world. Mathematics secures the network and empowers individuals to control their own finances.
3. **Bytecoin (BCN):** Bytecoin is also a private, decentralized cryptocurrency where transaction is private and untraceable as well this is achieved using cryptographic algorithm. Its open source code that allows everyone to take part in development of network of Bytecoin it also incorporate privacy and security of its user. It uses CryptoNote Technology where transaction becomes untraceable and unlikable. Additionally the bytecoin API provides support for multi signature solution which will give an additional degree of security.
    Bytecoin encompass various features they are as follows:
    a. Bytecoin transaction
    b. Security and reliability
    c. Open source code base
    d. Multiple signature
    e. Powerful API

4. **Peercoin (PPC):** Peercoin is a cryptocurrency that launched in 2012. It holds value, offers complete anonymity, and can be sent over the internet without any central authority like a bank, just like Bitcoin, Dash, Litecoin, and the majority of other cryptocurrencies. Peercoin is different from bitcoin mining approach as it uses "Proof-of-stake" an alternative consensus protocol that was invented by Sunny King and Scott Nadal and first implemented in Peercoin in 2012. In a proof-of-stake based blockchain, coin owners are the ones who exert influence over the network, produce new blocks and secure the chain. Stakeholders of Peercoin effectively co-own the blockchain network, similar to how shareholders co-own a publicly traded corporation (Peercoin, 2019).

5. **Emercoin (EMC):** An open source cryptocurrency which originated from Bitcoin, Peercoin and Namecoin. Other than being a cryptocurrency, it is also a platform for secure distributed blockchain business services. The EMC coin is used for accessing the blockchain-based services provided by Emercoin. Emercoin inherits the reliability and security of Bitcoin, while at the same time putting more features to its own blockchain by leveraging several innovative technologies (emercoin.com, 2019).

6. **Ripple (XRP):** Ripple is a real-time gross settlement system (RTGS), currency exchange and remittance network created by Ripple Labs Inc. (US). It is built upon an open source distributed protocol it support tokens that represent cryptocurrency, commodities and other unit that represent value. Ripple network instantly enables free global financial transaction of any size incurring no additional costs.

    Ripple depends upon a common shared distributed database storing information of ripple accounts, the ripple network consists of validating servers that constantly compares their transactional records with very low latency

7. **Omni (MSC):** Omni is a digital currency and communication protocol built on bitcoin blockchain Omni is a platform for creating and trading custom digital assets and currencies. It is a software layer built on top of the most popular, most audited, most secure blockchain. Omni transactions are Bitcoin transactions that enable next-generation features on the Bitcoin Blockchain. Omni provide all feature of bicoin and also features of omni layers (omnilayer, 2019).

8. **Gridcoin (GRC):** Gridcoin is a decentralized, open-source, math-based digital asset (crypto-currency). Gridcoin implements a "Proof of Research" which rewards user with a Gridcoin on performing useful scientific computation on "BIONIC", while being energy-efficient, it is the first and only cryptocurrency that rewards individuals for scientific contributions and performs transactions peer-to-peer cryptographically - without the need for a central authority to distribute rewards (Gridcoin, 2019).

B. Business

-   **Insurance:** Claim Processing
-   **Payments:** Cross-Border Payments
-   **Asset Management:** Trade Processing and settlement
-   Copyright and Loyalty Protection
-   Tax Regulation and Compliances
-   Trading Equity

C. IOT'S Applications

- Smart Application
- Supply Chain Sensors

D. Smart Contracts

- Healthcare
- Government
- Music

E. Identity Applications

- Passports
- Personal Identification
- Birth certificate, wedding certificate and death certificates

CONCLUSION

Blockchain technology has revealed it's prospective for transmuting conventional business with its key features: anonymity decentralization, auditability, and persistency. Here, we have presented an overview over blockchain technology. We have also discussed the issues and challenges related to blockchain technology. Furthermore, the applications of blockchain technology with respect to various domains has also been discussed.

FUTURE DIRECTIONS

In this day and age blockchain technology centred applications are growing up day by day. Now our prospective effort would be to done comprehensive investigations on blockchain-centred applications in business, education. The issues and challenges will also be taken up comprehensively.

REFERENCES

Bytecoin.org. (n.d.). Retrieved from https://www.bytecoin.org/

Chen, G., Xu, B., Lu, M., & Chen, N. S. (2018). Exploring blockchain technology and its potential applications for education. Smart Learning Environments, 5(1), 1.

Emercoin.com. (n.d.). Retrieved from https://www.emercoin.com/

Gridcoin.org. (n.d.). Retrieved from https://www.gridcoin.org/

Gridcoin.us. (n.d.). Retrieved from https://www.gridcoin.us/

Kraft, D. (2016). Difficulty control for blockchain-based consensus systems. Peer-to-Peer Networking and Applications, 9(2), 397–413.

Nakamoto, S. (2019), Bitcoin: A peer-to-peer electronic cash system. Retrieved from https://bitcoin.org/bitcoin.pdf

Natchkebia, A. (2018), https://www.forexnewsnow.com/forex/analysis/cryptocurrency/ challenges-blockchain-technology/ (Retrieved on 15.03.2019)

Omnilayer.org. (n.d.). Retrieved from https://www.omnilayer.org/

https://ripple.com/(Retrieved on 20.03.2019)

Tschorsch, F., & Scheuermann, B. (2016). Bitcoin and beyond: A technical survey on decentralized digital currencies. IEEE Communications Surveys and Tutorials, 18(3), 2084–2123.

Yli-Huumo, J., Ko, D., Choi, S., Park, S., & Smolander, K. (2016). Where is current research on Blockchain technology?—A systematic review. PLoS One, 11(10).

Zheng, Z., Xie, S., Dai, H., Chen, X., & Wang, H. (2017). An overview of blockchain technology: Architecture, consensus, and future trends. In *2017 IEEE International Congress on Big Data (BigData Congress)* (pp. 557-564). IEEE. doi:10.1109/BigDataCongress.2017.8510.1109/BigDataCongress.2017.85

KEY TERMS AND DEFINITIONS

Bitcoin: Bitcoin is a cryptocurrency, a form of electronic cash. A purely peer-to-peer version of electronic cash would allow online payments to be sent directly from one party to another without going through a financial institution

Block: A block is a container data structure which contain series of transactions. Each transaction within a block is digitally signed and encrypted and verified by the peer node of blockchain network.

Blockchain: The Blockchain is a decentralized computation and information sharing platform that enables multiple authoritative domains, who don't trust each other, to cooperate, coordinate and collaborate in a rational decision making process.

Cryptocurrency: Cryptocurrency is a mechanism designed to work for the online secure payments system using cryptography.

Chapter 47
Security for IoT:
Challenges, Attacks, and Prevention

Anjum Nazir Qureshi Sheikh
Kalinga University, India

Asha Ambhaikar
Kalinga University, India

Sunil Kumar
Kalinga University, India

ABSTRACT

The internet of things is a versatile technology that helps to connect devices with other devices or humans in any part of the world at any time. Some of the researchers claim that the number of IoT devices around the world will surpass the total population on the earth after a few years. The technology has made life easier, but these comforts are backed up with a lot of security threats. Wireless medium for communication, large amount of data, and device constraints of the IoT devices are some of the factors that increase their vulnerability to security threats. This chapter provides information about the attacks at different layers of IoT architecture. It also mentions the benefits of technologies like blockchain and machine learning that can help to solve the security issues of IoT.

1. INTRODUCTION

Internet of Things (IoT) has become one of the emerging technologies which are set to revolutionize the lifestyle of people by enabling digital connectivity everywhere. Decades ago we connected computers using the internet but now all the devices, animals, and human beings can be connected wirelessly through this technology. IoT is a platform where every device will be connected, controlled through the internet, collect store data, and communicate data. It enables the exchange of information either from device to device or among a human and device. Many researchers have been working to upgrade the technology to increase its acceptability among the users. The reports Statista research department has

DOI: 10.4018/978-1-6684-7132-6.ch047

predicted a major boost in the number of IoT connected devices which reveals that there will be 75.44 billion IoT devices worldwide in 2025 which is approximately a fivefold increase as compared to the year 2015 which had 15.4 billion connected devices. Applicability scenario of IoT has evolved rapidly in the last decade due to which it is being deployed in different domains like smart home, smart cities, smart transportation, health care, agriculture, etc. Internet of Things instills connectivity and intelligence in the devices thereby enhancing power, precision, and availability of the existing devices. The primary objective of this chapter is to discuss the security and privacy issues faced by the IoT platforms. The popularity of IoT among the users had to lead to an increase in the number of IoT devices, applications as well as the data that is being sent or received on the network. The chapter will be arranged as follows:

There is a need to minimize the security risks on IoT platforms to make it widely acceptable so that more and more people adopt it to make their life easier. But there are few issues mainly the device constraints and the lack of encryption methods which are increasing the vulnerability of IoT. In section 2 authors will list out some of the factors that need attention to mitigate the effects of security attacks on the IoT devices and also on the communication paths. Ensuring the security of IoT needs to consider devices as well as the communication platforms that are being utilized for implementing a particular application. The essential security methods have to utilize after having an overview of applications, networks as well as the devices. A secure IoT environment is difficult to achieve if all these factors are not recognized appropriately.

Section 3 will discuss the various attacks that are faced while ensuring security for the Internet of Things. This section will give brief information about the five-layer architecture of IoT that includes the perception layer, network, processing, application, and business layer. All the five layers are susceptible to different types of attacks and therefore in this section will shed light on the attacks each layer of the five-layer architecture is subjected to.

Figure 1. Number of Connected IoT Devices (source: Statista 2020)

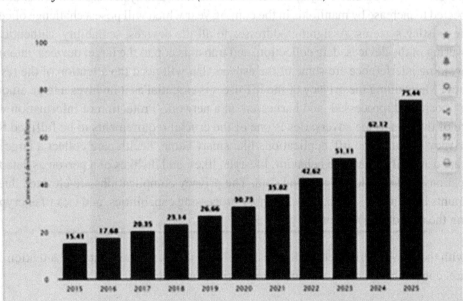

The security risks are increased proportionately with the number of IoT devices and their users. Some of the security threats can be avoided if the IoT end-users know how to keep their devices secure. Section 4 sheds light on the simple measures to be adopted by the IoT consumers to keep your data secure on the IoT devices, networks, clouds, and applications.

Efforts are being made to use techniques like Blockchain and machine learning to minimize security risks on these systems. In section 5 authors will discuss benefits of using the above-mentioned techniques for facing the challenges of security. This section will be followed by future scopes for the security techniques and conclusion.

1.2. Background

As numerous organizations are trying to integrate IoT for deriving additional benefits they are coming across numerous challenges. Some of the challenges faced by IoT that require more attention are:

A. **Security:** One of the fundamental problems that need to be addressed is the security of IoT devices. As the technology connects and controls the devices through the internet and as most of the applications support wireless connectivity, security concerns creep in automatically. With the significant increase in the number of IoT users, the risks of security threats will increase. Though there are a lot of algorithms or protocols available to protect the internet networks from breaching it is not possible to use those algorithms directly. The security architectures for the internet have been designed for human communication whereas the IoT networks are a combination of things, services, and networks due to which security of IoT must have additional features than the traditional networks.

B. **Connectivity:** The Internet of Things has created a network that enables people and devices to be connected anywhere with anyone at any time. Server –client model or centralized approach is being extensively used for connectivity of servers, work stations, and systems. The number of IoT devices is expected to increase by manifolds in the coming year which will pose a challenge of connectivity for the existing systems. Assigning addresses to all the devices, scalability, authenticate access, discovering of the devices, data collection, and transmission to the target devices, interoperability, and avoiding interference are some of the aspects that will need the attention of the researchers.

C. **Privacy:** Maintaining the privacy of the IoT users is essential as it involves a large amount of data being transmitted, processed, and harnessed on a network. Protection of information without exposure of the data to the adversaries is one of the crucial requirements to be fulfilled to maintain the privacy of data. The IoT applications like smart home, health care collect a large amount of data that can easily reveal the behavior, lifestyle, likes, and dislikes of a person as data from these applications contain a lot of personal data. The privacy complications are elevated due to device constraints like limited size, battery, memory processing capabilities, and lack of encryption while passing the data on the network.

Along with the above-mentioned challenges of IoT, some more issues that need attention are regarding hardware, compatibility, and government regulations or policies.

Figure 2. IoT Attacks Comparison (Source: SonicWall Cyber Threat Report 2019)

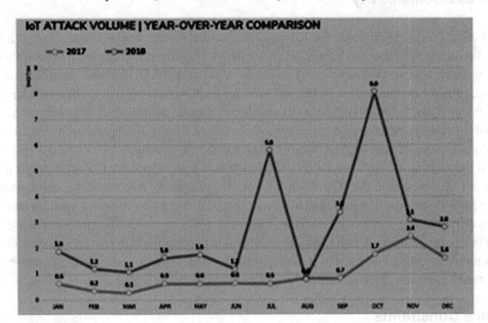

A report on IoT attacks by SonicWall released in 2019 provides a detailed comparison of IoT attacks in the years 2017 and 2018. The study indicates that the percentage of IoT attacks in 2018 has increased by 217.5% as compared to the year 2017. The number of attacks in 2017 was reported to be 10.3 million which steeply increased to 32.8 in 2018. Another study by the researchers of SonicWall in 2020 disclosed that there was a moderate increase of 5.7% attacks as compared to 2018 which were a total 34.3 million attacks. One of the primary reasons behind the increase in the number of attacks was that the manufacturers were unable to apply security methods to protect devices from the invaders. Besides this weak password, insecure networks, and lack of safe updates process are some common IoT weakness that helps the attackers to initiate attacks comfortably. Outdated software serves to be a prominent factor to increase the vulnerability of attacks on most of the devices that are used for applications like smart homes and healthcare. But with the flooding of fresh IoT devices every day it has become essential to come up with strategies for blocking these attacks rather than expecting attacks due to the shortcomings of the present IoT system.

2. FACTORS THAT MAKE IOT VULNERABLE TO SECURITY

Though IoT is being recognized as a versatile technology but overcoming its security concerns has become one of the primary issues to increase trustworthiness among the people. The security attacks on IoT can be minimized by taking care of the devices as well as the connectivity mediums that are being deployed for the various applications. In this section, we discuss some of the factors that increase vulnerability. The security issues of IoT can be classified depending upon devices, applications, connectivity, and storage/processing techniques.

2.1 Wireless Connectivity

The connectivity technologies used for IoT applications are mostly implemented through a wireless medium. According to Sadlier and Sabri (2017), wireless technologies can be classified into short-range networks and wide area networks. Bluetooth, Local Area Network (PAN), Personal Area Network (PAN), Zigbee, Near Field Communication (NFC) are used for localized connectivity while cellular networks and Low Power Wide Area (LWPA) networks are used to connect devices over large areas. The wireless connectivity technologies have enabled ubiquitous coverage for the IoT applications but the wireless medium comes with a disadvantage that they can be hacked very easily.

Most of the users now a day's use wi-fi on their mobile phones to monitor IoT applications like smart homes, smart transportation, etc. The wi-fi networks especially the free networks available at public places like railway stations, hospitals, and hotels are insecure. It uses open air as a medium due to which it becomes difficult to prevent passive sniffing. When you are using a wired connection you are sure that your data is passing through the wire but when a signal is passing through wi-fi any hacker can access your data and you just cannot prevent it. Compromising Bluetooth or spoofing MAC addresses on a Zigbee network are some of the activities that can be easily done by a hacker.

2.2 Device Constraints

The IoT devices consist of sensors, actuators, and microcontrollers and are basically battery operated. As the IoT devices are small in sizes, small size batteries are used which get discharged very soon owing to the electrochemical limitations of the battery. The IoT devices thus possess low processing capabilities, low memory, and storage space to fulfill the purpose of prolonging its battery lifetime. They lack significant processing and storage capacities to implement encryptions as well as the decryption algorithms. The process of encrypt- decrypt - re-crypt requires space for transmission and storage of information which is beyond the capacity of IoT devices. It is therefore challenging for the IoT device manufacturers and software developers to design security algorithms within a footprint of 64 kb to 640 kb.

2.3 Big Data

The smart devices or the IoT nodes collect sensitive information and are also able to process it for further use. Since these IoT devices are being controlled by the internet they are susceptible to security or cyber threats just like any other internet-enabled device. The explosion in the number of IoT devices being connected to the network has raised concerns for the data that is being transmitted or received through these networks. This large amount of data is quite difficult to manage with perspectives of data collection and networking. At such a high volume of data channelizing efforts to keep data secure has to be maintained as one of the primary objectives because along with the large information being transmitted a lot of personal data is going into these systems. Business enterprises for example may use IoT enabled printers, doorbells, security cameras, etc. In case these types of equipment are hacked by a cybercriminal the attacker can quickly observe the functioning of the enterprise. If this data gets leaked, hacked, or gets into the wrong hands it can lead to disastrous results.

2.4 Cloud Computing

Cloud computing is a technology that is being widely used to overcome the limitations of the storage and processing capabilities of IoT devices. Botta et. al. (2016) describes Cloud Computing as mature technology with virtually unlimited capacities in terms of storage and processing power. The growing rate of IoT users and data on the network requires more storage space for collecting and sharing valuable information needed by its users. Cloud computing has proved beneficial in handling large storage needs of the customers which can be further increased on users' demand. As more and more organizations are moving towards the cloud, security risks are about to increase not due to cloud insecurity but due to a lack of security awareness among the employees. Cloud computing according to Donno et. al. (2019) has provided benefits like flexibility, economic savings, and support of new services but security issues associated with it are hindering its widespread adoption. IoT users and organizations keep on updating their data on clouds. Most of the users do not have strong passwords while many of them do not regularly update their passwords. The tech companies manufacture IoT products but fail to pay attention to the probable security risks. Most of the IoT devices fail to receive enough updates due to insufficient knowledge of security risks among the users. All these factors maximize the data security and privacy risks associated with the furnishing of continuous data over the cloud. The attackers are more interested in data due to which security attacks that cause data breaching and data loss are being considered to be the biggest security risks of cloud computing.

3. SECURITY ISSUES FOR FIVE LAYERED ARCHITECTURE OF IOT

The extensive research on IoT led to the development of different types of architecture to foster a better understanding of the technology and to promote more research opportunities in this area. The basic three layered or three-tiered architecture proposed by Duan et.al (2011) consisted of a perception layer, a network layer, and an application layer. ITU-T (2012) mentions an IoT reference model with a four-layered architecture which includes management service layers in addition to the previous architecture. According to Rayes. A and Salem. S (2019)addition of one more layer to the existing structure provided benefits of solving problems on the interoperability of IoT devices, help vendors to develop joint solutions, facilitate the process of troubleshooting, design, and component development. Khan R. et.al (2012) proposed a five-layered architecture that includes an additional business layer. The five different layers have different functions or objectives due to which they are subjected to different kinds of attacks.

This section covers a brief description of the five layers and the common security threats at these layers.

Perception Layer: This layer sometimes referred to as a device or sensing layer mainly consists of sensors, devices actuators, and controllers. A sensor collects data from the surrounding environment by using a physical interface that is converted into an electrical signal so that it can be used by a computing device or can be interpreted to determine. There are numerous varieties of sensors available that can be deployed to attain the desired objectives. Some commonly used sensors are temperature sensors, humidity sensors, moisture sensors, pressure sensors, image sensors, and noise sensors. With the advancements in technology sensors with increased accuracy and decreased size as well as cost are readily available today. Another important content of the perception layer is the actuator that takes an electrical input to convert it into a physical quantity. The devices at this level may include smartphones, tablets, and single-board computers.

Figure 3. Five Layered Architecture of IoT

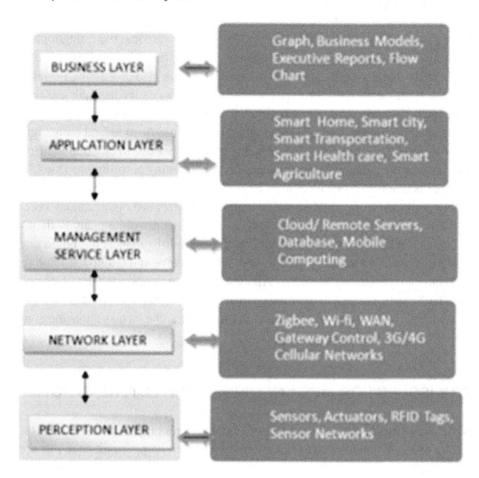

The attackers are interested in knowing the information being collected by the sensors for which they may replace it with fake devices. Wurn (2016) considers that gaining physical access to a remote IoT device is easier for an intruder as most of the devices available today lack basic security mechanisms. It happens because providing continuous protection and regular monitoring for a lightweight, low-cost device is not economically viable.

(Hany and Gary,2019; Deogiriakar and Vidhate 2017) has mentioned that some of the security threats at the perception layer are node capture, RF interference on RFID, node jamming, malicious code injection, physical damage, social engineering, sleep deprivation attack, and malicious code injection.

- **Node Capture/Tampering:** In this type of attack the intruder can have access to sensitive data, leak it with the help of important keys like encryption or cryptographic keys and also alter the data being transmitted from the sender to the receiver nodes. It is sometimes considered to be one of the hazardous attacks as the attacker can physically damage the node and also make either partial change in its hardware or alter the entire node. Two problems encountered after these types of attacks are DoS attack against availability by which a captured node can generate random queries on behalf of the attacker and attack against integrity through which the captured node transfers incorrect data to the authentic users.

- **RF interference on RFID:** Radio frequency identification (RFID) provides a great potential to the IoT applications but has a limitation that it is insecure due to its susceptibility to electromagnetic interference. The attackers use noise or electromagnetic interference from other RF devices to corrupt transmission.
- **Node Jamming:** Jamming is commonly called as a Dedicated Denial of Service (DDoS) in the field of cybersecurity. It is a destructive security attack in the WSNs based IoT as it jams the traffic in the network by blocking the channel. This attack causes a quick discharge of batteries for the target devices by disrupting data transmissions and allowing repeated retransmissions. It introduces noise in the carrier which reduces the signal to noise ratio considerably due to which the channels are unable to receive correct data. Jamming can be done permanently that will hamper all the communications in the region or can be done temporarily at regular intervals.
- **Fake node Injection:** The attacker controls data flow on the communicating path by injecting malicious nodes. A malicious node can stop all the data transmissions by dropping the entire packet that has to be forwarded to other nodes. These nodes avoid their detection at occasions by dropping a few packets on the communication path while allowing the remaining packets to the destination. It may at times receive data packets from the source nodes and forward it to other malicious nodes.
- **Malicious Code Injection:** In this type of attack the hacker introduces malicious code into the node or device's memory for achieving full control over the IoT system. Efficient code authentication techniques should be developed to overcome these attacks.
- **Sleep Deprivation:** The protocols or the algorithms developed for communication through the IoT nodes are developed by taking into account the limited available power of the battery-operated devices. Some of the algorithms keep the unused or idol nodes in sleeping mode to elongate the battery lifetime. Through sleep deprivation attacks the intruders keep on running the nodes continuously so that the batteries get discharged soon which results in shut down of the IoT system.
- **Social Engineering:** Most of the IoT users are ignorant about the security techniques required for the safety of their data and devices. This characteristic of the users is utilized by the attacker to sniff sensitive data from the devices without the knowledge of the users. The attacker can sniff data from the sender, manipulate it, and forward it to the receiver due to which the receiver may act according to the manipulated instructions received by it.
- **Physical Damage:** The attacker can destroy the nodes or the physical components by using electrical surge or physical force. The attacker has to reach the place where the IoT devices or nodes are located for accomplishing this type of attack. Physical damage can cause direct damage to the IoT system as for some of the topologies unavailability of a node can disrupt the whole communication path.

Network Layer: The function of the network layer or transport layer is to transmit the data collected from the perception layer to the upper layers of the IoT architecture. The upper layer can be an application layer in the case of three-layered architecture and management service/processing layers for the four and five-layered architecture. The data can be transferred through the internet, cellular networks, or any other reliable wireless sensor networks.

An IoT system is a combination of several adjoining networks that connect for exchanging information. The network layer uses routing algorithms for data communication over the network. A network layer is divided into two sub-layers known as routing and encapsulation layer. The routing layer delivers data packets from source to destination while the encapsulation layer forms the packets. Along with the transmission of data this layer is expected to provide reliability, avoid congestion, and ensure that all the data packets reach their assigned destinations within the designated time limits. This layer can be more appealing for the intruder as all the devices get connected to the network for either transferring or receiving data. At the network layer, the two protocols that are widely used for data transfer among connected devices are RPL and 6LoWPAN. According to Mayzaud et.al (2015), some of the routing attacks on IoT are flooding, routing table overload, increased rank, decreased rank, eavesdropping, sinkhole, wormhole, and black hole attack.

- **Sinkhole Attack:** It is considered to be the most destructive routing attacks as it compromises the authenticity and integrity of the information being transferred by the devices. The attacker attracts data traffic with a motive to prevent the reception of data by the destination nodes. The compromised node is then used by the attacker to launch an attack by sending fake information to the neighboring nodes about its link quality that is used in routing metrics for choosing the best possible routes for data transmission on the network. All the data packets thus pass through the comprised nodes due to which the destination node is unable to acquire accurate and complete sensing data from the nodes.

- **Wormhole attack:** Wormhole is an internal attack that is very hard to detect because the attacker listens to the activities of the network without any interference. It uses mostly more than one malicious node and these nodes have a tunnel between them. These malicious nodes communicate with each other at a slightly different frequency as compared to other nodes. In this attack, a malicious node receives all the data packets coming towards it and also captures packets from other nodes to forward it through the tunnel for the other malicious node. It disrupts the routing path by creating nonoptimized routes which may lead to early arrival, delayed arrival, or in some cases nonarrival of the data packets at the destined nodes.

Figure 4. Wormhole Attack

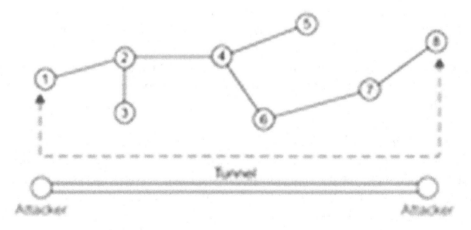

- **Blackhole Attacks:** Routing protocols use intermediate nodes for sending data packets over the network. An intruder utilizes this feature and inserts a fake node in the communication path. This fake node advertises itself to be the best possible route to attract data traffic towards it and thus a blackhole attack occurs. The fake node silently drops all the data packets coming towards it thus preventing transmission of data towards the destination nodes. It causes loss of data, exhaustion of energy resources, and increases transmission delay.

- **Flooding Attack:** Flooding or sometimes referred to as the HELLO flooding attack generates a large amount of traffic in the network which makes nodes and links unavailable for routing. A malicious node joins the network by broadcasting a HELLO message to all neighboring nodes. This node sends HELLO packets with high routing metrics or high energy due to which most of the nodes select it to be the parent node. All the messages are then transmitted through this malicious node which increases the transmission time of messages. As all the neighboring nodes select it to be parent node network traffic and delay increases considerably which in turn depletes the energy of nodes.

- **Routing Table Overload:** In this category of attack the intruder causes resource exhaustion by overloading the routing table. This attack is generally used for the proactive routing protocols as they maintain a routing table that gets regularly updated. For routing overload, the attacker generates fake routes that cause overloading of the routing table for the targeted nodes. This overloading prevents the formation of appropriated, affects the functioning of the network, and may result in memory overflow.

- **Increased Rank:** Routing protocols for low power lossy networks (RPL) use Destination oriented directed acrylic graph (DODAG) to identify and maintain a topology over a network. Every node is assigned a rank that corresponds to its position according to the root node on the graph. This rank characteristic is used by the attackers to launch an attack by altering the ranks. An Increased rank attack is launched by using a malfunctioning node that increases its rank to a value greater than its actual value to display that it is closer to the root node. The compromised nodes select a malicious node as its preferred parent. This process creates additional routes due to which the data packets either fail to reach their destination or do not forward all the data packets.

- **Version Number Attack:** The version number is a field that is propagated unaltered down the DODAG graph which can be incremented only by the root. An attacker uses a malicious node to change the version number and forwards it to the neighbors. When the nodes receive this new version number, the formation of a new DODAG tree starts. The successive rebuilding of trees will exhaust network resources, increase traffic congestion, and cause loss of data packets.

- **Eavesdropping Attack:** An intruder can launch an eavesdropping attack on an insecure network that is being used for data transfer. It includes activities like sniffing and traffic analysis of the network. These attacks are difficult to detect as no significant change is observed in the network transmissions. An attacker performs sniffing by listening to the exchange of information on the networks. It is a very common attack for a wired as well as the wireless medium which can be done through a compromised device or by capturing of data packets. In a traffic analysis attack, the intruder tries to collect routing information to know the partial view of topology. The attacker can gather information regarding the network through this attack and then decide the type of attack that can be used to disrupt the data transfer.

Figure 5. Attacks of Five Layered Architecture of IoT

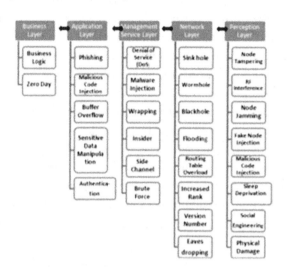

Management Service Layer: The three-layer architecture developed in the initial days of IoT did not consider security risks and the network layer was directly transferred to the application layer. The management service layer sometimes referred to as the processing layer or middleware layer performs the task of storing, analyzing, and processing the huge amount of data coming from the network layer. This layer mainly consists of remote servers placed on the cloud. As the cloud offers a large or virtually never-ending space more and more organizations are relying on the cloud for storing their data. Cloud provides security and privacy by using effective authentication and encryption techniques. But still, the cloud is not completely safe from the attackers or the security threats. As the cloud collects data from different networks and organizations the attackers consider it to be a source of enormous data that has increased the possibilities of attacks on the cloud. Adamou (2019) and Swamy et.al (2017) have explained some of the security threats to cloud storage that can take place at the management service layer like DoS attacks, Malware Injection attack, Wrapping attack, side-channel attack, and the malicious insider.

- **Denial of Service (DoS) attack:** In one of the works of literature by Deshmukh and Dewadkar (2015) among all the different kind of attacks on the cloud environment 14% of them are DDoS and according to a survey as the usage of cloud increases the rate of DDoS attacks will increase proportionately. An attacker overloads the target cloud with a large number of service requests due to which the cloud is unable to respond to the incoming requests from the users. This attack can reduce the performance of the cloud by damaging the virtual servers or in some cases may lead to the unavailability of resources to the users. The attackers scan the network for vulnerabilities and then use these vulnerable machines as agents to launch an attack.
- **Malware Injection Attack:** A malware injection attack is launched on a cloud; the attacker inserts a malicious service or virtual machine in the cloud. A malicious service implementation module or virtual machine instance is created by the attacker for adding it to the cloud. These attacks are implemented by the intruders to have control of the user's information. When the attacker is successful in hacking a cloud, its user's requests are diverted towards the hacker. The malicious code execution is initiated after which the invader can manipulate or steal data and cloud services go

through the problem of eavesdropping. The attacker can use a malware injection attack to perform data modifications and changes or reverse in functionality. It is considered to be a dominant attack that results in misusing service to a cloud environment.

- **Wrapping Attack:** One of the reasons that elevate the risk of wrapping attack on clouds is that most of the cloud users get connected to services through a web browser and the problems caused by the attackers are seen during the execution of the web service request. When a user makes a request it reaches the server through the browser which leads to the generation of a SOAP message. The XML documents are signed, canonicalization is done and signature values are added at the end of the document before passing the SOAP message. The attacker launches a wrapping attack during the translation of the SOAP message as the SOAP header contains all the required information about the destination. In cloud computing, a wrapping attack is launched by using XML (eXtensible Markup Language) signature wrapping through which the attacker can change the contents of the XML document that is being exchanged. XML signature is generally used for securing user's credentials from unauthorized access but it is not able to provide complete security to positions in the document. The attacker duplicates the SOAP message and transfers it to the server which in turn fails to check the integrity of the message owing to the duplication of the signature value. When a server fails to detect the duplication an attacker interferes with the working of the cloud by running malicious code.

- **Insider attack:** This kind of threat is initiated by a person who is a current or former employee of a cloud service provider, who has access to the organization's data, system, and functionality. The attacker in this case commonly called as malicious insider misuses his position to fulfill some offensive intentions that adversely affect the confidentiality, integrity, and availability of the company's information system. A malicious insider can attempt his attack in a shorter period as compared to an external attacker as he has complete knowledge regarding the system policies and functionality of the organization. Moreover, a company exercises most of its efforts for protection from external attackers without sensing security threats from the insiders. Some of the factors responsible for insider attacks are poor authentication, lack of techniques to observe user behavior, and deficiency of methods to protect devices. The attackers can steal data, share it with unauthorized parties, and inject malware/ viruses in the system that can severely affect a company's performance.

- **Side Channel Attack:** This attack is considered to be a threat to data security over the cloud. Highly sensitive data, encryption, or decryption keys are some of the targets of side-channel attacks. It creates a hidden channel by using hardware and software techniques that are utilized to obtain information and the information acquired through these hidden channels is called side-channel information. An attack that is initiated using the side-channel information is called a side-channel attack. This type of attack can be either passive or active. For active attacks, the attackers modify the contents of the target thereby forcing it to carry out some abnormal tasks. On the other hand, in a passive attack, the intruder keeps on examining the activities of the target to obtain information but does not make any changes.

- **Brute Force Attack:** Brute force attacks are used by cheap cloud providers to target users, organizations, and other cloud service providers. It is generally a trial and error method used for decoding data. Some of the common targets of this attack are passwords, encryption keys, and API keys. To implement a brute force attack the intruder does not use any intellectual strategy but keeps on trying different combinations of characters and evaluates the response until he is successful. This attack is easy to perform but the time required to complete it can be very long in some cases as the attackers have to check through all possible combinations of characters till the task is completed.

Application Layer: An application layer consists of several applications like smart home, smart city, smart health care, smart agriculture, a smart grid that uses IoT. These applications are regulated by the information obtained from the management service layer. It provides a virtual service layer to ensure data transport, security, and service discovery and device management without being dependent on technologies utilized for connectivity at the lower layers. The application layer furnishes the data received from the devices and performance of the actuators. This layer provides services and at the same time defines a set of protocols to interact directly with the users. Virtual reality, augmented reality, human-computer interface, and multimedia applications are some of the technologies used for connecting intelligent IoT applications with its users. The application layer is intended to be used by the people and therefore is considered to be a wide attack surface by the malicious users. Some of the security attacks on the application layer as mentioned by Molugu et.al. (2018) and Chen et.al (2018) are phishing attacks, malicious code injection, butter overflow, sensitive data manipulation, and authentication.

- **Phishing Attack:** One of the security risks associated with IoT is a phishing attack which is sometimes referred to as a social engineering attack as it targets human beings through devices rather than sending attacks on devices. The attacker gets involved in communication with the victim to gather some confidential data like user identity or passwords, which may become the source for bigger attacks. Another method used for a phishing attack is when an attacker persuades the victim for acting like that would support attacks like clicking on a link or going to a website. Phishing emails are the most common source of this attack.
- **Malicious Code Injection:** This attack destroys the IoT system's function by adding, removing, or modifying software by introducing malicious codes. Some of the different purposes the attackers try to fulfill through these attacks are to have unauthorized access to data, propagate worms, and to acquire system control. These attacks can cause the system to lose control by which the privacy of the user is lost and in some cases may lead to a complete shutdown.
- **Buffer Overflow Attack:** Ina buffer overflow attack, the attacker tries to exploit the program vulnerabilities by using software coding to place extra data in the buffer which is more than its storage capability. This causes an overflow of the excess data, which may get leaked to other buffers thereby corrupting or overwriting the data in those buffers. The extra data induced by the attacker consists of some specific instructions for the accomplishment of tasks like corrupting files, modifying data, and accessing some private information
- **Sensitive Data Manipulation:** This attack violates user privacy as the attacker gets illicit access to sensitive or confidential data to manipulate it. An attacker tries to analyze the defects in the permission model and obtain illicit access to data. An application is then controlled by the attacker who makes the applications operate in a way that is different from their tasks they have been originally assigned to do. For example, a smart device and smart App exchange a lot of sensitive data by using events. Lack of sufficient protection of events can cause leakage of the event. If the user input lacks sufficient protection, these attacks may cause a violation of the privacy of users and harm the users seriously.
- **Authentication/ Authorization:** Authentication is a process used in IoT to identify its users, devices, and applications to limit unauthorized access by the adversaries. Authentication thus

helps the users in having secure communication, avoid data leakage, and develop new services. But most of the authentication mechanisms are not perfect due to which they fail to provide firm security to the applications. Many of the IoT applications like the smart home, smart transportation, health care are being managed by mobile phones. The attackers introduce some malicious apps and tempt users to download it. The attackers are then able to remotely control these devices containing malicious apps and also gain access to their usernames, passwords and also launch attacks in varying degrees. Lack of two-factor authentication, weak passwords that are easy to be guessed, and no limit to failed attempts that allows the attackers to attempt access to a device number of times without getting blocked are some of the factors that increase the vulnerability of authentication attacks.

Business Layer: The business layer being at the top level of the five-layered IoT architecture symbolizes the purpose of an IoT application and at the same time plays a significant role in regulating the overall working of the IoT system. It is closely associated with the real-world in terms of handling the user's information. Some common security problems as mentioned by Burhan et.al (2018) are business logic attacks and zero-day attacks.

- **Business Logic Attack:** A business logic attack takes advantage of the loopholes in the programming which has been adopted to control data exchange among the users and application's supporting database. The attackers download the application to know about its weaknesses and then program bots called business logic bots (BLB) to launch attacks. Some of the business logic flaws are poor validation process for password recovery and inappropriate coding techniques used by the programmer in case of encryption as well as for input validation. These attacks are imperceptible as they arrive as regular requests and contain legitimate values. Attackers use business logic attacks to steal information, removing business-related crucial information, and perform server-based or application-level attacks.

- **Zero-Day Attack:** Zero-day attack is one more type of attack on the business layer that tries to take advantage of infirmity in the security algorithms which remain unattended by the vendors or developers owing to lack of awareness among them. It is called a zero-day attack because it occurs before the software developer comes to know about the problem. These attacks are launched by inserting malware or spyware to steal information from the companies without the knowledge of the software developers. The intruders target a software system with a malware which integrates with the existing system to prevent it from executing its normal operations. They send malware in the systems in the form of website links and as the user clicks the link the malicious software begins to download on the system. These attacks can prove to be very harmful if not detected at the proper time because it may lead to the failure of the entire network.

4. INTERNET OF THINGS SECURITY SOLUTIONS

The various attacks on the IoT system that occur at different levels of architecture raise an alarming situation for the users thereby making it essential for everyone to know the remedies or solutions to deal with these types of attacks. Most of the attacks that are being implemented by the invaders are happening due to the vulnerabilities with the device or networks or clouds or at the application level.

Inadequate information among the users related to the security solutions and lack of concern among the manufacturers or the vendors has increased the vulnerabilities of IoT. Security mechanisms should be devised for devices, networks, storage, and also the applications.

4.1 Solutions at Device Layer

The IoT devices should be smart enough to handle processes like encryption, authentication, time stamps, firewalls, and connection loss. Most of the IoT devices are microprocessor-based which hinders their ability to handle the intricacies involved in being connected through the internet. The IoT devices generally used can communicate with the cloud through Ethernet or Wi-Fi but due to their incapability to handle data and low storage space, all data has to be stored in the cloud which increases the risks of data breaching. Therefore we should opt for devices that can process data locally. An advantage of using such kind of devices will be that the forwarding of sensitive data to the cloud can be avoided.

The attackers keep on discovering new vulnerabilities in the existing system. At the same time, device manufacturers and service providers devote time to develop innovative methods to handle security risks. The users should keep on regularly updating their operating systems firmware, and application software. Along with these, the users should be careful about their passwords. Unique and strong passwords should be used and the same passwords for a long time or different applications should be avoided. Similarly, passwords that can be easily guessed should be avoided.

The users should read the privacy policies before downloading any applications and avoid the ones that appear to be harmful. Before the selection of devices try to know if the data on your devices is being collected by a third party and in that case, the manufacturers should be ready to inform about the protection policies envisaged regarding data breaches.

4.2 Solutions at Network Layer

According to Hameed et.al (2019), the network topology or the designs should be tolerant of any kind of malicious attack coming towards it. Early detection of unwanted intrusions is another desirable feature that can prevent major damage and the effect of attacks can be mitigated before it spreads across the network. The protocols must be able to recover quickly from network failures caused due to security threats as disruption of networks for a long time may prove to be disastrous in case of applications like disaster management. Hence algorithms or protocols or techniques used at the communication layer should be able to detect as well as recover from the threats.

Transfer of encrypted data over the networks is preferred so that even if it is intercepted, it will be of no use to the people who do not possess the appropriate encryption key to unlock the code. The process of data transfer between device and cloud or the remote server should be initiated by the devices. A bidirectional connection with the cloud can be allowed in specific circumstances to facilitate remote control of the devices. But it is preferred to avoid any incoming connections towards a device or connection from the internet to the device. Many of the field devices do not have to reconfigure, testing, or monitoring software that are applicable to cloud service. If incoming connections are allowed, individuals or network or field devices outside the communication network can enter to utilize its resources which can increase the security risks of a network.

It is essential to handle information exchange, either a transmitted message from a device or a received message with equal attention. A suitable security policy should be used for handling messages and techniques like double encryption, filtering, queuing should be used according to the purpose of communication. For example, if some confidential data is to be sent to the desired location, all the messages carrying client information can be double encrypted. Careful handling of the messages is a powerful tool to avoid inappropriate access at the communication or network layer.

Node location privacy algorithms have been discussed in some research works. Guangjie et.al (2019) has discussed the source location privacy algorithm that protects the privacy of source location from the adversaries. Similarly, Liu et.al (2017) has discussed the sink location privacy algorithm and Babu and Balasubadra (2018) have discussed an algorithm that preserves the location of the source as well as sink nodes. All these algorithms use different techniques to inject false packets or false nodes in the path between source and destination. The presence of false packets confuses the adversaries and they are unable to detect the exact location of the source and destination nodes and therefore fail to capture data on the networks.

a. Solutions on the Management Service layer

Connection to the cloud by the users or by the devices should be based on an authentication system. Research by Chouhan and Singh (2016) signifies the importance of a one-time password for authentication as the one-time passwords are immune to the man in the middle of eavesdropping attacks. Accessing the clouds can be done by using two-step authentications where a password and then a one-time password can be used to assure secure access to the cloud. Passwords can be used as an authentication mechanism for humans but to enhance the security environment for the cloud digital certificate can be used. An asymmetric, encryption-based system is used by the digital certificate to encrypt the communication path from device to cloud to verify data exchange. Cryptographic identification is another advantage that a digital certificate provides over the traditional access methods done with user identification and passwords. Some of the issues that need to be addressed are suitable time slots for loading data on the cloud, level of encryption required by data elements, and the kind of firewalls that are being used for the cloud.

In some of the authentication methods, the attacker can easily present themselves as legitimate users by knowing passwords. To overcome this problem Cirani et.al (2013) have suggested an open authorization method to determine the validity of the requesting user. The open authorization (OAuth) protocol uses four roles: Resources owner that grants access to an end-user, Resource server than maintains user-related information, a client or the third party that desires to achieve user's data, and authorization servers that accomplishes the task of authentication by issuing access tokens. OAuth process starts with the client sending an authorization request to the resources owner. Approval of the resource owner gets confirmed when the client receives an authorization grant. The client forwards this authorization grant to the Authorized server which in turn issues an access token only if the grant request if found valid. The access token is presented by the client to the resource server that provides the requested resources to the client after validation of the token. OAuth is thus an effective method to grant secure permission to the requesting users and also to restrict the access of a third party.

Figure 6. Open Authorization Protocol for IoT

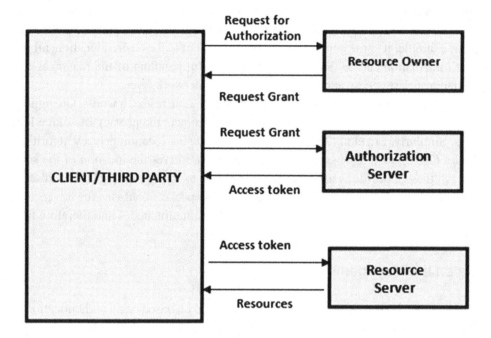

b. Solutions at Application Layer

Application layer security threats need to be handled cautiously as any amendments in the application level by the hackers can be dangerous for the users. If we consider a medical application a hacker can vary the limit of medicine dosage that can prove to be fatal and may deteriorate the health condition of the patient. To protect the application layer from the intruders it is essential to check if the maintenance activities make the applications susceptible to some new threats. Authenticated software should be used and it should be updated regularly. Access or privilege levels assigned to the users should be of optimum limits to avoid any undesirable changes by the users. A fundamental prerequisite for an application is that it should be able to control its associated devices through remote or far locations. The ability of remote control can facilitate sending commands to devices during its whole lifecycle, detecting problems that may arise during functioning, updating software, and include some new functions.

To aid the proper handling of devices without granting more privilege to the users and to encourage safe communication Gyory and Chuah (2017) have suggested IoTOne solutions. It is a technology that examines security weaknesses before publishing IoT Apps. IoTOne is a user-friendly platform that supports devices from different vendors thus providing its customer an opportunity to select a product that will correspond to their necessities at lower deployment costs. This platform allows all the devices to run the internet and supports third-party applications. IoTOne handles the risks associated with third-party integration by imposing restrictions on them to avoid any unreliable methodologies that may harm the system. The third-party developers have to submit their backend programs to IoTOne system for verification of any insecure parameters. A third-party app will be available in the IoTOne app store only if it is verified that the code provided by the third party has correct commands, uses safe programming techniques, and confirms that the endpoints have not allotted more privileges to the apps. All these restrictions on third-party apps reduce the risks of attacks on the IoT applications.

5. TECHNOLOGIES FOR SECURITY OF IOT

Machine learning and Blockchain are some of the emerging technologies that help to deal with security issues in IoT.

5.1 Machine learning (ML)

ML is an application of Artificial Intelligence that aims to turn our machines into intelligent gadgets without being programmed or without any human interference. The programmers do not need to worry about algorithms while working with ML. An appropriate dataset and the expected outputs are supplied to a computer which is then converted into a meaningful program for the users. It is like asking a computer to learn an algorithm according to the input and anticipated outputs. Four types of learning generally used are Supervised/Inductive Learning in which the training data includes expected outputs, Unsupervised Learning that does not include desired outputs in training data, Semi-supervised learning where the training data involves some of the expected outcomes, and Reinforcement learning which is utilized for making robots. ML can be used in IoT to provide intelligent services.

Machine learning can efficiently process large amounts of data generated by the IoT networks and at the same time enable IoT systems to make intelligent systems. ML is therefore envisaged to be a promising technique for better utilization of data. Some of the characteristics that make ML more flexible for IoT include its support for self-organizing operations, optimization of overall system performance by processing analytical data received from devices/users, and its distributed nature which eliminates the requirement of centralized information exchange for users and devices. Research by Hussain et. al (2019) shows that ML can be used for solving security issues like Authentication and access control, detection of attacks and to decrease its effects, DoS as well as DDoS attacks, intrusion detection, and analysis of malicious code that are injected by the invaders.

5.2 BlockChain

Blockchain consists of a group of blocks that are linked through cryptography. It is composed of a distributed digital ledger that cannot be altered and is shared by all the participants in the Blockchain network. A block consists of a cryptographic hash, a list of validated transactions, and a pointer to the cryptographic hash of the previous block. It uses a decentralized approach in which a node can verify if a participant is the real owner of the asset. Decentralized architecture, trustless peer to peer transactions, immutable transactions, the record of transactions, and consensus mechanism are the key characteristics that have made Blockchain a favorable technology for solving security or privacy issues.

Blockchain is another potential solution that can prove to be fruitful in handling the existing security aspects of IoT. It can help in the favorable processing of numerous transactions, tracking and managing the billions of connected smart IoT devices. In a centralized model used by IoT, several security threats are observed because devices are identified and connected through cloud services and need the internet to communicate even if they are located close to each other. Integration of Blockchain with IoT can improve the overall security of the IoT environment by (i) using powerful data encryptions that are difficult to be hacked (ii) decentralized approach which will reduce the risks of single-point failures in which the attackers target a single point through spoofing or DDoS attacks to disrupt network functioning (iii) mitigation of Man in the Middle attacks by using cryptographic signatures as it will be difficult to interrupt any communication (iv) ability to track the node status that will help in preventing data tampering by locking access for the IoT devices and shutting down the compromised devices.

6. FUTURE DIRECTIONS

The voluminous data being exchanged over the IoT platforms is a principal factor that draws the attention of the invaders. A lot of private data is exchanged through the communication networks there is a need to embrace innovative solutions to secure the data of the users. The storage facilities should be upgraded as there is no facility available to maintain the safety of the stored data. Authentication facilities are available but passwords are not sufficient to keep our data secure due to a large number of devices. Passwords can be guessed or obtained by victimizing the users so new systems ought to be developed that will use unique identification systems like fingerprint or iris scanning. IoT devices are away from the users and they have to access remotely due to which connectivity in IoT depends on wireless communication techniques for information transfer. There is a need to ensure more security at the network layer. The source and sink node location privacy algorithms provide security but the energy consumption increases due to the presence of false packets in the route which in turn reduces the network lifetime. As our IoT devices are battery-powered there is a need to develop algorithms that can balance the energy requirements of the network in the presence of security algorithms.

7. CONCLUSION

Attainment of security goals for the IoT system seems to be a herculean task due to many challenges like a large amount of data, heterogeneous environment, device constraints like low storage capacity and power, varying network topology, and lack of safe storage facility for data. This chapter has discussed security attacks at the five-layer architecture of IoT. Some of the common attacks observed at all the layers are Denial of Service (DoS), Eavesdropping attacks, and malicious code injection attack. The security requirements at all the levels are different and therefore techniques to deal with them are also different. It is not possible to achieve a safe IoT system by implementing security algorithms at any one of the layers. Machine learning and Blockchain are two technologies that can help to ensure security for the IoT system. Security algorithms should be updated regularly to keep IoT systems for a long time because as the developers bring up with new security solutions the attackers may try to find new vulnerabilities in the system. So whatever technology or protocol or algorithm is used it should be able to minimize security risks to satisfy the demands of users. Security is an important parameter to maintain trust among the consumers and at the same time increase the usability of the versatile technology.

REFERENCES

Ari, A.A., Ngangmo, O.K., Titouna, C., Thiare, O., Mohamadou, A., & Gueroui, A.M. (2019). Enabling privacy and security in Cloud of Things: Architecture, applications, security & privacy challenges. *Applied Computing and Informatics*.

Babu, S. S., & Balasaubadra, K. (2018). Chronic Privacy Protection from Source to Sink in Sensor Network Routing. *International Journal of Applied Engineering Research, 13*(5), 2798-2808.

Botta, A., Donato, W. D., Persico, V., & Pescape, A. (2016). Integration of Cloud computing and Internet of Things: A survey. In *Future Generation Computer Systems*. Elsevier.

Burhan, M., Rehman, R. A., Khan, B., & Kim, B. S. (2018). IoT Elements, Layered Architectures, and SecurityIssues: A Comprehensive Survey. *Mdpi Sensors*.

Chen, K., Zhang, S., Li, Z., Zhang, Y., Deng, Q., Ray, S., & Jin, Y. (2018). Internet-of-Things Security and Vulnerabilities: Taxonomy, Challenges, and Practice. *Journal of Hardware and Systems Security*, 2, 97–110.

Chouhan, P., & Singh, R. (2016). Security Attacks on Cloud Computing With Possible Solution. *International Journal of Advanced Research in Computer Science and Software Engineering, 6*(1).

Cirani, S., Ferrari, G., & Veltri, L. (2013). Enforcing security mechanisms in the IP-based Internet of things: An algorithmic overview. *Algorithms*, 197–226.

Deogirikar, J., & Vidhate, A. S. (2017). Security Attacks in IoT: A Survey. *International Conference on I-SMAC (IoT in Social, Mobile, Analytics, and Cloud, 32-37*.

Donno, M. D., Giaretta, A., Dragoni, N., Bucchiarone, A., & Mazzara, M. (2019). *Cyber-Storms Come from Clouds: Security of Cloud Computing in the IoT Era*. Future Internet.

Duan, R., Chen, X., & Xing, T. (2011). A QoS Architecture for IoT. *IEEE International Conferences on Internet of Things, and Cyber, Physical and Social Computing*.

Gyory, M., & Chuah, M. (2017). IoT One: Integrated Platform for Heterogeneous IoT Devices. *International Conference on Computing, Networking, and Communications (ICNC): Workshop*.

Hameed, S., Khan, F.I., & Hameed, B. (2019).Understanding Security Requirements and Challenges in The Internet of Things (IoT): A Review. *Hindawi, Journal of Computer Networks and Communication*.

Hany, F. A., & Gary, B. W. (2019). *IoT security, Privacy, Safety, and Ethics*. Springer Nature Switzerland.

He, Y., Han, G., Wang, H., Ansere, J. A., & Zhang, W. (2019). A Sector Based Random Routing Scheme for Protecting the Source Location Privacy in WSNs for the Internet of Things. *Elsevier Future Generation Computer Systems*.

Hussain, F., Hussain, R., Hassan, S. A., & Hossain, E. (2019). *Machine Learning in IoT Security: Current Solutions and Future Challenges*. Arxiv: 1904.05735v1 [cs.CR].

Khan, R., Khan, S. N., Zaheer, R., & Khan, S. (2012). Future Internet: The Internet of Things Architecture, Possible Applications, and Key Challenges. *10th International Conference on Frontiers of Information Technology (FIT): Proceedings.*

Liu, A., Liu, X., Tang, Z., Yang, L. T., & Shao, Z. (2017). Preserving Smart Sink-Location Privacy with Delay Guaranteed Routing Scheme for WSNs. *ACM Transactions on Embedded Computing Systems*, *16*(3), 68.

Mayzaud, A., Badonnel, R., Chrisment, I. (2016) A Taxonomy of Attacks in RPL-based Internet of Things. *International Journal of Network Security, 18*(3), 459 - 473.

Molugu, S. V., Bindu, S. M., Aishwarya, B., Dhanush, B. N., & Manjunath, R. K. (2018). Security and Privacy Challenges in Internet of Things. *Proceedings of the 2nd International Conference on Trends in Electronics and Informatics.*

Rayes, A., & Salem, S. (2019). *Internet of Things from Hype to Reality: The Road to digitization.* Springer.

Sadier, G., & Sabri, F. (2017). *Nanosatellite Communications: A Market Study for IoT/M2M applications.* London Economics, Market Sizing, and Requirements Report.

Sharma, R., Pandey, N., & Khatri, S. K. (2017). Analysis of IoT Security at Network Layer. *Proceedings of 6th International Conference on Reliability, Infocom Technologies and Optimization (ICRITO) (Trends and Future Directions),* 585-590.

Wurm, J., Jin, Y., Liu, Y., Hu, S., Heffner, K., Rahman, F., & Tehranipoor, M. (2016). *Introduction to cyber-physical system security: A cross-layer perspective. IEEE Transactions on Multi-Scale Computing Systems.*

Index

K

L

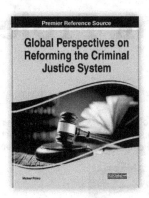

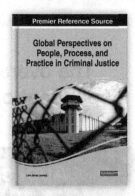

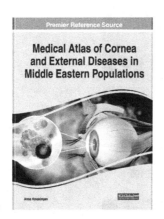

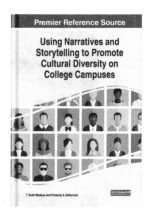

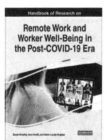

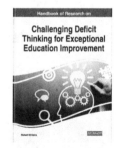

Printed in the United States
by Baker & Taylor Publisher Services

Printed in the United States
by Baker & Taylor Publisher Services